Why Do You Need This New Edition?

Six good reasons why you should buy this new Fourteenth Edition of *The American Nation!*

1. This edition is tied more closely than ever to the innovative website, MyHistoryLab, which helps you save time and improve results as you study history (www.myhistorylab.com). Improved MyHistoryLab icons appear in the textbook, alerting you to important connections between the textbook and MyHistoryLab resources. At the end of each chapter you will find a *MyHistoryLab Connections* table. These provide a checklist of the most important MyHistoryLab resources related to the chapter, facilitating the integrated study of the textbook and the website.

2. The new edition strengthens the guiding principle of the textbook—to survey American history in a way that bridges the present and the past, showing the relevance of history to contemporary readers. For example, the essays that open each chapter connect a major topic of the chapter to experiences that pertain to many readers. For the Fourteenth Edition these essays are either entirely new or have been thoroughly updated; nearly all pertain to events or developments since 2008.

3. Other elements designed to bridge the present and the past, such as the *American Lives* and *Re-Viewing the Past* essays, have also been thoroughly revised. Several of these essays are entirely new to the Fourteenth Edition.

4. The more than 100 maps in this book have been completely reworked to convey new ideas and to enhance comprehension. Many entirely new maps have been created to illuminate important themes, including a stronger global emphasis.

5. Each chapter has been revised to reflect new scholarship, to offer important new perspectives, and to streamline and sharpen the writing. For instance, the Prologue and first few chapters reflect new insights concerning the "pre-historic" period. These chapters also feature a more detailed comparison of the civilizations of the Americas with those of the "Old World"—Europe, Africa, and Asia. An almost entirely new chapter, "From Boomers to Millennials" (Chapter 31), draws an explicit comparison between the social and cultural foundations of young modern Americans and their parents; it especially explores the culture of consumption and the impact of the Internet.

6. To facilitate study and review, each chapter now ends with a list of key terms and definitions and a set of review questions. The key terms are also compiled in the glossary that appears at the end of the text.

PEARSON

The
American Nation

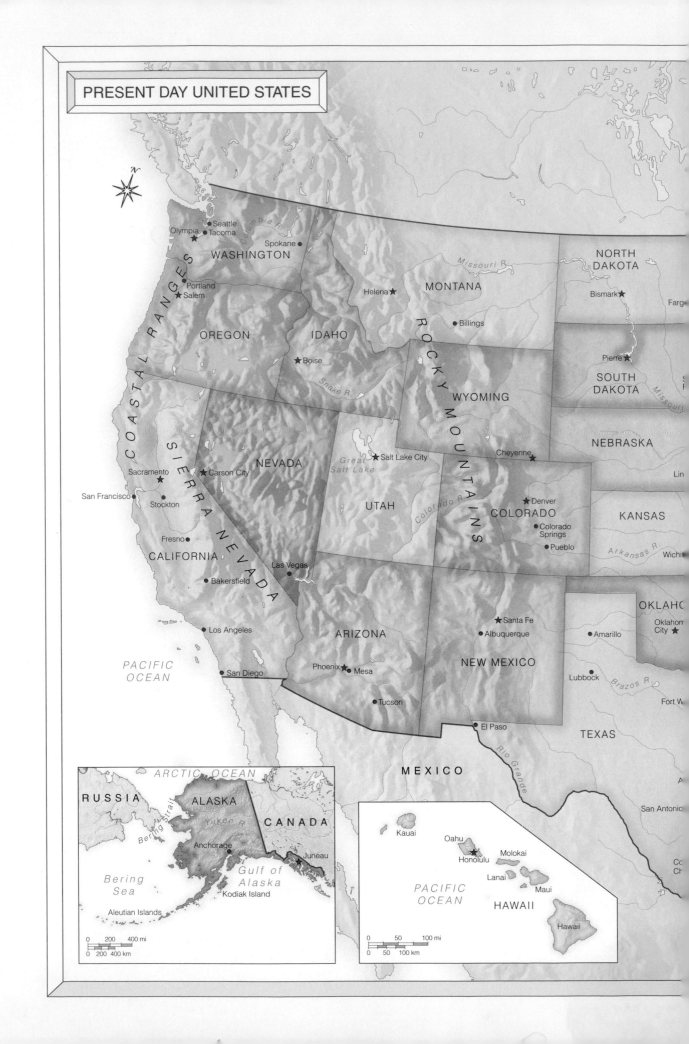

PRESENT DAY UNITED STATES

N

WASHINGTON • Seattle
Olympia ★ • Tacoma
• Spokane

Portland •
Salem •

OREGON

COASTAL RANGES

IDAHO
• Boise

Helena ★ **MONTANA**
• Billings

NORTH DAKOTA
Bismark ★
Far

Missouri R.

ROCKY MOUNTAINS

WYOMING

Pierre ★
SOUTH DAKOTA

Missouri

Snake R.

SIERRA NEVADA

NEVADA

Sacramento ★ ★ Carson City

San Francisco •
Stockton •

Fresno •

CALIFORNIA

★ Salt Lake City
Great Salt Lake

UTAH

Colorado R.

Cheyenne ★

★ Denver
COLORADO
• Colorado Springs
• Pueblo

NEBRASKA

Lin

KANSAS

Arkansas R. Wichi

Las Vegas •

Bakersfield •

Los Angeles •

• San Diego

ARIZONA

Phoenix ★ • Mesa

• Tucson

PACIFIC OCEAN

★ Santa Fe
• Albuquerque

NEW MEXICO

• Amarillo

OKLAHO
Oklahoma City ★

• Lubbock

Brazos R.

Fort W

El Paso •

Rio Grande

TEXAS

MEXICO

San Antonio

ARCTIC OCEAN
RUSSIA **ALASKA** **CANADA**
Bering Strait
Yukon R.
Anchorage •
Juneau ★
Bering Sea
Gulf of Alaska
Kodiak Island
Aleutian Islands

0 200 400 mi
0 200 400 km

Kauai
Oahu
Honolulu ★ Molokai
Lanai Maui

PACIFIC OCEAN

HAWAII

Hawaii

Co
Ch

0 50 100 mi
0 50 100 km

FOURTEENTH EDITION

VOLUME TWO

The American Nation

A HISTORY OF THE UNITED STATES

Mark C. Carnes

Ann Whitney Olin Professor of History
Barnard College, Columbia University

John A. Garraty

Gouverneur Morris Professor of History, Emeritus
Columbia University

Prentice Hall

Boston   Columbus   Indianapolis   New York   San Francisco   Upper Saddle River
Amsterdam   Cape Town   Dubai   London   Madrid   Milan   Munich   Paris   Montréal   Toronto
Delhi   Mexico City   São Paulo   Sydney   Hong Kong   Seoul   Singapore   Taipei   Tokyo

Editorial Director: Craig Campanella
Executive Editor: Ed Parsons
Senior Development Editor: Roberta Meyer
Editorial Assistant: Alex Rabinowitz
Supplements Editor: Emsal Hasan
Director of Marketing: Brandy Dawson
Senior Marketing Manager: Maureen E. Prado Roberts
Marketing Assistant: Marissa C. O'Brien
Senior Managing Editor: Ann Marie McCarthy
Senior Project Manager: Debra A. Wechsler
*Senior Manufacturing and Operations Manager
    for Arts & Sciences:* Nick Sklitsis
Operations Specialist: Christina Amato
Senior Art Director: Maria Lange
AV Project Manager: Mirella Signoretto

Text Design: GEX Publishing Services
Cover Design: dePinho Design
Manager, Visual Research: Beth Brenzel
Photo Researcher: Barbara S. Salz
Cover Art: Zakim Bridge illuminated at dusk, Boston,
    USA. © Allan Baxter/Photodisc/Getty Images
Director of Media and Assessment: Brian Hyland
Media Editor: Andrea Messineo
Media Project Manager: Tina Rudowski
Full-Service Project Management: GEX Publishing Services
Composition: GEX Publishing Services
Printer/Binder: R. R. Donnelley & Sons
Cover Printer: Lehigh-Phoenix Color/Hagerstown
Text Font: 10/12 Galliard

Credits and acknowledgments borrowed from other sources and reproduced, with permission, in this textbook appear on appropriate page within text (or starting on page C1).

Library of Congress Cataloging-in-Publication Data
Carnes, Mark C. (Mark Christopher),
 The American nation : a history of the United States / Mark C. Carnes, John A. Garraty. -- 14th ed.
   p. cm.
 Includes index.
 ISBN-13: 978-0-205-79044-9
 ISBN-10: 0-205-79044-5
 ISBN-13: 978-0-205-79042-5
 ISBN-10: 0-205-79042-9
 [etc.]
 1. United States--History--Textbooks. I. Garraty, John A. (John Arthur), 1920-2007. II. Title.
 E178.1.C27 2011
 973—dc22
                    2010039087

10 9 8 7 6 5 4 3 2 1

Prentice Hall
is an imprint of

www.pearsonhighered.com

Combined Volume
ISBN 10: 0-205-79044-5
ISBN 13: 978-0-205-79044-9

Examination Copy
ISBN 10: 0-205-84106-6
ISBN 13: 978-0-205-84106-6

Volume 1
ISBN 10: 0-205-79042-9
ISBN 13: 978-0-205-79042-5

Volume 1 à la carte
ISBN 10: 0-205-84200-3
ISBN 13: 978-0-205-84200-1

Volume 2
ISBN 10: 0-205-79043-7
ISBN 13: 978-0-205-79043-2

Volume 2 à la carte
ISBN 10: 0-205-84201-1
ISBN 13: 978-0-205-84201-8

Brief Contents

Contents

Maps and Graphs

Additional maps, arranged by topic, appear in the "Mapping the Past" features.

Features

■ American Lives

■ Re-Viewing the Past

■ Mapping the Past

■ Debating the Past

Preface

"RELEVANT HISTORY"

Many colleges and universities require the study of American history. The reasons are numerous, ranging from the need for informed citizens in a democracy to the centrality of history to other branches of knowledge.

But telling the story of "the American nation" in a single book—even one as big as this—is no easy matter. If the "Brief Contents" section can be regarded as a road map, the journey is long and demanding. Sometimes, too, the past is a strange land, bearing little resemblance to the world we know. Readers may ask: Why make a detour in their busy lives to visit "Jeffersonian Democracy" (Chapter 6) or "American Society in an Industrial Age" (Chapter 18)? The past is past. Why not just move on?

These questions are fair. The answer is simple. Though we live upon the shores of the present, the waves of the past, often originating far in the distance, continuously touch our lives. Sometimes they ebb and flow so gently we can scarcely perceive them. Sometimes they form huge breakers that come crashing down on us. We may ignore history; it will not ignore us.

This book seeks to prove this assertion.

Chapter Openers

To that end, every chapter opens with questions that pertain to many readers: Chapter 6—on Jeffersonian Democracy—begins: "Do you have too much debt?" The essay that follows examines the problem of credit card debt among college students today and shows how similar concerns occupied Jefferson and his followers. Chapter 18, on society and culture during the late nineteenth century, opens with: "Have you ever been kicked out of a mall?" The succeeding paragraphs show how much more of our lives are played out in public spaces compared to a century ago.

Other opening questions include:
"Do you rebel against authority?"
"Are you wearing anything made in the United States?"
"Do you space out during political debates?"
"Do you drink too much?"
"What will happen to you?"

Such questions bridge present and past; they connect our lives to those of our forebears.

Re-Viewing the Past

Because movies on historical themes often figure prominently in how we think about the past, eleven of the chapters include *Re-Viewing the Past* essays, which contrast Hollywood's rendering of history with what really happened. The selected movies range from those with obvious "historical" themes, such as *The Alamo* and *Saving Private Ryan*, to popular movies whose historical themes are less well known, such as *Chicago*, a musical based on the actual story of women who murdered their lovers, and *Titanic*, a movie that purports to describe courtship patterns among rich and poor in the early twentieth century.

American Lives

Eleven of the chapters include *American Lives* essays, ranging from Eunice Williams, a young girl who was captured and raised by Indians, to contemporary figures such as Bill Gates and Barack Obama. These essays focus on the young adulthood of such figures; we hope that readers of the same age will in this way find it easier to relate to them.

Artwork

We have also chosen much of the artwork to link past and present. For example, the discussion of the slave trade in Chapter 2 includes a photograph of the Cape Coast Castle in Ghana, which held slaves before they were shipped to the Americas. Juxtaposed with this picture is a photograph of President Barack Obama at the Cape Coast Castle delivering a speech on race. Chapter 5, on the American Revolution, shows the famous painting of Washington crossing the Delaware in a longboat; juxtaposed is a photograph of modern Americans, dressed in Patriot garb, struggling to re-enact his accomplishment more than two hundred years later. Chapter 13 includes Thomas Noble's 1867 painting of Margaret Garner, an escaped slave who, when captured, killed her daughter rather than return her to slavery—the story that inspired Toni Morrison's Pulitzer-prizewinning *Beloved* (1987). We chose many of the pictures not merely to illustrate the past but also to connect it to the present.

NEW TO THIS EDITION

- Each chapter has been revised to reflect new scholarship, offer new perspectives, and streamline and sharpen the prose. An almost entirely new chapter, "From Boomers to Millennials" (Chapter 31), draws an explicit comparison between the social and cultural foundations of young modern Americans and their parents; it especially explores the culture of consumption and the impact of the Internet.

- The essays that introduce each chapter are either entirely new or have been updated; nearly all pertain to events or developments since 2008. Chapter 20 includes a new *Debating the Past* essay—"Populism—Crusade of Cranks or Potent Grass-Roots Protest?"— and all of the other *Debating* essays are informed by recent scholarship.

- The Prologue and first few chapters reflect new insights unearthed (literally) by archaeologists and anthropologists concerning the "pre-historic" period. These chapters also feature a more detailed comparison of the civilizations of the Americas with those of the "Old World"—Europe, Africa, and Asia.

- This edition includes several new *American Lives*: Davy Crockett—perhaps the first person who became famous for being famous; Charlotte Perkins Gilman, a visionary who perceived that women's legal and political emancipation was largely dependent on their gaining paid work; civil rights leader Martin Luther King, Jr.; Barack Obama, the first African American to be elected president; and four randomly selected heroes who were killed in the recent wars in Afghanistan and Iraq.

- This edition also includes three new *Re-Viewing the Past* essays. *Black Robe* thoughtfully explores the interaction of Indians and colonists in the seventeenth century. Two versions of *The Alamo*: the first, released in 1960, stars John Wayne; the second (2004) tells a different story with Billy Bob Thornton as Davy Crockett. The widely acclaimed *There Will Be Blood* presents Daniel Day Lewis's searing performance as an unscrupulous wildcatting oilman loosely based on the life of Edward Doheny, who opened up the major oil fields of California and Mexico early in the twentieth century.

- The more than 100 maps in this book have been completely reworked to convey new ideas and to enhance comprehension. A new *Mapping the Past* in Chapter 20, "Agrarian Discontent and the Populist Challenge," features a new map on Populism in Texas in the 1890s. Many other new maps—unique to this book—have been created to illuminate important themes: the populations of Eurasian civilizations in 1500; the exchange of animals, bacteria, plants, and technologies caused by the linkage of the Americas with Eurasia after Columbus's voyage; Osceola's rebellion against the removal of the Seminole Indians from Florida; Socialist Party successes in rural Oklahoma and in Milwaukee, Wisconsin during the early twentieth century; rural African Americans' movement to cities in the South during the 1920s; white flight from downtown St. Louis to the suburbs in the 1950s; and the spread of AIDS in Ohio during the 1980s.

- Other maps focus on the Middle East: the dismantling of the Ottoman Empire in the 1920s and the wars in Iraq and Afghanistan in recent decades. This last point warrants expansion: the maps focusing on the Arab world are part of a more general emphasis on global themes and the Middle East in particular.

- Because artists often convey deep truths about the human experience, *The American Nation* has sought to incorporate art, broadly defined. This edition includes over 800 photographs of paintings, sculpture, movies, and architecture. Too often, however, art is added to history texts uncritically. Artistic renderings of the past do not always coincide with historical accounts. For that reason, most captions for the artwork in *The American Nation* examine the historical credibility of those works. This juxtaposition of "art" and "history" is most obvious in the *Re-Viewing the Past* essays, which show how film directors enhance (and often undermine) historical understanding. The *Debating the Past* essay in Chapter 3 examines the issue in some detail: "Do Artists Depict Historical Subjects Accurately?" Much of the art, too, is the work of actual participants or observers to the phenomena they depicted. Soldier artists, for example, painted many of the battle scenes in *The American Nation*; such portrayals may not be factually accurate but they are "primary sources" that reflect the views of historical participants.

- Sometimes historical "truths" are just as elusive to historians. Indeed, the *Debating the Past* feature shows how historians themselves disagree over fundamental issues of interpretation and fact. These disputes are so central to the historian's task that students may fairly ask the question posed in this book's final *Debating the Past* feature (Chapter 32): "Do Historians Ever Get It Right?" Readers of *The American Nation* must supply their own answer. What this long book argues, however, is that the exploration of the past itself is as important as any particular facts that may be discerned along the way.

- This edition of *The American Nation* concedes the difficulty of internalizing so many complex concepts and materials. To assist in this task, nearly every chapter includes at least one "conceptual" table illuminating its key themes and issues. For example, a table in Chapter 9

summarizes the chief elements of the *Second American Party System* by comparing the fundamental ideas of the Democrats and Whigs; a table in Chapter 31 outlines the "victories" of gender activists in the 1960s and 1970s and shows the subsequent conservative response to these events. These tables are not mere summaries but instruments to promote deeper learning and comprehension.

- To encourage and facilitate study and review, each chapter now ends with a list of key terms and definitions and a set of review questions. The key terms are also compiled in the glossary that appears at the end of the text.

Supplements for Instructors and Students

Supplements for Qualified College Adopters	Supplements for Students
MyHistoryLab (www.myhistorylab.com) Save Time. Improve Results. MyHistoryLab is a dynamic Web site that provides a wealth of resources geared to meet the diverse teaching and learning needs of today's instructors and students. MyHistoryLab's many accessible tools will encourage students to read their text and help them improve their grade in their course.	**MyHistoryLab (www.myhistorylab.com) Save Time. Improve Results.** MyHistoryLab is a dynamic Web site that provides a wealth of resources geared to meet the diverse teaching and learning needs of today's instructors and students. MyHistoryLab's many accessible tools will encourage you to read your text and help you improve your grade in your course.
Instructor's Resource Manual with Test Bank Available at the Instructor's Resource Center, at **www.pearsonhighered.com/irc**, the Instructor's Resource Manual with Test Bank contains chapter outlines, summaries, key points and vital concepts, and information on audio-visual resources that can be used in developing and preparing lecture presentations. The Test Bank includes multiple choice questions and essay questions and is text specific.	**CourseSmart www.coursemart.com** CourseSmart eTextbooks offer the same content as the printed text in a convenient online format—with highlighting, online search, and printing capabilities. You **save 60% over the list price** of the traditional book.
PowerPoint Presentation Available at the Instructor's Resource Center, at **www.pearsonhighered.com/irc**, the PowerPoints contain chapter outlines and full-color images of maps and arts. They are text specific and available for download.	**Books à la Carte** Books à la Carte editions feature the exact same content as the traditional printed text in a convenient, three-hole-punched, loose-leaf version at a discounted price—allowing you to take only what you need to class. You'll **save 35% over the net price** of the traditional book. **Vol. 1 - ISBN: 0205842003; ISBN-13: 9780205842001; Vol. 2 - ISBN: 0205842011; ISBN-13: 9780205842018**
MyTest Available at **www.pearsonmytest.com**, MyTest is a powerful assessment generation program that helps instructors easily create and print quizzes and exams. Questions and tests can be authored online, allowing instructors ultimate flexibility and the ability to efficiently manage assessments anytime, anywhere! Instructors can easily access existing questions and edit, create, and store using simple drag-and-drop and Word-like controls.	**Library of American Biography Series www.pearsonhighered.com/educator/series/Library-of-American-Biography/10493.page** Pearson's renowned series of biographies spotlighting figures who had a significant impact on American history. Included in the series are Edmund Morgan's *The Puritan Dilemma: The Story of John Winthrop*, B. Davis Edmund's *Tecumseh and the Quest for Indian Leadership*, J. William T. Young's, *Eleanor Roosevelt: A Personal and Public Life*, and John R. M. Wilson's *Jackie Robinson and the American Dilemma*.
Retreiving the American Past Available through the Pearson Custom Library (**www.pearsoncustom.com, keyword search | rtap**), the *Retrieving the American Past* (RTAP) program lets you create a textbook or reader that meets your needs and the needs of your course. RTAP gives you the freedom and flexibility to add chapters from several best-selling Pearson textbooks, in addition to *The American Nation, 14/e*, and/or 100 topical reading units written by the history department of Ohio State University, all under one cover. Choose the content you want to teach in depth, in the sequence you want, at the price you want your students to pay.	**Penguin Valuepacks www.pearsonhighered.com/penguin** A variety of Penguin-Putnam texts is available at discounted prices when bundled with *The American Nation, 14/e*. Texts include Benjamin Franklin's *Autobiography and Other Writings*, Nathaniel Hawthorne's *The Scarlet Letter*, Thomas Jefferson's *Notes on the State of Virginia*, and George Orwell's *1984*.
	A Short Guide to Writing About History, 7/e Written by Richard Marius, late of Harvard University, and Melvin E. Page, Eastern Tennessee State University, this engaging and practical text helps students get beyond merely compiling dates and facts. Covering both brief essays and the documented resource paper, the text explores the writing and researching processes, identifies different modes of historical writing, including argument, and concludes with guidelines for improving style. **ISBN: 0205673708; ISBN-13: 9780205673704**
	Longman American History Atlas This full-color historical atlas designed especially for college students is a valuable reference tool and visual guide to American history. This atlas includes maps covering the scope of American history from the lives of the Native Americans to the 1990s. Produced by a renowned cartographic firm and a team of respected historians, the *Longman American History Atlas* will enhance any American history survey course. **ISBN: 0321004868; ISBN-13: 9780321004864**
	Study Card for American History This timeline of major events in American social, political, and cultural history distills course information to the basics, helping you quickly master the fundamentals and prepare for exams. **ISBN: 0321292324; ISBN-13: 9780321292322**

Save TIME. Improve Results. MyHistoryLab is a dynamic Web site that provides a wealth of resources geared to meet the diverse teaching and learning needs of today's instructors and students. MyHistoryLab's many accessible tools will encourage students to read their text and help them improve their grade in their course.

Among the features to help you and your students save time and improve results are the following.

- Pearson eText/Audio Files—Just like the printed text, the Pearson eText allows students to highlight and add their own notes. The full audio of the entire book is also included to suit the varied learning styles of today's students. Students save time and improve results by having access to their book online.
- Gradebook—Students can follow their own progress and instructors can monitor the work of the entire class. Automated grading of quizzes and assignments helps both instructors and students save time and monitor their results throughout the course.
- History Bookshelf—Students may read, download, or print 100 of the most commonly assigned history works like Homer's *The Iliad* or Machiavelli's *The Prince*.
- PEARSON **mysearchlab**—This website provides students access to a number of reliable sources for online research, as well as clear guidance on the research and writing process.

New MyHistoryLab Icons integrated in the text lead to Web-based expansions on topics, directing students to access extra information, videos, and simulations. Although many more resources are available than those highlighted in the book, the icons draw attention to the most directly pertinent material available at www.myhistorylab.com.

Read the **Document**

Points students to primary and secondary source documents related to the chapter.

View the **Image**

Identifies primary and secondary source images, including photographs, fine art, and artifacts to provide students with a visual perspective on history.

See the **Map**

Directs students to atlas and interactive maps; these present both broad overviews and detailed examinations of historical developments.

Watch the **Video**

Notes pertinent archival videos and videos of Pearson History authors that probe various topics.

Hear the **Audio**

Marks audio clips from historically significant songs and speeches that enrich students' engagement with history.

Study and **Review**

Alerts students to study resources for each chapter of the textbook available online through www.myhistorylab.com. These resources include practice tests and flashcards.

New *MyHistoryLab Connections* tables appear at the end of each chapter. These provide a checklist of the most important MyHistoryLab resources related to the chapter, facilitating the integrated study of the textbook and the website.

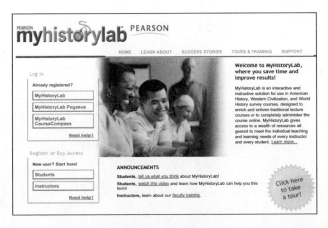

Acknowledgments

I thank the many friends, colleagues, and students who have helped me in writing this edition of *The American Nation*. My debt to John A. Garraty—teacher, colleague, co-author—warrants many paragraphs of acknowledgment. But his scorn for wordiness obliges me to acknowledge that he taught me the art of writing.

Mary Elin Korchinsky has lived this book (and nearly everything else) with me. My journey with her is a joy. For this edition, our particular challenge has been to relate the American nation's past to college students today. Much of the creativity in the chapters that follow—"Do you vote for *American Idol?*" "Do you illegally download?" "Do you space out during political debates?"—was a product of her special genius.

My daughter, Stephanie, read the book carefully and critically; her comments have proven invaluable. My goal of connecting with younger readers was surely influenced by her own immense capacity for sharing love with her parents. The dedication of this book is an acknowledgment of that special gift.

I especially thank E. Ward Smith for guidance through the murky depths of modern banking and finance. And I thank Prakhar Sharma for similarly leading me through the shrouded landscape of contemporary Iraq and Afghanistan.

Modern publishing, too, is a world of labyrinthine complexity. I thank the expert team at Pearson for sharing their mastery of its many arcane and demanding arts: Yolanda de Rooy, Roberta Meyer, Craig Campanella, Ed Parsons, Debra Wechsler, Mirella Signoretto, Maria Lange, Marisa Taylor, Brandy Dawson, Maureen Prado Roberts, and Alex Rabinowitz. Although they left me plenty of thread to find my way out, they also showed good sense in sometimes getting behind me and pushing. For that, and everything else, I am grateful. I also thank:

Armando C. Alonzo, Texas A & M University
Andrew Bagley, Phillips Community College
Mary E. Barnes, Blinn College
Mack Bean, Blinn College
Thomas Born, Blinn College
Robert Brooks, Tyler Junior College
Dale Carnagey, Blinn College
Carrie Coston, Blinn College
Shannon Cross, Tyler Junior College
Alan Harazin, Holyoke Community College
Billy Hathorn, Laredo Community College
Peter Jones, Tyler Junior College
Gene Kirkpatrick, Tyler Junior College
Martha Kline, Blinn College
Alan Lehman, Blinn College
Jan McCauley, Tyler Junior College
Nora McMillan, San Antonio College
Horacio Salinas, Jr., Laredo Community College
Malcolm Saunders, University of the South Pacific
Kenneth McCullough, Blinn College
Jeff Owens, Tyler Junior College
Kahne Parsons, Tyler Junior College
Madeleine Ross, Tyler Junior College
James R. Sisson, Central Texas College
Herbert Sloan, Barnard College
Isaac Solis, Navarro College
Brian Steele, University of Alabama at Birmingham
Quentin Taylor, Rogers State University
Tracy Teslow, University of Cincinnati
Hubert P. van Tuyll, Augusta State University
Larry Watson, Blinn College
Stan Watson, Tyler Junior College
Don Whatley, Blinn College
Geoffrey Willbanks, Tyler Junior College

And I thank the families of the American heroes, featured in Chapter 32, for sharing the stories of their children who served and died in the wars in Afghanistan and Iraq.

Mark C. Carnes
Barnard College, Columbia University

About the Authors

MARK C. CARNES received his undergraduate degree from Harvard and his PhD in history from Columbia University. He has chaired both the history and American studies departments at Barnard College, Columbia University, where he serves as the Ann Whitney Olin Professor of History. Carnes and Garraty were General Editors of the 26-volume *American National Biography*, for which they were awarded the Waldo Leland Prize of the American Historical Association. Carnes has published numerous books on American social and cultural history, including *Secret Ritual and Manhood in Victorian America* (1989), *Past Imperfect: History According to the Movies* (1995), *Novel History: Historians and Novelists Confront America's Past* (2001), and *Invisible Giants: 50 Americans That Shaped the Nation but Missed the History Books* (2002). Carnes also pioneered the *Reacting to the Past* pedagogy, winner of the Theodore Hesburgh Award, sponsored by TIAA-CREF, as the outstanding pedagogical innovation in the nation (2004). In *Reacting to the Past*, college students play elaborate games, set in the past, their roles informed by classic texts. (For more on *Reacting*, see: www.barnard.edu/reacting.) In 2005 the American Historical Association named Carnes the recipient of the William Gilbert Prize for the best article on teaching history.

The late **JOHN A. GARRATY**, formerly Gouverneur Morris Professor Emeritus of History at Columbia University, received his PhD from Columbia University and an LHD from Michigan State University. He authored and edited scores of books, among them biographies of Silas Wright, Henry Cabot Lodge, Woodrow Wilson, George W. Perkins, and Theodore Roosevelt. Garraty's *The New Commonwealth*, included in the new *American Nation* series, challenged earlier dismissals of what was commonly known as "the Gilded Age." His *The Great Depression* argued that political leaders throughout the world happened upon "solutions" much like those proposed by Franklin D. Roosevelt. Garraty was co-General Editor with Mark Carnes of the *American National Biography*.

■ Mark C. Carnes

The
American Nation

Has your family overcome adversity?

With nearly $3 billion in assets, Oprah Winfrey is the richest self-made woman in America. Her great-great-grandfather, Constantine Winfrey, was an illiterate slave in Sanford, Mississippi. On gaining his freedom in 1865, he owned little more than a strong back and a knowledge of cotton farming. But within fifteen years, he had learned to read and write and was owner of several farms and over 100 acres of land.

Whoopi Goldberg, another prominent black woman TV host and actress, is the great-great-granddaughter of William Washington and Elsa Tucker, slaves who were living in Alachua County, Florida when Lee surrendered at Appomattox. Over the next decade, the couple fulfilled the demanding provisions of the Southern Homestead Act, passed by the Republican-dominated Congress in 1866. They located an eligible plot of land, tracked down a federal registrar and paid the filing fees, enclosed the land with a fence, built a house, planted and harvested a crop, and paid property taxes.

Chris Rock, comedian and actor, is the great-great-grandson of Julius Caesar Tingman, a slave in South

Reconstruction and the South 15

((•—[Hear the Audio **Chapter 15 at www.myhistorylab.com**

- In *Dressing for the Carnival* (1877), Winslow Homer shows a family of former slaves dressing in gaudy strips of clothing to celebrate the West African festival of Jonkonnu—an illustration of the power of family ties and cultural traditions. Source: Winslow Homer,1836–1910, (American), *Dressing for the Carnival.* Oil on canvas. H. 20 in. W. 30 in. (50.8 × 76.2 cm.) Signed, inscribed and dated (lower right): Winslow Homer N.A./1877. The Metropolitan Museum of Art, Amelia B. Lazarus Fund, 1922 (22.220). Photograph ©1980 by The Metropolitan Museum of Art.

Carolina. In March 1865, a few weeks after Sherman had marched through South Carolina, Tingman joined the U.S. Colored Troops in the Union army. Three years later, at the age of twenty-four, he was elected to the "reconstructed" South Carolina legislature. The withdrawal of federal troops from the South in 1877 brought an end to Reconstruction—and to Tingman's career in politics. He, too, managed to buy a farm.

Such accounts add another dimension to the usual narrative of the Reconstruction era (1865–1877). The period began with the liberal readmission of southern states to the Union as proposed by Lincoln and his successor, Andrew Johnson. Once readmitted, southern states restricted the rights of former slaves through a series of "Black Codes." A furious Republican Congress responded by overturning white southern rule through a series of laws and constitutional amendments that empowered former slaves—and their Republican allies. A white backlash, often violent, followed Republican rule. Ultimately, white political power was restored, and a corrupt bargain secured the presidency for the Republican, Hayes. When Hayes removed Union troops from the South in 1877, Reconstruction was over.

Deprived of federal assistance, former slaves were obliged to make do on their own. Many failed. Only

10 percent of freed slaves acquired farms. But the ancestors of Oprah Winfrey, Whoopi Goldberg, Chris Rock, and many others prove that *some* former slaves succeeded, almost entirely through their own efforts. Harvard historian Louis Henry Gates, Jr., whose *In Search of Our Roots* (2009) recounted their stories and many similar ones, hoped that someday such accounts would move history "from our kitchens or parlors into the texts, ultimately changing the official narrative of American history itself." This chapter describes the era's bitter wrangles and recriminations, its political failures and disappointments, but it also shows that many survived and even flourished during these difficult years. ∎

The Assassination of Lincoln

On April 5, 1865, Abraham Lincoln visited Richmond. The fallen capital lay in ruins, sections blackened by fire, but the president was able to walk the streets unmolested and almost unattended.

Everywhere African Americans crowded around him worshipfully; some fell to their knees as he passed, crying "Glory, Hallelujah," hailing him as a messiah. Even white townspeople seemed to have accepted defeat without resentment.

A few days later, in Washington, Lincoln delivered an important speech on Reconstruction, urging compassion and open-mindedness. On April 14 he held a Cabinet meeting at which postwar readjustment was considered at length. That evening, while Lincoln was watching a performance of the play *Our American Cousin* at Ford's Theater, an actor, John Wilkes Booth, slipped into his box and shot him in the back of the head with a small pistol. Early the next morning, without having regained consciousness, Lincoln died.

The murder was part of a complicated plot organized by die-hard Southerners. One of Booth's accomplices went to the home of Secretary of State William Seward and stabbed him—Seward recovered from his wounds. A third conspirator, assigned to kill Vice President Andrew Johnson, changed his mind and fled Washington. Seldom have fanatics displayed so little understanding of their own

Richmond, Virginia lies in ruins in April, 1865 at the time of Lincoln's visit—and a few days before his assassination.

interests, for with Lincoln perished the South's best hope for a mild peace. After his body had been taken home to Illinois, the national mood hardened; apparently the awesome drama was still unfolding—retribution and a final humbling of the South were inevitable.

Presidential Reconstruction

Despite its bloodiness, the Civil War had caused less intersectional hatred than might have been expected. Although civilian property was often seized or destroyed, the invading armies treated the southern population with forbearance, both during the war and after Appomattox. While Confederate President Davis was ensconced in Richmond behind Lee's army, Northerners boasted that they would "hang Jeff Davis to a sour apple tree," and when he was captured in Georgia in May 1865 he was at once clapped into irons preparatory to being tried for treason and murder. But feeling against Davis subsided quickly. In 1867 the military turned him over to the civil courts, which released him on bail.

President Andrew Johnson poses regally with carefully manicured fingernails. Although Johnson hated southern aristocrats, he sometimes craved their approval.

Ben Wade, leader of the Radical Republicans, co-authored the Wade-Davis Bill (1864) to restrict readmission of southern states to the Union. Lincoln refused to sign the bill; Wade was subsequently accused of scheming to become president.

He was never brought to trial. (His wife, Varina Davis, eventually became a close friend of Julia Dent Grant, widow of Ulysses S. Grant.) A few other Confederate officials spent short periods behind bars, but the only Southerner executed for war crimes was Major Henry Wirz, the commandant of Andersonville military prison.

The legal questions related to bringing the defeated states back into the Union were extremely complex. Since Southerners believed that secession was legal, logic should have compelled them to argue that they were out of the Union and would thus have to be formally readmitted. Northerners should have taken the contrary position, for they had fought to prove that secession was illegal. Yet the people of both sections did just the opposite. Senator Charles Sumner and Congressman Thaddeus Stevens, who in 1861 had been uncompromising expounders of the theory that the Union was indissoluble, now insisted that the Confederate states had "committed suicide" and should be treated like "conquered provinces." Lincoln believed the issue a "pernicious abstraction" and tried to ignore it.

The process of readmission began in 1862, when Lincoln reappointed provisional governors for those parts of the South that had been occupied by federal troops. On December 8, 1863, he issued a proclamation setting forth a general policy. With the exception of high Confederate officials and a few other special groups, all Southerners could reinstate themselves as United States citizens by taking a simple loyalty oath. When, in any state, a number equal to 10 percent of those voting in the 1860 election had taken this oath, they could set up a state government. Under this **Ten Percent Plan**, such governments had to be republican in form, must recognize the "permanent freedom" of the slaves, and must provide for black education. The plan, however, did not require that blacks be given the right to vote.

The Ten Percent Plan reflected Lincoln's lack of vindictiveness and his political wisdom. He realized that any government based on such a small minority of the population would be, as he put it, merely "a tangible nucleus which the remainder . . . may rally around as fast as it can," a sort of puppet regime, like the paper government established in those sections of Virginia under federal control.[1] The regimes established under this plan in Tennessee, Louisiana, and Arkansas bore, in the president's mind, the same relation to finally reconstructed states that an egg bears to a chicken. "We shall sooner have the fowl by hatching it than by smashing it," he remarked. He knew that eventually representatives of the southern states would again be sitting in Congress, and he wished to lay the groundwork for a strong Republican party in the section. Yet he realized that Congress had no intention of seating representatives from the "10 percent" states at once.

The Radicals in Congress disliked the Ten Percent Plan, partly because of its moderation and partly because it enabled Lincoln to determine Union policy toward the recaptured regions. In July 1864 they passed the **Wade-Davis bill**, which provided for constitutional conventions only after a majority of the others in a southern state had taken a loyalty oath. Confederate officials and anyone who had "voluntarily borne arms against the United States" were barred

from voting in the election or serving at the convention. Besides prohibiting slavery, the new state constitutions would have to repudiate Confederate debts. Lincoln disposed of the Wade-Davis bill with a pocket veto and that's where matters stood when Andrew Johnson became president following the assassination.

Lincoln had picked Johnson for a running mate in 1864 because he was a border-state Unionist Democrat and something of a hero as a result of his courageous service as military governor of Tennessee. His political strength came from the poor whites and yeomen farmers of eastern Tennessee, and he was fond of extolling the common man and attacking "stuck-up aristocrats."

Thaddeus Stevens called Johnson a "rank demagogue" and a "damned scoundrel," and it is true that Johnson was a masterful rabble-rouser. But few men of his generation labored so consistently on behalf of small farmers. Free homesteads, public education, absolute social equality—such were his objectives. The father of communism, Karl Marx, a close observer of American affairs at this time, wrote approvingly of Johnson's "deadly hatred of the oligarchy."

Johnson was a Democrat, but because of his record and his reassuring penchant for excoriating southern aristocrats, the Republicans in Congress were ready to cooperate with him. "Johnson, we have faith in you," said Senator Ben Wade, author of the Wade-Davis bill, the day after Lincoln's death. "By the gods, there will be no trouble now in running the government!"

Johnson's reply, "Treason must be made infamous," delighted the Radicals, but the president proved temperamentally unable to work with them. Like Randolph of Roanoke, his antithesis intellectually and socially, opposition was his specialty; he soon alienated every powerful Republican in Washington.

Radical Republicans listened to Johnson's diatribes against secessionists and the great planters and assumed that he was anti-southern. Nothing could have been further from the truth. He had great respect for states' rights and he shared most of his poor white Tennessee constituents' contempt of blacks. "Damn the negroes, I am fighting these traitorous aristocrats, their masters," he told a friend during the war. "I wish to God," he said on another occasion, "every head of a family in the United States had one slave to take the drudgery and menial service off his family."

The new president did not want to injure or humiliate all white Southerners. He issued an amnesty proclamation only slightly more rigorous than Lincoln's. It

---

[1]By approving the separation of the western counties that had refused to secede, this government had provided a legal pretext for the creation of West Virginia in 1863.

assumed, correctly enough, that with the war over most southern voters would freely take the loyalty oath; thus it contained no 10 percent clause. More classes of Confederates, including those who owned taxable property in excess of $20,000, were excluded from the general pardon. By the time Congress convened in December 1865, all the southern states had organized governments, ratified the **Thirteenth Amendment** abolishing slavery, and elected senators and representatives. Johnson promptly recommended these new governments to the attention of Congress.

Republican Radicals

Peace found the Republicans in Congress no more united than they had been during the war. A small group of "ultra" Radicals were demanding immediate and absolute civil and political equality for blacks; they should be given, for example, the vote, a plot of land, and access to a decent education. Senator Sumner led this faction. A second group of Radicals, headed by Thaddeus Stevens in the House and Ben Wade in the Senate, agreed with the ultras' objectives but were prepared to accept half a loaf if necessary to win the support of less radical colleagues.

Nearly all Radicals distinguished between the "natural" God-given rights described in the Declaration of Independence, and social equality. "Equality," said Stevens, "does not mean that a negro shall sit in the same seat or eat at the same table with a white man. That is a matter of taste which every man must decide for himself." This did not reflect personal prejudice in Stevens's case. When he died, he was buried in a black cemetery. The moderate Republicans wanted to protect the former slaves from exploitation and guarantee their basic rights but were unprepared to push for full political equality. A handful of Republicans sided with the Democrats in support of Johnson's approach, but all the rest insisted at least on the minimal demands of the moderates. Thus Johnsonian Reconstruction was doomed.

Johnson's proposal had no chance in Congress for reasons having little to do with black rights. The Thirteenth Amendment had the effect of increasing the representation of the southern states in Congress because it made the Three-fifths Compromise meaningless (see Chapter 5). Henceforth those who had been slaves would be counted as whole persons in apportioning seats in the House of Representatives. If Congress seated the Southerners, the balance of power might swing to the Democrats. To expect the

Republicans to surrender power in such a fashion was unrealistic. Former Copperheads gushing with extravagant praise for Johnson put them instantly on guard.

Southern voters had further provoked northern resentment by their choice of congressmen. Georgia elected Alexander H. Stephens, vice president of the Confederacy, to the Senate, although he was still in a federal prison awaiting trial for treason! Several dozen men who had served in the Confederate Congress had been elected to either the House or the Senate, together with four generals and many other high officials. Voters in the South understandably selected locally respected and experienced leaders, but it was equally reasonable that these choices would sit poorly with Northerners.

Finally, the so-called **Black Codes** enacted by southern governments to control former slaves alarmed the North. These varied in severity from state to state, but all, as one planter admitted, set out to keep the blacks "as near to a state of bondage as possible."

When seen in historical perspective, even the strictest codes represented some improvement over slavery. Most permitted blacks to sue and to testify in court, at least in cases involving members of their own race. Blacks were allowed to own certain kinds of property. However, blacks could not bear arms, be employed in occupations other than farming and domestic service, or leave their jobs without forfeiting back pay. The Mississippi code required them to sign labor contracts for the year in January, and, in addition, drunkards, vagrants, beggars, "common night-walkers," "mischief makers," and persons who "misspend what they earn" and who could not pay the stiff fines assessed for such misbehavior were to be "hired out . . . at public outcry" to the white persons who would take them for the shortest period in return for paying the fines. Such laws, apparently designed to get around the Thirteenth Amendment, outraged Northerners.

Read the **Document** *The Mississippi Black Code* at www.myhistorylab.com

Congress Rejects Johnsonian Reconstruction

For all these reasons the Republicans in Congress rejected Johnsonian Reconstruction. Quickly they created a joint committee on Reconstruction, headed by Senator William P. Fessenden of Maine, a moderate, to study the question of readmitting the southern states.

SCENES IN MEMPHIS, TENNESSEE, DURING THE RIOT—SHOOTING DOWN NEGROES ON THE MORNING OF MAY 2, 1866.—[SKETCHED BY A. R. W.]

After Union troops seized Memphis in 1862, liberated slaves flocked to the city. By 1865, its black population had increased from 3,000 to 20,000. In May, 1866 racial tensions ignited a riot that killed forty-six blacks and two whites. The slaughter of so many blacks angered Republicans and weakened Johnson.

The committee held public hearings that produced much evidence of the mistreatment of blacks. Colonel George A. Custer, stationed in Texas, testified: "It is of weekly, if not of daily occurrence that Freedmen are murdered." The nurse Clara Barton told a gruesome tale about a pregnant woman who had been brutally whipped. Others described the intimidation of blacks by poor whites. The hearings strengthened the Radicals, who had been claiming all along that the South was perpetuating slavery under another name.

President Johnson's attitude speeded the swing toward the Radical position. While the hearings were in progress, Congress passed a bill expanding and extending the **Freedmen's Bureau**, which had been established in March 1865 to care for refugees. The bureau, a branch of the war department, was already exercising considerable coercive and supervisory power in the South. Now Congress sought to add to its authority in order to protect the black population.

Although the bill had wide support, Johnson vetoed it, arguing that it was an unconstitutional extension of military authority in peacetime. Congress then passed a Civil Rights Act that, besides declaring specifically that blacks were citizens of the United States, denied the states the power to restrict their rights to testify in court, to make contracts for their labor, and to hold property. In other words, it put teeth in the Thirteenth Amendment.

Once again the president refused to go along, although his veto was sure to drive more moderates into the arms of the Radicals. On April 9, 1866, Congress repassed the Civil Rights Act by a two-thirds majority, the first time in American history that a major piece of legislation became law over the veto of a president. This event marked a revolution in the history of Reconstruction. Thereafter Congress, not President Johnson, had the upper hand.

In the clash between the president and Congress, Johnson was his own worst enemy. His language was often intemperate, his handling of opponents inept, his analysis of southern conditions incorrect. He had assumed that the small southern farmers who made up the majority in the Confederacy shared his prejudices against the planter class. They did not, as their choices in the postwar elections demonstrated. In fact, Johnson's hatred of the southern aristocracy may have been based more on jealousy than on principle. Under the Reconstruction plan, persons excluded from the blanket amnesty could apply individually for the restoration of their rights. When wealthy and socially prominent Southerners flocked to Washington, hat in hand, he found their flattery and humility exhilarating. He issued pardons wholesale. "I did not expect to keep out all who were excluded from the amnesty," he explained. "I intended they should sue for pardon, and so realize the enormity of their crime."

The president misread northern opinion. He believed that Congress had no right to pass laws affecting the South before southern representatives had been readmitted to Congress. However, in the light of the refusal of most southern whites to grant any real power or responsibility to the freedmen (an attitude that Johnson did not condemn), the public would not accept this point of view. Johnson placed his own judgment over that of the overwhelming majority of northern voters, and this was a great error, morally and tactically. By encouraging white Southerners to resist efforts to improve the lot of blacks, Johnson played into the hands of the Radicals.

The Radicals encountered grave problems in fighting for their program. Northerners might object to the Black Codes and to seating "rebels" in Congress, but few believed in racial equality. Between 1865 and 1868, Wisconsin, Minnesota, Connecticut, Nebraska, New Jersey, Ohio, Michigan, and Pennsylvania all rejected bills granting blacks the vote.

The Radicals were in effect demanding not merely equal rights for freedmen but extra rights; not merely the vote but special protection of that right against the pressure that southern whites would surely apply to undermine it. This idea flew in the face of conventional American beliefs in equality before the law and individual self-reliance. Such protection would involve interference by the federal government in local affairs, a concept at variance with American practice. Events were to show that the Radicals were correct—that what amounted to a political revolution in state–federal relations was essential if blacks were to achieve real

equality. But in the climate of that day their proposals encountered bitter resistance, and not only from white Southerners.

Thus, while the Radicals sought partisan advantage in their battle with Johnson and sometimes played on war-bred passions in achieving their ends, they were taking large political risks in defense of genuinely held principles.

Read the **Document** *Southern Skepticism of the Freedmen's Bureau* at **www.myhistorylab.com**

The Fourteenth Amendment

In June 1866 Congress submitted to the states a new amendment to the Constitution. The **Fourteenth Amendment** was, in the context of the times, a truly radical measure. Never before had newly freed slaves been granted significant political rights. For example, in the British Caribbean sugar islands, where slavery had been abolished in the 1830s, stiff property qualifications and poll taxes kept freedmen from voting. The Fourteenth Amendment was also a milestone along the road to the centralization of political power in the United States because it reduced the power of all the states. In this sense it confirmed the great change wrought by the Civil War: the growth of a more complex, more closely integrated social and economic structure requiring closer national supervision. Few people understood this aspect of the amendment at the time.

First the amendment supplied a broad definition of American citizenship: "All persons born or naturalized in the United States, and subject to the jurisdiction thereof, are citizens of the United States and of the State wherein they reside." Obviously this included blacks. Then it struck at discriminatory legislation like the Black Codes: "No State shall make or enforce any law which shall abridge the privileges or immunities of citizens of the United States; nor shall any State deprive any person of life, liberty, or property, without due process of law." The next section attempted to force the southern states to permit blacks to vote. If a state denied the vote to any class of its adult male citizens, its representation was to be reduced proportionally. Under another clause, former federal officials who had served the Confederacy were barred from holding either state or federal office unless specifically pardoned by a two-thirds vote of Congress. Finally, the Confederate debt was repudiated.

While the amendment did not specifically outlaw segregation or prevent a state from disenfranchising blacks, the southern states would have none of it. Without them the necessary three-fourths majority of the states could not be obtained.

President Johnson vowed to make the choice between the Fourteenth Amendment and his own policy the main issue of the 1866 congressional elections. He embarked on "a swing around the circle" to rally the public to his cause. He failed dismally. Northern women objected to the implication in the amendment that black men were more fitted to vote than white women, but a large majority of northern voters was determined that African Americans must have at least formal legal equality. The Republicans won better than two-thirds of the seats in both houses, together with control of all the northern state governments. Johnson emerged from the campaign discredited, the Radicals stronger and determined to have their way. The southern states, Congressman James A. Garfield of Ohio said in February 1867, have "flung back into our teeth the magnanimous offer of a generous nation. It is now our turn to act."

●◆●─|Read the **Document** *13th, 14th, and 15th Amendments* at **www.myhistorylab.com**

◉─|See the **Map** *Reconstruction* at **www.myhistorylab.com**

The Reconstruction Acts

Had the southern states been willing to accept the Fourteenth Amendment, coercive measures might have been avoided. Their recalcitrance and continuing indications that local authorities were persecuting blacks finally led to the passage, on March 2, 1867, of the First Reconstruction Act. This law divided the former Confederacy—exclusive of Tennessee, which had ratified the Fourteenth Amendment—into five military districts, each controlled by a major general. It gave these officers almost dictatorial power to protect the civil rights of "all persons," maintain order, and supervise the administration of justice. To rid themselves of military rule, the former states were required to adopt new state constitutions guaranteeing blacks the right to vote and disenfranchising broad classes of ex-Confederates. If the new constitutions proved satisfactory to Congress, and if the new governments ratified the Fourteenth Amendment, their representatives would be admitted to Congress and military rule ended. Johnson's veto of the act was easily overridden.

Although drastic, the Reconstruction Act was so vague that it proved unworkable. Military control was easily established. But in deference to moderate Republican views, the law had not spelled out the process by which the new constitutions were to be drawn up. Southern whites preferred the status quo, even under army control, to enfranchising blacks and retiring their own respected leaders. They made no effort to follow the steps laid down in the law. Congress therefore passed a second act, requiring the military authorities to register voters and supervise the election of delegates to constitutional conventions. A third act further clarified procedures.

Still white Southerners resisted. The laws required that the constitutions be approved by a majority of the registered voters. Simply by staying away from the polls, whites prevented ratification in state after state. At last, in March 1868, a full year after the First Reconstruction Act, Congress changed the rules again. The constitutions were to be ratified by a majority of the voters. In June 1868 Arkansas, having fulfilled the requirements, was readmitted to the Union, and by July a sufficient number of states had ratified the Fourteenth Amendment to make it part of the Constitution. But it was not until July 1870 that the last southern state, Georgia, qualified to the satisfaction of Congress.

Congress Supreme

To carry out this program in the face of determined southern resistance required a degree of single-mindedness over a long period seldom demonstrated by an American legislature. The persistence resulted in part from the suffering and frustrations of the war years. The refusal of the South to accept the spirit of even the mild reconstruction designed by Johnson goaded the North to ever more overbearing efforts to bring the ex-Confederates to heel. President Johnson's stubbornness also influenced the Republicans. They became obsessed with the need to defeat him. The unsettled times and the large Republican majorities, always threatened by the possibility of a Democratic resurgence if "unreconstructed" southern congressmen were readmitted, sustained their determination.

These considerations led Republicans to attempt a kind of grand revision of the federal government, one that almost destroyed the balance between judicial, executive, and legislative power established in 1789. A series of measures passed between 1866 and 1868 increased the authority of Congress over the army, over the process of amending the Constitution, and over Cabinet members

Thaddeus Stevens is carried to an Andrew Johnson impeachment committee meeting in 1868. Stevens, a Radical Republican, insisted on being buried in a black cemetery. He wrote his own epitaph: "I repose in this quiet and secluded spot, not from any natural preference for solitude, but finding other cemeteries limited as to race, I have chosen this that I might illustrate in my death the principles which I advocated through a long life, equality of man before his Creator."

and lesser appointive officers. Even the Supreme Court was affected. Its size was reduced and its jurisdiction over civil rights cases limited. Finally, in a showdown caused by emotion more than by practical considerations, the Republicans attempted to remove President Johnson from office.

Johnson was a poor president and out of touch with public opinion, but he had done nothing to merit ejection from office. While he had a low opinion of African Americans, his opinion was so widely shared by whites that it is ahistorical to condemn him as a reactionary on this ground. Johnson believed that he was fighting to preserve constitutional government. He was honest and devoted to duty, and his record easily withstood the most searching examination. When Congress passed laws taking away powers granted him by the Constitution, he refused to submit.

The chief issue was the Tenure of Office Act of 1867, which prohibited the president from removing officials who had been appointed with the consent of the Senate without first obtaining Senate approval. In February 1868 Johnson "violated" this act by dismissing Secretary of War Edwin M. Stanton, who had been openly in sympathy with the Radicals for some time. The House, acting under the procedure set up in the Constitution for removing the president, promptly impeached him before the bar of the Senate, Chief Justice Salmon P. Chase presiding.

In the trial, Johnson's lawyers easily established that he had removed Stanton only in an effort to prove the Tenure of Office Act unconstitutional. They demonstrated that the act did not protect Stanton to begin with, since it gave Cabinet members tenure "during the term of the President by whom they may have been appointed," and Stanton had been appointed in 1862, during Lincoln's first term!

Nevertheless the Radicals pressed the charges (eleven separate articles) relentlessly. To the argument that Johnson had committed no crime, the learned Senator Sumner retorted that the proceedings were "political in character" rather than judicial. Thaddeus Stevens, directing the attack on behalf of the House, warned the senators that although "no corrupt or wicked motive" could be attributed to Johnson, they would "be tortured on the gibbet of everlasting obloquy" if they did not convict him. Tremendous pressure was applied to the handful of Republican senators who were unwilling to disregard the evidence.

Seven of them resisted to the end, and the Senate failed by a single vote to convict Johnson. This was probably fortunate. The trial weakened the presidency, but if Johnson had been forced from office on such flimsy grounds, the independence of the executive might have been permanently undermined. Then the legislative branch would have become supreme.

The Fifteenth Amendment

The failure of the impeachment did not affect the course of Reconstruction. The president was acquitted on May 16, 1868. A few days later, the Republican National Convention nominated General Ulysses S. Grant for the presidency. At the Democratic convention Johnson had considerable support, but the delegates nominated Horatio Seymour, a former governor of New York. In November Grant won an easy victory

Thomas Waterman Wood, a Northerner, painted this hopeful interpretation of Reconstruction, *His First Vote* (1868).

in the Electoral College, 214 to 80, but the popular vote was close: 3 million to 2.7 million. Although he would probably have carried the Electoral College in any case, Grant's margin in the popular vote was supplied by southern blacks enfranchised under the Reconstruction acts, about 450,000 of

whom supported him. A majority of white voters probably preferred Seymour. Since many citizens undoubtedly voted Republican because of personal admiration for General Grant, the election statistics suggest that a substantial white majority opposed the policies of the Radicals.

Racist depictions of Reconstruction were common. This one by Thomas Nast was entitled "Colored Rule in a Reconstructed (?) State" and appeared in *Harper's Weekly* (1874). In 1902 Columbia historian William A. Dunning similarly declared that free slaves were mere children, incapable of holding office. Under Reconstruction, the South was plunged into chaos and corruption. This view of Reconstruction prevailed in the public mind largely as a consequence of film director D. W. Griffith's *The Birth of a Nation* (1915), a triumph of cinematic art and racist caricature. In 1910 W. E. B. Du Bois, an African American scholar, was the first to applaud Reconstruction for broadening educational opportunities and democratizing government, but few historians concurred. In the 1960s, as the civil rights movement was gaining momentum, more scholars came out in support of Reconstruction. In 1965 Kenneth Stampp emphasized the Reconstruction governments' attempts to protect freedmen; that same year, Joel Williamson turned Dunning's thesis on its head and endorsed nearly all aspects of Reconstruction. More recent scholars have generally taken a moderate position: Reconstruction may have failed, but its accomplishments under difficult circumstances of white opposition were substantial; see, for example, Eric Foner (1988). In recent decades, scholars have shifted from these larger assessments to more focused work on particular regions and on issues of class and gender. Susan Eva O'Donovan (2007), for example, shows how slaves themselves developed survival strategies, including women's prominent role in devising a "free-labor" system for sharecropping. Certain facts are beyond argument. Black officeholders during Reconstruction were neither numerous nor inordinately influential. None was ever elected governor of a state; fewer than a dozen and a half during the entire period served in Congress.

Source: William A. Dunning, *Reconstruction and the Constitution* (1902), W. E. B. Du Bois, *Black Reconstruction in America* (1935), Kenneth Stampp, *The Peculiar Institution* (1965), Joel Williamson, *After Slavery* (1965), Eric Foner, *Reconstruction* (1988), Susan Eva O'Donovan, *Becoming Free in the Cotton South* (2007).

The Reconstruction acts and the ratification of the Fourteenth Amendment achieved the purpose of enabling black Southerners to vote. The Radicals, however, were not satisfied; despite the unpopularity of the idea in the North, they wished to guarantee the right of blacks to vote in every state. Another amendment seemed the only way to accomplish this objective, but passage of such an amendment appeared impossible. The Republican platform in the 1868 election had smugly distinguished between blacks voting in the South ("demanded by every consideration of public safety, of gratitude, and of justice") and in the North (where the question "properly belongs to the people").

However, after the election had demonstrated how important the black vote could be, Republican strategy shifted. Grant had carried Indiana by fewer than 10,000 votes and lost New York by a similar number. If blacks in these and other closely divided states had voted, Republican strength would have been greatly enhanced.

Suddenly Congress blossomed with suffrage amendments. After considerable bickering over details, the **Fifteenth Amendment** was sent to the states for ratification in February 1869. It forbade all the states to deny the vote to anyone "on account of race, color, or previous condition of servitude." Once again nothing was said about denial of the vote on the basis of sex, which caused feminists, such as Elizabeth Cady Stanton, to be even more outraged than they had been by the Fourteenth Amendment.

Most southern states, still under federal pressure, ratified the amendment swiftly. The same was true in most of New England and in some western states. Bitter battles were waged in Connecticut, New York, Pennsylvania, and the states immediately north of the Ohio River, but by March 1870 most of them had ratified the amendment and it became part of the Constitution.

The debates occasioned by these conventions show that partisan advantage was not the only reason why voters approved black suffrage at last. The unfairness of a double standard of voting in North and South, the contribution of black soldiers during the war, and the hope that by passing the amendment the strife of Reconstruction could finally be ended all played a part.

When the Fifteenth Amendment went into effect, President Grant called it "the greatest civil change and . . . the most important event that has occurred since the nation came to life." The American Anti-Slavery Society formally dissolved itself, its work apparently completed. "The Fifteenth Amendment confers upon the African race the care of its own destiny," Radical Congressman James A. Garfield wrote proudly after the amendment was ratified. "It places their fortunes in their own hands."

Many of the celebrants lived to see the amendment subverted in the South. That it could be evaded by literacy tests and other restrictions was apparent at the time and may even have influenced some persons who voted for it. But a stronger amendment—one, for instance, that positively granted the right to vote to all men and put the supervision of elections under national control—could not have been ratified.

"Black Republican" Reconstruction: Scalawags and Carpetbaggers

The Radicals had at last succeeded in imposing their will on the South. Throughout the region former slaves had real political influence; they voted, held office, and exercised the "privileges" and enjoyed the "immunities" guaranteed them by the Fourteenth Amendment. Nearly all voted Republican.

The spectacle of blacks not five years removed from slavery in positions of power and responsibility attracted much attention. But the real rulers of the "black Republican" governments were white: the **scalawags**—Southerners willing to cooperate with the Republicans because they accepted the results of the war and wished to advance their own interests—and the **carpetbaggers**—Northerners who went to the South as idealists to help the freed slaves as employees of the federal government, or more commonly as settlers hoping to improve themselves.

The scalawags were by far the more numerous. A few were prewar politicians or well-to-do planters, men such as the Mississippi planter John L. Alcorn and Joseph E. Brown, the Confederate governor of Georgia. General James Longstreet, one of Lee's most important lieutenants, was another prominent Southerner who cooperated with the Republicans. But most were people who had supported the Whig party before the secession crisis and who saw the Republicans as the logical successors of the Whigs.

The carpetbaggers were a particularly varied lot. Most had mixed motives for coming south and personal gain was certainly among them. But so were opposition to slavery and the belief that blacks deserved to be treated decently and given a chance to get ahead in the world.

Many northern blacks became carpetbaggers: former Union soldiers, missionaries from northern black churches, and also teachers, lawyers, and other members of the small northern black professional class. Many of these became officeholders, but like southern black politicians their influence was limited.

That blacks should fail to dominate southern governments is certainly understandable. They lacked experience in politics and were mostly poor and uneducated. They were nearly everywhere a minority. Those blacks who held office during Reconstruction tended to be better educated and more prosperous than most southern blacks. A disproportionate number had been free before the war. Of those freed by the Thirteenth Amendment, a large percentage had been house servants or artisans, not field hands. Mulatto politicians were also disproportionately numerous and (as a group) more conservative and economically better off than other black leaders.

In South Carolina and elsewhere, blacks proved in the main able and conscientious public servants: able because the best tended to rise to the top in such a fluid situation, and conscientious because most of those who achieved importance sought eagerly to demonstrate the capacity of their race for self-government. Even at the local level, where the quality of officials was usually poor, there was little difference in the degree of competence displayed by white and black officeholders. In power, the blacks were not vindictive; by and large they did not seek to restrict the rights of ex-Confederates.

Not all black legislators and administrators were paragons of virtue. In South Carolina, despite their control of the legislature, they broke up into factions repeatedly and failed to press for laws that would improve the lot of poor black farm workers. In *The Prostrate South* (1874), James S. Pike, a northern newspaperman, wrote, "The rule of South Carolina should not be dignified with the name of government. It is the installation of a huge system of brigandage." Like many northern commentators, Pike exaggerated the immorality and incompetence of the blacks, but waste and corruption were common during Reconstruction governments. Half the budget of Louisiana in some years went for salaries and "mileage" for representatives and their staffs. One Arkansas black took $9,000 from the state for repairing a bridge that had cost only $500 to build. A South Carolina legislator was voted an additional $1,000 in salary after he lost that sum betting on a horse race.

However, the corruption must be seen in perspective. The big thieves were nearly always white; blacks got mostly crumbs. Furthermore, graft and callous disregard of the public interest characterized government in every section and at every level during the decade after Appomattox. Big-city bosses in the North embezzled sums that dwarfed the most brazen southern frauds. The New York City Tweed Ring probably made off with more money than all the southern thieves, black and white, combined. While the evidence does not justify the southern corruption, it suggests that the unique features of Reconstruction politics—black suffrage, military supervision, and carpetbagger and scalawag influence—do not explain it.

In fact, the Radical southern governments accomplished a great deal. They spent money freely but not entirely wastefully. Tax rates zoomed, but the money financed the repair and expansion of the South's dilapidated railroad network, rebuilt crumbling levees, and expanded social services. Before the Civil War, southern planters possessed a disproportionate share of political as well as economic power, and they spent relatively little public money on education and public services of all kinds.

During Reconstruction an enormous gap had to be filled, and it took money to fill it. The Freedmen's Bureau made a major contribution. Northern religious and philanthropic organizations also did important work. Eventually, however, the state governments established and supported hospitals, asylums, and systems of free public education that, while segregated, greatly benefited everyone, whites as well as blacks. Much state money was also spent on economic development: land reclamation, repairing and expanding the war-ravaged railroads, maintaining levees.

The former slaves grasped eagerly at the opportunities to learn. Schools and other institutions were supported chiefly by property taxes, and these, of course, hit well-to-do planters hard. Hence much of the complaining about the "extravagance" of Reconstruction governments concealed traditional selfish objections to paying for public projects. Eventually the benefits of expanded government services to the entire population became clear, and when white supremacy was reestablished, most of the new services remained in force, and the corruption and inefficiency inherited from the carpetbagger governments continued.

Watch the Video *The Schools that the Civil War & Reconstruction created at* **www.myhistorylab.com**

The Politics of Reconstruction

Triumph of the Republican Party in the South, 1870

In the late 1860s the rise of the Republican party was due both to the weakness of the southern Democrats and to the enfranchisement of black men. African Americans voted solidly Republican—the party of Lincoln—and they exercised their vote diligently. In many elections, black voter turnout approached 90 percent. "It is the hardest thing in the world to keep a negro away from the polls," complained a white Alabama politician.

The power of the black vote in 1870 is demonstrated in the accompanying map. Of the fifteen congressional districts that encompassed the interior counties from Louisiana through South Carolina, it was in the Cotton Belt, where blacks comprised the majority, that Republican candidates

won fourteen seats. Throughout the South, Republicans took thirty-one of the fifty-seven seats in the House of Representatives. In the three states where blacks outnumbered whites—South Carolina, Mississippi, and Louisiana—the Republicans won every House seat.

Five blacks were among the Republican victors. With the exception of Josiah Walls, a former slave who had fought with the Union army and represented Florida, all of the blacks were from areas with a substantial black majority: three from South Carolina, the other from Alabama.

"Carpetbaggers," Republicans from the North, were also strong in the areas where blacks had a majority, especially Louisiana, Mississippi, and Virginia. Except for the two congressional districts in lower Louisiana, no "carpetbaggers" won House seats where blacks did not constitute a majority of the population.

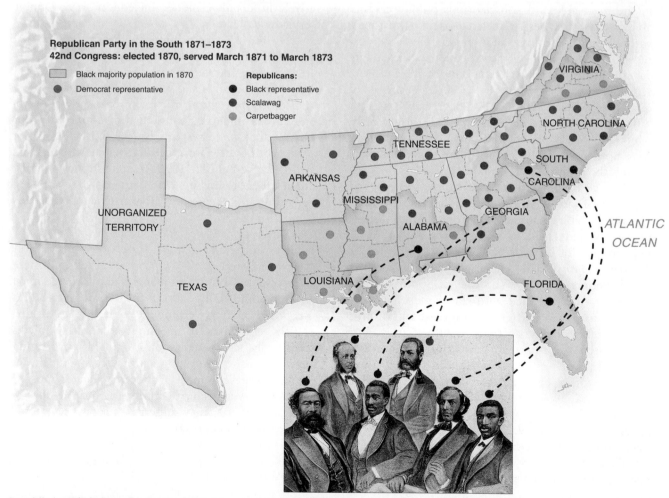

Republicans Win in Deep South The six black members of the House of Representatives in 1871 are from left to right: Benjamin Turner, Robert De Large, Josiah Wells, Jefferson Long, Joseph Rainey, Robert Brown Elliott. Each is linked to his district; the member in the blue coat—center—is not connected to a "black" dot. A special Republican primary replaced him with a scalawag.

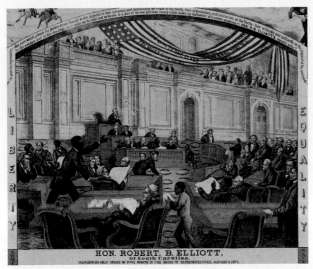

HON. ROBERT. B. ELLIOTT,
of South Carolina.

Robert Brown Elliott of South Carolina, addresses Congress in 1872.

The Freedmen's Bureau built 4,329 schools, attended by some 250,000 former slaves, in the postwar South. Many of the teachers in these schools were abolitionists or missionaries from New England. The schools drew African Americans of all ages, from children to grandparents, who were eager for the advantages offered by education.

"Scalawags," white Southerners who endorsed the Republican party, did take some seats in areas with white majorities. Usually these victories were in districts that had been Whig strongholds.

Collapse of the Republican Party in the South, 1878

With the Compromise of 1877 and subsequent withdrawal of Union troops, the Republican political power in the South collapsed. Tennessee, excluded from the Union military district, never experienced a period of Republican domination; in Virginia, the Democrats were firmly back in power by 1869.

Questions for Discussion

■ Which states had elected solely Republican representatives in 1870?

■ How did these states vote in 1878? What explains the shift?

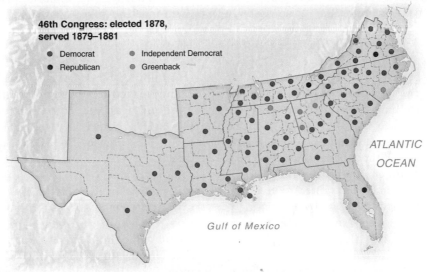

46th Congress: elected 1878, served 1879–1881

● Democrat   ● Independent Democrat
● Republican   ● Greenback

ATLANTIC OCEAN

Gulf of Mexico

Demise of the Republican Party in the South By 1878, Democrats, all of them white, recaptured seventy-seven of the eighty-three House seats in the South. All of the black House representatives had been defeated. No Republican was elected in Texas, Arkansas, Louisiana, Mississippi, Alabama, Georgia, South Carolina, or North Carolina. The South was not exactly "solid"—independent Democrats and Greenback representatives won a handful of seats. But the South would remain a Democratic bastion for over a century.

The Ravaged Land

The South's grave economic problems complicated the rebuilding of its political system. The section had never been as prosperous as the North, and wartime destruction left it desperately poor by any standard. In the long run the abolition of slavery released immeasurable quantities of human energy previously stifled, but the immediate effect was to create confusion. Freedom to move without a pass, to "see the world," was one of the former slaves' most cherished benefits of emancipation. Understandably, many at first equated legal freedom with freedom from having to earn a living, a tendency reinforced for a time by the willingness of the Freedmen's Bureau to provide rations and other forms of relief in war-devastated areas. Most, however, soon accepted the fact that they must earn a living; a small plot of land of their own ("40 acres and a mule") would complete their independence.

This objective was forcefully supported by the relentless Congressman Thaddeus Stevens, whose hatred of the planter class was pathological. "The property of the chief rebels should be seized," he stated. If the lands of the richest "70,000 proud, bloated and defiant rebels" were confiscated, the federal government would obtain 394 million acres. Every adult male ex-slave could easily be supplied with 40 acres. The beauty of his scheme, Stevens insisted, was that "nine-tenths of the [southern] people would remain untouched." Dispossessing the great planters would make the South "a safe republic," its lands cultivated by "the free labor of intelligent citizens." If the plan drove the planters into exile, "all the better."

Although Stevens's figures were faulty, many Radicals agreed with him. "We must see that the freedmen are established on the soil," Senator Sumner declared. "The great plantations, which have been so many nurseries of the rebellion, must be broken up, and the freedmen must have the pieces." Stevens, Sumner, and others who wanted to give land to the freedmen weakened their case by associating it with the idea of punishing the former rebels; the average American had too much respect for property rights to support a policy of confiscation.

Aside from its vindictiveness, the extremists' view was simplistic. Land without tools, seed, and other necessities would have done the freedmen little good. Congress did throw open 46 million acres of poor-quality federal land in the South to blacks under the Southern Homestead Act, but few settled on it. (Of the 3,000 former slaves who filed claims under its provisions in Florida, Whoopi Goldberg's great-great-grandparents were among the 300 who succeeded in fulfilling its terms.) Establishing former slaves on small farms with adequate financial aid would have been of incalculable benefit to them. This would have been practicable, but extremely expensive. It was not done.

The former slaves therefore had either to agree to work for their former owners or strike out on their own. White planters, influenced by the precipitous decline of sugar production in Jamaica and other Caribbean islands that had followed the abolition of slavery there, expected freed blacks to be incapable of self-directed effort. If allowed to become independent farmers, they would either starve to death or descend into barbarism. Of course the blacks did neither. True, the output of cotton and other southern staples declined precipitously after slavery was abolished. Observers soon came to the conclusion that a free black produced much less than a slave had produced. "You can't get only about two-thirds as much out of 'em now as you could when they were slaves," an Arkansas planter complained.

However, the decline in productivity was not caused by the inability of free blacks to work independently. They simply chose no longer to work like slaves. They let their children play instead of forcing them into the fields. Mothers devoted more time to childcare and housework, less to farm labor. Elderly blacks worked less.

Noting these changes, white critics spoke scornfully of black laziness and shiftlessness. "You cannot make the negro work without physical compulsion," was the common view. Even General Oliver O. Howard, head of the Freedmen's Bureau, used the phrase "wholesome compulsion" in describing the policy of forcing blacks to sign exploitive labor contracts. A leading southern magazine complained in 1866 that black women now expected their husbands "to support them in idleness." It would never have made such a comment about white housewives. Moreover, studies show that emancipated blacks earned almost 30 percent more than the value of the subsistence provided by their former masters.

The family life of ex-slaves was changed in other ways. Male authority increased when husbands became true heads of families. (Under slavery the ultimate responsibility for providing for women and children was the master's.) When blacks became citizens, the men acquired rights and powers denied to all women, such as the right to hold public office and serve on juries. Similarly, black women became more like white women, devoting themselves to separate "spheres" where their lives revolved around housekeeping and child rearing.

Many slaves understood that illiteracy was an implement of bondage: Here a young African American woman in Mt. Meigs, Alabama, teaches her mother to read.

Sharecropping and the Crop-Lien System

Before the passage of the Reconstruction acts, plantation owners tried to farm their land with gang labor, the same system as before, only now paying wages to the former slaves. But blacks did not like working for wages because it kept them under the direction of whites and thus reminded them of slavery. They wanted to be independent, to manage not merely their free time but their entire lives for themselves. "The colored people of this vicinity are so proud," a white Virginian noted, "that they think it is somewhat a second slavery to hire by the month or year." Since the voluntary withdrawal of so much black labor from the workforce had produced a shortage, the blacks had their way. "I had to yield," another white planter admitted, "or lose my labor."

Quite swiftly, a new agricultural system known as **sharecropping** emerged. Instead of cultivating the land by gang labor as in antebellum times, planters broke up their estates into small units and established on each a black family. The planter provided housing, agricultural implements, draft animals, seed, and other supplies, and the family provided labor. The crop was divided between them, usually on a fifty-fifty basis. If the landlord supplied only land and housing, the laborer got a larger share. This was called share tenancy.

Sharecropping gave blacks the day-to-day control of their lives that they craved and the hope of earning enough to buy a small farm. Many former slaves succeeded, as evidenced by the accounts narrated at the outset of this chapter. Oprah Winfrey's great-great-grandfather bought several plots of land and eventually moved a schoolhouse to his property so that black children in Sanford, Mississippi, could get an education. But not all managed to climb the first rungs into the middle class. As late as 1880 blacks owned less than 10 percent of the agricultural land in the South, although they made up more than half of the region's farm population.

Many white farmers in the South were also trapped by the sharecropping system and by white efforts to keep blacks in a subordinate position.

New fencing laws kept them from grazing livestock on undeveloped land, a practice common before the Civil War. But the main cause of southern rural poverty for whites as well as for blacks was the lack of enough capital to finance the sharecropping system. Like their colonial ancestors, the landowners had to borrow against October's harvest to pay for April's seed. Thus the **crop-lien system** developed.

Under the crop-lien system, both landowner and sharecropper depended on credit supplied by local bankers, merchants, and storekeepers for everything from seed, tools, and fertilizer to overalls, coffee, and salt. Crossroads stores proliferated, and a new class of small merchants appeared. The prices of goods sold on credit were high, adding to the burden borne by the rural population. The small southern merchants were almost equally victimized by the system, for they also lacked capital, bought goods on credit, and had to pay high interest rates.

Seen in broad perspective, the situation is not difficult to understand. The South, drained of every resource by the war, was competing for funds with the North and West, both vigorous and expanding and therefore voracious consumers of capital.

Sharecroppers pick cotton in the late 1800s.

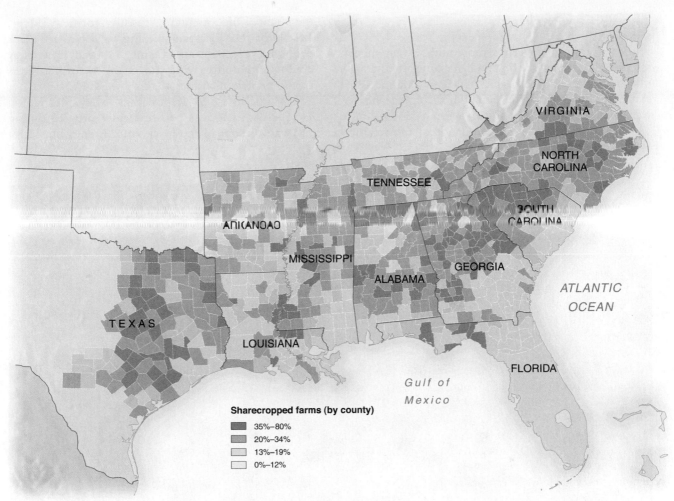

Sharecropping farms (by county)

- 35%–80%
- 20%–34%
- 13%–19%
- 0%–12%

Sharecropping, 1880 Sharecropping became especially common in areas outside of the cotton belt—eastern Texas, upland Alabama, and North Carolina.

Reconstruction, in the literal sense of the word, was accomplished chiefly at the expense of the standard of living of the producing classes. The crop-lien system and the small storekeeper were only agents of an economic process dictated by national, perhaps even worldwide, conditions.

Compared with the rest of the country, progress was slow. Just before the Civil War cotton harvests averaged about 4 million bales. During the conflict, output fell to about half a million, and the former Confederate states did not enjoy a 4-million-bale year again until 1870. In contrast, national wheat production in 1859 was 175 million bushels and in 1878, 449 million. About 7,000 miles of railroad were built in the South between 1865 and 1879; in the rest of the nation nearly 45,000 miles of track were laid.

But in the late 1870s, cotton production revived. It soon regained, and thereafter long retained, its title as "king" of the southern economy. This was true in large measure because of the crop-lien system.

The South made important gains in manufacturing after the war. The tobacco industry, stimulated by the sudden popularity of the cigarette, expanded rapidly. Virginia and North Carolina tobacco towns like Richmond, Lynchburg, and Durham flourished. The exploitation of the coal and iron deposits of northeastern Alabama in the early 1870s made a boomtown of Birmingham. The manufacture of cotton cloth increased, productive capacity nearly doubling between 1865 and 1880. Yet the mills of Massachusetts alone had eight times the capacity of the entire South in 1880. Despite the increases, the South's share of the national output of manufactured goods declined sharply during the Reconstruction era.

Read the Document *A Sharecrop Contract* at www.myhistorylab.com

View the Image *Five Generations of a Slave Family* at www.myhistorylab.com

The White Backlash

Radical southern governments could sustain themselves only as long as they had the support of a significant proportion of the white population, for except in South Carolina and Louisiana, the blacks were not numerous enough to win elections alone. The key to survival lay in the hands of the wealthy merchants and planters, mostly former Whigs. People of this sort had nothing to fear from black economic competition. Taking a broad view, they could see that improving the lot of the former slaves would benefit all classes.

Southern white Republicans used the Union League of America, a patriotic club founded during the war, to control the black vote. Employing secret

The Klu Klux Klan forces John Campbell, a black man, to beg for his life in Moore County, North Carolina (1871).

rituals, exotic symbols, and other paraphernalia calculated to impress unsophisticated people, they enrolled the freedmen in droves and marched them to the polls en masse.

Powerless to check the League by open methods, dissident Southerners established a number of secret terrorist societies, bearing such names as the **Ku Klux Klan**, the Knights of the White Camelia, and the Pale Faces. The most notorious of these organizations was the Klan, which originated in Tennessee in 1866. At first it was purely a social club, but by 1868 it had been taken over by vigilante types dedicated to driving blacks out of politics, and it was spreading rapidly across the South. Sheet-clad nightriders roamed the countryside, frightening the impressionable and chastising the defiant. Klansmen, using a weird mumbo jumbo and claiming to be the ghosts of Confederate soldiers, spread horrendous rumors and published broadsides designed to persuade the freedmen that it was unhealthy for them to participate in politics:

> *Niggers and Leaguers, get out of the way,*
> *We're born of the night and we vanish by day.*
> *No rations have we, but the flesh of man—*
> *And love niggers best—the Ku Klux Klan;*
> *We catch 'em alive and roast 'em whole,*
> *Then hand 'em around with a sharpened pole.*
> *Whole Leagues have been eaten, not leaving a man,*
> *And went away hungry—the Ku Klux Klan. . . .*

When intimidation failed, the Klansmen resorted to force. After being whipped by one group in Tennessee, a recently elected justice of the peace reported, "They said they had nothing particular against me . . . but they did not intend any nigger to hold office." In hundreds of cases the KKK murdered their opponents, often in the most gruesome manner.

Congress struck at the Klan with three **Force Acts** (1870–1871), which placed elections under federal jurisdiction and imposed fines and prison sentences on persons convicted of interfering with any citizen's exercise of the franchise. Troops were dispatched to areas where the Klan was strong, and by 1872 the federal authorities had arrested enough Klansmen to break up the organization.

Nevertheless the Klan contributed substantially to the destruction of Radical regimes in the South. Its depredations weakened the will of white Republicans (few of whom really believed in racial equality), and it intimidated many blacks. The fact that the army had to be called in to suppress it was a glaring illustration of the weakness of the Reconstruction governments.

Gradually it became respectable to intimidate black voters. Beginning in Mississippi in 1874, terrorism spread through the South. Instead of hiding behind masks and operating in the dark, these terrorists donned red shirts, organized into military companies, and paraded openly. Mississippi redshirts seized militant blacks and whipped them publicly. Killings were frequent. When blacks dared to fight back, heavily armed whites put them to rout. In other states similar results followed.

Terrorism fed on fear, fear on terrorism. White violence led to fear of black retaliation and thus to even more brutal attacks. The slightest sign of resistance came to be seen as the beginning of race war, and when the blacks suffered indignities and persecutions in silence, the awareness of how much they must resent the mistreatment made them appear more dangerous still. Thus self-hatred was displaced, guilt suppressed, aggression justified as self-defense, and individual conscience submerged in the animality of the mob.

Before long the blacks learned to stay home on election day. One by one, "Conservative" parties—Democratic in national affairs—took over southern state governments. Intimidation was only a partial explanation of this development. The increasing solidarity of whites, northern and southern, was equally significant.

The North had subjected the South to control from Washington while preserving state sovereignty in the North itself. In the long run this discrimination proved unworkable. Many Northerners had supported the Radical policy only out of irritation with President Johnson. After his retirement their enthusiasm waned. The war was fading into the past and with it the worst of the anger it had generated.

Northern voters could still be stirred by references to the sacrifices Republicans had made to save the Union and by reminders that the Democratic party was the organization of rebels, Copperheads, and the Ku Klux Klan. "If the Devil himself were at the helm of the ship of state," wrote the novelist Lydia Maria Child in 1872, "my conscience would not allow me to aid in removing him to make room for the Democratic party." Yet emotional appeals could not convince Northerners that it was still necessary to maintain a large army in the South. In 1869 the occupying forces were down to 11,000 men. After Klan disruption and intimidation had made a farce of the 1874 elections in Mississippi, Governor Ames appealed to Washington for help. President Grant's attorney general, Edwards Pierrepont, refused to act. "The whole public are tired out with these autumnal outbreaks in the South," he told Ames. "Preserve the peace by the forces of your own state."

Nationalism was reasserting itself. Had not Washington and Jefferson been Virginians? Was not Andrew Jackson Carolina-born? Since most Northerners had little real love or respect for African Americans, their interest in racial equality flagged once they felt reasonably certain that blacks would not be re-enslaved if left to their own devices in the South.

Another, much subtler force was also at work. The prewar Republican party had stressed the common interest of workers, manufacturers, and farmers in a free and mobile society, a land of equal opportunity where all could work in harmony. Southern whites had insisted that laborers must be disciplined if large enterprises were to be run efficiently. By the 1870s, as large industrial enterprises developed in the northern states, the thinking of business leaders changed—the southern argument began to make sense to them, and they became more sympathetic to the southern demand for more control over "their" labor force.

An 1872 Grant campaign poster of "Our Three Great Presidents" at best got it about two-thirds right.

●●●—**Read** the **Document** *Accounts from Victims of the Ku Klux Klan* at **www.myhistorylab.com**

Grant as President

Other matters occupied the attention of northern voters. The expansion of industry and the rapid development of the West, stimulated by a new wave of railroad building, loomed more important to many than the fortunes of the former slaves. Beginning in 1873, when a stock market panic struck at public confidence, economic difficulties plagued the country and provoked another debate over the tariff.

More damaging to the Republicans was the failure of Ulysses S. Grant to live up to expectations as president. Qualities that had made Grant a fine military leader for a democracy—his dislike of political maneuvering and his simple belief that the popular will could best be observed in the actions of Congress—made him a poor chief executive. When

Congress failed to act on his suggestion that the quality of the civil service needed improvement, he announced meekly that if Congress did nothing, he would assume the country did not want anything done. Grant was honest, but his honesty was of the naive type that made him the dupe of unscrupulous friends and schemers.

His most serious weakness as president was his failure to deal effectively with economic and social problems, but the one that injured him and the Republicans most was his inability to cope with government corruption. The worst of the scandals—such as the Whiskey Ring affair, which implicated Grant's private secretary (Orville E. Babcock) and cost the government millions in tax revenue, and the corruption of Secretary of War William W. Belknap in the management of Indian affairs—did not become public knowledge during Grant's first term. However, in 1872 Republican reformers, alarmed by rumors of corruption and disappointed by Grant's failure to press for civil service reform, organized the Liberal Republican party and nominated Horace Greeley, the able but eccentric editor of the *New York Tribune*, for president.

The Liberal Republicans were mostly well-educated, socially prominent types—editors, college presidents, economists, along with a sprinkling of businessmen and politicians. Their liberalism was of the laissez-faire variety; they were for low tariffs and sound money, and against what they called "class legislation,"

A major Reconstruction project was the development of Birmingham, Alabama as a center of the iron industry. Here iron moulders cast molten iron into rectangular blocks ("pigs").

meaning measures benefiting particular groups, whether labor unions or railroad companies or farm organizations. Nearly all had supported Reconstruction at the start, but by the early 1870s most were including southern blacks among the special interests that ought to be left to their own devices. Their observation of urban corruption and of unrestricted immigration led them to disparage universal suffrage, which, one of them said, "can only mean in plain English the government of ignorance and vice."

The Democrats also nominated Greeley in 1872, although he had devoted his political life to flailing the Democratic party in the *Tribune*. That surrender to expediency, together with Greeley's temperamental unsuitability for the presidency, made the campaign a fiasco for the reformers. Grant triumphed easily, with a popular majority of nearly 800,000.

Nevertheless, the defection of the Liberal Republicans hurt the Republican party in Congress. In the 1874 elections, no longer hampered as in the presidential contest by Greeley's notoriety and Grant's fame, the Democrats carried the House of Representatives. It was clear that the days of military rule in the South were ending. By the end of 1875 only three southern states—South Carolina, Florida, and Louisiana—were still under Republican control.

The Republican party in the South was "dead as a doornail," a reporter noted. He reflected the opinion of thousands when he added, "We ought to have a sound sensible republican . . . for the next President as a measure of safety; but only on the condition of absolute noninterference in Southern local affairs, for which there is no further need or excuse."

The Disputed Election of 1876

Against this background the presidential election of 1876 took place. Since corruption in government was the most widely discussed issue, the Republicans passed over their most attractive political personality, the dynamic James G. Blaine, Speaker of the House of Representatives, who had been connected with some chicanery involving railroad securities. Instead they nominated Governor Rutherford B. Hayes of Ohio, a former general with an untarnished reputation. The Democrats picked Governor Samuel J. Tilden of New York, a wealthy lawyer who had attracted national attention for his part in breaking up the Tweed Ring in New York City.

In November early returns indicated that Tilden had carried New York, New Jersey, Connecticut, Indiana, and all the southern states, including Louisiana, South Carolina, and Florida, where Republican regimes were still in control. This seemed to give him 203 electoral votes to Hayes's 165, and a popular plurality in the neighborhood of 250,000 out of more than 8 million votes cast. However, Republican leaders had anticipated the possible loss of Florida, South Carolina, and Louisiana and were prepared to use their control of the election machinery in those states to throw out sufficient Democratic ballots to alter the results if doing so would change the national outcome. Realizing that the electoral votes of those states were exactly enough to elect their man, they telegraphed their henchmen on the scene, ordering them to go into action. The local Republicans then invalidated Democratic ballots in wholesale lots and filed returns showing Hayes the winner. Naturally the local Democrats protested vigorously and filed their own returns.

The Constitution provides (Article II, Section 1) that presidential electors must meet in their respective states to vote and forward the results to "the Seat of the Government." There, it adds, "the President of the Senate shall, in the Presence of the Senate and House of Representatives, open all the Certificates, and the Votes shall then be counted." But who was to do the counting? The House was Democratic, the Senate Republican; neither would agree to allow the other to do the job. On January 29, 1877, scarcely a month before inauguration day, Congress created an electoral commission to decide the disputed cases. The commission consisted of five senators (three Republicans and two Democrats), five representatives (three Democrats and two Republicans), and five justices of the Supreme Court (two Democrats, two Republicans, and one "independent" judge, David Davis). Since it was a foregone conclusion that the others would vote for their party no matter what the evidence, Davis would presumably swing the balance in the interest of fairness.

But before the commission met, the Illinois legislature elected Davis senator! He had to resign from

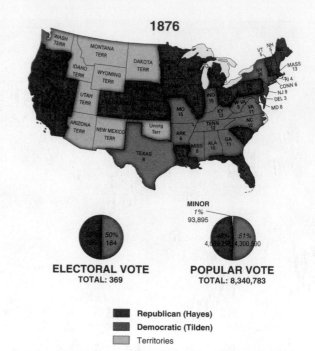

1876

MINOR
1%
93,895

ELECTORAL VOTE
TOTAL: 369

POPULAR VOTE
TOTAL: 8,340,783

■ Republican (Hayes)
■ Democratic (Tilden)
□ Territories

The Republicans Gain the Presidency, the White South Loses the Union Army, 1877 By 1876 white Democrats had regained political control in much of the South, giving Tilden 203 electoral votes to the Republican Hayes's 185. But Republican election officials in South Carolina, Florida, and Louisiana invalidated thousands of Democratic votes, which seemingly gave the election to Tilden. In 1877 a congressional commission finalized a deal giving the presidency to Hayes, who would withdraw the Union army from the South.

the Court and the commission. Since independents were rare even on the Supreme Court, no neutral justice was available to replace him. The vacancy went to Associate Justice Joseph P. Bradley of New Jersey, a Republican.

Evidence presented before the commission revealed a disgraceful picture of corruption. On the one hand, in all three disputed states Democrats had clearly cast a majority of the votes; on the other, it was unquestionable that many blacks had been forcibly prevented from voting.

In truth, both sides were shamefully corrupt. The governor of Louisiana was reported willing to sell his state's electoral votes for $200,000. The Florida election board was supposed to have offered itself to Tilden for the same price. "That seems to be the standard figure," Tilden remarked ruefully.

The Democrats had some hopes that Justice Bradley would be sympathetic to their case, for he was known to be opposed to harsh Reconstruction policies. On the eve of the commission's decision in the Florida controversy, he was apparently ready to vote in favor of Tilden. But the Republicans subjected him to tremendous political pressure. When he read his opinion on February 8, it was for Hayes. Thus, by a vote of eight to seven, the commission awarded Florida's electoral votes to the Republicans.

Grant, a Republican and a Union war hero, won easily in 1868 and 1872 because ex-Confederates, many of whom had voted Democratic, were barred from the polls. By 1876, however, white Democrats had regained political control in much of the South, creating the electoral stalemate that led to the Compromise of 1877.

The rest of the proceedings was routine. The commission assigned all the disputed electoral votes (including one in Oregon where the Democratic governor had seized on a technicality to replace a single Republican elector with a Democrat) to Hayes.

Democratic institutions, shaken by the South's refusal to go along with the majority in 1860 and by the suppression of civil rights during the rebellion, and further weakened by military intervention and the intimidation of blacks in the South during Reconstruction, seemed now a farce. According to Tilden's campaign manager, angry Democrats in fifteen states, chiefly war veterans, were readying themselves to march on Washington to force the inauguration of Tilden. Tempers flared in Congress, where some spoke ominously of a filibuster that would prevent the recording of the electoral vote and leave the country, on March 4, with no president at all.

The Compromise of 1877

Forces for compromise had been at work behind the scenes in Washington for some time. Although northern Democrats threatened to fight to the last ditch, many southern Democrats were willing to accept Hayes if he would promise to remove the troops and allow the southern states to manage their internal affairs by themselves. Ex-Whig planters and merchants who had reluctantly abandoned the carpetbag governments and who sympathized with Republican economic policies hoped that by supporting Hayes they might contribute to the restoration of the two-party system that had been destroyed in the South during the 1850s. Ohio Congressman James A. Garfield urged Hayes to find

"some discreet way" of showing these Southerners that he favored "internal improvements." Hayes replied, "Your views are so nearly the same as mine that I need not say a word."

Tradition has it that a great compromise between the sections was worked out during a dramatic meeting at the Wormley Hotel[2] in Washington on February 26. Actually the negotiations were drawn out and informal, and the Wormley conference was but one of many. With the tacit support of many Democrats, the electoral vote was counted by the president of the Senate on March 2, and Hayes was declared elected, 185 votes to 184.

Like all compromises, the **Compromise of 1877** was not entirely satisfactory; like most, it was not honored in every detail. Hayes recalled the last troops from South Carolina and Louisiana in April. He appointed a former Confederate general, David M. Key of Tennessee, postmaster general and delegated to him the congenial task of finding Southerners willing to serve their country as officials of a Republican administration. But the alliance of ex-Whigs and northern Republicans did not flourish; the South remained solidly Democratic. The major significance of the compromise, one of the great intersectional political accommodations of American history, was that it ended Reconstruction and inaugurated a new political order in the South. More than the Constitutional amendments and federal statutes, this new regime would shape the destinies of the four million freedmen.

For many former slaves, this future was to be bleak. Forgotten in the North, manipulated and then callously rejected by the South, rebuffed by the Supreme Court, voiceless in national affairs, they and their descendants were condemned in the interests of sectional harmony to lives of poverty, indignity, and little hope. But many other former slaves managed to thrive during the last third of the nineteenth century. Their hard work, discipline, and financial savvy elevated them into a property-owning middle class whose existence—more than Union armies—marked the end of slavery.

Watch the Video *The Promise and Failure of Reconstruction* at **www.myhistorylab.com**

---

[2]Ironically, the hotel was owned by James Wormley, reputedly the wealthiest black person in Washington.

Cold Mountain

Cold Mountain (2004), a movie based on Charles Frazier's novel, is a love story set during the Civil War. But this is an unusual love story. The lovers are seldom together; and the hero is a deserter.

Inman (Jude Law), a schoolteacher, and Ada (Nicole Kidman), the well-born daughter of a minister, meet in a town in western North Carolina in the shadows of Cold Mountain. They speak on several occasions, look searchingly at each other, and exchange a single resolute kiss. Then Inman enlists in the Confederate army. They send each other letters, many of which never arrive. They yearn for each other without knowing much about each other. In a world made ugly by war, they need something beautiful to love. Each cherishes photographs of the other.

Inman is wounded in the neck during the siege of Petersburg. While convalescing in a hospital, he receives a letter from Ada: "If you are fighting, stop fighting ... If you are marching, stop marching. Come back to me." He nods grimly and decides to desert. He sneaks out of the hospital and begins his long trek back to Cold Mountain.

The journey is an ordeal. He suffers from cold and hunger. Confederate soldiers chase, capture, and shoot him, leaving him for dead; rogues attack and rob him. If war is hell, leaving it is no picnic, either.

Ada suffers too. Her father dies and she sets the slaves free. A southern lady, she knows nothing about farming and goes hungry. A plucky female farmhand (Renée Zellweger) appears at the farm and sets it aright.

The movie reaches a climax when Inman staggers up Cold Mountain—and into the arms of Ada. He is closely pursued by ruffians in the Home Guard, a local militia on the lookout for deserters, who shoot him dead.

Can any of this be regarded as history?

There was a man named Inman, the brother of author Frazier's great-great-grandfather. The real Inman had been wounded in the neck at Petersburg, deserted, and was killed in a gunfight with the Home Guard near Cold Mountain. But the known facts of Inman's story, Frazier explained, "could be scrawled on the back of the envelope." Frazier made up everything else, doubtless inspired by Homer's *Odyssey*, another story of a soldier's return home from war.

But if much of the story is the product of Frazier's imagination, it nevertheless illuminates several historically significant themes. *Cold Mountain* examines the psychological effects of the loss of morale in the South, which many historians now regard as the best explanation for its defeat. (See Debating the Past, "Were Reconstruction Governments Corrupt?" p. 413.) Official statistics indicate that some 200,000 Union soldiers and 104,000 Confederates deserted. Many more simply walked unarmed into enemy camps and were arrested as "captured." When Robert E. Lee surrendered at Appomattox, his army had dwindled to 28,000 men; another 3,800 were reported as deserted and another 14,000 as captured.

The problem of desertion was especially acute in the mountain region of North Carolina, where support for secession had never been strong. In late 1863 and early 1864 the legislature of North Carolina passed laws penalizing sheriffs who failed to assist in capturing deserters and draft dodgers; it also created the Home Guard, local militias composed of men exempt from conscription, and charged them with the task of rounding up deserters. By early 1865, Lee was complaining that entire units were deserting; he especially regretted that "the greatest number of desertions have occurred among the North Carolina troops."

The movie accurately pinpoints the geography of desertion—North Carolina. But was its psychological explanation equally valid? Did southern women, like Ada, encourage their menfolk to desert?

The historical evidence is ambivalent.

On the one hand, the Confederacy made a concerted effort to enlist the support of white women. The South's surprisingly strong economic performance suggests that plenty of women, like Ada, learned how to manage farms and

Nicole Kidman as Ada in *Cold Mountain*.

The woman in *The Consecration* (1861) by George Cochran Lambdin was probably used as the model for Nicole Kidman's hair style and clothing. The movie was extraordinarily attentive to historical visual detail.

plantations. There is evidence, too, that southern women encouraged their men to fight. In 1862 and again the next year, a letter appeared in many Confederate newspapers in which "The Women of the South" called on their men to enlist and fight. "Never turn your backs on the flag," it advised soldiers, for cowardly behavior would disgrace themselves and their "children's children." When Sergeant Edwin Fay of Louisiana wrote to his wife saying that he wanted to leave "this horrid war," she responded that while she missed him terribly she could not countenance his becoming a deserter.

The Confederacy's appeal to women reflected their increasing importance in public life. Historian Drew Gilpin Faust (who in 2007 became the first woman president of Harvard University) argues that women's role shifted further as the Confederacy and its menfolk failed to defend white southern "womanhood." "Of necessity," such women assumed a larger role in the management of farms and plantations and they became more assertive in public matters. Some took the lead—as did Ada—in encouraging their men to desert.

"Though the ladies may not be willing to concede the fact," a Confederate official in North Carolina declared, "they are nevertheless responsible for the desertion in the army." James Fowler, a private from North Carolina who had been sentenced to death for desertion, cited his wife's pleas in his appeal for clemency. "I received a letter from my wife stating there [sic] condition and my two children was both at the point of Death and I made evry [sic] effort to get permission to go home honorably."

Cold Mountain is not history. But the movie illuminates the anguish of those who cling to life and love rather than to a war effort that will likely fail.

Questions for Discussion

- What causes soldiers to abandon a war?

- How do you think any soldiers reconcile their duties to their family and to their nation?

Table 15.1   Two Phases of Reconstruction: 1863–1877

Phase	Measure	Consequence
1. Presidential Reconstruction: Accommodation with white South		
	Lincoln's Ten-Percent Plan (1863)	Re-admits Southern states when 10 percent of 1860 voters profess loyalty to Union
	Lincoln vetoes Wade-Davis Bill (1864)	Retains 10 percent "easy-admission" policy
	Andrew Johnson pardons many Confederates and recommends admission of all former Confederate states	By 1866, all southern states are readmitted
	Southern states pass Black Codes (1864–1865) sharply restricting rights of former slaves	Outrages Republicans
2. Radical Reconstruction: Republicans gain power in Congress		
	Thirteenth Amendment (1865)	Ends Slavery
	Freedmen's Bureau (1865) established as branch of war department	Promotes education and economic opportunities for former slaves and destitute whites
	Congress passes Civil Rights Act over Johnson's veto (1866)	Republicans in Congress dominate federal government Washington
	Reconstruction Act of 1867	Divides South into five military districts, each under command of Union general
	Tenure of Office Act (1867)	Prohibits president from removing high officials
	Johnson impeached for firing Secretary of State Stanton	Johnson is tried but not removed from office
	Fourteenth Amendment (passed 1866, ratified 1868)	Requires that all citizens have "equal protection" of laws
	Republican Grant elected president (1868)	Further increases Republican domination
	Fifteenth Amendment (passed 1869, ratified 1870)	Prohibits voting restrictions on basis of race
	Force Acts (1870-1871)	Federal control of elections in South

Chapter Review

Milestones

1863	Lincoln announces "Ten Percent Plan" for Reconstruction
1865	Federal government sets up Freedmen's Bureau to ease transition from slavery to freedom
	General Lee surrenders at Appomattox Court House
	Abraham Lincoln is assassinated
	Andrew Johnson becomes president
	Johnson issues amnesty proclamation
	States ratify Thirteenth Amendment abolishing slavery
1865–1866	Southern states enact Black Codes
1866	Civil Rights Act passes over Johnson's veto
	Johnson campaigns for his Reconstruction policy
1867	First Reconstruction Act puts former Confederacy under military rule
	Tenure of Office Act protects Senate appointees
1868	House of Representatives impeaches Johnson
1868	Fourth Reconstruction Act requires a majority of Southern voters to ratify state constitutions

	Senate acquits Johnson
	States ratify Fourteenth Amendment extending rights to freed slaves
	Ulysses S. Grant is elected president
	Ku Klux Klan uses intimidation and force throughout South
1870	States ratify Fifteenth Amendment granting black suffrage
1870–1871	Force Act destroys Ku Klux Klan
1872	Liberal Republican party nominates Horace Greeley for president
	Grant is reelected president
1876	Rutherford B. Hayes runs against Samuel Tilden in disputed presidential election
1877	Electoral Commission awards disputed votes to Rutherford B. Hayes who becomes president
	Hayes agrees to Compromise of 1877 ending Reconstruction

Key Terms

Black Codes Special laws passed by southern state and municipal governments after the Civil War that denied free blacks many rights of citizenship, *407*

carpetbaggers A pejorative term for Northerners who went to the South after the Civil War to exploit the new political power of freed blacks and the disenfranchisement of former Confederates, *414*

Compromise of 1877 A brokered arrangement whereby Republican and Democratic leaders agreed to settle the disputed 1876 presidential election. Democrats allowed returns that ensured the election of Republican Rutherford B. Hayes; and Republicans agreed to withdraw federal troops from the South, ensuring an end to Reconstruction, *427*

crop-lien system A system of agriculture in which local landowners and merchants loaned money to farm workers in return for a portion of the harvest of cash crops. By forcing farmers to plant cash crops, the system discouraged diversified agriculture in the South, *420*

Fifteenth Amendment An amendment (1870), championed by the Republican party, that sought to guarantee the vote to blacks in the South following the Civil War, *414*

Force Acts Three laws passed by the Republican-dominated Congress in 1870–1871 to protect black voters in the South. The laws placed state elections under federal jurisdiction and imposed fines and imprisonment on those guilty of interfering with any citizen exercising his right to vote, *423*

Fourteenth Amendment An amendment, passed by Congress in 1866 and ratified in 1868, that prohibited states from depriving citizens of the due process or the equal protection of the laws. Although the amendment was a response to discriminatory laws against blacks in the South, it figured prominently in the expansion of individual rights and liberties during the last half of the twentieth century, *409*

Freedmen's Bureau A federal refugee agency to aid former slaves and destitute whites after the Civil War. It provided them food, clothing, and other necessities as well as helped them find work and set up schools, *408*

Ku Klux Klan   Founded as a social club in 1866 by a handful of former Confederate soldiers in Tennessee, it became a vigilante group that used violence and intimidation to drive African Americans out of politics. The movement declined in the late 1870s but resurfaced in the 1920s as a political organization that opposed all groups—immigrant, religious, and racial—that challenged Protestant white hegemony, *423*

Radical Republicans   A faction within the Republican party, headed by Thaddeus Stevens and Benjamin Wade, that insisted on black suffrage and federal protection of the civil rights of blacks. After 1867, the Radical Republicans achieved a working majority in Congress and passed legislation promoting Reconstruction, *406*

scalawags   White southern Republicans—mainly small landowning farmers and well-off merchants and planters—who cooperated with the congressionally imposed Reconstruction governments set up in the South following the Civil War, *414*

sharecropping   A type of agriculture, frequently practiced in the South during and after Reconstruction, in which landowners provided land, tools, housing, and seed to a farmer who provided his labor; the resulting crop was divided between them (i.e., shared), *420*

Ten Percent Plan   A measure drafted by President Abraham Lincoln in 1863 to readmit states that had seceded once 10 percent of their prewar voters swore allegiance to the Union and adopted state constitutions outlawing slavery, *406*

Thirteenth Amendment   Passed in 1865, this amendment declared an end to slavery and negated the Three-fifths Clause in the Constitution, thereby increasing the representation of the southern states in Congress, *407*

Wade-Davis bill   An 1864 alternative to Lincoln's "**Ten Percent Plan**," this measure required a majority of voters in a southern state to take a loyalty oath in order to begin the process of Reconstruction and guarantee black equality. It also required the repudiation of the Confederate debt. The president exercised a pocket veto, and it never became law, *406*

Review Questions

1. The introduction to this chapter—which cites the success of some randomly-chosen figures during Reconstruction—can be easily dismissed: Extraordinary people can prevail against any odds. What gains did most former slaves achieve during Reconstruction? Which federal policies and actions promoted their prospects?

2. What strategies did white Southerners use to control slaves after the Thirteenth Amendment had ended slavery?

3. Why did the Republicans in Congress disagree with Lincoln? With Andrew Johnson? In what sense did the Republican Congress come to "dominate" the political process?

4. What were the economic consequences of Reconstruction?

5. How did Reconstruction come to an end?

PEARSON
myhistorylab Connections

Reinforce what you learned in this chapter by studying the many documents, images, maps, review tools, and videos available at **www.myhistorylab.com**.

Read and Review

✓•┤**Study** and **Review** *Chapter 15*

•••┤**Read** the **Document** *The Mississippi Black Code,* p. 402

•••┤**Read** the **Document** *Southern Skepticism of the Freedmen's Bureau,* p. 409

•••┤**Read** the **Document** *13th, 14th, and 15th Amendments,* p. 410

👁┤**See** the **Map** *Reconstruction,* p. 410

•••┤**Read** the **Document** *A Sharecrop Contract,* p. 421

🔘┤**View** the **Image** *Five Generations of a Slave Family,* p. 421

•••┤**Read** the **Document** *Accounts from Victims of the Ku Klux Klan,* p. 424

Research and Explore

🔘┤**Watch** the **Video** *The Schools that the Civil War & Reconstruction created,* p. 415

🔘┤**Watch** the **Video** *The Promise and Failure of Reconstruction,* p. 427

((•••┤Hear the Audio

Hear the audio file for Chapter 15 at
www.myhistorylab.com.

Do you live on land stolen from Indians?

In 2010 the Census bureau reported that Buffalo County, South Dakota was the poorest in the nation, with well over half its residents below the poverty level. Buffalo County contains the Crow Creek Indian reservation. Six of the other ten poorest counties in the nation also consist of Indian reservations: Pine Ridge, Cheyenne River, Rosebud, and Standing Rock in South Dakota; and Navajo and Fort Apache in Arizona. Wade Hampton in Alaska is also among the ten poorest counties, and over 90 precent of its inhabitants are Native Americans, mostly Eskimo. Nationwide, nearly a quarter of all Indians live in poverty, twice the national average.

In 1988 Congress proposed to alleviate the plight of Native Americans with the Indian Gaming Regulatory Act. It allowed tribes to own casinos and other gambling operations. Within two decades, over 200 tribes had built 360 casinos and gaming establishments. By 2009, annual revenue from Indian casinos exceeded $25 billion, twice as much as the combined income of the National Football League (NFL) and Major League Baseball.

But little of the casino revenue has flowed to the poorest reservations. Foxwoods in Connecticut, the largest casino in the United States, generates about $1 billion

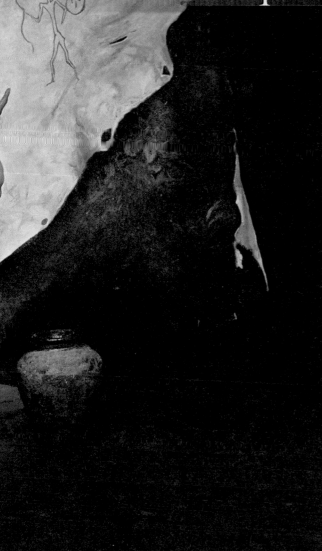

((•—[Hear the Audio **Chapter 16 at www.myhistorylab.com**

- In *The Picture Writer's Story* (1884), George de Forest Brush shows an older Mandan Indian documenting the story of a battle. The futility of the struggle is reflected in the young Indian's disinterested face.

annually, a windfall for the tiny Mashantucket Pequot tribe. But the Little Big Horn Casino, located in southeastern Montana near the battlefield where Custer lost his scalp, yielded a profit of only $100 a month during its first year of operation. Half of all reservation Indians live in Montana, Nevada, North and South Dakota, and Oklahoma, far from potential throngs of gamblers; those Indians remain mired in poverty.

The plight of most Indians today was determined by events that transformed the West after 1865. Ranchers and farmers acquired more Indian land. Railroad construction destabilized the habitat that sustained Indian life, especially the grazing lands of the buffalo, and brought still more settlers. The discovery of new deposits of gold, silver, and other valuable minerals caused miners and prospectors to swarm over and onto Indian lands. The federal government pushed Indians onto reservations, often on land unsuitable for cultivation, and sent troops to harass those who refused to abandon nomadic life. The new civilization that emerged in the West—initially the work of individual farmers, prospectors, ranchers, and businessmen—was increasingly controlled and organized by large-scale business enterprises.

By the turn of the twentieth century, the economic foundations of tribal life had been destroyed; relief, when it finally arrived many decades later, came in the form of slot machines. That so many Native Americans overcame the legacy of this past is testimony to their own initiative, and to traditional cultures characterized by both perseverance and adaptation. ∎

The West After the Civil War

Although the image of the West as the land of great open spaces is accurate enough, after the Civil War the region contained several bustling cities. San Francisco, with a population approaching 250,000 in the late 1870s, had long outgrown its role as a rickety boomtown where the forty-niners bought supplies and squandered whatever wealth they had sifted from the streams of the Sierras. Though still an important warehouse and supply center, it had become the commercial and financial heart of the Pacific Coast and a center of light manufacturing, food processing, and machine shops. Denver, San Antonio, and Salt Lake City were far smaller, but growing rapidly and equally "urban."

There was no one West, no typical Westerner. Although the economy was predominantly agricultural and extractive, commercial and industrial activities were expanding. The seeds of such large enterprises as Wells Fargo, Levi Strauss, and half a dozen important department store empires were sown in the immediate postwar decades.

Beginning in the mid-1850s a steady flow of Chinese migrated to the United States, most of them to the West Coast. About four or five thousand a year came, until the negotiation of the Burlingame Treaty of 1868, the purpose of which was to provide cheap labor for railroad construction crews. Thereafter the annual influx more than doubled, although before 1882 it exceeded 20,000 only twice. When the railroads were completed and the Chinese began to compete with native workers, a great cry of resentment went up on the west coast. Riots broke out in San Francisco in 1877. Chinese workers were called "groveling worms," "more slavish and brutish than the beasts that roam the fields." The California constitution of 1879 denied the right to vote to any "native of China" along with idiots, the insane, and persons convicted of "any infamous crime."

When Chinese immigration increased in 1882 to nearly 40,000, the protests reached such a peak that Congress passed the **Chinese Exclusion Act**, prohibiting all Chinese immigration for ten years. Later legislation extended the ban indefinitely.

Nevertheless, many parts of the West had as large a percentage of foreign-born residents as the populous eastern states—nearly a third of all Californians were foreign-born, as were more than 40 percent of Nevadans and more than half the residents of Idaho and Arizona. There were, of course, large populations of Spanish-speaking Americans of Mexican origin all over the Southwest. Chinese and Irish laborers were pouring into California by the thousands, and there were substantial numbers of Germans in Texas. Germans, Scandinavians, and other Europeans were also numerous on the High Plains east of the Rockies.

The Plains Indians

For 250 years the Indians had been driven back steadily, yet on the eve of the Civil War they still inhabited roughly half the United States. By the time of Hayes's inauguration in 1877, the Indians had been shattered as independent peoples, and in another decade the survivors were penned up on reservations, the government committed to a policy of extinguishing their way of life.

In 1860 the survivors of most of the eastern tribes were living peacefully in Indian Territory, what is now Oklahoma. In California the forty-niners had made short work of many of the local tribes. Elsewhere in the West—in the deserts of the Great Basin between the Sierras and the Rockies, in the mountains themselves, and on the semiarid, grass-covered plains between the Rockies and the edge of white civilization in eastern Kansas and Nebraska—nearly a quarter of a million Indians dominated the land.

By far the most important lived on the High Plains. From the Blackfoot of southwestern Canada and the Sioux of Minnesota and the Dakotas to the Cheyenne of Colorado and Wyoming and the Comanche of northern Texas, the plains tribes possessed a generally uniform culture. All lived by hunting the hulking American bison, or buffalo, which ranged over the plains by the millions. The buffalo provided the Indians with food, clothing, and even shelter, for the famous Indian tepee was covered with hides. On the treeless plains, dried buffalo dung was used for fuel. The buffalo was also an important symbol in Indian religion.

Although they seemed the epitome of freedom, pride, and self-reliance, the Plains Indians had begun to fall under the sway of white power. They eagerly adopted the products of the more technically advanced culture—cloth, metal tools, weapons, and cheap decorations. However, the most important thing the whites gave them had nothing to do with technology: It was the horse.

The horse was among the many large mammals that became extinct in the Western Hemisphere around 8000 BP. Cortés reintroduced the horse to America in the sixteenth century. Multiplying rapidly thereafter, the animals soon roamed freely from Texas to Argentina. By the eighteenth century the Indians of the plains had made them a vital part of their culture.

Horses thrived on the plains and so did their masters. Mounted Indians could run down buffalo instead of stalking them on foot. They could move more easily over the country and fight more effectively too. They could acquire and transport more

In Charles Russell's *Trail of the Iron Horse* (1910) the steel rails stretch nearly to the sun, while wispy brushstrokes depict the Indians almost as ghosts.

more important—to enable the government to negotiate separately with each tribe. It was the classic strategy of divide and conquer.

Although it made a mockery of diplomacy to treat Indian tribes as though they were European powers, the United States maintained that each tribe was a sovereign nation, to be dealt with as an equal in solemn treaties. Both sides knew that this was not the case. When Indians agreed to meet in council, they were tacitly admitting defeat. They seldom drove hard bargains or broke off negotiations. Moreover, tribal chiefs had only limited power; young braves frequently refused to respect agreements made by their elders.

possessions and increase the size of their tepees, for horses could drag heavy loads heaped on A-shaped frames (called *travois* by the French), whereas earlier Indians had only dogs to depend on as pack animals. The frames of the *travois*, when disassembled, served as poles for tepees. The Indians also adopted modern weapons: the cavalry sword, which they particularly admired, and the rifle. Both added to their effectiveness as hunters and fighters. However, like the whites' liquor and diseases, horses and guns caused problems. The buffalo herds began to diminish, and warfare became bloodier and more frequent.

After the start of the gold rush the need to link the East with California meant that the tribes were pushed aside. Deliberately the government in Washington prepared the way. In 1851 Thomas Fitzpatrick—an experienced mountain man, a founder of the Rocky Mountain Fur Company, scout for the first large group of settlers to Oregon in 1841 and for American soldiers in California during the Mexican War, and now an Indian agent—summoned a great "council" of the tribes. About 10,000 Indians, representing nearly all the plains tribes, gathered that September at Horse Creek, thirty-seven miles east of Fort Laramie, in what is now Wyoming.

The Indians respected Fitzpatrick, who had recently married a woman who was half-Indian. In the Fort Laramie Treaty of 1851 he persuaded each tribe to accept definite limits to its hunting grounds. For example, the Sioux nations were to stay north of the Platte River, and the Cheyenne and Arapaho were to confine themselves to the Colorado foothills. In return the Indians were promised gifts and annual payments. This policy, known as "concentration," was designed to cut down on intertribal warfare and—far

Indian Wars

The government showed little interest in honoring agreements with Indians. No sooner had the Kansas-Nebraska bill become law than the Kansas, Omaha, Pawnee, and Yankton Sioux tribes began to feel pressure for further concessions of territory. A gold rush into Colorado in 1859 sent thousands of greedy prospectors across the plains to drive the Cheyenne and Arapaho from land guaranteed them in 1851. By 1860 most of Kansas and Nebraska had been cleared. Other trouble developed in the Sioux country. Thus it happened that in 1862, after federal troops had been pulled out of the West for service against the Confederacy, most of the Plains Indians rose up against the whites. For five years intermittent but bloody clashes kept the entire area in a state of alarm.

This was guerrilla warfare, with all its horror and treachery. In 1864 a party of Colorado militia under the command of Colonel J. M. Chivington fell on an unsuspecting Cheyenne community at Sand Creek and killed several hundred Indians. A white observer described the scene: "They were scalped, their brains knocked out; the men used their knives, ripped open women, clubbed little children, knocked them in the head with their guns, beat their brains out, mutilated their bodies in every sense of the word." General Nelson A. Miles called this "Chivington massacre" the "foulest and most unjustifiable crime in the annals of America."

In turn the Indians slaughtered dozens of isolated white families, ambushed small parties, and fought many successful skirmishes against troops and militia. They achieved their most notable triumph in December 1866, when the Oglala Sioux, under their great chief

Robert Lindneux's *The Battle of Sand Creek*, 1864. Lindneux, born in 1871, did not witness what transpired at Sand Creek, Colorado. But although he used "battle" in the title of his painting, he depicted a massacre. "Kill and scalp all, big and little," Colonel J. M. Chivington, a minister in private life, told his men. The American flag (center right) was doubtless included as irony.

Red Cloud, wiped out a party of eighty-two soldiers under Captain W. J. Fetterman. Red Cloud fought ruthlessly, but only when goaded by the construction of the Bozeman Trail, a road through the heart of the Sioux hunting grounds in southern Montana.[1]

In 1867 the government tried a new strategy. The "concentration" policy had evidently not gone far enough. All the Plains Indians would be confined to two small reservations, one in the Black Hills of the Dakota Territory, the other in Oklahoma, and forced to become farmers. At two great conclaves held in 1867 and 1868 at Medicine Lodge Creek and Fort Laramie, the principal chiefs yielded to the government's demands and signed the 1868 Treaty of Fort Laramie.

Many Indians refused to abide by these agreements. With their whole way of life at stake, they raged across the plains like a prairie fire—and were almost as destructive.

That a relative handful of "savages," without central leadership, could hold off the cream of the army, battle-hardened in the Civil War, can be explained by the fact that the U.S. Army, usually with fewer than 20,000 soldiers, had to operate over a million square miles. Few Indian leaders were capable of organizing a campaign or following up an advantage. But the Indians made superb guerrillas. Every observer called them the best cavalry soldiers in the world. Armed with stubby, powerful bows capable of driving an arrow clear through a bull buffalo, they were a fair match for troops equipped with carbines and Colt revolvers. Expertly they led pursuers into ambushes, swept down on unsuspecting supply details, and stole up on small parties the way a mountain lion stalks a grazing lamb. They could sometimes be rounded up, as when General Philip Sheridan herded the tribes of the Southwest into Indian Territory in 1869. But once the troops withdrew, braves began to melt away into the surrounding grasslands. The distinction between "treaty" Indians, who had agreed to live on the new reservations, and the "nontreaty" variety shifted almost from day to day. Trouble flared here one week, and the next week somewhere else, perhaps 500 miles away. General William Tecumseh Sherman testified that a mere fifty Indians could often "checkmate" 3,000 soldiers.

If one concedes that no one could reverse the direction of history or stop the invasion of Indian lands, then some version of the "small reservation"

---

[1]Fetterman had boasted that with eighty cavalrymen he could ride the entire length of the Bozeman Trail. When he tried, however, he blundered into an ambush.

Indian Wars, 1860–1890 The frequent battles, involving nearly all tribes, show that the Indians did not cede their lands: The lands were taken in battle.

policy would probably have been best for the Indians. Had they been guaranteed a reasonable amount of land and adequate subsidies and allowed to maintain their way of life, they might have accepted the situation and ceased to harass the whites.

Whatever chance that policy had was weakened by the government's poor administration of Indian affairs. In dealing with Indians, nineteenth-century Americans displayed a grave insensitivity. After 1849 the Department of the Interior supposedly had charge of tribal affairs. Most of its agents systematically cheated the Indians. One, heavily involved in mining operations on the side, diverted goods intended for his charges to his private ventures. When an inspector looked into his records, he sold him

shares in a mine. That worthy in turn protected himself by sharing some of the loot with the son of the commissioner of Indian affairs. Army officers squabbled frequently with Indian agents over policy, and an "Indian Ring" in the Department of the Interior system typically stole funds and supplies intended for the reservation Indians. "No branch of the national government is so spotted with fraud, so tainted with corruption . . . as this Indian Bureau," Congressman Garfield charged in 1869.

At about this time a Yale paleontologist, Othniel C. Marsh, who wished to dig for fossils on the Sioux reservation, asked Red Cloud for permission to enter his domain. The chief agreed on condition that Marsh, whom the Indians called Big Bone Chief, take back with him samples of the moldy flour and beef that government agents were supplying to his people. Appalled by what he saw on the reservation, Professor Marsh took the rotten supplies directly to President Grant and prepared a list of charges against the agents. General Sherman, in overall command of the Indian country, claimed in 1875, "We could settle Indian troubles in an hour, but Congress wants the patronage of the Indian bureau, and the bureau wants the appropriations without any of the trouble of the Indians themselves." General Sheridan was no lover of Indians. "The only good Indians I ever saw," he said in an oft-quoted remark, "were dead." But he understood why they behaved as they did. "We took away their country and their means of support, broke up their mode of living, their habits of life, introduced disease and decay among them, and it was for this and against this that they made war. Could anyone expect less?"

In 1874 gold was discovered in the Black Hills Indian reservation. By the next winter thousands of miners had invaded the reserved area. Already alarmed by the approach of crews building the Northern Pacific Railroad, the Sioux once again went on the warpath. Joining with nontreaty tribes to the west, they concentrated in the region of the Bighorn River, in southern Montana Territory.

The summer of 1876 saw three columns of troops in the field against them. The commander of one column, General Alfred H. Terry, sent ahead a small detachment of the Seventh Cavalry under Colonel George A. Custer with orders to locate the Indians' camp and then block their escape route into the inaccessible Bighorn Mountains. Custer was vain and rash, and vanity and rashness were grave handicaps when fighting Indians. Grossly underestimating the number of the Indians, he decided to attack directly with his tiny force of 264 men. At the Little Bighorn late in June he found himself surrounded by 2,500 Sioux under Rain-in-the-Face, Crazy Horse, and Sitting Bull. He and all his men died on the field.

Because it was so one-sided, "Custer's Last Stand" was not a typical battle, although it may be taken as symbolic of the Indian warfare of the period in the sense that it was characterized by bravery, foolhardiness, and

a tragic waste of life. The battle greatly heartened the Indians, but it did not gain them their cause. That autumn, short of rations and hard-pressed by overwhelming numbers of soldiers, they surrendered and returned to the reservation.

Read the **Document** *Secretary of the Interior's Report on Indian Affairs* at **www.myhistorylab.com**

Read the **Document** *Red Cloud's Speech* at **www.myhistorylab.com**

The Destruction of Tribal Life

Thereafter, the fighting slackened. For this the building of transcontinental railroads and the destruction of the buffalo were chiefly responsible. An estimated 13–15 million head had roamed the plains in the mid-1860s. Then the slaughter began. Thousands were butchered to feed the gangs of laborers engaged in building the Union Pacific Railroad. Thousands more fell before the guns of sportsmen. Buffalo hunting became a fad, and a brisk demand developed for buffalo rugs and mounted buffalo heads. Railroads made the Army a far more efficient force. Troops and supplies could be moved swiftly when trouble with the tribes erupted. The lines also contributed to the decimation of the buffalo by running excursion trains for

A mound of buffalo skulls. In 1870 an estimated 30 million buffalo roamed the plains; by 1900, there were fewer than 1,000. During an eight-month period between 1867 and 1868, William F. Cody (Buffalo Bill) killed 4,280 buffalo, which fed construction crews for the Union Pacific railroad. Tourists also took up buffalo hunting, often shooting them from trains. The depletion of the buffalo, which provided the Plains Indians with meat and hides, was a major source of conflict with whites.

hunters; even the shameful practice of gunning down the beasts directly from the cars was allowed.

The discovery in 1871 of a way to make commercial use of buffalo hides completed the tragedy. In the next three years about 9 million head were killed; after another decade the animals were almost extinct. No more efficient way could have been found for destroying the Plains Indians. The disappearance of the bison left them starving and homeless.

By 1887 the tribes of the mountains and deserts beyond the plains had also given up the fight. Typical of the heartlessness of the government's treatment of these peoples was that afforded the Nez Percé of Oregon and Idaho, who were led by the remarkable Chief Joseph. After outwitting federal troops in a campaign across more than a thousand miles of rough country, Joseph finally surrendered in October 1877. The Nez Percé were then settled on "the malarial bottoms of the Indian Territory" in far-off Oklahoma. When Geronimo, leader of the Apache Indians of the Southwest, was captured in 1886, the Apache gave up, too.

By the 1880s, the advance of whites into the plains had become, in the words of one congressman, as irresistible "as that of Sherman's to the sea." Greed for land lay behind the pressure, but large numbers of disinterested people, including

most of those who deplored the way the Indians had been treated in the past, believed that the only practical way to solve the "Indian problem" was to persuade the Indians to abandon their tribal culture and live on family farms. The "wild" Indian must be changed into a "civilized" member of "American" society.

To accomplish this goal Congress passed the **Dawes Severalty Act of 1887**. Tribal lands were to be split up into individual allotments. To keep speculators from wresting the allotments from the Indians while they were adjusting to their new way of life, the land could not be disposed of for twenty-five years. Funds were to be appropriated for educating and training the Indians, and those who accepted allotments—took up residence "separate from any tribe," and "adopted the habits of civilized life"—were to be granted U.S. citizenship.

The sponsors of the Severalty Act thought they were effecting a fine humanitarian reform. "We must throw some protection over [the Indian]," Senator Henry L. Dawes declared. "We must hold up his hand." But no one expected all the Indians to accept allotments at once, and for some years little pressure was put on any to do so. The law was a statement of policy rather than a set of specific rules and orders. "Too great haste . . . should be avoided," Indian Commissioner

In 1879 an army officer founded the Carlisle School in Pennsylvania to "civilize" young Indians. These photographs are "before" and "after" renderings of three Lakota boys. No longer do they sit on the floor.

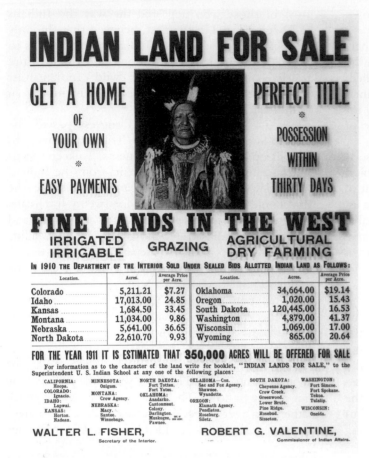

INDIAN LAND FOR SALE

GET A HOME
OF
YOUR OWN
*
EASY PAYMENTS

PERFECT TITLE
*
POSSESSION
WITHIN
THIRTY DAYS

FINE LANDS IN THE WEST
IRRIGATED   GRAZING   AGRICULTURAL
IRRIGABLE   DRY FARMING

IN 1910 THE DEPARTMENT OF THE INTERIOR SOLD UNDER SEALED BIDS ALLOTTED INDIAN LAND AS FOLLOWS:

Location.	Acres.	Average Price per Acre.	Location.	Acres.	Average Price per Acre.
Colorado	5,211.21	$7.27	Oklahoma	34,664.00	$19.14
Idaho	17,013.00	24.85	Oregon	1,020.00	15.43
Kansas	1,684.50	33.45	South Dakota	120,445.00	16.53
Montana	11,034.00	9.86	Washington	4,879.00	41.37
Nebraska	5,641.00	36.65	Wisconsin	1,069.00	17.00
North Dakota	22,610.70	9.93	Wyoming	865.00	20.64

FOR THE YEAR 1911 IT IS ESTIMATED THAT **350,000** ACRES WILL BE OFFERED FOR SALE

For information as to the character of the land write for booklet, "INDIAN LANDS FOR SALE," to the Superintendent U. S. Indian School at any one of the following places:

CALIFORNIA: MINNESOTA: NORTH DAKOTA: OKLAHOMA—Con.   SOUTH DAKOTA: WASHINGTON:
  Hoopa.   Onigum.   Fort Totten.   Sac and Fox Agency.   Cheyenne Agency.   Fort Simcoe.
COLORADO: MONTANA: Fort Yates.   Shawnee.   Crow Creek.   Fort Spokane.
  Ignacio.   Crow Agency. OKLAHOMA: Wyandotte.   Greenwood.   Tekoa.
IDAHO: Anadarko.   OREGON: Lower Brule.   Tulalip.
  Lapwai.   NEBRASKA: Cantonment.   Klamath Agency.   Pine Ridge.
KANSAS: Macy.   Colony.   Pendleton.   Rosebud.   WISCONSIN:
  Horton.   Santee.   Darlington.   Roseburg.   Sisseton.   Oneida.
  Nadeau.   Winnebago.   Muskogee, sec. &c   Siletz.
                                Pawnee.

WALTER L. FISHER,
Secretary of the Interior.

ROBERT G. VALENTINE,
Commissioner of Indian Affairs.

An ad for Indian land, offered for sale by the U.S. Department of the Interior. In 1889 alone, white settlers claimed 2 million acres of Indian Territory. By 1892, they had acquired some 30 million acres. During the 1890s, the white population of Oklahoma Territory—as it was called in 1890—increased from 60,000 to 400,000.

John Atkins explained. "Character, habits, and antecedents cannot be changed by enactment."

The Dawes Act had disastrous results in the long run. It assumed that Indians could be transformed into small agricultural capitalists by an act of Congress. It shattered what was left of the Indians' culture without enabling them to adapt to white ways. Moreover, unscrupulous white men systematically tricked many Indians into leasing their allotments for a pittance, and local authorities often taxed Indian lands at excessive rates. In 1934, after about 86 million of the 138 million acres assigned under the Dawes Act had passed into white hands, the government returned to a policy of encouraging tribal ownership of Indian lands.

The story of U.S.-Indian relations in the nineteenth century concludes, predictably, with a sad coda. In 1890 the Teton Sioux, suffering from cold and hunger, took heart from the words of Wovoka, a prophet, who had said that the whites would disappear if the Sioux performed their "ghost dance" rituals. When the Ghost Dance movement spread, federal military authorities resolved to stamp it out. On December 14 they attempted to arrest Chief Sitting Bull, a legendary Sioux warrior. When he resisted, shots rang out and Sitting Bull was killed. His people left the reservation at Pine Ridge and fled into the Badlands. The soldiers pursued them and the Indians surrendered. As they were being disarmed, however, a scuffle broke out and the troops opened fire. Some

Table 16.1   Key Federal Policies Affecting Indians

Policy	Year	Provisions	Consequences
Indian Removal Bill	1830	Indians surrender land east of Mississippi to settle in Oklahoma and elsewhere	Forcible removal of Indians from South
Treaty of Fort Laramie	1851	Indian tribes establish tribal boundaries over shared hunting grounds and ensure safe passage of westward-bound settlers through Indian territory	Discourages concerted action among Indian tribes; settlers encroach on Indian lands
Railroad land grants	1850–1871	Gives railroads lands to lay track throughout the West	Promotes settlement and further encroachment; hastens demise of buffalo
Treaty of Fort Laramie	1868	Concentrates Indians in reservations in the Dakotas and Oklahoma	Dissident Indians commence open warfare against U.S. government
Dawes Severalty Act	1887	Breaks Indian lands into small plots for Indian families or sale to whites	Weakens tribal authority; causes loss of Indian land
Indian Reorganization Act	1934	Rescinds Dawes	Increases tribal authority
Indian Gaming Regulatory Act	1988	Allows tribes to run federally regulated casinos and gambling operations	Generates huge revenue for a handful of eastern tribes, and little for the rest

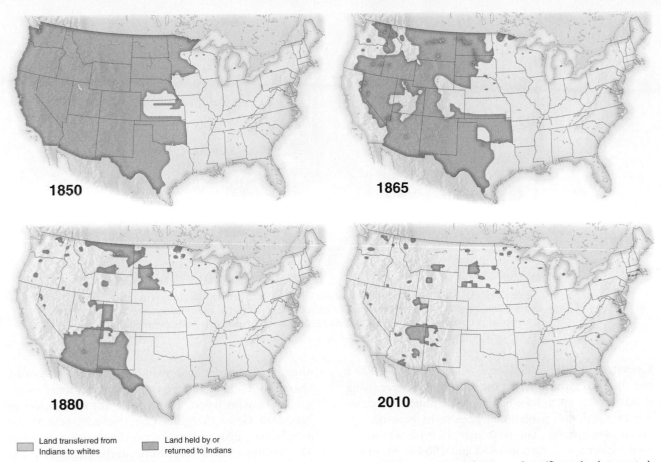

Loss of Indian Lands, 1850-2010 This chapter describes the specific government policies, economic tendencies, and specific treaties that wrested land from the Indians. But the simplest explanation is that an aggressive, acquisitive, and militarily powerful people craved the West and they took it.

150 Sioux were killed, including many women and children. Thirty federal soldiers also died during the fighting at Wounded Knee.

The Lure of Gold and Silver in the West

The natural resources of the nation were exploited in these decades even more ruthlessly and thoughtlessly than were its human resources. Americans had long regarded the West as a limitless treasure to be grasped as rapidly as possible, and after 1865 they acquired its riches still faster and in a wider variety of ways. From the mid-1850s to the mid-1870s thousands of gold-crazed prospectors fanned out through the Rockies, panning every stream and hacking furiously at every likely outcropping from the Fraser River country of British Columbia to Tucson in southern Arizona, from the eastern slopes of the Sierras to the Great Plains.

Gold and silver were scattered throughout the area, though usually too thinly to make mining profitable. Whenever anyone made a "strike," prospectors, the vast majority utterly without previous experience but driven by what a mining journal of

the period called an "unhealthy desire" for sudden wealth, flocked to the site, drawn by rumors of stream beds gleaming with gold-rich gravel and of nuggets the size of men's fists. For a few months the area teemed with activity. Towns of 5,000 or more sprang up overnight; improvised roads were crowded with people and supply wagons. Claims were staked out along every stream and gully. Then, usually, expectations faded in the light of reality: high prices, low yields, hardship, violence, and deception. The boom collapsed and the towns died as quickly as they had risen. A few found significant wealth, the rest only backbreaking labor and disappointment—that is, until tales of another strike sent them dashing feverishly across the land on another golden chase.

In the spring of 1858 it was on the Fraser River in Canada that the horde descended, 30,000 Californians in the vanguard. The following spring, Pikes Peak in Colorado attracted the pack, experienced California prospectors ("yonder siders") mixing with "greenhorns" from every corner of the globe. In June 1859 came the finds in Nevada, where the famous

Creede, Colorado, circa 1890, a mining town whose inhospitality to women is suggested by their absence. One reason is indicated in information compiled for another Colorado mining town, Leadville, which, with a population of 20,000, had 250 saloons, 120 gambling establishments, 100 brothels, and only 4 churches.

Comstock Lode yielded ores worth nearly $4,000 a ton. In 1861, while men in the settled areas were laying down their tools to take up arms, the miners were racing to the Idaho panhandle, hoping to become millionaires overnight. The next year the rush was to the Snake River valley, then in 1863 and 1864 to Montana. In 1874 to 1876 the Black Hills in the heart of the Sioux lands were inundated.

In a sense the Denvers, Aurarias, Virginia Cities, Orofinos, and Gold Creeks of the West during the war years were harbingers of the attitudes that flourished in the East in the age of President Grant and his immediate successors. The miners enthusiastically adopted the get-rich-quick philosophy, willingly enduring privations and laboring hard, always with the objective of striking it rich. The idea of reserving any part of the West for future generations never entered their heads.

The sudden prosperity of the mining towns attracted every kind of shady character—according to one forty-niner "rascals from Oregon, pickpockets from New York, accomplished gentlemen from Europe, interlopers from Lima and Chile, Mexican thieves, gamblers from no particular spot, and assassins manufactured in Hell." Gambling dens, dance halls, saloons, and brothels mushroomed wherever precious metal was found.

Law enforcement was a constant problem. Much of the difficulty lay in the antisocial attitudes of the miners themselves. Gold and silver dominated people's thoughts and dreams, and few paid much attention to the means employed in accumulating this wealth. Storekeepers charged outrageous prices; claim holders "salted" worthless properties with

nuggets in order to swindle gullible investors. Ostentation characterized the successful, mere swagger those who failed. During the administration of President Grant, Virginia City, Nevada, was at the peak of its vulgar prosperity, producing an average of $12 million a year in ore. Built on the richness of the Comstock Lode ($306 million in gold and silver was extracted from the Comstock in twenty years), it had twenty-five saloons before it had 4,000 people. By the 1870s its mountainside site was disfigured by ugly, ornate mansions where successful mine operators ate from fine china and swilled champagne as though it were water.

In 1873, after the discovery of the Big Bonanza, a seam of rich ore more than fifty feet thick, the future of Virginia City seemed boundless. Other discoveries shortly thereafter indicated to optimists that the mining boom in the West would continue indefinitely. The finds in the Black Hills district in 1875 and 1876, heralding deposits yielding eventually $100 million, led to the mushroom growth of Deadwood, home of Wild Bill Hickok, Deadwood Dick, Calamity Jane, and such lesser-known characters as California Jack and Poker Alice. The West continued to yield much gold and silver, especially silver, but big corporations produced nearly all of it. The mines around Deadwood were soon controlled by one large company, Homestake Mining. Butte, Montana, was similarly dominated by Anaconda Mining.

This is the culminating irony of the history of the mining frontier: Shoestring prospectors, independent and enterprising, made the key discoveries. They established local institutions and supplied the

West with much of its color and folklore. But the stockholders of large corporations, many of whom had never seen a mine, made off with the lion's share of the wealth. Those whose worship of gold was direct and incessant, the prospectors who peopled the mining towns and gave the frontier its character, mostly died poor, still seeking a prize as elusive if not as illusory as the pot of gold at the end of the rainbow.

The mining of gold and silver is not essentially different from the mining of coal and iron. To operate profitably, large capital investments were required. Tunnels had to be blasted deep into the earth and miniature railroads laid out to transport the ore-bearing rock to the surface. Heavy machinery had to be purchased and transported to remote regions to extract the precious metal. To do this work, hundreds of skilled miners (mostly "deep" miners from Cornwall, in England) had to be imported and paid. Henry Comstock, the prospector who gave his name to the Comstock Lode, was luckier than most, but he sold his claims to the lode for a pittance, disposing of what became one valuable mine for $40 and receiving only $10,000 for his share of the fabulous Ophir, the richest concentration of gold and silver ever found.

Though marked by violence, fraud, greed, and lost hopes, the gold rushes had valuable results. The most obvious was the new metal itself, which bolstered the financial position of the United States during and after the Civil War. Quantities of European goods needed for the war effort and for postwar economic development were paid for with the yield of the new mines. Gold and silver also caused a great increase of interest in the West. A valuable literature appeared, part imaginative, part reportorial, describing the mining camps and the life of the prospectors. These works fascinated contemporaries (as they have continued to fascinate succeeding generations when adapted to the motion picture and to television). Mark Twain's *Roughing It* (1872), based in part on his experiences in the Nevada mining country, is the most famous example of this literature.

The mines also speeded the political organization of the West. Colorado and Nevada became territories in 1861, Arizona and Idaho in 1863, and Montana in 1864. Although Nevada was admitted before it had 60,000 residents (in 1864, to ratify the Thirteenth Amendment and help reelect Lincoln), most of these territories did not become states for decades. But because of the miners, the framework for future development was early established.

Farmers Struggle to Keep Up

While miners were extracting the mineral wealth of the West, others were snapping up the region's choice farmland. Presumably the Homestead Act of 1862 was supposed to make it easier for poor families to acquire farms, thereby ending the reign of the speculator and the large landholder. An early amendment to the act even prevented husbands and wives from filing separate claims. The West, land reformers had assumed, would soon be dotted with 160-acre family farms.

They were doomed to disappointment. Most landless Americans were too poor to become farmers even when they could obtain land without cost. The expense of moving a family to the ever-receding frontier exceeded the means of many, and the cost of a plow, hoes and scythes, draft animals, a wagon, a well, fencing, and of building the simplest house, might come to $1,000—a formidable barrier. As for the industrial workers for whom the free land was supposed to provide a "safety valve," they had neither the skills nor the inclination to become farmers. Homesteaders usually came from districts not far removed from frontier conditions.

The first settlers in western Kansas, Nebraska, and the Dakotas took up land along the rivers and

A sod house in North Dakota, 1896. Individual "bricks" of sod were hewn from the ground and stacked in layers to build houses. The roof was made of timber packed with branches, twigs, straw, and more sod. This house was expanded with a room made of planed lumber (right). Sod houses were quite cool in summer and warm in winter, although excess moisture was always a problem.

Did the Frontier Promote Individualism and Democracy?

This 1887 photograph depicts a family in Custer County, Nebraska. They have begun to build a house (center), which suggests some optimism, yet their isolation and the rude dugout (upper left) illustrates their vulnerability. Were such people self-reliant individualists or needy dependents?

In 1893 historian Frederick Jackson Turner argued that the boundless expanses of the frontier gave rise to democracy, individualism, and "withal that buoyancy and exuberance which comes with freedom." Insofar as the frontier was then receding before the advance of urbanization and industrialization, Turner's readers had cause for alarm. Historians adopting the Turnerian analysis—and there were many—were generally pessimistic about the prospects for American democracy.

Philosopher John Dewey (1922) was among those who dissented. He argued that rather than promoting democracy, the frontier had a "depressing effect upon the free life of inquiry and criticism." Some historians insisted that democracy flourished not in the West but in urban and industrial areas. In recent decades scholars have challenged Turner's assertions that frontier peoples were self-sufficient and their democratic institutions vital.

Richard White (1991) insisted that the West, more so than any other region, had been "historically a dependency of the federal government." Donald Worster (1992) contended that its predominant economy—cattle-raising and irrigation agriculture—was developed mostly by large corporations.

During the past two decades, moreover, many scholars have asked the following question: How can anyone claim that the frontier promoted democratic sensibilities if it came at the cost of dispossessing the Indians—missing from the photograph—who had previously ranged over this land?

Source: Donald Worster, *Under Western Skies* (1992); Richard White, *It's Your Misfortune and None of My Own* (1991); Peggy Pascoe, *Relations of Rescue: The Search for Female Moral Authority in the American West, 1874–1939* (1990); Patricia Limerick, *Legacy of Conquest* (1988); and Elliot West, *The Contested Plains* (1998).

creeks, where they found enough timber for home building, fuel, and fencing. Later arrivals had to build houses of the tough prairie sod and depend on hay, sunflower stalks, and buffalo dung for fuel.

Frontier farm families had always had to work hard and endure the hazards of storm, drought, and insect plagues, along with isolation and loneliness. But all these burdens were magnified on the prairies and the High Plains. Life was particularly hard for farm women, who, in addition to childcare and housework, performed endless farm chores—milking cows, feeding livestock, raising vegetables, and so on. "I . . . am up and running every morning at half-past four o'clock, and run all day, often until half-past eleven P.M.," one farm woman explained. "Is it any wonder I have become slightly demoralized?"

Farming as Big Business

Immediately after the Civil War, Congress reserved 47.7 million acres of public land in the South for homesteaders, stopping all cash sales in the region. But in 1876 this policy was reversed and the land thrown open. Speculators flocked to the feast in such numbers that the Illinois Central Railroad ran special trains from Chicago to Mississippi and Louisiana. Between 1877 and 1888 over 5.6 million acres were sold; much of the land was covered with valuable pine and cypress.

The flat immensity of the land, combined with newly available farm machinery and the development of rail connections with the East, encouraged the growth of enormous corporation-controlled "bonanza" farms. One such organization was the railroad-owned empire managed by Oliver Dalrymple in the Dakota Territory, which cultivated 25,000 acres of wheat in 1880. Dalrymple employed 200 pairs of harrows to prepare his soil, 125 seeders to sow his seed, and 155 binders to harvest his crop.

Bonanza farmers could buy supplies wholesale and obtain concessions from railroads and processors, but even the biggest organizations could not cope with prolonged drought, and most of the bonanza outfits failed in the dry years of the late 1880s. Those wise farmers who diversified their crops and cultivated their land intensively fared better in the long run, although even they could not hope to earn a profit in really dry years.

Despite the hazards of plains agriculture, the region became the breadbasket of America in the decades following the Civil War. By 1889 Minnesota topped the nation in wheat production, and ten years later four of the five leading wheat states lay west of the Mississippi. The plains also accounted for heavy percentages of the nation's other cereal crops, together with immense quantities of beef, pork, and mutton.

Like other exploiters of the nation's resources, farmers took whatever they could from the soil with little heed for preserving its fertility and preventing erosion. The consequent national loss was less apparent because it was diffuse and slow to assume drastic proportions, but it was nonetheless real.

Western Railroad Building

Further exploitation of land resources by private interests resulted from the government's policy of subsidizing western railroads. Here was a clear illustration of the conflict between the idea of the West as a national heritage to be disposed of to deserving citizens and the concept of the region as a cornucopia pouring forth riches to be gathered up and carted off by anyone powerful and determined enough to take them. When it came to a choice between giving a particular tract to railroads or to homesteaders, the homesteaders nearly always lost out. On the other hand, the swift development of western railroads was essential if farmers, miners, and cattle ranchers were to prosper.

Unless the government had been willing to build the transcontinental lines itself—and this was unthinkable in an age dominated by belief in individual exploitation—some system of subsidy was essential. Private investors would not hazard the huge sums needed to lay tracks across hundreds of miles of rugged, empty country when traffic over the road could not possibly profit for many years. It might appear that subsidizing construction by direct outlays of public funds would have been adopted, but that idea had few supporters. Most voters were wary of entrusting the dispensing of large sums to politicians. Grants of land seemed a sensible way of financing construction. The method avoided direct outlays of public funds, for the companies could pledge the land as security for bond issues or sell it directly for cash.

In many cases the value of the land granted might be recovered by the government when it sold other lands in the vicinity, for such properties would certainly be worth more after transportation facilities to eastern markets had been constructed. "Why," the governor of one eastern state asked in 1867, "should private individuals be called upon to make a useless sacrifice of their means, when railroads can be constructed by the unity of public and private interests, and made profitable to all?"

Federal land grants to railroads began in 1850 with those allotted to the Illinois Central. Over the next two decades about 49 million acres were given to

Chinese work on a railway in the Far West. "Without them," Leland Stanford, president of the Central Pacific Railroad said, "it would be impossible to complete the western portion of this great national highway." Some Chinese were drawn from the gold fields farther north, and others were imported from China, under five-year contracts with the railroads, which paid them $10 or $12 a month.

various lines indirectly in the form of grants to the states, but the most lavish gifts of the public domain were those made directly to builders of intersectional trunk lines. These roads received more than 155 million acres, although about 25 million acres reverted to the government because some companies failed to lay the required miles of track. About 75 percent of this land went to aid the construction of four transcontinental railroads: the Union Pacific–Central Pacific line, running from Nebraska to San Francisco, completed in 1869; the Atchison, Topeka, and Santa Fe, running from Kansas City to Los Angeles by way of Santa Fe and Albuquerque, completed in 1883; the Southern Pacific, running from San Francisco to New Orleans by way of Yuma and El Paso, completed in 1883; and the Northern Pacific, running from Duluth, Minnesota, to Portland, Oregon, completed in 1883.

The Pacific Railway Act of 1862 established the pattern for these grants. It gave the builders of the Union Pacific and Central Pacific railroads five square miles of public land on each side of their right-of-way for each mile of track laid. The land was allotted in alternate sections, forming a pattern like a checkerboard: the squares of one color representing railroad property, the other government property. Presumably this arrangement benefited the entire nation since half the land close to the railroad remained in public hands.

However, whenever grants were made to railroads, the adjacent government lands were not opened to homesteaders—on the theory that free land in the immediate vicinity of a line would prevent the road from disposing of its properties at good prices. In addition to the land granted the railroads, a wide zone of "indemnity" lands was reserved to allow the roads to choose alternative sites to make up for lands that settlers had already taken up within the checkerboard. Thus, homesteading was in fact prohibited near land-grant railroads. More than twenty years after receiving its immense grant, the Northern Pacific was still attempting to keep homesteaders from filing in the indemnity zone. President Cleveland finally put a stop to this in 1887, saying that he could find "no evidence" that "this vast tract is necessary for the fulfillment of the grant."

Historians have argued at length about the fairness of the land-grant system. No railroad corporation waxed fat directly from the sale of its lands, which were sold at prices averaging between $2 and $5 an acre. Collectively the roads took in between $400 million and $500 million from this source, but only over the course of a century. Land-grant lines encouraged the growth of the West by advertising their property widely and by providing cheap transportation for prospective settlers and efficient shipping services for farmers. They were required by law to carry troops and handle government business free or at reduced rates, which saved the government millions over the years. At the same time the system imposed no effective restraints on how the railroads used the funds raised with federal aid. Being able to lay track with money obtained from land grants, the operators tended to be extravagant and often downright corrupt.

The construction of the Central Pacific in the 1860s illustrates how the system encouraged extravagance. The line was controlled by four businessmen: Collis P. Huntington, "scrupulously dishonest" but an excellent manager; Leland Stanford, a Sacramento grocer and politician; Mark Hopkins, a hardware merchant; and Charles Crocker, a hulking, relentless driver of men who had come to California during the gold rush and made a small fortune as a merchant. The Central Pacific and the Union Pacific were given, in addition to their land grants, loans in the form of government bonds—from $16,000 to $48,000 for each mile of track laid, depending on the difficulty of the terrain. The two competed with each other for the subsidies, the Central Pacific building eastward from Sacramento, the Union Pacific westward from Nebraska. They put huge crews to work grading and laying track, bringing up supplies over the already completed road. The Union Pacific employed Civil War veterans and Irish immigrants, while the Central employed Chinese immigrants.

This plan favored the Union Pacific. While the Central Pacific was inching up the gorges and granite of the mighty Sierras, the Union Pacific was racing across the level plains laying 540 miles of track between 1865 and 1867. Once beyond the Sierras, the Central Pacific would have easy going across the Nevada–Utah plateau country, but by then it might be too late to prevent the Union Pacific from making off with most of the government aid.

Crocker managed the Central Pacific construction crews. He wasted huge sums by working through the winter in the High Sierras. Often the men labored in tunnels dug through forty-foot snowdrifts to get at the frozen ground. To speed construction of the Summit Tunnel, Crocker had a shaft cut down from above so that crews could work out from the middle as well as in from each end. In 1866, over the most difficult terrain, he laid twenty-eight miles of track, at a cost of more than $280,000 a mile. Experts later estimated that 70 percent of this sum could have been saved had speed not been a factor. Such prodigality made economic sense to Huntington, Stanford, Hopkins, and Crocker because of the profits they were making through its construction company and because of the gains they could count on once they reached the flat country beyond the Sierras, where costs would amount to only half the federal aid.

Crocker's Herculean efforts paid off. The mountains were conquered, and then the crews raced across the Great Basin to Salt Lake City and beyond. The meeting of the rails—the occasion of a national celebration—took place at Promontory, north of Ogden, Utah, on May 10, 1869. Leland Stanford drove the final ceremonial golden spike with a silver hammer.[2]

The Union Pacific had built 1,086 miles of track, the Central 689 miles.

In the long run the wasteful way in which the Central Pacific was built hurt the road severely. It was ill-constructed, over grades too steep and around curves too sharp, and burdened with debts that were too large. Steep grades meant that heavier, more expensive locomotives burning more coal were needed to pull lighter loads—a sure way to lower profits. Such was the fate of nearly all the railroads constructed with the help of government subsidies.

The only transcontinental railroad built without land grants was the Great Northern, running from St. Paul, Minnesota, to the Pacific. Spending private capital, its guiding genius, James J. Hill, was compelled to build economically and to plan carefully. As a result, his was the only transcontinental line to weather the depression of the 1890s without going into bankruptcy.

The Cattle Kingdom

While miners were digging out the mineral wealth of the West and railroaders were taking possession of much of its land, another group was exploiting endless acres of its grass. For twenty years after the Civil War cattlemen and sheep raisers dominated huge areas of the High Plains, making millions of dollars by grazing their herds on lands they did not own.

Columbus brought the first cattle to the New World in 1493 on his second voyage, and later conquistadores took them to every corner of Spain's American empire. Mexico proved to be so well-suited to cattle raising that many were allowed to roam loose. They multiplied rapidly, and by the late eighteenth century what is now southern Texas harbored enormous herds. The beasts interbred with nondescript "English" cattle, brought into the area by settlers from the United States, to produce the Texas longhorn. Hardy, wiry, ill-tempered, and fleet, with horns often attaining a spread of six feet, these animals were far from ideal as beef cattle and almost as hard to capture as wild horses, but they existed in southern Texas by the millions, most of them unowned.

The lack of markets and transportation explains why Texas cattle were lightly regarded. But conditions were changing. Industrial growth in the East was causing an increase in the urban population and a consequent rise in the demand for food. At the same time, the expansion of the railroad network made it possible to move cattle cheaply over long distances. As the iron rails inched across the plains, astute cattlemen began to do some elementary figuring. Longhorns could be had locally for $3 and $4 a head.

---

[2]A mysterious "San Francisco jeweler" passed among the onlookers, taking orders for souvenir watch chains that he proposed to make from the spike at $5 each.

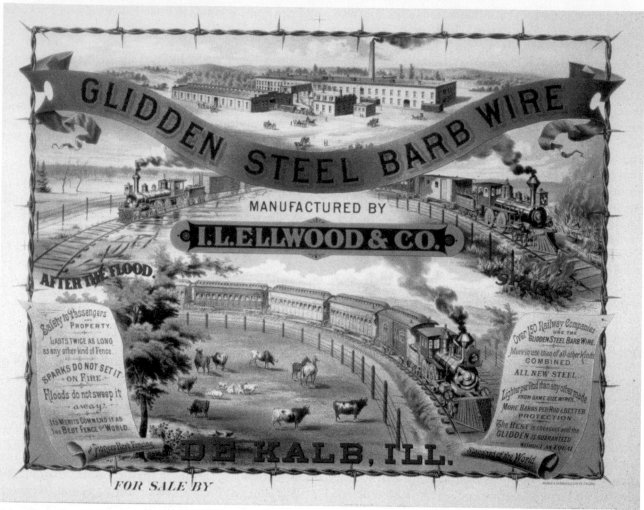

This ad for barbed wire depicts several scenes: A wooden fence has been swept away by a flood (left) and set afire (right). On the bottom, a barbed wire fence separates cattle from the railroad.

In the northern cities they would bring ten times that much, perhaps even more. Why not round them up and herd them northward to the railroads, allowing them to feed along the way on the abundant grasses of the plains? The land was unoccupied and owned by the federal government. Anyone could drive cattle across it without paying a fee or asking anyone's permission. The grass the cattle ate on the way swiftly renewed itself.

In 1866 a number of Texans drove large herds northward toward Sedalia, Missouri, railhead of the Missouri Pacific. This route took the herds through wooded and settled country and across Indian reservations, which provoked many difficulties. At the same time Charles Goodnight and Oliver Loving successfully drove 2,000 head in a great arc west to the New Mexico Territory and then north to Colorado.

The next year the drovers, inspired by a clever young Illinois cattle dealer named Joseph G. McCoy

and other entrepreneurs, led their herds north by a more westerly route, across unsettled grasslands, to the Kansas Pacific line at Abilene, Kansas, which McCoy described as "a very small, dead place, consisting of about one dozen log huts." They earned excellent profits, and during the next five years about 1.5 million head made the "long drive" over the Chisholm Trail to Abilene, where they were sold to ranchers, feedlot operators, and the agents of eastern meatpackers. Other shipping points sprang up as the railroads pushed westward. According to the best estimates 10 million head were driven north before the practice ended in the mid-1880s. (For the story of one cowboy, see the American Lives essay on "Nat Love," p. 452.)

Watch the **Video** *Cowboys and Cattle* at **www.myhistorylab.com**

Read the **Document** *Chisholm Trail* at **www.myhistorylab.com**

Open-Range Ranching

Soon cattlemen discovered that the hardy Texas stock could survive the winters of the northern plains. Attracted by the apparently limitless forage, they began to bring up herds to stock the vast regions where the buffalo had so recently roamed. Introducing pedigreed Hereford bulls, they improved the stock without weakening its resistance to harsh conditions. By 1880 some 4.5 million head had spread across the sea of grass that ran from Kansas to Montana and west to the Rockies.

The prairie grasses offered ranchers a bonanza almost as valuable as the gold mines. Open-range ranching required actual ownership of no more than a few acres along some watercourse. In this semiarid region, control of water enabled a rancher to dominate all the surrounding area back to the divide separating his range from the next stream without investing a cent in the purchase of land. His cattle, wandering freely on the public domain, fattened on grass owned by all the people, were to be turned into beefsteak and leather for the profit of the rancher.

Theoretically, anyone could pasture stock on the open range, but without access to water it was impossible to do so. "I have 2 miles of running water," a cattleman said in testifying before the Public Land

Squeezing the Indians Economically, 1850–1893 The construction of the railroads, the rise of mining and commercial farming, and vast open-range herding all weakened the Indians economically and drove them from their lands.

Nat Love, a slave, was born on a plantation in Davidson County, Tennessee sometime in 1854. Nat's father was a foreman on the plantation; his mother milked cows, cooked, and operated a loom. Although Love described his master as "kind and indulgent," his earliest memories were of begging for scraps "like a pet dog" from his master's table.

After the Civil War, Love's father rented twenty acres from his former master. Nat spent Sundays at a horse farm, where he learned how to ride. Soon he was earning ten cents for every colt he "broke."

When Nat's father died, the family's circumstances became dire. When they weren't working in the cornfield or garden, they collected nuts and berries. He and his siblings went shoeless and their clothes were in tatters. Nat longed to escape from it all and see the world. His opportunity came when he won a horse in a raffle. He sold the horse and bought clothing and food for his family. In February 1869, he set out for the frontier. He was fifteen years old.

Months later, he arrived in Dodge City, Kansas, "a typical frontier city, with a great many saloons, dance halls, and gambling houses, and very little of anything else." At a camp outside of town, he asked a group of cowboys for a job. Eager to have some fun with the black "tenderfoot," they agreed if he could prove he could ride; then they put him on the wildest horse in camp. Love clung to the bucking bronco, much to everyone's astonishment. The boss hired him at $30 a month. He also gave Nat a saddle, a Colt 45 pistol and a new name—"Love" being unsuitable for a cowboy. Nat was now "Red River Dick."

Three days after the cowboys left Dodge, they were attacked by scores of mounted Indians. "When I saw them coming after us and heard their blood curdling yell, I was too badly scared to run," Love recalled. Before the Indians were driven away by gunfire, they had killed one cowboy and made off with most of the horses and provisions. The cowboy was buried in a blanket beneath a pile of stones. Love and the others walked to Texas.

Nat Love, posed here with the requisite implements, claimed to have been the "Deadwood Dick" on whom a series of novels was based.
Source: *Life and Adventures of Nat Love, Better Known in the Cattle Country as "Deadwood Dick," by Himself; a True History of Slavery Days, Life on the Great Cattle Ranges and on the Plains of the "Wild and Woolly" West*, Los Angeles 1907.

Over the next three years, Love served with outfits that drove cattle to grazing ranges and markets throughout the West (see the map on p. 451). Every spring and fall the ranchers staged a great roundup, driving in all the cattle to a central place, separating them by the brands, and culling steers for shipment to market. Love specialized as a brand reader. He "cut out" those belonging to his employer and drove them back to that herd.

Disputes over horse and cattle ownership often led to gunfights. On Christmas Day, 1872, an argument over a horse in Holbrook, Arizona resulted in the deaths of several of Love's friends. In 1876, while Love was driving 500 steers from the Rio Grande to a ranch in the Shoshone mountains of Wyoming, Indians attacked and stampeded the cattle. The battle raged through the night. By morning, several score Indians were dead, most of them trampled by cattle. Several nights later, a buffalo stampede tore through the camp, scattering cattle and killing another cowboy. Another time, Love broke up a robbery of a Union Pacific railroad station. After he won a roping and riding competition in Deadwood, South Dakota, "Red River Dick" became known as "Deadwood Dick." Shortly afterward, while hunting strays, he was shot by Indians and captured. When he recovered, the chief offered him his daughter in marriage along with 100 ponies. Dick pretended to go along with the marriage, but then stole a horse and escaped.

By the late 1880s, however, the heyday of the cowboy had ended. Now railroads hauled cattle from the grazing ranges to slaughterhouses in Kansas City, Omaha, Chicago, and St. Louis. In 1889, Dick went to Denver and got married. The following year he found a job as a porter on the Pullman Railroad cars. He died in 1921.

This account of the life of Nat Love is based largely on his 1907 autobiography. In that book, Love claimed that he was the inspiration for the popular "Deadwood Dick" dime novels by Edward L. Wheeler, first published in the 1870s. Love also insisted that he had been shot fourteen times, could drink enormous volumes of whiskey without impairment, and had befriended "Buffalo Bill" Cody, Kit Carson, and Jesse James. His most surprising claim was to have never been a victim of racial prejudice. Perhaps that was because about a third of all cowboys were African Americans or Mexican *vaqueros*. Many of the rest were white Texans, Civil War veterans, former miners, and, in the words of Theodore Roosevelt, "wild spirits from every land." Love's life, like so much about the frontier West, was the stuff of legend. (Nat Love's autobiography is available online at http://docsouth.unc.edu/neh/natlove/natlove.html)

Questions for Discussion

- Which factors perhaps promoted racial equality among ranch hands?

- Which elements of Love's story ring true and which seem improbable?

Commission. "That accounts for my ranch being where it is. The next water from me in one direction is 23 miles; now no man can have a ranch between these two places. I have control of the grass, the same as though I owned it." By having his cowhands take out homestead claims along watercourses in his region, a rancher could greatly expand the area he dominated. In the late 1870s one Colorado cattle baron controlled an area roughly the size of Connecticut and Rhode Island even though he owned only 105 small parcels that totaled about 15,500 acres.

With the demand for meat rising and transportation cheap, princely fortunes could be made in a few years. Capitalists from the East and from Europe began to pour funds into the business. Eastern "dudes" like Theodore Roosevelt, a young New York assemblyman who sank over $50,000 in his Elkhorn Ranch in the Dakota Territory in 1883, bought up cattle as a sort of profitable hobby. (Roosevelt, clad in buckskin and bearing a small armory of rifles and six-shooters, made quite a splash in Dakota, but not as a rancher.) Soon large outfits such as the Nebraska Land and Cattle Company, controlled by British investors, and the Union Cattle Company of Wyoming, a $3 million corporation, dominated the business, just as large companies had taken over most of the important gold and silver mines.

Unlike other exploiters of the West's resources, cattle ranchers did not at first injure or reduce any public resource. Grass eaten by their stock annually renewed itself; droppings from the animals enriched the soil. Furthermore, ranchers poached on the public domain because there was no reasonable way for them to obtain legal possession of the large areas necessary to raise cattle on the plains. Federal land laws made no allowance for the special conditions of the semiarid West.

A system to take account for those conditions was soon devised by Major John Wesley Powell, later the director of the United States Geological Survey. His *Report on the Lands of the Arid Region of the United States* (1879) suggested that western lands be divided into three classes: irrigable lands, timber lands, and "pasturage" lands. On the pasturage lands the "farm unit" ought to be at least 2,560 acres (four sections), Powell urged. Groups of these units should be organized into "pasturage districts" in which the ranchers "should have the right to make their own regulations for the division of lands, the use of the water . . . and for the pasturage of lands in common or in severalty."

Barbed-Wire Warfare

Congress refused to change the land laws in any basic way, and this had two harmful effects. First, it encouraged fraud: Those who could not get title to enough land honestly turned to subterfuge. The Desert Land Act (1877) allowed anyone to obtain 640 acres in the arid states for $1.25 an acre provided the owner irrigated part of it within three years. Since the original claimant could transfer the holding, the ranchers set their cowboys and other hands to filing claims, which were then signed over to them. Over 2.6 million acres were taken up under the act, and according to the best estimate, 95 percent of the claims were fraudulent—no sincere effort was made to irrigate the land.

Second, overcrowding became a problem that led to serious conflicts, even killings, because no one had uncontestable title to the land. The leading ranchers banded together in cattlemen's associations to deal with overcrowding and with such problems as quarantine regulations, water rights, and thievery. In most cases these associations devised effective and sensible rules, but their functions would better have been performed by the government, as such matters usually are.

To keep other ranchers' cattle from those sections of the public domain they considered their own, the associations and many individuals began to fence huge areas. This was possible only because of the invention in 1874 of barbed wire by Joseph F. Glidden, an Illinois farmer. By the 1880s thousands of miles of the new fencing had been strung across the plains, often across roads and in a few cases around entire communities. "Barbed-wire wars" resulted, fought by rancher against rancher, cattleman against sheepman, herder against farmer. The associations tried to police their fences and to punish anyone who cut their wire. Posted signs gave dire warnings to trespassers. "The Son of a Bitch who opens this fence had better look out for his scalp," one such sign announced, another fine statement of the philosophy of the age.

By stringing so much wire the cattlemen were unwittingly destroying their own way of doing business. On a truly open range, cattle could fend for themselves, instinctively finding water during droughts, drifting safely downwind before blizzards. Barbed wire prevented their free movement. During winter storms these slender strands became as lethal as high-tension wires: the drifting cattle piled up against them and died by the thousands.

The boom times were ending. Overproduction was driving down the price of beef; expenses were on the rise; many sections of the range were badly overgrazed. The dry summer of 1886 left the stock in such poor condition as winter approached that the *Rocky Mountain Husbandman* urged its readers to sell their cattle despite the prevailing low prices rather than "endanger the whole herd by having the range overstocked."

Some ranchers took this advice; those who did not made a fatal error. Winter that year arrived early

In 1885 masked Nebraskans seeking access to water posed for photographer S. D. Butcher, who captioned the picture, "Settlers taking the law into their own hands: Cutting 15 miles of the Brighton Ranch fence."

and with unparalleled fury. Blizzards raged and temperatures plummeted far below zero. Cattle crowded into low places only to be engulfed in giant snowdrifts; barbed wire took a fearful toll. When spring finally came, the streams were choked with rotting carcasses. Between 80 and 90 percent of all cattle on the range were dead. "We have had a perfect smashup all through the cattle country," Theodore Roosevelt wrote sadly in April 1887 from Elkhorn Ranch.

That cruel winter finished open-range cattle-raising. The large companies were bankrupt; many independent operators, Roosevelt among them, became discouraged and sold out. When the industry

revived, it was on a smaller, more efficiently organized scale. The fencing movement continued, but now ranchers enclosed only the land they actually owned. It then became possible to bring in pedigreed bulls to improve the breed. Cattle-raising, like mining before it, ceased to be an adventure in rollicking individualism and became a business.

By the late 1880s the bonanza days of the West were over. No previous frontier had caught the imagination of Americans so completely as the Great West, with its heroic size, its awesome emptiness, its massive, sculptured beauty. Most of what Walter Prescott Webb, author of the classic study *The Great Plains* (1931) called the "primary windfalls" of the region—the furs, the precious metals, the forests, the cattle, and the grass—had been snatched up by first comers and by individuals already wealthy. Big companies were taking over all the West's resources. The frontier was no more.

But the frontier never existed except as an intellectual construction among white settlers and those who wrote about them. To the Indians, the land was simply home. The "conquest of the frontier" was thus an appealing evasion: It transformed the harmful actions and policies of the nation into an expression of human progress, the march westward of "civilization."

"Civilization," though, was changing. The nation was becoming more powerful, richer, and larger, and its economic structure more complex and diversified as the West yielded its treasures. But the East, and especially eastern industrialists and financiers, were increasingly dominating the economy of the entire nation.

●●─ See the Map *Resources and Conflict in the West* at www.myhistorylab.com

Chapter Review

Milestones

1859	Discovery of the Comstock Lode lures miners west
1864	Chivington massacre of Cheyenne
1869	Union Pacific Railroad completed
	Board of Indian Commissioners established
1873	Timber Culture Act encourages western forestation
1876	Sioux slaughter Custer's cavalry at Battle of Little Bighorn
1877	Desert Land Act favors ranchers
	U.S. troops capture Chief Joseph of Nez Percé after 1,000-mile retreat

1878	Timber and Stone Act favors lumber companies
1879	Major Powell's *Report on the Lands of the Arid Region* suggests division of West
1882	Chinese Exclusion Act bans Chinese immigrant workers for ten years
1886–1887	Blizzards end open-range ranching
1887	Dawes Severalty Act splits tribal lands

Key Terms

Chinese Exclusion Act   A law passed by Congress in 1882 that prohibited Chinese immigration to the United States; it was overturned in 1943, *436*

Comstock Lode   The first major vein of silver ore in the United States, discovered in the late 1850s, near Virginia City, Nevada, *444*

Dawes Severalty Act of 1887   An 1887 law terminating tribal ownership of land and allotting some parcels of land to individual Indians with the remainder of the land left open for white settlement. It included provisions for Indian education and eventual citizenship. The law led to corruption, exploitation, and the weakening of Indian tribal culture. It was reversed in 1934, *441*

Review Questions

1. The text suggests that if federal policy had been more tolerant, there would have been no need to drive Indians from so much of their land. What alternative policies might have succeeded and how?

2. In *The Comanche Empire* (2009), historian Pekka Hamalainen insists that the Comanche themselves managed to forge a mighty empire. Maps showing the steady loss of Indian lands (such as that on p. 443) deprive the Indians of their "agency" in history. In what ways did Indians leave their own imprint upon this period?

3. How did the treatment of African Americans during the last third of the nineteenth century compare with that of Indians?

4. The West has exerted a powerful hold on the American imagination. What explains the popularity of western themes in American life? How does the history compare with the popular image?

myhistorylab Connections

Reinforce what you learned in this chapter by studying the many documents, images, maps, review tools, and videos available at **www.myhistorylab.com**.

Read and Review

✔—Study and Review *Chapter 16*

○●●—Read the Document *Secretary of the Interior's Report on Indian Affairs*, p. 440

○●●—Read the Document *Red Cloud's Speech*, p. 440

○●●—Read the Document *Chisholm Trail*, p. 450

◉—See the Map *Resources and Conflict in the West*, p. 454

Research and Explore

◉—Watch the Video *Cowboys and Cattle*, p. 450

Hear the Audio

Hear the audio file for Chapter 16 at **www.myhistorylab.com**.

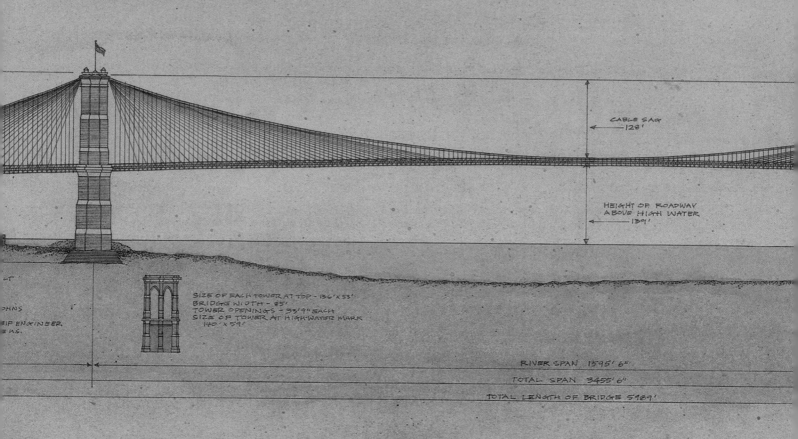

Within the illustration:

CABLE SAG — 128'

HEIGHT OF ROADWAY ABOVE HIGH WATER — 139'

SIZE OF EACH TOWER AT TOP — 136' × 53'
BRIDGE WIDTH — 85'
TOWER OPENINGS — 33'9" EACH
SIZE OF TOWER AT HIGH-WATER MARK
140' × 59'

RIVER SPAN 1595' 6"

TOTAL SPAN 3455' 6"

TOTAL LENGTH OF BRIDGE 5989'

THE BROOKLYN BRIDGE · OPENE

DESIGNED BY JOHN A. ROEBLING · CIVIL EN

Do you save money at big box stores?

In 2010 Walmart, with 2.1 million employees, was the largest corporation in the history of the world. Its revenues of $405 billion exceeded the gross domestic product of Sweden and Saudi Arabia. The company's clout made it a frequent target of popular satire. A 2008 episode of *The Simpsons* was set at "Sprawl-Mart," where Homer was offered a job as Executive Greeter. "Is there a chance for advancement?" he asks. "No," the manager says. "You get to work overtime without us paying you extra." In 2006 *Saturday Night Live* ran a satirical advertisement for "Sale-Mart," a big-box store that was "all about low prices." Toothless employees

expressed satisfaction with the company's dental plan. The announcer told shoppers to hurry to the pharmacy, "where generic prescription drugs are two handfuls for a dollar."

Real-world critics of Walmart leveled similar charges. A labor union website described Walmart as a "death star" that "destroys all other economic activity in its path." Others complained that many Walmart employees qualified for public assistance.

In 2009 Walmart, whose motto is "Save Money Live Better," claimed that it saved $3,100 per American household. Former CEO Lee Scott credited Walmart with

An Industrial Giant Emerges

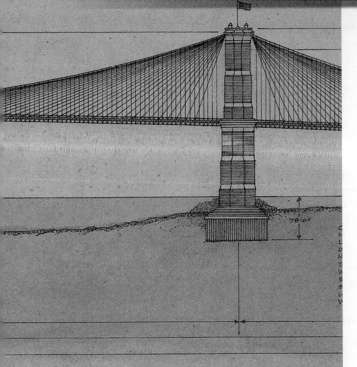

MAY 24, 1883

(((•—[Hear the Audio **Chapter 17 at www.myhistorylab.com**

■ John A. Roebling's design for the Brooklyn Bridge, then the longest suspension bridge in the world, was widely hailed as an artistic masterpiece, an illustration of the beauty of functional engineering.
Source: © 1993 E. Michael Beard www.errolgraphics.com.

having "democratized consumption" in the United States by enabling "working-class families to buy former luxuries like inexpensive flat-screen televisions, down comforters and porterhouse steaks." A retailer helps society best by lowering prices, or so the company contended.

The debate over the human costs of corporate efficiencies echoes the one that accompanied the rise of powerful industrial combinations during the last third of the nineteenth century. Then, the power of the railroads enabled them to bring substantial benefits to thousands of communities; but this power also enabled the railroads to ruin those who opposed their will. Industrial corporations followed suit, especially in steel, iron, oil,

and electricity, providing millions with new and improved products at lower prices. But the industrial behemoths also controlled political processes and often subjected workers to unsafe and exploitative conditions. Reformers and labor leaders denounced this concentration of wealth and power. Some advocated regulation; others called for revolution. Then as now, defenders of big business pointed out its benefits: new technology, better products, lower prices.

The question remains: Does the efficiency generated by economic concentration justify its threat to smaller businesses and communities—and to democratic institutions? ■

Essentials of Industrial Growth

When the Civil War began, the country's industrial output, while important and increasing, did not approach that of major European powers. By the end of the century the United States had become far and away the colossus among world manufacturers, dwarfing the production of Great Britain and Germany. The world had never seen such a remarkable example of rapid economic growth. The value of American manufactured products rose from $1.8 billion in 1859 to over $13 billion in 1899.

American manufacturing flourished for many reasons. New natural resources were discovered and exploited steadily, thereby increasing opportunities. These opportunities, in turn, attracted the brightest and most energetic of a vigorous and expanding population. The growth of the country added constantly to the size of the national market, and protective tariffs shielded that market from foreign competition. Foreign capital, however, entered the market freely, in part because tariffs kept out so many foreign goods.

The dominant spirit of the time encouraged businessmen to maximum effort by emphasizing progress, yet it also produced a generation of Robber Barons. The energetic search for wealth led to corrupt business practices such as stock manipulation, bribery, and cutthroat competition and ultimately to "combinations in restraint of trade," a kind of American euphemism for monopoly. European immigrants provided the additional labor needed by expanding industry; 2.5 million arrived in the 1870s, twice that number in the 1880s. These immigrants saw America as a land of opportunity, and for many, probably most, it was that indeed. But for others, emigrating to the United States meant a constant struggle for survival; dreary, often unhealthy living conditions; and grinding poverty.

The period witnessed rapid advances in basic science, and technicians created a bountiful harvest of new machines, processes, and power sources that increased productivity in many industries and created new industries as well. Agriculture was transformed by improved harvesters and binding machines, and combines capable of threshing and bagging 450 pounds of grain a minute. An 1886 report of the Illinois Bureau of Labor Statistics claimed that "new machinery has displaced fully 50 percent of the muscular labor formerly required to do a given amount of work in the manufacture of agricultural implements." Of course that also meant that many farm families were "displaced" from their homes and livelihoods, and it made farmers dependent on the vagaries of distant markets and powerful economic forces they could not control.

As a result of improvements in the milling of grain, packaged cereals appeared on the American breakfast table. The commercial canning of food, spurred by the "automatic line" canning factory, expanded so rapidly that by 1887 a writer in *Good Housekeeping* could say, "Housekeeping is getting to be ready made, as well as clothing." The Bonsack cigarette-rolling machine created a new industry that changed the habits of millions. George B. Eastman created still another with his development of mass-produced, roll photographic film and the simple but efficient Kodak camera. The perfection of the typewriter by the Remington company in the 1880s revolutionized office work. But even some of these inventions were mixed blessings. The harm done by cigarettes, for example, needs no explanation.

Railroads: The First Big Business

In 1866, returning from his honeymoon in Europe, thirty-year-old Charles Francis Adams Jr., (great-grandson of John Adams and grandson of John Quincy Adams), full of ambition and ready, as he put it, to confront the world "face to face," looked about in search of a career. "Surveying the whole field," he

The daily passenger train of the Union Pacific on its transcontinental line, crosses the Rocky Mountains. In 1869, just after the transcontinental line was completed, travel from New York City to San Francisco took nearly a week. First-class passengers, who rode in special cars such as those pictured, paid a fare of $150. Second-class passengers paid less than half as much, but they were crowded into cars that were attached to freight trains.

The Union Railroad Station in Montgomery, Alabama, was designed by Henry Hobson Richardson, the nation's foremost architect in the late nineteenth century. Richardson borrowed ideas from the past, including arches that evoked ancient Rome. The building's massiveness and horizontal lines suggested the power and reach of the railroads: the American empire as built on steel rails.

later explained, "I fixed on the railroad system as the most developing force and the largest field of the day, and determined to attach myself to it." Adams's judgment was acute: For the next twenty-five years the railroads were probably the most significant element in American economic development, railroad executives the most powerful people in the country.

Railroads were important first as an industry in themselves. Fewer than 35,000 miles of track existed when Lee laid down his sword at Appomattox. In 1875 railroad mileage exceeded 74,000 and the skeleton of the network was complete. Over the next two decades the skeleton was fleshed out. In 1890 the mature but still-growing system took in over $1 billion in passenger and freight revenues. (The federal government's income in 1890 was only $403 million.) The value of railroad properties and equipment was more than $8.7 billion. The national railroad debt of $5.1 billion was almost five times the national debt of $1.1 billion! By 1900 the nation had 193,000 miles of track.

The emphasis in railroad construction after 1865 was on organizing integrated systems. The lines had high fixed costs: taxes, interest on their bonds, maintenance of track and rolling stock, and salaries of office personnel. A short train with half-empty cars required almost as many workers and as much fuel to operate as a long one jammed with freight or passengers. To earn profits the railroads had to carry as much traffic as possible. They therefore spread out feeder lines to draw business to their main lines the way the root network of a tree draws water into its trunk.

Before the Civil War, passengers and freight could travel by rail from beyond Chicago and St. Louis to the Atlantic coast, but only after the war did true interregional trunk lines appear. In 1861, for example, the New York Central ran from Albany to Buffalo. One could proceed from Buffalo to Chicago, but on a different company's trains. In 1867 the New York Central passed into the hands of "Commodore" Cornelius Vanderbilt, who had made a large fortune in the shipping business. Vanderbilt already controlled lines running from Albany to New York City; now he merged these properties with the New York Central. In 1873 he integrated the Lake Shore and Michigan Southern into his empire and two years later the Michigan Central. At his death in 1877 the New York Central operated a network of over 4,500 miles of track between New York City and most of the principal cities of the Midwest.

While Vanderbilt was putting together the New York Central complex, Thomas A. Scott was fusing roads to Cincinnati, Indianapolis, St. Louis, and Chicago to his Pennsylvania Railroad, which linked

Pittsburgh and Philadelphia. In 1871 the Pennsylvania line obtained access to New York; soon it reached Baltimore and Washington. By 1869 another important system, the Erie, extended from New York to Cleveland, Cincinnati, and St. Louis. Soon thereafter it too tapped the markets of Chicago and other cities. In 1874 the Baltimore and Ohio rail line also obtained access to Chicago.

The transcontinentals were trunk lines from the start; the emptiness of the western country would have made short lines unprofitable, and builders quickly grasped the need for direct connections to eastern markets and thorough integration of feeder lines.

The dominant system builder of the Southwest was Jay Gould, a soft-spoken, unostentatious-looking man who was in fact ruthless, cynical, and aggressive. Another railroad president once called Gould a "perfect eel." Gould took over the Kansas Pacific, running from Denver to Kansas City, and consolidated it with the Union Pacific and the Missouri Pacific, a line from Kansas City to St. Louis. Often he put together such properties merely to unload them on other railroads at a profit, but his grasp of the importance of integration was sound.

In the Northwest, Henry Villard, a German-born former newspaperman, constructed another great complex based on his control of the Northern Pacific. James J. Hill controlled the Great Northern system, still another western network.

The Civil War had highlighted the need for thorough railroad connections in the South. Shortly after the conflict the Chesapeake and Ohio opened a direct line from Norfolk, Virginia, to Cincinnati, Ohio. By the late 1880s, the Richmond and West Point Terminal Company controlled an 8,558-mile network. Like other southern trunk lines such as the Louisville and Nashville and the Atlantic Coast Line, this system was controlled by northern capitalists.

The trunk lines interconnected and thus had to standardize many of their activities. This in turn led to the standardization of other aspects of life. The present system of time zones was developed in 1883 by the railroads. The standard track gauge (four feet eight and one-half inches) was established in 1886. Standardized car coupling and braking mechanisms, standard signal systems, even standard methods of accounting were essential to the effective functioning of the network.

The lines sought to work out fixed rates for carrying different types of freight, charge more for valuable manufactured goods than for bulky products like coal or wheat, and they agreed to permit rate concessions to shippers when necessary to avoid hauling empty cars. In other words, they charged what the traffic would bear. However, by the 1880s the men who ran the railroads had come to recognize the advantages of cooperating with one another to avoid "senseless" competition. Railroad management was becoming a kind of profession, with certain standard ways of doing things, its own professional journals, and with regional organizations such as the Eastern Trunk Line Association and the Western Traffic Association.

Because of their voracious appetite for traffic, railroads in sparsely settled regions and in areas with undeveloped resources devoted much money and effort to stimulating local economic growth. The Louisville and Nashville railroad, for instance, was a prime mover in the expansion of the iron industry in Alabama in the 1880s.

To speed the settlement of new regions, the land-grant railroads sold land cheaply and on easy terms, for sales meant future business as well as current income. They offered reduced rates to travelers interested in buying farms and set up "bureaus of immigration" that distributed brochures describing the wonders of the new country. Their agents greeted immigrants at the eastern ports and tried to steer them to railroad property. They sent agents who were usually themselves immigrants—often ministers—all over Europe to recruit prospective settlers.

Technological advances in railroading accelerated economic development in complex ways. In 1869 George Westinghouse invented the air brake. By enabling an engineer to apply the brakes to all cars simultaneously (formerly each car had to be braked separately by its own conductor or brakeman), this invention made possible revolutionary increases in the size of trains and the speed at which they could safely operate. The sleeping car, invented in 1864 by George Pullman, now came into its own.

To pull the heavier trains, more powerful locomotives were needed. They in turn produced a call for stronger and more durable rails to bear the additional weight. Steel, itself reduced in cost because of technological developments, supplied the answer, for steel rails outlasted iron by many years despite the use of much heavier equipment.

A close tie developed between the railroads and the nation's telegraph network, dominated by the Western Union Company. Commonly the railroads allowed Western Union to string wires along their rights-of-way, and they transported telegraphers and their equipment without charge. In return they received free telegraphic service, important for efficiency and safety.

See the **Map** *Railroads & New Transportation Systems* at **www.myhistorylab.com**

View the Image *J.P. Morgan* at **www.myhistorylab.com**

Iron, Oil, and Electricity

The transformation of iron manufacturing affected the nation almost as much as railroad development. Output rose from 920,000 tons in 1860 to 10.3 million tons in 1900, but the big change came in the development of ways to mass-produce steel. In its pure form (wrought iron) the metal is tough but relatively pliable: It bends under great stresses. Ordinary cast iron, which contains large amounts of carbon and other impurities, is hard but brittle. Steel, which contains 1 or 2 percent carbon, combines the hardness of cast iron with the toughness of wrought iron. For nearly every purpose—structural girders for bridges and buildings, railroad track, machine tools, boiler plate, barbed wire— steel is immensely superior to other kinds of iron.

ELECTRIC EFFECT BY MOONLIGHT.

Electric companies advertised the advantages of electric lights at regional exhibitions, such as these electrified renderings at the 1897 Tennessee Centennial Exposition. The lights evoke the Parthenon of ancient Athens and the pyramids of Egypt.

But steel was so expensive that it could not be used for bulky products until the invention in the 1850s of the Bessemer process, perfected independently by Henry Bessemer, an Englishman, and William Kelly of Kentucky. Bessemer and Kelly discovered that a stream of air directed into a mass of molten iron caused the carbon and other impurities to combine with oxygen and burn off. When measured amounts of carbon, silicon, and manganese were then added, the brew became steel. What had been a rare metal could now be produced by the hundreds and thousands of tons. The Bessemer process and the open-hearth method, a slower but more precise technique that enabled producers to sample the molten mass and thus control quality closely, were introduced

This 1900 photograph of steel factories at night in Duquesne, near Pittsburgh, was tinted by hand.
Source: North Wind Picture Archives.

Were the Railroads Indispensable?

In 1891 financier Sidney Dillon credited the railroads for the nation's impressive economic growth during the previous half century. Without them, he claimed, most of the nation's natural resources would have remained untouched, civilization would have "crept slowly" on, and the immense spaces from the Appalachians to the Pacific would have remained "an unknown and unproductive wilderness."

That the railroads were indispensable to the nation's economy during the nineteenth century has long been a commonplace of historical writing. One of the main reasons for it is summarized in the accompanying map, "The Railroads: Moving Agricultural Products to Eastern Markets, 1890."

This map shows that the urban areas of the nation, with a population density of over ninety people per square mile (shaded in blue), were chiefly located in New England, the Middle Atlantic seaboard, and the industrial regions surrounding Pittsburgh, Cleveland, Cincinnati, Detroit, and Chicago. This area needed to import massive amounts of grain—milled wheat and corn—to feed its people. The map also indicates that the main grain-growing regions were in the Midwest, the northern plains, and the South. The nation's basic economic geography presumed a transportation system to ship grain from the Midwest and South to the cities of the industrial Northeast.

By 1890, the map also suggests that the nation's railway system served this purpose. Railroads linked the major wheat markets of the upper Great Plains (principally Minneapolis and Duluth) and corn markets of the central Midwest (Chicago, St. Louis, and Kansas City) to the industrial cities of Ohio and Pennsylvania and the urban region along the Atlantic coast extending from Washington DC to Maine. The dense web of competing railway lines should have kept freight charges low, and it often did. Attempts to "pool" the available traffic and fix high rates usually collapsed. One reason the railways were the focus of much criticism was their centrality to the economy.

But in 1964 in *Railroads and American Economic Growth*, economic historian Robert Fogel challenged the assumption that the late nineteenth-century rail system was "indispensable" to economic growth. He asserted that if the nation had instead invested in building more canals and dredging more rivers, a water-based transportation system could have functioned nearly as effectively as the railways.

Counterfactual premises are often used by historians to examine the validity of causal statements. In this instance, Fogel argued that, in the absence of railroads, the economy still would have grown rapidly.

The map entitled "A Hypothetical Water-Based Transportation System, 1890" shows how the nation's navigable rivers, supplemented by existing and new canals, could have collected cereals from agricultural regions and moved them to eastern markets. This map also suggests how a water-based transportation system would have altered the relationship among regions. In the absence of the railroads, the dry upper Great Plains would have remained nearly undeveloped, while commercial agriculture would have been concentrated in the Mississippi, Ohio, and Missouri River valleys, and along the rivers that empty into the Gulf of Mexico and the Atlantic seaboard. The major centers of grain shipment would have been New Orleans, St. Louis, Cincinnati, Memphis, and Charleston. Minneapolis, Duluth, Chicago, and Kansas City would not have become major economic centers.

Shipment of grain, 1890, In thousand tons:
3450
1500
380

Over 90 people per sq mile
Wheat growing
Corn growing
Railroad
Wheat
Corn

The Railroads: Moving Agricultural Products to Eastern Markets, 1890 The railroad web links the grain-producing regions of the Midwest with the population centers of the Northeast.

Feasible commercial agriculture
— Navigable river
— Existing canal
— Proposed canal
⊙ Probable major center of grain shipment

A Hypothetical Water-Based Transportation System, 1890 If the nation's transportation system had been based on canal construction, the Mississippi River basin would have been the nation's breadbasket, and the central plains would have been less significant.

This "hypothetical" water-based transportation system might have been as efficient as the railroads. In 1890, the cost of transporting wheat from Chicago to New York City was 5.2 cents per ton-mile by rail, but only 1.4 cents by water. Fogel estimated that a water-based transportation system would have saved $38 million in carrying costs annually, though there would have been additional costs in warehouse construction and spoilage (boats are slower than trains). The railroads, in short, were not "indispensable" to move foodstuffs to eastern cities.

For decades, Fogel's argument was regarded by most historians as mathematical trickery: the fact is that railroads and industry emerged nearly simultaneously in all industrial nations: Is that not proof of the centrality of railroads to industrial development? In 2003, however, historian Richard White showed that in the late nineteenth century the railroad companies were engaged in massive fraud and deception—including controlling the news media in order to persuade investors to buy their stocks. This ensured enormous waste and inefficiency.

Yet the railroads stimulated economic development in other ways. Their demand for iron and steel jump-started the iron and steel industries, crucial for manufacturing and urban construction. The development of powerful locomotives gave rise to advances in steam and machine technology. Perhaps most important, the railroads promoted effective systems of corporate organization that stimulated economic development throughout the economy.

Questions for Discussion

■ Why was Chicago the largest center of grain shipment in 1890?

■ Why was Chicago not included as a "probable major center" of grain shipment in a "hypothetical water-based transportation system?"

■ Interior North Carolina, an important source of wheat and corn in 1890, would not have figured in a water-based system. Why?

■ How do counterfactual assertions promote historical understanding?

In this 1900 cartoon, oil baron John D. Rockefeller holds the White House in the palm of his hand while the U.S. Capitol building—labeled Standard Oil Refinery—belches smoke.

commercially in the 1860s. In 1870, 77,000 tons of steel were manufactured; by 1890, that had expanded to nearly 5 million tons. Such growth would have been impossible without the huge supplies of iron ore in the United States and the coal necessary to fire the furnaces that refined it. In the 1870s the great iron fields rimming Lake Superior began to yield their treasures. The enormous iron concentrations of the Mesabi region made a compass needle spin like a top. Mesabi ores could be mined with steam shovels, almost like gravel.

Pittsburgh, surrounded by vast coal deposits, became the iron and steel capital of the country, the Minnesota ores reaching it by way of steamers on the Great Lakes and rail lines from Cleveland. Other cities in Pennsylvania and Ohio were important producers, and a separate complex, centering on Birmingham, Alabama, developed to exploit local iron and coal fields.

The petroleum industry expanded even more spectacularly than iron and steel. Edwin L. Drake drilled the first successful well in Pennsylvania in 1859. During the Civil War, production ranged between 2 million and 3 million barrels a year. By 1890 the figure had leaped to about 50 million barrels.

Before the invention of the gasoline engine and the automobile, the most important petroleum product was kerosene, which was burned in lamps. Refiners heated crude oil in large kettles and, after the volatile elements had escaped, condensed the kerosene in coils cooled by water. The heavier petroleum tars were discarded.

Technological advances came rapidly. By the early 1870s, refiners had learned how to "crack" petroleum by applying high temperatures to the crude oil in order to rearrange its molecular structure, thereby increasing the percentage of kerosene yielded. By-products such as naphtha, gasoline (used in vaporized form as an illuminating gas), rhigolene (a local anesthetic), cymogene (a coolant for refrigerating machines), and many lubricants and waxes began to appear on the market. At the

same time a great increase in the supply of crude oil—especially after the German-born chemist Herman Frasch perfected a method for removing sulfur from low-quality petroleum—drove prices down.

These circumstances put a premium on refining efficiency. Larger plants using expensive machinery and employing skilled technicians became more important. In the mid-1860s only three refineries in the country could process 2,000 barrels of crude oil a week; a decade later plants capable of handling 1,000 barrels a day were common.

Two other important new industries were the telephone and electric light businesses. Both were typical of the period, being products of technical advances and intimately related to the growth of a high-speed, urban civilization that put great stress on communication. The telephone was invented in 1876 by Alexander Graham Bell, who had been led to the study of acoustics through his interest in the education of the deaf. The invention soon proved its value. By 1900 there were almost 800,000 telephones in the country, twice the total for all Europe. The American Telephone and Telegraph Company, a consolidation of over 100 local systems, dominated the business.

When Western Union realized the importance of the telephone, it tried for a time to compete with Bell by developing a machine of its own. The man it commissioned to devise this machine was Thomas A. Edison, but Bell's patents proved unassailable. Edison had already made a number of contributions toward solving what he called the "mysteries of electrical force," including a multiplex telegraph capable of sending four messages over a single wire at the same time. At Menlo Park, New Jersey, he built the prototype of the modern research laboratory, where specific problems could be attacked on a mass scale by a team of trained specialists. During his lifetime he took out more than 1,000 patents dealing with machines as varied as the phonograph, the motion-picture projector, the storage battery, and the mimeograph.

Edison's most significant achievement was the incandescent lamp, or electric lightbulb. Others before him had experimented with the idea of producing light by passing electricity through a filament in a vacuum. Always, however, the filaments quickly burned out. Edison tried hundreds of fibers before producing, in 1879, a carbonized filament that would glow brightly in a vacuum tube for as long as 170 hours without crumbling. At Christmastime he decorated the grounds about his laboratory with a few dozen of the new lights. People flocked by the thousands to see this miracle of the "Wizard of Menlo Park." The inventor boasted that soon he would be able to illuminate entire towns, even great cities like New York.

He was true to his promise. In 1882 his Edison Illuminating Company opened a power station in New York City and began to supply current for lighting to eighty-five consumers, including the *New York Times* and the banking house of J.P. Morgan and Company. Soon central stations were springing up everywhere until, by 1898, there were about 3,000 in the country.

The substitution of electric for steam power in factories was as liberating as that of steam for waterpower before the Civil War. Small, safe electric motors replaced dangerous and cumbersome mazes of belts and wheels. The electric power industry expanded rapidly. By the early years of the twentieth century almost 6 billion kilowatt-hours of electricity were being produced annually. Yet this was only the beginning.

⬤▸┤Read the Document Edison, *The Success of the Electric Light* at www.myhistorylab.com

Competition and Monopoly: The Railroads

During the post–Civil War era, expansion in industry went hand in hand with concentration. The principal cause of this trend, aside from the obvious economies resulting from large-scale production and the growing importance of expensive machinery, was the downward trend of prices after 1873. The deflation, which resulted mainly from the failure of the money supply to keep pace with the rapid increase in the volume of goods produced, affected agricultural goods as well as manufactures, and it lasted until 1896 or 1897.

Contemporaries believed that they were living through a "great depression." That label is misleading, for output expanded almost continuously, and at a rapid rate, until 1893, when production slumped and a true depression struck the country. Falling prices, however, kept a steady pressure on profit margins, and this led to increased production and thus to intense competition for markets.

According to the classical economists, competition advanced the public interest by keeping prices low and ensuring the most efficient producer the largest profit. Up to a point it accomplished these purposes in the years after 1865, but it also caused side effects that injured both the economy and society as a whole. Railroad managers, for instance, found it impossible to enforce "official" rate schedules and maintain their regional associations once competitive pressures mounted. In 1865 it had cost from ninety-six cents to $2.15 per 100 pounds, depending on the class of freight, to ship goods from New York to Chicago. In 1888 rates ranged from thirty-five cents to seventy-five cents.

Competition cut deeply into railroad profits, causing the lines to seek desperately to increase volume. It did so chiefly by reducing rates still more, on a selective basis. The competition gave rebates (secret reductions below the published rates) to large shippers in order to capture their business. Giving discounts to those who shipped in volume made economic sense: It was easier to handle freight in carload lots than in smaller units. So intense was the battle for business, however, that the railroads often made concessions to big customers far beyond what the economics of bulk shipment justified. In the 1870s the New York Central regularly reduced the rates charged to important shippers by 50–80 percent. One large Utica dry-goods merchant received a rate of nine cents while others paid thirty-three cents. Two big New York City grain merchants paid so little that they soon controlled the grain business of the entire city.

Railroad officials disliked rebating but found no way to avoid the practice. "Notwithstanding my horror of rebates," the president of a New England trunk line told one of his executives in discussing the case of a brick manufacturer, "bill at the usual rate, and rebate Mr. Cole 25 cents a thousand." In extreme cases the railroads even gave large shippers drawbacks, which were rebates on the business of the shippers' competitors. (For example, the same New England trunk line not only made Cole's competitors pay higher freight rates but also returned a percentage of the income from those rates to Mr. Cole!) Besides rebating, railroads issued passes to favored shippers, built sidings at the plants of important companies without charge, and gave freely of their landholdings to attract businesses to their territory.

To make up for losses forced on them by competitive pressures, railroads charged higher rates at waypoints along their tracks where no competition existed. Frequently it cost more to ship a product a short distance than a longer one. Rochester, New York, was served only by the New York Central. In the 1870s it cost thrity cents to transport a barrel of flour from Rochester to New York City, a distance of 350 miles. At the same time flour could be shipped from Minneapolis to New York, a distance of well over 1,000 miles, for only twenty cents a barrel. One Rochester businessman told a state investigating committee that he could save eighteen cents a hundredweight by sending goods to St. Louis by way of New York, where several carriers competed for the traffic, even though, in fact, the goods might come back through Rochester over the same tracks on the way to St. Louis!

Although cheap transportation stimulated the economy, few people benefited from cutthroat competition. Small shippers—and all businessmen in cities and towns with limited rail outlets—suffered; railroad discrimination speeded the concentration of industry in large corporations located in major centers. The instability of rates even troubled interests like the midwestern flour millers who benefited from the competitive situation, for it hampered planning. Nor could manufacturers who received rebates be entirely happy, since few could be sure that some other producer was not getting a larger reduction.

Probably the worst sufferers were the railroads themselves. The loss of revenue resulting from rate cutting, combined with inflated debts, put most of them in grave difficulty when faced with a downturn in the business cycle. In 1876 two-fifths of all railroad bonds were in default; three years later sixty-five lines were bankrupt. Wits called Samuel J. Tilden, the 1876 Democratic presidential candidate, "the Great Forecloser" because of his work reorganizing bankrupt railroads at this time.

Since the public would not countenance bankrupt railroads going out of business, these companies were placed in the hands of court-appointed receivers. The receivers, however, seldom provided efficient management and had no funds at their disposal for new equipment.

During the 1880s the major railroads responded to these pressures by building or buying lines in order to create interregional systems. These were the first giant corporations, capitalized in the hundreds of millions of dollars. Their enormous cost led to another wave of bankruptcies when a true depression struck in the 1890s.

The consequent reorganizations brought most of the big systems under the control of financiers, notably J. Pierpont Morgan and such other private bankers as Kuhn, Loeb of New York and Lee, Higginson of Boston.

Critics called the reorganizations "Morganizations." Representatives of the bankers sat on the board of every line they saved and their influence was predominant. They consistently opposed rate wars, rebating, and other competitive practices. In effect, control of the railroad network became centralized, even though the companies maintained their separate existences and operated in a seemingly independent manner. When Morgan died in 1913, "Morgan men" dominated the boards of the New York Central; the Erie; the New York, New Haven, and Hartford; the Southern; the Pere Marquette; the Atchison, Topeka, and Santa Fe; and many other lines.

Competition and Monopoly: Steel

The iron and steel industry was also intensely competitive. Despite the trend toward higher production, demand varied erratically from year to year, even from month to month. In good times producers built new

This early 1900 photograph shows how steel mills spread along the riverfront of Pittsburgh, Pennsylvania.

facilities, only to suffer heavy losses when demand declined. The forward rush of technology put a tremendous emphasis on efficiency; expensive plants quickly became obsolete. Improved transportation facilities allowed manufacturers in widely separated places to compete with one another.

The kingpin of the industry was Andrew Carnegie. Carnegie was born in Scotland and came to the United States in 1848 at the age of twelve. His first job, as a bobbin boy in a cotton mill, brought him $1.20 a week, but his talents perfectly fitted the times and he rose rapidly: to Western Union messenger boy, to telegrapher, to private secretary, to railroad manager. He saved his money, made some shrewd investments, and by 1868 had an income of $50,000 a year.

At about this time he decided to specialize in the iron business. Carnegie possessed great talent as a salesman, boundless faith in the future of the country, an uncanny knack of choosing topflight subordinates, and enough ruthlessness to survive in the iron and steel jungle. Where other steel men built new plants in good times, he preferred to expand in bad times, when it cost far less to do so. During the 1870s, he later recalled, "many of my friends needed money. . . . I bought out five or six of them. That is what gave me my leading interest in this steel business."

Carnegie grasped the importance of technological improvements. Slightly skeptical of the Bessemer process at first, once he became convinced of its practicality he adopted it enthusiastically. In 1875 he built the J. Edgar Thomson Steel Works, named after a president of the Pennsylvania Railroad, his biggest customer. He employed chemists and other specialists and was soon making steel from iron oxides that other manufacturers had discarded as waste. He was a merciless competitor. When a plant manager announced, "We broke all records for making steel last week," Carnegie replied, "Congratulations! Why not do it every week?" Carnegie sold rails by paying "commissions" to railroad purchasing agents, and he was not above reneging on a contract if he thought it profitable and safe to do so.

By 1890 the Carnegie Steel Company dominated the industry, and its output increased nearly tenfold during the next decade. Profits soared. Alarmed by his increasing control of the industry, the makers of finished steel products such as barbed wire and tubing considered pooling their resources and making steel themselves. Carnegie, his competitive temper aroused, threatened to manufacture wire, pipes, and other finished products. A colossal steel war seemed imminent.

J.P. Morgan, the financial genius, staved off ruinous competition among steel firms by combining most companies into a single huge firm, United States Steel.

However, Carnegie longed to retire in order to devote himself to philanthropic work. He believed that great wealth entailed social responsibilities and that it was a disgrace to die rich. When J.P. Morgan approached him through an intermediary with an offer to buy him out, he assented readily. In 1901 Morgan put together United States Steel, the "world's first billion-dollar corporation." (See the map on p. 468.) This combination included all the Carnegie properties, the Federal Steel Company (Carnegie's largest competitor), and such important fabricators of finished products as the American Steel and Wire Company, the American Tin Plate Company, and the National Tube Company. Vast reserves of Minnesota iron ore and a fleet of Great Lakes ore steamers were also included. U.S. Steel was capitalized at $1.4 billion, about twice the value of its component properties but not necessarily an overestimation of its profit-earning capacity. The owners of Carnegie Steel received $492 million, of which $250 million went to Carnegie himself.

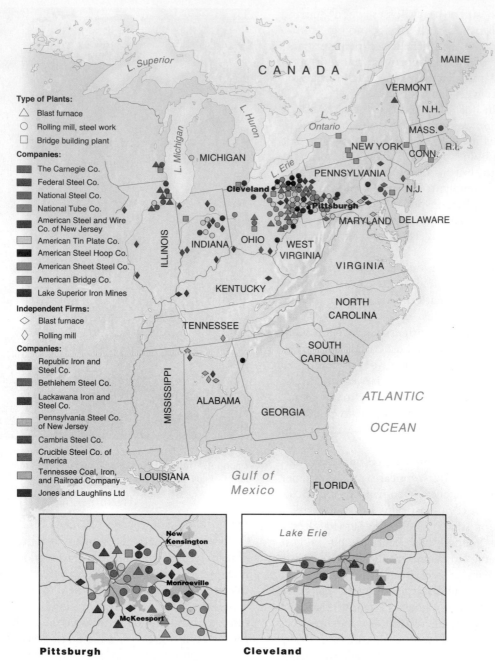

Type of Plants:
△ Blast furnace
○ Rolling mill, steel work
□ Bridge building plant

Companies:
■ The Carnegie Co.
■ Federal Steel Co.
■ National Steel Co.
■ National Tube Co.
■ American Steel and Wire Co. of New Jersey
■ American Tin Plate Co.
■ American Steel Hoop Co.
■ American Sheet Steel Co.
■ American Bridge Co.
■ Lake Superior Iron Mines

Independent Firms:
◇ Blast furnace
◇ Rolling mill

Companies:
■ Republic Iron and Steel Co.
■ Bethlehem Steel Co.
■ Lackawana Iron and Steel Co.
■ Pennsylvania Steel Co. of New Jersey
■ Cambria Steel Co.
■ Crucible Steel Co. of America
■ Tennessee Coal, Iron, and Railroad Company
■ Jones and Laughlins Ltd

Pittsburgh

Cleveland

Firms Incorporated into U. S. Steel J.P. Morgan's consolidation that created U.S. Steel.

Competition and Monopoly: Oil

The pattern of fierce competition leading to combination and monopoly is well illustrated by the history of the petroleum industry. Irresistible pressures pushed the refiners into a brutal struggle to dominate the business. Production of crude oil, subject to the uncertainties of prospecting and drilling, fluctuated constantly and without regard for need. In general, output surged far ahead of demand.

By the 1870s the chief oil-refining centers were Cleveland, Pittsburgh, Baltimore, and the New York City area. Of these Cleveland was the fastest growing, chiefly because the New York Central and Erie railroads competed fiercely for its oil trade and the Erie Canal offered an alternative route.

The Standard Oil Company of Cleveland, founded in 1870 by a thirty-one-year-old merchant named John D. Rockefeller, emerged as the giant among the refiners. Rockefeller exploited every possible technical advance and employed fair means and foul to persuade competitors either to sell out or to join forces. By 1879 he controlled 90 percent of the nation's oil-refining capacity along with a network of oil pipelines and large reserves of petroleum in the ground.

Standard Oil emerged victorious from the competitive wars because Rockefeller and his associates were the toughest and most imaginative fighters as well as the most efficient refiners in the business. In addition to obtaining from the railroads a 10 percent rebate and drawbacks on its competitors' shipments, Standard Oil cut prices locally to force small independents to sell out or face ruin. Since kerosene was sold in grocery stores, Standard supplied its own outlets with meat, sugar, and other products at artificially low prices to help crush the stores that handled other brands of kerosene. The company employed spies to track down the customers of independents and offer them oil at bargain prices. Bribery was also a Standard practice; the reformer Henry Demarest Lloyd quipped that the company had done everything to the Pennsylvania legislature except refine it.

Although a bold planner and a daring taker of necessary risks, Rockefeller was far too orderly and astute to enjoy the free-swinging battles that plagued his industry. Born in an upstate New York village in 1839, he settled in Cleveland in 1855 and became a produce merchant. During the Civil War he invested in a local refinery and by 1865 was engaged full time in the oil business.

Like Carnegie, Rockefeller was an organizer; he knew little about the technology of petroleum. His forte was meticulous attention to detail: Stories are told of his ordering the number of drops of solder used to seal oil cans reduced from forty to thirty-nine and of his insisting that the manager of one of his refineries account for 750 missing barrel caps. Not miserliness but a profound grasp of the economies of large-scale production explain this behavior.

Rockefeller competed ruthlessly not primarily to crush other refiners but to persuade them to join with him, to share the business peaceably and rationally so that all could profit. Competition was obsolescent, he argued, though no more effective competitor than he ever lived.

Having achieved his monopoly, Rockefeller stabilized and structured it by creating a new type of business organization, the trust. Standard Oil was an Ohio corporation, prohibited by local law from owning plants in other states or holding stock in out-of-state corporations. As Rockefeller and his associates took over dozens of companies with facilities scattered across the country, serious legal and managerial difficulties arose. How could these many organizations be integrated with Standard Oil of Ohio?

A rotund, genial little Pennsylvania lawyer named Samuel C. T. Dodd came up with an answer to this

THE KING OF THE COMBINATIONS.

A regally attired John D. Rockefeller poses on top of a barrel from his Standard Oil refinery, his crown encircled by the railroads he controlled. Rockefeller's actual clothing was considerably less conspicuous. Source: © Collection of The New-York Historical Society.

question in 1879.[1] The stock of Standard of Ohio and of all the other companies that the Rockefeller interests had swallowed up was turned over to nine trustees, who were empowered to "exercise general supervision" over all the properties. In exchange, stockholders received trust certificates, on which dividends were paid. This seemingly simple device brought order to the petroleum business. Competition almost disappeared, prices steadied, and profits skyrocketed. By 1892 John D. Rockefeller was worth over $800 million.

The Standard Oil Trust was not a corporation. It had no charter, indeed no legal existence at all. For many years few people outside the organization knew that it existed. The form they chose persuaded

---

[1]The trust formula was not "perfected" until 1882.

Rockefeller and other Standard Oil officials that without violating their consciences, they could deny under oath that Standard Oil of Ohio owned or controlled other corporations "directly or indirectly through its officers or agents." The trustees controlled these organizations—and Standard of Ohio too!

After Standard Oil's duplicity was revealed during a New York investigation in 1888, the word *trust,* formerly signifying a fiduciary arrangement for the protection of the interests of individuals incompetent or unwilling to guard them themselves, became a synonym for monopoly. However, from the company's point of view, monopoly was not the purpose of the trust—that had been achieved before the device was invented. Centralization of the management of diverse and far-flung operations in the interest of efficiency was its chief function. Standard Oil headquarters in New York became the brain of a complex network where information from salaried managers in the field was collected and digested, where top managerial decisions were made, and whence orders went out to armies of drillers, refiners, scientists, and salesmen.

Competition and Monopoly: Retailing and Utilities

That utilities such as the telephone and electric lighting industries tended to form monopolies is not difficult to explain, for in such fields competition involved costly duplication of equipment and, particularly in the case of the telephone, loss of service efficiency. However, competitive pressures were strong in the early stages of their development. Since these industries depended on patents, Bell and Edison had to fight mighty battles in the courts with rivals seeking to infringe on their rights. A patent, Edison said bitterly, was "simply an invitation to a lawsuit."

Competition in the electric lighting business raged for some years among Edison, Westinghouse, and another corporation, the Thomson-Houston Electric Company, which was operating 870 central lighting stations by 1890. In 1892 the Edison and Thomson-Houston companies merged, forming General Electric, a $35 million corporation. Thereafter, General Electric and Westinghouse maintained their dominance in the manufacture of bulbs and electrical equipment as well as in the distribution of electrical power.

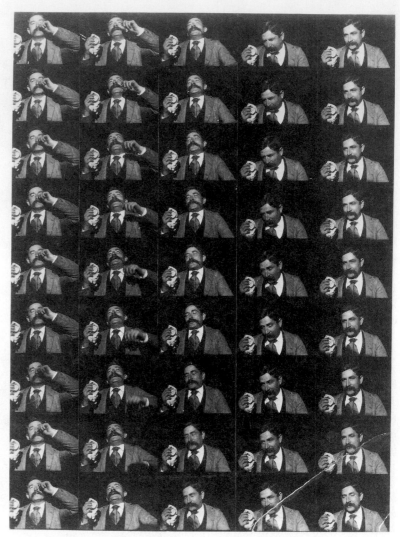

A sneeze is captured on film—the first copyrighted movie (1894). In 1889 Thomas A. Edison conceived of a machine that would do for the eye what the phonograph did for the ear. Over the next two years, Edison invented two separate devices—a camera to take a rapid sequence of pictures and a machine to view them, called a kinetoscope. In 1893 he developed reliable film for his camera. The motion picture industry was born.

The pattern of competition leading to dominance by a few great companies was repeated in many businesses. In life insurance an immense expansion took place after the Civil War. High-pressure salesmanship prevailed; agents gave rebates to customers by shaving their own commissions; companies stole crack agents from their rivals and raided new territories. They sometimes invested as much as 96 percent of the first year's premiums in obtaining new business. By 1900, after three decades of fierce competition, three giants dominated the industry—Equitable, New York Life, and Mutual Life, each with approximately $1 billion of insurance in force.

In retailing, the period saw the growth of urban department stores. In 1862 Alexander T. Stewart had built an eight-story emporium in New York City that covered an entire block and employed 2,000 persons. John Wanamaker in Philadelphia and Marshall Field in Chicago headed similar establishments by the 1880s, and there were others. These department stores advertised heavily, stressing low prices, efficient service, and money-back guarantees. High volume made for large profits. Here is how one of Field's biographers described his methods:

> His was a one-price store, with the price plainly marked on the merchandise. Goods were not misrepresented, and a reputation for quality merchandise and for fair and honest dealing was built up. . . . Courtesy toward customers was an unfailing rule.

Watch the Video *Rural Free Delivery Mail* at **www.myhistorylab.com**

American Ambivalence to Big Business

The expansion of industry and its concentration in fewer and fewer hands changed the way many people felt about the role of government in economic and social affairs. On the one hand, they professed to believe strongly in a government policy of noninterference, or **laissez-faire**. "'Things regulate themselves' . . . means, of course, that God regulates them by his general laws," Professor Francis Bowen of Harvard wrote in his *American Political Economy* (1870).

Certain intellectual currents encouraged this type of thinking. Charles Darwin's *The Origin of Species* was published in 1859, and by the 1870s his theory of evolution was beginning to influence opinion in the United States. That nature had ordained a kind of inevitable progress, governed by the natural selection of those individual organisms best adapted to survive in a particular environment, seemed eminently reasonable to most Americans, for it fitted well with their own experiences. "Let the buyer beware; that covers the whole business," the sugar magnate Henry O. Havemeyer explained to an investigating committee. "You cannot wet-nurse people from the time they are born until the time they die. They have to wade and get stuck, and that is the way men are educated."

This reasoning was similar to that of the classical economists and was thus at least as old as Adam Smith's *Wealth of Nations* (1776). But it appeared to

The Biltmore Estate in Asheville, North Carolina was built by George Vanderbilt, grandson of "The Commodore." Over 1,000 laborers worked on the mansion. With 250 rooms and 175,000 square feet, the Biltmore is the largest privately built home in the United States. Critics found the mansion ostentatious and offensive.

supply a hard scientific substitute for Smith's "invisible hand" as an explanation of why free competition advanced the common good.

Yale professor William Graham Sumner sometimes used the survival-of-the-fittest analogy in teaching undergraduates. "Professor," one student asked Sumner, "don't you believe in any government aid to industries?" "No!" Sumner replied, "It's root, hog, or die." The student persisted: "Suppose some professor of political science came along and took your job away from you. Wouldn't you be sore?" "Any other professor is welcome to try," Sumner answered promptly. "If he gets my job, it is my fault. My business is to teach the subject so well that no one can take the job away from me." Sumner's argument described what came to be known as **social Darwinism**, the belief that the activities of people, that is, their business and social relationships, were governed by the Darwinian principle that "the fittest" will always "survive" if allowed to exercise their capacities without restriction.

But the fact that Americans disliked powerful governments in general and strict regulation of the economy in particular had never meant that they objected to all government activity in the economic sphere. Banking laws, tariffs, internal-improvement legislation, and the granting of public land to railroads are only the most obvious of the economic regulations enforced in the nineteenth century by both the federal government and the states. Americans saw no contradiction between government activities of this type and the free enterprise philosophy, for such laws were intended to release human energy and thus increase the area in which freedom could operate. Tariffs stimulated industry and created new jobs, railroad grants opened up new regions for development, and so on.

The growth of huge industrial and financial organizations and the increasing complexity of economic relations frightened people yet made them at the same time greedy for more of the goods and services the new society was turning out. To many, the great new corporations and trusts resembled Frankenstein's monster—marvelous and powerful but a grave threat to society.

To some extent public fear of the industrial giants reflected concern about monopoly—much as some people today worry that Walmart may drive other retailers out of business. If Standard Oil dominated oil refining, it might raise prices inordinately at vast cost to consumers. Charles Francis Adams Jr., expressed this feeling in the 1870s: "In the minds of the great majority, and not without reason, the idea of any industrial combination is closely connected with that of monopoly, and monopoly with extortion."

In his classic autobiography *The Education of Henry Adams*, Adams said that he was staggered by the immense machines on display at the Columbian Exhibition in Chicago in 1893, such as this electricity-generating dynamo. The power of religious faith and works of art and literature had yielded to mechanical power. His world was a thing of the past.

Although in isolated cases monopolists did raise prices unreasonably, generally they did not. On the contrary, prices tended to fall until by the 1890s a veritable "consumer's millennium" had arrived. Far more important in causing resentment was the fear that the monopolists were destroying economic opportunity and threatening democratic institutions. It was not the wealth of tycoons like Carnegie and Rockefeller and Morgan so much as their influence that worried people. In the face of the growing disparity between rich and poor, could republican institutions survive? "The belief is common," wrote Charles Francis Adams's brother Henry as early as 1870, "that the day is at hand when corporations . . . will ultimately succeed in directing government itself."

As criticism mounted, business leaders rose to their own defense. Rockefeller described in graphic terms the chaotic conditions that plagued the oil industry before the rise of Standard Oil: "It seemed absolutely necessary to extend the market for oil . . . and also greatly improve the process of refining so that oil could be made and sold cheaply, yet with a profit. We proceeded to buy the largest and best refining concerns and centralized the administration of them with a view to securing greater economy and efficiency." Carnegie, in an essay published in 1889, insisted that the concentration of wealth was necessary if humanity was to progress, softening this "Gospel of Wealth" by insisting that the rich must use their money "in the manner which . . . is best calculated to produce the most beneficial results for the community." The rich man was merely a trustee for his "poorer brethren," Carnegie said, "bringing to their service his superior wisdom, experience, and ability to administer." Lesser tycoons echoed these arguments.

The voices of the critics were louder if not necessarily more influential. Many clergymen denounced unrestrained competition, which they considered un-Christian. The new class of professional economists (the American Economic Association was founded in 1885) tended to repudiate laissez-faire. State aid, Richard T. Ely of Johns Hopkins University wrote, "is an indispensable condition of human progress."

Read the Document Carnegie, *Wealth* at
www.myhistorylab.com

Reformers: George, Bellamy, Lloyd

The popularity of a number of radical theorists reflects public feeling in the period. In 1879 Henry George, a California journalist, published *Progress and Poverty*, a forthright attack on the uneven distribution of wealth in the United States. George argued that labor was the true and only source of

Edward Bellamy, author of the utopian novel *Looking Backward* (1888). Bellamy's socialism worried many. *The Household Encyclopedia* (1892) included this photograph of Bellamy in a section on phrenology, the "science" of ascertaining a person's character and intellectual traits from the shape of his or her cranium. Referring to Bellamy's, it concluded, "Large perceptive faculties; defective reasoning powers."

capital. Observing the speculative fever of the West, which enabled landowners to reap profits merely by holding property while population increased, George proposed a property tax that would confiscate this "unearned increment." The value of land depended on society and should belong to society; allowing individuals to keep this wealth was the major cause of the growing disparity between rich and poor, George believed.

George's "single tax," as others called it, would bring in so much money that no other taxes would be necessary, and the government would have plenty of funds to establish new schools, museums, theaters, and other badly needed social and cultural services. While the single tax on property was never adopted, George's ideas attracted enthusiastic attention. Single tax clubs sprang up throughout the nation, and *Progress and Poverty* became a best-seller.

Even more spectacular was the reception afforded *Looking Backward, 2000–1887*, a utopian novel written in 1888 by Edward Bellamy. This book, which sold over a million copies in its first few years, described a future America that was completely socialized, all economic activity carefully planned. Bellamy compared nineteenth-century society to a lumbering stagecoach upon which the favored few rode in comfort while the mass of the people hauled them along life's route. Occasionally one of the toilers managed to fight his way onto the coach; whenever a rider fell from it, he had to join the multitude dragging it along.

Such, Bellamy wrote, was the working of the vaunted American competitive system. He suggested that the ideal socialist state, in which all citizens shared equally, would arrive without revolution or violence. The trend toward consolidation would continue, he predicted, until one monster trust controlled all economic activity. At this point everyone would realize that nationalization was essential.

A third influential attack on monopoly was that of Henry Demarest Lloyd, whose *Wealth Against Commonwealth* appeared in 1894. Lloyd, a journalist of independent means, devoted years to preparing a denunciation of the Standard Oil Company. Marshaling masses of facts and vivid examples of Standard's evildoing, he assaulted the trust at every point. In his zeal, Lloyd sometimes distorted and exaggerated the evidence to make his indictment more effective. "Every important man in the oil, coal and many other trusts ought today to be in some one of our penitentiaries," he wrote in a typical overstatement—as a polemic his book was peerless. His forceful but uncomplicated arguments and his copious references to official documents made *Wealth Against Commonwealth* utterly convincing to thousands. The book was more than an attack on Standard Oil. Lloyd denounced the application of Darwin's concept of survival of the fittest to economic and social affairs, and he condemned laissez-faire policies as leading directly to monopoly.

The popularity of these books indicates that the trend toward monopoly in the United States worried many. But despite the drastic changes suggested in their pages, none of these writers questioned the underlying values of the middle-class majority. They insisted that reform could be accomplished without serious inconvenience to any individual or class. In *Looking Backward* Bellamy pictured the socialists of the future gathered around a radio-like gadget in a well-furnished parlor listening to a minister delivering an inspiring sermon.

Nor did most of their millions of readers seriously consider trying to apply the reformers' ideas. Henry George ran for mayor of New York City in 1886 and lost narrowly to Abram S. Hewitt, a wealthy iron manufacturer, but even if he had won, he would have been powerless to apply the single tax to metropolitan property. The national discontent was apparently not as profound as the popularity of these works might suggest. If John D. Rockefeller became the bogeyman of American industry because of Lloyd's attack, no one prevented him from also becoming the richest man in the United States.

●●●—⌐Read the Document Bellamy, from *Looking Backward* at **www.myhistorylab.com**

Reformers: The Marxists

By the 1870s the ideas of European socialists were beginning to penetrate the United States, and in 1877 a Socialist Labor party was founded. The first serious attempt to explain the ideas of German political philosopher Karl Marx to Americans was Laurence Gronlund's *The Cooperative Commonwealth*, which was published in 1884, two years before Marx's *Das Kapital* was translated into English.

Capitalism, Gronlund claimed, contained the seeds of its own destruction. The state ought to own all the means of production. Competition was "Established Anarchy," middlemen were "parasites," speculators "vampires." "Capital and Labor," he wrote in one of the rare humorous lines in his book,

Table 17.1   Defenders of Economic Consolidation

Defenders	Occupation	Argument
J. Pierpont Morgan	Wall Street financier	Excessive competition was wasteful and unstable; stable growth and efficiency required large business combinations
William Graham Sumner	Yale professor	Large corporations were those that were "fittest"—best-suited to prevail in the Darwinian world of capitalism
Andrew Carnegie	Steel manufacturer	Large corporations generated wealth, which could be channeled into charitable and other worthy causes

Table 17.2   Reformers Oppose Economic Consolidation

Reformers	Publication	Argument
Henry George	Author, *Progress and Poverty* (1879)	Labor was the source of wealth; but investors made money from *capital and property*. Governments should tax property, to help redistribute the unearned income of the wealthy.
Edward Bellamy	Author, *Looking Backward* (1888)	The trend toward industrial concentration would culminate in the government owning everything: an era of prosperity, stability, and cooperative planning would ensue.
Henry Demarest Lloyd	Author, *Wealth Against Commonwealth* (1894)	Concentration of power in corporations inevitably led to monopoly; the government must step in to prevent corporations from becoming behemoths.
Laurence Gronlund	Author, *The Cooperative Commonwealth* (1884)	Capitalism, including corporations, was doomed, as Marx had predicted; but the collapse of capitalism would not require a violent revolution.
Daniel De Leon	Editor, Socialist Labor, *The Weekly*	Capitalism, though doomed, would not fall without a fight; violent revolution was inevitable.

"are just as harmonious as roast beef and a hungry stomach." Yet like other harsh critics of that day, Gronlund expected the millennium to arrive in a peaceful, indeed orderly manner. The red flag of socialism, he said, "has no relation to blood." The movement could accommodate "representatives of all classes," even "thoughtful" middlemen parasites.

The leading voice of the Socialist Labor party, Daniel De Leon, editor of the party's weekly publication, *The People*, was a different type. He was born in the West Indies, son of a Dutch army doctor stationed in Curaçao, and educated in Europe. He emigrated to the United States in the 1870s, where he was progressively attracted by the ideas of Henry George, then Edward Bellamy and the Knights of Labor, and finally Marx. While personally mild-mannered and kindly, when he put pen to paper he became a doctrinaire revolutionary. He excoriated American labor unions in the *People*, insisting that industrial workers could improve their lot only by adopting socialism and joining the Socialist Labor party. He paid scant attention, however, to the practical needs or even to the opinions of rank-and-file working people. In 1891 he was the Socialist Labor party's candidate for governor of New York.

The Government Reacts to Big Business: Railroad Regulation

Political action related to the growth of big business came first on the state level and dealt chiefly with the regulation of railroads. Even before the Civil War, a number of New England states established railroad commissions to supervise lines within their borders; by the end of the century, twenty-eight states had such boards.

Strict regulation was largely the result of agitation by the **National Grange of the Patrons of Husbandry**. The Grange, founded in 1867 by Oliver H. Kelley, was created to provide social and cultural benefits for isolated rural communities. As it spread and grew in influence—fourteen states had Granges by 1872 and membership reached 800,000 in 1874—the movement became political too. "Granger" candidates, often not themselves farmers (many local businessmen resented such railroad practices as rebating), won control of a number of state legislatures in the West and South. Granger-controlled legislatures established "reasonable" maximum rates and outlawed "unjust" discrimination. The legislature also set up a commission to enforce the laws and punish violators.

The railroads protested, insisting that they were being deprived of property without due process of law. In *Munn v. Illinois* (1877), a case that involved a grain elevator whose owner had refused to comply with a state warehouse act, the Supreme Court upheld the constitutionality of this kind of act. Any business that served a public interest, such as a railroad or a grain warehouse, was subject to state control, the justices ruled. Legislatures might fix maximum charges; if the charges seemed unreasonable to the parties concerned, they should direct their complaints to the legislatures or to the voters, not to the courts.

Regulation of the railroad network by the individual states was inefficient, and in some cases the

A farmer with a pitchfork, wearing a hat identifying him as a Granger, warns of an oncoming railroad train. But the American people—one reads a newspaper, another smokes a cigar, but most doze—are oblivious of the danger that will soon crush them.

change them without due public notice. Most important, the law established an Interstate Commerce Commission (ICC), the first federal regulatory board, to supervise the affairs of railroads, investigate complaints, and issue cease and desist orders when the roads acted illegally.

The Interstate Commerce Act broke new ground, yet it was neither a radical nor a particularly effective measure. Its terms contradicted one another, some being designed to stimulate, others to penalize, competition. The chairman of the commission soon characterized the law as an "anomaly." It sought, he said, to "enforce competition" at the same time that it outlawed "the acts and inducements by which competition is ordinarily effected."

The new commission had less power than the law seemed to give it. It could not fix rates; it could only bring the roads to court when it considered rates unreasonably high. Such cases could be extremely complicated; applying the law "was like cutting a path through a jungle." With the truth so hard to determine and the burden of proof on the commission, the courts in nearly every instance decided in favor of the railroads.

Nevertheless, by describing so clearly the right of Congress to regulate private corporations engaged in interstate commerce, the Interstate Commerce Act challenged the philosophy of laissez-faire. Later legislation made the commission more effective. The commission also served as the model for a host of similar federal administrative authorities, such as the Federal Communications Commission (1934).

●●●—Read the **Document**   *Interstate Commerce Act* at
www.myhistorylab.com

The Government Reacts to Big Business: The Sherman Antitrust Act

As with railroad legislation, the first antitrust laws originated in the states, but they were southern and western states with relatively little industry, and most of the statutes were vaguely worded and ill-enforced.

commissions were incompetent and even corrupt. When the Supreme Court, in the case of *Wabash, St. Louis & Pacific Railroad v. Illinois* (1886), declared unconstitutional an Illinois regulation outlawing the long-and-short-haul evil, federal action became necessary. The railroad had charged twenty-five cents per 100 pounds for shipping goods from Gilman, Illinois, to New York City but only fifteen cents to ship goods from Peoria, which was eighty-six miles farther from New York. Illinois judges had held this to be illegal, but the Supreme Court decided that Illinois could not regulate interstate shipments.

Congress filled the gap created by the *Wabash* decision in 1887 by passing the **Interstate Commerce Act**. All charges made by railroads "shall be reasonable and just," the act stated. Rebates, drawbacks, the long-and-short-haul evil, and other competitive practices were declared unlawful, and so were their monopolistic counterparts—pools and traffic-sharing agreements. Railroads were required to publish schedules of rates and forbidden to

Federal action came in 1890 with the passage of the **Sherman Antitrust Act**. Any combination "in the form of trust or otherwise" that was "in restraint of trade or commerce among the several states, or with foreign nations" was declared illegal. Persons forming such combinations were subject to fines of $5,000 and a year in jail. Individuals and businesses suffering losses because of actions that violated the law were authorized to sue in the federal courts for triple damages.

Where the Interstate Commerce Act sought to outlaw the excesses of competition, the Sherman Act was supposed to restore competition. If businessmen joined together to "restrain" (monopolize) trade in a particular field, they should be punished and their deeds undone. "The great thing this bill does," Senator George Frisbie Hoar of Massachusetts explained, "is to extend the common-law principle . . . to international and interstate commerce." This was important because the states ran into legal difficulties when they tried to use the common law to restrict corporations engaged in interstate activities.

But the Sherman Act was rather loosely worded—Thurman Arnold, a modern authority, once said that it made it "a crime to violate a vaguely stated economic policy." Critics have argued that the congressmen were more interested in quieting the public clamor for action against the trusts than in actually breaking up any of the new combinations. Quieting the clamor was certainly one of their objectives. However, they were trying to solve a new problem and were not sure how to proceed. A law with teeth too sharp might do more harm than good. Most Americans assumed that the courts would deal with the details, as they always had in common law matters.

In fact, the Supreme Court quickly emasculated the Sherman Act. In *United States v. E. C. Knight Company* (1895) it held that the American Sugar Refining Company had not violated the law by taking over a number of important competitors. Although the Sugar Trust now controlled about 98 percent of all sugar refining in the United States, it was not restraining trade. "Doubtless the power to control the manufacture of a given thing involves in a certain sense the control of its disposition," the Court said in one of the greatest feats of judicial understatement of all time. "Although the exercise of that power may result in bringing the operation of commerce into play, it does not control it, and affects it only incidentally and indirectly."

If the creation of the Sugar Trust did not violate the Sherman Act, it seemed unlikely that any other combination of manufacturers could be convicted under the law. However, in several cases in 1898 and 1899 the Supreme Court ruled that agreements to fix prices or divide markets did violate the Sherman Act. These decisions precipitated a wave of outright mergers in which a handful of large companies swallowed up hundreds of smaller ones. Presumably mergers were not illegal. When, some years after his retirement, Andrew Carnegie was asked by a committee of the House of Representatives to explain how he had dared participate in the formation of the U.S. Steel Corporation, he replied, "Nobody ever mentioned the Sherman Act to me that I remember."

Table 17.3 Major Congressional and Supreme Court Decisions Concerning Corporations

Case/Act	Year	Decision/Action	Consequence
Munn v. Illinois	1877	State legislatures can regulate economic enterprises	Expansion of state powers against powerful corporations and trusts
Wabash, St. Louis & Pacific Railroad v. Illinois	1886	State legislatures can NOT regulate interstate economic activity; only federal government can do that	Congress passes Interstate Commerce Act 1887, regulating railroad behavior
Interstate Commerce Act	1887	Federal government can regulate railroad rates and practices	Sets precedent for federal intervention in national economic matters
Sherman Antitrust Act	1890	The federal government can break up economic enterprises that are so big and powerful that they have monopoly power	Originally used to weaken labor unions; eventually allows government to break up large corporations
United States v. E. C. Knight	1895	Huge corporations that dominated markets can not be broken up if they do not also behave badly	Weakens Sherman Antitrust Act

The Labor Union Movement

At the time of the Civil War only a small percentage of the American workforce was organized, and most union members were cigarmakers, printers, carpenters, and other skilled artisans, not factory hands. Aside from ironworkers, railroad workers, and miners, few industrial laborers belonged to unions. Nevertheless the union was the workers' response to the big corporation: a combination designed to eliminate competition for jobs and to provide efficient organization for labor.

After 1865 the growth of national craft unions, which had been stimulated by labor dissatisfaction during the Civil War, quickened perceptibly. In 1866 a federation of these organizations, the National Labor Union, was founded and by the early 1870s many new trades, notably in railroading, had been unionized.

Most of the leaders of these unions were visionaries who were out of touch with the practical needs and aspirations of workers. They opposed the wage system, strikes, and anything that increased the laborers' sense of being members of the working class. A major objective was the formation of worker-owned cooperatives.

Far more remarkable was the **Knights of Labor**, a curious organization founded in 1869 by a group of Philadelphia garment workers headed by Uriah S. Stephens. Like so many labor organizers of the period, Stephens was a reformer of wide interests rather than a man dedicated to the specific problems of industrial workers. He, his successor Terence V. Powderly, and many other leaders of the Knights would have been thoroughly at home in the labor organizations of the Jacksonian era. Like the Jacksonians, they supported political objectives that had no direct connection with working conditions, such as currency reform and the curbing of land speculation. They rejected the idea that workers must resign themselves to remaining wage earners. By pooling their resources, working people could advance up the economic ladder and enter the capitalist class. "There is no good reason," Powderly wrote in his autobiography, *The Path I Trod*, "why labor cannot, through cooperation, own and operate mines, factories, and railroads." The leading Knights saw no contradiction between their denunciation of "soulless" monopolies and "drones" like bankers and lawyers and their talk of "combining all branches of trade in one common brotherhood." Such muddled thinking led the Knights to attack the wage system and to frown on strikes as "acts of private warfare."

If the Knights had one foot in the past, they also had one foot in the future. They supported some startlingly advanced ideas. Rejecting the traditional grouping of workers by crafts, they developed a concept closely resembling modern industrial unionism. They welcomed blacks (though mostly in segregated locals), women, and immigrants, and they accepted unskilled workers as well as artisans. The eight-hour day was one of their basic demands, their argument being that increased leisure would give workers time to develop more cultivated tastes and higher aspirations. Higher pay would inevitably follow.

The growth of the union, however, had little to do with ideology. Stephens had made the Knights a secret organization with an elaborate initiatory ritual. Under his leadership, as late as 1879 it had fewer than 10,000 members. Under Powderly, secrecy was discarded. Between 1882 and 1886 successful strikes by local "assemblies" against western railroads, including one against the hated Jay Gould's Missouri Pacific, brought recruits by the thousands. The membership passed 42,000 in 1882, 110,000 in 1885, and in 1886 it soared beyond the 700,000 mark. Alas, sudden prosperity was too much for the Knights. Its national leadership was unable to control local groups. A number of poorly planned strikes failed dismally, and the public was alienated by sporadic acts of violence and intimidation. Disillusioned recruits began to drift away.

Circumstances largely fortuitous caused the collapse of the organization. By 1886 the movement for the eight-hour day had gained wide support among workers, including many who did not belong to unions. Several hundred thousand (estimates vary) were on strike in various parts of the country by May of that year. In Chicago, a center of the eight-hour movement, about 80,000 workers were involved, and a small group of anarchists was trying to take advantage of the excitement to win support.

When a striker was killed in a fracas at the McCormick Harvesting Machine Company, the anarchists called a protest meeting on May 4, at Haymarket Square. Police intervened to break up the meeting, and someone—his identity was never established—hurled a bomb into their ranks. Seven policemen were killed and many others injured.

View the Image *Terence Powderly at Knights of Labor Convention* at **www.myhistorylab.com**

The American Federation of Labor

Although the anarchists were the immediate victims of the resulting public indignation and hysteria—seven were condemned to death and four eventually executed—organized labor, especially the Knights, suffered heavily. No tie between the Knights and the bombing could be established, but the union had

On November 11, 1887, four anarchists were hanged in Chicago on charges they had thrown a bomb that had killed policemen at the Haymarket demonstration. The *Chicago Tribune* reported that after nooses were placed around the men's necks, and white hoods over their heads, "for a moment or two the men stood like ghosts." "Long live anarchy" one shouted.

been closely connected with the eight-hour agitation, and the public tended to associate it with violence and radicalism. Its membership declined as suddenly as it had risen, and soon it ceased to exist as a force in the labor movement.

The Knights' place was taken by the **American Federation of Labor (AFL)**, a combination of national craft unions established in 1886. In a sense the AFL was a reactionary organization. Its principal leaders, Adolph Strasser and Samuel Gompers of the Cigarmakers Union, were, like the founders of the Knights of Labor, originally interested in utopian social reforms. They even toyed with the idea of forming a workers' political party. Experience, however, soon led them to concentrate on organizing skilled workers and fighting for "bread-and-butter" issues such as higher wages and shorter hours. "Our organization does not consist of idealists," Strasser explained to a congressional committee. "We do not control the production of the world. That is controlled by the employers. . . . I look first to cigars."

The AFL accepted the fact that most workers would remain wage earners all their lives and tried to develop in them a sense of common purpose and pride in their skills and station. Strasser and Gompers paid great attention to building a strong organization of dues-paying members committed to unionism as a way of improving their lot. Rank-and-file AFL members were naturally eager to win wage increases and other benefits, but most also valued their unions for the companionship they provided,

the sense of belonging to a group. In other words, despite statements such as Strasser's, unions, in and out of the AFL, were a kind of club as well as a means of defending and advancing their members' material interests.

The chief weapon of the federation was the strike, which it used to win concessions from employers and to attract recruits. Gompers, president of the AFL almost continuously from 1886 until his death in 1924, encouraged workers to make "intelligent use of the ballot" in order to advance their interests. The federation worked for such things as eight-hour days, employers' liability, and mine-safety laws, but it avoided direct involvement in politics. "I have my own philosophy and my own dreams," Gompers once told a left-wing French politician, "but first and foremost I want to increase the workingman's welfare year by year. . . . The French workers waste their economic force by their political divisions."

Gompers's approach to labor problems produced solid, if unspectacular, growth for the AFL. Unions with a total of about 150,000 members formed the federation in 1886. By 1892 the membership had reached 250,000, and in 1901 it passed the million mark.

Labor Militancy Rebuffed

The stress of the AFL on the strike weapon reflected rather than caused the increasing militancy of labor. Workers felt themselves threatened from all sides: the growing size and power of their corporate employers; the substitution of machines for human skills; the invasion of foreign workers willing to accept substandard wages. At the same time they had tasted some of the material benefits of industrialization and had learned the advantages of concerted action.

The average employer behaved like a tyrant when dealing with his workers: He discharged them arbitrarily when they tried to organize unions; he hired scabs to replace strikers; he frequently failed to provide the most rudimentary protection against injury on the job. Some employers, Carnegie for example, professed to approve of unions, but almost none would bargain with labor collectively. To do so, they argued, would be to deprive workers of their freedom to contract for their own labor in any way they saw fit.

The industrialists of the period were not all ogres; they were as alarmed by the rapid changes of the times as their workers, and since they had more at stake materially, they were probably more frightened by the uncertainties. Deflation, technological change, and intense competition kept even the most successful under constant pressure.

The thinking of most employers was remarkably confused. They considered workers who joined unions "disloyal," and at the same time they treated labor as a commodity to be purchased as cheaply as possible. "If I wanted boiler iron," Henry B. Stone, a railroad official, explained, "I would go out on the market and buy it where I could get it cheapest, and if I wanted to employ men, I would do the same." Yet Stone was furious when the men he had "bought" joined a union. When labor was scarce, employers resisted demands for higher wages by arguing that the price of labor was controlled by its productivity; when it was plentiful, they justified reducing wages by referring to the law of supply and demand.

Thus capital and labor were often spoiling for a fight, frequently without fully understanding why. When labor troubles developed, they tended to be bitter, even violent. In 1877 a great railroad strike convulsed much of the nation. It began on the Baltimore and Ohio system in response to a wage cut and spread to other eastern lines and then throughout the West until about two-thirds of the railroad mileage of the country had been shut down. Violence broke out, rail yards were put to the torch, and dismayed and frightened businessmen formed militia companies to patrol the streets of Chicago and other cities. Eventually President Hayes sent federal troops to the trouble spots to restore order, and the strike collapsed. There had been no real danger of revolution, but the violence and destruction of the strike had been without precedent in America.

The disturbances of 1877 were a response to a business slump, those of the next decade a response to good times. Twice as many strikes occurred in 1886 as in any previous year. Even before the Haymarket bombing centered the country's attention on labor problems, the situation had become so disturbing that President Grover Cleveland, in the first presidential message devoted to labor problems, had urged Congress to create a voluntary arbitration board to aid in settling labor disputes—a remarkable

During the Pullman strike in Chicago, workers protesting wage cuts did $340,000 in property damage, chiefly by burning freight cars.

suggestion for a man of Cleveland's conservative, laissez-faire approach to economic issues.

In 1892 a violent strike broke out among silver miners at Coeur d'Alene, Idaho, and a far more important clash shook Andrew Carnegie's Homestead steel plant near Pittsburgh when strikers attacked 300 private guards brought in to protect strikebreakers. Seven guards were killed at Homestead and the rest forced to "surrender" and march off ignominiously. The Homestead affair was part of a struggle between capital and labor in the steel industry. Steel producers insisted that the workers were holding back progress by resisting technological advances, while the workers believed that the company was refusing to share the fruits of more efficient operation fairly. The strike was precipitated by the decision of company officials to crush the union at all costs. The final defeat, after a five-month walkout, of the 24,000-member Amalgamated Association of Iron and Steel Workers, one of the most important elements in the AFL, destroyed unionism as an effective force in the steel industry and set back the progress of organized labor all over the country.

As in the case of the Haymarket bombing, the activities of radicals on the fringe of the dispute turned the public against the steelworkers. The boss of Homestead was Henry Clay Frick, a tough-minded foe of unions who was determined to "teach our employees a lesson." Frick made the decision to bring in strikebreakers and to employ Pinkerton detectives to protect them. During the course of the strike, Alexander Berkman, an anarchist, burst into Frick's office and attempted to assassinate him. Frick was only slightly wounded, but the attack brought him much sympathy and unjustly discredited the strikers.

The most important strike of the period took place in 1894. It began when the workers at George Pullman's Palace Car factory outside Chicago walked out in protest against wage cuts. (While reducing wages, Pullman insisted on holding the line on rents in the company town of Pullman; when a delegation called on him to remonstrate, he refused to give in and had three of the leaders fired.) Some Pullman workers belonged to the American Railway Union, headed by Eugene V. Debs. After the strike had dragged along for weeks, the union voted to refuse to handle trains with Pullman cars. The union was perfectly willing to handle mail trains, but the owners refused to run trains unless they were made up of a full complement of cars.

When Pullman cars were added to mail trains, the workers refused to move them. The resulting railroad strike tied up trunk lines running in and out of Chicago. The railroad owners appealed to President Cleveland to send troops to preserve order. On the pretext that the soldiers were needed to ensure the movement of the mails, Cleveland agreed. When Debs defied a federal injunction to end the walkout, he was jailed for contempt and the strike was broken.

Whither America, Whither Democracy?

Each year more of the nation's wealth and power seemed to fall into fewer hands. As with the railroads, other industries were being influenced, if not completely dominated, by bankers. The firm of J.P. Morgan and Company controlled many railroads; the largest steel, electrical, agricultural machinery, rubber, and shipping companies; two life insurance companies; and a number of banks. By 1913 Morgan and the Rockefeller National City Bank group between them could name 341 directors to 112 corporations worth over $22.2 billion. The "Money Trust," a loose but potent fraternity of financiers, seemed fated to become the ultimate monopoly.

Centralization unquestionably increased efficiency, at least in industries that used a great deal of expensive machinery to turn out goods for the mass market, and in those where close coordination of output, distribution, and sales was important. The public benefited immensely from the productive efficiency of the new empires. Living standards rose.

But the trend toward giantism raised doubts. With ownership falling into fewer hands, what would be the ultimate effect of big business on American democracy? What did it mean for ordinary people when a few tycoons possessed huge fortunes and commanded such influence even on Congress and the courts?

The crushing of the Pullman strike demonstrated the power of the courts to break strikes by issuing injunctions. And the courts seemed only concerned with protecting the interests of the rich and powerful. Particularly ominous for organized labor was the fact that the federal government based its request for the injunction that broke the strike on the Sherman Antitrust Act, arguing that the American Railway Union was a combination in restraint of trade. An indirect result of the Pullman strike was that while serving his sentence for contempt, Eugene Debs was visited by a number of prominent socialists who sought to convert him to their cause. One gave him a copy of Karl Marx's *Capital,* which he found too dull to finish, but he did read *Looking Backward* and *Wealth Against Commonwealth.* In 1897 he became a socialist.

Chapter Review

Milestones

1859	First oil well is drilled in Pennsylvania
	Charles Darwin publishes *The Origin of Species*
1868	Carnegie Steel Company is formed
1869	George Westinghouse invents air brake
	Garment workers found Knights of Labor
1870– 1890	Railroad trunk lines are completed
1876	Alexander Graham Bell invents telephone
1877	Great railroad strike convulses nation
	Munn v. Illinois upholds state regulatory laws
1879	Thomas Edison invents electric light bulb
	Reformer Henry George publishes *Progress and Poverty*
1884	Marxist Laurence Gronlund publishes *The Cooperative Commonwealth*
1886	Anarchists clash with police in Chicago's Haymarket bombing
	Craft unions found American Federation of Labor (AFL)
1887	Interstate Commerce Act regulates railroads
1888	Edward Bellamy publishes utopian *Looking Backward*
1889	Philanthropist Andrew Carnegie publishes "Gospel of Wealth"
1890	Sherman Antitrust Act outlaws monopolies
1892	Seven Pinkerton guards are killed in Homestead steel strike
	General Electric Company is formed
1894	Eugene V. Debs leads American Railway Union in Pullman strike
	Henry Demarest Lloyd condemns laissez-faire in *Wealth Against the Commonwealth*
1895	*U.S. v. E.C. Knight Company* weakens Sherman Act
1901	J.P. Morgan forms U.S. Steel, "world's first billion-dollar corporation"

Key Terms

American Federation of Labor (AFL)   A union, formed in 1886, that organized skilled workers along craft lines. It focused on workplace issues rather than political or social reform, *479*

Interstate Commerce Act   Federal law establishing the Interstate Commerce Commission in 1887, the nation's first regulatory agency, *476*

Knights of Labor   A national labor organization, formed in 1869 and headed by Uriah Stephens and Terence Powderly, that promoted union solidarity, political reform, and sociability among members. Its advocacy of the eight-hour day led to violent strikes in 1886 and the organization's subsequent decline, *478*

laissez-faire   A French term—literally, "to let alone"—used in economic contexts to signify the absence of governmental interference in or regulation of economic matters, *471*

National Grange of the Patrons of Husbandry   A farmers' organization, founded in 1867 by Oliver H. Kelley, that initially provided social and cultural benefits but then supported legislation, known as the Granger laws, providing for railroad regulation, *475*

Sherman Antitrust Act   A federal law, passed in 1890, that outlawed monopolistic organizations that functioned to restrain trade, *477*

social Darwinism   A belief that Charles Darwin's theory of the evolution of species also applied to social and economic institutions and practices: The "fittest" enterprises or individuals prevailed, while those that were defective naturally faded away; society thus progressed most surely when competition was unrestricted by government, *472*

Review Questions

1. The introduction asked whether the benefits of economic concentration outweighed its social and political costs. List the benefits and costs: Which argument is stronger?
2. What factors contributed to the nation's extraordinarily rapid industrial growth during the last third of the nineteenth century?
3. What technological developments had the greatest economic impact? Greatest social impact?
4. Who were the major critics of economic concentration in the late nineteenth century and how did they differ?
5. How did Congress respond to critics of monopoly? How did the Supreme Court respond to attempts to regulate the economy?

myhistorylab Connections

Reinforce what you learned in this chapter by studying the many documents, images, maps, review tools, and videos available at **www.myhistorylab.com**.

Read and Review

✔—⌐Study and Review *Chapter 17*

◉—⌐See the Map *Railroads & New Transportation Systems*, p. 460

◉—⌐View the Image *J.P. Morgan*, p. 460

•◦•—⌐Read the Document Edison, *The Success of the Electric Light*, p. 465

•◦•—⌐Read the Document Carnegie, *Wealth*, p. 473

•◦•—⌐Read the Document Bellamy, from *Looking Backward*, p. 474

◉—⌐View the Image *Terence Powderly at Knights of Labor Convention*, p. 478

Research and Explore

◉—⌐Watch the Video *Rural Free Delivery Mail*, p. 471

•◦•—⌐Read the Document *Interstate Commerce Act*, p. 476

((•—⌐Hear the Audio

Hear the audio file for Chapter 17 at **www.myhistorylab.com**.

Have you been kicked out of a mall?

The Mall of America outside Minneapolis, Minnesota, is the largest enclosed mall in the United States. It is also the nation's most popular tourist destination, visited by 42.5 million people in 2009.

This mall, like many others, was also once a popular hangout for young people. On Friday and Saturday nights, as many as 10,000 teenagers would gather there. But this practice ended in 1996, when the Mall of America instituted a 6:00 PM weekend curfew for teenagers under sixteen unless accompanied by an adult. Since then, hundreds of malls have adopted similar curfews.

Teenagers, who in 2009 bought $170 billion in merchandise, spend much of their free time in malls—over fifty minutes a day on the average. Many resent the curfews. "We just want to be able to hang out at the mall," complains Kimberly Flanagan, sixteen, of Charlotte, North Carolina. Kary Ross, an attorney for the American Civil Liberties Union, sides with the teenagers: "We're opposed to curfews that treat all minors as if they're criminals."

Malls insist that as privately owned enterprises, they are exempt from First Amendment protections, such as

Contents

((●──[Hear the Audio **Chapter 18 at www.myhistorylab.com**

■ Lewis Hine's 1910 photograph shows a tenement alley in New York City. More famous for his "unsettling" photographs of the ills of the cities, Hine sought to depict urban life in all its fullness.

freedom of speech and the right to assemble. Malls are not public property.

Yet recent malls have been designed to evoke the public spaces of the nineteenth-century city. The Mall of America includes an exhibition gallery, amusement park, wedding chapel, assembly hall, school, medical clinic, and a central "Rotunda" for staging "public events" ranging from gardening shows to Hulk Hogan wrestling matches.

In the late nineteenth century, city life was played out in spaces that really were public. Factory workers walked to work along crowded streets or jammed into streetcars or subways. Courting couples strolled through shopping districts or public parks. Children played in streets. "Little

Italy" or "Chinatown" provided exotic attractions for all. Amusement parks and sporting events drew huge throngs. In New York City, a journalist reported in 1883, a "huge conglomerate mass" came together in public spaces to form a "vague and vast harmony."

But city life was not for all. In 1900, 50 percent more Americans lived in rural areas than in urban areas—even when "urban" was generously defined as holding more than 2,500 people. Why, asked sociologist Henry Fletcher in 1895, do "large masses of people, apparently against their own interests," abandon the nation's healthful and sociable rural areas and crowd into the nation's disease-ridden, anonymous cities?

Nineteenth-century cities, though noisy, chaotic, and often ill-governed, exerted a peculiar fascination. In cities, workers, even immigrants and young women, could more easily find jobs. Housing was cheap. Urban problems were daunting, but the immense aggregation of peoples and their resources constituted a limitless potential for uplift and reform. City life was a great spectacle, played out mostly in public spaces. ∎

Middle-Class Life

"This middle-class country had got a middle-class president, at last," Ralph Waldo Emerson had noted with satisfaction when Lincoln took office in 1861. Lincoln, in contrast to the presidents who had been wealthy planters or businessmen or high-ranking military men, was a self-made man who embraced middle-class values. Middle-class culture took the best aspects of romanticism—the enshrinement of human potential, the restless striving for personal betterment, the zest for competition and excitement—and tempered them with a passion for self-control and regularity.

But the Civil War sapped middle-class culture of its reforming zeal. The vital energy that invigorated antebellum reforms and had impelled the North to war became dissipated by that war. Afterwards, middle-class Americans focused their energies on building institutions. American society and culture underwent a process of "incorporation," as the predominant form of the business world seeped deep into the American consciousness.

No institution was more central to middle-class life than the family. After the Civil War, it lost some of its moral fervor but gained a new substantiality.

The Breakfast (1911), by William McGregor Paxton, shows a middle-class husband, absorbed in the newspaper and in the world beyond the home. His wife, in a gorgeous dress, sits—very much a "bird in a gilded cage," the title of a popular song in 1900. The servant girl, face unseen, cleans up the cage.
Source: *The Breakfast*, William McGregor Paxton, American, 1911 The Metropolitan Museum of Art, New York, NY, U.S.A. Image copyright ©The Metropolitan Museum of Art.

Increasingly family life was defined in terms of tangible goods: especially large houses, which were crowded with furniture, books, lamps, and all manner of decorative objects. Modern scholars have often indicted this "culture of consumption" for its superficiality, a criticism commonly aired by patrician elites at the time. But no attack on middle-class culture and its conspicuous consumption surpassed the venom of Thorstein Veblen's *Theory of the Leisure Class* (1899). Veblen contended that consumers derived little real pleasure from their big homes and gaudy purchases; they were simply showing off their wealth. Fashionable clothes, for example, induced "aesthetic nausea," prompting women to soon discard them. No one was ever satisfied with their wealth because everyone else was scrambling to get ahead of them. Everyone wanted more.

Middle-class people regarded the matter differently. They conceived of the family as a refuge from the increasingly chaotic and unsavory aspects of urban life: A beautiful house that was filled with books, paintings, and musical instruments would inculcate the finer sensibilities and elevate the minds of its occupants. Better for children to find stimulation at home than to visit the vice districts or unsupervised amusements downtown. The abundant material culture of the "Victorian age" reflected not its superficiality but its solidity.

Modern historians have often denounced the middle-class family as emotionally stiff and, in matters pertaining to sexuality, downright prudish. But diaries and letters provide ample proof that many couples experienced emotionally intense and sexually fulfilling relationships. Elaborate and protracted courtship rituals intensified the expression of love by delaying its gratification. Middle-class mothers at the end of the century had two or three children, four or five fewer than their grandmothers. Their families were smaller mostly because they married later in life and practiced abstinence, though during the last half of the century contraceptive devices were both more reliable and more available commercially.

While most women remained home to supervise their children and to preside over the private world of the family, men worked away from home, in shops and offices. Members of the professions and the large and diffuse groups of shopkeepers, small manufacturers, skilled craftsmen, and established farmers that made up the middle class lived in varying degrees of comfort. A family with an annual income of $1,000 in the 1880s would have no need to skimp on food, clothing, or shelter. When Professor Woodrow Wilson moved with his family to Wesleyan University in 1888, he was able to rent a large house and employ two full-time servants on his salary of $2,500 a year. Indeed, at this time, about a quarter of all urban families employed at least one servant.

The presence of servants showed that the middle-class family was never wholly "private." Husbands, of course, left the house each day to work in the businesses that provided the economic rationale for cities; but wives also made recurrent forays into the public world in order to shop, visit parks and museums, and participate in charitable and social organizations.

Skilled and Unskilled Workers

Wage earners, too, were drawn to urban areas. They felt the full force of the industrial tide, being affected in countless ways—some beneficial, others unfortunate. As manufacturing became more important, the number of manufacturing workers increased nearly ten-fold, from around 600,000 in 1860 to nearly 5 million in 1890. While workers lacked much sense of solidarity, they exerted a far larger influence on society at the turn of the century than they had in the years before the Civil War.

More efficient methods of production enabled them to increase their output, making possible a rise in their standard of living. The working day still tended to approximate the hours of daylight, but it was shortening perceptibly by the 1880s, at least in many occupations. In 1860 the average had been eleven hours, but by 1880 only one worker in four labored more than ten hours and radicals were beginning to talk about eight hours as a fair day's work.

This generalization, however, conceals some important differences. Skilled industrial workers—such types as railroad engineers and conductors, machinists, and iron molders—were relatively well-off in most cases. But it was still true that unskilled laborers could not earn enough to maintain a family decently by their own efforts alone.

Industrialization created problems for workers beyond the obvious one of earning enough money to support themselves. By and large, skilled workers improved their positions relatively, despite the increased use of machinery. Furthermore, when machines took the place of human skills, jobs became monotonous. Mechanization undermined both the artisans' pride and their bargaining power with employers. As expensive machinery became more important, the worker seemed of necessity less important. Machines more than workers controlled the pace of work and its duration. The time clock regulated the labor force more rigidly than the most exacting foreman. The length of the workday may have declined, but the pace of work and the danger involved in working around heavy, high-speed machinery increased accordingly.

As businesses grew larger, personal contact between employer and hired hand tended to disappear. Relations between them became less human, more businesslike, and ruthless. On the other hand, large enterprises usually employed a higher percentage of managerial and clerical workers than smaller companies, thus providing opportunities for more "blue-collar" workers to rise in the industrial hierarchy. But the trend toward bigness made it more difficult for workers to rise from the ranks of labor to become manufacturers themselves, as Andrew Carnegie, for example, had done during the Civil War era.

Another problem for workers was that industrialization tended to accentuate swings of the business cycle. On the upswing something approaching full employment existed, but in periods of depression unemployment became a problem that affected workers without regard for their individual abilities. It is significant that the word *unemployment* (though not, of course, the condition itself) was a late-nineteenth-century invention.

Read the **Document** *Massachusetts Bureau of Statistics of Labor* at **www.myhistorylab.com**

Working Women

Women continued to supply a significant part of the industrial working force. But now many more of them were working outside their homes; the factory had almost completely replaced the household as the seat of manufacturing.[1] Such women had no choice but to leave the "domestic sphere" to make a living. Textile mills and "the sewing trades" absorbed a large percentage of women, but in all fields women were paid substantially lower wages than men.

Women found many new types of work in these years, a fact commented on by *The New York Times* as early as 1869. They made up the overwhelming majority of salespersons and cashiers in the big new department stores. Store managers considered women more polite, easier to control, and more honest than male workers, all qualities especially valuable in the huge emporiums. Over half of the more than 1,700 employees in A. T. Stewart's New York store were women.

Educated, middle-class women also dominated the new profession of nursing that developed alongside the expanding medical profession and the establishment of large urban hospitals. To nearly all doctors, to most men, and indeed to many women of that day, nursing seemed the perfect female profession since it required the same characteristics that women were thought to

This girl ran four spinning machines in a cotton mill in Whitnel, North Carolina. Only four feet, three inches tall, she earned forty-eight cents a day. Photographer Lewis Hine hoped that pictures such as this one (1908) would generate public support for child labor laws.

have by nature: selflessness, cleanliness, kindliness, tact, sensitivity, and submissiveness to male control. Typical was this remark of a contemporary authority: "Since God could not care for all the sick, he made women to nurse." Why it had not occurred to God to make more women physicians, or for that matter members of other prestigious professions like law and the clergy, this man did not explain, probably because it had not occurred to him either.

Middle-class women did replace men as teachers in most of the nation's grade schools, and they also replaced men as clerks and secretaries and operators of the new typewriters in government departments and in business offices. Most men with the knowledge of spelling and grammar that these positions required had better opportunities and were uninterested in office work, so women high school graduates, of whom there was an increasing number, filled the gap.

Both department store clerks and "typewriters" (as they were called) earned more money than unskilled factory workers, and working conditions were more pleasant. Opportunities for promotion for women, however, were rare; managerial posts in these fields remained almost exclusively in the hands of men.

Working-Class Family Life

Early social workers who visited the homes of industrial laborers in this period reported enormous differences in the standard of living of people engaged in the same line of work, differences related to such variables as health, intelligence, the wife's ability as a homemaker, the degree of the family's commitment to middle-class values, and pure luck. Some families

---

[1]However, at least half of all working women were domestic servants.

spent most of their income on food; others saved substantial sums even when earning no more than $400 or $500 a year. Family incomes varied greatly among workers who received similar hourly wages, depending on the steadiness of employment and on the number of family members holding jobs.

Consider the cases of two Illinois coal miners, each a decent, hardworking union man with a large family, earning $1.50 a day in 1883. One was out of work nearly half the year; his income in 1883 was only $250. He, his wife, and their five children, ages three to nineteen, lived in a two-room tenement. They existed almost exclusively on a diet of bread and salt meat. Nevertheless, as an investigator reported, their home was neat and clean and three of the children were attending school.

The other miner, father of four children, worked full time and brought home $420 in 1883. He owned a six-room house and an acre of land, where the family raised vegetables. Their food bill for the year was more than ten times that of the family just described. These two solid families were probably similar in social attitudes and perhaps in political loyalties; but they had very different standards of living.

The cases of two families headed by railroad brakemen provide a different variation. One man brought home only $360 to house and feed a wife and eight children. Here is the report of a state official who interviewed the family: "Clothes ragged, children half-dressed and dirty. They all sleep in one room regardless of sex. . . . The entire concern is as wretched as could be imagined. Father is shiftless. . . . Wife is without ambition or industry."

The other brakeman and his wife had only two children, and he earned $484 in 1883. They owned a well-furnished house, kept a cow, and raised vegetables for home consumption. Although they were far from rich, they managed to put aside enough for insurance, reading matter, and a few small luxuries.

A mother died, a father lost his leg—such calamities shattered poor urban families. Orphaned street urchins formed roving bands that pilfered food and picked the pockets of the well-to-do. Rather than put such children in orphanages, the Children's Aid Society in New York sent them to live with, and work for, farming families. From the 1850s until 1929, over 200,000 orphans were put on trains such as this one and sent to the West.

Working-Class Attitudes

Social workers and government officials made many efforts in the 1880s and 1890s to find out how working people felt about all sorts of matters connected with their jobs. Their reports reveal a wide spectrum of opinion. To the question, asked of two Wisconsin carpenters, "What new laws, in your opinion, ought to be enacted?" one replied, "Keep down strikes and rioters. Let every man attend to his own business." But the other answered, "Complete nationalization of land and all ways of transportation. Burn all government bonds. A graduated income tax. . . . Abolish child labor and [pass] any other act that capitalists say is wrong."

Every variation of opinion between these extremes was expressed by working people in many sections and in many kinds of work. In 1881 a female textile worker in Lawrence, Massachusetts, said to an interviewer, "If you will stand by the mill, and see the people coming out, you will be surprised to see the happy, contented look they all have."

Despite such remarks and the general improvement in living standards, it is clear, if only from the large number of bitter strikes of the period, that there was a considerable dissatisfaction among industrial workers. Writing in 1885, the labor leader Terence V. Powderly reported that "a deep-rooted feeling of discontent pervades the masses."

The discontent had many causes. For some, poverty was still the chief problem, but for others, rising aspirations triggered discontent. Workers were confused about their destiny; the tradition that no one of ability need remain a hired hand died hard. They wanted to believe their bosses and the politicians when those worthies voiced the old slogans about a classless society and the community of interest of capital and labor. "Our men," William Vanderbilt of the New York Central said in 1877, "feel that, although I . . . may have my millions and they the rewards of their daily toil, still we are about equal in the end. If they suffer, I suffer, and if I suffer, they cannot escape." "The poor," another conservative said a decade later, "are not poor because the rich are rich." Instead "the service of capital" softened their lot and gave them many benefits. Statements such as these, though self-serving, were essentially correct. The rich were growing richer and more people were growing rich, but ordinary workers were better off too. However, the gap between the very rich and the ordinary citizen was widening. "The tendency . . . is toward centralization and aggregation," the Illinois Bureau of Labor Statistics reported in 1886. "This involves a separation of the people into classes, and the permanently subordinate status of large numbers of them."

Working Your Way Up

To study mobility in a large industrial country is extraordinarily difficult. Americans in the late nineteenth century believed their society offered great opportunities for individual advancement, and to prove it they pointed to men like Andrew Carnegie and to other poor boys who accumulated large fortunes. How general was the rise from rags to riches (or even to modest comfort) is another question.

Americans had been on the move, mostly, of course, in a westward direction, since the colonial period, but studies of census records show that there was considerable geographic mobility in urban areas throughout the last half of the nineteenth century and into the twentieth. Most investigations reveal that only about half the people recorded in one census were still in the same place ten years later. The nation had a vast reservoir of rootless people. For many, the way to move up in the world was to move on.

In most of the cities studied, mobility was accompanied by some economic and social improvement. On the average, about a quarter of the manual laborers traced rose to middle-class status during their lifetimes, and the sons of manual laborers were still more likely to improve their place in society. In New York City about a third of the Italian and Jewish immigrants of the 1890s had risen from unskilled to skilled jobs a decade later. Even in Newburyport, Massachusetts, a town that was something of an economic backwater, most laborers made some progress, though far fewer rose to skilled or white-collar positions than in more prosperous cities.

Such progress was primarily the result of the economic growth the nation was experiencing and of the energy and ambition of the people, native-born and immigrant alike, who were pouring into the cities in such numbers. The public education system gave an additional boost to the upwardly mobile.

The history of American education after about 1870 reflects the impact of social and economic change. Although Horace Mann, Henry Barnard, and others had laid the foundations for state-supported school systems in the 1840s and 1850s (see Chapter 10), most of these systems became compulsory only after the Civil War, when the growth of cities provided the concentration of population and financial resources necessary for economical mass education. In the 1860s about half the children in the country were getting some formal education, but this did not mean that half the children were attending school at any one time. Sessions were short, especially in rural areas, and many teachers were poorly trained. President Calvin Coolidge noted in his autobiography that the one-room school he attended in rural Vermont in the 1880s was open only in slack seasons

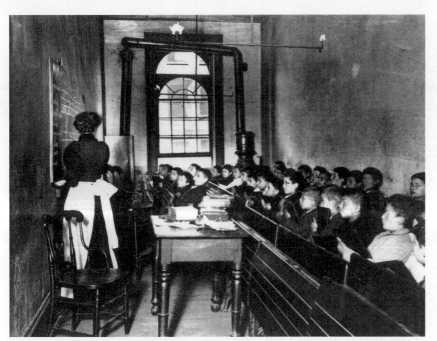

Jacob Riis's photograph of a class on the Lower East Side of New York City. At Riis's death, Theodore Roosevelt called him "the staunchest, most efficient, friend the children of New York City have ever had."

when the twenty-odd students were not needed in the fields. "Few, if any, of my teachers reached the standard now required," he wrote, adding that his own younger sister had obtained a teaching certificate and actually taught a class when she was only twelve.

Thereafter, steady growth and improvement took place. Attendance in the public schools increased from 6.8 million in 1870 to 15.5 million in 1900, a remarkable expansion even when allowance is made for the growth of the population. More remarkable still, during a time when prices were declining steadily, public expenditures for education nearly quadrupled. A typical elementary school graduate, at least in the cities, could count on having studied, besides the traditional "Three Rs," history, geography, a bit of science, drawing, and physical training.

Industrialization created many demands for vocational and technical training; both employers and unskilled workers quickly grasped the possibilities. Science courses were taught in some of the new high schools, but secondary education was still assumed to be only for those with special abilities and youths whose families did not require that they immediately become breadwinners. As late as 1890 fewer than 300,000 of the 14.3 million children attending public and private schools had progressed beyond the eighth grade and nearly a third of these were attending private institutions.

Education certainly helped young people to rise in the world, but progress from rags to real riches was far from common. Carnegies were rare. A study of the family backgrounds of 200 late-nineteenth-century business leaders revealed that nearly all of them grew up in well-to-do middle-class families. They were far better educated than the general run, and most were members of one or another Protestant church.

The unrealistic expectations inspired by the rags-to-riches myth more than the absence of real opportunity probably explains why so many workers, even when expressing dissatisfaction with life as it was, continued to subscribe to such middle-class values as hard work and thrift—that is, they continued to hope.

The "New" Immigration

Industrial expansion increased the need for labor, and this in turn powerfully stimulated immigration. Between 1866 and 1915 about 25 million foreigners entered the United States. Industrial growth alone does not explain the influx. The launching in 1858 of the English liner *Great Eastern*, which was nearly 700 feet from stem to stern and weighed about 19,000 tons, opened a new era in transatlantic travel. Although most immigrants traveled in steerage, which was cramped and almost totally lacking in anything that could be considered an amenity, the Atlantic crossing, once so hazardous, became safe and speedy with the perfection of the steamship. Competition between the great packet lines such as Cunard, North German Lloyd, and Holland-America drove down the cost of the passage, and advertising by the lines further stimulated traffic.

"Push" pressures as well as these "pull" factors had much to do with the new patterns of immigration. Improvements in transportation produced unexpected and disruptive changes in the economies of many European countries. Cheap wheat from the United States, Russia, and other parts of the world poured into Europe, bringing disaster to farmers throughout Europe. The spreading industrial revolution and the increased use of farm machinery led to the collapse of the peasant economy of central and southern Europe. For rural inhabitants this meant the loss of self-sufficiency, the fragmentation of landholdings, unemployment, and for many the decision to make a new start in the New World.

Political and religious persecutions pushed still others into the migrating stream, but the main reason

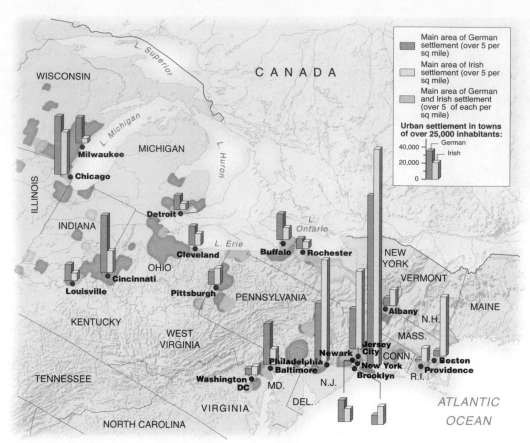

German and Irish Settlement in the Northeastern United States, 1870 In 1870, New York was the greatest immigrant city; its Irish population dwarfed that of Philadelphia or Boston. Its German population, too, greatly exceeded that of "German" cities such as Milwaukee and Chicago.

for immigration remained the desire for economic betterment. "In America," a British immigrant reported, "you get pies and puddings."

While immigrants continued to people the farms of America, industry absorbed an ever-increasing number of the newcomers. In 1870 one industrial worker in three was foreign-born. When congressional investigators examined twenty-one

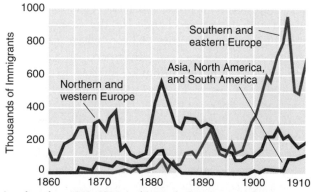

Immigration, 1860–1910 In this graph, Germany is counted as a part of northern and western Europe. Note the new immigration from southern and eastern Europe in the early 1900s.

major industries early in the new century, they discovered that well over half of the labor force had not been born in the United States.

Before 1882, when—in addition to the Chinese—criminals, and persons adjudged mentally defective or liable to become public charges were excluded, entry into the United States was almost unrestricted. Indeed, until 1891 the Atlantic coast states, not the federal government, exercised whatever controls were imposed on newcomers. Even when federally imposed, medical inspection was perfunctory. Public health officials boasted that with "one glance" at each arrival, the inspectors could "take in six details, namely the scalp, face, neck, hands, gait and general condition, both mental and physical." Only those who failed this "test" were examined more closely. On average, only one immigrant in fifty was ultimately rejected.

Private agencies, philanthropic and commercial, served as a link between the new arrivals and employers looking for labor. Until the Foran Act of 1885 outlawed the practice, a few companies brought in skilled workers under contract, advancing them passage money and collecting it in installments from their paychecks, a system somewhat like the indentured servitude of colonial times. Numerous nationality groups assisted (and sometimes exploited) their compatriots by organizing "immigrant banks" that recruited labor in the old country, arranged transportation, and then housed the newcomers in boardinghouses in the United States while finding them jobs. The *padrone* system of the Italians and Greeks was typical. The *padrone,* a sort of contractor who agreed to supply gangs of unskilled workers to companies for a lump sum, usually signed on immigrants unfamiliar with American wage levels at rates that ensured him a healthy profit.

Beginning in the 1880s, the spreading effects of industrialization in Europe caused a shift in the sources of American immigration from northern and western to southern and eastern sections of the continent. In 1882, 789,000 immigrants entered the United States; more than 350,000 came from Great Britain and Germany, only 32,000 from Italy, and fewer than 17,000 from Russia. In 1907—the all-time peak year, with 1,285,000 immigrants—Great Britain and Germany supplied fewer than half as many as they had twenty-five years earlier, while the **new immigration** from southern and eastern Europe was supplying eleven times as many as then. Up to 1880, only about 200,000 southern and eastern Europeans had migrated to America. Between 1880 and 1910, approximately 8.4 million arrived.

View the Image *Health Check at Ellis Island* at
www.myhistorylab.com

New Immigrants Face New Nativism

The "new" immigrants, like the "old" Irish of the 1840s and 1850s, were mostly peasants. They also seemed more than ordinarily clannish; southern Italians typically called all people outside their families *forestieri,* "foreigners." Old-stock Americans thought them harder to assimilate, and in fact many were. Some Italian immigrants, for example, were unmarried men who had come to the United States to earn enough money to buy a farm back home. Such people made hard and willing workers but were not much concerned with being part of an American community.

These "birds of passage" were a substantial minority, but the immigrant who saved in order to bring his wife and children or his younger brothers and sisters to America was more typical. In addition, thousands of immigrants came as family groups and intended to remain. Some, like the eastern European Jewish migrants, were refugees who were almost desperately eager to become Americans, although of course they retained and nurtured much of their traditional culture.

Many "older" Americans concluded, wrongly but understandably, that the new immigrants were incapable of becoming good citizens and should be kept out. During the 1880s, large numbers of social workers, economists, and church leaders, worried by the problems that arose when so many poor immigrants flocked into cities already bursting at the seams, began to believe that some restriction should be placed on the incoming human tide. The directors of charitable organizations, which bore the burden of aiding the most unfortunate immigrants, complained that their resources were being exhausted by the needs of the flood.

Social Darwinists and people obsessed with pseudoscientific ideas about "racial purity" also found the new immigration alarming. Misunderstanding the findings of the new science of genetics, they attributed the social problems associated with mass immigration to supposed physiological characteristics of the newcomers. Forgetting that earlier Americans had accused pre-Civil War Irish and German immigrants of similar deficiencies, they decided that the peoples of southern and eastern Europe were racially (and therefore permanently) inferior to "Nordic" and "Anglo-Saxon" types and ought to be kept out.

Workers, fearing the competition of people with low living standards and no bargaining power, spoke out against the "enticing of penniless and unapprised immigrants . . . to undermine our wages and social welfare." In 1883 the president of the Amalgamated Iron and Steel Workers told a Senate committee that Hungarian, Polish, Italian, and other immigrants "can live where I think a decent man would die; they can live on . . . food that other men would not touch." A Wisconsin iron worker put it this way: "Immigrants work for almost nothing and seem to be able to live on wind—something I can not do."

Employers were not disturbed by the influx of people with strong backs willing to work hard for low wages. Nevertheless, by the late 1880s many employers were alarmed about the supposed radicalism of the immigrants. The Haymarket bombing focused attention on the handful of foreign-born extremists in the country and loosed a flood of unjustified charges that "anarchists and communists" were dominating the labor movement. **Nativism,** which had grown in the 1850s under the Know-Nothing banner and faded during the Civil War, now flared up again, and for similar reasons. Denunciations of "longhaired, wild-eyed, bad-smelling, atheistic, reckless foreign wretches," of "Europe's human and inhuman rubbish," of the "cutthroats of Beelzebub from the Rhine, the Danube, the Vistula and the Elbe" crowded the pages of the nation's press. The Grand Army of the Republic, an organization of Civil War veterans, grumbled about foreign-born radicals.

DEBATING THE PAST
Did Immigrants Assimilate?

In this 1909 photograph, immigrant children at Ellis Island hold American flags as they share a ride in an "Uncle Sam" wagon. Did they and their parents readily adjust to life in the United States?

In 1951 historian Oscar Handlin thought not. He asserted that immigrants were "uprooted" from the lives they had known and "replanted" in "strange ground, among strangers, where strange manners prevailed." Many were shattered by the experience, which accounted for rampant crime, ruptured families, and social disorder in tenement districts.

But subsequent studies found that many immigrants adapted well. John Bodnar (1985) pointedly described immigrants as "transplanted" rather than "uprooted." When challenged by new situations, they "forged a culture, a constellation of behavioral and thought patterns which would offer them explanations, order, and a prescription for how to live with their lives." Sometimes they modified traditional institutions to serve new purposes; sometimes they

created new ones, such as ethnic clubs and parochial schools. The diversity of immigrant experiences was reflected in the *Harvard Encyclopedia of American Ethnic Groups* (1980), edited by Handlin and Stephen Thernstrom. In 2010 Ira Berlin argued that African Americans who made their way north after the Civil War were also "immigrants," but of a type entirely distinct from all other immigrant groups. This emphasis on the distinctiveness of each immigrant group had prompted Arthur M. Schlesinger Jr. (1992) to bemoan his profession's role in the "disuniting of America." By stressing our ethnic differences, we too readily forget that we remain citizens of a single nation.

In short, each of the children in "Uncle Sam's" wagon experienced life differently; but they were in for the ride together.

Source: Oscar Handlin, *The Uprooted* (1951); John Bodnar, *The Transplanted* (1985); Arthur M. Schlesinger Jr., *The Disuniting of America* (1992); Ira Berlin, *The Making of African America* (2010).

WHERE THE BLAME LIES.

APRIL 4, 1891

JUDGE (to Uncle Sam)—"If Immigration was properly Restricted you would no longer be troubled with Anarchy, Socialism, the Mafia and such kindred evils!"

An 1891 cartoon blames immigrants for the ills of American society: anarchy, socialism, mayhem, and organized crime.

These nativists, again like the pre-Civil War variety, disliked Catholics and other minority groups more than immigrants as such. The largest nativist organization of the period, the American Protective Association, founded in 1887, existed primarily to resist what its members called "the Catholic menace." The Protestant majority treated "new" immigrants as underlings, tried to keep them out of the best jobs, and discouraged their efforts to climb the social ladder. This prejudice functioned only at the social and economic level. But nowhere in America did prejudice lead to interference with religious freedom in the narrow sense. And neither labor leaders nor important industrialists, despite their misgivings about immigration, took a broadly antiforeigner position.

After the Exclusion Act of 1882 and the almost meaningless 1885 ban on importing contract labor, no further restrictions were imposed on immigration until the twentieth century. Strong support for a literacy test for admission developed in the 1890s, pushed by a new organization, the Immigration Restriction League. Since there was much more illiteracy in the southeastern quarter of Europe than in the northwestern, such a test would discriminate without seeming to do so on national or racial grounds. A literacy test bill passed both houses of Congress in 1897, but President Cleveland vetoed it. Such a "radical departure" from the "generous and free handed policy" of the past, Cleveland said, was unjustified. He added, perhaps with tongue in cheek, that a literacy requirement would not keep out "unruly agitators," who were only too adept at reading and writing.

Watch the **Video** *Ellis Island Immigrants, 1903* at www.myhistorylab.com

View the **Image** *Looking Backward at Immigrant Origins* at www.myhistorylab.com

See the **Map** *Foreign-Born Population, 1890* at www.myhistorylab.com

The Expanding City and Its Problems

Americans who favored restricting immigration made much of the fact that so many of the newcomers crowded into the cities, aggravating problems of housing, public health, crime, and immorality. Immigrants concentrated in the cities because the jobs created by expanding industry were located there. So, of course, did native-born Americans; the proportion of urban dwellers had been steadily increasing since about 1820.

Industrialization does not entirely explain the growth of nineteenth-century cities. All the large American cities began as commercial centers, and the development of huge metropolises like New York and Chicago would have been impossible without the national transportation network. But by the final decades of the century, the expansion of industry had become the chief cause of city growth. Thus the urban concentration continued; in 1890 one person in three lived in a city, by 1910 nearly one in two.

A steadily increasing proportion of the urban population was made up of immigrants. In 1890 the foreign-born population of Chicago almost equaled the total population of Chicago in 1880; a third of all Bostonians and a quarter of all Philadelphians were immigrants; and four out of five residents of New York City were either foreign-born or the children of immigrants.

After 1890 the immigrant concentration became even more dense. The migrants from eastern and southern Europe lacked the resources to travel to the agriculturally developing regions (to say nothing of the sums necessary to acquire land and farm equipment). As the concentration progressed it fed

upon itself, for all the eastern cities developed many ethnic neighborhoods, in each of which immigrants of one nationality congregated. Lonely, confused, often unable to speak English, the Italians, the Greeks, the Polish and Russian Jews, and other immigrants tended to settle where their predecessors had settled.

Most newcomers intended to become U.S. citizens, to be absorbed into the famous American "melting pot." But they also wanted to maintain their traditional culture. They supported "national" churches and schools. Newspapers in their native languages flourished, as did social organizations of all sorts. Each great American city became a Europe in microcosm. New York City, the great *entrepôt*, had a Little Italy; Polish, Greek, Jewish, and Bohemian quarters; and even a Chinatown.

Although ethnic neighborhoods were crowded, unhealthy, and crime-ridden, and many of the residents were desperately poor, they were not ghettos in the European sense, for those who lived there were not compelled by law to remain. Thousands "escaped" yearly to better districts. American ghettos were places where hopes and ambitions were fulfilled,

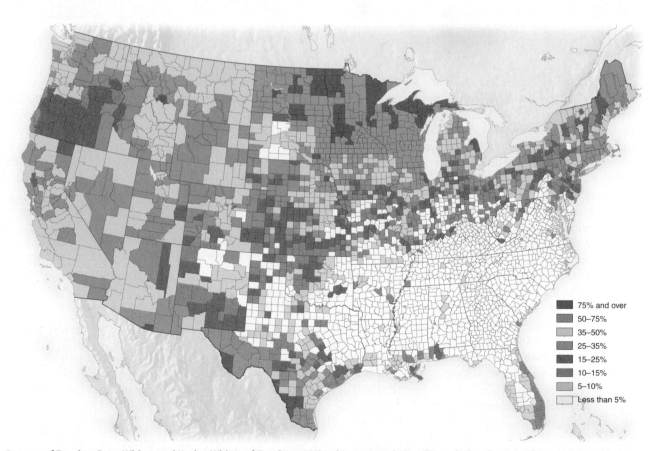

Percent of Foreign-Born Whites and Native Whites of Foreign or Mixed Parentage in Total Population, by Counties, 1910 In 1910, the South had the lowest proportion of immigrants; in Minnesota, Wisconsin, North Dakota, Massachusetts, Connecticut, Rhode Island, in the regions bordering Mexico, and in parts of the Rocky Mountains, over half of the population was immigrant.

where people worked hard and endured hardships in order to improve their own and their children's lot.

Observing the immigrants' attachment to "foreign" values and institutions, numbers of "natives" accused the newcomers of resisting Americanization and blamed them for urban problems. The immigrants were involved in these problems, but the rapidity of urban expansion explains the troubles associated with city life far more fully than the high percentage of foreigners.

Teeming Tenements

The cities were suffering from growing pains. Sewer and water facilities frequently could not keep pace with skyrocketing needs. By the 1890s the tremendous growth of Chicago had put such a strain on its sanitation system that the Chicago River had become virtually an open sewer, and the city's drinking water contained such a high concentration of germ-killing chemicals that it tasted like creosote. In the 1880s all the sewers of Baltimore emptied into the sluggish Back Basin, and according to the journalist H. L. Mencken, every summer the city smelled "like a billion polecats." Fire protection became less and less adequate, garbage piled up in the streets faster than it could be carted away, and the streets themselves crumbled beneath the pounding of heavy traffic. Urban growth proceeded with such speed that new streets were laid out more rapidly than they could be paved. Chicago had more than 1,400 miles of dirt streets in 1890.

People poured into the great cities faster than housing could be built to accommodate them. The influx into areas already densely packed in the 1840s became unbearable as rising property values and the absence of zoning laws conspired to make builders use every possible foot of space, squeezing out light and air ruthlessly in order to wedge in a few additional family units.

Substandard living quarters aggravated other evils such as disease and the disintegration of family life, with its attendant mental anguish, crime, and juvenile delinquency. The bloody New York City riots of 1863, though sparked by dislike of the Civil War draft and of blacks, reflected the bitterness and frustration of thousands jammed together amid filth and threatened by disease. A citizens' committee seeking to discover the causes of the riots expressed its amazement after visiting the slums "that so much misery, disease, and wretchedness can be huddled together and hidden . . . unvisited and unthought of, so near our own abodes."

New York City created a Metropolitan Health Board in 1866, and a state tenement house law the following year made a feeble beginning at regulating city housing. Another law in 1879 placed a limit on the percentage of lot space that could be covered by new construction and established minimal standards of plumbing and ventilation. The magazine *Plumber and Sanitary Engineer* sponsored a contest to pick the best design for a **tenement** that met these specifications. The winner of the competition was James E. Ware, whose plan for a "dumbbell" apartment house managed to crowd from twenty-four to thirty-two four-room apartments on a plot of ground only 25 by 100 feet.

Despite these efforts in 1890 more than 1.4 million persons were living on Manhattan Island, and in some sections the population density exceeded 900 persons per acre. Jacob Riis, a reporter, captured the horror of the crowded warrens in his classic study of life in the slums, *How the Other Half Lives* (1890):

> Be a little careful, please! The hall is dark and you might stumble. . . . Here where the hall turns and dives into utter darkness is . . . a flight of stairs. You can feel your way, if you cannot see it. Close? Yes! What would you have? All the fresh air that enters these stairs comes from the hall-door that is forever slamming. . . . The sinks are in the hallway, that all the tenants may have access—and all be poisoned alike by their summer stenches. . . . Here is a door. Listen! That short, hacking cough, that tiny, helpless wail—what do they mean? . . . The child is dying of measles. With half a chance it might have lived; but it had none. That dark bedroom killed it.

Impoverished immigrant families, like the one in this 1889 Jacob Riis photograph, often lived in tiny windowless rooms in crowded tenement districts. Riis devised a "flash bulb" for indoor photographs in poorly illuminated rooms like this one.
Source: Jacob A. Riis, *In Poverty Gap: An English Coal-Heaver's Home.* Courtesy of Museum of the City of New York.

Cholera: A New Disease Strikes the Nation

Urbanization during the nineteenth century contributed to the modernization of the nation, but it also brought an ancient disease to the United States: cholera. Cholera did not kill as many people as malaria or tuberculosis, but it was probably the most terrifying disease of the century. Cholera was new to the United States, and its symptoms were gruesome. People were stricken, sometimes in mid-stride, with severe abdominal cramps. Unremitting diarrhea followed, often culminating in dehydration and kidney failure. About half of those who contracted the disease died.

The disease had centuries earlier originated on the overcrowded banks of the Ganges River in India. In early 1831 the disease appeared in eastern Europe and moved steadily westward. In January 1832 it surfaced in England. Health officials in the United States then braced for an onslaught. In June an outbreak of cholera in Montreal prompted wealthy New Yorkers to flee. On June 26 cases appeared in New York City. Soon afterward the disease spread westward along the Erie Canal and then into cities in the Great Lakes region and along the Ohio and Mississippi rivers. Simultaneously it struck Charleston, South Carolina, and New Orleans, Louisiana.

In this cartoon, Boss Tweed welcomes cholera—a skeletal figure of death carrying a handbag from "Asia"—into the rat-infested and filthy slums of New York. Fear of cholera and other diseases led to the creation of powerful public bodies, relatively free from political interference, to promote sanitation and clean water.

During the next fifty years cholera outbreaks were fairly common during summer. In 1849 and 1866 it swept through the nation, taking tens of thousands of lives. Most people believed that cholera spread directly from one person to another by bodily contact. When it hit a city, neighboring communities would close the roads and governors called out militias to keep infected persons away. Because cholera outbreaks often appeared first in impoverished tenement districts, immigrants were often blamed for the disease.

But after a cholera epidemic killed nearly 14,000 people in London in 1849, John Snow, a physician, determined that most of those who contracted cholera drew their drinking water from the lower Thames River; people served by an upriver pumping station rarely fell ill from the disease. Snow concluded that infected people with diarrhea passed a "poison" into the Thames, which people downriver ingested. (In 1883 Robert Koch identified Snow's "poison": it was a comma-shaped bacterium.)

Physicians, meanwhile, struggled to treat the disease. Some prescribed opium or whiskey, others chloroform or strychnine. One physician claimed that a sick patient rallied after drinking four or five glasses of champagne. Scholars doubt that any treatment did much good. Prevention was the only way to fight cholera.

In 1866, in response to another cholera outbreak, New York City established a Metropolitan Board of Health to clean up cisterns and garbage. The success of these measures prompted the city to build an extensive network of aqueducts to bring clean water from distant reservoirs and watersheds. The city's clean water became one of its main assets.

Elsewhere, the situation was less encouraging. In February 1873 cholera hit New Orleans and spread up the Mississippi River, ravaging low-lying urban areas where drinking water had been contaminated with sewage.

Nashville was one such city. The city's pumping station was originally located upriver, far to the east of the city. But

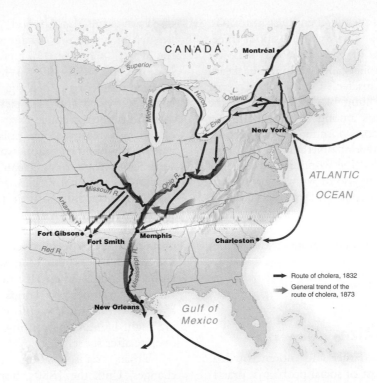

The Routes of Cholera, 1832, 1873 In 1832, cholera initially spread inland from port cities—New York, Charleston, and New Orleans; in 1873, cholera spread down the Ohio and Mississippi river valleys.

as the city rapidly filled out a forty-block region east of city hall and the state capitol, sewage seeped into the Cumberland River above the pumping station. In 1873 a cholera epidemic swept through the area. The prison was especially hard hit. The Capitol Hill district, on high ground to the west of Brown's Creek, had few cholera cases. In all, 647 people from Nashville died of cholera that summer.

Question for Discussion

■ At the time, many people chafed at the broad new powers and the higher taxes that city governments claimed in order to address health problems. What arguments can be derived both in support of those expanded powers and against them?

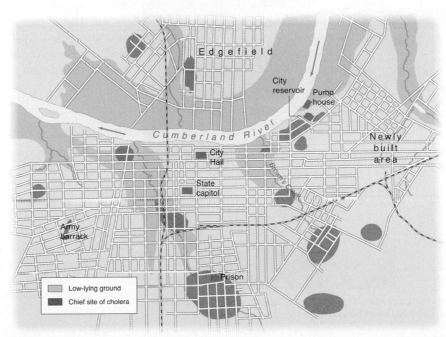

The Cholera Epidemic in Nashville, 1873 Most cholera cases in Nashville were in low-lying areas where sewage seeped into water supplies.

The unhealthiness of the tenements was notorious. No one knows exactly, but as late as 1900 about three-quarters of the residents of New York City's Lower East Side lacked indoor toilets and had to use backyard outhouses to relieve themselves. One noxious corner became known as the "lung block" because of the prevalence of tuberculosis among its inhabitants. In 1900 three out of five babies born in one poor district of Chicago died before their first birthday.

Slums bred criminals—the wonder was that they did not breed more. They also drove well-to-do residents into exclusive sections and to the suburbs. From Boston's Beacon Hill and Back Bay to San Francisco's Nob Hill, the rich retired into their cluttered mansions and ignored conditions in the poorer parts of town.

View the Image *New York City Tenements* at **www.myhistorylab.com**

The Cities Modernize

As American cities grew larger and more crowded, thereby aggravating a host of social problems, practical forces operated to bring about improvements. Once the relationship between polluted water and disease was fully understood, everyone saw the need for decent water and sewage systems. (See Mapping the Past, "Cholera: A New Disease Strikes the Nation," pp. 498–499.) While some businessmen profited from corrupt dealings with the city machines, more of them wanted efficient and honest government in order to reduce their tax bills. City dwellers of all classes resented dirt, noise, and ugliness, and in many communities public-spirited groups formed societies to plant trees, clean up littered areas, and develop recreational facilities. When one city undertook improvements, others tended to follow suit, spurred on by local pride and the booster spirit.

Gradually the basic facilities of urban living were improved. Streets were paved, first with cobblestones and wood blocks and then with smoother, quieter asphalt. Gaslight, then electric arc lights, and finally Edison's incandescent lamps brightened the cities after dark, making law enforcement easier, stimulating night life, and permitting factories and shops to operate after sunset.

Urban transportation underwent enormous changes. Until the 1880s, horse-drawn cars running on tracks set flush with the street were the main means of urban public transportation. In 1860 New York City's horsecars were carrying about 100,000 passengers a day. But horsecars had serious drawbacks. Enormous numbers of horses were needed, and feeding and stabling the animals was costly. Their droppings (ten pounds per day per horse) became a major source of urban pollution. That is why the invention of the electric trolley car in the 1880s put an end to horsecar transportation. Trolleys were cheaper and less unsightly than horsecars and quieter than steam-powered trains.

A retired naval officer, Frank J. Sprague, installed the first practical electric trolley line in Richmond, Virginia, in 1887–1888. At once other cities seized on the trolley. Lines soon radiated outward from the city centers, bringing commuters and shoppers from the residential districts to the business district. Without them the big-city department stores could not have flourished as they did. By 1895 some 850 lines were busily hauling city dwellers over 10,000 miles of track, and mileage tripled in the following decade. As with other new enterprises, ownership of street railways quickly became centralized until

On Sundays in the late nineteenth century, city people crowded into streetcars and headed to the countryside. Enticed by this taste of bucolic splendor, many chose to live in the suburbs and take the streetcars to work downtown. Soon, the population density of the suburbs resembled that of the cities.

The opening of the Brooklyn Bridge in 1883 was a community spectacle.

passengers a year over the East River between Manhattan and Brooklyn.

Even the high cost of urban real estate, which spawned the tenement, produced some beneficial results in the long run. Instead of crowding squat structures cheek by jowl on twenty-five-foot lots, architects began to build upward. Stone and brick apartment houses, sometimes elegantly known as "French flats," replaced many dumbbell tenements. The introduction of the iron-skeleton type of construction, which freed the walls from bearing the immense weight of a tall building, was the work of a group of Chicago architects who had been attracted to the metropolis of the Midwest by opportunities to be found amid the ashes of the great fire of 1871. The group included William Le Baron Jenney, John A. Holabird, Martin Roche, John W. Root, Louis H. Sullivan, and Daniel Burnham. Jenney's Home

a few big operators controlled the trolleys of more than 100 eastern cities and towns.

Streetcars changed the character of big-city life. Before their introduction urban communities were limited by the distances people could conveniently walk to work. The "walking city" could not easily extend more than twenty-one-and-a-half miles from its center. Streetcars increased this radius to six miles or more, which meant that the area of the city expanded enormously. Dramatic population shifts resulted as the better-off moved away from the center in search of air and space, abandoning the crumbling, jam-packed older neighborhoods to the poor. Thus economic segregation speeded the growth of ghettos. Older peripheral towns that had maintained some of the self-contained qualities of village life were swallowed up, becoming metropolitan centers.

As time passed, each new area, originally peopled by rising economic groups, tended to become crowded and then deteriorated. By extending their tracks beyond the developed areas, the streetcar companies further speeded suburban growth because they assured developers, bankers, builders, and middle-class home buyers of efficient transport to the center of town. By keeping fares low (five cents a ride was standard) the lines enabled poor people to "escape" to the countryside on holidays.

Advances in bridge design, notably the perfection of the steel-cable suspension bridge by John A. Roebling, aided the ebb and flow of metropolitan populations. The Brooklyn Bridge described by a poet as "a weird metallic Apparition . . . the cables, like divine messages from above . . . cutting and dividing into innumerable musical spaces the nude immensity of the sky," was Roebling's triumph. Completed in 1883 at a cost of $15 million, it was soon carrying more than 33 million

Daniel Burnham's Flatiron Building (1902) was one of the first to use steel girders to hold up the building; this allowed the outside masonry to be decorative stone. In mid-century, architects eliminated the outside wall entirely, encasing steel-framed buildings in walls of glass.

Insurance Building (completed in 1885) was the first metal-frame edifice. Height alone, however, did not satisfy these innovators; they sought a form that would reflect the structure and purpose of their buildings.

Their leader was Louis Sullivan. Architects must discard "books, rules, precedents, or any such educational impediments" and design functional buildings, he argued. A tall building "must be every inch a proud and soaring thing, rising in sheer exultation . . . from bottom to top . . . a unit without a single dissenting line." Sullivan's Wainwright Building in St. Louis and his Prudential Building in Buffalo, both completed in the early 1890s, combined spare beauty, modest construction costs, and efficient use of space in path-breaking ways. Soon a "race to the skies" was on in the great cities of America, and the words *skyscraper* and *skyline* entered the language. Daniel Burnham, another of the Chicago-school architects, designed the twenty-two-story Flatiron Building in New York which, when completed in 1902, was one of the tallest in the city.

Leisure Activities: More Fun and Games

By bringing together large numbers of people, cities made possible many kinds of social activity difficult or impossible to maintain in rural areas. Cities remained unsurpassed as centers of artistic and intellectual life. New York was the outstanding example, as seen in its many theaters and in the founding of the American Museum of Natural History (1870), the Metropolitan Museum of Art (1870), and the Metropolitan Opera (1883), but other cities were equally hospitable to such endeavors. Boston's Museum of Fine Arts, for example, was founded in 1870 and the Boston Symphony in 1881.

Of course less sophisticated forms of recreation also flourished in the urban environment. From 1865 to 1885 the number of breweries in Massachusetts quadrupled. It is only a slight exaggeration to say that in crowded urban centers there was a saloon on every corner; during the last third of the century the number of saloons in the country tripled. Saloons were strictly male working-class institutions, usually decorated with pictures and other mementos of sports heroes, the bar perhaps under the charge of a retired pugilist.

For workingmen the saloon was a kind of club, a place to meet friends; exchange news; and gossip, gamble, eat, and drink beer and whiskey. Saloons also flourished because factory owners and other employers of large numbers of workers tended to forbid the consumption of alcohol on their premises. In addition, the gradual reduction of the workday left men with more free time, which may explain why vaudeville and burlesques, the latter described by one straightlaced critic as a "disgraceful spectacle of padded legs juggling and tight-laced wriggling," also proliferated.

Calvinist-inspired opposition to sports as a frivolous waste of valuable time was steadily evaporating, replaced among the upper and middle classes by the realization that games like golf and tennis were "healthy occupation[s] for mind and body." Bicycling became a fad, both as a means of getting from place to place in the ever-expanding cities and as a form of exercise and recreation.

Many of the new streetcar companies built picnic grounds and amusement parks at their outer limits. In good weather thousands seeking to relax after a hard day's work flocked to these "trolley parks" to enjoy a fresh-air meal or patronize the shooting galleries, merry-go-rounds, and "freak shows."

The postwar era also saw the first important development of spectator sports, again because cities provided the concentrations of population necessary to support them. Curious relationships developed between upper- and working-class interests and between competitive sports as pure enjoyment for players and spectators and sports as something to bet on. Horse racing had strictly upper-class origins, but racetracks attracted huge crowds of ordinary people more intent on picking a winner than on improving the breed.

Professional boxing offers an even better example. It was in a sense a hobby of the rich, who sponsored favorite gladiators, offered prizes, and often wagered large sums on the matches. But the audiences were made up overwhelmingly of young working-class males, from whose ranks most of the fighters emerged. The gambling and also the brutality of the bloody, bare-knuckle character of the fights caused many communities to outlaw boxing, a fact that added to the appeal of the sport for some.

The first widely popular pugilist was the legendary "Boston Strong Boy," John L. Sullivan, who became heavyweight champion in 1882 by disposing of one Paddy Ryan in nine rounds. Sullivan was an immensely powerful man whose idea of fighting, according to his biographer, "was simply to hammer his opponent into unconsciousness," something he did repeatedly during his ten-year reign. Sullivan became an international celebrity and made and lost large sums during this period. He was also the beneficiary of patronage in such forms as a diamond belt worth $10,000 presented to him by some of his admirers. Yet boxing remained a raffish, clandestine occupation. One of Sullivan's important fights took place in France, on the estate of Baron Rothschild, yet when it ended both he and his opponent were arrested.

Three major team games—baseball, football, and basketball—developed in something approaching

Luna Park at Coney Island was a vast living theater in which the strollers were both spectators and actors. At night, a quarter of a million electric lights turned Luna Park into what its designer, Frederic Thompson, called "a different world—a dream world, perhaps a nightmare world—where all is bizarre and fantastic."

their modern form during the last quarter of the century. Various forms of what became baseball were played long before that time. Organized teams, in most cases made up of upper-class amateurs, first emerged in the 1840s, but the game only became truly popular during the Civil War, when it was a major form of camp recreation for the troops.

After the war professional teams began to appear (the first, the Cincinnati Red Stockings, paid players between $800 and $1,400 for the season), and in 1876 teams in eight cities formed the National League. The American League followed in 1901. After a brief period of rivalry, the two leagues made peace in 1903, the year of the first World Series.

Organized play led to codification of the rules and improvements in technique and strategy: for example, the development of "minor" leagues; impartial umpires calling balls and strikes and ruling on close plays; the use of catcher's masks and padded gloves; the invention of various kinds of curves and other erratic pitches (often enhanced by "doctoring" the ball). As early as the 1870s, baseball was being called "the national game" and losing all upper-class connotations. Important games attracted crowds in the tens of thousands; betting became a problem. Despite its urban origins, its broad green fields and dusty base paths gave the game a rural character that only recently has begun to fade away.

Nobody "invented" baseball, but both football and basketball owe their present form to individuals. James Naismith's invention of basketball is undisputed. In 1891, while a student at a YMCA school, he attached peach baskets to the edge of an elevated running track in the gymnasium and drew up what are still the basic rules of the game. The first basketball was a soccer ball. The game was popular from the start, but because it was played indoors it was not an important spectator sport until much later.

Football was not created by one person in the way that basketball was; it evolved out of English rugby. For many decades it remained almost entirely a college sport (and thus played almost entirely by upper- and middle-class types). Organized collegiate sports dated back to before the Civil War; the first intercollegiate matches were rowing races between Harvard and Yale students. The first intercollegiate football game occurred when Rutgers defeated

A football game pits Yale and Princeton in 1879. The field was not lined or bounded, and play consisted mostly of disorganized scrums.

Princeton in 1869, and by the 1880s college football had become extremely popular.

Much of the game's modern character, however, was the work of Walter Camp, the athletic director and football coach of Yale. Camp cut the size of teams from fifteen to eleven, and he invented the scrimmage line, the four-down system, and the key position of quarterback. He publicized the game in a series of books, ranging from *How to Coach a Team* (1886) to *Jack Hall at Yale* (1909). Camp's prestige was such that when he named his first All-American team after the 1889 season, no one challenged his judgment. Well into the twentieth century, the players that Camp selected were the All-Americans.

Spectator sports had little appeal to women at this time and indeed for decades thereafter. And few women participated in organized athletics. Sports were "manly" activities; a woman might ride a bicycle, play croquet, and perhaps play a little tennis, but to display any concentrated interest in excelling in a sport was considered unfeminine.

●●●─ Read the **Document** Fox, from *Coney Island Frolics* at
www.myhistorylab.com

Christianity's Conscience and the Social Gospel

The modernization of the great cities was not solving most of the social problems of the slums. As this fact became clear, a number of urban religious leaders began to take a hard look at the situation. Traditionally, American churchmen had insisted that where sin was concerned there were no extenuating circumstances. To the well-to-do they preached the virtues of thrift and hard work; to the poor they extended the possibility of a better existence in the next world; to all they stressed one's responsibility for one's own behavior—and thus for one's own salvation. Such a point of view brought meager comfort to residents of slums. Consequently, the churches lost influence in the poorer sections. Furthermore, as better-off citizens followed the streetcar lines out from the city centers, their church leaders followed them.

In New York, seventeen Protestant congregations abandoned the depressed areas of Lower Manhattan between 1868 and 1888. Catering thereafter almost entirely to middle-class and upper-class worshippers, the pastors tended to become even more conservative. No more strident defender of reactionary ideas existed than the pastor of Brooklyn's fashionable Plymouth Congregational Church, Henry Ward Beecher. Beecher, a younger brother of Harriet Beecher Stowe, the author of *Uncle Tom's Cabin*, attributed poverty to the improvidence of laborers who, he claimed, squandered their wages on liquor and tobacco. "No man in this land suffers from poverty," he said, "unless it be more than his fault—unless it be his sin." The best check on labor unrest was a plentiful supply of cheap immigrant labor, he told President Hayes. Unions were "the worst form of despotism and tyranny in the history of Christendom."

An increasing proportion of the residents of the blighted districts were Catholics, and the Roman church devoted much effort to distributing alms, maintaining homes for orphans and old people, and other forms of social welfare. But church leaders seemed unconcerned with the social causes of the blight; they were deeply committed to the idea that sin and vice were personal, while poverty was an act of God. They deplored the rising tide of crime, disease, and destitution among their coreligionists, yet they failed to see the connection between these evils and the squalor of the slums. "Intemperance is the great evil we have to overcome," wrote the president of the leading Catholic charitable organization, the Society of St. Vincent de Paul. "It is the source of the misery for at least three-fourths of the families we are called upon to visit and relieve."

The conservatism of most Protestant and Catholic clergymen did not prevent some earnest preachers from working directly to improve the lot of the city poor. Some followed the path blazed by Dwight L. Moody, a lay evangelist who became famous throughout America and Great Britain in the 1870s. A gargantuan figure weighing nearly 300 pounds, Moody conducted a vigorous campaign to persuade the denizens of the slums to cast aside their sinful ways. He went among them full of enthusiasm and God's love and made an impact no less powerful than that of George Whitefield during the Great Awakening of the eighteenth century or Charles Grandison Finney in the first part of the nineteenth. The evangelists founded mission schools in the slums and tried to provide spiritual and recreational facilities for the unfortunate. They were prominent in the establishment of American branches of the YMCA (1851) and the Salvation Army (1880).

However, many evangelists paid little heed to the causes of urban poverty and vice, believing that faith in God would enable the poor to transcend the material difficulties of life. For a number of

Dwight L. Moody, a lay preacher, saw the church he had built destroyed by the Chicago fire of 1871. But the fire also intensified his faith. His conversational manner appealed to working people, and his adherence to the literal word of the Bible provided them with an anchor in a sea of change.

Protestant clergymen who had become familiar with the slums, a different approach seemed called for. Slum conditions caused the sins and crimes of the cities; the wretched human beings who committed them could not be blamed, these ministers argued. They began to preach a **Social Gospel** that focused on improving living conditions rather than on saving souls. If people were to lead pure lives, they must have enough to eat, decent homes, and opportunities to develop their talents. Social Gospelers advocated civil service reform, child labor legislation, regulation of big corporations, and heavy taxes on incomes and inheritances.

The most influential preacher of the Social Gospel was probably Washington Gladden. At first, Gladden, who was raised on a Massachusetts farm, had opposed all government interference in social and economic affairs, but his experiences as a minister in Springfield, Massachusetts, and Columbus, Ohio, exposed him to the realities of life in industrial cities, and his views changed. In *Applied Christianity* (1886) and in other works he defended laborers' right to organize and strike and denounced the idea that supply and demand should control wage rates. He favored factory inspection laws, strict regulation of public utilities, and other reforms.

Nothing so well reveals the receptivity of the public to the Social Gospel as the popularity of Charles M. Sheldon's novel *In His Steps* (1896), one of America's all-time best-sellers. Sheldon, a minister in Topeka, Kansas, described what happened in the mythical city of Raymond when a group of leading citizens decided to live truly Christian lives, asking themselves "What would Jesus do?" before adopting any course of action. Naturally the tone of Raymond's society was immensely improved, but basic social reforms followed quickly. The Rectangle, a terrible slum area, "too dirty, too coarse, too sinful, too awful for close contact," became the center of a great reform effort. One of Raymond's "leading society heiresses" undertook a slum clearance project, and a concerted attack was made on drunkenness and immorality. The moral regeneration of the entire community was soon accomplished.

The Settlement Houses

Although millions read *In His Steps,* its effect, and that of other Social Gospel literature, was merely inspirational. On the practical level, a number of earnest souls began to grapple with slum problems by organizing what were known as **settlement houses**. These were community centers located in poor districts that provided guidance and services to all who would use them. The settlement workers, most of them idealistic, well-to-do young people, lived in the houses and were active in neighborhood affairs.

The prototype of the settlement house was London's Toynbee Hall, founded in the early 1880s; the first American example was the Neighborhood Guild, opened on the Lower East Side of New York in 1886 by Dr. Stanton Coit. By the turn of the century 100 had been established, the most famous being Jane Addams's Hull House in Chicago (1889), Robert A. Woods's South End House in Boston (1892), and Lillian Wald's Henry Street Settlement in New York (1893).

While some men were active in the movement, the most important settlement house workers were women fresh from college—the first generation of young women to experience the trauma of having developed their capacities only to find that society offered them few opportunities to use them. The settlements provided an outlet for their hopes and energies, and they seized upon the work avidly.

The settlement workers tried to interpret American ways to the new immigrants and to create a community spirit in order to teach, in the words of one of them, "right living through social relations." Unlike most charity workers, who acted out of a sense of upper-class responsibility toward the unfortunate, they expected to benefit morally and intellectually themselves by experiencing a way of life far different from their own and by obtaining "the first-hand knowledge the college classroom cannot give." Lillian Wald, a nurse by training, explained the concept succinctly in *The House on Henry Street* (1915): "We were to live in the neighborhood . . . identify ourselves with it socially, and, in brief, contribute to it our citizenship."

Lillian Wald and other settlement workers soon discovered that practical problems absorbed most of their energies. They agitated for tenement house

Prostitution was not only an urban phenonmenon. "The Club" was one of 100 brothels in Creede, Colorado, a frontier town in the 1880s.

laws, the regulation of the labor of women and children, and better schools. They employed private resources to establish playgrounds in the slums, along with libraries, classes in everything from child nutrition and home management to literature and arts and crafts, social clubs, and day-care centers. When they observed that many poor families were so occupied with the struggle to survive that they were neglecting or even abandoning their children, they tried to place the children in foster homes in the country.

In Boston Robert A. Woods organized clubs to get the youngsters of the South End off the streets, helped establish a restaurant where a meal could be had for five cents, acted as an arbitrator in labor disputes, and lobbied for laws tightening up the franchises of public utility companies. In Chicago Jane Addams developed an outstanding cultural program that included classes in music and art and an excellent "little theater" group. Hull House soon boasted a gymnasium, a day nursery, and several social clubs. Addams also worked tirelessly and effectively for improved public services and for social legislation of all kinds. She even got herself appointed garbage inspector in her ward and hounded local landlords and the garbage contractor until something approaching decent service was established.

A few critics considered the settlement houses mere devices to socialize the unruly poor by teaching them the "punctilios of upper-class propriety," but almost everyone appreciated their virtues. By the end of the century the Catholics, laggard in entering the arena of practical social reform, were joining the movement, partly because they were losing many communicants to socially minded Protestant churches. The first Catholic-run settlement house was founded in 1898 in an Italian district of New York. Two years later Brownson House in Los Angeles, catering chiefly to Mexican immigrants, threw open its doors.

With all their accomplishments, the settlement houses seemed to be fighting a losing battle. "Private beneficence," Jane Addams wrote of Hull House, "is totally inadequate to deal with the vast numbers of the city's disinherited." Much as a tropical forest grows faster than a handful of men armed with machetes can cut it down, so the slums, fed by an annual influx of hundreds of thousands, blighted new areas more rapidly than settlement house workers could clean up old ones. It became increasingly apparent that the wealth and authority of the state must be brought to bear in order to keep abreast of the problem.

Civilization and Its Discontents

As the nineteenth century died, the majority of the American people, especially those comfortably well-off, the residents of small towns, the shopkeepers, and some farmers and skilled workers, remained confirmed optimists and uncritical admirers of their civilization. However, blacks, immigrants, and others who failed to share equitably in the good things of life, along with a growing number of humanitarian reformers, found little to cheer about and much to lament in their increasingly industrialized society. Giant monopolies flourished despite federal restrictions. The gap between rich and poor appeared to be widening while the slum spread its poison and the materially successful made a god of their success. Human values seemed in grave danger of being crushed by impersonal forces typified by the great corporations.

In 1871 Walt Whitman, usually so full of extravagant praise for everything American, had called his

Table 18.1   Reformers and the Urban Poor

Person	Occupation	Action	Consequences
Jacob Riis, Lewis Hine	Photojournalists	Increased public awareness of poor immigrants' living conditions	Stimulated reform movements
Horace Mann	Educator	Favored state laws that supported public education	Increased proportion of young people in school
Dwight L. Moody	Lay evangelist	Encouraged people to consult the Bible for moral guidance and refrain from vice	Promoted spread of YMCA (1850) and Salvation Army (1880) in immigrant districts
Washington Gladden	Congregationalist minister	Persuaded people that they are obliged as Christians to improve conditions in the slums	Advanced the "social gospel"
Jane Addams, Robert Woods, and Lillian Wald	Settlement house organizers	Showed immigrants and impoverished people how to cope with urban conditions	Constructed playgrounds and provided social clubs, day-care centers, and schools

fellow countrymen the "most materialistic and money-making people ever known":

> I say we had best look our times and lands searchingly in the face, like a physician diagnosing some deep disease. Never was there, perhaps, more hollowness of heart than at present, and here in the United States.

By the late 1880s a well-known journalist could write to a friend, "The wheel of progress is to be run over the whole human race and smash us all." Others noted an alarming jump in the national divorce rate and an increasing taste for all kinds of luxury. "People are made slaves by a desperate struggle to keep up appearances," a Massachusetts commentator declared, and the economist David A. Wells expressed concern over statistics showing that heart disease and mental illness were on the rise. These "diseases of civilization," Wells explained, were "one result of the continuous mental and nervous activity which modern high-tension methods of business have necessitated."

Wells was a prominent liberal, but pessimism was no monopoly of liberals. A little later, Senator Henry Cabot Lodge of Massachusetts, himself a millionaire, complained of the "lawlessness" of "the modern and recent plutocrat" and his "disregard of the rights of others." Lodge spoke of "the enormous contrast

between the sanguine mental attitude prevalent in my youth and that, perhaps wiser, but certainly darker view, so general today." His one-time Harvard professor, Henry Adams, was still more critical of the way his contemporaries had become moneygrubbers. "All one's friends," he complained, along with church and university leaders and other educated people, "had joined the banks to force submission to capitalism."

Of course intellectuals often tend to be critical of the world they live in, whatever its nature; Thoreau denounced materialism and the worship of progress in the 1840s as vigorously as any late-nineteenth-century prophet of gloom. But the voices of the dissatisfied were rising. Despite the many benefits that industrialization had made possible, it was by no means clear around 1900 that the American people were really better off under the new dispensation.

That the United States was fast becoming a modern nation no one disputed. Physician George M. Beard contended that "modern civilization" overloaded the human nervous system the way burning too many of Thomas Edison's lightbulbs overloaded an electrical circuit. On the other hand, Edward Bellamy saw the future as a "paradise of order, equity, and felicity." Most took a more balanced view, believing that the modern world encompassed new possibilities as well as perils. The future beckoned, and yet it also menaced.

Chapter Review

Milestones

1858	English launch transatlantic liner *Great Eastern*
1870	Metropolitan Museum of Art and American Museum of Natural History open in New York City
1876	Eight teams form National Baseball League
1880	American branch of Salvation Army is founded
1880s	New immigration begins
1882	John L. Sullivan wins heavyweight boxing championship
	Exclusion Act bans Chinese immigrants
1883	Roebling completes Brooklyn Bridge
1885	Foran Act outlaws importing contract skilled labor

1887	Nativists found American Protective Association
1888	Richmond, Virginia, opens first urban electric streetcar system
1889	Jane Addams founds Hull House
	Yale's Walter Camp names first All-American football team
1890s	Louis Sullivan's skyscrapers rise
1890	Jacob Riis publishes *How the Other Half Lives*
1896	Charles M. Sheldon asks "What would Jesus do?" in best-selling *In His Steps*
1897	Cleveland vetoes Congress's literacy test bill

Key Terms

Nativism   A fear or hatred of immigrants, ethnic minorities, or alien political movements, *493*

new immigration   Reference to the influx of immigrants to the United States during the late nineteenth and early twentieth century predominantly from southern and eastern Europe, *493*

settlement houses   Community centers, founded by reformers such as Jane Addams and Lillian Wald beginning in the 1880s, that were located in poor urban districts of major cities; the centers sought to Americanize immigrant families and provide them with social services and a political voice, *506*

Social Gospel A doctrine preached by many urban Protestant ministers during the early 1900s that focused on improving living conditions for the city's poor rather than on saving souls; proponents advocated civil service reform, child labor laws, government regulation of big business, and a graduated income tax, *505*

tenement Four- to six-story residential apartment house, once common in New York and certain other cities, built on a tiny lot with little regard for adequate ventilation or light, *497*

Review Questions

1. The introduction to this chapter contrasts the appeal of cities in the late nineteenth century with their failures and limitations. Did people move into cities because they had no choice or because they wanted to do so? Were their lives better or worse in doing so?

2. What is the relationship between the rise of industry and economic consolidation, described in Chapter 17, to the rapid growth of cities described in this chapter?

3. How did the influx of immigrants into the cities affect relations among ethnic groups? Between immigrants and "natives"—nonimmigrant Americans?

4. How did the new forms of amusement and leisure differ from those in earlier, predominantly rural settings?

5. Which urban problems were most acute and what different solutions were proposed by the leading religious figures and social reformers?

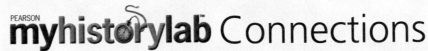

PEARSON **myhistorylab** Connections

Reinforce what you learned in this chapter by studying the many documents, images, maps, review tools, and videos available at **www.myhistorylab.com**.

Read and Review

✓• Study and Review *Chapter 18*

Read the Document *Massachusetts Bureau of Statistics of Labor,* p. 488

View the Image *Health Check at Ellis Island,* p. 493

View the Image *Looking Backward at Immigrant Origins,* p. 495

See the Map *Foreign-Born Population, 1890,* p. 495

View the Image *New York City Tenements,* p. 500

Research and Explore

Watch the Video *Ellis Island Immigrants, 1903,* p. 495

Read the Document Fox, from *Coney Island Frolics,* p. 504

Source: Jane Addams Memorial Collection (JAMC neg. 20), Special Collections, The University Library, University of Illinois at Chicago.

((•• Hear the Audio

Hear the audio file for Chapter 18 at
www.myhistorylab.com.

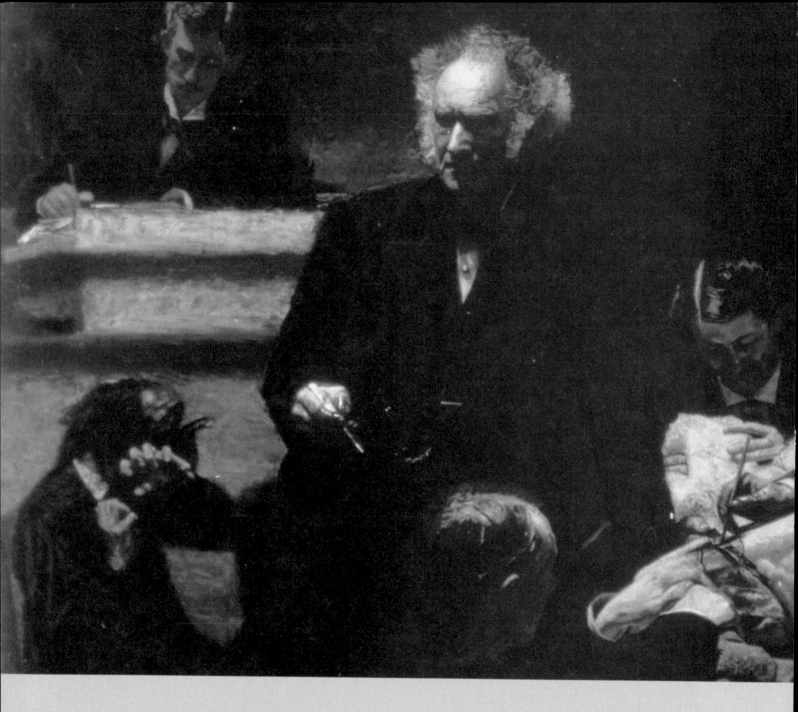

Is winning everything?

In 2010 the state of California cut funding for the University of California at Berkeley by several hundred million dollars, raised student fees 10 percent, and forced faculty and staff to take unpaid furloughs. Despite this, the university covered the nearly $6.4 million deficit generated by its intercollegiate athletics program. Campus supporters of the football program noted that two-thirds of the top NCAA football teams ran even larger deficits; the average was about $8 million.

Although some of Berkeley's faculty endorsed an "Academics First" petition, others applauded the chancellor's decision to pursue "competitive excellence" in all aspects of campus life. Berkeley's football team was mandated to compete "at the top levels of the Pacific Ten conference and in postseason and national championship play." To that end, Berkeley paid its head coach $1.5 million, about average for a Division I head coach.

This insistence on winning intercollegiate football originated in the late nineteenth century. At that time, a few colleges decided to pay coaches, recruited star prep school athletes, and charged spectators to watch the games. The game became faster and rougher. Soon the spectacle attracted huge audiences. Action often got out

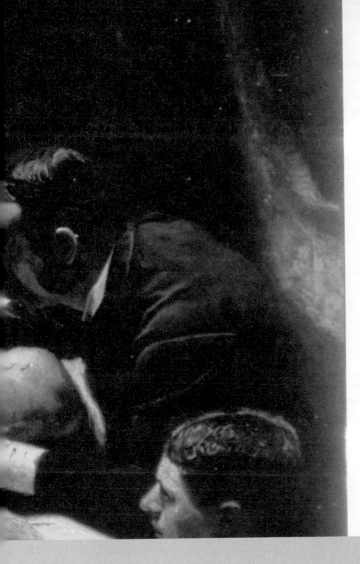

((•—[Hear the Audio **Chapter 19 at www.myhistorylab.com**

■ In painter Thomas Eakins's *The Gross Clinic* (1875), Professor Samuel Gross's team of surgeons cuts through flesh to repair bone, an examination of the bare essentials of life devoid of sentiment or moralism. The foremost intellectuals of the age regarded life in much the same way.
Source: Thomas Cowperthwait Eakins (1844–1916). *The Gross Clinic*, 1875. Oil on Canvas. Jefferson College, Philadelphia, PA, USA. Bridgeman Art Library.

of hand and, lacking satisfactory protective equipment, many football players sustained serious injuries; each year, some were killed.

In 1892, William Rainey Harper, president of the University of Chicago, defended the high cost of winning football. "If the world can afford to sacrifice lives for commercial gain"—a reference to the victims of industrial accidents—"it can more easily afford to make similar sacrifices on the altar of vigorous and unsullied manhood." In 1896 Massachusetts Senator Henry Cabot Lodge told Harvard students that "the injuries incurred on the playing-field are part of the price which the English-speaking race has paid for being world-conquerors."

The rise of football in the 1890s symbolized a profound transformation in cultural and intellectual life. The religious sensibilities and gentlemanly precepts of an earlier age were yielding to a tougher, "more manly" mind-set. Life was a struggle, Darwin had proclaimed, in which the fittest prevailed and the losers vanished. In this "competition" for survival, power trounced sentiment. Ideas were valuable not because they espoused truths or evinced beauty, but because they left an imprint on the world. Art and literature functioned not to transcend life or prettify it but to lay bare its grim reality. This stern ethos unsettled many but also invigorated those who yearned to confront the world as it was. ■

Colleges and Universities

Industrialization altered the way Americans thought at the same time that it transformed their ways of making a living. Technological advances revolutionized the communication of ideas more drastically than they did the transportation of goods or the manufacture of steel. The materialism that permeated American attitudes toward business also affected contemporary education and literature, while Charles Darwin's theory of evolution influenced American philosophers, lawyers, and historians profoundly. This was especially true of the nation's institutions of higher education.

Between 1878 and 1898, the number of colleges and universities increased from about 350 to 500, and the student body roughly tripled. Despite this growth, less than 2 percent of the college-age population attended college, but the aspirations of the nation's youth were rising, and more and more parents had the financial means necessary for fulfilling them.

More significant than the expansion of the colleges were the alterations in their curricula and in the atmosphere permeating the average campus. In 1870 most colleges remained what they had been in the 1830s: small, limited in their offerings, and intellectually stagnant. The ill-paid professors were seldom scholars of stature. Thereafter, change came like a flood tide: State universities proliferated; the federal government's land-grant program in support of training in "agriculture and the mechanic arts," established under the Morrill Act of 1862, came into its own; wealthy philanthropists poured fortunes into old institutions and founded new ones; educators introduced new courses and adopted new teaching methods; professional schools of law, medicine, education, business, journalism, and other specialties increased in number.

In the forefront of reform was Harvard, the oldest and most prestigious college in the country. In the 1860s it possessed an excellent faculty, but teaching methods were antiquated and the curriculum had remained almost unchanged since the colonial period. In 1869, however, a dynamic president, the chemist Charles W. Eliot, undertook a transformation of the college. Eliot introduced the elective system, gradually eliminating required courses and expanding offerings in such areas as modern languages, economics, and the laboratory sciences. For the first time, students were allowed to borrow books from the library! Eliot also encouraged the faculty to experiment with new teaching methods, and he brought in professors with original minds and new ideas.

An even more important development in higher education was the founding of Johns Hopkins in 1876. This university was one of many established in the period by wealthy industrialists; its benefactor, the Baltimore merchant Johns Hopkins, had made his fortune in the Baltimore and Ohio Railroad. Its distinctiveness, however, was due to the vision of Daniel Coit Gilman, its first president.

Gilman modeled Johns Hopkins on the German universities, where meticulous research and freedom of inquiry were the guiding principles. In staffing the institution, he sought scholars of the highest reputation, scouring Europe as well as America in his search for talent and offering outstanding men high salaries for that time—up to $5,000 for a professor, roughly ten times the income of a skilled artisan. Johns Hopkins specialized in graduate education. In the generation after its founding, it churned out a remarkable percentage of the most important scholars in the nation, including Woodrow Wilson in political science, John Dewey in philosophy, Frederick Jackson Turner in history, and John R. Commons in economics.

The success of Johns Hopkins did not stop the migration of American scholars to Europe; more than 2,000 matriculated at German universities during the 1880s. But as Hopkins graduates took up professorships at other institutions and as scholars trained elsewhere adopted the Hopkins methods, true graduate education

W. A. Rogers's engraving, "Out of the Game," showed one injured boy tending to another. It appeared in the October 31, 1891 issue of *Harper's Weekly*, which included an essay by Walter Camp. Camp claimed that football cultivated the man "of executive ability." If all life was "survival of the fittest," then colleges were right to promote such aggressive pastimes.

became possible in most sections of the country.

The example of Johns Hopkins encouraged other wealthy individuals to endow universities offering advanced work. Clark University in Worcester, Massachusetts, founded by Jonas Clark, a merchant and real estate speculator, opened its doors in 1889. Its president, G. Stanley Hall, had been a professor of psychology at Hopkins, and he built the new university in that institution's image. More important was John D. Rockefeller's creation, the University of Chicago (1892), whose first president, William Rainey Harper, was a brilliant biblical scholar—he received his PhD from Yale at the age of eighteen—an imaginative administrator, and a football enthusiast, as noted at the outset of this chapter. The new university, he told Rockefeller, should be designed "with the example of Johns Hopkins before our eyes."

A physics lecture, circa 1890, at the University of Michigan. Note that women are segregated from men; but in the men's section white and black men are sitting together. Many of the Morrill Act universities admitted women.

Like Daniel Coit Gilman, Harper sought topflight scholars for his faculty. He offered such high salaries that he was besieged with over 1,000 applications. Armed with Rockefeller dollars, he "raided" the best institutions in the nation. He decimated the faculty of the new Clark University—"an act of wreckage," the indignant President Hall complained, "comparable to anything that the worst trust ever attempted against its competitors." Chicago offered first-class graduate and undergraduate education. During its first year there were 120 instructors for fewer than 600 students, and despite fears that the mighty tycoon Rockefeller would enforce his social and economic views on the institution, academic freedom was the rule.

State and federal aid to higher education expanded rapidly. The Morrill Act, granting land to each state at a rate of 30,000 acres for each senator and representative, provided the endowments that gave many important modern universities, such as Illinois, Michigan State, and Ohio State, their start. While the federal assistance was earmarked for specific subjects, the land-grant colleges offered a full range of courses, and all received additional state funds. The land-grant universities adopted new ideas quickly. They were coeducational from the start, and most developed professional schools and experimented with extension work and summer programs.

Typical of the better state institutions was the University of Michigan, which reached the top rank among the nation's universities during the presidency of James B. Angell (1871–1909). Like Eliot at Harvard, Angell expanded the undergraduate curriculum and strengthened the law and medical schools. He encouraged graduate studies, seeking to make Michigan "part of the great world of scholars," and sought ways in which the university could serve the general community.

Important advances were made in women's higher education. Beginning with Vassar College, which opened its doors to 300 women students in 1865, the opportunity for young women to pursue serious academic work gradually expanded. Wellesley and Smith, both founded in 1875, completed the so-called Big Three women's colleges. Together with the already established Mount Holyoke (1837), and with Bryn Mawr (1885), Barnard (1889), and Radcliffe (1893), they became known as the Seven Sisters.

The only professional careers easily available to women were nursing, teaching, and the new area called social work. Nevertheless, the remarkable women that these institutions trained were conscious of their uniqueness and determined to demonstrate their capabilities. They provided most of the leaders of the early-twentieth-century drive for equal rights for women.

Not all the changes in higher education were beneficial. The elective system led to superficiality; students gained a smattering of knowledge of many subjects and mastered none. For example, 55 percent of the Harvard class of 1898 took elementary courses and no others during their four years of study. Intensive graduate work often produced narrowness of outlook and research monographs on trivial subjects. Attempts to apply the scientific method in fields such as history and economics often enticed students into making smug (and preposterous) claims to objectivity and definitiveness.

The gifts of rich industrialists sometimes came with strings, and college boards of trustees tended to be dominated by businessmen who sometimes attempted to impose their own social and economic beliefs on faculty members. Although few professors lost their positions because their views offended trustees, at many institutions trustees exerted constant nagging pressures that limited academic freedom and scholarly objectivity. At state colleges, politicians often interfered in academic affairs, even treating professorships as part of the patronage system.

Thorstein Veblen pointed out in his caustic study of *The Higher Learning in America* (1918) that "the intrusion of businesslike ideals, aims and methods" harmed the universities in countless, subtle ways. Size alone—the verbose Veblen called it "an executive weakness for spectacular magnitude"—became an end in itself, and the practical values of education were exalted over the humanistic. When universities grew bigger, administration became more complicated and the prestige of administrators rose inordinately. At many institutions professors came to be regarded as mere employees of the governing boards. In 1893 the members of the faculty of Stanford University were officially classified as personal servants of Mrs. Leland Stanford, widow of the founder. This was done in good cause—the Stanford estate was tied up in probate court and the ruling made it possible to pay professors out of Mrs. Stanford's allowance for household expenses—but that such a procedure was even conceivable must have appalled the scholarly world.

As the number of college graduates increased, and as colleges ceased being primarily training institutions for clergymen, the influence of alumni on educational policies began to make itself felt, not always happily. Campus social activities became more important. Fraternities proliferated. Interest in organized sports first appeared as a laudable outgrowth of the general expansion of the curriculum, but soon athletic contests were playing a role all out of proportion to their significance. After football evolved as the leading intercollegiate sport (over 50,000 attended the Yale-Princeton game in 1893), it became a source of revenue that many colleges dared not neglect. Since students, alumni, and the public demanded winning teams, college administrators stooped to subsidizing student athletes, in extreme cases employing players who were not students at all. One exasperated college president quipped that the BA degree was coming to mean Bachelor of Athletics.

Thus higher education reflected American values, with all their strengths and weaknesses. A complex society required a more professional and specialized education for its youth; the coarseness and the rampant materialism and competitiveness of the era inevitably found expression in the colleges and universities.

⊙ Read the **Document** *The Morrill Act* at www.myhistorylab.com

⊙ Watch the **Video** *College Football (1903)* at www.myhistorylab.com

Revolution in the Social Sciences

In the social sciences a close connection existed between the practical issues of the age and the achievements of the leading thinkers. The application of the theory of evolution to every aspect of human relations, the impact of industrialization on society—such topics were of intense concern to American economists, sociologists, and historians. An understanding of Darwin increased the already strong interest in studying the development of institutions and their interactions with one another. Controversies over trusts, slum conditions, and other problems drew scholars out of their towers and into practical affairs.

Social scientists were impressed by the progress being made in the physical and biological sciences. They eagerly applied the scientific method to their own specialties, hoping thereby to arrive at objective truths in fields that by nature were essentially subjective.

Among the economists something approaching a revolution took place in the 1880s. The classical school, which maintained that immutable natural laws governed all human behavior and which used the insights of Darwin only to justify unrestrained competition and laissez-faire, was challenged by a group of young economists who argued that as times changed, economic theories and laws must be modified in order to remain relevant. Richard T. Ely, another of the scholars who made Johns Hopkins a font of new ideas in the 1880s, summarized the thinking of this group in 1885. "The state [is] an educational and ethical agency whose positive aid is an indispensable condition of human progress," Ely proclaimed. Laissez-faire was outmoded and dangerous. Economic problems were basically moral problems; their solution required "the united efforts of Church, state and science." The proper way to study these problems was by analyzing actual conditions, not by applying abstract laws or principles.

This approach produced the so-called institutionalist school of economics, whose members made detailed, on-the-spot investigations of labor unions, sweatshops, factories, and mines. The study of institutions would lead both to theoretical insights and to practical social reform, they believed. John R. Commons, one of Ely's students at Johns Hopkins and later professor of economics at the University of Wisconsin, was the outstanding member of this school. His ten-volume *Documentary History of*

American Industrial Society (1910–1911) reveals the institutionalist approach at its best.

A similar revolution struck sociology in the mid-1880s. Prevailing opinion up to that time rejected the idea of government interference with the organization of society. The influence of the English social Darwinist, Herbert Spencer, who objected even to public schools and the postal system, was immense. Spencer and his American disciples, among them Edward L. Youmans, editor of *Popular Science Monthly*, twisted the ideas of Darwin to mean that society could be changed only by the force of evolution, which moved with cosmic slowness. "You and I can do nothing at all," Youmans told the reformer Henry George. "It's all a matter of evolution. Perhaps in four or five thousand years evolution may have carried men beyond this state of things."

•••Read the Document Herbert Spencer, *Social Darwinism* at **www.myhistorylab.com**

Progressive Education

Traditionally, American teachers had emphasized the three Rs and relied on strict discipline and rote learning. Typical of the pedagogues of the period was the Chicago teacher, described by a reformer in the 1890s, who told her students firmly, "Don't stop to think, tell me what you know!" Yet new ideas were attracting attention. According to a German educator, Johann Friedrich Herbart, teachers could best arouse the interest of their students by relating new information to what they already knew; good teaching called for professional training, psychological insight, enthusiasm, and imagination, not merely facts and a birch rod. At the same time, evolutionists were pressing for a kind of education that would help children to "survive" by adapting to the demands of their rapidly changing urban environment.

Forward-looking educators seized on these ideas because dynamic social changes were making the old system increasingly inadequate. Settlement house workers discovered that slum children needed training in handicrafts, citizenship, and personal hygiene as much as in reading and writing. They were appalled by the local schools, which suffered from the same disease, filth, overcrowding, rickety construction that plagued the tenements, and by school systems that were controlled by machine politicians who doled out teaching positions to party hacks and other untrained persons. They argued that school playgrounds, nurseries, kindergartens, and adult education programs were essential in communities where most women worked and many people lacked much formal education. "We are impatient with the schools which lay all stress on reading and writing," Jane Addams declared. This type of education "fails to give the child any clew

to the life about him." The philosopher who summarized and gave direction to these forces was John Dewey, a professor at the University of Chicago. Dewey was concerned with the implications of evolution—indeed, of all science—for education.

"Education," Dewey insisted in *The School and Society* (1899), was "the fundamental method of social progress and reform." To seek to improve conditions merely by passing laws was "futile." Moreover, in an industrial society the family no longer performed many of the educational functions it had carried out in an agrarian society. Farm children learn about nature, about work, about human character in countless ways denied to children in cities. The school can fill the gap by becoming "an embryonic community . . . with types of occupations that reflect the life of the larger society." At the same time, education should center on the child, and new information should be related to what the child already knows. Children's imagination, energy, and curiosity are tools for broadening their outlook and increasing their store of information. Finally, the school should become an instrument for social reform, "saturating [the child] with the spirit of service" and helping to produce a "society which is worthy, lovely, and harmonious." Education, in other words, ought to build character and teach good citizenship as well as transmit knowledge.

The School and Society created a stir, and Dewey immediately assumed leadership of what in the next generation was called progressive education. Although the gains made in public education before 1900 were more quantitative than qualitative and the philosophy dominant in most schools was not very different at the end of the century from that prevailing in Horace Mann's day, change was in the air. The best educators of the period were full of optimism, convinced that the future was theirs.

Law and History

Even jurisprudence, by its nature conservative and rooted in tradition, felt the pressure of evolutionary thought and the new emphasis on studying institutions as they actually are. In 1881 Oliver Wendell Holmes Jr. published *The Common Law*. Rejecting the ideas that judges should limit themselves to the mechanical explication of statutes and that law consisted only of what was written in law books, Holmes argued that "the felt necessities of the time" rather than precedent should determine the rules by which people are governed. "The life of the law has not been logic; it has been experience," he wrote. "It is revolting," he added on another occasion, "to have no better reason for a rule of law than that so it was laid down in the time of Henry IV."

Charlotte Perkins Gilman

In 1885, severe depression gripped twenty-five-year-old Charlotte Perkins Stetson. "Every morning the same helpless waking," she confided in her journal. "Retreat impossible, escape impossible." She had married the previous year and had just given birth to a daughter. But the infant gave her no pleasure. "I would hold her close—that lovely child!—and instead of love and happiness, feel only pain. The tears ran down my breast." Over the next few years, her depression worsened. She feared she was approaching "the edge of insanity."

Charlotte's life had not been easy. Shortly after she was born, her father abandoned the family. He visited every couple of years, and occasionally sent a check, but

Charlotte Perkins Stetson, shortly after her marriage, wrote, "You were called to serve humanity, and you cannot serve yourself. No good as a wife, no good as a mother, no good at anything. And you did it yourself!"

Charlotte, her brother, and her mother lacked regular income and lived with relatives, moving frequently.

When Charlotte was fifteen she tracked down her father at the Boston Public Library, where he worked as a librarian, and kissed him. "He put me away from him and said I must not do that sort of thing there," she recalled. "What I do know is that my childhood had no father," she wrote.

Charlotte's relationship with her mother was not much better. Shattered by her husband's abandonment, she refused to cuddle Charlotte as an infant lest the child become dependent on affection. They never were close.

At the time of the incident at the library, Charlotte and her mother lived in a cooperative run by a spiritualist, a woman who claimed to communicate with spirits. One day Charlotte saw her taking grapes that were meant for the whole group. The woman accused Charlotte of thinking evil thoughts about her. Charlotte's mother insisted that Charlotte apologize for her thoughts; Charlotte refused. "And what are you going to do about it?" she taunted. Her mother hit her. At that moment, "I was born," Charlotte recalled. "Neither she, nor any one, could *make* me do anything."

Charlotte devised a stern regimen to ensure her future independence. Every day she ran a mile and educated herself by drawing, reading, and writing. Never would she depend on anyone—especially a man. "I am not domestic and I don't want to be," she told a female confidante.

Her resolve weakened when she was courted by an aspiring young writer, though not an especially talented one. They married and the baby soon followed. Charlotte's bouts of depression became more frequent and incapacitating. Finally she agreed to consult with neurologist S. Weir Mitchell, the nation's foremost expert on neurasthenia, a disease that especially afflicted well-to-do young women. Its chief symptoms were depression, listlessness, and invalidism.

Mitchell believed that women's nervous systems were attuned to childbearing and childrearing. Women who pursued education and careers would exhaust their nervous energy and become neurasthenic. Charlotte's condition, Mitchell assured her, resulted from her intellectual labors. His prescription was simple:

Live as domestic a life as possible. Have your child with you all the time. Lie down an hour after each meal. Have but two hours' intellectual life a day. And never touch pen, brush, or pencil as long as you live.

John Singer Sargent painted this imposing portrait of S. Weir Mitchell (1903). Mitchell, who devised "the rest cure" for neurasthenics, wrote several successful novels.

For a time, Charlotte accepted his regimen. "I went home, followed those directions rigidly for months, and came perilously close to losing my mind," she noted. Then she decided to "cast off Dr. Mitchell bodily" and "do exactly as I pleased."

She separated from her husband, took her child to Pasadena, California, and wrote essays, editorials, and fiction.

In 1890 she finished "The Yellow Wallpaper," a story about a young wife who, suffering from depression, was confined by her doctor-husband to bed in an upstairs room, with servants tending to her every need. As she endlessly stared at her surroundings, the designs on the wallpaper changed shape; a figure appeared and wandered in and out of her consciousness. The wallpaper then grew bars that locked her, and the shadowy figure, into the room. Unable to escape through the bars, the woman chewed at the bed, fleeing ultimately into madness. The story was well-received as a literary horror story reminiscent of Edgar Allan Poe.

Having at last purged Mitchell from her psyche, Charlotte wrote incessantly and supported herself by giving lectures. She developed close and even intimate relationships with several women. When she sent her daughter to live with her father, newspapers denounced her for neglecting woman's proper function. Then she fell in love with Houghton Gilman, who accepted her refusal to embrace domesticity. "I *must not* focus on 'home duties' and entangle myself with them," she told him. They married in 1900.

Charlotte's first book, *Women and Economics* (1898), was a work of extraordinary creativity. A thoroughgoing Social Darwinist, Charlotte explained that while women once were indispensable providers, they had become economically dependent on men who performed important and lucrative work; women's dependence obliged them to exaggerate their sexuality and domesticity so as to attract the men who would provide for them. Marriage was founded on women's economic subjugation. Marx was wrong: Gender, not class, was the fundamental social distinction. The most important revolution would promote women's independence by allowing them to work outside the home.

In this and subsequent books and articles, Charlotte Perkins Gilman insisted that the domestic ideal had deprived society of women's creativity and ideas. Her own life was a case in point. With only four years of education, none after the age of fifteen, she achieved economic independence through her own heroic effort. Lacking alternative child-care arrangements, she sent her young child to live with her father so that she could pursue her life and work as an intellectual. The decision would psychologically scar both her and her daughter, but her work anticipated many of the themes of modern feminism.

Holmes went on to a long and brilliant judicial career, during which he repeatedly stressed the right of the people, through their elected representatives, to deal with contemporary problems in any reasonable way, unfettered by outmoded conceptions of the proper limits of government authority. Like the societies they regulated, laws should evolve as times and conditions changed, he said.

This way of reasoning caused no sudden reversal of judicial practice. Holmes's most notable opinions as a judge tended to be dissents. But his philosophy reflected the advanced thinking of the late nineteenth century, and his influence grew with every decade of the twentieth.

The new approach to knowledge did not always advance the cause of liberal reform. Historians in the graduate schools became intensely interested in studying the origins and evolution of political institutions. They concluded, after much "scientific" study of old charters and law codes, that the roots of democracy were to be found in the customs of the ancient tribes of northern Europe. This theory of the "Teutonic origins" of democracy, which has since been thoroughly discredited, fitted well with the prejudices of people of British stock, and it provided ammunition for those who favored restricting immigration and for those who argued that blacks were inferior beings.

Out of this work, however, came an essentially democratic concept, the frontier thesis of Frederick Jackson Turner, still another scholar trained at Johns Hopkins. Turner's essay "The Significance of the Frontier in American History" (1893) argued that the frontier experience, through which every section of the country had passed, had affected the thinking of the people and the shape of American institutions. The isolation of the frontier and the need during each successive westward advance to create civilization anew, Turner wrote, account for the individualism of Americans and the democratic character of their society. Nearly everything unique in our culture could be traced to the existence of the frontier, he claimed.

Turner, and still more his many disciples, made too much of his basic insights. Life on the frontier was not as democratic as Turner believed, and it certainly does not "explain" American development as completely as he said it did. Nevertheless, his work showed how important it was to investigate the evolution of institutions, and it encouraged historians to study social and economic, as well as purely political, subjects. If the claims of the new historians to objectivity and definitiveness were absurdly overstated, their emphasis on thoroughness, exactitude, and impartiality did much to raise standards in the profession. Perhaps the finest product of the new scientific school, a happy combination of meticulous

scholarship and literary artistry, was Henry Adams's nine-volume *History of the United States During the Administrations of Jefferson and Madison.*

Read the **Document** Frederick Jackson Turner, *The Significance of the Frontier in American History (1893)* at **www.myhistorylab.com**

Realism in Literature

When what Mark Twain called the Gilded Age began, American literature was dominated by the romantic mood. All the important writers of the 1840s and 1850s, except Hawthorne, Thoreau, and Poe, were still living. Longfellow stood at the height of his fame, and the lachrymose Susan Warner—"tears on almost every page"—continued to turn out stories in the style of her popular *The Wide, Wide World.* Romanticism, however, had lost its creative force; much of the popular writing in the decade after 1865 was sentimental trash pandering to the preconceptions of middle-class readers. Magazines like the *Atlantic Monthly* overflowed with stories about fair ladies worshiped from afar by stainless heroes, women coping selflessly with drunken husbands, and poor but honest youths rising through various combinations of virtue and diligence to positions of wealth and influence. Most writers of fiction tended to ignore the eternal conflicts inherent in human nature and the social problems of the age; polite entertainment and pious moralizing appeared to be their only objectives.

The patent unreality, even dishonesty, of contemporary fiction eventually caused a reaction. The most important forces giving rise to the Age of Realism were those that were transforming every other aspect of American life: industrialism, with its associated complexities and social problems; the theory of evolution, which made people more aware of the force of the environment and the basic conflicts of existence; the new science, which taught dispassionate, empirical observation. Novelists undertook the examination of social problems such as slum life, the conflict between capital and labor, and political corruption. They created multidimensional characters, depicted persons of every social class, used dialect and slang to capture the flavor of particular types, and fashioned painstaking descriptions of the surroundings into which they placed their subjects. The romantic novel did not disappear. General Lew Wallace's *Ben Hur* (1880) and Frances Hodgson Burnett's *Little Lord Fauntleroy* (1886) were bestsellers. But by 1880 realism was the point of view of the finest literary talents in the country.

Read the **Document** Mark Twain, *Incident in the Philippines (1924)* at **www.myhistorylab.com**

Read the **Document** Mark Twain, *To the Person Sitting in Darkness (1901)* at **www.myhistorylab.com**

Mark Twain

While it was easy to romanticize the West, that region lent itself to the realistic approach. Almost of necessity, novelists writing about the West described coarse characters from the lower levels of society and dealt with crime and violence. It would have been difficult indeed to write a genteel romance about a mining camp. The outstanding figure of western literature, the first great American realist, was Mark Twain.

Twain, whose real name was Samuel L. Clemens, was born in 1835. He grew up in Hannibal, Missouri, on the banks of the Mississippi. After mastering the printer's trade and working as a riverboat pilot, he went west to Nevada in 1861. The wild, rough life of Virginia City fascinated him, but prospecting got him nowhere, and he became a reporter for the *Territorial Enterprise*. Soon he was publishing humorous stories about the local life under the nom de plume Mark Twain. In 1865, while working in California, he wrote "The Celebrated Jumping Frog of Calaveras County," a story that brought him national recognition. A tour of Europe and the Holy Land in 1867 to 1868 led to *The Innocents Abroad* (1869), which made him famous.

Twain's greatness stemmed from his keen reportorial eye and ear, his eagerness to live life to the full, his marvelous sense of humor, and his ability to be at once in society and outside it, and to love humanity yet be repelled by human vanity and perversity. He epitomized the zest and adaptability of his age and also its materialism. No contemporary pursued the almighty dollar more zealously. An inveterate speculator, he made a fortune with his pen and lost it in foolish business ventures. He was equally at home and equally successful on the Great River of his childhood, in the mining camps, and in the eastern bourgeois society of his mature years. But every prize slipped through his fingers. Twain died a dark pessimist, surrounded by adulation yet alone, an alien and a stranger in the land he loved and knew so well.

Twain excelled every contemporary in the portrayal of character. In his biting satire, *The Gilded Age* (1873), he created that magnificent mountebank Colonel Beriah Sellers, purveyor of eyewash ("the Infallible Imperial Oriental Optic Liniment") and false hopes, ridiculous, unscrupulous, but lovable. In *Huckleberry Finn* (1884), his masterpiece, his portrait of the slave Jim, loyal, patient, naive, yet withal a man, is unforgettable. When Huck takes advantage of Jim's credulity merely for his own amusement, the slave turns from him coldly and says, "Dat truck dah is trash; en trash is what people is dat puts dirt on de head er dey fren's en makes 'em ashamed." And there is Huck Finn himself, full of devilry, romantic, amoral (up to a point), and at bottom the complete realist. When Miss Watson tells him he can get anything he wants by praying for it, he makes the effort, is disillusioned, and concludes, "If a body can get anything they pray for, why don't Deacon Winn get back the money he lost on pork? . . . Why can't Miss Watson fat up? No, I says to myself, there ain't nothing in it."

Whether directly, as in *The Innocents Abroad* and in his fascinating account of the world of the river pilot, *Life on the Mississippi* (1883), or when transformed by his imagination in works of fiction such as *Tom Sawyer* (1876) and *A Connecticut Yankee in King Arthur's Court* (1889), Mark Twain always put much of his own experience and feeling into his work. A story, he told a fellow author, "must be written with the blood out of a man's heart." His innermost confusions, the clash between his recognition of the pretentiousness and meanness of human beings and his wish to be accepted by society, added depths and overtones to his writing that together with his comic genius give it lasting appeal. He could not rise above

A sidewheeler on the Mississippi. In 1856 Samuel Clemens became an apprentice to a steamboat pilot and spent the next four years—among the most carefree in his life—plying the waters of the Mississippi River. In his writings, the river was a metaphor for a journey of discovery. A century later, the highway would function in a similar way for many American novelists.

the sentimentality and prudery of his generation entirely, for these qualities were part of his nature. He never dealt effectively with sexual love, for example, and often—even in *Huckleberry Finn*—contrived to end his tales on absurdly optimistic notes that ring false after so many brilliant pages portraying life as it is. On balance Twain's achievement was magnificent. Rough and uneven like the man himself, his works catch more of the spirit of the age he named than those of any other writer.

Read the **Document**   Mark Twain, from *The Gilded Age* at www.myhistorylab.com

William Dean Howells

Twain's realism was far less self-conscious than that of his longtime friend William Dean Howells. Like Twain, Howells, who was born in Ohio in 1837, had little formal education. He learned the printer's trade from his father and became a reporter for the *Ohio State Journal*. After the Civil War he worked briefly for *The Nation* in New York and then moved to Boston, where he became editor of the *Atlantic Monthly*. In 1886 he returned to New York as editor of *Harper's*.

A long series of novels and much literary criticism poured from Howells's pen over the next thirty years. While he insisted on treating his material honestly, he was not at first a critic of society, being content to write about what he called "the smiling aspects" of life. Realism to Howells meant concern for the complexities of individual personalities and faithful description of the genteel, middle-class world he knew best.

Besides a sharp eye and an open mind, Howells had a real social conscience. Gradually he became aware of the problems that industrialization had created. In 1885, in *The Rise of Silas Lapham*, he dealt with some of the ethical conflicts faced by businessmen in a competitive society. The harsh public reaction to the Haymarket bombing in 1886 stirred him, and he threw himself into a futile campaign to prevent the execution of the anarchist suspects. Thereafter he moved rapidly toward the left. In *A Hazard of New Fortunes* (1890), he attempted to portray the whole range of metropolitan life, weaving the destinies of a dozen interesting personalities from diverse sections and social classes. The book represents a triumph of realism in its careful descriptions of various sections of New York and the ways of life of rich and poor, in the intricacy of its characters, and in its rejection of sentimentality and romantic love.

His own works were widely read, and Howells was also the most influential critic of his time. He helped bring the best contemporary foreign writers, including Tolstoy, Dostoevsky, Ibsen, and Zola, to the attention

In 1891 William Dean Howells championed the poetry of Emily Dickinson: "This poetry is as characteristic of our life as our business enterprise, our political turmoil, our demagogism, or our millionaires." Yet few of her poems appeared during her lifetime; arguably the most important poet of her age was unknown to that age.

of readers in the United States, and he encouraged many important young American novelists, among them Stephen Crane, Theodore Dreiser, Frank Norris, and Hamlin Garland.

Some of these writers went far beyond Howells's realism to what they called naturalism. Many, like Twain and Howells, began as newspaper reporters. Working for a big-city daily in the 1890s was sure to teach anyone a great deal about the dark side of life. Naturalist writers believed that the human being was essentially an animal, a helpless creature whose fate was determined by environment. Their world was Darwin's world—mindless, without mercy or justice. They wrote chiefly about the most primitive emotions—lust, hate, and greed. In *Maggie, A Girl of the Streets* (1893), Stephen Crane described the seduction, degradation, and eventual suicide of a young woman, all set against the background of a sordid slum; in *The Red Badge of Courage* (1895), he captured the pain and humor of war. In *McTeague* (1899), Frank Norris told the story of a brutal, dull-witted dentist who murdered his greed-crazed wife with his bare fists.

Such stuff was too strong for Howells, yet he recognized its importance and befriended the younger writers in many ways. He found a publisher for *Maggie* after it had been rejected several times, and he wrote appreciative reviews of the work of Garland and Norris. Even Theodore Dreiser, who was contemptuous of Howells's writings and considered him hopelessly middle-class in point of view, appreciated his aid and praised his influence on American literature. Dreiser's first novel, *Sister Carrie* (1900), treated sex so forthrightly that it was withdrawn after publication.

Henry James

Henry James was very different in spirit and background from the tempestuous naturalists. Born to wealth, reared in a cosmopolitan atmosphere, twisted in some strange way while still a child and unable to achieve satisfactory relationships with women, James spent most of his mature life in Europe, writing novels, short stories, plays, and volumes of criticism. Although far removed from the world of practical affairs, he was preeminently a realist, determined, as he once said, "to leave a multitude of pictures of my time" for the future to contemplate.

Although he preferred living in the cultivated surroundings of London high society, James yearned for the recognition of his fellow Americans almost as avidly as Mark Twain. However, he was incapable of modifying his rarefied, overly subtle manner of writing. Most serious writers of the time admired his books, and he received many honors, but he never achieved widespread popularity. His major theme was the clash of American and European cultures, his primary interest the close-up examination of wealthy, sensitive, yet often corrupt persons in a cultivated but far from polite society.

James dealt with social issues such as feminism and the difficulties faced by artists in the modern world, but he subordinated them to his interest in his subjects as individuals. *The American* (1877) told the story of the love of a wealthy American in Paris for a French noblewoman who rejected him because her family disapproved of his commercial background. *The Portrait of a Lady* (1881) described the disillusionment of an intelligent woman married to a charming but morally bankrupt man and her eventual decision to remain with him nonetheless. *The Bostonians* (1886) was a complicated and psychologically sensitive study of the varieties of female behavior in a seemingly uniform social situation.

James's reputation, greater today than in his lifetime, rests more on his highly refined accounts of the interactions of individuals and their environment and his masterful commentaries on the novel as a literary form than on his ability as a storyteller. Few major writers have been more long-winded, more prone to circumlocution. Yet few have been so dedicated to their art, possessed of such psychological penetration, or so successful in producing a large body of important work.

Realism in Art

American painters responded to the times as writers did, but with this difference: Despite the new concern for realism, the romantic tradition retained its vitality. Preeminent among the realists was Thomas Eakins, who was born in Philadelphia in 1844. Eakins studied in Europe in the late 1860s and was influenced by the great realists of the seventeenth century, Velasquez and Rembrandt. Returning to America in 1870, he passed the remainder of his life teaching and painting in Philadelphia.

The scientific spirit of the age suited Eakins perfectly. He mastered human anatomy; some of his finest paintings, such as *The Gross Clinic* (1875), as seen on page 510, are graphic illustrations of surgical operations. He was an early experimenter with motion pictures, using the camera to capture exactly the attitudes of human beings and animals in action. Like his friend Walt Whitman, whose portrait is one of his greatest achievements, Eakins gloried in the ordinary. But he had none of Whitman's weakness for sham and self-delusion. His portraits are monuments to his integrity and craftsmanship: Never would he touch up or soften a likeness to please his sitter. His study of six men bathing (*The Swimming Hole*) is a stark portrayal of nakedness; his surgical scenes catch the tenseness of a situation without descending into sensationalism.

Winslow Homer, a Boston-born painter best known for his brilliant watercolors, was also influenced by realist ideas. Homer was a lithographer as well as a master of the watercolor medium, yet he had had almost no formal training. Indeed, he had contempt for academicians and refused to go abroad to study. Aesthetics seemed not to concern him at all; he liked to shock people by referring to his profession as "the picture line." "When I have selected [a subject]," he said, "I paint it exactly as it appears."

During the Civil War, Homer worked as an artist-reporter for *Harper's Weekly*, and he continued to do magazine illustrations for some years thereafter. He roamed America, painting scenes of southern farm life, Adirondack campers, and, after about 1880, magnificent seascapes and studies of fishermen and sailors.

The careers of Eakins and Homer show that the late-nineteenth-century American environment was not uncongenial to first-rate artists. Nevertheless, at least two major American painters abandoned native shores for Europe. One was James A. McNeill Whistler, whose portrait of his mother, which he called *Arrangement in Grey and Black*, is probably the most famous canvas ever painted by an American. Whistler left the United States in 1855 when he was twenty-one and spent most of his life in Paris and London. "I shall

Thomas Eakins's interest in science was as great as his interest in art. In the early 1880s he collaborated with photographer Eadweard Muybridge in serial-action photographic experiments and later devised a special camera for his anatomical studies. The accompanying picture (top) was taken with the Marey wheel. The impact of Eakins's photographic experiments is evident in *The Swimming Hole* (bottom), painted in 1883. At that time Eakins was director of the art school at the Pennsylvania Academy of the Fine Arts.

Source: (top) Philadelpia Museum of Art. Gift of Charles Bregler.

James McNeill Whistler's *Arrangement in Grey and Black* (1872) was nearly rejected at the Royal Academy showing of that year, but in later years viewers and critics were beguiled by the contrast between the painter's somber composition and the heartfelt emotion. *Whistler's Mother* became arguably the most famous painting in the United States.
Source: James Abbott McNeill Whistler, *Arrangement in Black and Gray: The Artist's Mother.* 1871. Oil on Canvas. 57' × 64 1/2" (144.8 × 163.8 cm). Musee d'Orsay, Paris. RMN Reunion des Musees Nationaux/Art Resource, NY.

Mary Cassatt's *Children Playing on the Beach* (1884). Now widely recognized as one of America's finest impressionist painters, Cassatt's talent was ignored in this country during her lifetime.
Source: National Gallery of Art, Ailsa Mellon Bruce Collection.

come to America," he announced grandly, "when the duty on works of art is abolished!"

Whistler made a profession of eccentricity, but he was a talented and versatile artist. Some of his portraits are triumphs of realism, whereas his misty studies of the London waterfront—which the critic John Ruskin characterized as pots of paint flung in the face of the beholder and which Whistler conceived as visual expressions of poetry—are thoroughly romantic in conception. Paintings such as *Whistler's Mother* represent still another expression of his talent. Spare and muted in tone, they are more interesting as precise arrangements of color and space than as images of particular objects; they had considerable influence on the course of modern art.

The second important expatriate artist was Mary Cassatt, daughter of a wealthy Pittsburgh banker and sister of Alexander J. Cassatt, who was president of the Pennsylvania Railroad around the turn of the century. She went to Paris as a tourist and dabbled in art like many conventional young socialites, then was caught up in the impressionist movement and decided to become a serious painter. Her work is more French than American and was little appreciated in the United States before World War I. When once she returned to America for a visit, the *Philadelphia Public Ledger* reported, "Mary Cassatt, sister of Mr. Cassatt, president of the Pennsylvania Railroad, returned from Europe yesterday. She has been studying painting in Paris, and owns the smallest Pekinese dog in the world."

The Pragmatic Approach

It would have been remarkable indeed if the intellectual ferment of the late nineteenth century had not affected contemporary ideas about the meaning of life, the truth of revealed religion, moral values, and similar fundamental problems. In particular the theory of evolution, so important in altering contemporary views of science, history, and social relations, produced significant changes in American thinking about religious and philosophical questions.

Evolution posed an immediate challenge to religion: If Darwin was correct, the biblical account of the creation was apparently untrue and the idea that the human race had been formed in God's image was highly unlikely. A bitter controversy erupted, described by President Andrew D. White of Cornell in *The Warfare of Science with Theology in Christendom* (1896). While millions continued to believe in the literal truth of the Bible, among intellectuals, lay and clerical, victory went to the evolutionists because, in addition to the arguments of the geologists and the biologists, scholars were throwing light on the historical origins of the Bible, showing that its words were of human rather than divine inspiration.

Evolution did not undermine the faith of any large percentage of the population. If the account of the creation in Genesis could not be taken literally, the Bible remained a repository of wisdom and inspiration. Such books as John Fiske's *The Outlines of Cosmic Philosophy* (1874) provided religious persons with the comforting thesis that evolution, while true, was merely God's way of ordering the universe—as the liberal preacher Washington Gladden put it, "a most impressive demonstration of the presence of God in the world."

The effects of Darwinism on philosophy were less dramatic but in the end more significant. Fixed systems and eternal truths were difficult to justify in a world that was constantly evolving. By the early 1870s a few philosophers had begun to reason that ideas and theories mattered little except when applied to specifics.

"Nothing justifies the development of abstract principles but their utility in enlarging our concrete knowledge of nature," wrote Chauncey Wright, secretary of the American Academy of Arts and Sciences. This startling philosophy, known as **pragmatism**, was further developed by William James, brother of the novelist. James was one of the most remarkable persons of his generation. Educated in London, Paris, Bonn, and Geneva—as well as at Harvard—he studied painting, participated in a zoological expedition

to South America, earned a medical degree, and was a professor at Harvard, successively of comparative anatomy, psychology, and finally philosophy. His *Principles of Psychology* (1890) may be said to have established that discipline as a modern science. His *Varieties of Religious Experience* (1902), which treated the subject from both psychological and philosophical points of view, helped thousands of readers reconcile their religious faith with their increasing knowledge of psychology and the physical universe.

James's wide range and his verve and imagination as a writer made him by far the most influential philosopher of his time. He rejected the deterministic interpretation of Darwinism and all other one-idea explanations of existence. Belief in free will was one of his axioms; environment might influence survival, but so did the *desire* to survive, which existed independent of surrounding circumstances. Even truth was relative; it did not exist in the abstract but *happened* under particular circumstances. What a person thought helped to make thought occur, or come true. The mind, James wrote in a typically vivid phrase, has "a vote" in determining truth. Religion was true, for example, because people were religious.

The pragmatic approach inspired much of the reform spirit of the late nineteenth century and even more of that of the early twentieth. James's hammer

Table 19.1 Key Figures and Intellectual Currents

Intellectual	Chief Accomplishment	Major Ideas
Charles W. Eliot	Elective system at Harvard	Encouraged development of college majors and hiring of specialized faculty
Daniel Coit Gilman	Graduate education at Johns Hopkins	Brought German standards of research to the United States
Richard Ely	Founded "institutional school of economics"	Challenged theorists who focused on markets and advocated laissez-faire governmental policy
John Dewey	*The School and Society* (1899)	Insisted that meaningful social change was impossible without educational change
Oliver Wendell Holmes, Jr.	*The Common Law* (1881)	Demonstrated that law was not founded on historical precedent; legal principles evolved with society
Frederick Jackson Turner	"The Significance of the Frontier in American History" (1893)	Frontier conditions explained the individualism and democracy that characterized American society
Mark Twain	*Huckleberry Finn* (1884)	Lampooned the sentimentality and hypocrisy of Victorian culture
Charlotte Perkins Gilman	*Women and Economics* (1898)	Maintained that society was unjustly built upon women's economic dependence on men; social change depended on women finding meaningful paid work
William Dean Howells	*A Hazard of New Fortunes* (1890)	Promoted a realistic, nonsentimental look at society
Henry James	*The Portrait of a Lady* (1881)	Showed how literature could probe the depths and complexities of human relationships
Thomas Eakins	*The Gross Clinic* (1875)	Applied realistic perspectives to art
William James	*The Principles of Psychology* (1890)	Contended that the will, as influenced by psychological factors, was an independent force in human affairs

blows shattered the laissez-faire extremism of Herbert Spencer. In "Great Men and Their Environment" (1880) James argued that social changes were brought about by the actions of geniuses whom society had selected and raised to positions of power, rather than by the impersonal force of the environment. Such reasoning fitted the preconceptions of rugged individualists yet encouraged those dissatisfied with society to work for change. Educational reformers like John Dewey, the institutionalist school of economists, settlement house workers, and other reformers adopted pragmatism eagerly. James's philosophy did much to revive the buoyant optimism that had characterized the pre-Civil War reform movement.

Yet pragmatism brought Americans face-to-face with somber problems. While relativism made them optimistic, it also bred insecurity, for there could be no certainty, no comforting reliance on any eternal value in the absence of absolute truth. Pragmatism also seemed to suggest that the end justified the means, that what worked was more important than what ought to be. At the time of James's death in 1910, the *Commercial and Financial Chronicle* pointed out that the pragmatic philosophy was helpful to businessmen in making decisions. By emphasizing practice at the expense of theory, the new philosophy encouraged materialism, anti-intellectualism, and other unlovely aspects of the American character. And what place had conventional morality in such a system? Perhaps pragmatism placed too much reliance on the free will of human beings, ignoring their capacity for selfishness and self-delusion.

The people of the new century found pragmatism a heady wine. They would quaff it freely and enthusiastically—down to the bitter dregs.

The Knowledge Revolution

Improvements in public education and the needs of an increasingly complex society for every type of intellectual skill caused a veritable revolution in how knowledge was discovered, disseminated, and put to use. Observing the effects of formal education on their children, many older people were eager to experience some of its benefits. Nothing so well illustrates the desire for new information as the rise of the Chautauqua movement, founded by John H. Vincent, a Methodist minister, and Lewis Miller, an Ohio manufacturer of farm machinery. Vincent had charge of Sunday schools for the Methodist church. In 1874 he and Miller organized a two-week summer course for Sunday school teachers on the shores of Lake Chautauqua in New York. Besides instruction, they offered good meals, evening songfests around the campfire, and a relaxing atmosphere—all for $6 for the two weeks.

The forty young teachers who attended were delighted with the program, and soon the leafy shore of Lake Chautauqua became a city of tents each summer as thousands poured into the region from all over the country. The founders expanded their offerings to include instruction in literature, science, government, and economics. Famous authorities, including, over the years, six presidents of the United States, came to lecture to open-air audiences on every subject imaginable. Eventually Chautauqua supplied speakers to reading circles throughout the country; it even offered correspondence courses leading over a four-year period to a diploma, the program designed, in Vincent's words, to give "the college outlook" to persons who had not had the opportunity to obtain a higher education. Books were written specifically for the program, and a monthly magazine, the *Chautauquan*, was published.

Such success provoked imitation, and by 1900 there were about 200 Chautauqua-type organizations. Intellectual standards in these programs varied greatly; in general they were very low. Entertainment was as important an objective as enlightenment. Musicians (good and bad), homespun humorists, inspirational lecturers, and assorted quacks shared the platform with prominent preachers and scholars. Moneymaking undoubtedly motivated many of the entrepreneurs who operated the centers, all of which, including the original Chautauqua, reflected the prevailing tastes of the American people—diverse, enthusiastic, uncritical, and shallow. Nevertheless the

The first commercially successful typewriter, manufactured in quantity beginning in 1874. It used the QWERTY keyboard found on later typewriters—and eventually found on computer keyboards.

movement provided opportunities for thousands seeking stimulation and intellectual improvement.

Still larger numbers profited from the proliferation of public libraries. By the end of the century nearly all the states supported libraries. Private donors, led by the steel industrialist Andrew Carnegie, contributed millions to the cause. In 1900 over 1,700 libraries in the United States had collections of more than 5,000 volumes.

Publishers tended to be conservative, but reaching the masses meant lowering intellectual and cultural standards, appealing to emotions, and adopting popular, sometimes radical, causes. Cheap, mass-circulation papers had first appeared in the 1830s and 1840s, the most successful being the *Sun*, the *Herald*, and the *Tribune* in New York; the *Philadelphia Public Ledger*; and the *Baltimore Sun*. None of them much exceeded a circulation of 50,000 before the Civil War. The first publisher to reach a truly massive audience was Joseph Pulitzer, a Hungarian-born immigrant who made a first-rate paper of the *St. Louis Post-Dispatch*. In 1883 Pulitzer bought the *New York World*, a sheet with a circulation of perhaps 20,000. Within a year he was selling 100,000 copies daily, and by the late 1890s the *World*'s circulation regularly exceeded 1 million.

"The *World* is the people's newspaper," Pulitzer boasted, and in the sense that it appealed to men and women of every sort, he was correct. Pulitzer's methods were quickly copied by competitors, especially William Randolph Hearst, who purchased the *New York Journal* in 1895 and soon outdid the *World* in sensationalism. But no other newspaperman of the era approached Pulitzer in originality, boldness, and the knack of reaching the masses without abandoning seriousness of purpose and basic integrity.

Growth and ferment also characterized the magazine world. In 1865 there were about 700 magazines in the country, and by the turn of the century more than 5,000. Until the mid-1880s, few of the new magazines were in any way unusual. A handful of serious periodicals, such as the *Atlantic Monthly*, *Harper's*, and the *Century*, dominated the field. They were staid in tone and conservative in politics. Although they had great influence, none approached mass circulation because of the limited size of the upper-middle-class audience they aimed at.

Magazines directed at the average citizen were of low quality. The leading publisher of this type in the 1860s and 1870s was Frank Leslie, whose periodicals bore such titles as *Frank Leslie's Chimney Corner*, *Frank Leslie's Illustrated Newspaper*, and *Frank Leslie's Jolly Joker*. Leslie specialized in illustrations of current events (he put as many as thirty-four engravers to work on a single picture in order to bring it out quickly) and on providing what he frankly admitted was "mental pabulum"—a combination of cheap romantic fiction, old-fashioned poetry, jokes, and advice columns. Some of his magazines sold as many as 300,000 copies per issue.

Popular magazines rarely discussed the great issues that preoccupied intellectuals—the impact of Darwinism on law, sociology, and anthropology; the theories of John Dewey and the progressive educators; the import of realism in literature and art; the implications of pragmatism to psychology, philosophy, and theology. But some phenomena—such as the mania for college football—pressed forward because they represented so powerful a convergence of popular culture and intellectual trends.

Chapter Review

Milestones

1862	Morrill Act establishes land-grant colleges
1865	Vassar College is founded for women
1869	Charles W. Eliot becomes Harvard's president
1874	Chautauqua movement begins
1876	Johns Hopkins University is founded to specialize in graduate education
1881	Oliver Wendell Holmes Jr. publishes *The Common Law*
	Henry James publishes *The Portrait of a Lady*
1883	Joseph Pulitzer purchases *New York World*
1884	Mark Twain publishes *Huckleberry Finn*
1886	Ottmar Mergenthaler invents linotype machine
	William Dean Howells becomes editor of *Harper's*
1889	Edward W. Bok becomes editor of the *Ladies' Home Journal*
1890	William James publishes *Principles of Psychology*
1893	Frederick Jackson Turner publishes "Significance of the Frontier in American History"
1895	William Randolph Hearst purchases the *New York Journal*
1898	Charlotte Perkins Gilman publishes *Women and Economics*
1899	John Dewey publishes *The School and Society*

Key Terms

pragmatism A philosophical system, chiefly associated with William James, that deemphasized abstraction and assessed ideas and cultural practices based on their practical effects; it helped inspire political and social reform during the late nineteenth century, *524*

Review Questions

1. The introductory essay argues that football was embraced by colleges and universities in the late nineteenth century because it reflected hard-nosed Darwinian concepts. What other aspects of late nineteenth-century intellectual and cultural life were influenced by Darwinism? What intellectual trends and movements rejected social Darwinism?

2. What institutional developments transformed higher education during the last third of the nineteenth century?

3. How was popular culture at odds with intellectual trends in literature and the arts?

4. How did pragmatism—the belief that ideas must be judged by their consequences—challenge earlier outlooks on philosophy and morality?

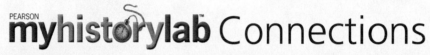

PEARSON
myhistorylab Connections

Reinforce what you learned in this chapter by studying the many documents, images, maps, review tools, and videos available at **www.myhistorylab.com**.

Read and Review

✓● Study and Review *Chapter 19*

●●●● Read the Document *The Morrill Act,* p. 514

●●●● Read the Document Herbert Spencer, *Social Darwinism,* p. 515

●●●● Read the Document Mark Twain, *Incident in the Philippines (1924),* p. 518

●●●● Read the Document Mark Twain, *To the Person Sitting in Darkness (1901),* p. 518

●●●● Read the Document Mark Twain, from *The Gilded Age,* p. 520

Research and Explore

◉ Watch the Video *College Football (1903),* p. 514

●●●● Read the Document Frederick Jackson Turner, *The Significance of the Frontier in American History (1893),* p. 518

((●●── Hear the Audio

Hear the audio file for Chapter 19 at
www.myhistorylab.com.

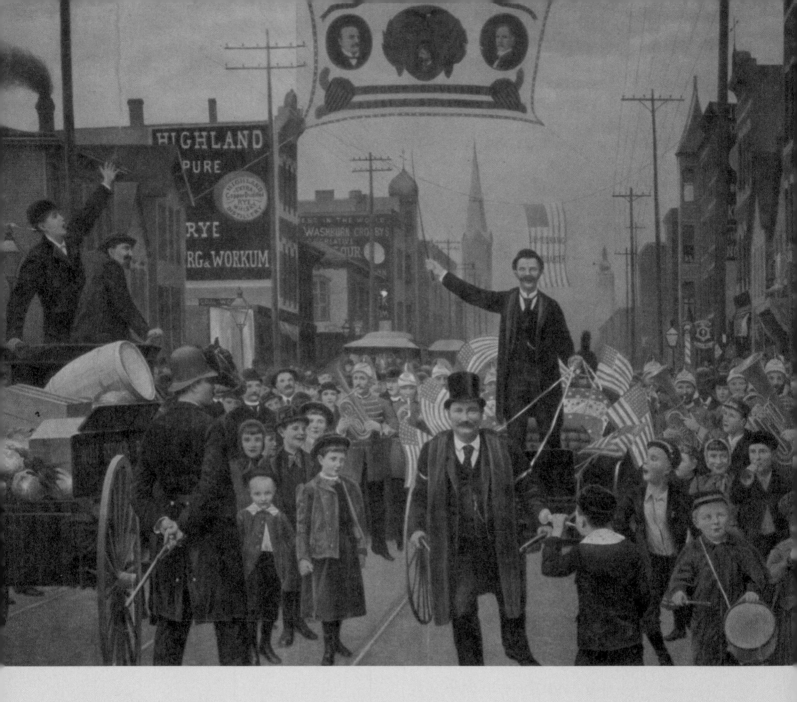

Did you vote for an American Idol?

On May 20, 2009, twenty-three-year-old guitar-strumming Kris Allen captivated the audience of *American Idol* with his rendition of Keith Urban's "Kiss a Girl" and Bill Withers's "Ain't No Sunshine." By receiving a majority of the nearly 100 million "votes"—by telephone and text message—Allen became the *American Idol* for 2009.

Although pundits had for years grumbled that Americans cared more about pop stars on *American Idol* than about their president, this may not have been true in 2009. The producers of the show did not release the exact number of votes for Allen, but they did say the vote was close; probably he received no more than 55 million. Six months earlier, presidential candidates Barack Obama and John McCain received more votes than Allen, with 69 million and 60 million respectively.

The comparison, of course, is unsound. *American Idol* fans often cast multiple votes for their favorite; some spent hundreds of dollars in phone and texting fees. A better comparison is of voter turnout for presidential elections nowadays and during the late nineteenth century. Since 1946, fewer than half of the eligible voters have on the average voted in presidential elections. By contrast, over three-fourths of eligible

From Smoke-Filled Rooms to Prairie Wildfire: 1877–1896

((•—[Hear the Audio **Chapter 20 at www.myhistorylab.com**

■ A parade for Grover Cleveland in Chicago in 1892, by John Klir. Music, mirth, real drama—a presidential election was perhaps even better entertainment than *American Idol*.

voters did so in presidential campaigns from 1876 to 1896—the highest rates in the nation's history.

This puzzles scholars, because the issues of that time seem inconsequential: Civil War soldiers' pensions, the tariff, paper money vs. gold and silver coins, and civil service reform. Perhaps the most volatile issue—the plight of former slaves—never attracted much notice because most politicians looked the other way. The other key issue—the minimal role of the federal government in the nation's industrial ascent—went without saying and, being unsaid, generated little controversy.

Why, then, did so many people vote? Local issues seem to have loomed large in most people's thinking.

Public health, municipal services, and corruption all dominated the headlines. Then, during the 1890s, a nationwide industrial depression crushed many local manufacturing firms, just as an agricultural crisis was sweeping through the midsection of the nation.

Because the nation had become more tightly integrated, these economic upheavals jolted nearly every community. National policy and local issues converged, culminating in the extraordinary election of 1896, which brought over 80 percent of the electorate to the polls. In Illinois, Indiana, Iowa, Michigan, and Ohio (important farm states) over 95 percent of those eligible to vote did so. In these years, politics had become the greatest show around. ■

Congress Ascendant

A succession of weak presidents occupied the White House during the last quarter of the nineteenth century. Although the impeachment proceedings against Andrew Johnson had failed, Congress dominated the government. Within Congress, the Senate generally overshadowed the House of Representatives. In his novel *Democracy* (1880), the cynical Henry Adams wrote that the United States had a "government of the people, by the people, for the benefit of Senators." Critics called the Senate a "rich man's club," and it did contain many millionaires, among them Leland Stanford, founder of the Central Pacific Railroad; the mining tycoon James G. "Bonanza" Fair of Nevada; Philetus Sawyer, a self-made Wisconsin lumberman; and Nelson Aldrich of Rhode Island, whose wealth derived from banking and a host of corporate connections. However, the true sources of the Senate's influence lay in the long tenure of many of its members (which enabled them to master the craft of politics), in the fact that it was small enough to encourage real debate, and in its long-established reputation for wisdom, intelligence, and statesmanship.

The House of Representatives, on the other hand, was one of the most disorderly and inefficient legislative bodies in the world. "As I make my notes," a reporter wrote in 1882 while sitting in the House gallery,

> I see a dozen men reading newspapers with their feet on their desks. . . . "Pig Iron" Kelley of Pennsylvania has dropped his newspaper and is paring his fingernails. . . . The vile odor of . . . tobacco . . . rises from the two-for-five-cents cigars in the mouths of the so-called gentlemen below. . . . They chew, too! Every desk has a spittoon of pink and gold china beside it to catch the filth from the statesman's mouth.

An infernal din rose from the crowded chamber. Desks slammed; members held private conversations, hailed pages, shuffled from place to place, clamored for the attention of the Speaker—and all the while some poor orator tried to discuss the question of the moment. Speaking in the House, one writer said, was like trying to address the crowd on a passing Broadway bus from the curb in front of the Astor House in New York. On one occasion in 1878 the adjournment of the House was held up for more than

An 1887 cartoon indicting the Senate for closely attending to the Big (read, fat) Trusts rather than to the needs of the public (whose "entrance" to the Senate is "closed"). Drawn by Joseph Keppler, a caricaturist who was born and trained in Germany, this type of grotesque satire greatly influenced late-nineteenth-century American comic arts.

twelve hours because most of the members of an important committee were too drunk to prepare a vital appropriations bill for final passage.

The great political parties professed undying enmity to each other, but they seldom took clearly opposing positions on the questions of the day. Democrats were separated from Republicans more by accidents of geography, religious affiliation, ethnic background, and emotion than by economic issues. Questions of state and local importance, unrelated to national politics, often determined the outcome of congressional elections and thus who controlled the federal government.

The fundamental division between Democrats and Republicans was sectional, a result of the Civil War. The South, after the political rights of blacks had been drastically circumscribed, became heavily Democratic. Most of New England was solidly Republican. Elsewhere the two parties stood in fair balance, although the Republicans tended to have the advantage. A preponderance of the well-to-do, cultured Northerners were Republicans. Perhaps in reaction to this concentration, immigrants, Catholics, and other minority groups—except for blacks—tended to vote Democratic. But the numerous exceptions weakened the applicability of these generalizations. German and Scandinavian immigrants usually voted Republican; many powerful business leaders supported the Democrats.

The bulk of the people—farmers, laborers, shopkeepers, white collar workers—distributed their ballots fairly evenly between the two parties in most elections; the balance of political power after 1876 was almost perfect. Between 1856 and 1912 the Democrats elected a president only twice (1884 and 1892), but most contests were extremely close. Majorities in both the Senate and the House fluctuated continually. Between 1876 and 1896 the "dominant" Republican party controlled both houses of Congress and the presidency at the same time for only a single two-year period.

Recurrent Issues

Four questions obsessed politicians in these years. One was the "bloody shirt." The term, which became part of the language after a Massachusetts congressman dramatically displayed to his colleagues in the House the bloodstained shirt of an Ohio carpetbagger who had been flogged by terrorists in Mississippi, referred to the tactic of reminding the electorate of the northern states that the men who had precipitated the Civil War had been Democrats. Should Democrats regain power, former rebels would run the government and undo all the work

accomplished at such sacrifice during the war. "Every man that endeavored to tear down the old flag," a Republican orator proclaimed in 1876, "was a Democrat. Every man that tried to destroy this nation was a Democrat. . . . The man that assassinated Abraham Lincoln was a Democrat. . . . Soldiers, every scar you have on your heroic bodies was given you by a Democrat." And every scoundrel or incompetent who sought office under the Republican banner waved the bloody shirt in order to divert the attention of northern voters from his own shortcomings. The technique worked so well that many decent candidates could not resist the temptation to employ it in close races. Nothing, of course, so effectively obscured the real issues of the day.

Waving the bloody shirt was related intimately to the issue of the rights of African Americans. Throughout this period Republicans vacillated between trying to build up their organization in the South by appealing to black voters—which required them to make sure that blacks in the South could vote—and trying to win

The 1860 dollar, minted in gold, front and back.

conservative white support by stressing economic issues such as the tariff. When the former strategy seemed wise, they waved the bloody shirt with vigor; in the latter case, they piously announced that the blacks' future was "as safe in the hands of one party as it is in the other."

The question of veterans' pensions also bore a close relationship to the bloody shirt. Following the Civil War, Union soldiers founded the Grand Army of the Republic (GAR). By 1890 the organization had a membership of 409,000. The GAR put immense pressure on Congress, first for aid to veterans with service-connected disabilities, then for those with any disability, and eventually for all former Union soldiers. Republican politicians played on the emotions of the former soldiers by waving the bloody shirt, but the tough-minded leaders of the GAR demanded that they prove their sincerity by treating in open-handed fashion the warriors whose blood had stained the shirt.

The tariff was another perennial issue in post-Civil War politics. Despite considerable loose talk about free trade,

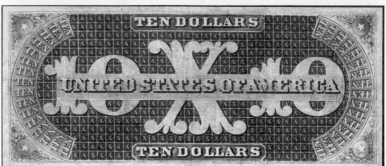

When the supply of gold became perilously low during the Civil War, the U.S. Treasury printed Demand Notes, usually in green ink. These "greenbacks" were withdrawn after the Civil War and the "gold standard" was restored. But not enough gold dollars were minted to keep up with the growth of the economy.

almost no one in the United States except for a handful of professional economists, most of them college professors, believed in eliminating duties on imports. Manufacturers desired protective tariffs to keep out competing products, and a majority of their workers were convinced that wage levels would fall if goods produced by cheap foreign labor entered the United States untaxed. Many farmers supported protection, although almost no competing agricultural products were being imported. Congressman William McKinley of Ohio, who reputedly could make reciting a tariff schedule sound like poetry, stated the majority opinion in the clearest terms: high tariffs foster the growth of industry and thus create jobs. "Reduce the tariff and labor is the first to suffer," he said.

The tariff could have been a real political issue because American technology was advancing so rapidly that many industries no longer required protection from foreign competitors. A powerful argument could have been made for scientific rate making that would adjust duties to actual conditions and avoid overprotection. The Democrats professed to believe in moderation, yet whenever party leaders tried to revise the tariff downward, Democratic congressmen from Pennsylvania, New York, and other industrial states sided with the

Republicans. Many Republicans endorsed tariff reform in principle, but when particular schedules came up for discussion, most of them demanded the highest rates for industries in their own districts and traded votes shamelessly with colleagues representing other interests in order to get what they wanted. Every new tariff bill became an occasion for logrolling, lobbying, and outrageous politicking rather than for sane discussion and careful evaluation of the public interest.

A third political question in this period was currency reform. During the Civil War, the government, faced with obligations it could not meet by taxing or borrowing, suspended specie payments and issued about $450 million in paper money, originally printed in green ink. This currency, called greenbacks, did not command the full confidence of a people accustomed to money readily convertible into gold or silver. Greenbacks seemed to encourage inflation, for how could one trust the government not to print them in wholesale lots to avoid passing unpopular tax laws? Thus, when the war ended, strong sentiment developed for withdrawing the greenbacks from circulation and returning to a bullion standard—to coining money from silver and gold.

In fact, beginning during Reconstruction, prices declined sharply. The deflation increased the real income of bondholders and other creditors but injured debtors. Farmers were particularly hard-hit, for many of them had borrowed heavily during the wartime boom to finance expansion.

Here was a question of real significance. Many groups supported some kind of currency inflation. A National Greenback party nominated Peter Cooper, an iron manufacturer, for president in 1876. Cooper received only 81,000 votes, but a new Greenback Labor party polled over a million in 1878, electing fourteen congressmen. However, the major parties refused to confront each other over the currency question. While Republicans professed to be the party of sound money, most western Republicans favored expansion of the currency. And while one wing of the Democrats flirted with the Greenbackers, the conservative, or "Bourbon," Democrats favored deflation as much as Republicans did. Under various administrations steps were taken to increase or decrease the amount of money in circulation, but the net effect on the economy was not significant.

The final major political issue of these years was civil service reform. That the federal bureaucracy needed overhauling nearly everyone agreed. As American society grew larger and more complex, the government necessarily took on more functions. The need for professional administration increased. The number of federal employees rose from 53,000 in 1871 to 256,000 at the end of the century. Corruption flourished; waste and inefficiency were the normal state of affairs. The collection of tariff duties offered perhaps the greatest opportunity for venality. The New York Custom House, one observer wrote in 1872, teemed with "corrupting merchants and their clerks and runners, who think that all men can be bought, and . . . corrupt swarms [of clerks], who shamelessly seek their price."

With a succession of relatively ineffective presidents and a Congress that squandered its energies on private bills, pork-barrel projects, and other trivia, the administration of the government was strikingly inefficient.

Every honest observer could see the need for reform, but the politicians refused to surrender the power of dispensing government jobs to their lieutenants without regard for their qualifications. They argued that patronage was the lifeblood of politics, that parties could not function without armies of loyal political workers, and that the workers expected and deserved the rewards of office when their efforts were crowned with victory at the polls. Typical was the attitude of the New York assemblyman who, according to Theodore Roosevelt, had "the same idea about Public Life and the Civil Service that a vulture

has of a dead sheep." When reformers suggested establishing the most modest kind of professional, nonpartisan civil service, politicians of both parties subjected them to every kind of insult and ridicule even though both the Democratic and Republican parties regularly wrote civil service reform planks into their platforms.

Party Politics: Sidestepping the Issues

With the Democrats invincible in the South and the Republicans predominant in New England and most of the states beyond the Mississippi, the outcome of presidential elections was usually determined in a handful of populous states: New York (together with its satellites, New Jersey and Connecticut), Ohio, Indiana, and Illinois. The fact that opinion in these states on important questions such as the tariff and monetary policy was divided and that every imaginable religious and ethnic interest was represented in the electorate goes far to explain why the parties hesitated to commit themselves on issues. In every presidential election, Democrats and Republicans concentrated their heaviest guns on these states. Of the eighteen Democrats and Republicans nominated for president in the nine elections between 1868 and 1900, only three were not from New York, Ohio, Indiana, or Illinois, and all three lost.

Partisanship was intense in these states. Campaigns were conducted in a carnival atmosphere, entertainment being substituted for serious debate. Large sums were spent on brass bands, barbecues, uniforms, and banners. Speakers of national reputation were imported to attract crowds, and spellbinders noted for their leather lungs—this was before the day of the loudspeaker—and their ability to rouse popular emotions were brought in to address mass meetings.

With so much depending on so few, the level of political morality was abysmal. Mudslinging, character assassination, and plain lying were standard practice; bribery was routine. Drifters and other dissolute citizens were paid in cash—or more often in free drinks—to vote the party ticket. The names of persons long dead were solemnly inscribed in voting registers, their suffrages exercised by impostors. During the 1880 campaign the Democratic national chairman, hearing that the Republicans were planning to transport Kentuckians into Indiana to vote illegally in that crucial state, urged Indiana Democrats to "check this outrageous fraud." Then, perhaps seeking an easier solution to the problem, he added, "If necessary . . . keep even with them."

Lackluster Presidents: From Hayes to Harrison

The leading statesmen of the period were disinterested in important contemporary questions, powerless to influence them, or content with things the way they were. Consider the presidents.

Rutherford B. Hayes, president from 1877 to 1881, came to office with a distinguished record. He attended Kenyon College and Harvard Law School before settling down to practice in Cincinnati. Although he had a family to support, he volunteered for service in the Union army within weeks after the first shell fell on Fort Sumter. "A just and necessary war," he called it in his diary. "I would prefer to go into it if I knew I was to die . . . than to live through and after it without taking any part."

Hayes was wounded at South Mountain on the eve of Antietam and later served under Sheridan in the Shenandoah Valley campaign of 1864. Entering the army as a major, he emerged a major general. In 1864 he was elected to Congress; four years later he became governor of Ohio, serving three terms altogether. The Republicans nominated him for president

FARMER GARFIELD
Cutting a Swath to the White House.

In this 1880 campaign lithograph by Currier & Ives, "Farmer Garfield" uses a scythe made of honesty, ability, and patriotism to cut a swath to the White House through brush infested by snakes like Falsehood and Malice. One snake bears the countenance of Garfield's predecessor, Hayes.

in 1876 because of his reputation for honesty and moderation, and his election, made possible by the Compromise of 1877, seemed to presage an era of sectional harmony and political probity.

Outwardly Hayes had a sunny disposition; inwardly, in his own words, he was sometimes "nervous to the point of disaster." Despite his geniality, he was utterly without political glamour. He played down the tariff issue. On the money question he was conservative. He cheerfully approved the resumption of gold payments in 1879 and vetoed bills to expand the currency. He accounted himself a civil service reformer, being opposed to the collection of political contributions from federal officeholders.

Hayes complained about the South's failure to treat blacks decently after the withdrawal of federal troops, but he took no action. He worked harder for civil service reform, yet failed to achieve the "thorough, rapid, and complete" change he had promised. In most matters, he was content to "let the record show that he had made the requests."

Hayes's successor, James A. Garfield, fought at Shiloh and later at Chickamauga. In two years he rose from lieutenant colonel to major general. In 1863 he won a seat in Congress, where his oratorical and managerial skills brought him to prominence in the affairs of the Republican party.

Garfield had been a compromise choice at the 1880 Republican convention. His election precipitated a great battle over patronage, the new president standing in a sort of no-man's land between contending factions within the party. In July 1881 an unbalanced office-seeker named Charles J. Guiteau shot Garfield in the Washington railroad station. After lingering for weeks, the president died on September 19.

The assassination of Garfield elevated Chester A. Arthur to the presidency. A New York lawyer and abolitionist, Arthur became an early convert to the Republican party and rose rapidly in its local councils. In 1871 Grant gave him the juiciest political plum in the country, the collectorship of the Port of New York, which he held until removed by Hayes in 1878 for refusing to keep his hands out of party politics.

The vice presidency was the only elective position that Arthur had ever held. Before Garfield's death, he had paid little attention to questions like the tariff and monetary policy, being content to take in fees ranging upward of $50,000 a year as collector of the port and to oversee the operations of the New York customs office, with its hordes of clerks and laborers. (During Arthur's tenure, the novelist Herman Melville was employed as an "outdoor inspector" by the customhouse.) Of course, Arthur was an unblushing defender of the spoils system, though in fairness it must be said that he was personally honest and an excellent administrator.

The tragic circumstances of his elevation to the presidency sobered Arthur. Although he was a genial, convivial man, perhaps overly fond of good food and flashy clothes, he comported himself with dignity as president. He handled patronage matters with restraint, and he gave at least nominal support to the movement for civil service reform, which had been strengthened by the public's indignation at the assassination of Garfield. In 1883 Congress passed the **Pendleton Act**, "classifying" about 10 percent of all government jobs and creating the bipartisan Civil Service Commission to administer competitive examinations for these positions. The law made it illegal to force officeholders to make political contributions and empowered the president to expand the list of classified positions at his discretion.

As an administrator Arthur was systematic, thoughtful, businesslike, and at the same time cheerful and considerate. Just the same, he too was a political failure. He made relatively little effort to push his program through Congress. He did not seek a second term in 1884.

The election of 1884 brought the Democrat Grover Cleveland to the White House. Cleveland grew up in western New York. After studying law, he settled in Buffalo. Although somewhat lacking in the social graces and in intellectual pretensions, he had a basic integrity that everyone recognized; when a group of reformers sought a candidate for mayor in 1881, he was a natural choice. His success in Buffalo led to his election as governor of New York in 1882.

In the governor's chair his no-nonsense attitude toward public administration endeared him to civil service reformers at the same time that his basic conservatism pleased businessmen. When he vetoed a popular bill to force a reduction of the fares charged by the New York City elevated railway on the ground that it was an unconstitutional violation of the company's franchise, his reputation soared. Here was a man who cared more for principle than for the adulation of the multitude, a man who was courageous, honest, hardworking, and eminently sound. The Democrats nominated him for president in 1884.

The election revolved around personal issues, for the platforms of the parties were almost identical. On the one hand, the Republican candidate, the dynamic James G. Blaine, had an immense following, but his reputation had been soiled by the publication of the "Mulligan letters," which connected him with the corrupt granting of congressional favors to the Little

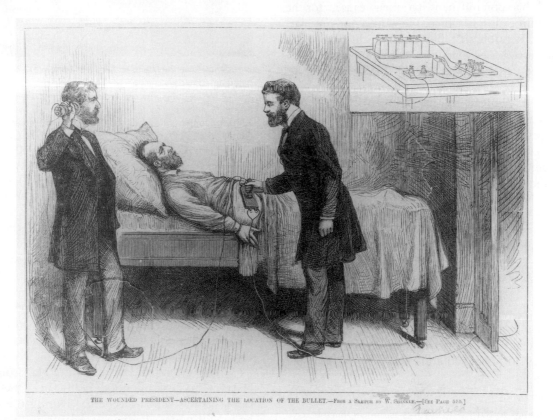

THE WOUNDED PRESIDENT—ASCERTAINING THE LOCATION OF THE BULLET.—From a Sketch by W. Shinkle.—[See Page 535.]

James A. Garfield lies mortally wounded. After failing to locate the bullet, surgeons called in Alexander Graham Bell, the famous inventor. Bell conceived of a device, pictured here, that anticipated the mine detector. Bell's machine failed to locate the bullet, however, perhaps because the metal bed springs interfered with its operation. Garfield died, either from the bullet or the surgeon's unsuccessful attempts to extricate it.

Rock and Fort Smith Railroad. On the other hand, it came out during the campaign that Cleveland, a bachelor, had fathered an illegitimate child. Instead of debating public issues, the Republicans chanted the ditty,

Ma! Ma! Where's my pa?
Gone to the White House,
Ha! Ha! Ha!

to which the Democrats countered,

Blaine, Blaine, James G. Blaine,
The continental liar from the State of Maine.

Blaine lost more heavily in the mudslinging than Cleveland, whose quiet courage in saying "Tell the truth" when his past was brought to light contrasted favorably with Blaine's glib and unconvincing denials. A significant group of eastern Republicans, known as **mugwumps**, campaigned for the Democrats.[1] However, Blaine ran a strong race against a general pro-Democratic trend; Cleveland won the election by fewer than 25,000 votes. The change of 600 ballots in New York would have given that state, and the presidency, to his opponent.

As a Democrat, Cleveland had no stomach for refighting the Civil War. Civil service reformers overestimated his commitment to their cause, for he believed in rotation in office. He would not summarily dismiss Republicans, but he thought that when they had served four years, they "should as a rule give way to good men of our party." He did, however, insist on honesty and efficiency regardless of party. As a result, he made few poor appointments.

Cleveland had little imagination and too narrow a conception of his powers and duties to be a dynamic president. His appearance perfectly reflected his character: A squat, burly man weighing well over 200 pounds, he could defend a position against heavy odds, yet he lacked flexibility. He took a fairly broad view of the powers of the federal government, but he thought it unseemly to put pressure on Congress, believing in "the entire independence of the executive and legislative branches."

Toward the end of his term Cleveland bestirred himself and tried to provide constructive leadership on the tariff question. The government was embarrassed by a large revenue surplus, which Cleveland hoped to reduce by cutting the duties on necessities and on raw materials used in manufacturing. He devoted his entire

President Grover Cleveland and Frances Folsom in 1888. The couple had married two years earlier; he was 48, and she, 21, the youngest First Lady. Her popularity blunted criticisms that Cleveland, a bachelor, had earlier fathered an illegitimate child. When he lost the 1888 election, his wife predicted that she would return as First Lady. Four years later, she did.

annual message of December 1887 to the tariff, thereby focusing public attention on the subject. When worried Democrats reminded him that an election was coming up and that the tariff might cause a rift in the organization, he replied simply, "What is the use of being elected or re-elected, unless you stand for something?"

In that contest, Cleveland obtained a plurality of the popular vote, but his opponent, Benjamin Harrison, grandson of President William Henry Harrison, carried most of the key northeastern industrial states by narrow margins, thereby obtaining a comfortable majority in the electoral college, 233 to 168.

Although intelligent and able, Harrison was too reserved to make a good politician. One observer called him a "human iceberg." During the Civil War he fought under Sherman at Atlanta and won a reputation as a stern, effective disciplinarian. In 1876 he ran unsuccessfully for governor of Indiana, but in 1881 was elected to the Senate.

---

[1]The mugwumps considered themselves reformers, but on social and economic questions nearly all of them were very conservative. They were sound-money proponents and advocates of laissez-faire. Reform to them consisted almost entirely of doing away with corruption and making the government more efficient.

Harrison believed ardently in protective tariffs. His approach to fiscal policy was conservative, though he was freehanded in the matter of veterans' pensions. No more flamboyant waver of the bloody shirt existed. Harrison professed to favor civil service reform, but fashioned an unimpressive record on the question. He appointed the vigorous young reformer Theodore Roosevelt to the Civil Service Commission and then proceeded to undercut him systematically. Before long the frustrated Roosevelt was calling the president a "cold blooded, narrow minded, prejudiced, obstinate, timid old psalm singing Indianapolis politician."

Under Harrison, Congress distinguished itself by expending, for the first time in a period of peace, more than $1 billion in a single session. It raised the tariff to an all-time high. The Sherman Antitrust Act was also passed.

Harrison had little to do with the fate of any of these measures. The Republicans lost control of Congress in 1890, and two years later Grover Cleveland swept back into power, defeating Harrison by more than 350,000 votes.

Read the Document Pendleton Civil Service Act at www.myhistorylab.com

View the Image Harrison and Morton Campaign Ad at www.myhistorylab.com

African Americans in the South After Reconstruction

Perhaps the most important issue of the last quarter of the nineteenth century was the fate of the former slaves after the withdrawal of federal troops from the South. Shortly after his inauguration in 1877, President Hayes made a goodwill tour of the South and he urged blacks to trust southern whites. A new Era of Good Feelings had dawned, he announced. Some southern leaders made earnest attempts to respect the civil rights of African Americans. That same year Governor Wade Hampton of South Carolina proposed to "secure to every citizen, the lowest as well as the highest, black as well as white, full and equal protection in the enjoyment of all his rights under the Constitution."

But the pledge was not kept. By December, Hayes was sadly disillusioned. "By state legislation, by frauds, by intimidation, and by violence of the most atrocious character, colored citizens have been deprived of the right of suffrage," he wrote in his diary. However, he did nothing to remedy the situation. Frederick Douglass called Hayes's policy "sickly conciliation."

Hayes's successors in the 1880s did no better. "Time is the only cure," President Garfield said, thereby confessing that he had no policy at all. President Arthur gave federal patronage to antiblack groups in an effort to split the Democratic South. In President Cleveland's day African Americans had scarcely a friend in high places, North or South. In 1887 Cleveland explained to a correspondent why he opposed "mixed [integrated] schools." Expert opinion, the president said, believed "that separate schools were of much more benefit for the colored people." Hayes, Garfield, and Arthur were Republicans, and Cleveland a Democrat; party made little difference. Both parties subscribed to hypocritical statements about equality and constitutional rights, and neither did anything to implement them.

For a time blacks were not totally disenfranchised in the South. Rival white factions tried to manipulate them, and corruption flourished as widely as in the machine-dominated wards of the northern cities. In the 1890s, however, the southern states, led by Mississippi, began to deprive blacks of the vote despite the Fifteenth Amendment. Poll taxes raised a formidable economic barrier, one that also disenfranchised many poor whites. Literacy tests completed the work; a number of states provided a loophole for illiterate whites by including an "understanding" clause whereby an illiterate person could qualify by demonstrating an ability to explain the meaning of a section of the state constitution when an election official read it to him. Blacks who attempted to take the test were uniformly declared to have failed it.

In Louisiana, 130,000 blacks voted in the election of 1896. Then the law was changed. In 1900 only 5,000 votes were cast by blacks. "We take away the Negroes' votes," a Louisiana politician explained, "to protect them just as we would protect a little child and prevent it from injuring itself with sharp-edged tools." Almost every Supreme Court decision after 1877 that affected blacks somehow nullified or curtailed their rights. The **civil rights cases** (1883) declared the Civil Rights Act of 1875 unconstitutional. Blacks who were refused equal accommodations or privileges by hotels, theaters, and other privately owned facilities had no recourse at law, the Court announced. The Fourteenth Amendment guaranteed their civil rights against invasion by the states, not by individuals.

Finally, in *Plessy v. Ferguson* (1896), the Court ruled that even in places of public accommodation, such as railroads and, by implication, schools, segregation was legal as long as facilities of equal quality were provided: "If one race be inferior to the other socially, the Constitution of the United States cannot put them upon the same plane." In a noble dissent in the Plessy case, Justice John Marshall Harlan protested this line of argument. "Our Constitution is color-blind," he said. "The arbitrary separation of citizens, on the basis of race . . . is a badge of servitude wholly inconsistent with civil freedom. . . . The two

A cartoon from *Judge* magazine in 1892 depicts Ku Klux Klansmen barring a black voter from the polls.

races in this country are indissolubly linked together, and the interests of both require that the common government of all shall not permit the seeds of race hatred to be planted under the sanction of law."

More than half a century was to pass before the Court came around to Harlan's reasoning and reversed the *Plessy* decision. Meanwhile, total segregation was imposed throughout the South. Separate schools, prisons, hospitals, recreational facilities, and even cemeteries were provided for blacks, and these were almost never equal to those available to whites.

Most Northerners supported the government and the Court. Newspapers presented a stereotyped, derogatory picture of blacks, no matter what the circumstances. Northern magazines, even high-quality publications such as *Harper's*, *Scribner's*, and the *Century*, repeatedly made blacks the butt of crude jokes.

The restoration of white rule abruptly halted the progress in public education for blacks that the Reconstruction governments had made. Church groups and private foundations such as the Peabody Fund and the Slater Fund, financed chiefly by northern philanthropists, supported black schools after 1877. Among them were two important experiments in vocational training, Hampton Institute and Tuskegee Institute.

These schools had to overcome considerable resistance and suspicion in the white community; they survived only because they taught a docile philosophy, preparing students to accept second-class citizenship and become farmers and craftsmen. Since proficiency in academic subjects might have given the lie to the southern belief that blacks were intellectually inferior to whites, such subjects were avoided.

The southern insistence on segregating the public schools, buttressed by the separate but equal decision of the Supreme Court in *Plessy v. Ferguson*, imposed a crushing financial burden on poor, sparsely settled communities, and the dominant opinion that blacks were not really educable did not encourage these communities to make special efforts in their behalf.

View the Image *Plessy v. Ferguson*, 1896 at **www.myhistorylab.com**

Booker T. Washington: A "Reasonable" Champion for African Americans

Since nearly all contemporary biologists, physicians, and other supposed experts on race were convinced that African Americans were inferior, white Americans generally accepted black inferiority as fact. Most did not especially wish blacks ill; they simply consigned them complacently to oblivion, along with the Indians. A vicious circle was established. By denying blacks decent educational opportunities and good jobs, the dominant race could use the blacks' resultant ignorance and poverty to justify the inferior facilities offered them.

Southern blacks reacted to this deplorable situation in a variety of ways. Some sought redress in racial pride and what would later be called black nationalism. Some became so disaffected that they tried to revive the African colonization movement. "Africa is our home," insisted Bishop Henry M. Turner, a huge, plainspoken man who had served as an army chaplain during the war and as a member of the Georgia legislature during Reconstruction. Another militant, T. Thomas Fortune, editor of the New York *Age* and founder of the Afro-American League (1887), called on blacks to demand full civil rights, better schools, and fair wages and to fight against discrimination of every sort. "Let us stand up like men in our own organization," he urged. "If others use . . . violence to combat our peaceful arguments, it is not for us to run away from violence."

For a time, militancy and black separatism won few adherents among southern blacks. For one thing, life was better than it had been under slavery. Segregation actually helped southern blacks who became barbers, undertakers, restaurateurs, and shopkeepers because whites were reluctant to supply such services to blacks. Even when whites competed with black businesses, the resentment caused by segregation led blacks to patronize establishments run by people of their own race. According to the most conservative estimates, the living standard of the average southern black more than doubled between 1865 and 1900. But this only made many southern whites more angry and vindictive.

This helps explain the tactics of Booker T. Washington, one of the most extraordinary Americans of that generation. Washington had been born a slave in Virginia in 1856. Laboriously he obtained an education, supporting himself while a student by working as a janitor. In 1881, with the financial help of northern philanthropists, he founded Tuskegee Institute in Alabama. His experiences convinced Washington that blacks must lift themselves up by their own bootstraps but that they must also accommodate themselves to white prejudices. A persuasive speaker and a brilliant fundraiser, he soon developed a national reputation as a "reasonable" champion of his race. (In 1891 Harvard awarded him an honorary degree.)

In 1895 Washington made a now-famous speech to a mixed audience at the Cotton States International Exposition in Atlanta. To the blacks he said, "Cast

Booker T. Washington in his office at Tuskegee Institute, 1900. Washington chose a policy of accommodation. Washington did not urge blacks to accept inferiority and racial slurs but to ignore them. His own behavior was indeed subtle, even devious. In public he minimized the importance of civil and political rights. Behind the scenes he lobbied against restrictive measures, marshaled large sums of money to fight test cases in the courts, and worked hard in northern states to organize the black vote and make sure that black political leaders got a share of the spoils of office.

down your bucket where you are," by which he meant stop fighting segregation and second-class citizenship and concentrate on learning useful skills "Dignify and glorify common labor," he urged. "Agitation of questions of racial equality is the extremest folly." Progress up the social and economic ladder would come not from "artificial forcing" but from self-improvement. "There is as much dignity in tilling a field as in writing a poem."

Washington asked the whites of what he called "our beloved South" to lend the blacks a hand in their efforts to advance themselves. If you will do so, he promised, you will be "surrounded by the most patient, faithful, law-abiding, and unresentful people that the world has seen."

This **Atlanta Compromise** delighted white Southerners and won Washington financial support in every section of the country. He became one of the most powerful men in the United States, consulted by presidents, in close touch with business and philanthropic leaders, and capable of influencing in countless unobtrusive ways the fate of millions of blacks.

Blacks responded to the compromise with mixed feelings. Accepting Washington's approach might relieve them of many burdens and dangers. Being obsequious might, like discretion, be the better part of valor. But Washington was asking them to give up specific rights in return for vague promises of future help. The cost was high in surrendered personal dignity and lost hopes of obtaining real justice.

Washington's career illustrates the terrible dilemma that American blacks have always faced: the choice between confrontation and accommodation. This choice was particularly difficult in the late nineteenth century.

City Bosses

Outside of the South, the main issue concerned municipal government. This was complicated by the religious and ethnic character of the city dwellers and by the special problems of late-nineteenth-century urban life: rapid, helter-skelter growth; the influx of European immigrants; the need to develop costly transportation, sanitation, and other public utility systems; and the crime and corruption that the size, confusion, and anonymity incidental to urban existence fostered.

The immigrants who flocked into American cities in the 1880s and early 1890s were largely of peasant stock, and having come from societies unacquainted with democracy, they had no experience with representative government. The tendency of urban workers to move frequently in search of better jobs further lessened the likelihood that they would develop political influence independently.

Furthermore, the difficulties of life in the slums bewildered and often overwhelmed newcomers, both native- and foreign-born. Hopeful, but passive and naive, they could hardly be expected to take a broad view of social problems when so beset by personal ones. This enabled shrewd urban politicians—most of them in this period of Irish origin, since the Irish being the first-comers among the migrants and, according to mobility studies, more likely to stay put—to take command of the city masses and march them in obedient phalanxes to the polls.

Most city machines were loose-knit neighborhood organizations headed by ward bosses, not tightly geared hierarchical bureaucracies ruled by a single leader. "Big Tim" Sullivan of New York's Lower East Side and "Hinky Dink" Kenna of Chicago were typical of the breed. Sullivan, Kenna, and others like them performed many useful services for people they liked to think of as their constituents. They found jobs for new arrivals and distributed food and other help to all in bad times. Anyone in trouble with the law could obtain at least a hearing from the ward boss, and often, if the crime was minor or due to ignorance, the difficulty was quietly "fixed" and the culprit was sent off with a word of caution. Sullivan provided turkey dinners for 5,000 or more homeless people each Christmas, distributed new shoes to the poor children of his district on his birthday, and arranged summer boat rides and picnics for young and old alike. At any time of year the victim of some sudden disaster could turn to the local clubhouse for help. Informally, probably without consciously intending to do so, the bosses educated the immigrants in the complexities of American civilization, helping them to leap the gulf between the almost medieval society of their origins and the modern industrial world.

The price of such aid—the bosses were not altruists—was unquestioning political support, which the bosses converted into cash. In New York, Sullivan levied tribute on gambling, had a hand in the liquor business, and controlled the issuance of peddlers' licenses. When he died in 1913, he was reputedly worth $1 million. Yet he and others like him were immensely popular; 25,000 grieving constituents followed Big Tim's coffin on its way to the grave.

The more visible and better-known city bosses played even less socially justifiable roles than the ward bosses. Their principal technique for extracting money from the public till was the kickback. To get city contracts, suppliers were made to pad their bills and, when paid for their work with funds from the city treasury, turn over the excess to the politicians. Similarly, operators of streetcar lines, gas and electricity companies, and other public utilities were compelled to pay huge bribes to obtain favorable franchises.

The most notorious of the nineteenth-century city bosses was William Marcy Tweed, whose "Tweed Ring" extracted tens of millions of dollars from New York City during the brief period of 1869–1871. Tweed was swiftly jailed. More typical was Richard Croker, who ruled New York's Tammany Hall organization from the mid-1880s to the end of the century. Croker held a number of local offices, but his power rested on his position as chairman of the Tammany Hall finance committee. Although more concerned than Tweed with the social and economic services that machines provided, Croker was primarily a corrupt political manipulator; he accumulated a large fortune and owned a mansion and a stable of racehorses, one of which was good enough to win the English Derby.

Despite their welfare work and their popularity, most bosses were essentially thieves. Efforts to romanticize them as the Robin Hoods of industrial society grossly distort the facts. However, the system developed and survived because too many middle-class city dwellers were indifferent to the fate of the poor. Except during occasional reform waves, few tried to check the rapaciousness of the politicos.

Many substantial citizens shared at least indirectly in the corruption. The owners of tenements were interested in crowding as many rent payers as possible into their buildings. Utility companies seeking franchises preferred a system that enabled them to buy favors. Honest citizens who had no selfish stake in the system and who were repelled by the sordidness of city government were seldom sufficiently concerned to do anything about it. When young Theodore Roosevelt decided to seek a political career in 1880, his New York socialite friends laughed in his face. They told him, Roosevelt wrote in his autobiography, "that politics were 'low'; that the organizations were not controlled by 'gentlemen'; that I would find them run by saloonkeepers, horse-car conductors, and the like."

Many so-called urban reformers resented the boss system mainly because it gave political power to people who were not "gentlemen" or, as one reformer put it, to a "proletarian mob" of "illiterate peasants, freshly raked from Irish bogs, or Bohemian mines, or Italian robber nests." A British visitor in Chicago struck at the root of the urban problem of the era. "Everybody is fighting to be rich," he said, "and nobody can attend to making the city fit to live in."

Crops and Complaints

The vacuity of American politics may well have stemmed from the complacency of the middle-class majority. The country was growing; no foreign enemy threatened it; the poor were mostly recent immigrants, blacks, and others with little influence, who were easily ignored by those in comfortable circumstances. However, one important group in society suffered increasingly as the years rolled by: the farmers. Out of their travail came the force that finally, in the 1890s, brought American politics face to face with the problems of the age.

After the Civil War, however, farmers did well. Harvests were bountiful and wheat prices high at over a dollar a bushel in the early 1870s. Well into the 1880s farmers on the plains experienced boom conditions. In that decade the population of Kansas increased by 43 percent, that of Nebraska by 134 percent, and that of the Dakotas by 278 percent. Land prices rose and farmers borrowed money to expand their farms.

A farm family in Custer, Nebraska, in 1888, a region where Populist sentiment was strong.

In the 1890s disaster struck. First came a succession of dry years and poor harvests. Then farmers in Australia, Canada, Russia, and Argentina took advantage of improvements in transportation to sell their produce in European markets that had relied on American foodstuffs. The price of wheat fell to about sixty cents a bushel. Cotton, the great southern staple, which sold for more than thirty cents a pound in 1866 and fifteen cents in the early 1870s, at times in the 1890s fell below six cents.

The tariff on manufactured goods appeared to aggravate the farmers' predicament, and so did the domestic marketing system, which enabled a multitude of middlemen to gobble up a large share of the profits of agriculture. The shortage of credit, particularly in the South, was an additional burden.

The downward swing of the business cycle in the early 1890s completed the devastation. Settlers who had paid more for their lands than they were worth and borrowed money at high interest rates to do so found themselves squeezed relentlessly. Thousands lost their farms and returned eastward, penniless and dispirited. The population of Nebraska increased by fewer than 4,000 persons in the entire decade of the 1890s.

The Populist Movement

The agricultural depression triggered a new outburst of farm radicalism, the Alliance movement. Alliances were organizations of farmers' clubs, most of which had sprung up during the bad times of the late 1870s. The first Knights of Reliance group was founded in 1877 in Lampasas County, Texas. As the Farmers' Alliance, this organization gradually expanded in northeastern Texas, and after 1885 it spread rapidly throughout the cotton states. Alliance leaders stressed cooperation. Their co-ops bought fertilizer and other supplies in bulk and sold them at fair prices to members. They sought to market their crops cooperatively but could not raise the necessary capital from banks, with the result that some of them began to question the workings of the American financial and monetary system. They became economic and social radicals in the process. A similar though less influential Alliance movement developed in the North.

Although the state alliances of the Dakotas and Kansas joined the Southern Alliance in 1889, for a time local prejudices and conflicting interests prevented the formation of a single national organization. But the farm groups emerged as a potent force in the 1890 elections.

In the South, Alliance-sponsored gubernatorial candidates won in Georgia, Tennessee, South Carolina, and Texas; eight southern legislatures fell under Alliance control, and forty-four representatives and three senators committed to Alliance objectives were sent to Washington. In the West, Alliance candidates

In Kansas in 1893 a Populist governor and a Populist-controlled Senate invalidated the election of some Republicans in the Kansas House of Representatives, giving the Populists control of that body, too. The displaced Republicans, denied seats, smashed their way into the capitol building with this sledgehammer and ousted the Populists, who decided to meet in a separate building. Each proclaimed itself to be the true legislature and passed its own laws. Eventually the Kansas Supreme Court decided in favor of the Republican legislature and disbanded the Populist gathering. Source: Kansas State Historical Society.

swept Kansas, captured a majority in the Nebraska legislature, and accumulated enough seats in Minnesota and South Dakota to hold the balance of power between the major parties.

Such success, coupled with the reluctance of the Republicans and Democrats to make concessions to their demands, encouraged Alliance leaders to create a new national party. By uniting southern and western farmers, they succeeded in breaking the sectional barrier erected by the Civil War. If they could recruit industrial workers, perhaps a real political revolution could be accomplished. In February 1892, farm leaders, representatives of the Knights of Labor, and various professional reformers, some 800 in all, met at St. Louis. They organized the **People's (Populist) party**, and issued a call for a national convention to meet at Omaha in July.

Mary Elizabeth Lease was a prominent Populist, noted for her rallying cry to "raise less corn and more hell."
Source: Kansas State Historical Society.

That convention nominated General James B. Weaver of Iowa for president (with a one-legged Confederate veteran as his running mate) and drafted a platform that called for a graduated income tax and national ownership of railroads, the telegraph, and telephone systems. It also advocated a "subtreasury" plan that would permit farmers to keep nonperishable crops off the market when prices were low. Under this proposal the government would make loans in the form of greenbacks to farmers, secured by crops held in storage in federal warehouses. When prices rose, the farmers could sell their crops and repay the loans. To combat deflation further, the platform demanded the unlimited coinage of silver and an increase in the money supply "to no less than $50 per capita."

To make the government more responsive to public opinion, the Populists urged the adoption of the initiative and referendum procedures and the election of U.S. senators by popular vote. To win the support of industrial workers, their platform denounced the use of Pinkerton detectives in labor disputes and backed the eight-hour day and the restriction of "undesirable" immigration.

The Populists saw themselves not as a persecuted minority but as a victimized majority betrayed by what would a century later be called the establishment. They were at most ambivalent about the free enterprise system, and they tended to attribute social and economic injustices not to built-in inequities in the system but to nefarious conspiracies organized by selfish interests in order to subvert the system.

The appearance of the new party was the most exciting and significant aspect of the presidential campaign of 1892, which saw Harrison and Cleveland refighting the election of 1888. The Populists put forth a host of colorful spellbinders: Tom Watson, a Georgia congressman whose temper was such that on one occasion he administered a beating to a local planter with the man's own riding crop; William A. Peffer, a senator from Kansas whose long beard and grave demeanor gave him the look of a Hebrew prophet; "Sockless Jerry" Simpson of Kansas, unlettered but full of grassroots shrewdness and wit, a former Greenbacker, and an admirer of the single tax doctrine of Henry George; and Ignatius Donnelly, the "Minnesota Sage," who claimed to be an authority on science, economics, and Shakespeare. (He believed that Francis Bacon wrote the plays.)

In the one-party South, Populist strategists sought to wean black farmers away from the ruling Democratic organization. Southern black farmers had their own Colored Farmers' Alliance, and even before 1892 their leaders had worked closely with the white alliances. Nearly 100 black delegates had attended the Populist convention at St. Louis. Of course, the blacks would be useless to the party if they could not vote; therefore, white Populist leaders opposed the southern trend toward disfranchising African Americans and called for full civil rights for all.

The results proved disappointing. Tom Watson lost his seat in Congress, and Donnelly ran a poor third in the Minnesota gubernatorial race. The Populists did sweep Kansas. They elected numbers of local officials in other western states and cast over a million votes for General Weaver. But the effort to unite white and black farmers in the South failed miserably. Conservative Democrats, while continuing with considerable success to attract black voters, played on racial fears cruelly, insisting that the Populists sought to undermine white supremacy. Since most white Populists saw the alliance with blacks as at best a marriage of convenience, this argument had a deadly effect. Elsewhere, even in the old centers of the Granger movement, the party made no significant impression. Urban workers remained aloof.

By standing firmly for conservative financial policies, Cleveland attracted considerable Republican support and won a solid victory over Harrison in the electoral college, 277 to 145. Weaver received twenty-two electoral votes.

•••—**Read** the **Document** *Mary Elizabeth Lease, the Populist Crusader* at **www.myhistorylab.com**

•••—**Read** the **Document** *The People's Party Platform* at **www.myhistorylab.com**

Showdown on Silver

One conclusion that politicians reached after analyzing the 1892 election was that the money question, particularly the controversy over the coinage of silver, was of paramount interest to the voters. Despite the wide-ranging appeal of the Populist platform, most of Weaver's strength came from the silver-mining states.

In truth, the issue of gold versus silver was superficial; the important question was what, if anything, should be done to check the deflationary spiral. The declining price level benefited people with fixed incomes and injured most others. Industrial workers profited from deflation except when depression caused unemployment.

By the early 1890s, discussion of federal monetary policy revolved around the coinage of silver. Traditionally, the United States had been on a bimetallic standard. Both gold and silver were coined, the number of grains of each in the dollar being adjusted periodically to reflect the commercial value of the two metals. The discovery of numerous gold mines in California in the 1840s and 1850s depressed the price of gold relative to silver. By 1861, a silver dollar could be melted down and sold for $1.03. No miner took silver to the mint to be stamped into coin. In a short time, silver dollars were withdrawn and only gold dollars circulated. However, an avalanche of silver from the mines of Nevada and Colorado gradually depressed the price until, around 1874, it again became profitable for miners to coin their bullion. Alas, when they tried to do so, they discovered that the Coinage Act of 1873, taking account of the fact that no silver had been presented to the mint in years, had demonetized the metal.

Silver miners denounced this as the "Crime of '73." Inflationists joined them in demanding a return to bimetallism. They knew that if more dollars were put into circulation, the value of each dollar would decline; that is, prices and wages would rise. Conservatives, still fighting the battle against inflationary greenback paper money, resisted strongly. The result was a series of compromises. In

L. Frank Baum, author of *The Wonderful Wizard of Oz* (1900) and a fan of William Jennings Bryan, perhaps wrote his story as an allegory of the 1896 election. Dorothy, wearing "silver" slippers (in the original), follows a "yellow brick road" (gold) on a crusade to free the Munchkins (the oppressed little people) from the Wicked Witch of the East (the rapacious corporations and financiers). Liberation is to come in Emerald City (greenbacks) through the intervention of a kindly, but ultimately ineffective wizard (Bryan). Only the entire people—Dorothy and entourage—can prevail against wickedness. Judy Garland starred as Dorothy in the film version of *The Wizard of Oz* (1939).
Source: *The Wizard of Oz* ©1939 The Kobal Collection/ MGM. Warner Brothers Motion Picture Titles.

1878 the **Bland-Allison Silver Purchase Act** authorized the buying of between $2 million and $4 million of silver a month at the market price, but this had little inflationary effect because the government consistently purchased the minimum amount. The commercial price of silver continued to fall. In 1890 the **Sherman Silver Purchase Act** required the government to buy 4.5 million *ounces* of silver monthly, but in the face of increasing supplies the price of silver fell still further. By 1894, a silver coin weighed thirty-two times more than a gold one.

The compromise satisfied no one. Silver miners grumbled because their bullion brought in only half what it had in the early 1870s. Debtors noted angrily that because of the general decline in prices, the dollars they used to meet their obligations were worth more than twice as much as in 1865. Advocates of the gold standard feared that unlimited silver coinage would be authorized, "destroying the value of the dollar."

The Depression of 1893

Both the silverites and "gold bugs" warned of economic disaster if their policies were not followed. Then, in 1893, after the London banking house of Baring Brothers collapsed, a financial panic precipitated a worldwide industrial depression. In the United States hundreds of cotton mills and iron foundries closed, never to reopen. During the harsh winter of 1893–1894, millions were without jobs. Discontented industrial workers added their voices to the complaints of the midwestern farmers.

President Cleveland believed that the controversy over silver had caused the depression by shaking the confidence of the business community and that all would be well if the country returned to a single gold standard. He summoned a special session of Congress, and by exerting immense political pressure he obtained the repeal of the Sherman Silver Purchase Act in October 1893. All that this accomplished was to split the Democratic party, its southern and western wings deserting him almost to a man.

During 1894 and 1895, while the nation floundered in the worst depression it had ever experienced, a series of events further undermined public confidence. In the spring of 1894 several "armies" of the unemployed, the most imposing led by Jacob S. Coxey, an eccentric Ohio businessman, marched on Washington to demand relief. Coxey wanted the government to undertake a program of federal public works and other projects to hire unemployed workers to build roads.

When Coxey's group of demonstrators, perhaps 500 in all, reached Washington, he and two other leaders were arrested for trespassing on the grounds of the Capitol. Their followers were dispersed by club-wielding policemen. This callous treatment convinced many Americans that the government had little interest in the suffering of the people, an opinion strengthened when Cleveland, in July 1894, used federal troops to crush the Pullman strike.

The next year the Supreme Court handed down several reactionary decisions. In *United States v. E. C. Knight Company* it refused to employ the Sherman Antitrust Act to break up the Sugar Trust. The Court also denied a writ of habeas corpus to Eugene V. Debs of the American Railway Union, who was languishing in prison for disobeying a federal injunction during the Pullman strike.

On top of these indications of official conservatism came a desperate financial crisis. Throughout 1894 the Treasury's supply of gold dwindled as worried citizens exchanged greenbacks (now convertible into gold) for hard money and foreign investors cashed in large amounts of American securities. The government tried to sell bonds for gold

Table 20.1   The Supreme Court Supports Racial Segregation and Corporate Power

Civil Rights Cases	1883	Overturned Civil Rights Act of 1875	Limited Fourteenth Amendment to protecting blacks from deprivation of rights by *states*; allowed individuals to do so
Plessy v. Ferguson	1896	Upheld principle of "separate but equal" in public accommodations	Allowed southern states and municipalities to pass laws enforcing separation of whites and blacks
U.S. v. E. C. Knight Co.	1895	Refused to break up the Sugar Trust for being a monopoly	Rendered the Sherman Antitrust Act of 1890 nearly meaningless
In Re Debs	1895	Refused to free Eugene V. Debs, president of the American Railway Union who had been jailed for leading a strike	Enabled the government to use injunctions to stop strikes, thereby depriving union leaders of the chance to plead their case in court

to bolster the reserve, but the gold reserve continued to melt away. Early in 1895 it touched a low point of $41 million.

At this juncture a syndicate of bankers headed by J. P. Morgan turned the tide by underwriting a $62 million bond issue, guaranteeing that half the gold would come from Europe. This caused a great public outcry; the spectacle of the nation being saved from bankruptcy by a private banker infuriated millions.

As the presidential election of 1896 approached, with the Populists demanding unlimited coinage of silver, the major parties found it impossible to continue straddling the money question. The Populist vote had increased by 42 percent in the 1894 congressional elections. Southern and western Democratic leaders feared that they would lose their following unless Cleveland was repudiated. Western Republicans, led by Senator Henry M. Teller of Colorado, were threatening to bolt to the Populists unless their party came out for silver coinage. After a generation of political equivocation, the major parties had to face an important issue squarely.

The Republicans, meeting to choose a candidate at St. Louis in June 1896, announced for the gold standard. "We are unalterably opposed to every measure calculated to debase our currency or impair the credit of our country," the platform declared. "We are therefore opposed to the free coinage of silver. . . . The existing gold standard must be maintained." The party then nominated Ohio's William McKinley for president. McKinley, best known for his staunch advocacy of the protective tariff yet highly regarded by labor, was expected to run strongly in the Midwest and the East.

The Democratic convention met in July in Chicago. The pro-gold Cleveland element made a hard fight, but the silverites swept them aside. The high point came when a youthful Nebraskan named William Jennings Bryan spoke for silver against gold, for western farmers against the industrial East. Bryan's every sentence provoked ear-shattering applause:

> We have petitioned and our petitions have been scorned; we have entreated, and our entreaties have been disregarded; we have begged, and they have mocked when our calamity came. We beg no longer; we entreat no more; we petition no more. We defy them!

The crowd responded like a great choir to Bryan's oratorical cues. "Burn down your cities and leave our farms," he said, "and your cities will spring up again as if by magic; but destroy our farms and the grass will grow in the streets of every city in the country." He ended with a marvelous figure of speech that set the tone for the coming campaign. "You shall not press down upon the brow of labor this crown of thorns," he warned, bringing his hands down suggestively to his temples. "You shall not crucify mankind upon a cross of gold!" Dramatically, he extended his arms to the side, the very figure of the crucified Christ.

The convention promptly adopted a platform calling for "the free and unlimited coinage of both silver and gold at the present legal ratio of 16 to 1" and went on to nominate Bryan, who was barely thirty-six, for president.

This action put tremendous pressure on the Populists. If they supported the Democrat Bryan, they risked losing their party identity; if they nominated another candidate, they would ensure McKinley's election. In part because the delegates could not find a person of stature willing to become a candidate against Bryan, the Populist convention nominated him, seeking to preserve the party identity by substituting Watson for the Democratic vice-presidential nominee, Arthur Sewall of Maine.

●●●—**Read** the **Document**   William Jennings Bryan, *Cross of Gold* Speech at **www.myhistorylab.com**

The Election of 1896

Never did a presidential campaign raise such intense emotions. The Republicans from the silver-mining states swung solidly behind Bryan. But many solid-money Democrats, especially in the Northeast, refused to accept the decision of the Chicago convention. Cleveland professed to be "so dazed by the political situation that I am in no condition for speech or thought on the subject." Many others adopted the policy of Governor David B. Hill of New York, who said, "I am a Democrat still—very still." The extreme gold bugs, calling themselves National Democrats, nominated their own candidate, seventy-nine-year-old Senator John M. Palmer of Illinois. Palmer ran only to injure Bryan. "Fellow Democrats," he announced, "I will not consider it any great fault if you decide to cast your vote for William McKinley."

At the start the Republicans seemed to have everything in their favor. Bryan's youth and relative lack of political experience—two terms in the House—contrasted unfavorably with McKinley's distinguished war record, his long service in Congress and as governor of Ohio, and his reputation for honesty and good judgment. The severe depression operated in favor of the party out of power, although

Populism—Crusade of Cranks or Potent Grass-Roots Protest?

In February 2010 the National Tea Party held its first convention. Sarah Palin, Republican candidate for Vice President in 2008, delivered the keynote address. "This movement is about the people," she added, "and Washington has broken trust with the people." Palin's broad definition of "populism" evoked the grass-roots insurgency of farmers and industrial workers that culminated in the Populist party of the 1890s.

Back then, well-educated Americans generally dismissed the Populists as ill-informed and simple-minded, and this disdain persisted well into the twentieth century. But in 1931 historian John D. Hicks championed the Populists as far-sighted reformers who sought to protect small farmers from the excesses of rapacious railroad barons and eastern financiers. Although the Populist movement swiftly collapsed, Hicks insisted that its ideas showed "an amazing vitality."

But as Hitler seized power later in the 1930s by appealing to the prejudices of the German masses, American intellectuals returned to their skepticism toward grass-roots populism. Historian Richard Hofstadter charged the Populists with bigotry and derided their nostalgia for the past.

In 1976 Lawrence Goodwyn countered Hofstadter's criticisms. The Populists were not backward-looking cranks, but activists in a "cooperative crusade" whose main goal— weakening the monopoly power of the corporations—was sound. But Goodwyn's assertion raised another question: If the Populists were on the right track, why did their movement die out?

In 2006 Michael Kazin declared that Bryan had not failed. On the contrary, the Populist movement had laid the foundations of Franklin Roosevelt's New Deal. Central to Kazin's analysis was Bryan's mastery of an impassioned rhetorical style that appealed to the common person and mobilized the masses.

Palin's oratory and the Tea Party protests in some ways resemble Bryan's combative rhetoric style. But Palin's critics note that few common people could have afforded the $349 cost of a ticket to hear her speech in Nashville, which helped pay her $100,000 fee. Perhaps the most important point is that Palin's supporters and critics alike seek to lay claim to a "populist" label dating back to the 1880s and 1890s.

Source: John D. Hicks, *The Populist Revolt* (1931); Richard Hofstadter, *The Age of Reform* (1955); Lawrence Goodwyn, *Democratic Promise* (1976); Michael Kazin, *A Godly Hero: The Life of William Jennings Bryan* (2006).

Sarah Palin, latter-day proponent of populism at a Tea Party convention in Nashville (2010), sought to "go back to our roots as a God-fearing nation" that would "start seeking some divine intervention."

A William Jennings Bryan poster alludes to religion: "no crown of thorns" and "no cross of gold."

William Jennings Bryan's "Cross of Gold" speech inspired this cartoonist's caricature of it as "plagiarized from the Bible." Bryan's speech in favor of bimetallism was, in fact, studded with religious references. He described the unlimited coinage of silver and gold as a "holy cause" supported by those who built churches "where they praise their Creator."

by repudiating Cleveland the Democrats escaped much of the burden of explaining away his errors. The newspapers came out almost unanimously for the Republicans. The *New York Times* accused Bryan of being insane, his affliction being variously classified as "paranoia querulenta," "graphomania," and "oratorical monomania." The Democrats had very little money and few well-known speakers to fight the campaign.

But Bryan proved a formidable opponent. Casting aside tradition, he took to the stump personally, traveling 18,000 miles and making over 600 speeches. He was one of the greatest of orators. A big, handsome man with a voice capable of carrying without strain to the far corners of a great hall yet equally effective before a cluster of auditors at a rural crossroads, he projected an image of absolute sincerity without appearing fanatical or argumentative. At every major stop on his tour, huge crowds assembled. In Minnesota he packed the 10,000-seat St. Paul Auditorium, while thousands milled in the streets outside. His energy was amazing, and his charm and good humor were unfailing. At one whistle-stop, while he was shaving in his compartment, a small group outside the train began clamoring for a glimpse of him. Flinging open the window and beaming through the lather, he shook hands cheerfully with each of the admirers. Everywhere he hammered away at the money question. Yet he did not totally neglect other issues. He was defending, he said, "all the people who suffer from the operations of trusts, syndicates, and combines."

McKinley's campaign was managed by a new type of politician, Marcus Alonzo Hanna, an Ohio businessman. In a sense Hanna was a product of the Pendleton Civil Service Act. When deprived of the contributions of officeholders, the parties turned to business for funds, and Hanna was one of the first leaders with a foot in both camps. Politics fascinated him, and despite his wealth and wide interests, he was willing to labor endlessly at the routine work of political organization.

Hanna aspired to be a kingmaker and early fastened on McKinley, whose charm he found irresistible, as the vehicle for satisfying his ambition. He spent about $100,000 of his own money on the preconvention campaign. His attitude toward the candidate, one mutual friend observed, was "that of a big, bashful boy toward the girl he loves."

Before most Republicans realized how effective Bryan was on the stump, Hanna perceived the danger and sprang into action.

Certain that money was the key to political power, he raised an enormous campaign fund. When businessmen hesitated to contribute, he pried open their purses by a combination of persuasiveness and intimidation. Banks and insurance companies were "assessed" a percentage of their assets, big corporations a share of their receipts, until some $3.5 million had been collected.

Hanna disbursed these funds with efficiency and imagination. He sent 1,500 speakers into the doubtful districts and blanketed the land with 250 million pieces of campaign literature, printed in a dozen languages. "He has advertised McKinley as if he were a patent medicine," Theodore Roosevelt, never at a loss for words, exclaimed.

Incapable of competing with Bryan as a swayer of mass audiences, McKinley conducted a "front-porch campaign." This technique dated from the first Harrison-Cleveland election, when Harrison regularly delivered off-the-cuff speeches to groups of visitors representing special interests or regions in his hometown of Indianapolis. The system conserved the candidate's energies and enabled him to avoid the appearance of seeking the presidency too openly—which was still considered bad form—and at the same time allowed him to make headlines throughout the country.

Guided by the masterful Hanna, McKinley brought the front-porch method to perfection. Superficially the proceedings were delightfully informal. From every corner of the land, groups representing various regions, occupations, and interests descended on McKinley's unpretentious frame house in Canton, Ohio. Gathering on the lawn—the grass was soon reduced to mud, the fence stripped of pickets by souvenir hunters—the visitors paid their compliments to the candidate and heard him deliver a brief speech, while beside him on the porch his aged mother and adoring invalid wife listened with rapt attention. Then there was a small reception, during which the delegates were given an opportunity to shake their host's hand.

Despite the air of informality, these performances were carefully staged. The delegations arrived on a tightly coordinated schedule worked out by McKinley's staff and the railroads, which operated cut-rate excursion trains to Canton from all over the nation. McKinley was fully briefed on the special interests and attitudes of each group, and the speeches of delegation leaders were submitted in advance. Often his secretary amended these remarks, and on occasion McKinley wrote the visitors' speeches himself. His own talks were carefully prepared, each calculated to make a particular point. All were reported fully in the newspapers. Thus without moving from his doorstep, McKinley met thousands of people from every section of the country.

These tactics worked admirably. On election day McKinley collected 271 electoral votes to Bryan's 176, the popular vote being 7,036,000 to 6,468,000.

⚙️ **View the Image** *McKinley and Hobart Campaign Poster* at
www.myhistorylab.com

The Meaning of the Election

During the campaign, some frightened Republicans had laid plans for fleeing the country if Bryan were elected, and belligerent ones, such as Theodore Roosevelt, then police commissioner of New York City, readied themselves to meet the "social revolutionaries" on the battlefield. Victory sent such people into transports of joy. Most conservatives concluded that the way of life they so fervently admired had been saved for all time.

However heartfelt, such sentiments were not founded on fact. With workers standing beside capitalists and with the farm vote split, it cannot be said that the election divided the nation class against class or that McKinley's victory saved the country from revolution.

Far from representing a triumph for the status quo, the election marked the coming of age of modern America. The battle between gold and silver, which everyone had considered so vital, had little real significance. The inflationists seemed to have been beaten, but new discoveries of gold in Alaska and South Africa and improved methods of extracting gold from low-grade ores soon led to a great expansion of the money supply. In any case, within two decades the system of basing the volume of currency on bullion had been abandoned. Bryan and the "political" Populists who supported him, supposedly the advance agents of revolution, were oriented more toward the past than the future; their ideal was the rural America of Jefferson and Jackson.

McKinley, for all his innate conservatism, was capable of looking ahead toward the new century. His approach was national where Bryan's was basically parochial. Though never daring and seldom imaginative, McKinley was able to deal pragmatically with current problems. Before long, as the United States became increasingly an exporter of manufactures, he would even modify his position on the tariff. And no one better reflected the spirit of the age than Mark Hanna, the outstanding political realist of his generation. Far from preventing change, the outcome of the election of 1896 made possible still greater changes as the United States moved into the twentieth century.

Campaign buttons for McKinley and Bryan in 1896. Bryan sought to expand the money supply through the coinage of silver dollars; McKinley sought to remain with the gold standard.

Agrarian Discontent and the Populist Challenge

Falling Prices and Farm Tenancy

After 1870 the falling price of wheat and cotton (see the graph, below) spelled disaster to farmers who were obliged to make fixed payments on their mortgages. Beleaguered farmers joined the Farmers' Alliance and similar organizations to pool resources and negotiate better deals with railroads, banks, and grain merchants. Nevertheless, many farmers fell behind in their mortgage payments; millions became bankrupt and lost their farms, obliging them to work as sharecroppers, tenant farmers, or hired hands in the fields.

To avert bankruptcy, farmers increasingly formed political groups whose chief goal was to drive up farm prices. Many blamed falling prices on the federal government's return to hard money after the Civil War. Not enough gold had been minted into dollars during the subsequent decades of economic expansion. As more goods were produced with a constant or slowly-rising supply of gold dollars, prices fell. Thus the farmers lobbied for an infusion of new currency—greenbacks as well as silver dollars—to raise prices. "We meet in the midst of a nation brought to the verge of moral, political and material ruin," declared the People's party in 1892. The nation must abandon the "gold standard."

The Rise of Populism in Texas

That Populism was fueled by agrarian discontent is reflected in the accompanying map of Texas in the 1890s. In Texas, the birthplace of the Knights of Reliance (Lampasas County) and the Southern Alliance, Populists made the most gains in the marginal cotton-growing counties, the drier counties near the western edge of the cotton-cultivating frontier, and the pine woods of east Texas. Conversely, the more prosperous farming lands of the Black and Grand prairies rarely voted Populist. Populism appealed most to marginal farmers.

Bryan versus McKinley in 1896

The depression of 1893, which lasted much of the decade, altered the geography of American politics. President Cleveland's defense of the gold standard fractured the Democrats. In the congressional election of 1894, Republicans seized control of both houses of Congress and

Sharecroping and Tenancy, 1880–1900 Sharecropping and farm tenancy, which had prevailed in the South since the Civil War, spread to other parts of the nation after 1880.

increased their delegation in the House by 100 votes. This defeat prompted Democrats from the West and South to reach out to the Populists in 1896; the Democratic party then adopted a platform that endorsed the free coinage of silver, and nominated William Jennings Bryan, a proponent of silver currency, for president.

The Republicans nominated William McKinley, whose endorsement of the gold standard, though ambiguously worded, ensured that the election of 1896 would be the most sharply defined since the Civil War.

On election day, Bryan won in the South, the Plains states, and the Rocky Mountain region. But McKinley carried the East;

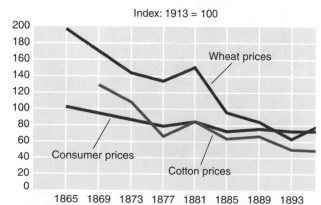

Wheat and Cotton Prices and Consumer Price Indexes, 1865–1896 Farm prices fell by about 50 percent after the Civil War; the Consumer Price Index declined, too, though less precipitously.

the Midwest, including even Iowa, Minnesota, and North Dakota; and the Pacific Coast states of Oregon and California.

The sharp sectional division marked the failure of the Populist effort to unite northern and southern farmers and also the triumph of the industrial part of the country over the agricultural. Business and financial interests voted solidly for the Republicans, fearing that a Bryan victory would bring economic chaos. When one Nebraska landowner tried to float a mortgage during the campaign, a loan company official wrote to him: "If McKinley is elected, we think we will be in the market, but we do not care to make any investments while there is an uncertainty as to what kind of money a person will be paid back in."

Other social and economic interests were far from being united. Many thousands of farmers voted for McKinley, as his success in states such as North Dakota, Iowa, and Minnesota proved. In the farm areas north of the Ohio and east of the Missouri Rivers, the agricultural depression was not severe, and farm radicalism was almost nonexistent.

A preponderance of the labor vote also went to the Republicans. In part this resulted from the tremendous pressures that many industrialists applied to their workers. "Men," one manufacturer announced, "vote as you please, but if Bryan is elected the whistle will not blow Wednesday morning." Some companies placed orders for materials subject to cancellation if the Democrats won. Yet coercion was not a major factor, for McKinley was highly regarded in labor circles. While governor of Ohio, he had advocated the arbitration of industrial disputes and backed a law fining employers who refused to permit workers to join unions. He had invariably based his advocacy of high tariffs on the argument that American wage levels would be depressed if foreign goods could enter the country untaxed. The Republicans carried nearly all the large cities, and in closely contested states such as Illinois and Ohio this made the difference between victory and defeat.

Questions for Discussion

■ What is the relationship between falling prices and sharecropping and farm tenancy? How do the maps of Populism in Texas and the election of 1896 confirm a correlation between agrarian discontents and Populist support?

Populism in Texas, 1892–1898 Populism was strongest in the cotton-farming region of Texas—east of the red-colored line. But the Populists carried few of the counties in the fertile Grande and Black prairies. The poorer cotton-farming counties, such as Lampasas (birthplace of the Knights of Reliance in 1877), were more likely to elect Populist candidates.

Bryan vs. McKinley, 1896 Democrat/Populist Bryan carried much of the South and West, and most of the farming regions of the plains. But he failed to win over enough industrial workers to take states in the North.

■ In the 1896 election, where were Bryan's strongest sources of support? McKinley's? What parts of Texas did Bryan carry?

Chapter Review

Milestones

1872	Ulysses Grant is reelected president
1873	Congress suspends the coining of silver ("Crime of '73")
1876	Rutherford B. Hayes is elected president
1877	Farmers' Alliance movement is founded
1878	Bland-Allison Act authorizes government silver purchases
1879	Specie payments resume
1880	James Garfield is elected president
1881	Garfield is assassinated; Grover Cleveland becomes president
1881	Booker T. Washington founds Tuskegee Institute for blacks
1883	Pendleton Act creates Civil Service Commission
	Supreme Court Overturns Civil Rights Act of 1875 in the civil rights cases
1884	Republicans support Democrats during Mugwump Movement
	Grover Cleveland is elected president
1887	Interstate Commerce Act regulates railroad rates
	Cleveland delivers tariff message
1888	Benjamin Harrison is elected president
	Englishman James Bryce analyzes American politics in *The American Commonwealth*

1890	Sherman Silver Purchase Act requires government silver purchase
1890–1900	Blacks are deprived of the vote in the South
1892	People's (Populist) party is founded
	Cleveland is elected president a second time
1893	Sherman Silver Purchase Act is repealed
1893	Panic of 1893 causes industrial depression
1894	Coxey's Army marches to Washington to demand relief
1895	Supreme Court declares federal income tax unconstitutional (*Pollock v. Farmers' Loan and Trust Company*)
	Booker T. Washington urges self-improvement in Atlanta Compromise Speech
	J. P. Morgan raises $62 million in gold for the U.S. Treasury
1896	William Jennings Bryan delivers "Cross of Gold" speech
	William McKinley is elected president
	Supreme Court upholds "separate but equal" in *Plessy v. Ferguson*

Key Terms

Atlanta Compromise   A social policy, propounded by black leader Booker T. Washington in 1895, advocating that blacks concentrate on learning useful skills rather than agitate over segregation, disfranchisement, and discrimination. In Washington's view, black self-help and self-improvement was the surest way to economic advancement, *539*

Bland-Allison Silver Purchase Act   An 1878 compromise law that that provided for the limited coinage of silver, *545*

civil rights cases   A group of cases in 1883 in which the U.S. Supreme Court declared unconstitutional the Civil Rights Act of 1875, which had prohibited racial discrimination in hotels, theaters, and other privately owned facilities. The Court ruled that the **Fourteenth Amendment** barred state governments from discriminating on the basis of race but did not prevent private individuals, businesses, or organizations from doing so, *537*

mugwumps   A group of eastern Republicans, disgusted with corruption in the party, who campaigned for the Democrats in the 1884 elections. These anticorruption reformers were conservative on the money question and government regulation, *536*

Pendleton Act   An 1883 law bringing civil service reform to federal employment; it classified many government jobs and required competitive exams for these positions, *535*

People's (Populist) party   The People's party of America was an important "third party," founded in 1891, that sought to unite various disaffected groups, especially farmers. The party nominated James B. Weaver for president in 1892 and in 1896 joined with the Democratic party in support of William Jennings Bryan for president, *542*

Plessy v. Ferguson   Supreme Court ruling (1896) that held that racial segregation of public accommodations did not infringe on the "equal protection" clause of the Constitution; this "separate but equal" doctrine was overturned by *Brown v. Board of Education* in 1954, *537*

Sherman Silver Purchase Act   An 1890 law that obliged the federal government to buy and coin silver, thereby counteracting the deflationary tendencies of the economy at the time; its repeal in 1894, following the Depression of 1893, caused a political uproar, *545*

Review Questions

1. The introduction to this chapter suggests that Americans from 1877 to 1896 were as enthralled with politics as Americans are today with *American Idol*. And yet the chapter contends that the major parties took similar positions on the major issues. What explains the high voter turnouts of the era?
2. How did the urban bosses respond to the challenges confronting the cities?
3. How did the decisions of the Supreme Court aggravate race relations and give rise to political protest? What strategies did African American leaders consider in response to increased segregation?
4. Why did such a seemingly dull issue as currency reform generate such passion, culminating in William Jennings Bryan's crusade against "a cross of gold" in 1896? Why did the Populists fail to win the support of northern labor, and thus the election?
5. How has populism fared among historians? How is populism regarded by politicians today? Why?

PEARSON myhistorylab Connections

Reinforce what you learned in this chapter by studying the many documents, images, maps, review tools, and videos available at **www.myhistorylab.com**.

Read and Review

✓•—[Study and Review *Chapter 20*

•••—[Read the Document *Pendleton Civil Service Act,* p. 537

•••—[View the Image *Harrison and Morton Campaign Ad,* p. 537

•••—[View the Image *Plessy v. Ferguson, 1896,* p. 538

•••—[Read the Document *The People's Party Platform,* p. 543

•••—[View the Image *McKinley and Hobart Campaign Poster,* p. 549

Research and Explore

•••—[Read the Document *Mary Elizabeth Lease, the Populist Crusader,* p. 543

•••—[Read the Document *William Jennings Bryan, Cross of Gold Speech,* p. 546

((•—[Hear the Audio

Hear the audio file for Chapter 20 at
www.myhistorylab.com.

Are college students apathetic?

Some think so. In 2007 *New York Times* columnist Thomas Friedman proposed that they be known as Generation Q—for Quiet. That generation, he reported, was "too quiet, too online, for its own good, and for the country's own good." Others chimed in with alternative monikers: the Logged-In Generation, the Net Generation, the Turned-Off Generation.

In 2010 Gabrielle Grow, a senior at the University of California at Davis, offered an explanation in the *Huffington Post*: "From those who deem us apathetic, we have not only inherited a country up to its neck in debt but a society and lifestyle in which we are constantly expected to outperform each other. . . [An] intense course load combined with little free time leaves little room for political inquiry or investigation."

Other students challenged Friedman's stereotype through civic engagement of the old-fashioned sort, by rolling up their sleeves and helping out. In a 2009 UCLA survey, two-thirds of college seniors reported that they "occasionally" or "frequently" performed volunteer

The Age of Reform

((•─[Hear the Audio **Chapter 21 at www.myhistorylab.com**

■ Like garbage being tossed from a window, this family, evicted from their apartment by police, appears to be in the process of decomposing. Painted by Everett Shinn when he was in his late twenties, *Eviction* (1904) was characteristic of the so-called Ashcan School of artists, many of whom sought to promote social awareness.
Source: Smithsonian American Art Museum, Washington, DC / Art Resource, NY.

work. Over three-fourths said that they voted in the 2008 presidential election. In 2009 AmeriCorps, a federally sponsored public-service plan, received twice as many applications from college graduates as the previous year. That same year, more than 168,000 college students worked for Habitat for Humanity, far more than a decade earlier.

Today's college-age volunteers in many ways resemble their counterparts during the "age of reform" a century ago. Then, large numbers of young adults worked to improve society in various ways. They investigated tenements, factories, schools, municipal governments,

and consumer goods. They joined political movements to fight city bosses and to restrain the excessive influence of corporations on state, local, and federal governments. They promoted legislation to protect children from exploitative employers and to secure voting rights for women. They advocated conservation of natural resources. They swelled the ranks of the Socialist party, the Progressive party, and of more radical movements. In response to this sea change among younger voters, the Republican and Democrat parties embraced some reforms that earlier generations had regarded as wild-eyed radicalism. ■

Roots of Progressivism

The progressives were never a single group seeking a single objective. The movement sprang from many sources. One was the fight against corruption and inefficiency in government, which began with the Liberal Republicans of the Grant era and was continued by the mugwumps of the 1880s. The struggle for civil service reform was only the first skirmish in this battle; the continuing power of corrupt political machines and the growing influence of large corporations and their lobbyists on municipal and state governments outraged thousands of citizens and led them to seek ways of purifying politics and making the machinery of government at all levels responsive to the majority rather than to special-interest groups.

Progressivism also had roots in the effort to regulate and control big business, which characterized the Granger and Populist agitation of the 1870s and 1890s. The failure of the Interstate Commerce Act to end railroad abuses and of the Sherman Antitrust Act to check the growth of large

corporations became increasingly apparent after 1900. The return of prosperity after the depression of the 1890s encouraged reformers by removing the inhibiting fear, so influential in the 1896 presidential campaign, that an assault on the industrial giants might lead to the collapse of the economy.

Between 1897 and 1904 the trend toward concentration in industry accelerated. Such new giants as Amalgamated Copper (1899), U.S. Steel (1901), and International Harvester (1902) attracted most of the attention, but even more alarming were the overall statistics. In a single year (1899) more than 1,200 firms were absorbed in mergers, the resulting combinations being capitalized at $2.2 billion. By 1904 there were 318 industrial combinations in the country with an aggregate capital of $7.5 billion. People who considered bigness inherently evil demanded that the huge new "trusts" be broken up or at least strictly controlled.

Settlement house workers and other reformers concerned about the welfare of the urban poor made up a third battalion in the progressive army. This was an area in which women made the most important

Orchard Street, a tenement in lower Manhattan in New York City. The unpaved street, ankle-deep in mud, is lined with garbage. It resembles the scene painted by Everett Shinn shown at the opening of the chapter. But while reformers deplored life in such slums, many who lived there enjoyed the sociability of the congested streets.

contributions. The working and living conditions of slum dwellers remained abominable, and the child labor problem was particularly acute; in 1900 about 1.7 million children under the age of sixteen were working full time—more than the membership of the American Federation of Labor. In addition, laws regulating the hours and working conditions of women in industry were inadequate, and almost nothing had been done, despite the increased use of dangerous machinery in the factories, to enforce safety rules or to provide compensation or insurance for workers injured on the job. As the number of professionally competent social workers grew, the movement for social welfare legislation gained momentum.

America was becoming more urban, more industrial, more mechanized, more centralized—in short, more complex. This trend put a premium on efficiency and cooperation. It seemed obvious to the progressives that people must become more socially minded, and the economy more carefully organized.

By attracting additional thousands of sympathizers to the general cause of reform, the return of prosperity after 1896 fueled the progressive movement. Good times made people more tolerant and generous. As long as profits were on the rise, the average employer did not object if labor improved its position too. Middle-class Americans who had been prepared to go to the barricades in the event of a Bryan victory in 1896 became conscience-stricken when they compared their own comfortable circumstances with those of the "huddled masses" of immigrants and native-born poor.

Giant industrial and commercial corporations undermined not so much the economic well-being as the ambitions and sense of importance of the middle class. What owner of a small mill or shop could now hope to rise to the heights attained by Carnegie or merchants like John Wanamaker and Marshall Field? The growth of large labor organizations worried such types. In general, character and moral values seemed less influential; organizations—cold, impersonal, heartless—were coming to control business, politics, and too many other aspects of life.

Protestant pastors accustomed to the respect and deference of their flocks found their moral leadership challenged by materialistic congregations who did not even pay them decent salaries. College professors worried about their institutions falling under the sway of wealthy trustees who had little interest in or respect for learning. Lawyers had been "the aristocracy of the United States," James Bryce recalled in 1905; they were now merely "a part of the great organized system of industrial and financial enterprise."

The middle classes could support reform measures without feeling that they were being very radical because they were resisting change and because the intellectual currents of the time harmonized with their ideas of social improvement and the welfare state. The new doctrines of the social scientists, the Social Gospel religious leaders, and the philosophers of pragmatism provided a salubrious climate for progressivism. Many of the thinkers who had formulated these doctrines in the 1880s and 1890s turned to the task of putting them into practice in the new century. Their number included the economist Richard T. Ely, the philosopher John Dewey, and the Baptist clergyman Walter Rauschenbusch, a civic reformer who wrote many books extolling the Social Gospel.

The Muckrakers

As the diffuse progressive army gradually formed its battalions, a new journalistic fad brought the movement into focus. For many years magazines had been publishing articles discussing current political, social, and economic problems. Henry Demarest Lloyd's first blast at the Standard Oil monopoly appeared in the *Atlantic Monthly* in 1881. Over the years the tempo and forcefulness of this type of literature increased. Then, in the fall of 1902, *McClure's* began two particularly hard-hitting series of articles, one on Standard Oil by Ida Tarbell, the other on big-city political machines by Lincoln Steffens.

These children in Baltimore (1909) pull the stringy parts from beans in preparation for canning. Photographs such as this one were enlisted in support of laws preventing young children from being exploited as laborers.

These articles provoked much comment. When the editor, S. S. McClure, decided to include in the January 1903 issue an attack on labor gangsterism in the coal fields along with installments of the Tarbell and Steffens series, he called attention to the circumstance in a striking editorial.

Something was radically wrong with the "American character," McClure wrote. These articles showed that large numbers of American employers, workers, and politicians were fundamentally immoral. Lawyers were becoming tools of big business, judges were permitting evildoers to escape justice, the churches were materialistic, and educators seemed incapable of understanding what was happening. "There is no one left; none but all of us," McClure concluded. "We have to pay in the end."

McClure's editorial caused a sensation. The issue sold out quickly. Thousands of readers found their own vague apprehensions brought into focus. Some became active in progressive movements; still more lent passive support.

Other editors jumped to adopt the McClure formula. A small army of professional writers soon flooded the periodical press with denunciations of the insurance business, the drug business, college athletics, prostitution, sweatshop labor, political corruption, and dozens of other subjects. This type of article inspired Theodore Roosevelt, with his gift for vivid language, to compare the journalists to "the Man with the Muck-Rake" in John Bunyan's *Pilgrim's Progress*, whose attention was so fixed on the filth at his feet that he could not notice the "celestial crown" that was offered him in exchange. Roosevelt's characterization grossly misrepresented the literature of exposure, but the label *muckraking* was thereafter affixed to the type. Despite its literal connotations, **muckraker** became a term of honor.

The Progressive Mind

Progressives sought to arouse the conscience of "the people" in order to "purify" American life. They were convinced that human beings were by nature decent, well-intentioned, and kind. (After all, the words *human* and *humane* have the same root.) Unlike many earlier reformers, they believed that the source of society's evils lay in the structure of its institutions, not in the weaknesses or sinfulness of individuals. Therefore local, state, and national government must be made more responsive to the will of citizens who stood for the traditional virtues. In the South, many people who considered themselves progressives even argued that poll taxes and other measures designed to deny blacks the vote were reforms because they discouraged a class of people they considered unthinking and shiftless from voting.

When government had been thus reformed, then it must act; whatever its virtues, laissez-faire was obsolete. Businessmen, especially big businessmen, must be compelled to behave fairly, their acquisitive drives curbed in the interests of justice and equal opportunity for all. The weaker elements in society—women, children, the poor, the infirm—must be protected against unscrupulous power.

Despite its fervor and democratic rhetoric, progressivism was paternalistic, moderate, and often soft-headed. Typical reformers of the period oversimplified complicated issues and treated their personal values as absolute standards of truth and morality. Thus progressives often acted at cross-purposes; at times some were even at war with themselves. This accounts for the diffuseness of the movement.

The progressives never challenged the fundamental principles of capitalism, nor did they attempt a basic reorganization of society. They would have little to do with the socialist brand of reform. Wisconsin was the most progressive of states, but its leaders never cooperated with the Socialist party of Milwaukee. When Socialists threatened to win control of Los Angeles in 1911, California progressives made common cause with reactionary groups in order to defeat them. Many progressives were anti-immigrant, and only a handful had anything to offer blacks, surely the most exploited group in American society.

A good example of the relatively limited radicalism of most progressives is offered by the experiences of progressive artists. Early in the century a number of painters, including Robert Henri, John Sloan, and George Luks, tried to develop a distinctively American style. They turned to city streets and the people of the slums for their models, and they depended more on inspiration and inner conviction than on careful craftsmanship to achieve their effects.

These artists of the **Ashcan School** were individualists, yet they supported political and social reform and were caught up in the progressive movement. Sloan was a socialist; Henri claimed to be an anarchist. Most saw themselves as rebels. But artistically the Ashcan painters were not very advanced. Their idols were long-dead European masters such as Hogarth, Goya, and Daumier. They were uninfluenced by the outburst of postimpressionist activity then taking place in Europe. To their dismay, when they included canvases by Matisse, Picasso, and other European artists in a show of their own works at the Sixty-Ninth Regiment Armory in New York City in 1913, the "advanced" Europeans got all the attention.

THE VERDICT.

In 1900, Ashcan artist George Luks portrayed corporate monopolies and franchises as a monster preying on New York City.

"Radical" Progressives: The Wave of the Future

Some people espoused more radical views. The hard times of the 1890s and the callous reactions of conservatives to the victims of that depression pushed many toward Marxian socialism. In 1900 the labor leader Eugene V. Debs ran for president on the Socialist ticket. He polled fewer than 100,000 votes. When he ran again in 1904 he got more than 400,000, and in later elections still more. Labor leaders hoping to organize unskilled workers in heavy industry were increasingly frustrated by the craft orientation of the American Federation of Labor, and some saw in socialism a way to win rank-and-file backing.

In 1905 Debs, William "Big Bill" Haywood of the Western Federation of Miners, Mary Harris "Mother" Jones (a former organizer for the United Mine Workers), Daniel De Leon of the Socialist Labor party, and a few others organized a new union: the **Industrial Workers of the World (IWW)**. The IWW was openly anticapitalist. The preamble to its constitution began: "The working class and the employing class have nothing in common."

But the IWW never attracted many ordinary workers. Haywood, its most prominent leader, was usually a general in search of an army. His forte was attracting attention to spontaneous strikes by unorganized workers, not the patient recruiting of workers and the pursuit of practical goals. Shortly after the founding of the IWW, he was charged with complicity in the murder of an antiunion governor of Idaho after an earlier strike but was acquitted. In 1912 he was closely involved in a bitter and, at times, bloody strike of textile workers in Lawrence, Massachusetts, which was settled with some benefit to the strikers; he was also involved in a failed strike the following winter and spring by silk workers in Paterson, New Jersey.

Other "advanced" European ideas affected the thinking and behavior of some important progressive intellectuals. Sigmund Freud's psychoanalytical theories attracted numbers of Americans, especially after G. Stanley Hall invited Freud and some of his disciples to lecture at Clark University in 1909. Not many progressives actually read *The Interpretation of Dreams* or any of Freud's other works, none of which were translated into English before 1909, but many picked up enough of the vocabulary of psychoanalysis

JUNE. 1914   10 CENTS

The MASSES

IN THIS ISSUE
CLASS WAR IN COLORADO—Max Eastman
WHAT ABOUT MEXICO ?—John Reed

This issue of *The Masses*, a leading Socialist magazine, featured a cover by Ashcan artist John Sloan, as well as articles by Max Eastman and John Reed. Sloan depicted the conflagration that took the lives of women and children who lived in a tent city erected by miners who were striking near Ludlow, Colorado. The state militia, seeking to crush the strike, burned down the tent city.
Source: ©2011 Delaware Art Museum/Artists Rights Society (ARS), New York.

to discourse impressively about the significance of slips of the tongue, sublimation, and infant sexuality.

Some saw in Freud's ideas reason to effect a "revolution of manners and morals" that would have shocked (or at least embarrassed) Freud, who was personally quite conventional. They advocated easy divorce, trial marriage, and doing away with the double standard in all matters relating to sex. They rejected Victorian reticence and what they incorrectly identified as "puritan" morality out of hand, and they called for programs of sex education, especially the dissemination of information about methods of birth control.

Most large cities boasted groups of these "bohemian" thinkers, by far the most famous being the one centered in New York City's Greenwich Village. The dancer Isadora Duncan, the photographer Alfred Stieglitz, the novelist Floyd Dell, several of the Ashcan artists, and the playwright Eugene O'Neill rubbed shoulders with Big Bill Haywood of the IWW, the anarchist Emma Goldman, the psychoanalyst A. A. Brill, the militant feminist advocate of birth control Margaret Sanger, Max Eastman (editor of their organ, *The Masses*), and John Reed, a young Harvard graduate who was soon to become famous

for his eyewitness account of the Russian Revolution, *Ten Days That Shook the World*.

Goldman, Haywood, Sanger, and a few others in this group were genuine radicals who sought basic changes in bourgeois society, but most of the Greenwich Village intellectuals were as much concerned with aesthetic as social issues. *The Masses* described itself as "a revolutionary and not a reform magazine . . . a magazine whose final policy is to do as it pleases." Nearly all of them came from middle-class backgrounds. They found the far-different world of the Italian and Jewish immigrants of the Village and its surrounding neighborhoods charming. But they did not become involved in the immigrants' lives the way the settlement house workers did. Their influence on their own times, therefore, was limited. "Do as I say, not as I do" is not an effective way to change minds. They are historically important, however, because many of them were genuinely creative people and because many of the ideas and practices they advocated were adopted by later generations.

The creative writers of the era, applying the spirit of progressivism to the realism they had inherited from Howells and the naturalists, tended to adopt an optimistic tone. The poet Ezra Pound, for example, at this time talked grandly of an American renaissance and fashioned a new kind of poetry called imagism, which, while not appearing to be realistic, rejected all abstract generalizations and concentrated on concrete word pictures to convey meaning. "Little" magazines and experimental theatrical companies sprang to life by the dozen, each convinced that it would revolutionize its art. The poet Carl Sandburg, the best-known representative of

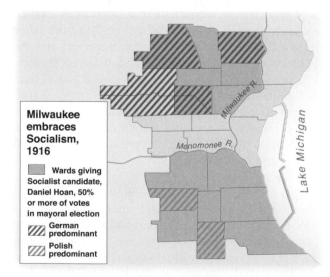

Milwaukee embraces Socialism, 1916

■ Wards giving Socialist candidate, Daniel Hoan, 50% or more of votes in mayoral election

▨ German predominant

▨ Polish predominant

Urban Socialism By 1912, Socialists had been elected mayor of dozens of cities, including Milwaukee. This map shows that Dan Hoan, the Socialist mayor, received strong support from the predominantly Polish and German wards. Opponents used such results to argue that socialism was a "foreign" concept.

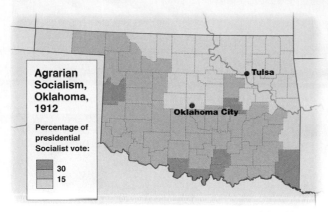

Rural Socialism Socialist strength extended far beyond the cities. Socialists in rural areas called for tenants to be allowed to work on state-owned plots of land. In 1912, Socialist candidates received nearly half the vote in southern Oklahoma.

the Chicago school, denounced the local plutocrats but sang the praises of the city they had made: "Hog Butcher for the World," "City of the Big Shoulders."

Most writers eagerly adopted Freudian psychology without understanding it. Freud's teachings seemed only to mean that they should cast off the restrictions of Victorian prudery; they ignored his essentially dark view of human nature. Theirs was an "innocent rebellion," exuberant and rather muddleheaded.

Political Reform: Cities First

To most "ordinary" progressives, political corruption and inefficiency lay at the root of the evils plaguing American society, nowhere more obvious than in the nation's cities. Urban life's anonymity and complexity help explain why slavery did not flourish in cities, but also why the previously named vices did flourish. As the cities grew, their antiquated and boss-ridden administrations became more and more disgraceful. Consider the example of San Francisco. After 1901, a shrewd lawyer named Abe Ruef ruled one of the most powerful and dissolute political machines in the nation. Only one kind of paving material was used on San Francisco's streets, and Ruef was the lawyer for the company that supplied it. When the gas company asked for a rate increase of ten cents per 100 cubic feet, Ruef, who was already collecting $1,000 a month from the company as a "retainer," demanded and got an outright bribe of $20,000. A streetcar company needed city authorization to install overhead trolley wires; Ruef's approval cost the company $85,000. Prostitution flourished, with Ruef and his henchmen sharing in the profits. There was a brisk illegal trade in liquor licenses and other favors. Similar conditions existed in dozens of communities. For his famous muckraking series in *McClure's*, Lincoln Steffens visited St. Louis, Minneapolis, Pittsburgh, New York, Chicago, and Philadelphia and found them all riddled with corruption.

Beginning in the late 1890s progressives mounted a massive assault on dishonest and inefficient urban governments. In San Francisco a group headed by Fremont Older, a newspaperman, and Rudolph Spreckels, a wealthy sugar manufacturer, broke the machine and lodged Ruef in jail. In Toledo, Ohio, Samuel M. "Golden Rule" Jones won election as mayor in 1897 and succeeded in arousing the citizenry against the corrupt officials. Other important progressive mayors were Tom L. Johnson of Cleveland (whose administration Lincoln Steffens called the best in the United States), Seth Low and John P. Mitchell of New York and Hazen S. Pingree of Detroit.

City reformers could seldom destroy the machines without changing urban political institutions. Some cities obtained "home rule" charters that gave them greater freedom from state control in dealing with local matters. Many created research bureaus that investigated government problems in a scientific and nonpartisan manner. A number of middle-sized communities (Galveston, Texas, was the prototype) experimented with a system that integrated executive and legislative powers in the hands of a small elected commission, thereby concentrating responsibility and making it easier to coordinate complex activities. Out of this experiment came the city manager system, under which the commissioners appointed a professional manager to administer city affairs on a nonpartisan basis. Dayton, Ohio, which adopted the plan after a flood devastated the town in 1913, offers the best illustration of the city manager system in the Progressive Era.

Once the political system had been made responsive to the desires of the people, the progressives hoped to use it to improve society itself. Many cities experimented with "gas and water socialism," taking over public utility companies and operating them as departments of the municipal government. Under "Golden Rule" Jones, Toledo established a minimum wage for city employees, built playgrounds and golf courses, and moderated its harsh penal code. Mayor Seth Low improved New York's public transportation system and obtained passage of the tenement house law of 1901. Mayor Tom Johnson forced a fare cut to three cents on the Cleveland street railways.

Political Reform: The States

To carry out this kind of change required the support of state legislatures since all municipal government depends on the authority of a sovereign state. Such approval was often difficult to obtain—local bosses were usually entrenched in powerful state machines, and rural majorities insensitive to urban needs controlled most legislatures. Therefore the progressives had to strike at inefficiency and corruption at the state level too.

Emma Goldman

In January 1886 a sixteen-year-old Jewish girl named Emma Goldman arrived in New York City from St. Petersburg, Russia, where her parents ran a grocery store. As soon as immigration officials had approved her entry into the United States, she hurried on to Rochester, New York, where her half-sister lived. Like most immigrants she expected the United States to be a kind of paradise on earth.

After moving in with her half-sister's family, Emma got a job in a factory sewing coats and earning $2.50 a week. She paid her sister $1.50 a week for room and board and spent sixty cents a week to get to her job. But when she asked her employer for more money he told her to "look for work elsewhere." She found a job at another factory that paid $4 a week.

In 1887 she married Jacob Kirshner, another Russian immigrant, but they soon divorced. In 1889 she took up with a group of radicals, most of them either socialists or anarchists. By this time Goldman was herself an ardent anarchist, convinced by her experiences that *all* governments repressed individual freedom and should be abolished.

In New York Emma fell in love with another Russian-born radical, Alexander Berkman. They started a kind of commune. Emma worked at home sewing shirts. Alexander found a job making cigars. They never married.

The couple moved to New Haven, where Emma started a cooperative dressmaking shop. Then they moved to Springfield, Massachusetts, where, with Berkman's cousin, an artist, they opened a photography studio. When this business failed, they opened an ice cream parlor.

Nearly all immigrants of that period retained their faith in the promise of American life even after they discovered that the streets were not paved with gold. But Emma was so disappointed that she became a radical.

In 1892 when she and Berkman learned of the bloody battle between Pinkertons and strikers during the Homestead steel strike, they closed the ice cream parlor and plotted to assassinate Henry Clay Frick, the archvillain of the Homestead drama. Berkman went to Pittsburgh, where, posing as a representative of an agency that provided strikebreakers, he got into Frick's office. Pulling a pistol, Berkman aimed for Frick's head but the shot went wide and hit Frick in the shoulder. Berkman then stabbed Frick, but still the Homestead boss survived. Convicted of the attempt on Frick's life, Berkman was imprisoned for fourteen years.

The next year Goldman was herself arrested and sentenced to a year in jail for making an "incendiary" speech urging unemployed workers to distrust politicians. Upon her release, Goldman went to Vienna, where she trained as a nurse. When she returned to America, she worked as a midwife among the New York poor, an experience that made her an outspoken advocate of birth control. She also helped organize a theatrical group, managed a touring group of Russian actors, and lectured on theatrical topics. In 1901, Goldman was arrested on charges of inspiring Leon Czolgosz to assassinate President McKinley. Czolgosz had attended one of

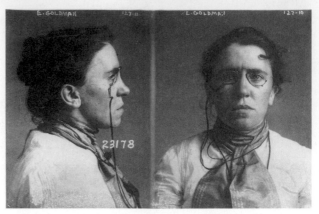

A "mug shot" of Emma Goldman, 1901. She was arrested so often that she took to carrying a book with her everywhere so that she would have something to read in jail if she were arrested.

Goldman's lectures, but there was no direct connection between the two, and the charges against her were dropped.

In 1906 Goldman founded *Mother Earth*, an anarchist journal. When Alexander Berkman was released from prison later that year, she made him its editor. *Mother Earth* denounced governments, organized religion, and private property. By this time Goldman had become a celebrity. "She was considered a monster, an exponent of free love and bombs," recalled Margaret Anderson, editor of a literary magazine.

Now Goldman campaigned for freedom of speech and lectured in support of birth control. In 1915, after Margaret Sanger was arrested for disseminating information on birth control, Goldman did the same in public speeches. She was arrested and spent two weeks in jail.

Goldman regarded the Great War—and especially American entry in it—as a calamity beyond measure. In 1917 Goldman and Berkman were convicted of conspiring to persuade men not to register for the draft. They served two years in federal prison. In 1919 they were deported to Russia. Two years later, disillusioned with the Bolsheviks, Goldman left the Soviet Union.

"Red Emma" Goldman was not a typical American, but she was in many ways a typical American immigrant. She learned English and quickly became familiar with American ways. She worked hard and developed valuable skills. Gradually she moved up the economic ladder. And while she was critical of the United States, she was a typical immigrant also in insisting that she was an American patriot. "The kind of patriotism we represent," she said during her trial in 1917, "is the kind of patriotism which loves America with open eyes."

Questions for Discussion

- Why did most immigrants, on learning of the gap between the promise of America and its reality, not become radicals?
- Was Goldman a radical by birth or by acculturation?

During the first decade of the new century, Robert M. La Follette, one of the most remarkable figures of the age, transformed Wisconsin, the progressive state par excellence. La Follette was born in Primrose, Wisconsin, in 1855. He had served three terms as a Republican congressman (1885–1891) and developed a reputation as an uncompromising foe of corruption before being elected governor in 1900. That the people would always do the right thing if properly informed and inspired was the fundamental article of his political faith. "Machine control is based upon misrepresentation and ignorance," La Follette said. "Democracy is based upon knowledge." His own career seemed to prove his point, for in his repeated clashes with the conservative Wisconsin Republican machine, he won battle after battle by vigorous grassroots campaigning.

Despite the opposition of railroad and lumbering interests, Governor La Follette obtained a direct primary system for nominating candidates, a corrupt practices act, and laws limiting campaign expenditures and lobbying activities. In power he became something of a boss himself. He made ruthless use of patronage, demanded absolute loyalty of his subordinates, and often stretched, or at least oversimplified, the truth when presenting complex issues to the voters.

La Follette was a consummate showman who never rose entirely above rural prejudices. He was prone to see a nefarious "conspiracy" organized by "the interests" behind even the mildest opposition to his proposals. But he was devoted to the cause of honest government. Realizing that some state functions called for specialized technical knowledge, he used commissions and agencies to handle such matters as railroad regulation, tax assessment, conservation, and highway construction. Wisconsin established a legislative reference library to assist lawmakers in drafting bills. For work of this kind, La Follette called on the faculty of the University of Wisconsin, enticing topnotch economists and political scientists into the public service and drawing freely on the advice of such outstanding social scientists as Richard T. Ely, John R. Commons, and E. A. Ross.

The success of these policies, which became known as the Wisconsin Idea, led other states to adopt similar programs. Reform administrations swept into office in Iowa and Arkansas (1901); Oregon (1902); Minnesota, Kansas, and Mississippi (1904); New York and Georgia (1906); Nebraska (1909); and New Jersey and Colorado (1910). In some cases the reformers were Republicans, in others Democrats, but in all the example of Wisconsin was influential. By 1910, fifteen states had established legislative reference services, most of them staffed by personnel trained in Wisconsin. The direct primary system, in which candidates were selected by voters than party bosses, became almost universal.

Some states went beyond Wisconsin in striving to make their governments responsive to the popular will. In 1902 Oregon began to experiment with the initiative, a system by which a bill could be forced on the attention of the legislature by popular petition, and the referendum, a method for allowing the electorate to approve measures rejected by their representatives and to repeal measures that the legislature had passed. Eleven states, most of them in the West, legalized these devices by 1914.

State Social Legislation

The first state laws aimed at social problems long preceded the Progressive Era, but most were either so imprecise as to be unenforceable or, like the Georgia law "limiting" textile workers to eleven hours a day, so weak as to be ineffective. In 1874 Massachusetts restricted the working hours of women and children to ten per day, and by the 1890s many other states, mostly in the East and Midwest, had followed suit. Illinois passed an eight-hour law for women workers in 1893. A New York law of 1882 struck at the sweatshops of the slums by prohibiting the manufacture of cigars on premises "occupied as a house or residence."

As part of this trend, some states established special rules for workers in hazardous industries. In the 1890s several states limited the hours of railroad workers on the grounds that fatigue sometimes caused railroad accidents. Utah restricted miners to eight hours in 1896. In 1901 New York finally enacted an effective tenement house law, greatly increasing the area of open space on building lots and requiring toilets for each apartment, better ventilation systems, and more adequate fireproofing.

Before 1900 the collective impact of such legislation was not impressive. Powerful manufacturers and landlords often succeeded in defeating the bills or rendering them innocuous. The federal system further complicated the task of obtaining effective legislation.

The Fourteenth Amendment to the Constitution, although enacted to protect the civil rights of blacks, imposed a revolutionary restriction on the states by forbidding them to "deprive any person of life, liberty, or property without due process of law." Since much state social legislation represented new uses of coercive power that conservative judges considered dangerous and unwise, the Fourteenth Amendment gave such judges an excuse to overturn the laws that deprived employers of the "liberty" to choose how long their employees should work or the conditions of the workplace.

On March 25, 1911, as scores of young factory girls leaped to their deaths from the eighth, ninth, and tenth stories of the Triangle Shirtwaist Factory in New York City, eighteen-year-old Victor Gatto watched in horror. Thirty-three years later he painted this rendering of his nightmare, the bodies of the dead girls placed in order at the base of the building.
Source: Victor Joseph Gatto (1893–1965), *Triangle Fire: March 25, 1911.* c. 1944 (depicting 1911), oil on canvas, 19 × 28", Gift of Mrs. Henry L. Moses, 54.75. The Museum of the City of New York.

As stricter and more far-reaching laws were enacted, many judges, fearing a trend toward socialism and regimentation, adopted an increasingly narrow interpretation of state authority to regulate business. In 1905 the U.S. Supreme Court declared in the case of *Lochner v. New York* that a New York ten-hour act for bakers deprived the bakers of the liberty of working as long as they wished and thus violated the Fourteenth Amendment. Justice Oliver Wendell Holmes, Jr., wrote a famous dissenting opinion in this case. If the people of New York believed that the public health was endangered by bakers working long hours, he reasoned, it was not the Court's job to overrule them.

Nevertheless, the progressives continued to battle for legislation to use state power against business. Women played a particularly important part in these struggles. Sparked by the National Child Labor Committee, organized in 1904, reformers over the next ten years obtained laws in nearly every state banning the employment of young children and limiting the hours of older ones. Many of these laws were poorly enforced, yet when Congress passed a federal child labor law in 1916, the

Supreme Court, in *Hammer v. Dagenhart* (1918), declared it unconstitutional.[1]

By 1917 nearly all the states had placed limitations on the hours of women industrial workers, and about ten had set minimum wage standards for women. But once again federal action that would have extended such regulation to the entire country did not materialize. A minimum wage law for women in the District of Columbia was overturned by the Court in *Adkins v. Children's Hospital* (1923).

Many states also enacted laws protecting workers against on-the-job accidents. Disasters like the 1911 fire in New York City, in which nearly 150 women perished because the Triangle Shirtwaist Factory had no fire escapes, led to the passage of stricter municipal building codes and factory inspection acts. By 1910 most states had modified the common-law principle that a worker accepted the risk of accident as a condition of employment and was not entitled to compensation if injured unless it could be proved that the

---

[1]A second child labor law, passed in 1919, was also thrown out by the Court, and a child labor amendment, submitted in 1924, failed to achieve ratification by the necessary three-quarters of the states.

employer had been negligent. Gradually the states adopted accident insurance plans, and some began to grant pensions to widows with small children. Most manufacturers favored such measures, if for no other reason than that they regularized procedures and avoided costly lawsuits.

The passage of so much state social legislation sent conservatives scurrying to the Supreme Court for redress. Such persons believed that no government had the power to deprive either workers or employers of the right to negotiate any kind of labor contract they wished. The decision of the Supreme Court in *Lochner v. New York* seemed to indicate that the justices would adopt this point of view. When an Oregon law limiting women laundry workers to ten hours a day was challenged in *Muller v. Oregon* (1908), Florence Kelley and Josephine Goldmark of the Consumers' League persuaded Louis D. Brandeis to defend the statute before the Court.

The Consumers' League, whose slogan was "investigate, agitate, legislate," was probably the most effective of the many women's reform organizations of the period. With the aid of league researchers, Brandeis prepared a remarkable brief stuffed with economic and sociological evidence indicating that long hours damaged both the health of individual women and the health of society. This nonlegal evidence greatly impressed the justices, who upheld the constitutionality of the Oregon law. "Woman's physical structure, and the functions she performs in consequence thereof, justify special legislation," they concluded. After 1908 the right of states to protect women, children, and workers performing dangerous and unhealthy tasks by special legislation was widely accepted. The use of the "Brandeis brief" technique to demonstrate the need for such legislation became standard practice.

View the **Image** *Little Spinner in Globe Cotton Mill* at www.myhistorylab.com

Political Reform: The Woman Suffrage Movement

On the national level the Progressive Era saw the culmination of the struggle for **woman suffrage**. The shock occasioned by the failure of the Fourteenth and Fifteenth Amendments to give women the vote after the Civil War continued to embitter most leaders of the movement. But it resulted in a split among feminists. One group, the American Woman Suffrage Association (AWSA), focused on the vote question alone. The more radical National Woman Suffrage Association (NWSA), led by Elizabeth Cady Stanton and Susan B. Anthony, concerned itself with many issues of importance to women as well as suffrage. The NWSA put the

Another argument in support of woman suffrage claimed that women were intrinsically *better* than men. Note that this woman in the turn-of-the-century poster, crowned by a halo, has her clothes arranged in the shape of a cross.

immediate interests of women ahead of everything else. It was deeply involved in efforts to unionize women workers, yet it did not hesitate to urge women to be strikebreakers if they could get better jobs by doing so.

Aside from their lack of unity, feminists were handicapped in the late nineteenth century by widely held Victorian ideals: Sex was a taboo topic, and women were to be "pure" guardians of home and family. Even under the best of circumstances, dislike of male-dominated society is hard enough to separate from dislike of men. Most feminists, for example, opposed contraception, insisting that birth control by any means other than continence would encourage what they called masculine lust. And the trend of nineteenth-century scientific thinking influenced by the Darwinian concept of biological adaptation led to the conclusion that the female personality was different from that of the male and that the differences were inherent, not culturally determined.

These ideas and prejudices enticed feminists into a logical trap. If women were morally superior to men— a tempting conclusion—giving women the vote would

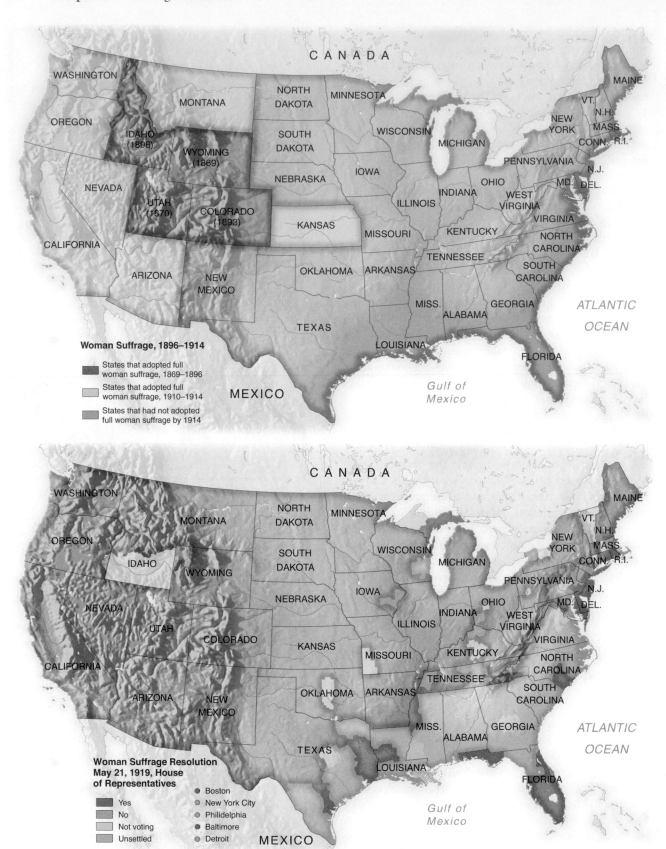

Woman Suffrage, 1896–1914

- States that adopted full woman suffrage, 1869–1896
- States that adopted full woman suffrage, 1910–1914
- States that had not adopted full woman suffrage by 1914

Woman Suffrage Resolution May 21, 1919, House of Representatives

- Yes
- No
- Not voting
- Unsettled

- Boston
- New York City
- Philidelphia
- Baltimore
- Detroit

The Advance of Woman Suffrage   In 1869 Wyoming, still a territory, voted to give women the vote. The next year, after Mormon leader Brigham Young endorsed woman suffrage, Utah followed. Then came Colorado (1893) and Idaho (1896), frontier states that sought to attract women settlers. In 1911, by a margin of 3,587 votes, California endorsed woman suffrage, and within three years the remainder of the western states had done so, too. World War I stimulated support for the Woman Suffrage (Nineteenth) Amendment. The May 21, 1919, vote in the House of Representatives shows that most of the opposing votes came from southern congressmen who believed that woman suffrage would be the first step toward securing the vote for blacks.

Vice President Thomas R. Marshall complained that the "everlasting clatter of the militant suffragettes" was keeping Congress from transacting other business. This was an overstatement, but in any case the amendment finally won congressional approval in 1919. By 1920 the necessary three-quarters of the states had ratified the Nineteenth Amendment; the long fight was over.

⊙ See the Map *Woman Suffrage Before the 19th Century* at www.myhistorylab.com

Theodore Roosevelt: Cowboy in the White House

On September 6, 1901, an anarchist named Leon Czolgosz shot President McKinley during a public reception at the Pan-American Exposition at Buffalo, New York. Eight days later McKinley died and Theodore Roosevelt became president of the United States. His ascension to the presidency marked the beginning of a new era in national politics.

Although only forty-two, by far the youngest president in the nation's history up to that time, Roosevelt brought solid qualifications to the office. Son of a well-to-do New York merchant, he had graduated from Harvard in 1880 and studied law briefly at Columbia, though he did not obtain a degree. In addition to political experience that included three terms in the New York assembly, six years on the U.S. Civil Service Commission, two years as police commissioner of New York City, another as assistant secretary of the navy, and a term as governor of New York, he had been a rancher in the Dakota Territory and a soldier in the Spanish-American War. He was also a well-known historian: His *Naval War of 1812* (1882), begun during his undergraduate days at Harvard, and his four-volume *Winning of the West* (1889–1896) were valuable works of scholarship, and he had written two popular biographies and other books as well. Politically, he had always been a loyal Republican. He rejected the mugwump heresy in 1884, and during the tempestuous 1890s he vigorously denounced populism, Bryanism, and "labor agitators."

Nevertheless, Roosevelt's elevation to the presidency alarmed many conservatives, and not without reason. He did not fit their conception, based on a composite image of the chief executives from Hayes to McKinley, of a president. He seemed too undignified, too energetic, too outspoken, too unconventional. It was one thing to have operated a cattle ranch, another to have captured a gang of rustlers at gunpoint; one thing to have run a metropolitan police force, another to have roamed New York slums in the small hours to catch patrolmen fraternizing with thieves and prostitutes; and one thing to have commanded a regiment, another to have killed a Spaniard personally.

improve the character of the electorate. Society would benefit because politics would become less corrupt, war a thing of the past. "City housekeeping has failed," said Jane Addams of Hull House in arguing for the reform of municipal government, "partly because women, the traditional housekeepers, have not been consulted."

The trouble with this argument (aside from the fact that opponents could easily demonstrate that in states where women did vote, governments were no better or worse than elsewhere) was that it surrendered the principle of equality. In the long run this was to have serious consequences for the women's movement, although the immediate effect of the purity argument was probably to advance the suffragists' cause.

By the early twentieth century there were signs of progress. In 1890 the two major women's groups combined as the **National American Woman Suffrage Association (NAWSA)**. Stanton and Anthony were the first two presidents of the association, but new leaders were emerging, the most notable being Carrie Chapman Catt, a woman who combined superb organizing abilities and political skills with commitment to broad social reform. The NAWSA made winning the right to vote its main objective and concentrated on a state-by-state approach. Wyoming gave women the vote in 1869, and Utah, Colorado, and Idaho had been won over to woman suffrage by 1896.

The burgeoning of the progressive movement helped as middle-class recruits of both sexes adopted the suffrage cause. The 1911 referendum in California was crucial. Fifteen years earlier, California voters had rejected the measure. But in 1911, despite determined opposition from saloonkeepers, the proposal barely passed. Within three years, most other Western states fell into line. For the first time, large numbers of working-class women began to agitate for the vote. In 1917, bosses at New York City's Tammany Hall, who had engineered the defeat of woman suffrage in that state two years earlier, concluded that passage was inevitable and threw their support to the measure, which passed. The suffragists then shifted the campaign back to the national level, the lead taken by a new organization, the Congressional Union, headed by Alice Paul and the wealthy reformer Alva Belmont. When President Wilson refused to support the idea of a constitutional amendment granting women the vote, militant women picketed the White House. A number of them, including the daughter of Thomas Bayard, a former senator and secretary of state, were arrested and sentenced to sixty days in the workhouse. This roused a storm of criticism, and Wilson quickly pardoned the picketers. After some hesitation the NAWSA stopped concentrating on the state-by-state approach and began to campaign for a constitutional amendment. Pressure on Congress mounted steadily. Later,

Theodore Roosevelt addressing a crowd in Evanston, Illinois, in the early 1900s.

Roosevelt had been a sickly child, plagued by asthma and poor eyesight, and he seems to have spent much of his adult life compensating for the sense of inadequacy that these troubles bred in him. He repeatedly carried his displays of physical stamina and personal courage and his love of athletics and big-game hunting to preternatural lengths. Henry Adams, who watched Roosevelt's development over the years with a mixture of fear and amusement, said that he was "pure act."

Once, while fox hunting, Roosevelt fell from his horse, cutting his face severely and breaking his left arm. Instead of waiting for help or struggling to some nearby house to summon a doctor, he clambered back on his horse and resumed the chase. "I was in at the death," he wrote next day. "I looked pretty gay, with one arm dangling, and my face and clothes like the walls of a slaughter house." That evening, after his arm had been set and put in splints, he attended a dinner party.

Roosevelt worshiped aggressiveness and was extremely sensitive to any threat to his honor as a gentleman. When another young man showed some slight interest in Roosevelt's fiancée, he sent for a set of French dueling pistols. His teachers found him an interesting student, for he was intelligent and imaginative, if annoyingly argumentative. "Now look here, Roosevelt," one Harvard professor finally said to him, "let me talk. I'm running this course."

Few individuals have rationalized or sublimated their feelings of inferiority as effectively as Roosevelt

and to such good purpose. And few have been more genuinely warmhearted, more full of spontaneity, more committed to the ideals of public service and national greatness. As a political leader he was energetic and hard-driving. Conservatives and timid souls, sensing his aggressiveness even when he held it in check, distrusted Roosevelt's judgment, fearing he might go off half-cocked in some crisis. In fact his judgment was nearly always sound; responsibility usually tempered his aggressiveness.

When Roosevelt was first mentioned as a running mate for McKinley in 1900, he wrote, "The Vice Presidency is a most honorable office, but for a young man there is not much to do." As president it would have been unthinkable for him to preside over a caretaker administration devoted to maintaining the status quo. However, the reigning Republican politicos, basking in the sunshine of the prosperity that had contributed so much to their victory in 1900, distrusted anything suggestive of change.

Had Roosevelt been the impetuous hothead that conservatives feared, he would have plunged ahead without regard for their feelings and influence. Instead he moved slowly and often got what he wanted by using his executive power rather than by persuading Congress to pass new laws. His domestic program included some measure of control of big corporations, more power for the Interstate Commerce Commission (ICC), and the conservation of natural resources. By consulting congressional leaders and following their advice not to bring up controversial matters like the tariff and currency reform, he obtained a modest budget of new laws.

The Newlands Act (1902) funneled the proceeds from land sales in the West into federal irrigation projects. The Department of Commerce and Labor, which was to include a Bureau of Corporations with authority to investigate industrial combines and issue reports, was established. The Elkins Railroad Act of 1903 strengthened the ICC's hand against the railroads by making the receiving as well as the granting of rebates illegal and by forbidding the roads to deviate in any way from their published rates.

Roosevelt and Big Business

Roosevelt soon became known as a trustbuster, and in the sense that he considered the monopoly problem the most pressing issue of the times, this was accurate to an extent. But he did not believe in breaking up big corporations indiscriminately. Regulation seemed the best way to deal with large corporations because, he said, industrial giantism "could not be eliminated unless we were willing to turn back the wheels of modern progress."

DEBATING THE PAST
Were the Progressives Forward-Looking?

Jack and the Wall Street Giants shows a diminutive Teddy Roosevelt taking on the titans of Wall Street, among them railroad barons James J. Hill and Jay Gould and financier J. P. Morgan. The cartoon anticipates the familiar argument—that the progressives challenged the "monied interests." By the 1930s, when the nation was mired in depression, many blamed the progressives. In 1932 John Chamberlain published a *Farewell to Reform* that excoriated progressive leaders for failing to check the power of the trusts. That failure, Richard Hofstadter (1955) declared, was rooted in their psychology. The progressives, mostly members of the middle class and the declining old elites, felt threatened by the increasing power and status of the new tycoons, many of them coarse, domineering, and fond of vulgar display. Progressive reformers sought to restore "familiar and traditional ideals," and their solutions were as old-fashioned as their goals. Revisionist historians such as Gabriel Kolko (1963) pushed Hofstadter's argument still further: The progressives failed to change society because they never meant to promote meaningful change. They endorsed government regulation to prevent anarchic economic competition, and they hoped to ameliorate the plight of workers to forestall revolution. Their "progressivism" was in fact the "triumph of conservatism." Daniel Rodgers (1998) was among the many who insisted that this portrait was overdrawn. The progressives in the United States were not much different from reformers at that time in Europe. All shared a dynamic rhetoric; all sought to counteract the increasing concentration of industrial power; none met with great success. In 2003 Michael McGerr went further still: Progressivism was not simply a political movement, but a far-reaching moral project aimed at reinvigorating American life more generally. In the cartoon TR is armed only with the sword of "Public Service." Was his cause noble—or irrelevant?

Source: John Chamberlain, *Farewell to Reform* (1932); Richard Hofstadter, *The Age of Reform* (1955); Gabriel Kolko, *The Triumph of Conservatism* (1963); Allen Weinstein, *The Decline of Socialism in America* (1967); Robert Wiebe, *The Search for Order* (1967); Daniel Rodgers, *Atlantic Crossings* (1998); Michael McGerr, *A Fierce Discontent* (2003).

■ ■ ■ ■ ■

With Congress unwilling to pass a stiff regulatory law, Roosevelt resorted to the Sherman Act to get at the problem. Although the Supreme Court decision in the Sugar Trust case (*E.C. Knight* [1895], see p. 477) seemed to have emasculated that law, in 1902 he ordered the Justice Department to bring suit against the Northern Securities Company.

He chose his target wisely. The Northern Securities Company controlled three different railroad companies. It had been created in 1901 after a titanic battle on the New York Stock Exchange between the forces of J. P. Morgan and James J. Hill and those of E. H. Harriman, who was associated with the Rockefeller interests. In their efforts to obtain control of the Northern Pacific, the rivals had forced its stock up to $1,000 a share, ruining many speculators and threatening to cause a panic.

Neither side could win a clear-cut victory, so they decided to put the stock of all three railroads in a holding company owned by the two groups. Since Harriman already controlled the Union Pacific and the Southern Pacific, the plan resulted in a virtual monopoly of western railroads. The public had been alarmed, for the merger seemed to typify the rapaciousness of the tycoons.

The announcement of the suit caused consternation in the business world. Morgan rushed to the White House. "If we have done anything wrong," he said to the president, "send your man to my man and they can fix it up." Roosevelt was not fundamentally opposed to this sort of agreement, but it was too late to compromise in this instance. Attorney General Philander C. Knox pressed the case vigorously, and in 1904 the Supreme Court ordered the dissolution of the Northern Securities Company.

Roosevelt then ordered suits against the meat packers, the Standard Oil Trust, and the American Tobacco Company. His stock among progressives rose, yet he had not embarrassed the conservatives in Congress by demanding new antitrust legislation.

The president went out of his way to assure cooperative corporation magnates that he was not against size per se. At a White House conference in 1905, Roosevelt and Elbert H. Gary, chairman of the board of U.S. Steel, reached a "gentlemen's agreement" whereby Gary promised "to cooperate with the Government in every possible way." The Bureau of Corporations would conduct an investigation of U.S. Steel, Gary allowing it full access to company records. Roosevelt in turn promised that if the investigation revealed any corporate malpractices, he would allow Gary to set matters right voluntarily, thereby avoiding an antitrust suit. He reached a similar agreement with the International Harvester Company two years later.

There were limits to the effectiveness of such arrangements. Standard Oil agreed to a similar détente and then reneged, refusing to turn over vital records to the bureau. The Justice Department brought suit against the company under the Sherman Act, and eventually the company was broken up at the order of the Supreme Court. Roosevelt would have preferred a more binding kind of regulation, but when he asked for laws giving the government supervisory authority over big combinations, Congress refused to act.

Roosevelt and the Coal Strike

Roosevelt made remarkable use of his executive power during the anthracite coal strike of 1902. In June the United Mine Workers (UMW), led by John Mitchell, laid down their picks and demanded higher wages, an eight-hour day, and recognition of the union. Most of the anthracite mines were owned by railroads. Two years earlier the miners had won a 10 percent wage increase in a similar strike, chiefly because the owners feared that labor unrest might endanger the election of McKinley. Now the coal companies were dead set against further concessions; when the men walked out, they shut down the mines and prepared to starve the strikers into submission.

The strike dragged on through summer and early fall. The miners conducted themselves with great restraint, avoiding violence and offering to submit their claims to arbitration. As the price of anthracite soared with the approach of winter, sentiment in their behalf mounted.

The owners' spokesman, George F. Baer of the Reading Railroad, proved particularly inept at public relations. Baer stated categorically that God was on the side of management, but when someone suggested asking an important Roman Catholic prelate to arbitrate the dispute, he replied icily: "Anthracite mining is a business and not a religious, sentimental or academic proposition."

Roosevelt shared the public's sympathy for the miners, and the threat of a coal shortage alarmed him. Early in October he summoned both sides to a conference in Washington and urged them as patriotic Americans to sacrifice any "personal consideration" for the "general good." His action enraged the coal owners, for they believed he was trying to force them to recognize the union. They refused even to speak to the UMW representatives at the conference and demanded that Roosevelt end the strike by force and bring suit against the union under the Sherman Act. Mitchell, aware of the immense prestige that Roosevelt had conferred on the union by calling the conference, cooperated fully with the president.

The attitudes of management and of the union further strengthened public support for the miners. Even former president Grover Cleveland, who had used federal troops to break the Pullman strike, said

Table 21.1   Major Supreme Court Rulings during the Progressive Era

Northern Securities Case	1904	Upheld antitrust ruling against railroad conglomerate
Lochner v. New York	1905	Overturned (progressive) New York law restricting the hours bakers could work; invoked the Fourteenth Amendment to protect bakers' "right" to work as long as they wished
Muller v. Oregon	1908	Affirmed the right of Oregon to limit the hours worked by women in laundries

that he was "disturbed and vexed by the tone and substance of the operators' deliverances." Encouraged by this state of affairs, Roosevelt took a bold step: He announced that unless a settlement was reached promptly, he would order federal troops into the anthracite regions, not to break the strike but to seize and operate the mines.

The threat of government intervention brought the owners to terms. A Cabinet member, Elihu Root, worked out the details with J. P. Morgan, whose firm had major interests in the Reading and other railroads, while cruising the Hudson River on Morgan's yacht. The miners would return to the pits and all issues between them and the coal companies would be submitted for settlement to a commission appointed by Roosevelt. Both sides accepted the arrangement, and the men went back to work. In March 1903 the commission granted the miners a 10 percent wage increase and a nine-hour workday.

To the public the incident seemed a perfect illustration of the progressive spirit—in Roosevelt's words, everyone had received a **Square Deal**. In fact the results were by no means so clear-cut. The miners gained relatively little and the companies lost still less. The president was the main winner. The public acclaimed him as a fearless, imaginative, public-spirited leader. Without calling on Congress for support, he had expanded his own authority and hence that of the federal government. His action marked a major forward step in the evolution of the modern presidency.

TR's Triumphs

By reviving the Sherman Act, settling the coal strike, and pushing moderate reforms through Congress, Roosevelt ensured that he would be reelected president in 1904. Progressives, if not captivated, were at least pleased by his performance. Conservative Republicans offered no serious objection. Sensing that Roosevelt had won over the liberals, the Democrats nominated a conservative, Judge Alton B. Parker of New York, and bid for the support of eastern industrialists.

This strategy failed, for businessmen continued to eye the party of Bryan with intense suspicion. They preferred, as the *New York Sun* put it, "the impulsive candidate of the party of conservatism to the conservative candidate of the party which the business interests regard as permanently and dangerously impulsive." Despite his resentment at Roosevelt's attack on the Northern Securities Company, J. P. Morgan contributed $150,000 to the Republican campaign. Other tycoons gave with equal generosity. Roosevelt swept the country, carrying even the normally Democratic border states of Maryland and Missouri.

Encouraged by the landslide and the increasing militancy of progressives, Roosevelt pressed for more reform legislation. His most imaginative proposal was a plan to make the District of Columbia a model progressive community. He suggested child labor and factory inspection laws and a slum clearance program, but Congress refused to act. Likewise, his request for a minimum wage for railroad workers was rejected.

Early in the twentieth century, when malnutrition was common, companies such as this one advertised that its pills could make people fatter. The Pure Food and Drug Act of 1906 fined manufacturers who made false claims for their products. A century later, in 2010, the *Seattle Post Intelligencer*, under the headline "Too Fat to Fight," reported that over a fourth of eighteen to twenty-four year-old potential army recruits were rejected as unfit.

He had greater success when he proposed still another increase in the power of the Interstate Commerce Commission. Rebating remained a serious problem. With progressive state governors demanding federal action and farmers and manufacturers, especially in the Midwest, clamoring for relief against discriminatory rates, Roosevelt was ready by 1905 to make railroad legislation his major objective. The ICC should be empowered to fix rates, not merely to challenge unreasonable ones. It should have the right to inspect the private records of the railroads since fair rates could not be determined unless the true financial condition of the roads were known.

Because these proposals struck at rights that businessmen considered sacrosanct, many congressmen balked. But Roosevelt applied presidential pressure, and in June 1906 the Hepburn bill became law. It gave the commission the power to inspect the books of railroad companies, to set maximum rates (once a complaint had been filed by a shipper), and to control sleeping car companies, owners of oil pipelines, and other firms engaged in transportation. Railroads could no longer issue passes freely—an important check on their political influence. In all, the **Hepburn Act** made the ICC a more powerful and more active body. Although it did not outlaw judicial review of ICC decisions, thereafter those decisions were seldom overturned by the courts.

Congress also passed meat inspection and pure food and drug legislation. In 1906 Upton Sinclair published *The Jungle*, a devastating exposé of the filthy conditions in the Chicago slaughterhouses. Sinclair was more interested in writing a socialist tract than he was in meat inspection, but his book, a best seller, raised a storm against the packers. After Roosevelt read *The Jungle* he sent two officials to Chicago to investigate. Their report was so shocking, he said, that its publication would "be well-nigh ruinous to our export trade in meat." He threatened to release the report unless Congress acted. After a hot fight, the meat inspection bill passed. The Pure Food and Drug Act, forbidding the manufacture and sale of adulterated and fraudulently labeled products, rode through Congress on the coattails of this measure.

Roosevelt has probably received more credit than he deserves for these laws. He had never been deeply interested in pure food legislation, and he considered Dr. Harvey W. Wiley, chief chemist of the Department of Agriculture and the leader of the fight for this reform, something of a crank. He compromised with opponents of meat inspection cheerfully, despite his loud denunciations of the evils under attack. Nevertheless, the end results were positive and in line with his conception of the public good.

To advanced liberals Roosevelt's achievements seemed limited when placed beside his professed objectives and his smug evaluations of what he had done. How could he be a reformer and a defender of established interests at the same time? Roosevelt found no difficulty in holding such a position. As one historian has said, "He stood close to the center and bared his teeth at the conservatives of the right and the liberals of the extreme left."

Read the **Document** "Inside the Packinghouse" from Upton Sinclair's *The Jungle* at **www.myhistorylab.com**

Roosevelt Tilts Left

As the progressive movement advanced, Roosevelt advanced with it. He never accepted all the ideas of what he called its "lunatic fringe," but he took steadily more liberal positions. He always insisted that he was not hostile to business interests, but when those interests sought to exploit the national domain, they had no more implacable foe. **Conservation** of natural resources was dear to his heart and probably his most significant achievement as president. He placed some 150 million acres of forest lands in federal reserves, and he strictly enforced the laws governing grazing, mining, and lumbering.

As Roosevelt became more liberal, conservative Republicans began to balk at following his lead. The sudden panic that struck the financial world in October 1907 speeded the trend. Government policies had no direct bearing on the panic, which began with a run on several important New York trust companies and spread to the Stock Exchange when speculators found themselves unable to borrow money to meet their obligations. In the emergency Roosevelt authorized the deposit of large amounts of government cash in New York banks. He informally agreed to the acquisition of the Tennessee Coal and Iron Company by U.S. Steel when the bankers told him that the purchase was necessary to end the panic. In spite of his efforts, conservatives insisted on referring to the financial collapse as "Roosevelt's panic," and they blamed the president for the depression that followed on its heels.

Roosevelt, however, turned left rather than right. In 1908 he came out in favor of federal income and inheritance taxes, stricter regulation of interstate corporations, and reforms designed to help industrial workers. He denounced "the speculative folly and the flagrant dishonesty" of "malefactors of great wealth," further alienating conservative, or Old Guard, Republicans, who resented the attacks on their integrity implicit in Roosevelt's statements. When the president began criticizing the courts, the last bastion of conservatism, he lost all chance of obtaining further reform legislation. As he said himself, during his last months in office "stagnation continued to rage with uninterrupted violence."

William Howard Taft: The Listless Progressive, or More Is Less

But Roosevelt remained popular and politically powerful; before his term ended, he chose William Howard Taft, his secretary of war, to succeed him and easily obtained Taft's nomination. William Jennings Bryan was again the Democratic candidate. Campaigning on Roosevelt's record, Taft carried the country by well over a million votes, defeating Bryan 321 to 162 in the Electoral College.

Taft was intelligent, experienced, and public spirited; he seemed ideally suited to carry out Roosevelt's policies. Born in Cincinnati in 1857, educated at Yale, he had served as an Ohio judge, as solicitor general of the United States under Benjamin Harrison, and then as a federal circuit court judge before accepting McKinley's assignment to head the Philippine Commission in 1900. His success as civil governor of the Philippines led Roosevelt to make him secretary of war in 1904.

Taft supported the Square Deal loyally. This, together with his mentor's ardent endorsement, won him the backing of most progressive Republicans. Yet the Old Guard liked him too; although outgoing, he had none of the Roosevelt impetuosity and aggressiveness. His genial personality and his obvious desire to avoid conflict appealed to moderates.

However, Taft lacked the physical and mental stamina required of a modern chief executive. Although not lazy, he weighed over 300 pounds and needed to rest this vast bulk more than the job allowed. He liked to eat in leisurely fashion, to idle away mornings on the golf course, to take an afternoon nap. Campaigning bored him; speech making seemed a useless chore. The judicial life was his real love; intense partisanship dismayed and confused him. He was too reasonable to control a coalition and not ambitious enough to impose his will on others. He found extremists irritating and persistent people (including his wife) difficult to resist. He supported many progressive measures, but he never absorbed the progressive spirit.

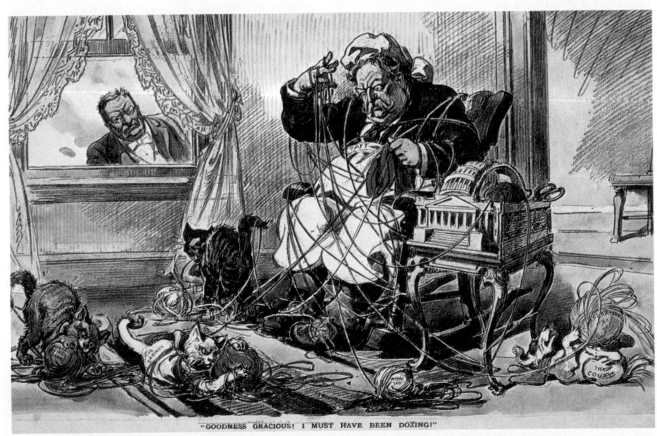

"GOODNESS GRACIOUS! I MUST HAVE BEEN DOZING!"

A hapless Taft is entangled in governmental yarn, while a disapproving Roosevelt looks on. "Goodness gracious! I must have been dozing," reads the caption, a reference to Taft's penchant for naps.

Taft honestly wanted to carry out most of Roosevelt's policies. He enforced the Sherman Act vigorously and continued to expand the national forest reserves. He signed the Mann-Elkins Act of 1910, which empowered the ICC to suspend rate increases without waiting for a shipper to complain and established the Commerce Court to speed the settlement of railroad rate cases. An eight-hour day for all persons engaged in work on government contracts, mine safety legislation, and several other reform measures received his approval. He even summoned Congress into special session specifically to reduce tariff duties—something that Roosevelt had not dared to attempt.

But Taft had been disturbed by Roosevelt's sweeping use of executive power. "We have got to work out our problems on the basis of law," he insisted. Whereas Roosevelt had excelled at maneuvering around congressional opposition and at finding ways to accomplish his objectives without waiting for Congress to act, Taft adamantly refused to use such tactics. His restraint was in many ways admirable, but it reduced his effectiveness.

In 1910 Taft got into difficulty with the conservationists. Although he believed in husbanding natural resources carefully, he did not like the way Roosevelt had circumvented Congress in adding to the forest reserves. He demanded, and eventually obtained, specific legislation to accomplish this purpose. The issue that aroused the conservationists concerned the integrity of his secretary of the interior, Richard A. Ballinger. A less than ardent conservationist, Ballinger returned to the public domain certain waterpower sites that the Roosevelt administration had withdrawn on the legally questionable ground that they were to become ranger stations. Ballinger's action alarmed Chief Forester Gifford Pinchot, the darling of the conservationists. When Pinchot learned that Ballinger intended to validate the shaky claim of mining interests to a large tract of coal-rich land in Alaska, he launched an intemperate attack on the secretary.

In the Ballinger-Pinchot controversy Taft felt obliged to support his own man. The coal lands dispute was complex, and Pinchot's charges were exaggerated. It was certainly unfair to call Ballinger "the most effective opponent the conservation policies have yet had." When Pinchot, whose own motives were partly political, persisted in criticizing Ballinger, Taft dismissed him. He had no choice under the circumstances, but a more adept politician might have found some way of avoiding a showdown.

Breakup of the Republican Party

One ominous aspect of the Ballinger-Pinchot affair was that Pinchot was a close friend of Theodore Roosevelt. After Taft's inauguration, Roosevelt had gone off to hunt big game in Africa, bearing in his baggage an autographed photograph of his protégé and a touching letter of appreciation, in which the new president said, "I can never forget that the power I now exercise was a voluntary transfer from you to me." For months, as he trudged across Africa, guns blazing, Roosevelt was out of touch with affairs in the United States. As soon as he emerged from the wilderness in March 1910, bearing more than 3,000 trophies, including nine lions, five elephants, and thirteen rhinos, he was caught up in the squabble between the progressive members of his party and its titular head. Pinchot met him in Italy, laden with injured innocence and a packet of angry letters from various progressives. TR's intimate friend Senator Henry Cabot Lodge, essentially a conservative, barraged him with messages, the gist of which was that Taft was lazy and inept and that Roosevelt should prepare to become the "Moses" who would guide the party "out of the wilderness of doubt and discontent" into which Taft had led it.

Roosevelt hoped to steer a middle course, but Pinchot's complaints impressed him. Taft had decided to strike out on his own, he concluded. "No man must render such a service as that I rendered Taft and expect the individual . . . not in the end to become uncomfortable and resentful," he wrote Lodge sadly. Taft sensed the former president's coolness and was offended. He was egged on by his ambitious wife, who wanted him to stand clear of Roosevelt's shadow and establish his own reputation.

Perhaps the resulting rupture was inevitable. The Republican party was dividing into two factions, the progressives and the Old Guard. Forced to choose between them, Taft threw in his lot with the Old Guard. Roosevelt backed the progressives. Speaking at Osawatomie, Kansas, in August 1910 he came out for a comprehensive program of social legislation, which he called the **New Nationalism**. Besides attacking "special privilege" and the "unfair money-getting" practices of "lawbreakers of great wealth," he called for a broad expansion of federal power. "The betterment we seek must be accomplished," he said, "mainly through the National Government."

The final break came in October 1911 when Taft ordered an antitrust suit against U.S. Steel. "The effort at prohibiting all combination has substantially failed," Taft said. "The way out lies . . . in completely controlling them." He was prepared to enforce the Sherman Act "or die in the attempt." But this initiative angered Roosevelt because the lawsuit focused on U.S. Steel's absorption of the Tennessee Coal and Iron Company, which Roosevelt had unofficially authorized during the panic of 1907. The government's antitrust brief made Roosevelt appear to have been either a proponent of the monopoly or, far worse, a fool who had been duped by the steel corporation. Early in 1912 he declared himself a candidate for the Republican presidential nomination.

Roosevelt plunged into the preconvention campaign with typical energy. He was almost uniformly victorious in states that held presidential primaries, carrying even Ohio, Taft's home state. However, the president controlled the party machinery and entered the national convention with a small majority of the delegates. Since some Taft delegates had been chosen under questionable circumstances, the Roosevelt forces challenged the right of 254 of them to their seats. The Taft-controlled credentials committee, paying little attention to the evidence, gave all but a few of the disputed seats to the president, who then won the nomination on the first ballot.

Roosevelt was understandably outraged by the ruthless manner in which the Taft "steamroller" had overridden his forces. When his leading supporters urged him to organize a third party, and when two of them, George W. Perkins, formerly a partner of the banker J. P. Morgan, and the publisher Frank Munsey, offered to finance the campaign, Roosevelt agreed to make the race.

In August, amid scenes of hysterical enthusiasm, the first convention of the Progressive party met at Chicago and nominated him for president. Announcing that he felt "as strong as a bull moose," Roosevelt delivered a stirring "confession of faith," calling for strict regulation of corporations, a tariff commission, national presidential primaries, minimum wage and workers' compensation laws, the elimination of child labor, and many other reforms.

Watch the Video *Bull Moose Campaign Speech* at
www.myhistorylab.com

The Election of 1912

The Democrats made the most of the opportunity offered by the Republican schism. Had they nominated a conservative or allowed Bryan a fourth chance, they would probably have ensured Roosevelt's election. Instead, after battling through forty-six ballots at their convention in Baltimore, they nominated Woodrow Wilson, who had achieved a remarkable liberal record as governor of New Jersey. Incidentally, Wilson, a Virginia native, was one of three southern candidates for the nomination, further evidence that the sectional conflicts of Reconstruction had been forgotten.

Although as a political scientist Wilson had criticized the status quo and taken a pragmatic

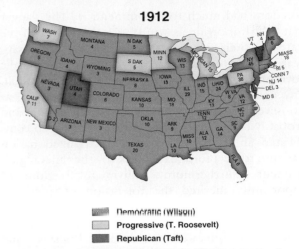

1912

- ▨ Democratic (Wilson)
- ▢ Progressive (T. Roosevelt)
- ▨ Republican (Taft)

1912: Divided Republicans, Democratic Victory In 1912, when Theodore Roosevelt chose to run as a Progressive, he took away millions of votes from the Republican Taft. This ensured Democrat Woodrow Wilson's landslide election.

approach to the idea of government regulation of the economy, he had objected strongly to Bryan's brand of politics. In 1896 he voted for the Gold Democratic party candidate instead of Bryan. But by 1912, influenced partly by ambition and partly by the spirit of the times, he had been converted to progressivism. He called his brand of reform the **New Freedom**.

The federal government could best advance the cause of social justice, Wilson reasoned, by eradicating the special privileges that enabled the "interests" to flourish. Where Roosevelt had lost faith in competition as a way of protecting the public against monopolies, Wilson insisted that competition could be restored. The government must break up the great trusts, establish fair rules for doing business, and subject violators to stiff punishments. Thereafter, the free enterprise system would protect the public from exploitation without destroying individual initiative and opportunity. "If America is not to have free enterprise, then she can have freedom of no sort whatever," he said. Although rather vague, this argument appealed to thousands of voters who found the growing power of large corporations disturbing, but who hesitated to make the thoroughgoing commitment to government control of business that Roosevelt was advocating.

Roosevelt's reasoning was perhaps theoretically more sound. He called for a New Nationalism. Laissez-faire made less sense than it had in earlier times. The complexities of the modern world seemed to call for a positive approach, a plan, the close application of human intelligence to social and economic problems.

But being more in line with American experience than the New Nationalism, Wilson's New

Freedom had much to recommend it. The danger that selfish individuals would use the power of the state for their own ends had certainly not disappeared, despite the efforts of progressives to make government more responsive to popular opinion. Any considerable expansion of national power, as Roosevelt proposed, would increase the danger and probably create new difficulties. Managing so complicated an enterprise as an industrialized nation was sure to be a formidable task for the federal government. Furthermore, individual freedom of opportunity merited the toleration of a certain amount of inefficiency.

To choose between the New Nationalism and the New Freedom, between the dynamic Roosevelt and the idealistic Wilson, was indeed difficult. Thousands grappled with this problem before going to the polls, but partisan politics determined the outcome of the election. Taft got the hard-core Republican vote but lost the progressive wing of the GOP to Roosevelt. Wilson had the solid support of both conservative and liberal Democrats. As a result, Wilson won an easy victory in the Electoral College, receiving 435 votes to Roosevelt's 88 and Taft's 8. The popular vote was Wilson, 6,286,000; Roosevelt, 4,126,000; and Taft, 3,484,000.

If partisan politics had determined the winner, the election was nonetheless an overwhelming endorsement of progressivism. The temper of the times was shown by the 897,000 votes for Eugene Debs, who was again the Socialist candidate. Altogether, professed liberals amassed over 11 million of the 15 million ballots cast. Wilson was a minority president, but he took office with a clear mandate to press forward with further reforms.

••• Read the Document Roosevelt, *The New Nationalism* at www.myhistorylab.com

Wilson: The New Freedom

No one ever rose more suddenly or spectacularly in American politics than Woodrow Wilson. In the spring of 1910 he was president of Princeton University; he had never held or even run for public office. In the fall of 1912 he was president-elect of the United States. Yet if his rise was meteoric, in a very real sense he had devoted his life to preparing for it. He was born in Staunton, Virginia, in 1856, the son of a Presbyterian minister. As a student he became interested in political theory, dreaming of representing his state in the Senate. He studied law solely because he thought it the best avenue to public office, and when he discovered that he did not like legal work, he took a doctorate at Johns Hopkins in political science.

For years Wilson's political ambitions appeared doomed to frustration. He taught at Bryn Mawr, then at Wesleyan, and finally at his alma mater, Princeton. He wrote several influential books, among them *Congressional Government* and *The State*, and achieved an outstanding reputation as a teacher and lecturer. In 1902 he was chosen president of Princeton and soon won a place among the nation's leading educators. He revised the curriculum, introducing many new subjects and insisting that students pursue an organized and integrated course of study. He instituted the preceptorial system, which placed the students in close intellectual and social contact with their teachers. He attracted outstanding young scholars to the Princeton faculty.

In time Wilson's educational ideas and his overbearing manner of applying them got him in trouble with some of Princeton's alumni and trustees. Although his university career was wrecked, the controversies, in which he appeared to be championing democracy and progress in the face of reactionary opponents, brought him at last to the attention of the politicians. Then, in a great rush, came power and fame.

Wilson was an immediate success as president. Since Roosevelt's last year in office, Congress had been almost continually at war with the executive branch and with itself. Legislative achievements had been few. Now a small avalanche of important measures received the approval of the lawmakers. In October 1913 the **Underwood Tariff** brought the first significant reduction of duties since before the Civil War. To compensate for the expected loss of revenue, the act provided for a graduated tax on personal incomes.

Two months later the **Federal Reserve Act** gave the country a central banking system for the first time since Jackson destroyed the Bank of the United States. The measure divided the nation into twelve banking districts, each under the supervision of a Federal Reserve bank, a sort of bank for bankers. All national banks in each district and any state banks that wished to participate had to invest 6 percent of their capital and surplus in the reserve bank, which was empowered to exchange (the technical term is *rediscount*) paper money, called Federal Reserve notes, for the commercial and agricultural paper that member banks took in as security from borrowers. The volume of currency was no longer at the mercy of the supply of gold or any other particular commodity.

The crown and nerve center of the system was the Federal Reserve Board in Washington, which appointed a majority of the directors of the Federal Reserve banks and had some control over rediscount rates (the commission charged by the reserve banks for performing the rediscounting function). The

Woodrow Wilson, presiding over the 1906 Princeton commencement, walks beside steel magnate and educational philanthropist Andrew Carnegie.

board provided a modicum of public control over the banks, but the effort to weaken the power of the great New York banks by decentralizing the system proved ineffective. Nevertheless, a true central banking system was created.

When inflation threatened, the reserve banks could raise the rediscount rate, discouraging borrowing and thus reducing the amount of money in circulation. In bad times it could lower the rate, making it easier to borrow and injecting new dollars into the economy. Much remained to be learned about the proper management of the money supply, but the nation finally had a flexible yet safe currency.

In 1914 Congress passed two important laws affecting corporations. One created the Federal Trade Commission (FTC) to replace Roosevelt's Bureau of Corporations. In addition to investigating corporations and publishing reports, this nonpartisan board could issue cease-and-desist orders against "unfair" trade practices brought to light through its research. The law did not define the term *unfair*, and the commission's rulings could be taken on appeal to the federal courts, but the FTC was nonetheless a powerful instrument for protecting the public against the trusts.

The second measure, the **Clayton Antitrust Act**, made certain specific business practices illegal, including price discrimination that tended to foster monopolies; "tying" agreements, which forbade retailers from handling the products of a firm's competitors; and the creation of interlocking directorates as a means of controlling competing companies. The act

exempted labor unions and agricultural organizations from the antitrust laws and curtailed the use of injunctions in labor disputes. The officers of corporations could be held individually responsible if their companies violated the antitrust laws.

The Democrats controlled both houses of Congress for the first time since 1890 and were eager to make a good record, but Wilson's imaginative and aggressive use of presidential power was decisive. He called the legislators into special session in April 1913 and appeared before them to lay out his program; he was the first president to address Congress in person since John Adams. Then he followed the course of administration bills closely. He had a private telephone line installed between the Capitol and the White House. Administration representatives haunted the cloakrooms and lobbies of both houses. Cooperative congressmen began to receive notes of praise and encouragement, whereas recalcitrant ones received stern demands for support, often pecked out on the president's own portable typewriter.

Wilson explained his success by saying, only half humorously, that running the government was child's play for anyone who had managed the faculty of a university. Responsible party government was his objective; he expected individual Democrats to support the decisions of the party majority, and his idealism never prevented him from awarding the spoils of office to city bosses and conservative congressmen, as long as they supported his program. Nor did his career as a political theorist make him rigid and doctrinaire. In practice the differences between his New Freedom and Roosevelt's New Nationalism tended to disappear. The FTC and the Federal Reserve system represented steps toward the kind of regulated economy that Roosevelt advocated.

There were limits to Wilson's progressivism, limits imposed partly by his temperament and partly by his philosophy. He objected as strenuously to laws granting special favors to farmers and workers as to those benefiting the tycoons. When a bill was introduced in 1914 making low-interest loans available to farmers, he refused to support it. "It is unwise and unjustifiable to extend the credit of the Government to a single class of the community," he said. He considered the provision exempting unions from the antitrust laws equally unsound. Nor would he push for a federal law prohibiting child labor;

Table 21.2 Progressive Legislation (Federal)

Newlands Act	1902	Funneled revenues from sale of public lands to irrigation projects
Elkins Act	1903	Strengthened the ICC by making it illegal for railroads to deviate from published rates, such as by granting rebates
Hepburn Act	1906	Gave ICC the power to fix rates of railroads and other corporations involved in interstate commerce (such as corporations operating oil pipelines)
Pure Food and Durg Act	1906	Prohibited the fraudulent advertising, manufacturing, and selling of impure foods and drugs
Mann-Elkins Act	1910	Empowered ICC to suspend rate increases for railroads or telephone companies
Underwood Tariff	1913	Lowered tariff rates; introduced graduated tax on personal incomes
Federal Reserve Act	1913	Established federal supervision of banking system
Sixteenth Amendment	1913	Authorized federal income tax
Clayton Antitrust Act	1914	Exempted labor unions from antitrust laws and curtailed injunctions against labor leaders
Nineteenth Amendment	1920	Established woman suffrage

such a measure would be unconstitutional, he believed. He also refused to back the constitutional amendment giving the vote to women.

By the end of 1914 Wilson's record, on balance, was positive but distinctly limited. The president believed that the major progressive goals had been achieved; he had no plans for further reform. Many other progressives thought that a great deal more remained to be done.

The Progressives and Minority Rights

On one important issue, race relations, Wilson was distinctly reactionary. With a mere handful of exceptions, the progressives exhibited strong prejudices against nonwhite people and against certain categories of whites as well. Many were as unsympathetic to immigrants from Asia and eastern and southern Europe as any of the "conservative" opponents of immigration in the 1880s and 1890s. The Gentlemen's Agreement excluding Japanese immigrants was reached in 1907 at the height of the progressive movement. In the same year, Congress appointed a commission headed by Senator William Dillingham of Vermont to study the immigration question. The Dillingham Commission labored for more than two years and brought forth a forty-one-volume report that led in 1913 to a bill restricting the number of newcomers to be admitted and reducing especially the influx from eastern and southern Europe. Only the outbreak of war in Europe in 1914, which cut immigration to a trickle, prevented the passage of this measure.

American Indians were also affected by the progressives' racial attitudes. Where the sponsors of the Dawes Act (1887) had assumed that Indians were inherently capable of adopting the ways of "civilized"

people, in the progressive period the tendency was to write Indians off as fundamentally inferior and to assume that they would make second-class citizens at best. Francis Leupp, Theodore Roosevelt's commissioner of Indian affairs, put it this way in a 1905 report: "If nature has set a different physical stamp upon different races of men it is fair to assume that the variation . . . is manifested in mental and moral traits as well. . . . Nothing is gained by trying to undo nature's work." A leading muckraker, Ray Stannard Baker, who was far more sympathetic to blacks than most progressives, dismissed Indians as pathetic beings, "eating, sleeping, idling, with no more thought of the future than a white man's child."

In 1902 Congress passed the Dead Indian Land Act, which made it easier for Indians to sell allotments that they had inherited, and in 1906 another law further relaxed restrictions on land sales. Efforts to improve the education of Indian children continued, but most progressives assumed that only vocational training would help them. Theodore Roosevelt knew from his experiences as a rancher in the Dakota Territory that Indians could be as energetic and capable as whites, but he considered these "exceptional." As for the rest, it would be many generations before they could be expected to "move forward" enough to become "ordinary citizens," Roosevelt believed.

To say that African Americans did not fare well at the hands of progressives would be a gross understatement. White southerners, furious at Populist efforts to unite white and black farmers, imposed increasingly repressive measures after 1896. Segregation became more rigid, white opposition to black voting more monolithic. In 1900 the body of a Mississippi black was dug up by order of the state legislature and reburied in a segregated cemetery; in Virginia in 1902 the daughter of Robert E. Lee was arrested for riding in the black section of a railroad car. "Insult is being added to injury continually," a black journalist in Alabama complained. "Have those in power forgotten that there is a God?"

Many progressive women, still smarting from the insult to their sex entailed in the Fourteenth and Fifteenth Amendments and eager to attract southern support for their campaign for the vote, adopted racist arguments. They contrasted the supposed corruption and incompetence of black voters with their own "purity" and intelligence. Southern progressives of both sexes argued that disfranchising blacks would reduce corruption by removing from unscrupulous white politicians the temptation to purchase black votes!

On May 15, 1916, after deliberating for one hour, an all-white jury in Waco, Texas, found seventeen-year-old Jesse Washington guilty of bludgeoning a white woman to death. A mob rushed him out of the courtroom, chained him to a tree, and burned him to death. The story was chronicled by Patricia Bernstein in *The First Waco Horror* (2005).

The typical southern attitude toward the education of blacks was summed up in a folk proverb: "When you educate a Negro, you spoil a good field hand." In 1910 only about 8,000 black children in the entire South were attending high schools. Despite the almost total suppression of black rights, lynchings persisted; between 1900 and 1914 more than 1,100 blacks were murdered by mobs, most (but not all) in the southern states. In the rare cases in which local prosecutors brought the lynchers to trial, juries almost without exception brought in verdicts of not guilty.

Booker T. Washington was shaken by this trend, but he could find no way to combat it. The times were passing him by. He appealed to his white southern "friends" for help but got nowhere. Increasingly he talked about the virtues of rural life, the evils of big cities, and the uselessness of higher education for black people. By the turn of the century a number of young, well-educated blacks, most of them Northerners, were breaking away from his accommodationist leadership.

Read the **Document** "Events in Paris, Texas," from Ida B. Wells, *A Red Record* at **www.myhistorylab.com**

Black Militancy

William E. B. Du Bois was the most prominent of the militants. Du Bois was born in Great Barrington, Massachusetts, in 1868. His father, a restless wanderer of Negro and French Huguenot stock, abandoned the family, and young William grew up on the edge of poverty. Neither accepted nor openly rejected by the overwhelmingly white community, he devoted himself to his studies, showing such brilliance that his future education was ensured by scholarships: to Fisk University, then to Harvard, and then to the University of Berlin. In 1895 Du Bois became the first American black to earn a PhD in history from Harvard; his dissertation, *The Suppression of the African Slave Trade* (1896), remains a standard reference.

Personal success and "acceptance" by whites did not make the proud and sensitive Du Bois complacent. Outraged by white racism and the willingness of many blacks to settle for second-class citizenship, he set out to make American blacks proud of their color—"Beauty is black," he said—and of their African origins and culture.

Like Washington, Du Bois wanted blacks to lift themselves up by their own bootstraps. They must establish their own businesses, run their own newspapers and colleges, and write their own literature; they must preserve their identity rather than seek to amalgamate themselves into a society that offered them only crumbs and contempt. At first he cooperated with Washington, but in 1903, in the essay "Of Mr. Booker T. Washington and Others," he subjected

A striking likeness of W.E.B. Du Bois drawn by Winold Reiss when Du Bois was in his fifties.

continually survives and persists, continually aspires, continually shows itself in thrift and ability and character." Du Bois, moreover, prided himself on being of mixed races.

Whatever his prejudices, Du Bois exposed both the weaknesses of Washington's strategy and the callousness of white American attitudes. Accommodation was not working. Washington was praised, even lionized by prominent southern whites, yet when Theodore Roosevelt invited him to a meal at the White House they exploded with indignation, and Roosevelt, although not personally prejudiced, meekly backtracked, never repeating his "mistake." He defended his record by saying, "I have stood as valiantly for the rights of the negro as any president since Lincoln." That, sad to relate, was true enough.

Not mere impatience but despair led Du Bois and a few like-minded blacks to meet at Niagara Falls in July 1905 and to issue a stirring list of demands: the unrestricted right to vote, an end to every kind of segregation, equality of economic opportunity, higher education for the talented, equal justice in the courts, and an end to trade-union discrimination. This **Niagara movement** did not attract mass support, but it did stir the consciences of some whites, many of them the descendants of abolitionists, who were also becoming disenchanted by the failure of accommodation to provide blacks with real opportunity.

In 1909, the centennial of the birth of Abraham Lincoln, a group of these liberals, including the newspaperman Oswald Garrison Villard (grandson of William Lloyd Garrison), the social worker Jane Addams, the philosopher John Dewey, and the novelist William Dean Howells, founded the **National Association for the Advancement of Colored People (NAACP).** The organization was dedicated to the eradication of racial discrimination. Its leadership was predominantly white in the early years, but Du Bois became a national officer and the editor of its journal, *The Crisis.*

A turning point had been reached. After 1909 virtually every important leader, white and black alike, rejected the Washington approach. More and more, blacks turned to the study of their past in an effort to stimulate pride in their heritage. In 1915 Carter G. Woodson founded the Association for the Study of Negro Life and History; the following year he began editing the *Journal of Negro History*, which became the major publishing organ for scholarly studies on the subject.

This militancy produced few results in the Progressive Era. Theodore Roosevelt behaved no differently than earlier Republican presidents; he courted blacks when he thought it advantageous, and turned

Washington's "attitude of adjustment and submission" to polite but searching criticism. Washington had asked blacks to give up political power, civil rights, and the hope of higher education, not realizing that "voting is necessary to modern manhood, that . . . discrimination is barbarism, and that black boys need education as well as white boys." Washington "apologizes for injustice," Du Bois charged. "He belittles the emasculating effects of caste distinctions, and opposes the higher training and ambitions of our brightest minds." Du Bois deemed this totally wrong: "The way for a people to gain their reasonable rights is not by voluntarily throwing them away."

Du Bois was not an uncritical admirer of the ordinary American black. He believed that "immorality, crime, and laziness" were common vices. Quite properly he blamed the weaknesses of blacks on the treatment afforded them by whites, but his approach to the solution of racial problems was frankly elitist. "The Negro race," he wrote, "is going to be saved by its exceptional men," what he called the "talented tenth" of the black population. After describing in vivid detail how white mistreatment had corrupted his people, Du Bois added loftily, "A saving remnant his back when he did not. When he ran for president on the Progressive ticket in 1912, he pursued a "lily-white" policy, hoping to break the Democrats' monopoly in the South. By trusting in "[white] men of justice and of vision," Roosevelt argued in the face of decades of experience to the contrary, "the colored men of the South will ultimately get justice."

The southern-born Wilson was actively hostile to blacks. During the 1912 campaign he appealed to them for support and promised to "assist in advancing the interest of their race" in every possible way. Once elected, he refused even to appoint a privately financed commission to study the race problem. Southerners dominated his administration and Congress; as a result, blacks were further degraded. No fewer than thirty-five blacks in the Atlanta post office lost their jobs. In Washington employees in many government offices were rigidly segregated, and those who objected were summarily discharged.

These actions stirred such a storm that Wilson backtracked a little, but he never abandoned his belief that segregation was in the best interests of both races. "Wilson . . . promised a 'new freedom,'" one newspaperman complained. "On the contrary we are given a stone instead of a loaf of bread." Even

Booker T. Washington admitted that his people were more "discouraged and bitter" than at any time in his memory.

Du Bois, who had supported Wilson in 1912, attacked administration policy in *The Crisis* In November 1914 the militant editor of the *Boston Guardian*, William Monroe Trotter, a classmate of Du Bois at Harvard and a far more caustic critic of the Washington approach, led a delegation to the White House to protest the segregation policy of the government. When Wilson accused him of blackmail, Trotter lost his temper, and an ugly confrontation resulted. The mood of black leaders had changed completely.

By this time the Great War had broken out in Europe. Soon every American would feel its effects, blacks perhaps more than any other group. In November 1915, a year almost to the day after Trotter's clash with Wilson, Booker T. Washington died. One era had ended; a new one was beginning.

Many of the young Americans who had participated in the various crusades of the "age of reform" would soon embark on another crusade—but one of a very different character.

Watch the **Video** *The conflict between Booker T. Washington & W.E.B Du Bois* at **www.myhistorylab.com**

Chapter Review

Milestones

1890	National American Woman Suffrage Association is founded
1900	Robert La Follette is elected governor of Wisconsin
	McKinley is reelected president
1901	McKinley is assassinated; Theodore Roosevelt becomes president
1902	Roosevelt helps settle anthracite coal strike
	Oregon adopts initiative system for proposing legislation
1904	Northern Securities case revives Sherman Antitrust Act
	National Child Labor Committee is established
	Theodore Roosevelt is elected president
1905	Anticapitalist Industrial Workers of the World (IWW) is founded
1906	Hepburn Act strengthens Interstate Commerce Commission
	Upton Sinclair exposes Chicago slaughterhouses in *The Jungle*
1907	U.S. Steel absorbs Tennessee Coal and Iron Company
1908	Theodore Roosevelt convenes National Conservation Conference

	Muller v. Oregon upholds law limiting women's work hours
	William Howard Taft is elected president
1909	NAACP is founded
1910	Ballinger-Pinchot Affair deepens Roosevelt-Taft rift
1911	Roosevelt gives New Nationalism speech
1912	Roosevelt runs for president on Progressive ticket
	Woodrow Wilson is elected president
1913	Sixteenth Amendment authorizes federal income taxes
	Seventeenth Amendment provides for direct election of U.S. senators
	Underwood Tariff Act reduces duties and imposes personal income tax
	Federal Reserve Act gives the United States a central banking system again
1914	Federal Trade Commission is created to protect against trusts
	Clayton Antitrust Act regulates business
1920	Nineteenth Amendment guarantees women the right to vote

582 Chapter 21 The Age of Reform

Key Terms

Ashcan School Artists in the early twentieth century who used as their subject matter the things and people found in city streets and slums. Ashcan artists often supported progressive political and social reform, *558*

Clayton Antitrust Act Legislation that strengthened antitrust laws. Passed in 1914, it outlawed interlocking directorates, exempted labor unions from antitrust laws, and limited the use of injunctions in labor disputes, *577*

Conservation The efficient management and use of natural resources, such as forests, grasslands, and rivers; it represents a "middle-of-the-road" policy as opposed to the uncontrolled exploitation of such resources or the preservation those resources from any human exploiters, *572*

Federal Reserve Act A 1913 law establishing a Federal Reserve Board, which controlled the rediscount rate and thus the money supply; this helped regularize the national banking system, *576*

Hepburn Act Federal legislation, passed in 1906, that gave the Interstate Commerce Commission sufficient power to inspect railroad companies' records, set maximum rates, and outlaw free passes, *572*

Industrial Workers of the World (IWW) A militant labor organization, founded in 1905 and inspired by European anarchists, that advocated "abolition of the wage system" and called for a single union of all workers, regardless of trade or skill level; it was repressed during and after World War I, *559*

muckraker A term for progressive investigative journalists who exposed the seamy side of American life at the turn of the twentieth century by "raking up the muck," *558*

National American Woman Suffrage Association (NAWSA) An organization, founded in 1890, that united the National Woman Suffrage Association, headed by Elizabeth Cady Stanton and Susan B. Anthony, and the American Woman Suffrage Association, headed by Lucy Stone. After ratification of the Nineteenth Amendment granting women the vote in 1920, the NAWSA became the League of Women Voters, *567*

National Association for the Advancement of Colored People (NAACP) A national interracial organization, founded in 1909, that promoted the rights of African Americans. Initially it fought against lynching, but from 1955 through 1977, under the leadership of Roy Wilkins, it launched the campaign that overturned legalized segregation and it backed civil rights legislation. The NAACP remains the nation's largest African American organization, *580*

New Freedom Democratic candidate Woodrow Wilson's term in the 1912 presidential campaign for a proposed policy that would restore competition by breaking up the trusts and punishing corporations that violated rules of business conduct, *575*

New Nationalism Progressive candidate Theodore Roosevelt's term in the 1912 presidential election for an expansion of federal power to regulate big business and enact legislation to promote social justice, *574*

Niagara movement A response by W. E. B. Du Bois and other blacks, following a meeting in Niagara Falls in 1905, in opposition to Booker T. Washington's advocacy of black accommodation to white prejudice; these leaders drafted a political program to achieve equal opportunity, equal justice, and an end to segregation that led to the founding of the **National Association for the Advancement of Colored People (NAACP)**, *580*

Progressivism A cluster of movements for various forms of social change—some of them contradictory—during the early twentieth century; progressives generally opposed corruption and inefficiency in government, monopoly power among corporations, and wayward behavior among immigrants and others, *556*

Square Deal The phrase, initially employed by President Theodore Roosevelt in 1904, to describe an arbitrated settlement between workers and an employer, but more generally employed as a goal to promote fair business practices and to punish "bad" corporations that used their economic clout unfairly, *571*

Underwood Tariff A 1913 reform law that lowered tariff rates and levied the first regular federal income tax, *576*

woman suffrage The right of women to vote, ensured by the passage and ratification of the Nineteenth Amendment (1920), *565*

Review Questions

1. The introduction to this chapter compares volunteers today to young reformers early in the twentieth century. What were the similarities and differences?
2. List the ideas of the various progressive-thinking leaders and their movements. What attitudes and values did they share? Were these sufficiently coherent to constitute a "Progressive movement"?
3. How did the attitudes of the reformers and political activists compare with those of the people whose lives they meant to improve? How did immigrants, Native Americans, and workers respond to Progressive reforms?
4. In what ways was the Progressive Era especially challenging for African Americans?
5. How did the relationship between business and government change during the presidencies of Roosevelt, Taft, and Wilson? Did business oppose government regulation or favor it as a means of controlling competition and weakening radicalism?

PEARSON myhistorylab Connections

Reinforce what you learned in this chapter by studying the many documents, images, maps, review tools, and videos available at **www.myhistorylab.com**.

Read and Review

✓ **Study** and **Review** *Chapter 21*

View the **Image** *Little Spinner in Globe Cotton Mill*, p. 565

See the **Map** *Woman Suffrage Before the 19th Century*, p. 567

Read the **Document** *"Inside the Packinghouse" from Upton Sinclair's The Jungle*, p. 572

Read the **Document** *Roosevelt, The New Nationalism*, p. 576

Read the **Document** *"Events in Paris, Texas," from Ida B. Wells, A Red Record*, p. 579

Research and Explore

Watch the **Video** *Bull Moose Campaign Speech*, p. 575

Watch the **Video** *The conflict between Booker T. Washington & W.E.B Du Bois*, p. 581

 ((•—**Hear** the **Audio**

Hear the audio file for Chapter 21 at
www.myhistorylab.com.

Can you find Afghanistan on a map?

During the presidential campaign of 2000, Republican candidate George W. Bush chastised the Clinton administration for sending troops to Haiti and the Balkans. "If we don't stop extending our troops all around the world in nation-building missions," Bush declared, "then we're going to have a serious problem coming down the road."

Few could have imagined that within two years, following the 9/11 attacks on the World Trade Center and the Pentagon, thousands of American troops would be patrolling the high mountains of the Hindu Kush, fighting enemies at places named Tora Bora and Mazar-e

Sharif, and working to install a new government in Afghanistan. A National Geographic Society survey found that nearly half of Americans aged 18 to 24 knew that the fictional island for the *Survivor* TV series was located in the South Pacific, but five in six could not find Afghanistan on a map—even after the United States had invaded the country.

Yet by the summer of 2010, President Barack Obama had increased American troops in Afghanistan to nearly 100,000. "If I thought for a minute that America's vital interests were not at stake here in Afghanistan," he told

From Isolation to Empire

((●─ Hear the Audio **Chapter 22 at www.myhistorylab.com**

■ American troops engage Filipino nationalists near Manila in 1899. The gunboats that carried the soldiers appear in the distance.

American soldiers, "I would order all of you home right away." These vital interests in many ways originated during the late nineteenth and early twentieth centuries.

Until then, Americans had given little thought to foreign affairs. In 1888 Benjamin Harrison articulated a widely held belief when he said that the United States was "an apart nation" and should remain so. That year James Bryce, the British political theorist, made the same point in *The American Commonwealth*. "Happy America," he wrote, stood "apart in a world of her own . . . safe even from menace."

But sentiment was shifting. Intellectuals and many others cited "Darwinian" principles, such as "survival of the fittest," to justify American expansion abroad. Missionaries called on Americans to help impoverished and ill-educated peoples elsewhere in the world. American businessmen, increasingly confident of their own powers, craved access to foreign resources and markets. Such factors converged in Cuba, prompting the United States to go to war with Spain.

In 1898 tens of thousands of American troops were dispatched to Cuba and, within a year, to the Philippines. For years thereafter, Americans at home would struggle to locate on globes and in atlases battle sites in places such as Balangiga, Pulang Lupa, and Kandahar. They still do. ■

Isolation or Imperialism?

If Americans had little concern for what was going on far beyond the seas, their economic interest in Latin America was great and growing, and in East Asia only somewhat less so. Shifts in foreign commerce resulting from industrialization strengthened this interest with every passing year. Whether one sees isolation or expansion as the hallmark of American foreign policy after 1865 depends on what part of the world one looks at.

The disdain of the people of the United States for Europe rested on several historical foundations. Faith in the unique character of American civilization—and the converse of that belief, suspicion of Europe's supposedly aristocratic and decadent society—formed the chief basis of this **isolationism**. Bitter memories of indignities suffered during the Revolution and the Napoleonic Wars and anger at the hostile attitude of the great powers toward the United States during the Civil War strengthened it. Also important was the undeniable truth that the United States, in an era before airplanes, was virtually invulnerable to European attack and at the same time incapable of mounting an offensive against any European power. In turning their backs on Europe, Americans were taking no risk and passing up few opportunities—hence their indifference.

When occasional conflicts with one or another of the great powers erupted, the United States pressed its claims hard. It insisted, for example, that Great Britain pay for the loss of some 100,000 tons of American shipping sunk by Confederate cruisers that had been built in British yards during the rebellion. Some politicians even demanded that the British pay for the entire cost of the war after the Battle of Gettysburg—some $2 billion—on the grounds that without British backing the Confederacy would have collapsed at about that point. However, the controversy never became critical, and in 1871 the two nations signed the Treaty of Washington, agreeing to arbitrate the so-called *Alabama* claims. The next year the judges awarded the United States $15.5 million for the ships and cargoes that had been destroyed. Such incidents never amounted to much.

Origins of the Large Policy: Coveting Colonies

The nation's interests elsewhere in the world gradually increased. During the Civil War, France had established a protectorate over Mexico, installing the

Midway Island, an inhospitable atoll acquired in 1867, was valuable as a military base located midway between Pearl Harbor, another naval station, and East Asia. The acquisition of a Pacific empire during these years was a reason why Pearl Harbor and Midway became pivotal during the war in the Pacific in World War II.

Archduke Maximilian of Austria as emperor. In 1866 Secretary of State William H. Seward demanded that the French withdraw, and the United States moved 50,000 soldiers to the Rio Grande. While fear of American intervention was only one of many reasons for their action, the French pulled their troops out of Mexico during the winter of 1866–1867. Mexican nationalists promptly seized and executed Maximilian. In 1867, at the instigation of Seward, the United States purchased Alaska from Russia for $7.2 million, thereby ridding the continent of another foreign power.

In 1867 the aggressive Seward acquired the Midway Islands in the western Pacific, which had been discovered in 1859 by an American naval officer, N. C. Brooks. Seward also made overtures toward annexing the Hawaiian Islands, and he looked longingly at Cuba. In 1870 President Grant submitted to the Senate a treaty annexing the Dominican Republic. He applied tremendous pressure in an effort to obtain ratification, thus forcing a "great debate" on extracontinental expansion. Expansionists stressed the wealth and resources of the country, the markets it would provide, and even its "salubrious climate." But the arguments of the opposition proved more persuasive. The distance of the Dominican Republic from the continent and its crowded, dark-skinned population of what one congressman called "semi-civilized, semi-barbarous men who cannot speak our language" made annexation unattractive. The treaty was rejected. Seward had to admit that there was no significant support in the country for his expansionist plans.

The internal growth that preoccupied Americans eventually led them to look outward. By the late

1880s the country was exporting a steadily increasing share of its agricultural and industrial output. Exports, only $450 million in 1870, passed the billion-dollar mark early in the 1890s. Imports increased at a rate only slightly less spectacular.

The character of foreign trade was also changing: Manufactures loomed ever more important among exports until in 1898 the country shipped abroad more manufactured goods than it imported. By this time American steelmakers could compete with producers anywhere in the world. In 1900 one American firm received a large order for steel plates from a Glasgow shipbuilder, and another won contracts for structural steel to be used in constructing bridges for the Uganda Railroad in British East Africa. When American industrialists became conscious of their ability to compete with Europeans in far-off markets, they took more interest in world affairs, particularly during periods of depression.

Shifting intellectual currents further altered the attitudes of Americans. Darwin's theories, applicable by analogy to international relations, gave the concept of manifest destiny a new plausibility. Darwinists like the historian John Fiske argued that the American democratic system of government was so clearly the world's "fittest" that it was destined to spread peacefully over "every land on the earth's surface." In *Our Country* (1885) Josiah Strong found racist and religious justifications for American expansionism, again based on the theory of evolution. The Anglo-Saxon race, centered now in the United States, possessed "an instinct or genius for colonization," Strong claimed. "God, with infinite wisdom and skill is training the Anglo-Saxon race for . . . the final competition of races." "Can anyone doubt," Strong asked, "that the result of this . . . will be 'the survival of the fittest'?"[1]

The completion of the conquest of the American West encouraged Americans to consider expansion beyond the seas. "For nearly 300 years the dominant fact in American life has been expansion," declared Frederick Jackson Turner, propounder of the frontier thesis. "That these energies of expansion will no longer operate would be a rash prediction." Turner and writers who advanced other expansionist arguments were much influenced by foreign thinking. European liberals had tended to disapprove of colonial ventures, but in the 1870s and 1880s many of them were changing their minds. English liberals in particular began to talk and write about the "superiority" of English culture, to describe the virtues of the "Anglo-Saxon race," to stress a "duty" to spread Christianity among the heathen, and to advance economic arguments for overseas expansion.

European ideas were reinforced for Americans by their observation of the imperialist activities of the European powers in what would today be called underdeveloped areas. "While the great powers of Europe are steadily enlarging their colonial domination in Asia and Africa," James G. Blaine said in 1884, "it is the especial province of this country to improve and expand its trade with the nations of America." While Blaine emphasized commerce, the excitement and adventure of overseas enterprises appealed to many people even more than the economic possibilities or any sense of obligation to fulfill a supposed national, religious, or racial destiny.

Finally, military and strategic arguments were advanced to justify adopting a "large" policy. The powerful Union army had been demobilized rapidly after Appomattox; in the 1880s only about 25,000 men were under arms, their chief occupation fighting Indians in the West.

Half the navy, too, had been scrapped after the war, and the remaining ships were obsolete. While other nations were building steam-powered iron warships, the United States still depended on wooden sailing vessels. In 1867 a British naval publication accurately described the American fleet as "hapless, broken-down, tattered [and] forlorn."

Although no foreign power menaced the country, the decrepit state of the navy vexed many of its officers and led one of them, Captain Alfred Thayer Mahan, to develop a startling theory about the importance of sea power. He explained his theory in two important books, *The Influence of Sea Power Upon History* (1890) and *The Influence of Sea Power Upon the French Revolution and Empire* (1892). According to Mahan, history proved that a nation with a powerful navy and the overseas bases necessary to maintain it would be invulnerable in war and prosperous in time of peace. Applied to the current American situation, this meant that in addition to building a modern fleet, the United States should obtain a string of coaling stations and bases in the Caribbean, annex the Hawaiian Islands, and cut a canal across Central America. A more extensive colonial empire might follow, but these bases and the canal they would protect were essential first steps to ensure America's future as a great power.

Writing at a time when the imperialist-minded European nations showed signs of extending their influence in South America and the Pacific islands, Mahan attracted many influential disciples. One was Congressman Henry Cabot Lodge of Massachusetts, a prominent member of the Naval Affairs Committee.

---

[1]In later writings Strong insisted that by "fittest" he meant "social efficiency," not "mere strength."

Lodge had married into a navy family and was close with the head of the new Naval War College, Commodore Stephen B. Luce. In 1883 he helped push through Congress an act authorizing the building of three steel warships, and he consistently advocated expanding and modernizing the fleet. Elevated to the Senate in 1893, Lodge pressed for expansionist policies, basing his arguments on the strategic concepts of Mahan. "Sea power," he proclaimed, "is essential to the greatness of every splendid people." Lodge's friend Theodore Roosevelt was another ardent supporter of the "large" policy, but he had little influence until McKinley appointed him assistant secretary of the navy in 1897.

View the Image *Uncle Sam Teaching the World* at
www.myhistorylab.com

Toward an Empire in the Pacific

The interest of the United States in the Pacific and East Asia began in the late eighteenth century, when the first American merchant ship dropped anchor in Canton harbor. After the Treaty of Wanghia (1844), American merchants in China enjoyed many privileges and trade expanded rapidly. Missionaries began to flock into the country—in the late 1880s, over 500 were living there.

The Hawaiian Islands were an important way station on the route to China, and by 1820 merchants and missionaries were making contacts there. As early as 1854 a movement to annex the islands existed, although it foundered because Hawaii insisted on being admitted to the Union as a state. Commodore Perry's expedition to Japan led to the signing of a commercial treaty (1858) that opened several Japanese ports to American traders.

The United States pursued a policy of cooperating with the European powers in expanding commercial opportunities in East Asia. In Hawaii the tendency was to claim a special position but to accept the fact that Europeans also had interests in the islands. This state of affairs did not change radically following the Civil War. Despite Chinese protests over the exclusion of their nationals from the United States after 1882, American commercial privileges in China were not disturbed.

American influence in Hawaii increased steadily; the descendants of missionary families, most of them engaged in raising sugar, dominated the Hawaiian monarchy. While they made no overt effort to make the islands an American colony, all the expansionist ideas

of the era—manifest destiny, Darwinism, Josiah Strong's racist and religious assumptions, and the relentless force of American commercial interests—pointed them in that direction. In 1875 a reciprocity treaty admitted Hawaiian sugar to the United States free of duty in return for a promise to yield no territory to a foreign power. When this treaty was renewed in 1887, the United States obtained the right to establish a naval base at Pearl Harbor. In addition to occupying Midway, America obtained a foothold in the Samoan Islands in the South Pacific.

During the 1890s American interest in the Pacific area steadily intensified. Conditions in Hawaii had much to do with this. The McKinley Tariff Act of 1890, discontinuing the duty on raw sugar and compensating American producers of cane and beet sugar by granting them a bounty of two cents a pound, struck Hawaiian sugar growers hard, for it destroyed the advantage they had gained in the reciprocity treaty.

The following year the death of the complaisant King Kalakaua brought Queen Liliuokalani, a determined nationalist, to the throne. Placing herself at

Queen Liliuokalani (1838–1917) succeeded her brother as ruling monarch of Hawaii in 1891. In 1893 she was deposed by a consortium of American and European business interests.

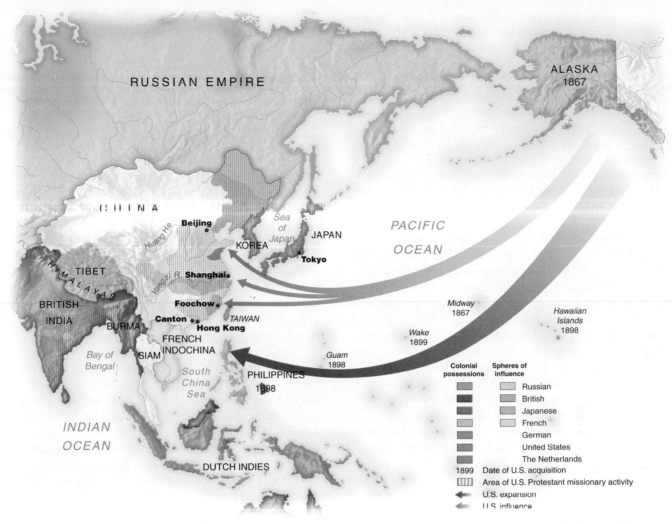

The Course of Empire, 1867–1901 China was the focus of American imperial visions: Missionaries, most of them women, flocked into China, and American manufacturers craved access to the huge China market.

the head of a "Hawaii for the Hawaiians" movement, she abolished the existing constitution under which the white minority had pretty much controlled the islands and attempted to rule as an absolute monarch. The resident Americans then staged a coup. In January 1893, with the connivance of the U.S. minister, John L. Stevens, who ordered 150 marines from the cruiser *Boston* into Honolulu, they deposed Queen Liliuokalani and set up a provisional government. Stevens recognized their regime at once, and the new government sent a delegation to Washington to seek a treaty of annexation.

In the closing days of the Harrison administration such a treaty was negotiated and sent to the Senate, but when Cleveland took office in March, he withdrew it. The new president disapproved of the way American troops had been used to overthrow the monarchy and attempted to restore Queen Liluokalani. But by now the new regime, backed by American businessmen, was firmly entrenched. Cleveland found himself unable to do anything.

Finally, in July 1898, after the outbreak of the Spanish-American War, Congress annexed the islands by joint resolution, a procedure requiring only a simple majority vote.

View the Image *Iolani Palace, Hawaii* at **www.myhistorylab.com**

Toward an Empire in Latin America

Most of the arguments for extending American influence in the Pacific applied more strongly to Central and South America, where the United States had much larger economic interests and where the strategic importance of the region was clear. Furthermore, the Monroe Doctrine had long conditioned the American people to the idea of acting to protect national interests in the Western Hemisphere.

As early as 1869 President Grant had come out for an American-owned canal across the isthmus of Panama, in spite of the fact that the United States had agreed in the Clayton-Bulwer Treaty with Great Britain (1850) that neither nation would "obtain or maintain for itself any exclusive control" over an inter-oceanic canal. In 1880, when the French engineer Ferdinand de Lesseps organized a company to build a canal across the isthmus, President Hayes announced that the United States would not permit a European power to control such a waterway. "The policy of the country is a canal under American control," he announced, another blithe disregard of the Clayton-Bulwer agreement.

When Cleveland returned to power in 1893, the possibility of trouble in Latin America seemed remote, for he had always opposed imperialistic ventures. Yet scarcely two years later the United States was again on the verge of war in South America as a result of a crisis in Venezuela, and before this issue was settled Cleveland had made the most powerful claim to American hegemony in the hemisphere ever uttered. The tangled borderland between Venezuela and British Guiana had long been in dispute, Venezuela demanding more of the region than it was entitled to and Great Britain making exaggerated claims and imperiously refusing to submit the question to arbitration. What made a crisis of the controversy was the political situation in the United States. With his party rapidly deserting him because of his stand on the silver question, and with the election of 1896 approaching, President Cleveland desperately needed a popular issue.

There was considerable latent anti-British feeling in the United States. By taking the Venezuelan side in the boundary dispute, Cleveland would be defending a weak neighbor against a great power, a position certain to evoke a popular response. "Turn this Venezuela question up or down, North, South, East or West, and it is a winner" one Democrat advised the president.

Cleveland did not resist the temptation to intervene. In July 1895 he ordered Secretary of State Richard Olney to send a near ultimatum to the British. By occupying the disputed territory, Olney insisted, Great Britain was invading Venezuela and violating the Monroe Doctrine. Quite gratuitously, he went on to boast, "Today the United States is practically sovereign on this continent, and its fiat is law upon the subjects to which it confines its interposition." Unless Great Britain responded promptly by agreeing to arbitration, the president would call the question to the attention of Congress.

The note threatened war, but the British ignored it for months. They did not take the United States seriously as a world power, and with reason, for the American navy, although expanding, could not hope to stand up against the British, who had fifty battleships, twenty-five armored cruisers, and many smaller vessels. When Lord Salisbury, the prime minister and foreign secretary, finally replied, he rejected outright the argument that the Monroe Doctrine had any status under international law and refused to arbitrate what he called the "exaggerated pretensions" of the Venezuelans.

If Olney's note had been belligerent, this reply was supercilious. Cleveland was furious. On December 17, 1895, he asked Congress for authority to appoint an American commission to determine the correct line between British Guiana and Venezuela. When that had been done, he added, the United States should "resist by every means in its power" the appropriation by Great Britain of any territory "we have determined of right belongs to Venezuela." Congress responded at once, unanimously appropriating $100,000 for the boundary commission. Popular approval was almost universal.

In Great Britain government and people suddenly awoke to the seriousness of the situation. No one wanted a war with the United States over a remote patch of tropical real estate. In Europe, Britain was concerned about German economic competition and the increased military power of that nation. In addition Canada would be terribly vulnerable to American attack in the event of war. The immense potential strength of the United States could no longer be ignored. Why make an enemy of a nation of 70 million, already the richest industrial power in the world? To fight with the United States, the British colonial secretary realized, "would be an absurdity as well as a crime."

Great Britain agreed to arbitrate the boundary. The war scare subsided; soon Olney was talking about "our inborn and instinctive English sympathies" and offering "to stand side by side and shoulder to shoulder with England in . . . the defense of human rights." When the boundary tribunal awarded nearly all the disputed region to Great Britain, whatever ill feeling the surrender may have occasioned in that country faded away. Instead of leading to war, the affair marked the beginning of an era of Anglo-American friendship. It had the unfortunate effect, however, of adding to the long-held American conviction that the nation could get what it wanted in international affairs by threat and bluster—a dangerous illusion.

The Cuban Revolution

On February 10, 1896, scarcely a week after Venezuela and Great Britain had signed the treaty ending their dispute, General Valeriano Weyler arrived in Havana from Spain to take up his duties as governor of Cuba. His assignment to this post was occasioned by the guerrilla warfare that Cuban nationalist rebels had been waging for almost a year. Weyler, a tough and ruthless soldier, set out to administer Cuba with "a salutary rigor." He began herding the rural population into wretched **"reconcentration" camps** to deprive the rebels of food and recruits. Resistance in Cuba hardened.

The United States had been interested in Cuba since the time of John Quincy Adams and, were it not for Northern opposition to adding more slave territory, might well have obtained the island one way or another before 1860. When the Cubans revolted against Spain in 1868, considerable support for intervening on their behalf developed. Hamilton Fish, Grant's secretary of state, resisted this sentiment, and Spain managed to pacify the rebels in 1878 by promising reforms. But change was slow in coming—slavery was not abolished until 1886. The worldwide depression of the 1890s hit the Cuban economy hard, and when an American tariff act in 1894 jacked up the rate on Cuban sugar by 40 percent, thus cutting off Cuban growers from the American market, the resulting distress precipitated another revolt.

Public sympathy in the United States went to the Cubans, who seemed to be fighting for liberty and democracy against an autocratic Old World power. Most newspapers supported the rebels; labor unions, veterans' organizations, many Protestant clergymen, a great majority of American blacks, and important politicians in both major parties demanded that the United States aid their cause. Rapidly increasing American investments in Cuban sugar plantations, now approaching $50 million, were endangered by the fighting and by the social chaos sweeping across the island.

Cuban propagandists in the United States played on American sentiments cleverly. When reports, often exaggerated, of the cruelty of "Butcher" Weyler and the horrors of his reconcentration camps filtered into America, the cry for action intensified. In April 1896 Congress adopted a resolution suggesting that the revolutionaries be granted the rights of belligerents. Since this would have been akin to formal recognition, Cleveland would not go that far, but he did exert diplomatic pressure on Spain to remove the causes of the rebels' complaints, and he offered the services of his government as mediator. The Spanish rejected the suggestion. For a time the issue subsided. The election of 1896 deflected American attention from Cuba, and then McKinley refused to take any action that might disturb Spanish-American relations. Business interests—except those with holdings in Cuba—backed McKinley, for they feared that a crisis would upset the economy, which was just beginning to pick up after the depression. In Cuba General Weyler made some progress toward stifling rebel resistance.

American expansionists, however, continued to demand intervention, and the press, especially Joseph Pulitzer's *New York World* and William Randolph Hearst's *New York Journal*, competing fiercely to increase circulation, kept resentment alive with tales of Spanish atrocities. McKinley remained adamant. Although he warned Spain that Cuba must be pacified, and soon, his tone was friendly and he issued no ultimatum. A new government in Spain relieved the situation by recalling Weyler and promising partial self-government to the Cubans. In a message to Congress in December 1897, McKinley urged that Spain be given "a reasonable chance to realize her expectations" in the island. McKinley was not insensible to Cuba's plight—while far from being a rich man, he made an anonymous contribution of $5,000 to the Red Cross Cuban relief fund—but he genuinely desired to avoid intervention.

His hopes were doomed, primarily because Spain failed to "realize her expectations." The fighting in Cuba continued. When riots broke out in Havana in January 1898, McKinley ordered the battleship *Maine* to Havana harbor to protect American citizens.

Shortly thereafter Hearst's *New York Journal* printed a letter written to a friend in Cuba by the Spanish minister in Washington, Dupuy de Lôme. The letter had been stolen by a spy. De Lôme, an experienced but arrogant diplomat, failed to appreciate McKinley's efforts to avoid intervening in Cuba. In the letter he characterized the president as a *politicastro*, or "small-time politician," which was a gross error, and a "bidder for the admiration of the crowd," which was equally insulting though somewhat closer to the truth. Americans were outraged, and de Lôme's hasty resignation did little to soothe their feelings.

Then, on February 15, the *Maine* exploded and sank in Havana harbor, 260 of the crew perishing in the disaster. Interventionists in the United States accused Spain of having destroyed the ship and clamored for war. The willingness of Americans to blame Spain indicates the extent of anti-Spanish opinion in the United States by 1898. No one has ever discovered what actually happened. A naval court of inquiry decided that the vessel had been sunk by a submarine mine, but it now seems more likely that an internal explosion destroyed the *Maine*. The Spanish government could hardly have been foolish enough to commit an act that would probably bring American troops into Cuba.

With admirable courage, McKinley refused to panic; but he could not resist the wishes of millions of citizens that something be done to stop the fighting

The explosion of the *Maine* in Havana harbor, killing 260 men, caused much speculation in the newspapers and across the nation. Many Americans accused Spain of destroying the ship, a reaction that typified American sentiment toward the Spanish in 1898. What really caused the explosion remains unknown.

McKinley spent a succession of sleepless nights; sedatives brought him no repose. Finally, early in April, the president drafted a message asking for authority to use the armed forces "to secure a full and final termination of hostilities" in Cuba.

At the last moment the Spanish government seemed to yield; it ordered its troops in Cuba to cease hostilities. McKinley passed this information on to Congress along with his war message, but he gave it no emphasis and did not try to check the march toward war. To seek further delay would have been courageous but not necessarily wiser. Merely to stop fighting was not enough. The Cuban nationalists now insisted on full independence, and the Spanish politicians were unprepared to abandon the last remnant of their once-great American empire. If the United States took Cuba by force, the Spanish leaders might save their political skins; if they meekly surrendered the island, they were done for.

Watch the Video   Burial of the *Maine* Victims at www.myhistorylab.com

and allow the Cubans to determine their own fate. Spanish pride and Cuban patriotism had taken the issue of peace or war out of the president's hands. Spain could not put down the rebellion, and it would not yield to the nationalists' increasingly extreme demands. To have granted independence to Cuba might have caused the Madrid government to fall, or might even have led to the collapse of the monarchy, for the Spanish public was in no mood to surrender. The Cubans, sensing that the continuing bloodshed aided their cause, refused to give the Spanish regime room to maneuver. After the *Maine* disaster, Spain might have agreed to an armistice had the rebels asked for one, and in the resulting negotiations it might well have given up the island. The rebels refused to make the first move. The fighting continued, bringing the United States every day closer to intervention.

The president faced a dilemma. Most of the business interests of the country, to which he was particularly sensitive, opposed intervention. His personal feelings were equally firm. "I have been through one war," he told a friend. "I have seen the dead piled up, and I do not want to see another." Congress, however, seemed determined to act. When he submitted a restrained report on the sinking of the *Maine*, the Democrats in Congress, even most of those who had supported Cleveland's policies, gleefully accused him of timidity. Vice President Garret A. Hobart warned him that the Senate could not be held in check for long; should Congress declare war on its own, the administration would be discredited.

The "Splendid Little" Spanish-American War

On April 20, 1898, Congress, by joint resolution, recognized the independence of Cuba and authorized the use of the armed forces to drive out the Spanish. An amendment proposed by Senator Henry M. Teller disclaiming any intention of adding Cuban territory to the United States passed without opposition. Four days after passage of the **Teller Amendment**, Spain declared war on the United States.

The Spanish-American War was fought to free Cuba, but the first action took place on the other side of the globe, in the Philippine Islands. Weeks earlier, Theodore Roosevelt, at the time assistant secretary of the navy, had alerted Commodore George Dewey, who was in command of the United States Asiatic Squadron located at Hong Kong, to move against the Spanish base at Manila if war came. Dewey had acted promptly, drilling his gun crews, taking on supplies, giving his gleaming white ships a coat of battle-gray paint, and establishing secret contacts with the Filipino nationalist leader, Emilio Aguinaldo. When word of the declaration of war

Sailors on the USS *Oregon* watch the destruction of the Spanish cruiser, *Cristobal Colon*, during the Battle of Santiago, Cuba, July 3, 1898.

reached him, Dewey steamed from Hong Kong across the South China Sea with four cruisers and two gunboats. On the night of April 30 he entered Manila Bay, and at daybreak he opened fire on the Spanish fleet at 5,000 yards. His squadron made five passes, each time reducing the range; when the smoke had cleared, all ten of Admiral Montojo's ships had been destroyed. Not a single American was killed in the engagement.

Dewey immediately asked for troops to take and hold Manila, for now that war had been declared, he could not return to Hong Kong or put in at any other neutral port. McKinley took the fateful step of dispatching some 11,000 soldiers and additional naval support. On August 13 these forces, assisted by Filipino irregulars under Aguinaldo, captured Manila.

Meanwhile, in Cuba, the United States had won a swift and total victory, though more because of the weakness of the Spanish armed forces than because of the power or efficiency of the Americans. When the war began, the U.S. regular army consisted of about 28,000 men. This tiny force was bolstered by 200,000 hastily enlisted volunteers. In May an expeditionary force gathered at Tampa, Florida. That hamlet was inundated by the masses of men and supplies that descended upon it. Entire regiments sat without uniforms or weapons while hundreds of freight cars jammed with equipment lay forgotten on sidings. Army management was abominable, rivalry between commanders a serious problem. Aggressive units like the regiment of "Rough Riders" raised by Theodore Roosevelt, who had resigned his Navy Department post to become a lieutenant colonel of volunteers, scrambled for space and supplies, shouldering aside other units to get what they needed. "No words could describe . . . the confusion and lack of system and the general mismanagement of affairs here," the angry Roosevelt complained.

Since a Spanish fleet under Admiral Pascual Cervera was known to be in Caribbean waters, no invading army could safely embark until the fleet could be located. On May 29 American ships found

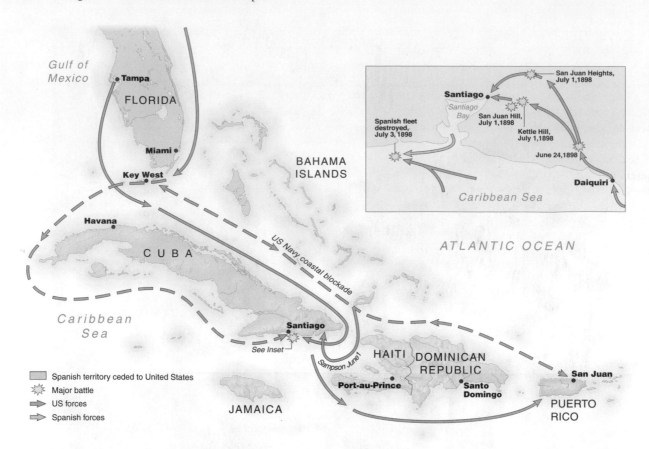

Spanish-American War: Caribbean Theater, 1898 After boarding in Tampa, American soldiers landed near Santiago, Cuba. They swiftly overran Spanish fortifications on the heights to the east of the city. When U.S. troops came within artillery range of Santiago Bay, the Spanish fleet fled. Soon the Spanish ships were intercepted and destroyed by the American navy.

Cervera at Santiago harbor, on the eastern end of Cuba, and established a blockade. In June a 17,000-man expeditionary force commanded by General William Shafter landed at Daiquiri, east of Santiago, and pressed quickly toward the city, handicapped more by its own bad staff work than by the enemy, though the Spanish troops resisted bravely. The Americans sweated through Cuba's torrid summer in heavy wool winter uniforms, ate "embalmed beef" out of cans, and fought mostly with old-fashioned rifles using black powder cartridges that marked the position of each soldier with a puff of smoke whenever he pulled the trigger. On July 1 they broke through undermanned Spanish defenses and stormed San Juan Hill, the intrepid Roosevelt in the van. ("Are you afraid to stand up while I am on horseback?" Roosevelt demanded of one soldier.)

With Santiago harbor in range of American artillery, Admiral Cervera had to run the blockade. On July 3 his black-hulled ships, flags proudly flying, steamed forth from the harbor and fled westward along the coast. Like hounds after rabbits, five American battleships and two cruisers, commanded by Rear Admiral William T. Sampson and Commodore

Winfield Scott Schley, ran them down. In four hours the entire Spanish force was destroyed by a hail of eight-inch and thirteen-inch projectiles (the size of artillery shells refers to their diameter). Damage to the American ships was superficial; only one American seaman lost his life in the engagement.

The end then came abruptly. Santiago surrendered on July 17. A few days later, other U.S. troops completed the occupation of Puerto Rico. On August 12, one day before the fall of Manila, Spain agreed to get out of Cuba and to cede Puerto Rico and an island in the Marianas (Guam) to the United States. The future of the Philippines was to be settled at a formal peace conference, convening in Paris on October 1.

🔊 ▶ **Watch** the **Video**   *Roosevelt's Rough Riders* at www.myhistorylab.com

Developing a Colonial Policy

Although the Spanish resisted surrendering the Philippines at Paris, they had been so thoroughly defeated that they had no choice. The decision hung rather on the outcome of a conflict over policy within the United States. The war, won at so little cost militarily, produced problems far larger than those it solved.[2] The nation had become a great power in the world's eyes. As a French diplomat wrote a few years later, "[The United States] is seated at the table where the great game is played, and it cannot leave it." European leaders had been impressed by the forcefulness of Cleveland's diplomacy in the Venezuela boundary dispute and by the efficiency displayed by the navy in the war. The annexation of Hawaii and other overseas bases intensified their conviction that the United States was determined to become a major force in international affairs.

But were the American people determined to exercise that force? The debate over taking the Philippine Islands throws much light on their attitudes. The imagination of Americans had been captured by the trappings of empire, not by its essence. It was titillating to think of a world map liberally sprinkled with American flags and of the economic benefits that colonies might bring, but most citizens were not prepared to join in a worldwide struggle for power and influence. They entered blithely on adventures in far-off regions without facing the implications of their decision.

---

[2]More than 5,000 Americans died as a result of the conflict, but fewer than 400 fell in combat. The others were mostly victims of yellow fever, typhoid, and other diseases.

Since the United States (in the Teller Amendment) had abjured any claim to Cuba, even though the island had long been desired by expansionists, logic dictated that a similar policy be applied to the Philippines, a remote land few Americans had ever thought about before 1898. But expansionists were eager to annex the entire archipelago. Even before he had learned to spell the name, Senator Lodge was saying that "the Phillipines [sic] mean a vast future trade and wealth and power," offering the nation a greater opportunity "than anything that has happened . . . since the annexation of Louisiana."

President McKinley adopted a more cautious stance, but he too favored "the general principle of holding on to what we can get." A speaking tour of the Midwest in October 1898, during which he experimented with varying degrees of commitment to expansionism, convinced him that the public wanted the islands. Business opinion had shifted dramatically during the war. Business leaders were now calling the Philippines the gateway to the markets of East Asia.

The Anti-Imperialists

The war had produced a wave of unifying patriotic feeling. It greatly furthered reconciliation between the North and the South; two major generals, for example, were Confederate veterans. But victory raised new

While the good children (the states) sit at their seats, with the Indian off to the side, the unruly blacks—"Cuba," "Puerto Rico," "Hawaii," and "Philippines"—are lectured by Uncle Sam. Racist anti-imperialists argued, as did this cartoon in *Puck* in 1899, that the inclusion of other peoples would weaken the American nation.

divisive questions. An important minority objected strongly to the U.S. acquisition of overseas possessions. Those opposed to annexing the Philippines included such diverse persons as the tycoon Andrew Carnegie and the labor leader Samuel Gompers, the venerable Republican Senator George Frisbie Hoar of Massachusetts and the southern Democratic firebrand "Pitchfork Ben" Tillman, writers Mark Twain and William Dean Howells, the reformers Lincoln Steffens and Jane Addams, and the educators Charles W. Eliot of Harvard and David Starr Jordan of Stanford.

The anti-imperialists insisted that since no one would consider statehood for the Philippines, it would be unconstitutional to annex them. It was a violation of the spirit of the Declaration of Independence to govern a foreign territory without the consent of its inhabitants, Senator Hoar argued; by taking over "vassal states" in "barbarous archipelagoes" the United States was "trampling . . . on our own great Charter, which recognizes alike the liberty and the dignity of individual manhood."

McKinley was not insensitive to this appeal to idealism and tradition, which was the fundamental element in the anti-imperialist argument. But he rejected it for several reasons.

Public opinion would not sanction restoring Spanish authority in the Philippines or allowing some other power to have them. That the Filipinos were sufficiently advanced and united socially to form a stable government if granted independence seemed unlikely. Senator Hoar believed that "for years and for generations, and perhaps for centuries, there would have been turbulence, disorder and revolution" in the islands if they were left to their own devices.

Strangely—for he was a kind and gentle man—Hoar faced this possibility with equanimity. McKinley was unable to do so. The president searched the depths of his soul and could find no solution but annexation. Of course the state of public feeling made the decision easier, and he probably found the idea of presiding over an empire appealing. Certainly the commercial possibilities did not escape him. In the end it was with a heavy sense of responsibility that he ordered the American peace commissioners to insist on acquiring the Philippines. To salve the feelings of the Spanish the United States agreed to pay $20 million for the archipelago, but it was a forced sale, accepted by Spain under duress.

The peace treaty faced a hard battle in the U.S. Senate, where a combination of partisan politics and anticolonialism made it difficult to amass the two-thirds majority necessary for ratification. McKinley had shrewdly appointed three senators, including one Democrat, to the peace commission. This predisposed many members of the upper house to approve the treaty, but the vote was close. William Jennings Bryan, titular head of the Democratic party, could probably have prevented ratification had he urged his supporters to vote nay. Although he was opposed to taking the Philippines, he did not do so. To reject the treaty would leave the United States technically at war with Spain and the fate of the Philippines undetermined; better to accept the islands and then grant them independence. The question should be decided, Bryan said, "not by a minority of the Senate but by a majority of the people" at the next presidential election. Perplexed by Bryan's stand, a number of Democrats allowed themselves to be persuaded by the expansionists' arguments and by McKinley's judicious use of patronage; the treaty was ratified in February 1899 by a vote of fifty-seven to twenty-seven.

The Philippine Insurrection

The national referendum that Bryan had hoped for never materialized. Bryan himself confused the issue in 1900 by making free silver a major plank in his platform, thereby driving conservative anti-imperialists into McKinley's arms. Moreover, early in 1899 the Filipino

Emilio Aguinaldo, shown here with his young son, commanded Filipino insurgents who worked with Commodore Dewey to help overthrow Spanish rule of the Philippines in 1898. He later took up arms against the United States in a brutal three-year struggle when President McKinley opposed granting independence to the islands.

Fighting the insurgents in the Philippines proved unpopular and enlistments declined as the war dragged on. This poster was used to attract recruits in 1900.

nationalists under Aguinaldo, furious because the United States would not withdraw, took up arms. A savage guerrilla war resulted, one that cost far more in lives and money than the "splendid little" Spanish-American conflict.

Like all conflicts waged in tangled country chiefly by small, isolated units surrounded by a hostile civilian population, neither side displayed much regard for the "rules" of war. Goaded by sneak attacks and instances of cruelty to captives, American soldiers, most of whom had little respect for Filipinos to begin with, responded in kind. (See American Lives, "Frederick Funston," p. 600.) Civilians were rounded up, prisoners tortured, and property destroyed. Horrifying tales of rape, arson, and murder by U.S. troops filtered into the country, providing ammunition for the anti-imperialists. "You seem to have about finished your work of civilizing the Filipinos," Andrew Carnegie wrote angrily to one of the American peace commissioners. "About 8,000 of them have been completely civilized and sent to Heaven. I hope you like it." In fact, far more than 8,000 Filipinos lost their lives during the conflict, which raged for three years. More than 70,000 American soldiers had to be sent to the islands before the resistance was crushed, and about as many of them lost their lives as had perished in the Cuban conflict.

In 1900 McKinley sent a commission headed by William Howard Taft, a federal judge, to establish a government. Taft, a warmhearted, affable man, took an instant liking to the Filipinos, and his policy of encouraging them to participate in the territorial government attracted many converts. In July 1901 he became the first civilian governor of the Philippines.

Actually, the reelection of McKinley in 1900 settled the Philippine question so far as most Americans were concerned. Anti-imperialists still claimed that it was unconstitutional to take over territories without the consent of the local population. Their reasoning, while certainly not unsound, was unhistorical. No American government had seriously considered the wishes of the American Indians, the French and Spanish settlers in Louisiana, the Eskimos of Alaska, or the people of Hawaii when it had seemed in the national interest to annex new lands.

Read the Document   Twain, *Incident in the Philippines* at www.myhistorylab.com

View the Image   *Filipino Guerrillas* at www.myhistorylab.com

Cuba and the United States

Nevertheless, grave constitutional questions arose as a result of the acquisitions that followed the Spanish-American War. McKinley acted with remarkable independence in handling the problems involved in expansion. He set up military governments in Cuba, Puerto Rico, and the Philippines without specific congressional authority. The Supreme Court, in what became known as the "insular cases," granted Congress permission to act toward the colonies much as it pleased. A colony, one dissenting justice said, could be kept "like a disembodied shade, in an indeterminate state of ambiguous existence for an indefinite period."

While the most heated arguments raged over Philippine policy, the most difficult colonial problems concerned the relationship between the United States and Cuba. Despite the desire of most Americans to get out of Cuba, an independent government could not easily be created.

The insurgent government was feeble, corrupt, and oligarchic, the Cuban economy in a state of collapse, and life was chaotic. The first Americans entering Havana found the streets littered with garbage and the corpses of horses and dogs. All public services were at a standstill; it seemed essential for the United States, as McKinley said, to give "aid and direction" until "tranquillity" could be restored.

When McKinley established a military government for Cuba late in 1898, it was soon embroiled with local leaders. Then an eager horde of American promoters descended on Cuba in search of profitable franchises and concessions. Congress put a stop to this exploitation by forbidding all such grants as long as the occupation continued.

The problems were indeed knotty, for no strong local leader capable of uniting Cuba appeared. Even Senator Teller, father of the Teller Amendment, expressed concern lest "unstable and unsafe" elements gain control of the country. European leaders expected that the United States would eventually annex Cuba; and many Americans, including General Leonard Wood, who became military governor in December 1899, considered this the best solution. The desperate state of the people, the heavy economic stake of Americans in the region, and its strategic importance militated against withdrawal.

In the end the United States did withdraw, after doing a great deal to modernize sugar production, improve sanitary conditions, establish schools, and restore orderly administration. In November 1900 a Cuban constitutional convention met at Havana and proceeded without substantial American interference or direction to draft a frame of government. The chief restrictions imposed by this document on Cuba's freedom concerned foreign relations; at the insistence of the United States, it authorized American intervention whenever necessary "for the preservation of Cuban independence" and "the maintenance of a government adequate for the protection of life, property, and individual liberty." Cuba had to promise to make no treaty with a foreign power compromising its independence and to grant naval bases on its soil to the United States.

The Cubans, after some grumbling, accepted this arrangement, known as the **Platt Amendment**. It had

the support of most American opponents of imperialism. The amendment was a true compromise: It safeguarded American interests while granting to the Cubans real self-government on internal matters. In May 1902 the United States turned over the reins of government to the new republic. The next year the two countries signed a reciprocity treaty tightening the economic bonds between them.

True friendship did not result. Although American troops occupied Cuba only once more, in 1906, and then at the specific request of Cuban authorities, the United States repeatedly used the threat of intervention to coerce the Cuban government. American economic penetration proceeded rapidly and without regard for the well-being of the Cuban peasants, many of whom lived in a state of peonage on great sugar plantations. Nor did the Americans' good intentions make up for their tendency to consider themselves innately superior to the Cubans and to overlook the fact that Cubans did not always wish to adopt American customs and culture.

Read the **Document** *The Platt Amendment* at www.myhistorylab.com

The United States in the Caribbean and Central America

If the purpose of the Spanish-American War had been to bring peace and order to Cuba, the Platt Amendment was a logical step. The same purpose soon necessitated a further extension of the principle, for once the United States accepted the role of protector and stabilizer in parts of the Caribbean and Central America, it seemed desirable, for the same economic, strategic, and humanitarian reasons, to supervise the entire region.

The Caribbean and Central American countries were economically underdeveloped, socially backward, politically unstable, and desperately poor. Everywhere a few families owned most of the land and dominated social and political life. Most of the people were uneducated peasants, many of whom were little better off than slaves. Rival cliques of wealthy families struggled for power, force being the usual method of effecting a change in government. Most of the meager income of the average Caribbean state was swallowed up by the military or diverted into the pockets of the current rulers.

Cynicism and fraud poisoned the relations of most of these nations with the great powers. European merchants and bankers systematically cheated their Latin American customers, who in turn frequently refused to honor their obligations. Foreign bankers floated bond issues on outrageous terms, while revolutionary

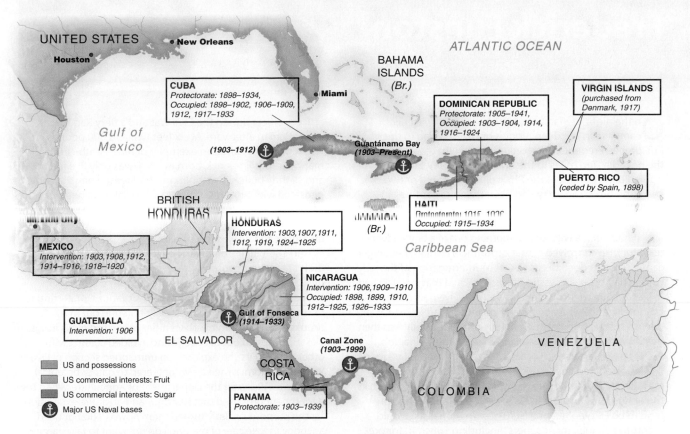

The United States in the Caribbean and Central America Puerto Rico was ceded by Spain to the United States after the Spanish-American War; the Virgin Islands were bought from Denmark; the Canal Zone was leased from Panama. The ranges of dates shown for Cuba, the Dominican Republic, Haiti, Nicaragua, and Panama cover those years during which the United States either had troops in occupation or in some other way (such as financial) had a protectorate relationship with that country.

governments in the region annulled concessions and repudiated debts with equal disdain for honest business dealing.

In 1902, shortly after the United States had pulled out of Cuba, trouble erupted in Venezuela, where a dictator, Cipriano Castro, was refusing to honor debts owed the citizens of European nations. To force Castro to pay up, Germany and Great Britain established a blockade of Venezuelan ports and destroyed a number of Venezuelan gunboats and harbor defenses. Under American pressure the Europeans agreed to arbitrate the dispute. For the first time, European powers had accepted the broad implications of the Monroe Doctrine. By this time Theodore Roosevelt had become president of the United States, and he quickly capitalized on the new European attitude. In 1903 the Dominican Republic defaulted on bonds totaling some $40 million. When European investors urged their governments to intervene, Roosevelt announced that under the Monroe Doctrine the United States could not permit foreign nations to intervene in Latin America. But, he added, Latin American nations should not be allowed to escape their obligations. "If we intend to say 'Hands

off' . . . sooner or later we must keep order ourselves," he told Secretary of War Elihu Root.

The president did not want to make a colony of the Dominican Republic. "I have about the same desire to annex it as a gorged boa constrictor might have to swallow a porcupine wrong-end-to," he said. He therefore arranged for the United States to take charge of the Dominican customs service—the one reliable source of revenue in that poverty-stricken country. Fifty-five percent of the customs duties would be devoted to debt payment, the remainder turned over to the Dominican government to care for its internal needs. Roosevelt defined his policy, known as the Roosevelt Corollary to the Monroe Doctrine, in a message to Congress in December 1904. "Chronic wrongdoing" in Latin America, he stated with his typical disregard for the subtleties of complex affairs, might require outside intervention. Since, under the Monroe Doctrine, no other nation could step in, the United States must "exercise . . . an international police power."

In the short run this policy worked. Dominican customs were honestly collected for the first time and the country's finances put in order. The presence of

Frederick Funston

On the night of March 22, 1901, as rain battered his campsite in the deep jungles of Luzon Island in the Philippines, Frederick Funston pondered what awaited him the next day. Ten miles to the north lay his prey, Emilio Aguinaldo, President of the Philippine Republic. For two years, the American army had been trying to capture Aguinaldo. But repeatedly Aguinaldo had slipped away. This time Funston was close. His ruse was working.

It had been a wild idea, something out of a boy's adventure story. He conceived it after capturing a Filipino messenger carrying coded documents. Funston's interrogation of the courier had been successful. (It was later said that Funston had subjected him to the "water cure," an effective new aid to military intelligence whereby several gallons of water were forced down a suspect's throat; his painfully distended belly was then beaten with logs.) The courier confirmed that Aguinaldo's secret headquarters was located in a remote area of Luzon.

Funston had chosen eighty Filipino scouts from the Macabebes, a tribe hostile to Aguinaldo. He outfitted them in the uniforms of Aguinaldo's army and trained them to pretend to be Filipino nationalists. These "nationalists" would escort five American "prisoners" (including Funston) for presentation to Aguinaldo. When Funston outlined his scheme to his superior, General Arthur MacArthur had deep misgivings. "Funston, this is a desperate undertaking," he said as they parted. "I fear I shall never see you again."

The words pleased Funston, who longed to be a hero. Ever since he was a child, he worried that he failed to measure up to his father. Edward "Foghorn" Funston had been an artillery officer during the Civil War and a fiery Republican congressman afterward. At six feet two and 200 pounds, he was regarded by all as an exemplar of nineteenth-century manhood. But Frederick, born in 1864, was only five feet four and slightly built. His schoolmates had teased him. He compensated with bravado displays of martial manliness. He craved a military career, but though his father was a congressman, West Point rejected him: His grades were mediocre, and he was too small.

In 1886 he enrolled at the University of Kansas but didn't fit in. He devoted himself to the pursuit of the most desirable women on campus, all of whom spurned him. Increasingly he retreated from social situations, preferring to drink alone in his room, periodically bursting out in a drunken rage, screaming obscenities at the top of his lungs.

He dropped out of college and avoided contact with other people. First, he explored an unmapped section of Death Valley in California. Then he volunteered to gather botanical samples in Alaska for the Department of Agriculture. When the department proposed that he command an entire expedition for the purpose, he flatly turned them down. "I do not need anybody to take care of me, and I do not want to take care of anybody." Alone, he trekked into the frigid wastes of northern Alaska and remained there for the better part of a year. When he ran out of food he ate his sled dogs.

During those long, silent nights, Funston realized that he could hardly prove that he measured up if no one were around to take the measurements. He decided to become a soldier, not caring much against whom he fought. In 1895 he contacted a recruiter for the cause of Cuban independence and accepted a commission as an artillery officer in the rebel army.

In Cuba he was given command of a Hotchkiss cannon; he made up for his lack of gunnery skill by sneaking his cannon absurdly close to Spanish fortifications at night, often within 400 yards. As the sun rose, the Spaniards, aghast at what was sitting on their doorstep, fired everything they had at Funston's cannon. Funston calmly adjusted the sights, pulled the lanyard, and climbed upon the parapet, shouting "Viva Cuba libre!" He was repeatedly wounded; once, a bullet pierced his lungs. When a severe hip wound became infected, he returned to the United States for medical assistance.

But he was not done with war. In 1898 Funston was given command of the Kansas regiments that had volunteered against Spain. To his dismay, they were sent to the Philippines, where the Spaniards had already ceased fighting. But after President McKinley decided to annex the Philippines, war broke out between the Americans and the Filipino nationalists. Funston finally got what he craved: sweeping charges, glorious victories, and newspaper feature stories. Yet the jokes persisted. Behind his back, his men called him the "Bantam General." The *New York Times*, in its coverage of a battle in which he won a Congressional Medal of Honor, ran the headline: "Daring Little Colonel Funston." The opening

Frederick Funston: hero or antihero?

paragraph attributed Funston's courage to the fact that he was too small to hit.

But now, if he captured Aguinaldo, Funston, the little man, would become a great one.

On March 23, 1901, Funston's Macabebes and their five American "prisoners" met up with a contingent of Aguinaldo's army. Deceived, Aguinaldo's troops escorted Funston's band into the town of Palanan. Aguinaldo watched from a window above. When shots rang out, thinking the troops were firing a salute, he shouted, "Stop that foolishness. Don't waste ammunition!"

Then Funston burst into Aguinaldo's compound: "I am General Funston. You are a prisoner of war of the Army of the United States of America."

Dazed, Aguinaldo replied, "Is this not some joke?" Funston seized Aguinaldo, dragged him through the jungle to the coast, where the USS *Vicksburg* was waiting. It took them to American headquarters in Manila.

After being subjected to intense pressure by American officials, Aguinaldo renounced the Filipino revolution, swore

Cartoon of Uncle Sam drowning in pursuit of Aguinaldo.

allegiance to the United States, and called on his followers to do likewise. The Philippine-American conflict was virtually over. Frederick Funston had almost single-handedly won the war.

For a time, Funston was a sensation. He was promoted to brigadier general. Newspaper editors and politicians championed him for governor of Kansas or for vice president on a ticket headed by Theodore Roosevelt in 1904. But within a few years Funston all but vanished. Anti-imperialists pointed out that Funston's men had surrendered and then fired their weapons, and that the Macabebes had been wearing enemy uniforms; both actions violated international law. Worse, several reporters and some of his soldiers claimed that Funston had ordered the execution of Filipino prisoners. He was ordered to an inconsequential command in San Francisco.

One hundred years after Funston's capture of Aguinaldo, U.S. troops would again be tracking a rebel fugitive: Osama bin Laden, mastermind of the September 11, 2001, attacks on the World Trade Center and Pentagon. That virtually no one recalled Funston's single-handed pursuit and capture of Aguinaldo was one measure of how completely he had slipped from view.

But Funston's name resurfaced in 2010, after major earthquakes had triggered widespread looting in Haiti and Chile. The *New York Times* observed that when the 1906 earthquake destroyed much of San Francisco, General Frederick Funston had immediately marched his troops into the city and taken charge; sometimes, the *Times* noted, leaders must act decisively.

The Defeat of the Filipinos and Capture of Aguinaldo, 1899–1901
Aguinaldo's flight, and Funston's pursuit and capture.

Question for Discussion

■ To catch Aguinaldo, Funston employed tactics of doubtful legality. A century later Americans have been accused of using torture and other unsavory methods to win "the war on terror." Are such techniques morally or legally wrong? Why or why not?

American warships in the area provided a needed measure of political stability. In the long run, however, the Roosevelt Corollary caused a great deal of resentment in Latin America, for it added to nationalist fears that the United States wished to exploit the region for its own benefit.

◉━**See** the **Map**   *Activities of the United States in the Caribbean* at www.myhistorylab.com

The Open Door Policy in China

The insular cases, the Platt Amendment, and the Roosevelt Corollary established the framework for American policy both in Latin America and in East Asia. Coincidental with the Cuban rebellion of the 1890s, a far greater upheaval had convulsed the ancient empire of China. In 1894–1895 Japan easily defeated China in a war over Korea. Alarmed by Japan's aggressiveness, the European powers hastened to carve out for themselves new spheres of influence along China's coast. After the annexation of the Philippines, McKinley's secretary of state, John Hay, urged on by business leaders fearful of losing out in the scramble to exploit the Chinese market, tried to prevent the further absorption of China by the great powers.

For the United States to join in the dismemberment of China was politically impossible because of anti-imperialist feeling, so Hay sought to protect American interests by clever diplomacy. In a series of "Open Door" notes (1899) he asked the powers to agree to respect the trading rights of all countries and to impose no discriminatory duties within their spheres of influence.

The replies to the Open Door notes were at best noncommittal, yet Hay blandly announced in March 1900 that the powers had "accepted" his suggestions! Thus he could claim to have prevented the breakup of the empire and protected the right of Americans to do business freely in its territories. In reality nothing had been accomplished; the imperialist nations did not extend their political control of China only because they feared that by doing so they might precipitate a major war among themselves. Nevertheless, Hay's action marked a revolutionary departure

from the traditional American policy of isolation, a bold advance into the complicated and dangerous world of international power politics.

Within a few months of Hay's announcement the **Open Door policy** was put to the test. Chinese nationalists, angered by the spreading influence of foreign governments, launched the so-called Boxer Rebellion. They swarmed into Peking and drove foreigners behind the walls of their legations, which were placed under siege. For weeks, until an international rescue expedition (which included 2,500 American soldiers) broke through to free them, the fate of the foreigners was unknown. Fearing that the Europeans would use the rebellion as a pretext for further expropriations, Hay sent off another round of Open Door notes announcing that the United States believed in the preservation of "Chinese territorial and administrative entity" and in "the principle of equal and impartial trade with all parts of the Chinese Empire." This broadened the Open Door policy to include all China, not merely the European spheres of influence.

Hay's diplomacy was superficially successful. Although the United States maintained no important military force in East Asia, American business and commercial interests there were free to develop and

Grace Service, a YMCA missionary, explained that these porters worked at the base of Mount Omei in Szechwan, China, a favorite site for Buddhist pilgrims. Upper-class Chinese women's feet were bound to keep them small. The deformities that resulted limited the distance they could walk, so they hired men such as these to carry them to the summit.

to compete with Europeans. But once again European jealousies and fears rather than American cleverness were responsible. When the Japanese, mistrusting Russian intentions in Manchuria, asked Hay how he intended to implement his policy, he replied meekly that the United States was "not prepared . . . to enforce these views." The United States was being caught up in the power struggle in East Asia without having faced the implications of its actions.

In time the country would pay a heavy price for this unrealistic attitude, but in the decade following 1900 its policy of diplomatic meddling unbacked by bayonets worked fairly well. Japan attacked Russia in a quarrel over Manchuria, smashing the Russian fleet in 1905 and winning a series of battles on the mainland. Japan was not prepared for a long war, however, and suggested to President Roosevelt that an American offer to mediate would be favorably received.

Eager to preserve the nice balance of power in East Asia, which enabled the United States to exert influence without any significant commitment of force, Roosevelt accepted the hint. In June 1905 he invited the belligerents to a conference at Portsmouth, New Hampshire. At the conference the Japanese won title to Russia's sphere around Port Arthur and a free hand in Korea, but when they demanded Sakhalin Island and a large money indemnity, the Russians balked. Unwilling to resume the war, the Japanese settled for half of Sakhalin and no money.

The Treaty of Portsmouth was unpopular in Japan, and the government managed to place the blame on Roosevelt, who had supported the compromise. Ill feeling against Americans increased in 1906 when the San Francisco school board, responding to local opposition to the influx of cheap labor from Japan, instituted a policy of segregating Asian children in a special school. Japan protested, and President Roosevelt persuaded the San Franciscans to abandon segregation in exchange for his pledge to cut off further Japanese immigration. He accomplished this through a "Gentlemen's Agreement" (1907) in which the Japanese promised not to issue passports to laborers seeking to come to America. Discriminatory legislation based specifically on race was thus avoided. However, the atmosphere between the two countries remained charged. Japanese resentment at American racial prejudice was great; many Americans talked fearfully of the "yellow peril."

Theodore Roosevelt was preeminently a realist in foreign relations. "Don't bluster," he once said. "Don't flourish a revolver, and never draw unless you intend to shoot." In East Asia he failed to follow his own advice. He considered the situation in that part of the world fraught with peril. The Philippines, he said, were "our heel of Achilles," indefensible in case of a Japanese attack. He suggested privately that the United States ought to "be prepared for giving the islands independence . . . much sooner than I think advisable from their own standpoint."

Yet while Roosevelt did not appreciably increase American naval and military strength in East Asia, neither did he stop trying to influence the course of events in the area, and he took no step toward withdrawing from the Philippines. He sent the fleet on a world cruise to demonstrate its might to Japan but knew well that this was mere bluff. "The 'Open Door' policy," he advised his successor, "completely disappears as soon as a powerful nation determines to disregard it." Nevertheless he allowed the belief to persist in the United States that the nation could influence the course of East Asian history without risk or real involvement.

The Panama Canal

In the Caribbean region American policy centered on building an interoceanic canal across Central America. Expanding interests in Latin America and East Asia made a canal necessary, a truth pointed up during the war with Spain by the two-month voyage of USS *Oregon* around South America from California waters to participate in the action against Admiral Cervera's fleet at Santiago. The first step was to get rid of the old Clayton-Bulwer Treaty with Great Britain, which barred the United States from building a canal on its own. In 1901 Lord

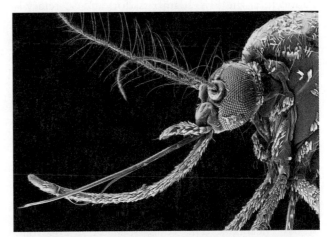

An electron microscopic photo of a mosquito that carried yellow fever. Major Walter Reed of the U.S. army proved that yellow fever was not spread directly among humans, but from the bites of infected mosquitoes. The virus then multiplied in the human bloodstream. Headache, backache, fever, and vomiting ensued. Liver cells were destroyed, resulting in jaundice—thus the name "yellow fever." American surgeon William Crawford Gorgas worked to eliminate yellow fever by destroying the breeding grounds of these mosquitoes. The last yellow fever outbreak in the United States struck New Orleans and parts of the South in 1905.

The grand opening of the huge Miraflores lock on the Panama Canal in October, 1914. The locks were big enough to allow passage of the largest American warships.

Pauncefote, the British ambassador, and Secretary of State John Hay negotiated an agreement abrogating the Clayton-Bulwer pact and giving the United States the right to build and defend a canal connecting the Pacific Ocean with the Caribbean Sea.

One possible canal route lay across the Colombian province of Panama, where the French-controlled New Panama Canal Company had taken over the franchise of the old De Lesseps company. Only fifty miles separated the oceans in Panama. The terrain, however, was rugged and unhealthy. While the French company had sunk much money into the project, it had little to show for its efforts aside from some rough excavations. A second possible route ran across Nicaragua. This route was about 200 miles long but was relatively easy since much of it traversed Lake Nicaragua and other natural waterways.

President McKinley appointed a commission to study the alternatives. It reported that the Panamanian route was technically superior, but recommended building in Nicaragua because the New Panama Canal Company was asking $109 million for its assets, which the commission valued at only $40 million. Lacking

another potential purchaser, the French company lowered its price to $40 million, and after a great deal of clever propagandizing by Philippe Bunau-Varilla, a French engineer with heavy investments in the company, President Roosevelt settled on the Panamanian route.

In January 1903 Secretary of State Hay negotiated a treaty with Colombia. In return for a ninety-nine-year lease on a zone across Panama six miles wide, the United States agreed to pay Colombia $10 million and an annual rent of $250,000. The Colombian senate, however, unanimously rejected this treaty. It demanded $15 million directly from the United States, plus one-fourth of the $40 million U.S. payment to the New Panama Canal Company.

A little more patience might have produced a mutually satisfactory settlement, but Roosevelt looked on the Colombians as highwaymen who were "mad to get hold of the $40,000,000 of the Frenchmen." ("You could no more make an agreement with the Colombian rulers," Roosevelt later remarked, "than you could nail currant jelly to a wall.") When Panamanians, egged on by the French company, staged a revolution against Colombia in November 1903, he ordered the cruiser *Nashville* to Panama. Colombian government forces found themselves looking down the barrels of the guns of the *Nashville* and shortly thereafter eight other American warships. The revolution succeeded.

Roosevelt instantly recognized the new Republic of Panama. Secretary Hay and the new "Panamanian" minister, Bunau-Varilla, then negotiated a treaty granting the United States a zone ten miles wide in perpetuity, on the same terms as those rejected by Colombia. Within the Canal Zone the United States could act as "the sovereign of the territory . . . to the entire exclusion of . . . the Republic of Panama." The United States guaranteed the independence of the republic. The New Panama Canal Company then received its $40 million, including a substantial share for Bunau-Varilla.

Historians have condemned Roosevelt for his actions in this shabby affair, and with good reason. It was not that he fomented the Panamanian revolution, for he did not. Separated from the government at Bogotá by an impenetrable jungle, the people of Panama province had long wanted to be free of Colombian rule. He sinned, rather, in his disregard of Latin American sensibilities. He referred to the Colombians as "dagoes" and insisted smugly that he was defending "the interests of collective civilization" when he overrode their opposition to his plans. "They cut their own throats," he said. "They tried to hold us up; and too late they have discovered their criminal error."

If uncharitable, Roosevelt's analysis was not entirely inaccurate, yet it did not justify his haste in taking Panama under his wing. "Have I defended myself?" Roosevelt asked Secretary of War Root. "You certainly have, Mr. President," Root retorted. "You were accused of seduction and you have conclusively proved that you were guilty of rape." Throughout Latin America, especially as nationalist sentiments grew stronger, Roosevelt's intolerance and aggressiveness in the canal incident bred resentment and fear.[3]

The first vessels passed through the canal in 1914 and American hegemony in the Caribbean expanded. Yet even in that strategically vital area there was more show than substance to American strength. The navy ruled Caribbean waters largely by default, for it lacked adequate bases in the region. In 1903, as authorized by the Cuban constitution, the United

---

[3]In 1921 the United States made amends by giving Colombia $25 million. Colombia in turn recognized the independence of the Republic of Panama.

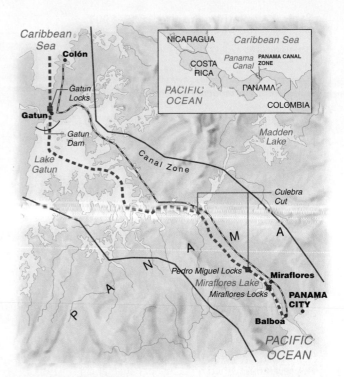

The U.S. Panama Canal Following many negotiations, construction of the Panama Canal began in 1904. After many delays and hardships, it was completed in 1914.

States obtained an excellent site for a base at Guantanamo Bay, but before 1914 Congress appropriated only $89,000 to develop it.

The tendency was to try to influence outlying areas without actually controlling them. Roosevelt's successor, William Howard Taft, called this policy **dollar diplomacy**, his reasoning being that economic penetration would bring stability to underdeveloped areas and power and profit to the United States without the government's having to commit troops or spend public funds.

Under Taft the State Department won a place for American bankers in an international syndicate engaged in financing railroads in Manchuria. When Nicaragua defaulted on its foreign debt in 1911, the department arranged for American bankers to reorganize Nicaraguan finances and manage the customs service. Although the government truthfully insisted that it did not "covet an inch of territory south of the Rio Grande," dollar diplomacy provoked further apprehension in Latin America. Efforts to establish similar arrangements in Honduras, Costa Rica, and Guatemala all failed. In Nicaragua orderly administration of the finances did not bring internal peace. In 1912, 2,500 American marines and sailors had to be landed to put down a revolution.

Economic penetration proceeded briskly. American investments in Cuba reached $500 million by 1920,

Table 22.1 Path to Empire, 1885–1901

Josiah Strong, *Our Country*	1885	Applied social Darwinism—"survival of the fittest"—to justify American expansion
A.T. Mahan, *The Influence of Seapower upon History*	1890	Endorsed naval power to ensure prosperity and national security
United States helped sugar planters depose Queen Liliuokalani	1893	Major step toward annexation of Hawaii
United States intervened in British dispute with Venezuela over land claims	1895	Reaffirmed the Monroe Doctrine claim to American supervision of Latin America
USS *Maine* exploded in Havana harbor	1898	Generated public pressure for war against Spain
Defeat of Spain	1898	Opened former Spanish colonies to U.S. annexation and economic penetration
U.S. annexation of Philippines	1899	United States became formal empire
"Open Door" Policy	1899	United States asserted trading rights in China
Roosevelt intervened on behalf of Panamanian independence	1903	Advanced expansive rights in Central America
Roosevelt Corollary	1904	Asserted U.S. right to military intervention in Latin America
Taft's Dollar Diplomacy	1909–1913	Encouraged U.S. government-supported investment abroad
Panama Canal opened	1914	Allowed U.S. warships to travel swiftly between Atlantic and Pacific

and smaller but significant investments were made in the Dominican Republic and in Haiti. In Central America the United Fruit Company accumulated large holdings in banana plantations, railroads, and other ventures. Other firms plunged heavily into Mexico's rich mineral resources.

Imperialism without Colonies

The United States deserves fair marks for effort in its foreign relations following the Spanish-American War, barely passable marks for performance, and failing marks for the results. If one defines imperialism narrowly as a policy of occupying and governing foreign lands, American imperialism lasted for an extremely short time. With trivial exceptions, all the American colonies—Hawaii, the Philippines, Guam, Puerto Rico, the Guantanamo base, and the Canal Zone—were obtained between 1898 and 1903. In retrospect it seems clear that the urge to own colonies was only fleeting; the legitimate questions raised by

the anti-imperialists and the headaches connected with the management of overseas possessions soon produced a change of policy.

The objections of protectionists to the lowering of tariff barriers, the shock of the Philippine insurrection, and a growing conviction that the costs of colonial administration outweighed the profits affected American thinking. Hay's Open Door notes (which anti-imperialists praised highly) marked the beginning of the retreat from imperialism as thus defined, while the Roosevelt Corollary and dollar diplomacy signaled the consolidation of a new policy. Elihu Root summarized this policy as it applied to the Caribbean nations (and by implication to the rest of the underdeveloped world) in 1905: "We do not want to take them for ourselves. We do not want any foreign nations to take them for themselves. We want to help them."

Yet imperialism can be given a broader definition. Although the United States did not seek colonies, it pursued a course that promoted American economic penetration of underdeveloped areas without the trouble of owning and controlling them. American statesmen regarded American expansion as beneficial to all concerned. They genuinely believed that they were exporting democracy along with capitalism and industrialization. But U.S. economic penetration has had many unfortunate results for the nonindustrial nations. Americans were particularly, though not uniquely, unimpressed by the different social and cultural patterns of people in far-off lands and insensitive to their wish to develop in their own way.

Both the U.S. government and American businessmen showed little interest in finding out what the people of Cuba wanted from life. They assumed that the Cubans wanted what everybody (read "Americans") wanted and, if by some strange chance this was not the case, that it was best to give it to them anyway. Dollar diplomacy had two main objectives, the avoidance of violence and the economic development of Latin America; it paid small heed to how peace was maintained and how the fruits of development were distributed. The policy was self-defeating, for in the long run stability depended on the support of local people, and this was seldom forthcoming.

By the eve of World War I the United States had become a world power and had assumed what it saw as a duty to guide the development of many countries with traditions far different from its own. The American people, however, did not understand what world power involved. While they stood ready to extend their influence into distant lands, they did so with little awareness of the implications of their behavior for themselves or for other peoples. The national psychology, if such a term has any meaning, remained fundamentally isolationist. Americans understood that their wealth and numbers made their nation strong and that geography made it virtually invulnerable. Thus they proceeded to do what they wanted to do in foreign affairs, limited more by their humanly flexible consciences than by any rational analysis of the probable consequences. This policy seemed safe enough—in 1914.

See the Map *World Colonial Empires, 1900* at www.myhistorylab.com

Chapter Review

Milestones

1850	Britain and United States sign Clayton-Bulwer Treaty concerning interoceanic canal
1858	Commercial treaty with Japan opens several ports to American trade
1867	United States buys Alaska from Russia
1871	Treaty of Washington settles *Alabama* claims
1875	Reciprocity treaty increases U.S. influence in Hawaii
1885	Josiah Strong justifies expansionism in *Our Country*
1890	A. T. Mahan fuels American imperialism in *The Influence of Sea Power*
1893	United States helps sugar planters depose Queen Liliuokalani of Hawaii
1895	United States supports Venezuela in European border dispute over British Guiana
1898	*Maine* explodes in Havana harbor
	Spanish-American war breaks out
	Dewey defeats Spanish fleet at Manila Bay
	Theodore Roosevelt leads Rough Riders at Battle of San Juan Hill
	United States annexes Hawaii
1899	Hay's Open Door policy safeguards United States' access to China trade
1899	United States annexes Philippines and becomes an empire
1900	Platt Amendment gives United States naval stations and right to intervene in Cuba
1901	Hay-Pauncefote Treaty gives United States rights to build interoceanic canal
	Supreme Court's insular cases give Congress free reign over colonies
1902	Europeans accept Monroe Doctrine during Venezuela bond dispute
1904	Roosevelt Corollary to Monroe Doctrine gives United States "international police power"
1907	"Gentlemen's Agreement" curtails Japanese immigration
1914	Panama Canal opens

Key Terms

dollar diplomacy   A policy of President William Taft to promote American economic penetration to underdeveloped nations, especially in Latin America; it sought to strengthen American influence without requiring the presence of U.S. troops, *605*

isolationism   A national policy that eschews foreign alliances, such as was propounded by George Washington in his **"Farewell Address."** Isolationism was also embraced by part of the **Monroe Doctrine** of 1823 and after the First World War, when the United States refused to join the **League of Nations** and sought to distance itself during the 1930s from the rumblings of another world war. Isolationism ended as national policy when Japan attacked Pearl Harbor on December 7, 1941, *586*

Open Door policy   A policy, propounded by Secretary of State John Hay in 1899, affirming the

territorial integrity of China and a policy of free trade, *602*

Platt Amendment   A law, passed in 1901 and superseding the **Teller Amendment**, which stipulated the conditions for the withdrawal of American forces from Cuba; it also transferred ownership of the naval base at Guantanamo Bay to the United States, *598*

"reconcentration" camps   A term that referred to the Spanish refugee camps into which Cuban farmers were herded in 1896 to prevent them from providing assistance to rebels fighting for Cuban independence from Spain, *591*

Teller Amendment   A rider to the 1898 war resolution with Spain whereby Congress pledged that it did not intend to annex Cuba and that it would recognize Cuban independence from Spain, *592*

Review Questions

1. The introduction to this chapter holds that American soldiers are fighting in Afghanistan in part because of American imperialism after 1890. Could Americans then have avoided imperial expansion? What factors impelled them to support imperialism?

2. On what issues did the anti-imperialists and the imperialists agree? And how did they differ?

3. How did American involvement in the Caribbean differ from the United States' approach to China and East Asia?

4. Why did McKinley choose to annex the Philippines? Was his decision a wise one?

5. How did the Roosevelt Corollary modify the Monroe Doctrine? How did Taft's policies differ from those of Roosevelt?

6. Was American imperialism from 1890–1910 chiefly beneficial or harmful to other nations? To the United States?

myhistorylab Connections

PEARSON

Reinforce what you learned in this chapter by studying the many documents, images, maps, review tools, and videos available at **www.myhistorylab.com**.

Read and Review

✓• Study and Review   *Chapter 22*

View the Image   *Uncle Sam Teaching the World, p. 588*

View the Image   *Iolani Palace, Hawaii, p. 589*

Read the Document   *Twain, Incident in the Philippines, p. 597*

View the Image   *Filipino Guerillas, p. 597*

Read the Document   *The Platt Amendment, p. 598*

See the Map   *Activities of the United States in the Caribbean, p. 602*

See the Map   *World Colonial Empires, 1900, p. 607*

Research and Explore

Watch the Video   *Burial of the Maine Victims, p. 592*

Watch the Video   *Roosevelt's Rough Riders, p. 594*

((•• Hear the Audio

Hear the audio file for Chapter 22 at
www.myhistorylab.com.

Do you know someone with TBI?

In 2008 Toggle, a character in Gary Trudeau's *Doonesbury* comic strip, was driving a Humvee in Iraq when it was blown up by an improvised explosive device (IED). Toggle was hospitalized with traumatic brain injury (TBI), a buffeting of the brain caused by the shock waves of an explosion. Trudeau, who had visited VA hospitals to gather material about another character who lost a leg in the Iraq war, was astonished by how many American wounded suffered from TBI. By 2010 over 5,000 service members had been diagnosed with TBI, about a quarter of all combat casualties. "The Iraq war," the *Washington Post* observed, "has brought back one of the worst afflictions of World War I trench warfare: shell shock."

During World War I millions of men hunkered down in trenches surrounded by thickets of barbed wire. Before a major offensive, attacking armies hurled millions of artillery shells to pulverize such defenses. The casualties were staggering; many of the wounded suffered from shell shock—some 80,000 in the British army alone. Most never returned to active duty.

Woodrow Wilson and the Great War

CONTENTS

((•● [Hear the Audio **Chapter 23 at www.myhistorylab.com**

■ Colin Unwin Gill went to France to serve in World War I. He was twenty-three. Four years later, he completed this painting that depicted the carnage caused by an exploding artillery shell on a headquarters ("protected" by corrugated metal). The man, seated on a chair in the lower right, a victim of shell shock, holds his head.

Just as American soldiers at the outset of the twenty-first century could not have imagined that they would be the victims of powerful explosions in Afghanistan and Iraq, few Americans in the early twentieth century thought it possible that they would get caught up in a war in Europe. To be sure, in the early 1900s Americans heard ominous rumblings from across the Atlantic Ocean. But even as European rivals spoke of war, none of it had much to do with American imperial interests in the Pacific and the Caribbean. But history unfolds in unpredictable ways.

In 1914 a spark ignited the powder keg of ethnic tensions in the Balkans. Soon, much of Europe was in flames.

As the armies of the major powers became bogged down in a bloody stalemate, nonbelligerent nations were drawn into the conflagration. Woodrow Wilson, who had campaigned as a peace candidate, later called on the United States to go to war. Eventually he embraced it with an almost religious zeal. He recruited workers, farmers, financiers, manufacturers, minorities, and women to help in the war effort. He stamped out dissent. He also sought to take advantage of the transformations wrought by the war to promote various reforms—including creation of an international body to mediate future conflicts. The tragedy of the Wilson years was that none of it turned out quite as he had imagined. ■

Wilson's "Moral" Diplomacy

Wilson did not lead the nation to war; both he and the nation stumbled into it without meaning to. Part of the reason was that Wilson's foreign relations, though well-intentioned, were often confused. He knew that the United States had no wish to injure any foreign state and assumed that all nations would recognize this fact and cooperate. Like nineteenth-century Christian missionaries, he wanted to spread the gospel of American democracy, to lift and enlighten the unfortunate and the ignorant—but in his own way. "I am going to teach the South American republics to elect good men!" he told one British diplomat.

Wilson set out to raise the moral tone of American foreign policy by denouncing dollar diplomacy. Encouraging bankers to lend money to countries like China, he said, implied the possibility of "forcible interference" if the loans were not repaid, and that would be "obnoxious to the principles upon which the government of our people rests." To seek special economic concessions in Latin America was "unfair" and "degrading." The United States would deal with Latin American nations "upon terms of equality and honor."

Yet Wilson sometimes failed to live up to his promises. Because of the strategic importance of the Panama Canal, he was unwilling to tolerate "unrest" anywhere in the Caribbean. Within months of his inauguration he was pursuing the same tactics employed by Roosevelt and Taft. The Bryan-Chamorro Treaty of 1914, which gave the United States an option to build a canal across Nicaragua, made that country virtually an American protectorate and served to maintain in power an unpopular dictator, Adolfo Díaz.

A much more serious example of missionary diplomacy occurred in Mexico. In 1911 a liberal coalition overthrew the dictator Porfirio Díaz, who had been exploiting the resources and people of Mexico for the benefit of a small class of wealthy landowners, clerics, and military men since the 1870s. Francisco Madero became president.

Perhaps inspired by progressive reforms in the United States, Madero proposed a liberal constitution for Mexico. But British oil magnates, who controlled most of Mexico's chief export, conspired with Victoriano Huerta, a general in Madero's army. In 1913 Huerta assassinated Madero and seized power. Britain promptly recognized Huerta's government.

The American ambassador urged Wilson to do so too, but he refused. His sympathies were with the government of Madero, whose murder had horrified him. "I will not recognize a government of butchers," he said. Wilson instead brought enormous pressure to bear against Huerta. He demanded that

Juan O'Gorman, a famous Mexican painter, did this mural (left) celebrating Francisco Madero, leader of the Mexican revolution. In 1913, Madero was murdered by his top general, Victoriano Huerta (right). Chaos ensued.

Huerta hold free elections as the price of American mediation in the continuing civil war. Huerta refused. The tense situation exploded in April 1914, when a small party of American sailors was arrested in the port of Tampico, Mexico. Wilson used the affair as an excuse to send troops into Mexico.

The invasion took place at Veracruz, where Winfield Scott had launched the assault on Mexico City in 1847. Instead of surrendering the city, the Mexicans resisted tenaciously, suffering 400 casualties before falling back. This bloodshed caused dismay throughout Latin America. Huerta, hard-pressed by Mexican opponents, fled from power.

Wilson now made a monumental blunder. He threw his support to Francisco "Pancho" Villa, one of Huerta's generals. But Villa was little more than an ambitious bandit whose only objective was personal power. In October 1915, realizing his error, Wilson abandoned Villa and backed another Mexican rebel, who drove Villa to the northern border of Mexico. In 1916 Villa stopped a train in northern Mexico and killed sixteen American passengers in cold blood. Then he crossed into New Mexico and burned the town of Columbus, killing nineteen.

Having learned the perils of intervening in Mexican politics, Wilson would have preferred to bear even this assault in silence; but public opinion forced him to send American troops under General John J. Pershing across the border in pursuit of Villa.

Villa proved impossible to catch. Cleverly he drew Pershing deeper and deeper into Mexico, which challenged Mexican sovereignty. Several clashes occurred between Pershing's men and Mexican regulars, and for a brief period in June 1916 war seemed imminent. Wilson now acted bravely and wisely. Early in 1917 he recalled Pershing's force, leaving the Mexicans to work out their own destiny.

Missionary diplomacy in Mexico had produced mixed, but in the long run beneficial, results. His bungling bred anti-Americanism in Mexico; but his opposition to Huerta strengthened the real revolutionaries, enabling the constitutionalists to consolidate power.

Europe Explodes in War

On June 28, 1914, in the Austro-Hungarian provincial capital of Sarajevo, Gavrilo Princip, a young student, assassinated the Archduke Franz Ferdinand, heir to the imperial throne. Princip was a member of the Black Hand, a Serbian terrorist organization. He was seeking to further the cause of Serbian nationalism. Instead his rash act precipitated a general European war. Within little more than a month, following a complex series of diplomatic challenges and responses, two great coalitions, the **Central Powers** (chiefly Germany, Austria-Hungary, and Ottoman Turkey) and the **Allied Powers** (chiefly Great Britain, France, and Russia), were locked in a brutal struggle that brought one era in world history to a close and inaugurated another.

The outbreak of this Great War caught Americans psychologically unprepared; few understood its significance. President Wilson promptly issued a proclamation of neutrality and asked the nation to be "impartial in thought." Of course, not even the president had the superhuman self-control that this request called for, but the almost unanimous reaction of Americans, aside from dismay, was that the conflict did not concern them.

The United States had good reason to remain neutral. Over a third of its 92 million inhabitants were either European-born or the children of European immigrants. Sentimental ties bound them to the lands of their ancestors. American involvement would create new internal stresses in a society already strained by the task of assimilating so many diverse groups. War was also an affront to the prevailing progressive spirit, which assumed that human beings were reasonable, high-minded, and capable of settling disputes peaceably. Along with the traditional American fear of entanglement in European affairs, these were ample reasons for remaining aloof.

Although most Americans hoped to keep out of the war, nearly everyone was partial to one side or the other. People of German or Austrian descent, about 8 million in number, and the nation's 4.5 million Irish Americans, motivated chiefly by hatred of the British, sympathized with the Central Powers. The majority of the people, however, influenced by bonds of language and culture, preferred an Allied victory, and when the Germans launched a mighty assault across neutral Belgium in an effort to outflank the French armies, many Americans were outraged.

As the war progressed, the Allies—especially Britain—cleverly exploited American prejudices by publishing exaggerated tales of German atrocities against Belgian civilians. A supposedly impartial study of these charges by the widely respected James Bryce, author of *The American Commonwealth*, portrayed the Germans as ruthless barbarians. The Germans also conducted a propaganda campaign in the United States, but they labored under severe handicaps and won few converts.

Watch the **Video** *The outbreak of WWI at*
www.myhistorylab.com

Titanic

James Cameron's *Titanic* (1997) was a blockbuster. He made audiences feel what it was like to be on the ship. When the deck tilted to the right, viewers leaned to the left; many gasped as the ship plunged into the icy depths. What sent a shiver down the spine was the knowledge that real people had experienced what was being depicted on the screen.

Cameron well understood the audience's craving to relive a true story. The movie opens with footage of the actual HMS *Titanic* on the floor of the Atlantic, fish gliding silently through its barnacle-encrusted wreckage. Cameron also spent scores of millions of dollars devising computer-enhanced techniques to ensure that his *Titanic* looked like the one that went down in the North Atlantic on the night of April 14–15, 1912.

But Cameron's *Titanic* was more than a disaster movie. It was also the story of two young people who fall in love. The romance begins when Jack (Leonardo DiCaprio), a struggling artist, spots Rose (Kate Winslet), a wealthy socialite, climbing over the railing and peering despondently into the water below. Obliged to marry a contemptuous (and contemptible) snob, she is miserable. Jack, from a lower deck, scrambles up and persuades her to forgo the plunge.

As a reward for saving Rose, Jack is invited to dine with Rose's table. At dinner, Rose appraises Jack more carefully—and is impressed. He looks good in a tuxedo, displays plenty of moxie, and possesses artistic talent ("Jack, you see things!"). She proposes that she pose for him in the nude. A few hours later they venture below decks and, in anticipation of the courtship rituals of future decades, locate an automobile, climb inside,

and rip off each other's clothes. The windows steam up, and a hand leaves an imprint, fingers outstretched in ecstasy.

Minutes later they are cooled off when the ship has its close encounter of the icy kind. Jack—young, vital, alive—perishes in the frigid waters; but he has imparted to Rose a gift of love, and thus of life. This tale of young lovers, held apart by society, is a nautical "Romeo and Juliet," a brief, pure instant of love, tragically ended by death.

If Cameron's *Titanic* is a love story for the ages, it was also frozen in a particular place and in a particular time. Much as Cameron spent millions to show the ship as it really was, he took similar pains to give a convincing rendering of New York society, especially its clothing, silverware, and social conventions.

Of the latter, the most significant for the story are the elaborate rituals of Victorian courtship. Rose seeks to break free from her impending marriage partly because she despises her fiancé, but also because marriage to him constitutes the final, irreversible step into the gilded cage of a society lady. Jack's presence at dinner with the "best" of society underscores the shallow materialism of this upper crust and its preoccupation with wealth, its absurd rules of etiquette, and its repressive attitudes toward sexuality. Viewers of the movie, looking through Rose's eyes, may wonder how such rituals ever came to be.

Some had existed for centuries. The idealization of courtly love and pure womanhood was a commonplace of medieval literature. In the early nineteenth century novelist Jane Austen described the subtle interplay of money and romance in England. But the rituals of New York society in the Gilded Age were characterized by sumptuous and public displays of wealth—glittering balls and extravagant "Grand Tours" of Europe.

This new mode of courtship was largely the creation of Mrs. John Jacob Astor, wife of one of New York's wealthiest businessmen, and her friends. After the Civil War, industrialization and urbanization were generating new wealth and destroying the old at a dizzying pace. While prominent businessmen and investment bankers were devising institutions to impose order on this creative industrial chaos, their wives were regulating its social elite. They endeavored to determine who should be admitted to New York's "best" families—and who should not. They concluded that it was not enough to be rich; the elite of the nation must also adhere to high standards of etiquette and decorum.

Leonardo DiCaprio and Kate Winslet as lovers on the *Titanic*.

A society couple of the new type: Edith Stokes, heiress to a shipping fortune and her husband, an architect. The portrait was painter John Singer Sargent's wedding gift to the couple.

Source: John Singer Sargent (1856–1925), *Mr. and Mrs. Isaac Newton Phelps Stokes*. Oil on Canvas. 85 ¼" × 39 ¾" (214 × 101 cm). Signed and dated (upper right): John S. Sargent 1897. The Metropolitan Museum of Art, Bequest of Edith Minturn Phelps Stokes (Mrs. I.N.), 1938. (38.104). Photograph ©1992. The Metropolitan Museum of Art, NY.

By controlling entrance into society, women such as Mrs. Astor (and her imitators in nearly every city in the nation) also determined the disposition, through marriage and inheritance, of the nation's largest fortunes. Society women possessed immense power.

Although the system was created and supervised by mature women, it demanded the compliance of adolescent girls. The process began when a wealthy mother took her daughter on a round of visits to society women, to whom they would present their "calling cards." If mother and daughter were judged suitable, they would be invited in for tea; if the girl behaved with decorum (and if her father's assets proved sound), she would be invited to balls and other formal events. At or near her sixteenth birthday, her parents would hold a ball in her honor—in New York the event usually took place at Delmonico's restaurant—marking her "debut" into society. She wore a white gown symbolizing her virginity. A male relative presented her formally to the prominent women. Now she could accept male suitors from "society."

This highly stylized—almost tribal—ritual brought young women to the threshold of womanhood. Marriage awaited beyond the door. Many eagerly anticipated the acquisition of adult status and the social power it entailed. Others regarded this rite with terror. (Novelist Edith Wharton remembered her debut as a "long cold agony of shyness.") In the early twentieth century, some young women began to rebel. Elsie Clews, daughter of a Wall Street banker, refused to wear corsets. When her mother wasn't looking, she took off her veil and white gloves. She subsequently scandalized Newport—the fashionable Rhode Island summer resort for society's wealthy—by going swimming with a young man without a chaperone (but not without a bathing suit). To her mother's dismay, Clews delayed marriage and went to Barnard College; eventually she became a respected anthropologist (Elsie Clews Parsons).

Kate Winslet's "Rose" was, like Elsie Clews, a prematurely "modern" woman. But Clews tore off only her veil and white gloves, not all her clothes; she dispensed with the rituals of courtship, not its substance. Even in the waning years of the Victorian era, few wealthy young women succumbed to impoverished men, however earnest and appealing.

Victorian courtship was necessarily protracted. Young women did not unburden themselves to strangers; and even to friends, especially of the opposite sex, the process of revealing one's inner feelings unfolded slowly, often after a series of tests and trials. One person's tentative disclosure invited a reciprocal response. Letters and diaries show that, over time, these personal revelations often led to sexual intimacies. Nowadays many people regard Victorian marriages as unfeeling and stiff, but many Victorians maintained that their personal intimacies were the more delicious for having been long delayed.

Cameron's *Titanic* looks like the past; but the heart of the movie is Jack and Rose's whirlwind romance. While Rose's story addresses some of the anxieties of young society women, it more closely resembles the courtship patterns of Hollywood today than the experiences of young people at the beginning of the last century.

Questions for Discussion

- Jack and Rose "hooked up," to use modern slang. Why was such behavior improbable among young women of wealthy families in the late nineteenth century?

- What other behaviors in the film seem anachronistic?

During World War I, advancing armies unloosed ferocious artillery barrages to destroy deeply entrenched enemy positions. Before the Third Battle of Ypres, the British fired 4.5 million shells at German defenses, pulverizing the landscape. But as the British moved forward they became mired in mud; they lost 300,000 men in the action. Few Americans perceived the special horrors of this type of warfare.

Freedom of the Seas

Propaganda did not basically alter American attitudes; far more important were questions arising out of trade and commerce. Under international law, neutrals could trade freely with any belligerent. Americans were prepared to do so, but because the British fleet dominated the North Atlantic, they could not. The situation was similar to the one that had prevailed during the Napoleonic Wars. The British declared nearly all commodities, even foodstuffs, to be contraband of war. They forced neutral merchant ships into British or French ports in order to search them for goods headed for the enemy. Many cargoes were confiscated, often without payment. American firms that traded with the Central Powers were "blacklisted," which meant that no British subject could deal with them. When Americans protested, the British answered that in a battle for survival, they dared not adhere to old-fashioned rules of international law.

Had the United States insisted that Great Britain abandon these "illegal" practices, as the Germans demanded, no doubt it could have had its way. The British foreign secretary, Sir Edward Grey, later admitted, "The ill-will of the United States meant certain defeat. The object of diplomacy, therefore,

was to secure the maximum of blockade that could be enforced without a rupture with the United States." It is ironic that an embargo, which failed so ignominiously in Jefferson's day, would have been almost instantly effective if applied at any time after 1914, for American supplies were vital to the Allies.

Although British tactics frequently exasperated Wilson, they did not result in the loss of innocent lives. He never considered taking as drastic a step as an embargo. He faced a dilemma. To allow the British to make the rules meant siding against the Central Powers. Yet to insist on the old rules (which had never been strictly obeyed in wartime) meant siding against the Allies because that would have deprived them of much of the value of their naval superiority. *Nothing* the United States might do would be truly impartial.

Wilson's own sentiments made it doubly difficult for him to object strenuously to British practices. No American admired British institutions and culture more extravagantly. "Everything I love most in the world is at stake," he confessed privately to the British ambassador. A German victory "would be fatal to our form of Government and American ideals."

In any event, the immense expansion of American trade with the Allies made an embargo unthinkable.

NOTICE!

TRAVELLERS intending to embark on the Atlantic voyage are reminded that a state of war exists between Germany and her allies and Great Britain and her allies; that the zone of war includes the waters adjacent to the British Isles; that, in accordance with formal notice given by the Imperial German Government, vessels flying the flag of Great Britain, or of any of her allies, are liable to destruction in those waters and that travellers sailing in the war zone on ships of Great Britain or her allies do so at their own risk.

IMPERIAL GERMAN EMBASSY
WASHINGTON, D. C., APRIL 22, 1915.

Three weeks before the *Lusitania* was torpedoed, this notice appeared in the classified sections of Washington newspapers.

While commerce with the Central Powers fell to a trickle, that with the Allies soared from $825 million in 1914 to over $3.2 billion in 1916. An attempt to limit this commerce would have raised a storm; to have eliminated it would have caused a catastrophe. Munitions makers and other businessmen did not want the United States to enter the war. Neutrality suited their purposes admirably.

Britain and France soon exhausted their ready cash, and by early 1917 they had borrowed well over $2 billion. Although these loans violated no principle of international law, they fastened the United States more closely to the Allies' cause.

During the first months of the Great War, the Germans were not especially concerned about neutral trade or American goods because they expected to crush the Allied armies quickly. When their first swift thrust into France was blunted along the Marne River, only twenty miles from Paris, and the war became a bloody stalemate, they began to challenge the Allies' control of the seas. Unwilling to risk their battleships and cruisers against the much larger British fleet, they resorted to a new weapon, the submarine, commonly known as the U-boat (for *Unterseeboot*). German submarines played a role in World War I not unlike that of American privateers in the Revolution and the War of 1812: They ranged the seas stealthily in search of merchant ships. However, submarines could not operate under the ordinary rules of war, which required that a raider stop its prey, examine its papers and cargo, and give the crew and passengers time to get off in lifeboats before sending it to the bottom. U-boats when surfaced were vulnerable to the deck guns that many merchant ships carried; they could even be sunk by ramming, once they had stopped and put out a boarding party. Therefore, they commonly launched their torpedoes from below the surface without warning, often resulting in a heavy loss of life.

In February 1915 the Germans declared the waters surrounding the British Isles a zone of war and announced that they would sink without warning all enemy merchant ships encountered in the area. Since Allied vessels sometimes flew neutral flags to disguise their identity, neutral ships entering the zone would do so at their own risk. This statement was largely bluff, for the Germans had only a handful of submarines at sea; but they were feverishly building more.

Wilson—perhaps too hurriedly, considering the importance of the question—warned the Germans that he would hold them to "strict accountability" for any loss of American life or property resulting from violations of "acknowledged [neutral] rights on the high seas." He did not distinguish clearly between losses incurred through the destruction of *American* ships and those resulting from the sinking of other vessels. If he meant to hold the Germans responsible for injuries to Americans on *belligerent* vessels, he was changing international law as arbitrarily as the Germans were. Secretary of State Bryan, who opposed Wilson vigorously on this point, stood on sound legal ground when he said, "A ship carrying contraband should not rely upon passengers to protect her from attack—it would be like putting women and children in front of an army."

Correct or not, Wilson's position reflected the attitude of most Americans. It seemed barbaric to them that defenseless civilians should be killed without warning; Americans refused to surrender their "rights" as neutrals to cross the North Atlantic on any ship they wished. The depth of their feeling was demonstrated when, on May 7, 1915, the submarine *U–20* sank the British liner *Lusitania* off the Irish coast. The torpedoing of the *Lusitania* caused a profound and emotional

The *Titanic* carried only twenty lifeboats, a reason why so many perished in 1912. The *Lusitania* (above) carried forty-eight lifeboats, but it sank so quickly that many went unused.

reaction in the United States. The sinking of the *Lusitania* evoked the sinking of HMS *Titanic* three years earlier, after it had struck an iceberg in the northern Atlantic; first-person accounts rendered the tragedy all the more vivid to Americans. When it was learned that nearly 1,200 persons, including 128 Americans, lost their lives when the *Lusitania* went down (nearly as many as had perished on the *Titanic*), Americans were outraged. (For more on the *Titanic*, see Re-Viewing the Past, pp. 614–615.)

Wilson was shocked, but he kept his head. He demanded that Germany disavow the sinking, indemnify the victims, and promise to stop attacking passenger vessels. When the Germans quibbled about these points, he responded with further diplomatic correspondence rather than with an ultimatum.

In one sense this was sound policy. The Germans pointed out that they had published warnings in American newspapers saying they considered the *Lusitania* subject to attack, that the liner was carrying munitions, and that on past voyages it had flown the American flag to deceive German U-boat captains. However, after dragging the controversy out for nearly a year, Germany apologized and agreed to pay an indemnity. After the torpedoing of the French channel steamer *Sussex* in March 1916 had produced another stiff American protest, the Germans at last promised, in the *Sussex* pledge, to stop sinking merchant ships without warning.

Theodore Roosevelt urged Wilson to commit the United States to war with Germany; Wilson's refusal to do so incensed him. In November 1915 Wilson, in a belated nod to such criticisms, pressed for increased military and naval expenditures.

Read the **Document** Adolf K.G.E. Von Spiegal, *U-boat 202 (1919)* at **www.myhistorylab.com**

The Election of 1916

Wilson had won the presidency in 1912 only because the Republican party had split in two. In late 1915 he sought to broaden his support by winning over the progressives. In January 1916 he appointed Louis D. Brandeis to the Supreme Court. In addition to being an advanced progressive, Brandeis was the first Jewish Justice appointed to the Court. Wilson's action won him many friends among people who favored fair treatment for minority groups. In July Wilson bid for the farm vote by signing the Farm Loan Act to provide low-cost loans based on agricultural credit. Shortly thereafter, he approved the Keating-Owen Child Labor Act barring goods manufactured by the labor of children under 16 from interstate commerce, and a workers' compensation act for federal employees. He persuaded Congress to pass the Adamson Act, establishing an eight-hour day for railroad workers, and he modified his position on the tariff by approving the creation of a tariff commission.

Each of these actions represented a sharp reversal. In 1913 Wilson had considered Brandeis too radical even for a Cabinet post. The new farm, labor, and tariff laws were all examples of the kind of "class legislation" he had refused to countenance in 1913 and 1914. Wilson was putting into effect much of the progressive platform of 1912. Although the progressive convention came out for the Republican nominee, Associate Justice Charles Evans Hughes, who had compiled a record as a progressive governor of New York, many other progressives supported Wilson.

The key issue in the campaign was American policy toward the warring powers. Wilson intended to stress preparedness, which he was now wholeheartedly supporting. However, during the Democratic convention, the delegates shook the hall with cheers whenever orators referred to the president's success in keeping the country out of the war. One spellbinder, referring to the *Sussex* pledge, announced that the president had "wrung from the most militant spirit that ever brooded above a battlefield an acknowledgement of American rights and an agreement to American demands," and the convention erupted in a demonstration that lasted more than twenty minutes. Thus "He Kept Us Out of War" became the Democratic slogan.

To his credit, Wilson made no promises. "I can't keep the country out of war," he told one member of his Cabinet. "Any little German lieutenant can put us into the war at any time by some calculated outrage." His attitude undoubtedly cost him the votes of extremists on both sides, but it won the backing of thousands of moderates.

The combination of progressivism and the peace issue placed the Democrats on substantially equal terms with the Republicans. In the end, personal factors probably tipped the balance. Hughes was very stiff (Theodore Roosevelt called him a bearded Woodrow Wilson) and an ineffective speaker; he offended a number of important politicians, especially in crucial California, where he inadvertently snubbed the popular progressive governor, Hiram Johnson; and he equivocated on a number of issues. Nevertheless, on election night he appeared to have won, having carried nearly all the East and Midwest. Late returns gave Wilson California, however, and with it victory by the narrow margin of 277 to 254 in the Electoral College. He led Hughes in the popular vote, 9.1 million to 8.5 million.

The Road to War

Encouraged by his triumph, appalled by the continuing slaughter on the battlefields, fearful that the United States would be dragged into the conflagration, Wilson made one last effort to end the war by negotiation. In 1915 and again in 1916 he had sent his friend Colonel Edward House on secret missions to London, Paris, and Berlin to try to mediate among the belligerents. Each had proved fruitless, but after another long season of bloodshed, perhaps the powers would listen to reason.

Wilson's own feelings were more genuinely neutral than at any other time during the war, for the Germans had stopped sinking merchant ships without warning and the British had irritated him repeatedly by their arbitrary restrictions on neutral trade. He drafted a note to the belligerents asking them to state the terms on which they would agree to lay down their arms. Unless the fighting ended soon, he warned, neutrals and belligerents alike would be so ruined that peace would be meaningless.

When neither side responded encouragingly, Wilson, on January 22, 1917, delivered a moving speech aimed at "the people of the countries now at war" more than at their governments. Any settlement imposed by a victor, he declared, would breed hatred and more wars. There must be "peace without victory," based on the principles that all nations were equal and that every nationality should determine its own form of government. He mentioned, albeit vaguely, disarmament and freedom of the seas, and he suggested the creation of some kind of international organization to preserve world peace. "There must be not a balance of power, but a community of power," he said, and he added, "I am speaking for the silent mass of mankind everywhere."

This noble appeal met a tragic fate. The Germans had already decided to renounce the *Sussex* pledge and unleash their submarines against all vessels headed for Allied ports. After February 1, any ship in the war zone would be attacked without warning. Possessed now of more than 100 U-boats, the German military leaders had convinced themselves that they could starve the British people into submission and reduce the Allied armies to impotence by cutting off the flow of American supplies. The United States would probably declare war, but the Germans believed that they could overwhelm the Allies before the Americans could get to the battlefields in force. In 1917, after the German military leaders had made this decision, events moved relentlessly, almost uninfluenced by the actors who presumably controlled the fate of the world:

> *February 3: Housatonic* is torpedoed. Wilson announces to Congress that he has severed diplomatic relations with Germany.
>
> *February 24:* Walter Hines Page, United States ambassador to Great Britain, transmits to the State Department an intercepted German dispatch (the "Zimmermann telegram") revealing that Germany has proposed a secret alliance with Mexico; Mexico will receive, in the event of war with the United States, "the lost territory in Texas, New Mexico, and Arizona."
>
> *February 25:* Cunard liner *Laconia* is torpedoed; two American women perish.
>
> *February 26:* Wilson asks Congress for authority to arm American merchant ships.
>
> *March 1:* Zimmermann telegram is released to the press.
>
> *March 4:* President Wilson takes oath of office, beginning his second term.
>
> *March 9:* Wilson, acting under his executive powers, orders the arming of American merchantmen.
>
> *March 12:* Revolutionary provisional government is established in Russia. *Algonquin* is torpedoed.
>
> *March 15:* Czar Nicholas II of Russia abdicates.
>
> *March 16: City of Memphis, Illinois,* and *Vigilancia* are torpedoed.
>
> *March 21: New York World,* a leading Democratic newspaper, calls for declaration of war on Germany. Wilson summons Congress to convene in a special session on April 2.
>
> *March 25:* Wilson calls up the National Guard.
>
> *April 2:* Wilson asks Congress to declare war. Germany is guilty of "throwing to the winds all scruples of humanity," he says. America must fight, not to conquer, but for "peace and justice. . . . The world must be made safe for democracy."
>
> *April 4, 6:* Congress declares war—the vote, 82–6 in the Senate, 373–50 in the House.

The bare record conceals Wilson's agonizing search for an honorable alternative to war. To admit that Germany posed a threat to the United States meant confessing that interventionists had been right all along. To go to war meant, besides sending innocent Americans to their deaths, allowing "the spirit of ruthless brutality [to] enter into the very fibre of our national life."

The president's Presbyterian conscience tortured him. He lost sleep, appeared gray and drawn. When someone asked him which side he hoped would win, he answered petulantly, "Neither." "He was resisting," Secretary of State Lansing recorded, "the irresistible logic of events." In the end Wilson could salve his conscience only by giving intervention an idealistic purpose: the war had become a threat to humanity. Unless the United States threw its weight into the balance, Western civilization itself might be destroyed. Out of the long bloodbath must come a new and better world. The war must be fought to end, for all time, war itself. Thus in the name not of vengeance and victory but of justice and humanity he sent his people into battle.

Read the **Document** *United States Declaration of War (1917)* at **www.myhistorylab.com**

Read the **Document** *President Wilson's War Message to Congress (1917)* at **www.myhistorylab.com**

Watch the **Video** *American entry into WWI* at **www.myhistorylab.com**

Mobilizing the Economy

America's entry into the Great War determined its outcome. The Allies were running out of money and supplies; their troops, decimated by nearly three years in the trenches, were exhausted, disheartened, and rebellious. In February and March 1917, U-boats sent over a million tons of Allied shipping to the bottom of the Atlantic. The outbreak of the Russian Revolution in March 1917, at first lifting the spirits of the Western democracies, led to the Bolshevik takeover under Lenin. The Russian armies collapsed; by December 1917 Russia was out of the war and the Germans were moving masses of men and equipment from the eastern front to France. Without the aid of the United States, the Allies would likely have sued for peace according to terms dictated from Berlin. Instead American men and supplies helped contain the Germans' last drives and then push them back to final defeat.

It was a close thing, for the United States entered the war little better prepared to fight than it had been in 1898. The conversion of American industry to war production had to be organized and carried out without prearrangement. Confusion and waste resulted. The hurriedly designed shipbuilding program was an almost total fiasco. The gigantic Hog Island yard in Maine, which employed at its peak over 34,000 workers, completed its first vessel only after the war ended. Airplane, tank, and artillery construction programs developed too slowly to affect the war. The big guns that backed up American soldiers in 1918 were made in France and Great Britain; of the 8.8 million rounds of artillery ammunition fired by American troops, a mere 8,000 were manufactured in the United States.

"Enlist"—a poster by Fred Spear, published in June 1915 by the Boston Committee of Public Safety—evoked the drowning deaths of women and children on the *Lusitania*.

Congress authorized the manufacture of 20,000 airplanes, but only a handful, mostly British-designed planes made in America, got to France.

American pilots such as the great "ace" Captain Eddie Rickenbacker flew British Sopwiths and De Havillands or French Spads and Nieuports. Theodore Roosevelt's son Quentin was shot down while flying a Spad over Château-Thierry in July 1918.

The problem of mobilization was complicated. It took Congress six weeks of hot debate merely to decide on conscription. Only in September 1917, nearly six months after the declaration of war, did the first draftees reach the training camps, and it is hard to see how Wilson could have speeded this process appreciably. He wisely supported the professional soldiers, who insisted that he resist the appeals of politicians who wanted to raise volunteer units, even rejecting, at considerable political cost, Theodore Roosevelt's offer to raise an entire army division.

Wilson was a forceful and inspiring war leader once he grasped what needed to be done. He displayed both determination and unfailing patience in the face of frustration and criticism. Raising an army was only a small part of the job. The Allies had to be supplied with food and munitions, and immense amounts of money had to be collected.

After several false starts, Wilson placed the task in the hands of the **War Industries Board (WIB)**. The board was given almost dictatorial power to allocate scarce materials, standardize production, fix prices, and coordinate American and Allied purchasing. Evaluating the mobilization effort raises interesting historical questions. The antitrust laws were suspended and producers were encouraged, even compelled, to cooperate with one another. Government regulation went far beyond what the New Nationalists had envisaged in 1912.

As for the New Freedom variety of laissez-faire, it had no place in a wartime economy. The nation's railroads, strained by immensely increased traffic, became progressively less efficient. A monumental tie-up in December and January 1917–1918 finally persuaded Wilson to appoint Secretary of the Treasury William G. McAdoo director-general of the railroads, with power to run the roads as a single system. McAdoo's Railroad Administration pooled all railroad equipment, centralized purchasing, standardized accounting practices, and raised wages and passenger rates.

Wilson accepted the kind of government-industry agreement developed under Theodore Roosevelt that he had denounced in 1912. Prices were set by the WIB at levels that allowed large profits—U.S. Steel, for example, despite high taxes, cleared over half a billion dollars in two years. It is at least arguable that producers would have turned out just as much even if compelled to charge lower prices.

At the start of the war, army procurement was decentralized and inefficient—as many as eight bureaus were purchasing material in competition with one another. One official bought 1,200 typewriters, stacked them in the basement of a government building, and announced proudly to his superior, "There is going to be the greatest competition for typewriters around here, and I have them all."

Mobilization required close cooperation between business and the military. However, the army, suspicious of civilian institutions, resisted cooperating with them. Wilson finally compelled the War Department to place officers on WIB committees, laying the foundation for what was later to be known as the "industrial-military complex," an alliance between business and military leaders.

The history of industrial mobilization was the history of the entire home-front effort in microcosm: Marvels were performed, but the task was so gigantic and unprecedented that a full year passed before an efficient system had been devised, and many unforeseen results occurred.

The problem of mobilizing agricultural resources was solved more quickly, and this was fortunate because in April 1917 the British had on hand only a six-week supply of food Wilson appointed as food administrator Herbert Hoover; Hoover, a mining engineer, had headed the Belgian Relief Commission earlier in the war. Acting under powers granted by the Lever Act of 1917, Hoover set the price of wheat at $2.20 a bushel in order to encourage production. He established a government corporation to purchase the entire American and Cuban sugar crops, which he then doled out to American and British refiners. To avoid rationing he organized a campaign to persuade consumers to conserve food voluntarily. One slogan ran "If U fast U beat U boats"; another, "Serve beans by all means."

"Wheatless Mondays" and "meatless Tuesdays" were the rule, and although no law compelled their observance, the public responded patriotically. Boy Scouts dug up backyards and vacant lots to plant vegetable gardens; chefs devised new recipes to save on scarce items; restaurants added horsemeat, rabbit, and whale steak to their menus and doled out butter and sugar to customers in minuscule amounts. Mothers pressured their children to "Hooverize" their plates. Chicago residents were so successful in making use of leftovers that the volume of raw garbage in the city declined from 12,862 tons to 8,386 tons per month.

Without subjecting its own citizens to serious inconvenience, the United States increased food exports from 12.3 million tons to 18.6 million tons. Farmers, of course, profited greatly. Their real income went up nearly 30 percent between 1915 and 1918.

Workers in Wartime

With the army siphoning so many men from the labor market and with immigration reduced to a trickle, unemployment disappeared and wages rose. Although the cost of living soared, imposing hardships on people with fixed incomes, the boom produced unprecedented opportunities.

Americans, always a mobile people, pulled up their roots in record numbers. Disadvantaged groups, especially African Americans, were particularly attracted by jobs in big-city factories. Early in the conflict, the government began regulating the wages and hours of workers building army camps and manufacturing uniforms. In April 1918 Wilson created the National War Labor Board, headed by former president Taft and Frank P. Walsh, a prominent lawyer, to settle labor disputes. The board considered more than 1,200 cases and prevented many strikes. The War Labor Policies Board, chaired by Felix Frankfurter of the Harvard Law School, set wages-and-hours standards for each major war industry. Since these were determined in consultation with employers and representatives of labor, they speeded the unionization of workers by compelling management, even in antiunion industries like steel, to deal with labor leaders. Union membership rose by 2.3 million during the war.

However, the wartime emergency roused the public against strikers; some conservatives even demanded that war workers, like soldiers, be conscripted. While he opposed strikes that impeded the war effort, Wilson set great store in preserving the individual worker's freedom of action. It would be "most unfortunate . . . to relax the laws by which safeguards have been thrown about labor," he said. "We must accomplish the results we desire by organized effort rather than compulsion."

Paying for the War

Wilson managed the task of financing the war effectively. The struggle cost the United States about $33.5 billion, not counting pensions and other postwar expenses. About $7 billion of this was lent to the Allies,[1] but since this money was spent largely in America, it contributed to the national prosperity.

Over two-thirds of the cost of the war was met by borrowing. Five Liberty and Victory Loan drives, spurred by advertising, parades, and other appeals to patriotism, persuaded people to open their purses. Industrialists, eager to instill in their employees a sense of personal involvement in the war effort, conducted campaigns in their plants. Some went so far as to threaten "A Bond or Your Job," but more typical was the appeal of the managers of the Gary, Indiana, plant of U.S. Steel, who published bond advertisements in six languages in order to reach its immigrant workers.

In addition to borrowing, the government collected about $10.5 billion in taxes during the war. A steeply graduated income tax took more than 75 percent of the incomes of the wealthiest citizens. A 65 percent excess-profits tax and a 25 percent inheritance tax were also enacted. Thus although many individuals made fortunes from the war, its cost was distributed far more equitably than during the Civil War.

Americans also contributed generously to philanthropic agencies engaged in war work. Most notable, perhaps, was the great 1918 drive of the United War Work Council, an interfaith religious group, which

---

[1]In 1914 Americans owed foreigners about $3.8 billion. By 1919 Americans *were owed* $12.5 billion by Europeans alone.

raised over $200 million mainly to finance recreational programs for the troops overseas.

Propaganda and Civil Liberties

Wilson was preeminently a teacher and preacher, a specialist in the transmission of ideas and ideals. He excelled at mobilizing public opinion and inspiring Americans to work for the better world he hoped would emerge from the war. In April 1917 he created the Committee on Public Information (CPI), headed by the journalist George Creel. Soon 75,000 speakers were deluging the country with propaganda prepared by hundreds of CPI writers. They pictured the war as a crusade for freedom and democracy, the Germans as a bestial people bent on world domination.

A large majority of the nation supported the war enthusiastically. But thousands of persons—German Americans and Irish Americans, for example; people of pacifist leanings such as Jane Addams, the founder of Hull House; and some who thought both sides in the war were wrong—still opposed American involvement. Creel's committee and a number of unofficial "patriotic" groups allowed their enthusiasm for the conversion of the hesitant to become suppression of dissent. People who refused to buy war bonds were often exposed to public ridicule and even assault. Those with German names were persecuted without regard for their views; some school boards outlawed the teaching of the German language; sauerkraut was renamed "liberty cabbage." Opponents of the war were subjected to coarse abuse. A cartoonist pictured Senator Robert La Follette, who had opposed entering the war, receiving an Iron Cross from the German militarists, and the faculty of his own University of Wisconsin voted to censure him.

Although Wilson spoke in defense of free speech, his actions opposed it. He signed the **Espionage Act** of 1917, which imposed fines of up to $10,000 and jail sentences ranging to twenty years on persons convicted of aiding the enemy or obstructing recruiting, and he authorized the postmaster general to ban

Eugene V. Debs ("Convict #9653") was imprisoned for speaking against the war. In 1920 he ran as the Socialist candidate for president from the Atlanta federal prison, receiving nearly a million votes.

from the mails any material that seemed treasonable or seditious.

In May 1918, again with Wilson's approval, Congress passed the **Sedition Act**, which made "saying anything" to discourage the purchase of war bonds a crime, with the proviso that investment counselors could still offer "bona fide and not disloyal advice" to clients. The law also made it illegal to "utter, print, write, or publish any disloyal, profane, scurrilous, or abusive language" about the government, the Constitution, or the uniform of the army or navy. Socialist periodicals such as *The Masses* were suppressed, and Eugene V. Debs, formerly a candidate for president, was sentenced to ten years in prison for making an antiwar speech. Ricardo Flores Magón, an anarchist, was sentenced to twenty years in jail for publishing a statement criticizing Wilson's Mexican policy, an issue that had nothing to do with the war.

These laws went far beyond what was necessary to protect the national interest. Citizens were jailed

Table 23.1 Suppression of Liberties during World War I

Federal Action	Year	Consequence
Espionage Act	1917	Prohibited words or actions that would aid the enemy or obstruct recruiting efforts
Sedition Act	1918	Prohibited people from "saying anything" that might discourage purchase of war bonds or otherwise undermine the federal government or the Constitution
Schenck v. United States	1919	Supreme Court upheld limitations on free speech during times of "clear and present danger" to the nation

for suggesting that the draft law was unconstitutional and for criticizing private organizations like the Red Cross and the YMCA. One woman was sent to prison for writing, "I am for the people, and the government is for the profiteers."

The Supreme Court upheld the constitutionality of the Espionage Act in *Schenck v. United States* (1919), a case involving a man who had mailed circulars to draftees urging them to refuse to report for induction into the army. Free speech has its limits, Justice Oliver Wendell Holmes, Jr., explained. No one has the right to cry, "Fire!" in a crowded theater. When there is a "clear and present danger" that a particular statement would threaten the national interest, it can be repressed by law. In peacetime Schenck's circulars would be permissible, but not in time of war.

The "clear and present danger" doctrine did not prevent judges and juries from interpreting the espionage and sedition acts broadly, and although in many instances higher courts overturned their decisions, this usually did not occur until after the war. The wartime repression far exceeded anything that happened in Great Britain and France. In 1916 the French novelist Henri Barbusse published *Le Feu (Under Fire)*, a graphic account of the horrors and purposelessness of trench warfare. In one chapter Barbusse described a pilot flying over the trenches on a Sunday, observing French and German soldiers at Mass in the open fields, each worshiping the same God. Yet *Le Feu* circulated freely in France and even won the coveted Prix Goncourt.

•❖•❘Read the Document Buffington, *Friendly Words to the Foreign Born* at www.myhistorylab.com

Wartime Reforms

The American mobilization experience was part and product of the Progressive Era. The work of the progressives at the national and state levels in expanding government functions in order to deal with social and economic problems provided precedents and conditioned the people for the all-out effort of 1917 and 1918. Social and economic planning and the management of huge business operations by public boards and committees got their first practical tests. College professors, technicians, and others with complex skills entered government service en masse. The federal government for the first time actively entered such fields as housing and labor relations.

Many progressives believed that the war was creating the sense of common purpose that would stimulate the people to act unselfishly to benefit the poor and to eradicate social evils. Patriotism and public service seemed at last united. Secretary of War Newton D. Baker, a prewar urban reformer, expressed this attitude in supporting a federal child labor law: "We cannot afford, when we are losing boys in France, to lose children in the United States."

Men and women of this sort worked for a dozen causes only remotely related to the war effort. The women's suffrage movement was brought to fruition, as was the campaign against alcohol. Both the Eighteenth Amendment, outlawing alcoholic beverages, and the Nineteenth, giving women the vote, were adopted at least in part because of the war. Reformers began to talk about health insurance. The progressive campaign against prostitution and venereal disease gained strength, winning the enthusiastic support both of persons worried about inexperienced local girls being seduced by the soldiers and of those concerned lest prostitutes lead innocent soldiers astray. One of the latter type claimed to have persuaded "over 1,000 fallen women" to promise not to go near any army camps.

The effort to wipe out prostitution around military installations was a cause of some misunderstanding with the Allies, who provided licensed facilities for their troops as a matter of course. When the premier of France graciously offered to supply prostitutes for American units in his country, Secretary Baker is said to have remarked, "For God's sake . . . don't show this to the President or he'll stop the war." Apparently Baker had a rather peculiar sense of humor. After a tour of the front in France, he assured an American women's group that life in the trenches was "far less uncomfortable" than he had thought and that not a single American doughboy was "living a life which he would not be willing to have [his] mother see him live."

Women and Blacks in Wartime

Although a number of prominent feminists were pacifists, most supported the war enthusiastically, moved by patriotism and the belief that opposition to the war would doom their hopes of gaining the vote. They also expected that the war would open up many kinds of high-paying jobs to women. To some extent it did; about a million women replaced men in uniform, but the numbers actually engaged in war industries were small (about 6,000 found jobs making airplanes, for example), and the gains were fleeting. When the war ended, most women who were engaged in industrial work either left their jobs voluntarily or were fired to make room for returning veterans. Some women went overseas as nurses, and a few served as ambulance drivers and YMCA workers.

Most unions were unsympathetic to the idea of enrolling women, and the government did little to encourage women to do more for the war effort than prepare bandages, knit warm clothing for

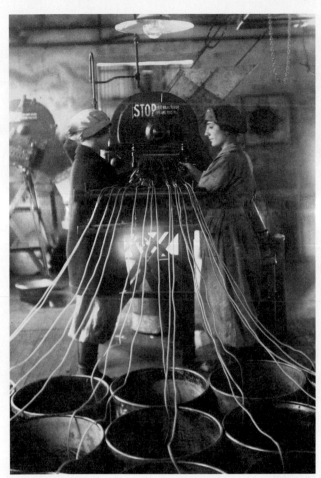

Women workers at the Dupont factory in Old Hickory, Tennessee, in 1917, form smokeless gunpowder into long strips, which will then be cut for use in artillery shells and other armaments.

population of New York City, for example, fell from over 10 percent in 1800 to under 2 percent in 1900.

Around the turn of the century, as the first post-slavery generation reached maturity and as southern repression increased, the northward movement quickened—about 200,000 blacks migrated between 1890 and 1910. Then, after 1914, the war boom drew blacks north in a flood. Agents of northern manufacturers flocked into the cotton belt to recruit them in wholesale lots. "Leave the benighted land," urged the *Chicago Defender*, a black-owned newspaper with a considerable circulation in southern states. "Get out of the South." Half a million made the move between 1914 and 1919. The African American population of New York City rose from 92,000 to 152,000; that of Chicago from 44,000 to 109,000; and that of Detroit from 5,700 to 41,000.

Life for the newcomers was difficult; many whites resented them; workers feared them as potential strikebreakers yet refused to admit them into their unions. In East St. Louis, Illinois, where employers had brought in large numbers of blacks in an attempt to discourage local unions from striking for higher wages, a bloody riot erupted during the summer of 1917 in which nine whites and an undetermined number of blacks were killed. As in peacetime, the Wilson administration was at worst antagonistic and at best indifferent to blacks' needs and aspirations.

Nevertheless, the blacks who moved north during the war were, as a group, infinitely better off, materially and psychologically, than those they left behind. Many

soldiers, participate in food conservation programs, and encourage people to buy war bonds. There was a Women in Industry Service in the Department of Labor and a Woman's Committee of the Council of National Defense, but both served primarily as window dressing for the Wilson administration. The final report of another wartime agency, issued in 1919, admitted that few women war workers had been paid as much as men and that women had been promoted more slowly than men, were not accepted by unions, and were discharged promptly when the war ended.

The wartime "great migration" of southern blacks to northern cities where jobs were available brought them important economic benefits. Actually, the emigration of blacks from the former slave states began with emancipation, but the mass exodus that many people had expected was slow to materialize. Between 1870 and 1890 only about 80,000 blacks moved to northern cities. Compared with the influx from Europe and from northern farms, this number was inconsequential. The black proportion of the

When manufacturers in East St. Louis (Illinois) sought to weaken labor unions by hiring African American workers from Mississippi and western Tennessee, the white workers went on a rampage. Much of East Saint Louis was destroyed by fire, and several dozen blacks and a few whites were dead. Here National Guardsmen lead a black man to safety.

A recruiting poster for the "True Sons of Freedom" encouraged African Americans to enlist. In fact, some 350,000 black Americans served in segregated units during the Great War. Several such units fought alongside French units, and 171 African Americans were awarded the French Legion of Honor, an award for courageous military service.

black soldiers killed seventeen white civilians, black recruits were dispersed among many camps for training to lessen the possibility of trouble.

In the military service, all blacks were placed in segregated units. Only a handful were commissioned as officers. Despite the valor displayed by black soldiers in the Civil War and the large role they played in the Spanish-American War, where five blacks had won the Congressional Medal of Honor, most even those sent overseas, were assigned to labor battalions working as stevedores and common laborers. But many fought and died for their country. Altogether about 200,000 served overseas.

W. E. B. Du Bois supported the war wholeheartedly. He praised Wilson for making, at last, a strong statement against lynching, which had increased to a shocking extent during the previous decade. He even went along with the fact that the handful of black officer candidates were trained in a segregated camp. "Let us," he wrote in the *Crisis*, "while the war lasts, forget our special grievances and close ranks shoulder to shoulder with our fellow citizens and the allied nations that are fighting for democracy."

Many blacks condemned Du Bois's accommodationism (which he promptly abandoned when the war ended), but most saw the war as an opportunity to demonstrate their patriotism and prove their worth. For the moment the prevailing mood was one of optimism. "We may expect to see the walls of prejudice gradually crumble"—this was the common attitude of blacks in 1917 and 1918. If winning the war would make the world safe for democracy, surely blacks in the United States would be better off when it was won. Whether or not this turned out to be so was (and still is) a matter of opinion.

Watch the **Video** *The Great Migration* at www.myhistorylab.com

Americans: To the Trenches and Over the Top

All activity on the home front had one ultimate objective: defeating the Central Powers on the battlefield. This was accomplished. The navy performed with special distinction. In April 1917, German submarines sank more than 870,000 tons of Allied shipping; after April 1918, monthly losses never reached

earned good wages and were accorded at least some human rights. They were not treated by the whites as equals, or even in most cases entirely fairly, but they could vote, send their children to decent schools, and within reasonable limits do and say what they pleased without fear of humiliation or physical attack.

There were two black regiments in the regular army and a number of black national guard units when the war began, and once these outfits were brought up to combat strength, no more volunteers were accepted. Indeed, at first no blacks were conscripted; Southerners in particular found the thought of giving large numbers of guns to blacks and teaching them how to use them most disturbing. However, blacks were soon drafted, and once they were, a larger proportion of them were taken than whites. One Georgia draft board exempted more than 500 of 815 white registrants and only 6 of the 202 blacks in its jurisdiction before its members were relieved of their duties. After a riot in Texas in which

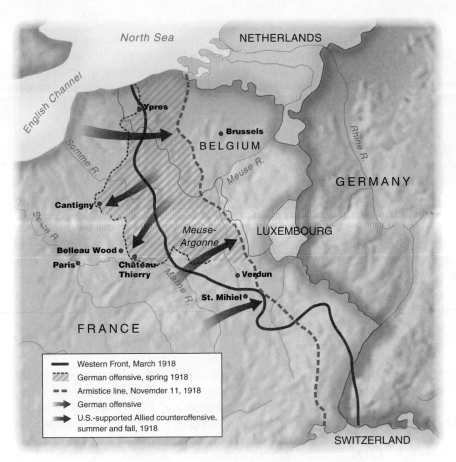

The Western Front, 1918 The Germans launched their great offensive in the spring and summer of 1918 with the goal of taking Paris. American troops helped hold the line at Château-Thierry and Belleau Woods. Several months later, a half million American soldiers participated in the counteroffensive that drove the Germans back to the Meuse River.

Legend:
- Western Front, March 1918
- German offensive, spring 1918
- Armistice line, November 11, 1918
- German offensive
- U.S.-supported Allied counteroffensive, summer and fall, 1918

mere presence boosted French and British morale.

Pershing insisted on maintaining his troops as independent units; he would not allow them to be filtered into the Allied armies as reinforcements. This was part of a perhaps unfortunate general policy that reflected America's isolationism. (Wilson always referred to the other nations fighting Germany as "associates," not as "allies.")

In March 1918 the Germans launched a great spring offensive, their armies strengthened by thousands of veterans who had been freed from the eastern front by the collapse of Russia. By late May they had reached a point on the Marne River near the town of Château-Thierry, only fifty miles from Paris. Early in June the AEF fought its first major engagements, driving the Germans back from Château-Thierry and Belleau Wood.

In this fighting only about 27,500 Americans saw action, and they suffered appalling losses. Nevertheless, when the Germans advanced again in the direction of the Marne in mid-July, 85,000 Americans were in the lines that withstood their charge. Then, in the major turning point of the war, the Allied armies counterattacked. Some 270,000 Americans participated, helping to flatten the German bulge between Reims and Soissons. By late August the American First Army, 500,000 strong, was poised before the Saint-Mihiel bulge, a deep extension of the German lines southeast of Verdun. On September 12 this army, buttressed by French troops, struck and in two days wiped out the salient.

Late in September began the greatest American engagement of the war. No fewer than 1.2 million doughboys plunged into the Argonne Forest. For over a month of indescribable horror they inched ahead through the tangle of the Argonne and the formidable defenses of the Hindenburg line, while to the west, French and British armies staged similar drives. In this one offensive the AEF suffered 120,000 casualties. Finally, on November 1, they broke the German center and raced toward the vital Sedan-Mézières railroad. On November 11, with Allied armies advancing on all fronts, the Germans signed the armistice, ending the fighting.

300,000 tons. The decision to send merchant ships across the Atlantic in convoys screened by destroyers made the reduction possible. Checking the U-boats was essential because of the need to transport American troops to Europe. Slightly more than 2 million soldiers made the voyage safely. Those who crossed on fast ocean liners were in little danger as long as the vessel maintained high speed and followed a zigzag course, a lesson learned from the *Lusitania*, whose captain had neglected both precautions. Those who traveled on slower troop transports benefited from the protection of destroyers and also from the fact that the Germans concentrated on attacking supply ships. They continued to believe that inexperienced American soldiers would not be a major factor in the war.

The first units of the American Expeditionary Force (AEF), elements of the regular army commanded by General John J. Pershing, reached Paris on Independence Day, 1917. They took up positions on the front near Verdun in October. Not until the spring of 1918, however, did the "doughboys" play a significant role in the fighting, though their

Preparing for Peace

The fighting ended on November 11, 1918, but the shape of the postwar world remained to be determined. European society had been shaken to its foundations. Confusion reigned. People wanted peace yet burned for revenge. Millions faced starvation. Other millions were disillusioned by the seemingly purposeless sacrifices of four years of horrible war. Communism—to some an idealistic promise of human betterment, to others a commitment to rational economic and social planning, to still others a danger to individual freedom, toleration, and democracy—having conquered Russia, threatened to envelop Germany and much of the defunct Austro-Hungarian Empire, perhaps even the victorious Allies. How could stability be restored? How could victory be made worth its enormous cost?

Woodrow Wilson had grasped the significance of the war while most statesmen still thought that triumph on the battlefield would settle everything automatically. As early as January 1917 he had realized that victory would be wasted if the winners permitted themselves the luxury of vengeance. Such a policy would disrupt the balance of power and lead to economic and social chaos. The victors must build a better society, not punish those they believed had destroyed the old one.

In a speech to Congress on January 8, 1918, Wilson outlined a plan, known as the **Fourteen Points**, designed to make the world "fit and safe to live in." The peace treaty should be negotiated in full view of world opinion, not in secret. It should guarantee the freedom of the seas to all nations, in war as in peacetime. It should tear down barriers to international trade, provide for a drastic reduction of armaments, and establish a colonial system that would take proper account of the interests of the native peoples concerned. European boundaries should be redrawn so that no substantial group would have to live under a government not of its own choosing.

More specifically, captured Russian territory should be restored, Belgium evacuated, Alsace-Lorraine returned to France, the heterogeneous nationalities of Austria-Hungary accorded autonomy. Italy's frontiers should be adjusted "along clearly recognizable lines of nationality," the Balkans made free, Turkey divested of its subject peoples, and an independent Polish state (with access to the Baltic Sea) created. To oversee the new system, Wilson insisted, "a general association of nations must be formed under specific covenants for the purpose of affording mutual guarantees of political independence and territorial integrity to great and small states alike."

Wilson's Fourteen Points for a fair peace lifted the hopes of people everywhere. After the guns fell silent, however, the vagueness and inconsistencies in his list became apparent. Complete national self-determination was impossible in Europe; there were too many regions of mixed population for every group to be satisfied. Self-determination, like the war itself, also fostered the spirit of nationalism that Wilson's dream of international organization, a league of nations, was designed to

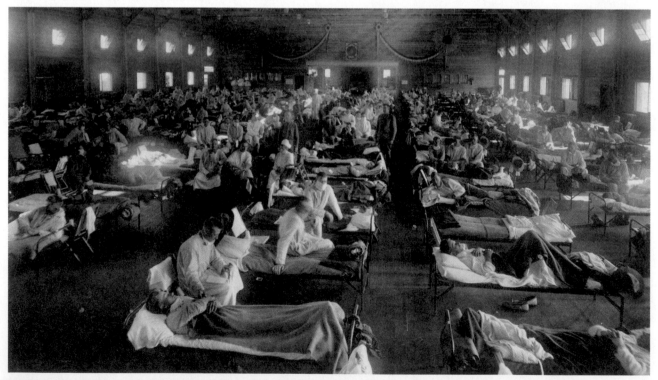

Hundreds of soldiers in a Spanish flu ward at Camp Funston, Kansas (named for Frederick Funston, see American Lives, Chapter 22).

de-emphasize. Furthermore, the Allies had made territorial commitments to one another in secret treaties that ran counter to the principle of self-determination, and they were not ready to give up all claims to Germany's colonies. Freedom of the seas in wartime posed another problem; the British flatly refused to accept the idea. In every Allied country, millions rejected the idea of a peace without indemnities. They expected to make the enemy pay for the war, hoping, as Sir Eric Geddes, first lord of the Admiralty, said, to squeeze Germany "as a lemon is squeezed—until the pips squeak."

Wilson assumed that the practical benefits of his program would compel opponents to fall in line. He had the immense advantage of seeking nothing for his own country and the additional strength of being leader of the one important nation to emerge from the war richer and more powerful than it had been in 1914.

Yet this combination of altruism, idealism, and power was his undoing; it intensified his tendency to be overbearing and undermined his judgment. He had never found it easy to compromise. Once, when he was president of Princeton, he got into an argument over some abstract question with a professor while shooting a game of pool. To avoid acrimony, the professor finally said: "Well, Doctor Wilson, there are two sides to every question." "Yes," Wilson answered, "a right side and a wrong side." Now, believing that the fate of humanity hung on his actions, he was unyielding. Always a preacher, he became in his own mind a prophet—almost, one fears, a kind of god.

In the last weeks of the war Wilson proved to be a brilliant diplomat, first dangling the Fourteen Points before the German people to encourage them to overthrow Kaiser Wilhelm II and sue for an armistice, then sending Colonel House to Paris to persuade Allied leaders to accept the Fourteen Points as the basis for the peace. When the Allies raised objections, House made small concessions, but by hinting that the United States might make a separate peace with Germany, he forced them to agree. Under the armistice, Germany had to withdraw behind the Rhine River and surrender its submarines, together with quantities of munitions and other materials. In return it received the assurance of the Allies that the Wilsonian principles would prevail at the Paris peace conference.

Wilson then came to a daring decision: He would personally attend the conference as a member of the United States Peace Commission. This was a precedent-shattering step, for no president had ever left American territory while in office. (Taft, who had a summer home on the St. Lawrence River in Canada, never vacationed there during his term, believing that to do so would be unconstitutional.)

Wilson probably erred in going to Paris, but not because of the novelty or possible illegality of the act. By going, he was turning his back on obvious domestic problems. Western farmers believed that they had been discriminated against during the war, since wheat prices had been controlled while southern cotton had been allowed to rise unchecked from seven cents a pound in 1914 to thirty-five cents in 1919. The administration's drastic tax program had angered many businessmen. Labor, despite its gains, was restive in the face of reconversion to peacetime conditions.

Wilson had increased his political difficulties by making a partisan appeal for the election of a Democratic Congress in 1918. Republicans, who had in many instances supported his war program more loyally than the Democrats, considered the action a gross affront. The appeal failed; the Republicans won majorities in both houses. Wilson appeared to have been repudiated at home at the very moment that he set forth to represent the nation abroad. Most important, Wilson intended to break with the isolationist tradition and bring the United States into a league of nations. Such a revolutionary change would require explanation; he should have undertaken a major campaign to convince the American people of the wisdom of this step.

The Paris Peace Conference and the Versailles Treaty

Wilson arrived in Europe a world hero. He toured England, France, and Italy briefly and was greeted ecstatically almost everywhere. The reception tended

The "Big Four" world leaders meet at the Hotel Crillon in Paris, 1919. From left to right (front row): Vittorio Emanuele Orlando of Italy, David Lloyd George of Great Britain, Georges Clemenceau of France, and Woodrow Wilson of the United States.

Europe before the Great War In 1914, five countries dominated Europe: the German Empire, France, Great Britain, Austria-Hungary, and Russia.

to increase his sense of mission and to convince him, in the fashion of a typical progressive, that whatever the European politicians might say about it, "the people" were behind his program.

When the conference settled down to its work, control quickly fell into the hands of the so-called Big Four: Wilson, Prime Minister David Lloyd George of Great Britain, Premier Georges Clemenceau of France, and Prime Minister Vittorio Orlando of Italy. Wilson stood out in this group but did not dominate it. His principal advantage in the negotiations was his untiring industry. He alone of the leaders tried to master all the complex details of the task.

The seventy-eight-year-old Clemenceau cared only for one thing: French security. He viewed Wilson cynically, saying that since mankind had been unable to keep God's Ten Commandments, it was unlikely to do better with Wilson's Fourteen Points. Lloyd George's approach was pragmatic and almost cavalier. He sympathized with much that Wilson was trying to accomplish but found the president's frequent sermonettes about "right being more important than might, and justice being more eternal than force" incomprehensible. "If you want to succeed in politics," Lloyd George advised a British statesman, "you must keep your conscience well under control." Orlando, clever, cultured, a believer in international cooperation but inflexible where Italian national interests were concerned, was

not the equal of his three colleagues in influence. He left the conference in a huff when they failed to meet all his demands.

The conference labored from January to May 1919 and finally brought forth the Versailles Treaty. American liberals whose hopes had soared at the thought of a peace based on the Fourteen Points found the document abysmally disappointing.

The peace settlements failed to carry out the principle of self-determination completely. They gave Italy a large section of the Austrian Tyrol, though the area contained 200,000 people who considered themselves Austrians. Other German-speaking groups were incorporated into the new states of Poland and Czechoslovakia.

The victors forced Germany to accept responsibility for having caused the war—an act of senseless vindictiveness as well as a gross oversimplification—and to sign a "blank check," agreeing to pay for all damage to civilian properties and even future pensions and other indirect war costs. This reparations bill, as finally determined, amounted to $33 billion. Instead of attacking imperialism, the treaty attacked German imperialism; instead of seeking a new international social order based on liberty and democracy, it created a great-power entente designed to crush Germany and to exclude Bolshevik Russia from the family of nations.

Europe after the Great War The Versailles Treaty and other postwar settlements punished the losers, especially Germany and Austria-Hungary, transferring their lands to newly-created nations in eastern Europe, such as Poland, Czechoslovakia, and Yugoslavia.

Wilson himself backtracked on his pledge to honor the right of self-determination. The fate of Arab peoples eventually proved to be of particular significance to Americans, especially after the events of September 11, 2001. For centuries, most Arabs had lived under the Turkish rulers of the Ottoman Empire. When the Ottoman Empire joined Germany and Austria-Hungary in World War I, Arab nationalists looked to the Allies and eventually worked out a deal with Britain. In return for Arab military support against the Ottoman Empire and the Germans, Britain would endorse Arab independence after the war. Wilson seemingly concurred, for Point Twelve of his Fourteen Points called for the "autonomous development" of Arab peoples. But in 1917 the British issued the Balfour Declaration in support of "a national home" for the Jewish people in Palestine, land mostly occupied by Palestinian Arabs. How could Palestinian Arabs be granted independence if Palestine was to become the home of Jewish settlers?

In the postwar negotiations, Britain retreated from its earlier promise to the Arabs. Wilson, too, had second thoughts about granting the Arab peoples self-determination. Secretary of State Lansing worried about the "danger of putting such ideas into the minds of certain races," particularly the "Mohammedans [Muslims] of Syria and Palestine."

Wilson reluctantly deleted explicit references to self-determination from the postwar settlements. Rather than grant the Arab peoples independence, Britain and France themselves seized Arab lands that had been ruled by the Turks. This land grab was "legalized" through the device of a mandate to rule the region issued by the League of Nations.

Similarly, Ho Chi Minh, a young Vietnamese nationalist, was embittered by the failure at Versailles to deliver his people from French colonial rule. He decided to become a communist revolutionary. The repercussions of Arab and Vietnamese discontent, though far removed from American interests at the time, would be felt in full force much later.

To those who had taken Wilson's "peace without victory" speech and the Fourteen Points literally, the Versailles Treaty seemed an abomination. The complaints of the critics were individually reasonable, yet their conclusions were not entirely fair. The new map of Europe left fewer people on "foreign" soil than in any earlier period of history. Although the Allies seized the German colonies, they were required, under the mandate system, to render the **League of Nations** annual accounts of their stewardship and to prepare the inhabitants for eventual independence. Above all, Wilson had persuaded the powers to incorporate the League of Nations in the treaty.

Wilson expected the League of Nations to make up for all the inadequacies of the Versailles Treaty. Once the League had begun to function, problems like freedom of the seas and disarmament would solve themselves, he argued, and the relaxation of trade barriers would surely follow. The League would arbitrate international disputes, act as a central body for registering treaties, and employ military and economic sanctions against aggressor nations. Each member promised (Article 10) to protect the "territorial integrity" and "political independence" of all other members. No nation could be made to go to war against its will, but Wilson emphasized that all were *morally* obligated to carry out League decisions. By any standard, Wilson had achieved a remarkably moderate peace, one full of hope for the future. Except for the war guilt clause and the heavy reparations imposed on Germany, he could be justly proud of his work.

Ottoman Empire and the Arab World, 1914 In 1914, the Ottoman Empire, also known as Turkey, controlled much of the Arab world, stretching from the Persian Gulf to the Red Sea.

Dismantling the Ottoman Empire, 1919–1920 The Ottoman Empire was the biggest loser at Versailles: It lost everything apart from Turkey itself; but the Arab nationalists lost as well, because Britain and France, through League-appointed mandates, took control of Syria, Transjordan, Palestine, and Mesopotamia (Iraq).

The Senate Rejects the League of Nations

When Wilson returned from France, he finally directed his attention to the task of winning public approval of his handiwork. A large majority of the people probably favored the League of Nations in principle, though few understood all its implications or were entirely happy with every detail. Wilson had persuaded the Allies to accept certain changes in the original draft to mollify American opposition. No nation could be forced to accept a colonial mandate, and "domestic questions" such as tariffs, the control of immigration, and the Monroe Doctrine were excluded from League control.

Many senators found these modifications insufficient. Even before the peace conference ended, thirty-seven Republican senators signed a manifesto, devised by Henry Cabot Lodge of Massachusetts, opposing Wilson's League and demanding that the question of an international organization be put off until "the urgent business of negotiating peace terms with Germany" had been completed. Wilson rejected this suggestion icily. Further alterations were out of the question. "Anyone who opposes me . . . I'll crush!" he told

one Democratic senator. "I shall consent to nothing. The Senate must take its medicine." Thus the stage was set for a monumental test of strength between the president and the Republican majority in the Senate.

Partisanship, principle, and prejudice clashed mightily in this contest. A presidential election loomed. Should the League prove a success, the Republicans wanted to be able to claim a share of the credit, but Wilson had refused to allow them to participate in drafting the document. This predisposed all of them to favor changes. Politics aside, genuine alarm at the possible sacrifice of American sovereignty to an international authority led many Republicans to urge modification of the League covenant, or constitution. Personal dislike of Wilson and his high-handed methods motivated others. Yet the noble purpose of the League made many reluctant to reject it entirely. The intense desire of the people to have an end to the long war made Republican leaders hesitate before voting down the Versailles Treaty, and they could not reject the League without rejecting the treaty.

Wilson could count on the Democratic senators almost to a man, but he had to win over many Republicans to obtain the two-thirds majority necessary for ratification. Republican opinion divided roughly into three segments. At one extreme were some dozen "irreconcilables," led by the shaggy-browed William E. Borah of Idaho, an able and kindly person of progressive leanings but an uncompromising isolationist. Borah claimed that he would vote against the League even if Jesus Christ returned to earth to argue in its behalf, and most of his followers were equally inflexible. At the other extreme stood another dozen "mild" reservationists who were in favor of the League but who hoped to alter it in minor ways, chiefly for political purposes. In the middle were the "strong" reservationists, senators willing to go along with the League only if American sovereignty were fully protected and if it were made clear that their party had played a major role in fashioning the final document.

Senator Lodge, the leader of the Republican opposition, was a haughty, rather cynical, intensely partisan individual. He possessed a keen intelligence,

Despite Wilson's serving as mother hen, the League of Nations never hatched.

a mastery of parliamentary procedure, and, as chairman of the Senate Foreign Relations Committee, a great deal of power. Although not an isolationist, he had little faith in the League. He also had a profound distrust of Democrats, especially Wilson, whom he considered a hypocrite and a coward. The president's pious idealism left him cold. While perfectly ready to see the country participate actively in world affairs, Lodge insisted that its right to determine its own best interests in every situation be preserved. He had been a senator since 1893 and an admirer of senatorial independence since early manhood. When a Democratic president tried to ram the Versailles Treaty down the Senate's throat, he fought him with every weapon he could muster.

Lodge belonged to the strong reservationist faction. His own proposals, known as the Lodge Reservations, fourteen in number to match Wilson's Fourteen Points, limited U.S. obligations to the League and stated in unmistakable terms the right of Congress to decide when to honor these obligations. Some of the reservations were mere quibbles. Others, such as the provision that the United States would not endorse Japan's seizure of Chinese territory, were included mainly to embarrass Wilson by pointing out compromises he had made at Versailles. The most important reservation applied to Article Ten of the League covenant, which committed signatories to protect the political independence and territorial integrity of all member nations. Wilson had rightly called Article Ten "the heart of the Covenant." One of Lodge's reservations made it inoperable so far as the United States was concerned

"unless in any particular case the Congress . . . shall by act or joint resolution so provide."

Lodge performed brilliantly, if somewhat unscrupulously, in uniting the three Republican factions behind his reservations. He got the irreconcilables to agree to them by conceding their right to vote against the final version in any event, and he held the mild reservationists in line by modifying some of his demands and stressing the importance of party unity. Reservations—as distinct from amendments—would not have to win the formal approval of other League members. In addition, the Lodge proposals dealt forthrightly with the problem of reconciling traditional concepts of national sovereignty with the new idea of world cooperation. Supporters of the League could accept them without sacrifice of principle. Wilson, however, refused to agree. "Accept the Treaty with the Lodge reservations?" the president snorted when a friendly senator warned him that he must accept a compromise. "Never! Never!"

This foolish intransigence seems almost incomprehensible in a man of Wilson's intelligence and political experience. In part his hatred of Lodge accounts for it, in part his faith in his League. His physical condition in 1919 also played a role. At Paris he had suffered a violent attack of indigestion that was probably a symptom of a minor stroke. Thereafter, many observers noted small changes in his personality, particularly increased stubbornness and a loss of good judgment. Instead of making concessions, the president set out early in September on a nationwide speaking crusade to rally support for the League. In three weeks, Wilson traveled some 10,000 miles by train and gave forty speeches, some of them brilliant. But they had little effect on senatorial opinion, and the effort drained his last physical reserves. On September 25, after an address in Pueblo, Colorado, he collapsed. The rest of the trip had to be canceled. A few days later, in Washington, he suffered a severe stroke that partially paralyzed his left side.

For nearly two months the president was almost totally cut off from affairs of state, leaving supporters of the League leaderless while Lodge maneuvered the reservations through the Senate. Gradually, popular attitudes toward the League shifted. Organized groups of Italian, Irish, and German Americans, angered by what they considered unfair treatment of their native lands in the Versailles Treaty, clamored for outright rejection. The arguments of the irreconcilables persuaded many citizens that Wilson had made too sharp a break with America's isolationist past and that the Lodge Reservations were therefore necessary. Other issues connected with the reconversion of society to a peacetime basis increasingly occupied the public mind.

This 1920 photograph of Wilson, with his second wife, Edith, was the first taken since his stroke.

A coalition of Democratic and moderate Republican senators could easily have carried the treaty. That no such coalition was organized was Wilson's fault. Lodge obtained the simple majority necessary to add his reservations to the treaty merely by keeping his own party united. When the time came for the final roll call on November 19, Wilson, bitter and emotionally distraught, urged the Democrats to vote for rejection. "Better a thousand times to go down fighting than to dip your colors to dishonorable compromise," he explained to his wife. Thus the amended treaty failed, thirty-five to fifty-five, the irreconcilables and the Democrats voting against it. Lodge then allowed the original draft without his reservations to come to a vote. Again the result was defeat, thirty-eight to fifty-three. Only one Republican cast a ballot for ratification.

Dismayed but not yet crushed, friends of the League in both parties forced reconsideration of the treaty early in 1920. Neither Lodge nor Wilson would yield an inch. Lodge, who had little confidence in the effectiveness of any league of nations, was under no compulsion to compromise. Wilson, who believed that the League was the world's best hope, did have such a compulsion. Yet he would not compromise either, and this ensured the treaty's defeat.

Wilson's behavior is further evidence of his physical and mental decline. Had he died or stepped down, the treaty, with reservations, would almost certainly have been ratified. When the Senate balloted again in March, half the Democrats voted for the treaty with the Lodge Reservations. The others, mostly southern party regulars, joined the irreconcilables. Together they mustered thirty-five votes, seven more than the one-third that meant defeat.

Read the **Document** *Henry Cabot Lodge's Objections to the Treaty of Versailles* at **www.myhistorylab.com**

The Red Scare

Business boomed in 1919 as consumers spent wartime savings on cars, homes, and other goods that had been in short supply during the conflict. But temporary shortages caused inflation; by 1920 the cost of living stood at more than twice the level of 1913. Workers demanded that their wages be increased as well. The unions, grown strong during the war, struck for wage increases. Over four million workers, one in five in the labor force, were on strike at some time during 1919.

The activities of radicals in the labor movement led millions of citizens to associate unionism and strikes with the new threat of communist world revolution. Although there were only a relative handful of communists in the United States, Russia's experience persuaded many that a tiny minority of ruthless revolutionaries could take over a nation of millions if conditions were right. Communists appointed themselves the champions of workers; labor unrest attracted them magnetically. When strikes broke out, some accompanied by violence, many people interpreted them as communist-inspired preludes to revolution.

But organized labor in America had seldom been truly radical. The Industrial Workers of the World (IWW) had made little impression in most industries. But some labor leaders had been attracted to socialism, and many Americans failed to distinguish between the common ends sought by communists and socialists and the entirely different methods by which they proposed to achieve those ends. When a general strike paralyzed Seattle in February 1919, the fact that a procommunist had helped organize it sent shivers down countless conservative spines. When the radical William Z. Foster began a drive to organize the steel industry at about this time, the fears became more intense. In September 1919 a total of 343,000 steelworkers walked off their jobs, and in the same month the Boston police went on strike. Violence marked the steel strike, and the suspension of police protection in Boston led to looting and fighting that ended only when Governor Calvin Coolidge called out the National Guard.

During the same period a handful of terrorists caused widespread alarm by attempting to murder various prominent persons, including John D. Rockefeller, Justice Oliver Wendell Holmes Jr., and

"UNGRATEFUL SCUM!"

The "red scare" that followed the Great War caused panic and new racial violence throughout the nation. Paranoid delusions of "dangerous aliens" and "foreign subversives" were prevalent, as this cartoon demonstrates.

Attorney General A. Mitchell Palmer. Although the terrorists were anarchists and anarchism had little in common with communism, many citizens lumped all extremists together and associated them with a monstrous assault on society.

What aroused the public even more was the fact that most radicals were not American citizens. Wartime fear of alien saboteurs easily transformed itself into peacetime terror of foreign radicals. In place of Germany, the enemy became the lowly immigrant, usually an Italian or a Jew or a Slav and usually an industrial worker. In this muddled way, radicalism, unionism, and questions of racial and national origins combined to make many Americans believe that their way of life was in imminent danger. That few immigrants were radicals, that most workers had no interest in communism, and that the extremists themselves were faction-ridden and irresolute did not affect conservative thinking. From all over the country came demands that radicals be ruthlessly suppressed. Thus the **"red scare"** was born.

Attorney General Palmer was the key figure in the resulting purge. He had been a typical progressive, a supporter of the League of Nations and such reforms as woman suffrage and child labor legislation. But pressure from Congress and his growing conviction that the communists really were a menace led him to join the "red hunt." Soon he was saying of the radicals,

"Out of the sly and crafty eyes of many of them leap cupidity, cruelty, insanity, and crime; from their lopsided faces, sloping brows, and misshapen features may be recognized the unmistakable criminal type."

In August 1919, Palmer established within the Department of Justice the General Intelligence Division, headed by J. Edgar Hoover, to collect information about clandestine radical activities. In November, Justice Department agents in a dozen cities swooped down on the meeting places of an anarchist organization known as the Union of Russian Workers. More than 650 persons, many of them unconnected with the union, were arrested but in only forty-three cases could evidence be found to justify deportation.

Nevertheless, the public reacted so favorably that Palmer, thinking now of winning the 1920 Democratic presidential nomination, planned an immense roundup of communists. He obtained 3,000 warrants, and on January 2, 1920, his agents, reinforced by local police and self-appointed vigilantes, struck simultaneously in thirty-three cities.

About 6,000 persons were taken into custody, many of them citizens and therefore not subject to the deportation laws, many others unconnected with any radical cause. Some were held incommunicado for weeks while the authorities searched for evidence against them. In a number of cases, individuals who went to visit prisoners were themselves thrown behind bars on the theory that they too must be communists. Hundreds of suspects were jammed into filthy "bullpens," beaten, and forced to sign "confessions."

The public tolerated these wholesale violations of civil liberties because of the supposed menace of communism. Gradually, however, protests began to be heard, first from lawyers and liberal magazines, then from a wider segment of the population. No revolutionary outbreak had taken place. Of 6,000 seized in the Palmer raids, only 556 proved liable to deportation. The widespread ransacking of communists' homes and meeting places produced mountains of inflammatory literature but only three pistols.

Palmer, attempting to maintain the crusade, announced that the radicals planned a gigantic terrorist demonstration for May Day, 1920. In New York and other cities thousands of police were placed on round-the-clock duty; federal troops stood by anxiously. But the day passed without even a rowdy meeting. Suddenly Palmer appeared ridiculous. The red scare swiftly subsided.

The Election of 1920

Wilson still hoped for vindication at the polls in the presidential election, which he sought to make a "great and solemn referendum" on the League. He would have liked to run for a third term, but in his enfeebled condition he attracted no support among Democratic leaders. The party nominated James M. Cox of Ohio.

Cox favored joining the League, but the election did not produce the referendum on the new organization that Wilson desired. The Republicans, whose candidate was another Ohioan, Senator Warren G. Harding, equivocated shamelessly on the issue. The election turned on other matters, largely emotional. Disillusioned by the results of the war, many Americans had their fill of idealism. They wanted, apparently, to end the long period of moral uplift and reform agitation that had begun under Theodore Roosevelt and return to what Harding called "normalcy."

To the extent that the voters were expressing opinions on Wilson's League, their response was overwhelmingly negative. Senator Harding, a strong reservationist, swept the country, winning over 16.1 million votes to Cox's 9.1 million. In July 1921,

Congress formally ended the war with the Central Powers by passing a joint resolution.

The defeat of the League was a tragedy both for Wilson, whose crusade for a world order based on peace and justice ended in failure, and for the world, which was condemned to endure another, still more horrible and costly war. Perhaps this dreadful outcome could not have been avoided. Had Wilson compromised and Lodge behaved like a statesman instead of a politician, the United States would have joined the League, but it might well have failed to respond when called on to meet its obligations. As events soon demonstrated, the League powers acted timidly and even dishonorably when challenged by aggressor nations.

Yet it might have been different had the Senate ratified the Versailles Treaty. What was lost when the treaty failed was not peace but the possibility of peace, a tragic loss indeed.

Chapter Review

Milestones

1914	United States invades Veracruz, Mexico
	Great War begins in Europe
1915	German U-boat torpedoes *Lusitania*
1916	Wilson appoints Louis D. Brandeis to Supreme Court
	Adamson Act gives railroad workers eight-hour day
	"Pancho" Villa burns Columbus, New Mexico
	Wilson is reelected president
1917	Germany resumes unrestricted submarine warfare
	Russian Revolution begins
	United States declares war on Central Powers
	Bernard Baruch heads War Industries Board
	Former President Taft heads War Labor Board
1918	Sedition Act limits freedom of speech
	Wilson announces Fourteen Points

	Republicans gain control of both houses of Congress
	Armistice ends the Great War
1918– 1919	Flu epidemic kills 600,000 Americans
1919	Steel workers strike
	Red scare culminates in Palmer raids
	Big Four meet at Paris Peace Conference
	Senate rejects Versailles Treaty and League of Nations
	Wilson wins Nobel Peace Prize, suffers massive stroke
1920	Senate again rejects Versailles Treaty and League of Nations
	Warren Harding is elected president

Key Terms

Allied Powers   The military alliance during World War I, chiefly consisting of Britain, France, Russia, and Italy, that opposed the **Central Powers**, chiefly Germany, Austria-Hungary, and Turkey, *613*

Central Powers   Germany and its World War I allies—Austria-Hungary, Turkey, and Bulgaria, *613*

Espionage Act   A law passed in 1917 that made it a crime to obstruct the nation's effort to win World War I, *623*

Fourteen Points   A comprehensive plan, proposed by President Woodrow Wilson in January 1918, to negotiate an end to World War I. It called for

freedom of the seas, free trade, arms reduction, national self-determination and an end to colonial rule and secret diplomacy, *628*

League of Nations   A worldwide assembly of nations, proposed by President Woodrow Wilson, that was included in the Treaty of Versailles ending World War I. The refusal of the United States to join the League limited its effectiveness, *631*

"red scare"   Public hysteria over Bolshevik influence in the United States after World War I; it led to the arrest or deportation of thousands of radicals, labor activists, and ethnic leaders, *635*

Sedition Act   Federal legislation, first passed in 1798 and expired in 1801, that placed limits on freedom of speech during wartime. Another such act was passed in 1918 and led to the imprisonment of Socialist Eugene V. Debs and others during World War I, *623*

War Industries Board (WIB)   A federal agency, established during World War I, that reorganized industry for maximum efficiency and productivity, *621*

Review Questions

1. The chapter's introduction draws a parallel between the American efforts to fight terrorism in Afghanistan and Iraq and Woodrow Wilson's crusade to make the world "safe for democracy." Does the history of American involvement in World War I teach any "lessons" about foreign wars?

2. Why did Woodrow Wilson recommend neutrality at the outset of the European war and why did he change his mind?

3. Did progressivism play a role in leading the United States into World War I? Did it shape how the war was waged?

4. What problems did the United States encounter in mobilizing for war? How did the war effort contribute to the growth of the American state?

5. How did the war affect minorities and women? How did it restrict dissent and labor?

6. What were the arguments for and against American ratification of the League of Nations?

PEARSON myhistorylab Connections

Reinforce what you learned in this chapter by studying the many documents, images, maps, review tools, and videos available at **www.myhistorylab.com**.

Read and Review

✔ **Study** and **Review** *Chapter 23*

Read the Document Adolf K.G.E. Von Spiegal, *U-boat 202 (1919)*, p. 618

Read the Document *United States Declaration of War (1917)*, p. 620

Read the Document *President Wilson's War Message to Congress (1917)*, p. 620

Read the Document Buffington, *Friendly Words to the Foreign Born*, p. 624

Read the Document *Henry Cabot Lodge's Objections to the Treaty of Versailles*, p. 634

Research and Explore

Watch the Video *The outbreak of WWI*, p. 613

Watch the Video *American entry into WWI*, p. 620

Watch the Video *The Great Migration*, p. 626

He is keeping the World safe for Democracy
Enlist and help him

(((•— Hear the Audio

Hear the audio file for Chapter 23 at
www.myhistorylab.com.

Do you drink too much?

Many college students drink—a lot. In 2008 the National Center on Addiction and Substance Abuse (CASA) at Columbia University found that 44 percent of college students were binge-drinkers and that nearly one in four fulfilled the medical criteria for substance abuse. In 2010 the National Institute on Alcohol Abuse and Alcoholism reported that alcohol annually caused nearly 100,000 sexual assaults and date rapes and 1,700 deaths of college students.

"It's time to get the 'high' out of higher education," declared Joseph A. Califano, president of CASA and former U.S. secretary of health, education, and welfare. He blamed college administrators for condoning a "college culture of abuse." Campaigns to promote responsible drinking accomplished little, he noted. The only effective strategy was campus-wide prohibition.

But such words caused many to bristle. In 2010, after Iowa City banned those under twenty-one from bars, the *Daily Iowan* at the University of Iowa claimed that "harsh restrictions on alcohol drive the behavior underground, pushing young people to use more hard liquor in unsupervised private house parties." "Let's not repackage the Prohibition Era of the 1920s," the article concluded. When the University of Hawaii considered

Postwar Society and Culture: Change and Adjustment

24

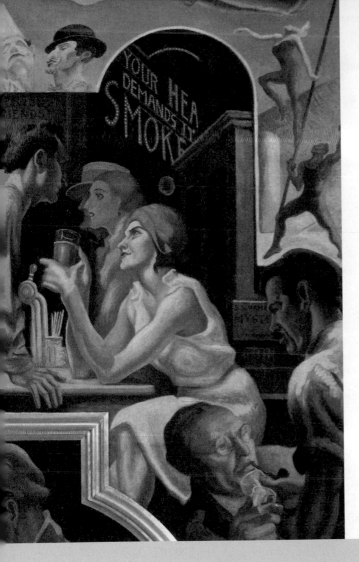

((•—[Hear the Audio **Chapter 24 at www.myhistorylab.com**

■ In *America Today: City Activities with Dance Hall* (1929), Thomas Hart Benton chronicled the glitz and glamour of the "jazz age"—dirty dancing, illicit drinking, cigarette smoking, and, above it all, a broker studying the ticker tape with the stock results.
Source: Thomas Hart Benton, *City Activities with Dance Hall* from America Today, 1930, distemper and egg tempera with oil glaze on gessoed linen, 92 × 134 ½ inches. Collection, The Equitable Life Assurance Society of the United States. Photo 1988 by Dorothy Zeidman.

banning alcohol at the football stadium, another professor cited the nation's experience with Prohibition eighty years earlier. "You cannot root out the drinking of alcohol by outlawing it," he added.

The mural accompanying this introduction provides some support for this view. Painted by Thomas Hart Benton in 1929 and entitled *America Today*, it shows that drinking—though illegal—was an integral part of popular culture. It also suggests that flaunting Prohibition contributed to a more general loosening of social and cultural conventions.

Such changes unsettled many. The recent flood of immigration had strained the nation's social fabric, especially in cities. Young women were challenging traditional gender roles. African Americans were leaving the South in droves and demanding rights that had been long deferred. Gays were becoming visible—at least to each other. Movies and radio, and even artists and writers, stimulated a rebellious youth culture. Advertising encouraged people to lose themselves in the delights of consumption.

These transformations also elicited opposition. The federal government curtailed immigration and cracked down on foreign-born radicals. The Ku Klux Klan reemerged to intimidate immigrants and blacks. Traditionalists inveighed against the enticements of popular culture and decline in faith. Prohibition was only the most visible expression of a reaction against social and cultural change. ■

Closing the Gates to New Immigrants

One indication of this was a tightening of immigration rules. In 1921 Congress, reflecting a widespread prejudice against a huge influx of eastern and southern Europeans, passed an emergency act establishing a quota system. Each year 3 percent of the number of foreign-born residents of the United States in 1910 (about 350,000 persons) might enter the country. Each country's quota was based on the number of its nationals in the United States in 1910. This meant that only a relative handful of the total would be from southern and eastern Europe. In 1924 the quota was reduced to 2 percent and the base year shifted to 1890, thereby lowering further the proportion of southern and eastern Europeans admitted.

In 1929 Congress established a system that allowed only 150,000 immigrants a year to enter the country. (In recent years, that annual number of legal immigrants has been increased to 700,000.) Each national quota was based on the supposed origins of the entire white population of the United States in 1920, not merely on the foreign-born. Here is an example of how the system worked:

$$\frac{\text{Italian quota}}{150,000} = \frac{\text{Italian-origin population, 1920}}{\text{White population, 1920}}$$

$$\frac{\text{Italian quota}}{150,000} = \frac{3,800,000}{95,500,000}$$

$$\text{Italian quota} = 6,000 \text{ (approximately)}$$

The system was complicated and unscientific, for no one could determine with accuracy the "origins" of millions of citizens. More seriously, it ignored America's long history of constantly changing ethnic diversity. The motto *E Pluribus Unum*—Out of Many, One—conceived to represent the unity of the original thirteen states, applied even more appropriately to the blending of different cultures into one nationality. The new law sought to freeze the mix, to turn the American melting pot into a kind of gigantic ice cube.

The law reduced actual immigration to far below 150,000 a year. Between 1931 and 1939, for example, only 23,000 British immigrants came to the United States, far below Britain's annual quota of 65,000. Meanwhile, hundreds of thousands of southern and eastern Europeans waited for admission.

The United States had closed the gates. The **National Origins Act** caused the foreign-born percentage of the population to fall from about 13 percent in 1920 to 4.7 percent in 1970. (In 2010, the foreign-born population had again increased to about 13 percent.) Instead of an open, cosmopolitan society eager to accept, in Emma Lazarus's stirring line, the "huddled

"Give me your tired, your poor, your huddled masses yearning to breathe free, the wretched refuse of your teeming shore"—these words of Emma Lazarus, inscribed at the base of the Statue of Liberty, tell only part of the story. Most immigrants were young and hopeful, like this family at Ellis Island; many were resolute and ambitious. The restriction of immigration during the 1920s, conceived to exclude misfits, also deprived the nation of people such as these.

masses yearning to breathe free," America now became committed to preserving a homogeneous, "Anglo-Saxon" population.

Distaste for the "new" immigrants from eastern Europe, many of whom were Jewish, expanded into a more general anti-Semitism in the 1920s. American Jews, whether foreign-born or native, were subjected to increasing discrimination, not because they were slow in adopting American ways but because (being ambitious and hardworking, as immigrants were supposed to be) many of them were getting ahead in the world somewhat more rapidly than expected. Prestigious colleges like Harvard, Yale, and Columbia that had in the past admitted Jews based on their academic records now imposed unofficial but effective quotas. Medical schools also established quotas, and no matter how talented, most young Jewish lawyers and bankers could find places only in so-called "Jewish" firms.

New Urban Social Patterns

The census of 1920 revealed that for the first time a majority of Americans (54 million in a population of 106 million) lived in "urban" rather than "rural" places. These figures are somewhat misleading when applied to the study of social attitudes because the census classified anyone in a community of 2,500 or more as urban. Of the 54 million "urban" residents in 1920, over 16 million lived in villages and towns of fewer than 25,000 persons and the evidence suggests strongly that a large majority of them held ideas and values more like those of rural citizens than like those of city dwellers. But the truly urban Americans, the one person in four who lived in a city of 100,000 or more—and particularly the nearly 16.4 million who lived in metropolises of at least half a million—were increasing steadily in number and influence. More than 19 million persons moved from farms to cities in the 1920s, and the population living in centers of 100,000 or more increased by about a third.

The urban environment transformed family structure, educational opportunities, and dozens of other aspects of human existence. Indeed, since most of the changes in the relations of husbands, wives, and children that had occurred in the nineteenth century were related to the fact that people were leaving farms to work in towns and cities, these trends continued and were intensified in the early twentieth century as more and more people settled in urban centers. In addition, couples continued to marry more because of love and physical attraction than because of social position, economic advantage, or the wishes of their parents. In each decade, people married slightly later in life and had fewer children.

Earlier differences between working-class and middle-class family structures persisted. In 1920 about a quarter of the American women who were working were married, but less than 10 percent of all married women were working. Middle-class married women who worked were nearly all either childless or highly paid professionals who were able to employ servants. Most male skilled workers now earned enough to support a family in modest comfort so long as they could work steadily, but an unskilled laborer still could not. Wives in most such families helped out, usually by taking in laundry or doing piecework sewing for jobbers.

By the 1920s the idea of intrafamily democracy had emerged. In such families, husbands and wives would deal with each other as equals; given existing conditions, this meant sharing housework and child-care, downplaying male authority, and stressing mutual satisfaction in sexual and other matters. On the one hand, they should be friends and lovers, not merely housekeepers, earners of money, and producers of children. On the other hand, advocates of these companionate relationships believed that there was nothing particularly sacred about marriage; divorce should be made easier for couples that did not get along, provided they did not have children.

In *The Companionate Marriage* (1927), Benjamin B. Lindsey, a juvenile court judge, suggested a kind of trial marriage, a period during which a young couple could get used to each other before undertaking to raise a family. By practicing contraception such couples could separate without doing serious damage to anyone if they decided to end the relationship. If the relationship remained firm and loving, it would become a traditional marriage and their children would grow up in a loving environment that would help them to become warm, well-adjusted adults.

Much attention was given to "scientific" child-rearing. Childcare experts (a new breed) agreed that routine medical examinations and good nutrition were of central importance, but they were divided about how the socialization and psychological development of the young should be handled. One school stressed rigid training. Children could be "spoiled" by

In Howard Thain's 1925 painting of New York's Times Square, the people are inconsequential gray blurs beneath the luminous wonders of consumption and pleasure.

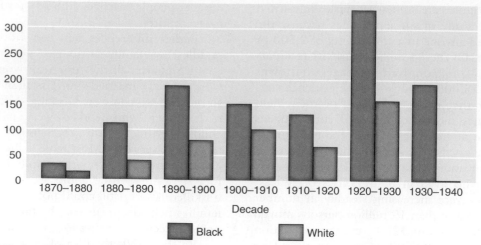

Black and White Out-Migration from Virginia and North and South Carolina, 1870–1940

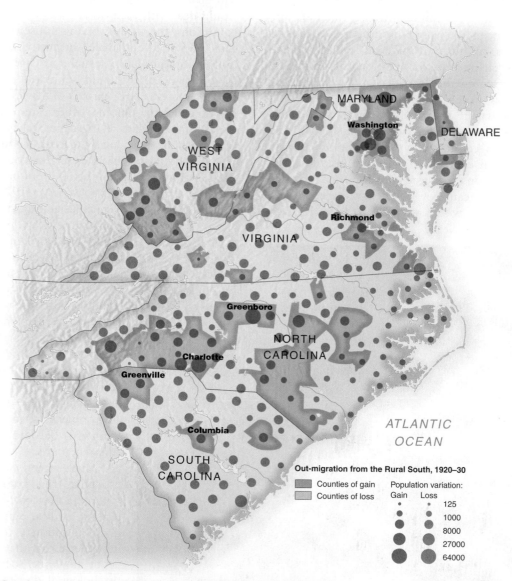

Out-migration from the Rural South, 1920–30

Population Losses in the South The graph shows that whites and especially blacks were leaving the South in large numbers, especially during the 1920s. The map shows that while many urban areas in the South gained population, most rural areas lost population.

indulgence; toilet training should begin early in infancy; thumb sucking should be suppressed; too much kissing could turn male youngsters into "mama's boys." "Children are made not born," John B. Watson, a former president of the American Psychological Association who was also a vice president of the J. Walter Thompson advertising agency, explained in *The Psychological Care of Infant and Child* (1928). "Never hug and kiss them, never let them sit in your lap. If you must, kiss them once on the forehead when they say good night."

Another school favored a more permissive approach. Toilet training could wait; parents should pay attention to their children's expressed needs, not impose a generalized set of rules on them.

The growth of large cities further loosened social constraints on sexuality. Amidst the sea of people that surged down the streets or into the subways, the solitary individual acquired a freedom derived from anonymity. (For further perspective on urban life, see Re-Viewing the Past *Chicago*, pp. 644–645.) Homosexuals, in particular, developed a set of identifying signals and fashioned a distinctive culture in parks, cafeterias, nightclubs, and rooming houses of big cities. Because most others wrongly assumed that male homosexuality was characterized by effeminacy, they were unaware of the extent of the emerging gay culture. But by the late 1920s and early 1930s homosexual parades, dances, and nightclub acts had become public events.

The Younger Generation

The Great War profoundly affected the generation born around the turn of the century. It had raised and then dashed their hopes for the future. Now the narrowness and prudery of so many of their elders and the stuffy conservatism of nearly all politicians seemed not merely old-fashioned but ludicrous. The actions of red-baiters and reactionaries led them to exaggerate the importance of their right to express themselves in bizarre ways. Their models and indeed some of their leaders were the prewar Greenwich Village bohemians.

The 1920s has been described as the Jazz Age, the era of "flaming youth," when young people danced to syncopated "African" rhythms, careened about the countryside in automobiles in search of pleasure and forgetfulness, and made gods of movie stars and professional athletes. This view of the period bears a superficial resemblance to reality. "Younger people," one observer noted in 1922, were attempting "to create a way of life free from the bondage of an authority that has lost all meaning." But if they differed from their parents and grandparents, it was primarily because young people were adjusting to more profound and more rapid changes in their world than their grandparents could have imagined.

Beliefs that only the avant-garde had held before the war became commonplace; trends that were barely perceptible during the Progressive Era now reached avalanche proportions. This was particularly noticeable in relationships between the sexes. Courtship, for example, was transformed. In the late nineteenth century, a typical young man "paid a call" on a female friend. He met and conversed with her parents, perhaps over coffee and cookies. The couple remained at home, the parents nearby if not actually participating in what was essentially a social (one might say, public) event held in a private place.

By the 1920s paying calls was being replaced by *dating*; the young man called only to "pick up" his "date," to go off, free of parental supervision, to whatever diversion they wished. Many dating conventions counteracted the trend toward freedom in sexual matters. A man asked a woman "for a date" because dating meant going somewhere and spending money, and the man was expected to do the transporting and pay the bill. This made the woman doubly dependent; under the old system, *she* provided the refreshments, and there was no taboo against her doing the inviting.

But for young people of the 1920s, relations between the sexes were becoming more relaxed and uninhibited. Respectable young women smoked cigarettes, something previously done in public only by prostitutes and bohemian types. They cast off heavy corsets, wore lipstick and "exotic" perfumes, and shortened both their hair and their skirts, the latter rising steadily from instep to ankle to calf to knee and beyond as the decade progressed. For decades female dressmakers and beauty salon proprietors had sold their own beauty products and potions. By 1920, however, new cosmetic corporations, managed primarily by men, appropriated the products and marketing strategies of local women entrepreneurs and catered to national mass markets.

Freudian psychology and the more accessible ideas of the British "sexologist" Havelock Ellis reached steadily deeper into the popular psyche. According to A. A. Brill, the chief American popularizer of Freud's theories, the sex drive was irrepressible. "Love and sex are the same thing," he wrote. "The urge is there, and whether the individual desires it or no, it always manifests itself." Since sex was "the central function of life," Ellis argued, it must be "simple and natural and pure and good." Bombarded by

RE-VIEWING THE PAST
Chicago

Chicago (2003) is a tale of illicit sex, booze, and "all that jazz." The characters played by Renée Zellweger and Catherine Zeta-Jones aspire to cabaret stardom. Each is married, each is jilted, and each shoots her wayward lover because "he had it coming." The newspapers gleefully promote the stories. From prison, while awaiting trial for murder, the women compete to garner the most headlines, courting the fame that will boost their careers. Richard Gere, who plays their celebrity lawyer, "razzle dazzles" all Chicago (including the juries) and gets the women acquitted. *Chicago* is a musical. It does not claim to be history. Trial lawyers do not tap dance upon the judge's bench, nor do prisoners tango on death row. The movie, however, is based on a true story; and both the movie and the story illuminate important aspects of the Roaring Twenties.

On March 11, 1924, Walter Law, an automobile salesman, was found slumped against the steering wheel of a car in downtown Chicago. He was dead from a gunshot wound to the head. A pistol and an empty bottle of gin were on the floor. The car was registered to Belva Gaertner, a twice-divorced cabaret singer known as Belle Brown. Police hurried to her rooming house and peppered her with questions.

"We went driving, Mr. Law and I," she told them. She explained that they had stopped at the Bingham "café," bought a bottle of gin (illegally, since this was during Prohibition), and drove around town. "I don't know what happened next," she declared. During the interrogation Gaertner paced nervously, perhaps for good reason: Her clothes were soaked with blood. The police charged her with murder.

On April 3, police received a phone call from Beulah Annan, a young married woman who worked in a laundry. She said that a man had attempted to rape her and that she had shot him. Police raced to her apartment, where they found Harry Kalstedt dead from a gunshot wound. Annan insisted that she had acted in self-defense, and her husband supported her story. But police hammered away at the fact that Kalstedt had worked at the same laundry as Annan, and that he had been shot in the back. Annan eventually confessed that the two had been having an affair and that, when he threatened to dump her, she shot him. For two hours, as he lay dying, she drank cocktails and listened to a recording of "Hula Lou," a foxtrot about a Hawaiian girl "with more sweeties than a dog has fleas."

Maurine Watkins, a young reporter, covered both stories for the Chicago *Tribune*. Murder had long been a staple of local journalism, but Watkins recognized the extraordinary appeal of this story: jazz, booze, and two comely "lady murderesses," as Watkins termed them. While awaiting trial in prison, the women provided Watkins with delicious quotes.

Gaertner told Watkins that she was innocent. "No woman can love a man enough to kill him," she explained. "There are always plenty more." She added, "Gin and guns—either one is bad enough, but together they get you in a dickens of a mess." When the grand jury ruled that she could be tried for murder, Gaertner was irritated. "That was bum," she snapped. She called the jurors "narrow-minded old birds—bet they never heard a jazz band in their lives. Now, if I'm tried, I

Catherine Zeta-Jones and Renée Zellweger from the movie *Chicago*.

Beulah Annan and Belva Gaertner, "lady murderesses."

want worldly men, broad-minded men, men who know what it is to get out a bit. Why, no one like that would convict me!"

Watkins described Gaertner as "stylish" and "classy" but called Annan the "prettiest woman ever accused of murder in Chicago"—"young, slender, with bobbed auburn hair; wide set, appealing blue eyes, upturned nose; translucent skin, faintly, very faintly, rouged, an ingenuous smile. Refined features, intelligent expression—an 'awfully nice girl.'" This account appeared on the front page.

During the trial, Annan's attorney pointed to "this frail little girl, struggling with a drunken brute." On May 25, after deliberating less than two hours, the all-male jury acquitted her of the crime. (Justice in those days was swift; in Illinois, too, it was devoid of women, who did not gain the right to serve on juries until 1939.) Two weeks after Annan's trial, Gaertner was also found not guilty. "Another pretty woman gone free," muttered the prosecutor. Watkins noted that four other women remained on death row, but none were as "stylish" or "pretty" as Gaertner and Annan.

Unlike the movie's "lady murderesses," Annan and Gaertner did not team up in a cabaret act. Annan had a nervous breakdown, was institutionalized, and died in 1928. Of Gaertner's subsequent life, little is known. Watkins abandoned journalism and entered Yale drama school. In 1926 she wrote *Chicago*, a comedy derived from the Gaertner and Annan trials, and it ran on Broadway for 172 performances. The next year Cecil B. De Mille adapted the play as a silent movie. In 1975 director Bob Fosse bought the rights to *Chicago* and created the Broadway musical on which the 2003 movie was based.

The "lady murderesses" became part of the lore of the Roaring Twenties; the story seemed to confirm the fears of traditionalists. One minister warned about jazz's "wriggling movement and sensuous stimulation" of the body's "sensory center." Short, bobbed, or marcelled hair was similarly worrisome, because it signified a young woman's break from convention. Silk stockings, skirts that exposed knees, and straight dresses that de-emphasized the waist further suggested that

women's bodies were not meant solely for childbirth. The movie makes all of these points with suitable salaciousness.

The movie also reiterates widespread concerns about city life. Several months after the acquittal of Gaertner and Annan, *Literary Digest* warned "country girls" of the moral dangers of large cities. Such fears echoed the judgments of sociologists, especially those of "the Chicago school" of urban sociology, headed by Robert Park of the University of Chicago. The Chicago sociologists contended that large cities disrupted traditional bonds of family and community and fostered crime and deviance. In *The Gold Coast and the Slum* (1929), sociologist Harvey Zorbaugh maintained that life in much of downtown Chicago was "the direct antithesis of all we are accustomed to think of as normal in society." Big-city life was characterized by a "laxity of conventional standards, and of personal and social disorganization."

Scholars now recognize that the portrait of urban city life as propounded by "the Chicago school"—and by movies such as *Chicago*—was overdrawn. Urbanization did not shatter family and ethnic ties. Neighborliness and community persisted even in blighted tenement districts. Few people cast off social conventions, much less succumbed to murderous impulses. In short, Belva Gaertner and Beulah Annan were good copy, and stories such as theirs helped make that celebrated decade roar, but most folks painted the town less vividly, if at all.

Questions for Discussion

- Compare the photographs of Beulah Annan and Belva Gaertner with those of actresses Catherine Zeta-Jones and Renée Zellweger. What are the similarities and differences and what do they suggest about Hollywood's rendering of the past?

- Why would Hollywood take pains to depict the visual aspects of the past accurately?

these exciting ideas, to say nothing of their own inclinations, young people found casting off their inhibitions more and more tempting.

Conservatives bemoaned what they described as the breakdown of moral standards, the fragmentation of the family, and the decline of parental authority—all with some reason. Nevertheless, society was not collapsing. Much of the rebelliousness of the young, like their particular style of dress, was faddish in nature, in a sense a kind of youthful conformity. This was particularly true of college students. Elaborate rituals governed every aspect of their extracurricular life, which was consuming a steadily larger share of most students' time and energy. Fraternity and sorority initiations, "proms," attendance at Saturday afternoon football games, styles of dress, and college slang, seemingly aspects of independence and free choice, were nearly everywhere shaped and controlled by peer pressure.

But young people's new ways of relating to one another, while influenced by the desire to conform, were not mere fads and were not confined to people under thirty. This can be seen most clearly in the birth control movement, the drive to legalize the use of contraceptives.

The "New" Woman

The young people of the 1920s were more open about sex and perhaps more sexually precocious than the young had been before the war. This does not mean that most of them engaged in sexual intercourse before marriage or that they tended to marry earlier. Single young people might "believe in" birth control, but relatively few (at least by modern standards) had occasion to practice it. Contraception was a concern of married people, and particularly of married women.

The leading American proponent of birth control in the 1920s, actually the person who coined the term, was Margaret Sanger, one of the less self-centered Greenwich Village bohemians. Before the war she was a political radical, a friend of Eugene Debs, "Big Bill" Haywood, and the anarchist Emma Goldman. Gradually, however, her attention focused on the plight of the poor women she encountered while working as a nurse; many of these women, burdened by large numbers of children, knew nothing about contraception. Sanger began to write articles and pamphlets designed to enlighten them, but when she did so she ran afoul of the Comstock Act of 1873, an anti-obscenity law that banned the distribution of information about contraception from the mail. She was frequently in trouble with the law,

The shape of Flapper sundresses minimized hips and breasts, and the gossamer thinness of the fabric showed that the wearer was not wearing a corset.

but she was persistent to the edge of fanaticism. In 1921 she founded the American Birth Control League and two years later a research center. (Not until the 1960s, however, did the Supreme Court determine that the right to use contraceptives was guaranteed by the Constitution.)

Other gender-based restrictions and limitations of particular importance to women also seemed to be breaking down. The divorce laws had been modified in most states. More women were taking jobs, attracted by the expanding demand for clerks, typists, salespeople, receptionists, telephone operators, and similar service-oriented occupations. Over 10.6 million women were working by the end of the decade, in contrast with 8.4 million in 1920. The Department of Labor's Women's Bureau, outgrowth of a wartime agency, was founded in 1920 and was soon conducting investigations of the working conditions women faced in different industries and how various laws affected them.

But most of these gains were illusory. Relaxation of the strict standards of sexual morality did not eliminate the double standard. More women worked, but most of the jobs they held were still menial or of a kind that few men wanted: domestic service, elementary school teaching, clerical work, selling behind a counter. When they competed for jobs with men, women usually received much lower wages. Women's Bureau studies demonstrated this repeatedly; yet when the head of the bureau, Mary Anderson, tried to get employers to raise women's wages, most of them first claimed that the men had families to support, and when she reminded them that many female employees also had family responsibilities, they told her that there was a "tacit understanding" that women were to make less than men. "If I paid them the same," one employer said, "there would be a revolution." Efforts to get the American

This photograph of Margaret Sanger was taken during her trial in January 1917. Having opened the nation's first birth control clinic in Brooklyn, New York, she was convicted of disseminating information on contraception and served thirty days in prison. Friends had advised Sanger to dress conservatively and affect a persona of motherhood. Despite her demure clothing, her eyes express her characteristic assertiveness.

Federation of Labor to take up the issue failed; few of the unions in the federation admitted women.

More women graduated from college, but the colleges placed more emphasis on subjects like home economics that seemed designed to make them better housewives rather than professional nutritionists or business executives. As one Vassar College administrator (a woman!) said, colleges should provide "education for women along the lines of their chief interests and responsibilities, motherhood and the home."

The 1920s proved disillusioning to feminists, who now paid a price for their single-minded pursuit of the right to vote in the Progressive Era. After the ratification of the Nineteenth Amendment, Carrie Chapman Catt was exultant: "We are no longer petitioners," she announced, "but free and equal citizens." Many activists, assuming the battle won, lost interest in agitating for change. They believed that

the suffrage amendment had given them the one weapon needed to achieve whatever women still lacked. In fact, it soon became apparent that women did not vote as a bloc. Many married women voted for the candidates their husbands supported.

When radical feminists discovered that voting did not automatically bring true equality, they founded the National Woman's Party (NWP) and began campaigning for an equal rights amendment. Their dynamic leader, Alice Paul, disdained specific goals such as disarmament, ending child labor, and liberalized birth control. Total equality for women was the one objective. The party considered protective legislation governing the hours and working conditions of women discriminatory. This caused the so-called social feminists, who believed that children and working women needed the protection provided by such laws, to break away.

The NWP never attracted a wide following, but only partly because of the split with the social feminists. Many of the younger radical women, like the bohemians of the Progressive Era, were primarily concerned with their personal freedom to behave as they wished; politics did not interest them. But a more important reason was that nearly all the radicals failed to see that questions of gender—the attitudes that men and women *were taught* to take toward each other, not immutable physical or psychological differences—stood in the way of sexual equality. Many more women joined the more moderate League of Women Voters, which attempted to mobilize support for a broad spectrum of reforms, some of which had no specific connection to the interests of women as such. The entire women's movement lost momentum. The battle for the equal rights amendment persisted through the 1930s, but it was lost. By the end of that decade the movement was moribund.

●●●▬ **Read** the **Document** Margaret Sanger, *Happiness in Marriage* at **www.myhistorylab.com**

Popular Culture: Movies and Radio

The postwar decade saw immense changes in popular culture. Unlike the literary flowering of the era (see pp. 654–656), these changes seemed in tune with the times, not a reaction against them. This was true in part because they were products as much of technology as of human imagination.

The first motion pictures were made around 1900, but the medium only came into its own after the Great War. The early films, such as the eight-minute epic *The Great Train Robbery* (1903), were brief, action-packed, and unpretentious. Professional actors and most educated people viewed them with amused

This cover of *Life* (1925) offered a stereotypical rendering of the new generation: a young couple dressing alike, sharing the indulgence of smoking, and completely wrapped up in themselves. Was this a fair portrait youth during the Roaring Twenties?

Frederick Lewis Allen claimed that it was in *Only Yesterday* (1931), an immediate bestseller. In his view young people believed that "life was futile and nothing much mattered." So they occupied themselves with "tremendous trifles" such as mah-jong, jazz, and illicit booze. Of the wider world, they cared little. In 1937 Samuel Eliot Morison and Henry Steele Commager added a political gloss to Allen's cultural pessimism. Because people were "weary of reform and disillusioned by the crusade of democracy," they drifted toward conservatism.

Two important works were published in 1955. John Higham referred to the "tribal twenties" as a time when Americans attempted to "close the gates" of immigration, and Richard Hofstadter derided the decade as an insignificant *"entr'acte"* (intermission) bracketed by the more consequential eras of progressivism and New Deal reform.

William Leuchtenburg (1958) sought to balance these assessments: There was much more to the decade than "raccoon coats and bathtub gin." While conceding that politicians had failed to solve problems of state authority, industrial concentration, and mass culture, they had not done much worse than the progressives. (Recall Debating the Past "Were the Progressives Forward-Looking?" in Chapter 21, p. 569.)

In later decades leftist scholars such as Roland Marchand (1985) associated the 1920s with the triumph of advertising and consumption, part of a "cultural hegemony" that promoted sales to ensure corporate profits. On the other hand, Kathy Peiss (1998) was among a group of scholars who insisted that consumption could add depth and richness to life. She found, for example, that in purchasing cosmetics women partook of the "pleasures of fantasy and desire."

George Chauncey (1994) championed the self-absorption—self-expression?—of gays who, left mostly to

themselves, exulted in a remarkably open homosexual culture in many big cities.

Source: Frederick Lewis Allen, *Only Yesterday* (1931); Samuel Eliot Morison and Henry Steele Commager, *The Growth of the American Republic* (1937); John Higham, *Strangers in the Land* (1955); Richard Hofstadter, *The Age of Reform* (1955); William Leuchtenburg, *The Perils of Prosperity* (1958); Roland Marchand, *Advertising the American Dream* (1985); T. J. Jackson Lears, *Fables of Abundance* (1995); Warren I. Susman, *Culture as History* (1984); Kathy Peiss, *Hope in a Jar* (1998); George Chauncey, *Gay New York* (1994).

■ ■ ■ ■ ■

contempt. But their success was instantaneous with recent immigrants and many other slum dwellers. In 1912 there were nearly 13,000 movie houses in the United States, more than 500 in New York City alone. Many of these places were converted stores called nickelodeons because the admission charge was only five cents.

In the beginning the mere recording of movement seemed to satisfy the public, but success led to rapid technical and artistic improvements and consequently to more cultivated audiences. D. W. Griffith's twelve-reel *Birth of a Nation* (1915) was a particularly important breakthrough in both areas, although his sympathetic treatment of the Ku Klux Klan of Reconstruction days angered blacks and white liberals.

By the mid-1920s the industry, centered in Hollywood, California, was the fourth largest in the nation in capital investment. Films moved from the nickelodeons to converted theaters. So large was the audience that movie "palaces" seating several thousand people sprang up in the major cities. Daily ticket sales averaged more than 10 million.

With the introduction of talking movies, *The Jazz Singer* (1927) being the first of significance, and color films a few years later, the motion picture reached technological maturity. Costs and profits mounted; by the 1930s million-dollar productions were common.

Many movies were still tasteless trash catering to the prejudices of the multitude. Sex, crime, war, romantic adventure, broad comedy, and luxurious living were the main themes, endlessly repeated in predictable patterns. Popular actors and actresses tended to be either handsome, talentless sticks or so-called character actors who were typecast over and over again as heroes, villains, or comedians. The stars attracted armies of adoring fans and received thousands of dollars a week for their services. Critics charged that the movies were destroying the legitimate stage (which underwent a sharp decline), corrupting the morals of youth, and glorifying the materialistic aspects of life.

Nevertheless the motion picture made positive contributions to American culture. Beginning with the work of Griffith, filmmakers created an entirely new theatrical art, using close-ups to portray character and heighten tension and broad, panoramic shots to transcend the limits of the stage. They employed, with remarkable results, special lighting effects, the fade-out, and other techniques impossible in the live theater. Movies enabled dozens of established actors to reach wider audiences and developed many first-rate new ones. As the medium matured, it produced many dramatic works of high quality. At its best the motion picture offered a breadth and power of impact superior to anything on the traditional stage.

Charlie Chaplin was the greatest film star of the era. His characterization of the sad-eyed little tramp with his toothbrush moustache and cane, tight frock coat, and baggy trousers became famous throughout the world. Chaplin's films were superficially unpretentious; they seemed even in the 1920s old-fashioned, aimed at the lower-class audiences that had first found the movies magical. But his work proved both universally popular and enduring; he was perhaps the greatest comic artist of all time. The animated cartoon, perfected by Walt Disney in the 1930s, was a lesser but significant cinematic achievement; Mickey Mouse, Donald Duck, and other Disney cartoon characters gave endless delight to millions of children.

Even more pervasive than the movies in its effects on the American people was radio. Wireless transmission of sound was developed in the late nineteenth century by many scientists in Europe and the United States. During the war radio was put to important military uses and was strictly controlled, but immediately thereafter the airwaves were thrown open to everybody.

Radio was briefly the domain of hobbyists, thousands of "hams" broadcasting in indiscriminate fashion. Even under these conditions, the manufacture of radio equipment became a big business. In 1920 the first commercial station (KDKA in Pittsburgh) began broadcasting, and by the end of 1922 over 500 stations were in operation. In 1926 the National Broadcasting Company, the first continent-wide network, was created.

It took little time for broadcasters to discover the power of the new medium. When one pioneer interrupted a music program to ask listeners to phone in requests, the station received 3,000 calls in an hour. The immediacy of radio explained its tremendous impact. As a means of communicating the latest news, it had no peer; beginning with the broadcast of the 1924 presidential nominating conventions, all major public events were covered live. Advertisers seized on radio too; it proved to be as effective a way to sell soap as to transmit news.

Advertising had mixed effects on broadcasting. The sums paid by businesses for airtime made possible elaborate entertainments performed by the finest actors and musicians, all without cost to listeners. However, advertisers hungered for mass markets. They preferred to sponsor programs of little intellectual content, aimed at the lowest tastes and utterly uncontroversial. And good and bad alike, programs were constantly interrupted by irritating pronouncements extolling the supposed virtues of one commercial product or another.

In 1927 Congress limited the number of stations and parceled out wavelengths to prevent interference. Further legislation in 1934 established the Federal Communications Commission (FCC), with power to revoke the licenses of stations that failed to operate in the public interest. But the FCC placed no effective controls on programming or on advertising practices.

Read the Document *Advertisements from 1925 and 1927* at www.myhistorylab.com

The Golden Age of Sports

The extraordinary popularity of sports in the postwar period can be explained in a number of ways. People had more money to spend and more free time to fill. Radio was bringing suspenseful, play-by-play accounts of sports contests into millions of homes, thus encouraging tens of thousands to want to see similar events. New means of persuasion developed by advertisers to sell lipstick, breakfast cereal, and refrigerators were applied with equal success to sporting events and to the athletes who participated in them.

There had been great athletes before; indeed probably the greatest all-around athlete of the twentieth century was Jim Thorpe, a Sac and Fox Indian

Newly built Yankee Stadium on opening day of the 1923 baseball season. Babe Ruth hit his first home run and soon Yankee Stadium was dubbed "the House that Ruth Built." That year, perhaps his best, Ruth hit forty-one home runs, batted .393, and drew 170 walks. He got on base more than half the times he appeared at the plate. Ruth's feats matched the colossal appearance of Yankee Stadium, whose arches evoked the imperial grandeur of ancient Rome.

who won both the pentathlon and the decathlon at the 1912 Olympic Games, made Walter Camp's All-American football team in 1912 and 1913, then played major league baseball for several years before becoming a pioneer founder and player in the National Football League. But what truly made the 1920s a golden age was a coincidence—the emergence in a few short years of a remarkable collection of what today would be called superstars.

In football there was the University of Illinois's Harold "Red" Grange, who averaged over ten yards a carry during his college career and who in one incredible quarter during the 1924 game between Illinois and Michigan carried the ball four times and scored a touchdown each time, gaining in the process 263 yards. In prize fighting, heavyweight champion Jack Dempsey, the "Manassas Mauler," knocked out a succession of challengers in bloody battles only to be deposed in 1927 by "Gentleman Gene" Tunney, who gave him a fifteen-round boxing lesson and then, according to Tunney's own account, celebrated by consuming "several pots of tea."

During the same years William "Big Bill" Tilden dominated tennis, winning the national singles title every year from 1920 to 1925 along with nearly every other tournament he entered. Beginning in 1923, Robert T. "Bobby" Jones ruled over the world of golf with equal authority, his climactic achievement being his capture of the amateur and open championships of both the United States and Great Britain in 1930.

A few women athletes dominated their sports during this golden age in similar fashion. In tennis Helen Wills was three times United States singles champion and the winner of the women's singles at Wimbledon eight times in the late 1920s and early 1930s. The swimmer Gertrude Ederle, holder of eighteen world records by the time she was seventeen, swam the English Channel on her second attempt, in 1926. She was not only the first woman to do so, but she did it faster than any of the four men who had previously made it across.

However, the sports star among stars was "the Sultan of Swat," baseball's Babe Ruth.[1] Ruth not only dominated baseball, he changed it from a game ruled by pitchers and low scores to one in which hitting was more greatly admired. Originally himself a brilliant pitcher, his incredible hitting ability made him more valuable in the outfield, where he could play every day. Before Ruth, John "Home Run" Baker was the most famous slugger; his greatest annual home run total was 12, achieved shortly before the Great War. Ruth hit twenty-nine in 1919 and fifty-four in 1920, his first year with the New York Yankees. By 1923 he was so feared that pitchers intentionally walked him more than half the times he appeared at the plate.

---

[1] His full name was George Herman Ruth, but the nickname, Babe, given to him early in his career, was what everyone called him.

The achievements of these and other outstanding athletes had a cumulative effect. New stadiums were built, and they were filled by "the largest crowds that ever witnessed athletic sports since the fall of Rome." Record crowds paying unprecedented sums attended all sorts of events.

Football was the preeminent school sport. At many colleges football afternoons came to resemble religious rites both in their formality, with their cheerleaders and marching bands, and in the fervor of the crowds. A national magazine entitled a 1928 article "The Great God Football," and the editor of a college newspaper denounced "disloyal" students who took seats in the grandstand where they could see what was happening on the field, rather than encouraging the team by doing their bit in the student cheering section in the end zone.

Tens of thousands of men and women took up tennis, golf, swimming, and calisthenics. Social dancing became more energetic. The turkey trot, a popular prewar dance, led in the next decade to the Charleston and what one historian called "an imitative swarm of hops, wriggles, squirms, glides and gallops named after all the animals in the menagerie."

Urban–Rural Conflicts: Fundamentalism

These were buoyant times for people in tune with the times—the young, the devil-may-care, factory workers with money in their pockets, many different types. But nearly all of them were city people. However, the tensions and hostilities of the 1920s exaggerated an older rift in American society—the conflict between urban and rural ways of life. To many among the scattered millions who tilled the soil and among the millions who lived in towns and small cities, the new city-oriented culture seemed sinful, overly materialistic, and unhealthy. To them change was something to be resented and resisted.

Yet there was no denying its fascination. Made even more aware of the appeal of the city by radio and the automobile, farmers and townspeople coveted the comfort and excitement of city life at the same time that they condemned its vices. Rural society proclaimed the superiority of its ways at least in part to protect itself from temptation. Change, omnipresent in the postwar world, must be resisted even at the cost of individualism and freedom.

One expression of this resistance was a resurgence of religious fundamentalism. Although it was especially prevalent among Baptists and Methodists, fundamentalism was primarily an attitude of mind, profoundly conservative, rather than a religious idea. Fundamentalists rejected the theory of evolution as well as advanced hypotheses on the origins of the universe.

What made crusaders of the fundamentalists was their resentment of modern urban culture. The teaching of evolution must be prohibited, they insisted. Throughout the 1920s they campaigned vigorously for laws banning discussion of Darwin's theory in textbooks and classrooms. By 1929 five southern states had passed laws prohibiting the teaching of evolution in the public schools.

Their greatest asset in this crusade was William Jennings Bryan. After leaving Wilson's Cabinet in 1915 he devoted much time to religious and moral issues, but without applying himself conscientiously to the study of these difficult questions. He went about the country charging that "they"—meaning the mass of educated Americans—had "taken the Lord away from the schools." He denounced the use of public money to undermine Christian principles, and he offered $100 to anyone who would admit to being descended from an ape. His immense popularity in rural areas assured him a wide audience, and no one came forward to take his money.

The fundamentalists won a minor victory in 1925, when Tennessee passed a law forbidding instructors in the state's schools and colleges to teach "any theory that denies the story of the Divine Creation of man as taught in the Bible." The bill passed both houses by big majorities; few legislators wished to expose themselves to charges that they did not believe the Bible. Governor Austin Peay, a liberal-minded man, feared to veto the bill lest he jeopardize other measures he was backing. "Probably the law will never be applied," he predicted when he signed it. Even Bryan, who used his influence to obtain passage of the measure, urged—unsuccessfully—that it include no penalties.

On learning of the passage of this act, the American Civil Liberties Union announced that it would finance a test case challenging its constitutionality if a Tennessee teacher would deliberately violate the statute. Urged on by friends, John T. Scopes, a young biology teacher in Dayton, reluctantly agreed to do so. He was arrested. A battery of nationally known lawyers came forward to defend him, and the state obtained the services of Bryan himself. The **Scopes trial,** also known as the "Monkey Trial," became an overnight sensation.

Clarence Darrow, chief counsel for the defendant, stated the issue clearly. "Scopes isn't on trial," he said, "civilization is on trial. No man's belief will be safe if they win." The comic aspects of the trial obscured this issue. Big-city reporters like H. L. Mencken of the *Baltimore Evening Sun* flocked to Dayton to make sport of the fundamentalists. Scopes's conviction was a foregone conclusion; after the jury rendered its verdict, the judge fined him $100.

The Scopes trial was a media sensation; it even gave rise to popular songs, such as this one by Billy Rose.

Nevertheless, the trial exposed the danger of the fundamentalist position. The high point came when Bryan agreed to testify as an expert witness on the Bible. In a sweltering courtroom, both men in shirtsleeves, the lanky, rough-hewn Darrow cross-examined the aging champion of fundamentalism, exposing his childlike faith and his disdain for the science of the day. Bryan admitted to believing that Eve had been created from Adam's rib and that a whale had swallowed Jonah. "I believe in a God that can make a whale and can make a man and make both do what He pleases," he explained.

The Monkey Trial ended badly for nearly everyone concerned. Scopes moved away from Dayton; the judge, John Raulston, was defeated when he sought reelection; Bryan died in his sleep a few days after the trial. But fundamentalism continued to flourish, not only in the nation's backwaters but also in many cities, brought there by rural people in search of work. In retrospect, even the heroes of the Scopes trial—science and freedom of thought—seem somewhat less stainless than they did to liberals at the time. The account of evolution in the textbook used by Scopes was hopelessly deficient and laced with bigotry, yet it was advanced as unassailable fact. In a section on the "Races of Man," for example, it described Caucasians as "the highest type of all . . . represented by the civilized white inhabitants of Europe and America."

Urban–Rural Conflicts: Prohibition

The conflict between the countryside and the city was fought on many fronts, and in one sector the rural forces achieved a quick victory. This was the Eighteenth Amendment, ratified in 1919, which prohibited the manufacture, transportation, and sale of alcoholic beverages. Although there were some big-city advocates of prohibition, the Eighteenth Amendment, in the words of one historian, marked a triumph of the "Corn Belt over the conveyor belt."

The temperance movement had been important since the age of Jackson; it was a major issue in many states during the Gilded Age, and by the Progressive Era powerful organizations like the Anti-Saloon League and the Women's Christian Temperance Union were seeking to have drinking outlawed entirely. Indeed, prohibition was a typical progressive reform, moralistic, backed by the middle class, and aimed at frustrating "the interests"—in this case the distillers.

Federal agents pour liquor into a sewer during Prohibition.

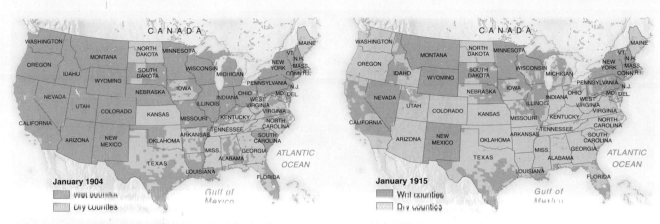

The Advance of Prohibition Prohibition had spread through much of the South and Midwest even before ratification of the Eighteenth (Prohibition) Amendment in 1919.

World War I aided the prohibitionists by increasing the need for food. The Lever Act of 1917 outlawed the use of grain in the manufacture of alcoholic beverages, primarily as a conservation measure. The prevailing dislike of foreigners helped the dry cause still more: Beer drinking was associated with Germans. State and local laws had made a large part of the country dry by 1917. National prohibition became official in January 1920.

This "experiment noble in purpose," as Herbert Hoover called it, achieved a number of socially desirable results. It reduced the annual national consumption of alcohol from 2.6 gallons per capita in the period just before the war to less than 1 gallon in the early 1930s. Arrests for drunkenness fell off sharply, as did deaths from alcoholism. Fewer workers squandered their wages on drink. If the drys had been willing to legalize beer and wine, the experiment might have worked. Instead, by insisting on total abstinence, they drove thousands of moderates to violate the law. Strict enforcement became impossible, especially in the cities.

In areas where sentiment favored prohibition strongly, liquor remained difficult to find. Elsewhere, anyone with sufficient money could obtain it easily. Smuggling became a major business, *bootlegger* a household word. Private individuals busied themselves learning how to manufacture "bathtub gin." Many druggists issued prescriptions for alcohol with a free hand. The manufacture of wine for religious ceremonies was legal, and consumption of sacramental wine jumped by 800,000 gallons during the first two years of prohibition. The saloon disappeared, replaced by the speakeasy, a supposedly secret bar or club operating under the benevolent eye of the local police.

That the law was often violated does not mean that it was ineffective any more than violations of laws against theft and murder mean that those laws are ineffective. Although gangsters such as Alphonse

"Scarface Al" Capone of Chicago were engaged in the liquor traffic, their "organizations" existed before the passage of the Eighteenth Amendment. But prohibition widened already serious rifts in the social fabric of the country. Organized crime became more powerful. Besides undermining public morality by encouraging hypocrisy, prohibition almost destroyed the Democratic party as a national organization. Democratic immigrants in the cities hated it, but southern Democrats sang its praises, often while continuing to drink (the humorist Will Rogers quipped that Mississippi would vote dry "as long as the voters could stagger to the polls").

The hypocrisy of prohibition had a particularly deleterious effect on politicians, a class seldom famous for candor. Members of Congress catered to the demands of the powerful lobby of the Anti-Saloon League yet failed to grant adequate funds to the Prohibition Bureau. Nearly all the prominent leaders, Democrat and Republican, from Wilson and La Follette to Hoover and Franklin D. Roosevelt, equivocated shamelessly on the liquor question. By the end of the decade almost every competent observer recognized that prohibition at least needed to be overhauled, but the well-organized and powerful dry forces rejected all proposals for modifying it.

(((•──Hear the Audio *Prohibition is a Failure* at **www.myhistorylab.com**

The Ku Klux Klan

The most horrible manifestation of the social malaise of the 1920s was the revival of the Ku Klux Klan. This new Klan, founded in 1915 by William J. Simmons, a former preacher, admitted only native-born white Protestants. The distrust of foreigners, blacks, Catholics, and Jews implicit in this regulation explains why it flourished in the social climate that spawned religious fundamentalism, immigration restriction,

A Ku Klux Klan initiation ceremony photographed in Kansas in the 1920s. During its peak influence at mid-decade, Klan endorsement was essential to political candidates in many areas of the West and Midwest. Campaigning for reelection in 1934, an Indiana congressman testified, "I was told to join the Klan, or else."
Source: Kansas State Historical Society.

and prohibition. In 1920 two unscrupulous publicity agents, Edward Y. Clarke and Elizabeth Tyler, got control of the movement and organized a massive membership drive, diverting a major share of the initiation fees into their own pockets. In a little over a year they enrolled 100,000 recruits, and by 1923 they claimed the astonishing total of 5 million.

Simmons gave his society trappings and mystery calculated to attract gullible and bigoted people who yearned to express their frustrations and hostilities without personal risk. Klansmen masked themselves in white robes and hoods and enjoyed a childish mumbo jumbo of magnificent-sounding titles and dogmas (kleagle, klaliff, kludd, kloxology, kloran). They burned crosses in the night, organized mass demonstrations to intimidate people they disliked, and put pressure on businessmen to fire black workers from better-paying jobs.

The Klan had relatively little appeal in the Northeast or in metropolitan centers in other parts of the country, but it found many members in mid-sized cities and in the small towns and villages of midwestern and western states. The scapegoats in such regions were immigrants, Jews, and especially Catholics. The rationale was an urge to return to an older, supposedly finer America and to stamp out all varieties of nonconformity. Klansmen "watched everybody," themselves safe from observation behind their masks and robes. They persecuted gamblers, "loose" women, violators of the prohibition laws, and anyone who happened to differ from them on religious questions or who belonged to a "foreign race."

The very success of the Klan led to its undoing. Factionalism sprang up, and rival leaders squabbled over the large sums that had been collected from the membership. The cruel and outrageous behavior of the organization roused both liberals and conservatives in every part of the country. And of course its victims joined forces against their tormentors. When the powerful leader of the Indiana Klan, a middle-aged reprobate named David C. Stephenson, was convicted of assaulting and causing the death of a young woman, the rank and file abandoned the organization in droves. The Klan remained influential for a number of years, contributing to the defeat of the Catholic Alfred E. Smith in the 1928 presidential election, but it ceased to be a dynamic force after 1924. By 1930 it had only some 9,000 members.

Read the **Document** *Creed of Klanswomen* at www.myhistorylab.com

Literary Trends

The literature of the 1920s reflects the disillusionment of the intellectuals. The prewar period had been an age of hopeful experimentation in the world of letters. But the Progressive Era writers, along with most other intellectuals, were beginning to abandon this view by about 1912. The wasteful horrors of the Great War and then the antics of the fundamentalists and the cruelty of the red-baiters and the Klan turned them into critics of society. Many intellectuals deplored the 1927 execution of Nicola Sacco and Bartolomeo Vanzetti, Italian immigrants (and anarchists) who were deprived of a fair trial in a murder case. They included the poet Edna St. Vincent Millay, the playwright Maxwell Anderson, and the novelists Upton Sinclair and John Dos Passos. After the war the poet Ezra Pound dropped his talk of an American Renaissance and wrote instead of a "botched civilization." The soldiers of the Great War, he said,

> *walked eye-deep in hell*
> *believing in old men's lies, then unbelieving*
> *came home, home to a lie,*
> *home to deceits,*
> *home to old lies and new infamy . . .*

Source: "Hugh Selwyn Mauberley IV" (excerpt of 5 lines) by Ezra Pound, from Personae, copyright ©1926 by Ezra Pound. Reprinted by permission of New Directions Publishing.

The symbol of what some called the "lost generation," in his own mind as well as to his contemporaries and to later critics, was F. Scott Fitzgerald. Born to modest wealth in St. Paul, Minnesota, in 1896, Fitzgerald attended Princeton and served in the army during the Great War. He rose to sudden fame in 1920 when he published *This Side of Paradise*, a somewhat sophomoric novel that appealed powerfully to college students and captured the fears and confusions of the lost generation. In *The Great Gatsby* (1925), a more mature work, Fitzgerald depicted a modern millionaire—coarse, unscrupulous, jaded, in love with another man's wife. Gatsby's tragedy lay in his dedication to a woman who, Fitzgerald made clear, did not merit his passion. He lived in "the service of a vast, vulgar, meretricious beauty," and in the end he understood this himself.

The tragedy of *The Great Gatsby* was related to Fitzgerald's own. Pleasure-loving and extravagant, he squandered the money earned by *This Side of Paradise*. When *The Great Gatsby* failed to sell as well, he turned to writing potboilers. "I really worked hard as hell last winter," he told the critic Edmund Wilson, "but it was all trash and it nearly broke my heart." While some of his later work, particularly *Tender Is the Night* (1934), is first-class, he descended into the despair of alcoholism and ended his days as a Hollywood scriptwriter.

Many young American writers and artists became expatriates in the 1920s. They flocked to Rome, Berlin, and especially Paris, where they could live cheaply and escape what seemed to them the "conspiracy against the individual" prevalent in their own country. The *quartier latin*—the Latin Quarter—along the left bank of the Seine was a large-scale Greenwich Village in those days. Writers, artists, and eccentrics of every sort lived there. Some made meager livings as journalists, translators, and editors, perhaps turning an extra dollar from time to time by selling a story or a poem to an American magazine or a painting to a tourist.

Ernest Hemingway was the most talented of the expatriates. He had served in the Italian army during

Nicola Sacco and Bartolomeo Vanzetti were electrocuted in 1927 for murdering a guard and paymaster during a robbery of a shoe factory. Although at least Sacco was likely guilty of the crime, the judge's prejudice against the men—he called them "those anarchist bastards"—caused intellectuals worldwide to condemn American justice.

the war and been grievously wounded (in spirit as well as in body). He settled in Paris in 1922 to write. His first novel, *The Sun Also Rises* (1926), portrayed the café world of the expatriate and the rootless desperation, amorality, and sense of outrage at life's meaninglessness that obsessed so many in those years. In *A Farewell to Arms* (1929) he drew on his military experiences to describe the confusion and horror of war.

Hemingway's books were best-sellers and he became a legend in his own time, but his style rather than his ideas explains his towering reputation. Few novelists have been as capable of suggesting powerful emotions and action in so few words. Mark Twain and Stephen Crane were his models; Gertrude Stein, a writer and revolutionary genius, his teacher. But his style was his own—direct, simple, taut, sparse:

> *I went out the door and down the hall to the room*
> *where Catherine was to be after the baby came. I sat*
> *in a chair there and looked at the room. I had the*
> *paper in my coat that I had bought when I went out*
> *for lunch and I read it. . . . After a while I stopped*
> *reading and turned off the light and watched it get*
> *dark outside. (A Farewell to Arms)*

Source: Reprinted with the permission of Scribner, a Division of Simon & Schuster, Inc., from *A Farewell to Arms* by Ernest Hemingway. Copyright © 1929 by Charles Scribner's Son's; copyright renewed 1956 by Ernest Hemingway. All rights reserved.

This kind of writing, evoking rather than describing emotion, fascinated readers and inspired hundreds of imitators; it made a permanent mark on world literature. What Hemingway had to say was of less universal interest—he was an unabashed, rather muddled romantic, an adolescent emotionally. He wrote about bullfights, hunting and fishing, and violence; while he did so with masterful penetration, these themes placed limits on his work that he never transcended. The critic

Alfred Kazin summed up Hemingway in a sentence: "He brought a major art to a minor vision of life."

Edith Wharton was of the New York aristocracy. She was educated by tutors and governesses and never went to college. To counteract what she called "the creeping darkness of neurasthenia," she traveled frequently to Europe, eventually chose to live there, and took up writing. After co-authoring a book on home decoration, she wrote novels on marriage and manners in some ways reminiscent of Henry James. In Paris at the outset of the Great War, she threw herself into war-related charities. But while the shock of the war jolted Fitzgerald and Hemingway into the vanguard of innovation, she retreated from the jangling energy of postwar life and culture. "I am steeping myself in the nineteenth century," she explained to a friend, "like taking refuge in a mighty temple." The product of her retreat, *The Age of Innocence* (1920), offered a penetrating portrait of an unsettlingly serene if vanished world. The *Nation* remarked that Wharton had described the wealthy of old New York "as familiarly as if she loved them and as lucidly as if she hated them." Though the younger novelists of the decade often dismissed her work as uninventive and dowdy, and she theirs as unformed and thin, her judgment has proven the more enduring.

Although neither was the equal of Hemingway, Fitzgerald, or Wharton, two other writers of the 1920s deserve mention: H. L. Mencken and Sinclair Lewis. Each reflected the distaste of intellectuals for the climate of the times. Mencken, a Baltimore newspaperman and founder of one of the great magazines of the era, the *American Mercury*, was a thoroughgoing cynic. He coined the word *booboisie* to define the complacent, middle-class majority, and he fired superbly witty broadsides at fundamentalists, prohibitionists, and "Puritans." "Puritanism," he once said, "is the haunting fear that someone, somewhere, may be happy."

But Mencken was never indifferent to the many aspects of American life that roused his contempt. Politics at once fascinated and repelled him, and he assailed the statesmen of his generation with magnificent impartiality:

> [On Bryan]: "If the fellow was sincere, then so was P. T. Barnum. . . . He was, in fact, a charlatan, a mountebank, a zany without sense or dignity."
>
> [On Wilson]: "The bogus Liberal. . . . A pedagogue thrown up to 1,000 diameters by a magic lantern."
>
> [On Coolidge]: "A cheap and trashy fellow, deficient in sense and almost devoid of any notion of honor—in brief, a dreadful little cad."
>
> [On Hoover]: "Lord Hoover is no more than a pious old woman, a fat Coolidge."

Source: H. L. Mencken [On excerpt of Bryan Obituary Source: *American Mercury*, October 1925, pp. 158–160.]

As these examples demonstrate, Mencken's diatribes, while amusing, were not profound. In perspective he seems more a professional iconoclast than a constructive critic; like both Fitzgerald and Hemingway, he was something of a perennial adolescent. However, he consistently supported freedom of expression of every sort.

Sinclair Lewis was probably the most popular American novelist of the 1920s. Like Fitzgerald, his first major work brought him instant fame and notoriety—and for the same reason. *Main Street* (1920) portrayed the smug ignorance and bigotry of the American small town so accurately that even Lewis's victims recognized themselves; his title became a symbol for provinciality and middle-class meanness of spirit. In *Babbitt* (1922), he created what many people considered the typical businessman of the 1920s, gregarious, a "booster," blindly orthodox in his political and social opinions, a slave to every cliché, and full of loud self-confidence, but under the surface a bumbling, rather timid fellow who would have liked to be better than he was but dared not try. Lewis went on to dissect the medical profession in *Arrowsmith* (1925), religion in *Elmer Gantry* (1927), and fascism in *It Can't Happen Here* (1935).

Read the **Document** *Bartolomeo Vanzetti, Court Statement* at www.myhistorylab.com

The "New Negro"

The postwar reaction brought despair for many blacks. Aside from the barbarities of the Klan, they suffered from the postwar middle-class hostility to labor (and from the persistent reluctance of organized

Zora Neale Hurston, a major figure of the Harlem Renaissance, wrote eighteen novels—many of which were made into movies.

A painting from Jacob Lawrence's *Migration Series* (1940–1941).
Source: Gift of Mrs. David M. Levy. (28.1942.20). ©The Museum of Modern Art/Artists Rights Society/Art Resource, NY.

labor to admit black workers into its ranks). The increasing presence of southern blacks in northern cities also caused conflict. Some 393,000 settled in New York, Pennsylvania, and Illinois in the 1920s, most of them in New York City, Philadelphia, and Chicago. The black population of New York City more than doubled between 1920 and 1930. In earlier periods blacks in northern cities had tended to live together, but in small neighborhoods scattered over large areas. Now the tendency was toward concentration in what came to be called ghettos.

Even in small northern cities where they made up only a tiny proportion of the population, blacks were badly treated. When Robert S. and Helen M. Lynd made their classic sociological analysis of "Middletown" (Muncie, Indiana), they discovered that although black and white children attended the same schools, the churches, the larger movie houses, and other places of public accommodation were segregated. The local YMCA had a gymnasium where high school basketball was played, but the secretary refused to allow any team with a black player to use it. Even the news in Muncie was segregated. Local papers chronicled the affairs of the black community—roughly 5 percent of the population—under the heading "In Colored Circles."

Coming after the hopes inspired by wartime gains, the disappointments of the 1920s produced a new militancy among many blacks. In 1919 W. E. B. Du Bois wrote in *The Crisis,* "We are cowards and jackasses if . . . we do not marshal every ounce of our brain and brawn to fight . . . against the forces of hell in our own land." He increased his commitment to black nationalism, organizing a series of Pan African Conferences in an effort—futile, as it turned out—to create an international black movement.

Du Bois never made up his mind whether to work for integration or black separatism. Such ambivalence never troubled Marcus Garvey, a West Indian whose Universal Negro Improvement Association attracted hundreds of thousands of followers in the early 1920s. Garvey had nothing but contempt for whites, for light-skinned blacks like Du Bois, and for organizations such as the NAACP, which sought to bring whites and blacks together to fight segregation and other forms of prejudice. "Back to Africa" was his slogan; the black man must "work out his salvation in his motherland." (Paradoxically, Garvey's ideas won the enthusiastic support of the Ku Klux Klan and other white racist groups.)

Garvey's message was naive, but it served to build racial pride among the masses of poor and unschooled blacks. He dressed in elaborate braided uniforms, wore a plumed hat, and drove about in a limousine. Both God and Christ were black, he

The Making of Black Harlem In 1911, African Americans lived mostly in a dozen-block region of Harlem; by 1930, they had created a predominantly black city of well over 100 city blocks.

insisted. He organized black businesses of many sorts, including a company that manufactured black dolls. He established a corps of Black Cross nurses and a Black Star Line Steamship Company to transport blacks back to Africa.

More sophisticated black leaders like Du Bois detested Garvey, whom they thought something of a charlatan. In 1923 Garvey's steamship line went into bankruptcy. He was convicted of defrauding the thousands of his supporters who had invested in its stock and was sent to prison. Nevertheless, his message, if not his methods, helped to create the "New Negro," proud of being black and prepared to resist both mistreatment and white ideas. Many were inspired by his exhortation, "Up you mighty race, you can accomplish what you will!"

The ghettos produced compensating advantages for blacks. One effect, not fully utilized until later, was to increase their political power by enabling them to elect representatives to state legislatures and Congress, and to exert considerable influence in closely contested elections. More immediately, city life stimulated self-confidence; despite their horrors, the ghettos offered economic opportunity, political

rights, and freedom from the everyday debasements of life in the South. The ghetto was a black world where black men and women could be themselves.

Black writers, musicians, and artists found in the ghettos both an audience and the "spiritual emancipation" that unleashed their capacities. Jazz, the great popular music of the age, was largely the creation of black musicians working in New Orleans before the turn of the century. By the 1920s it had spread throughout the country and to most of the rest of the world. White musicians and white audiences took it up—in a way it became a force for racial tolerance and understanding.

Jazz meant improvisation, and both players and audiences experienced in it a kind of liberation. Jazz was the music of the 1920s in part because it expressed the desire of so many people to break with tradition and throw off conventional restraints.

Harlem, the largest black community in the world, became in the 1920s a cultural capital, center of the **Harlem Renaissance**. Black newspapers and magazines flourished along with theatrical companies and libraries. Du Bois opened *The Crisis* to young writers and artists, and a dozen "little" magazines sprang up. Langston Hughes, one of the most talented poets of the era, described the exhilaration of his first arrival in this city within a city, a magnet for every black intellectual and artist: "Harlem! I . . . dropped my bags, took a deep breath, and felt happy again." In 1925 Zora Neale Hurston, who had worked in menial jobs while attending Howard University, came to New York, joined with Hughes to create a literary magazine, and celebrated the lives of ordinary black workers.

With some exceptions, African American writers like Hughes and Hurston did not share in the disillusionment that afflicted so many white intellectuals. The persistence of prejudice angered them and made them militant. But to be militant, one must be at some level hopeful. Sociologists and psychologists (for whom the ghettos were indispensable social laboratories) were demonstrating that environment rather than heredity was preventing black economic progress. Together with the achievements of creative blacks, which for the first time were being appreciated by large numbers of white intellectuals, these discoveries seemed to herald the eventual disappearance of racial prejudice. The black, Alain Locke wrote in *The New Negro* (1925), "lays aside the status of beneficiary and ward for that of a collaborator and participant in American civilization." Alas, as Locke and other black intellectuals were soon to discover, this prediction, like so many made in the 1920s, did not come to pass.

Watch the Video *The Harlem Renaissance* at www.myhistorylab.com

Economic Expansion

Despite the turmoil of the times and the dissatisfactions expressed by some of the nation's best minds, the 1920s was an exceptionally prosperous decade. Business boomed, real wages rose, unemployment declined. The United States was as rich as all Europe; perhaps 40 percent of the world's total wealth lay in American hands. Little wonder that business leaders and other conservatives described the period as a "new era."

The prosperity rested on many bases, one of which was the friendly, hands-off attitude of the federal government, which bolstered the confidence of the business community. The Federal Reserve Board kept interest rates low, a further stimulus to economic growth. Pent-up wartime demand helped to power the boom; the construction business in particular profited from a series of extremely busy years. The continuing mechanization and rationalization of industry provided a more fundamental stimulus to the economy. From heavy road-grading equipment and concrete mixers to devices for making cigars and glass tubes, from pneumatic tools to the dial telephone, machinery was replacing human hands at an ever more rapid rate. Industrial output almost doubled between 1921 and 1929 without any substantial increase in the industrial labor force. Greater use of power, especially of electricity, also encouraged expansion—by 1929 the United States was producing more electricity than the rest of the world combined.

Most important, American manufacturing was experiencing a remarkable improvement in efficiency. The method of breaking down the complex processes of production into many simple operations and the use of interchangeable parts were nineteenth-century innovations; in the 1920s they were adopted on an almost universal scale. The moving assembly line which carried the product to the worker, first devised by Henry Ford in his automobile plant in the decade before World War I, speeded production and reduced costs. In ten years the hourly output of Ford workers quadrupled. The time-and-motion studies of Frederick W. Taylor, developed early in the century, were applied in hundreds of factories after the war. Taylor's method was to make careful analyses of each step and movement in the manufacturing process. Then workers would be taught exactly how best to perform each function. Taylor described his system as "enforced standardization" made possible by the "enforced cooperation" of workers. "Taylorism" alarmed some union leaders, but no one could deny the effectiveness of "scientific shop management" methods.

The Age of the Consumer

The growing ability of manufacturers to produce goods meant that great effort had to be made to create new consumer demands. Advertising and salesmanship were raised almost to the status of fine arts. Bruce Barton, one of the advertising "geniuses" of the era, wrote a best-selling book, *The Man Nobody Knows* (1925), in which he described Jesus as the "founder of modern business," the man who "picked up twelve men from the bottom ranks . . . and forged them into an organization that conquered the world."

Producers concentrated on making their goods more attractive and on changing models frequently to entice buyers into the market. The practice of selling goods on the installment plan helped bring expensive items within the reach of the masses. Inventions and technological advances created new or improved products: radios, automobiles, electric appliances such as vacuum cleaners and refrigerators, gadgets like cigarette lighters, and new forms of entertainment like motion pictures. These influences interacted much as the textile industry in the early nineteenth century and the railroad industry after the Civil War had been the "multipliers" of their times.

FREE —*Send coupon for 8 x 10 Art Print of this beautiful painting—the Kissproof Girl. Printed in 12 colors, mailed flat for framing.*

Would women believe the claims of cosmetics advertisements? "Kissproof" promised to make a woman's lips "pulsate with the very spirit of reckless, irrepressible youth." In a 1927 survey of housewives in Columbus, Ohio, Pond's Company found that two-thirds of the women could not even recall the company's advertisements. Younger women, however, were more impressionable. When the J. Walter Thompson advertising agency asked Vassar students to describe cosmetics, they unconsciously used the exact phrases from advertising copy—proof of its power.

Undoubtedly the automobile had the single most important impact on the nation's economy in the 1920s. Although well over a million cars a year were being regularly produced by 1916, the real expansion of the industry came after 1921. Output reached 3.6 million in 1923 and fell below that figure only twice during the remainder of the decade. By 1929, 23 million private cars clogged the highways, an average of nearly one per family.

The auto industry created companies that manufactured tires and spark plugs and other products. It consumed immense quantities of rubber, paint, glass, nickel, and petroleum products. It triggered a gigantic road-building program: There were 387,000 miles of paved roads in the United States in 1921, and 662,000 miles in 1929. Thousands of persons found employment in filling stations, roadside stands, and other businesses catering to the motoring public. The tourist industry profited, and the shift of population from the cities to the suburbs accelerated.

The automobile made life more mobile yet also more encapsulated. It changed recreational patterns and family life. It created a generation of tinkerers and amateur mechanics and explorers. In addition, it profoundly affected the way Americans thought. It gave them a freedom never before imagined. The owner of the most rickety jalopy could travel farther, faster, and far more comfortably than a monarch of old with his pure-blooded steeds and gilded coaches.

These benefits were real and priceless. Cars also became important symbols. They gave their owners the feeling of power and status that a horse gave to a medieval knight. According to some authorities the typical American cared more about owning an automobile than a house.

In time there were undesirable, even dangerous results of the automotive revolution: roadside scenery disfigured by billboards, gas stations, and other enterprises aimed at satisfying the traveler's needs; horrendous traffic jams; soaring accident rates; air pollution; and the neglect of public transportation, which was an important cause of the deterioration of inner cities. All these disadvantages were noticed during the 1920s, but in the springtime of the new industry they were discounted. The automobile seemed an unalloyed blessing—part toy, part tool, part symbol of American freedom, prosperity, and individualism.

View the Image *Downtown Scene with Cars, 1911* at www.myhistorylab.com

Henry Ford

The person most responsible for the growth of the automobile industry was Henry Ford, a self-taught mechanic from Greenfield, Michigan. Ford was neither a great inventor nor one of the true automobile pioneers. He was not even the first person to manufacture a good low-priced car (that being the achievement of Ransom E. Olds, producer of the "Merry Oldsmobile"). Ford's first brilliant insight was to "get the prices down to the buying power." Through mass production, cars could be made cheaply enough to put them within reach of the ordinary citizen. In 1908 he designed the Model T Ford, a simple, tough box on wheels. In a year he proved his point by selling 11,000 Model Ts. Relentlessly cutting costs and increasing efficiency with the assembly line system, he expanded production at an unbelievable rate. By 1925 he was turning out more than 9,000 cars a day, one approximately every ten seconds, and the price of the Model T had been reduced below $300.

Ford's second insight was the importance of high wages in stimulating output (and selling more automobiles). The assembly line simplified the laborer's task and increased the pace of work; at the same time it made each worker much more productive. Jobs became boring and fatiguing, and absenteeism and labor turnover became serious problems. To combat this difficulty, in 1914 Ford established the $5 day, an increase of about $2 over prevailing wages. The rate of turnover in his plant fell 90 percent, and although critics charged that he recaptured his additional labor costs by speeding up the line, his policy had a revolutionary effect on wage rates. Later he raised the minimum to $6 and then to $7 a day.

Ford's profits soared along with sales; since he owned the entire company, he became a billionaire. He also became an authentic folk hero: his homespun style, his dislike of bankers and sophisticated society, and his intense individualism endeared him to millions. He stood as a symbol of the wonders of the American system—he had given the nation a marvelous convenience at a low price, at the same time enriching himself and raising the living standards of his thousands of employees.

Unfortunately, Ford had the defects of his virtues in full measure. He paid high wages but refused to deal with any union and he employed spies to investigate the private lives of his workers, and gangsters and thugs to enforce plant discipline. When he discovered a worker driving any car but a Ford, he had him dismissed. So close was the supervision in the factory that workers devised the "Ford whisper," a means of talking without moving one's lips.

Success made Ford stubborn. The Model T remained essentially unchanged for nearly twenty years. Other companies, notably General Motors, were soon turning out better vehicles for very little more money. Customers, increasingly affluent and style-conscious, began to shift to Chevrolets and Chryslers. Finally, in 1927, Ford shut down all operations for eighteen months in order to retool for the Model A.

His competitors rushed in during this period to fill the vacuum. Although his company continued to make a great deal of money, Ford never regained the dominant position he had held for so long.

Ford was enormously uninformed, yet—because of his success and the praise the world heaped on him—he did not hesitate to speak out on subjects far outside his area of competence, from the evils of drink and tobacco to medicine and international affairs. He developed political ambitions and published virulent anti-Semitic propaganda. He said he would not give five cents for all the art in the world.

While praising his talents as a manufacturer, historians have not dealt kindly with Ford the man, in part no doubt because he once said, "History is more or less the bunk."

Watch the **Video** *The rise and fall of the automobile economy* at **www.myhistorylab.com**

The Airplane

Henry Ford was also an early manufacturer of airplanes, and while the airplane industry was not economically important in the 1920s, its development in that decade laid the basis for changes in lifestyles and attitudes at least as momentous as those produced by the automobile. The invention of the internal combustion gasoline engine, with its extremely high ratio of power to weight, made the airplane possible, which explains why the early experiments with "flying machines" took place at about the same time that the prototypes of the modern automobile were being manufactured. Wilbur and Orville Wright made their famous flight at Kitty Hawk, North Carolina, in 1903, five years before Ford produced his Model T. Another pair of brothers, Malcolm and Haines Lockheed, built their Model G, one of the earliest commercial planes (commercial in the sense that they used it to take passengers up at $5 a ride) in 1913.

The Great War speeded the advance of airplane technology, and most of the planes built in the 1920s were intended for military use. Practical commercial air travel was long delayed. Aerial acrobats, parachute jumpers, wing walkers, and other daredevils who put on shows at county fairs and similar places where crowds gathered were the principal civilian aviators of the 1920s. They "barnstormed" from town to town, living the same kind of inbred, encapsulated lives that circus people did, their chief rewards being the sense of independence and pride that the successful performance of their highly skilled but risky trade provided.

The great event of the decade for aviation, still an achievement that must strike awe in the hearts of reflective persons, was Charles A. Lindbergh's nonstop flight from New York to Paris in May 1927. It

Wilbur Wright glides at Kitty Hawk, 1903, ushering in a century where airplanes would become the basis for military power as well as the preferred means of long distance travel. Wilbur and his brother Orville realized that any airborne vehicle would need to move on three axes: to climb or descend, to steer to either side, and to bank in either direction. This resulted in a bi-wing design with a steering rudder.

took more than thirty-three hours for Lindbergh's single-engine *Spirit of St. Louis* to cross the Atlantic, a formidable physical achievement for the pilot as well as an example of skill and courage. When the public learned that the intrepid "Lucky Lindy" was handsome, modest, uninterested in converting his new fame into cash, and a model of propriety (he neither drank nor smoked), his role as American hero was ensured. It was a role Lindbergh detested—one biographer has described him as "by nature solitary"—but could not avoid.

Lindbergh's flight enormously increased public interest in flying, but it was a landmark in aviation technology as well. The day of routine passenger flights was at last about to dawn. In July 1927, a mere two months after the *Spirit of St. Louis* touched down at Le Bourget Field in France, William E. Boeing of Boeing Air Transport began flying passengers and mail between San Francisco and Chicago, using the M–40, a plane of his own design and manufacture. Early in 1928 he changed the company name to United Aircraft and Transport. Two years later Boeing produced the first all-metal low-wing plane and, in 1933, the twin-engine 247, a prototype for many others.

In retrospect the postwar era seems even more a period of transition than it appeared to most people at the time. Rarely had change come so swiftly, and rarely had old and new existed side by side in such profusion. Creativity and reaction, hope and despair, freedom and repression—the modern world in all its unfathomable complexity was emerging.

Chapter Review

Milestones

1903	Wright brothers fly at Kitty Hawk, NC
1908	Henry Ford designs Model T automobile
1914	Ford establishes $5 day for autoworkers
1919	Eighteenth Amendment outlaws alcoholic beverages (Prohibition)
	Nineteenth Amendment gives women right to vote
1920	Sinclair Lewis publishes *Main Street*
	First commercial radio station, KDKA, Pittsburgh, begins broadcasting
1920s	Black culture flourishes in Harlem Renaissance
1921	Margaret Sanger founds American Birth Control League
1924	Ku Klux Klan membership peaks
1925	Scopes is convicted for teaching evolution

	F. Scott Fitzgerald publishes *The Great Gatsby*
1926	Gertrude Ederle swims English Channel
	Ernest Hemingway publishes *The Sun Also Rises*
1927	Charles Lindbergh flies solo across Atlantic
	Sacco and Vanzetti are executed
	The Jazz Singer, first motion picture with sound, is released
	Jack Dempsey loses heavyweight boxing title to Gene Tunney
	Babe Ruth hits sixty home runs
1928	John B. Watson publishes *The Psychological Care of Infant and Child*
1929	Capone's gang kills Moran's in Valentine's Day Massacre

Key Terms

Harlem Renaissance   A modern artistic and literary movement that celebrated African American life and culture in early twentieth-century Harlem, New York. Among its key figures were Langston Hughes, Richard Wright, and Zora Neale Hurston (literature); Duke Ellington (music); Jacob Lawrence (painting); and Aaron Douglas (sculpture), *658*

National Origins Act   A federal law, passed in 1929 that curtailed immigration, especially from southern and eastern Europe and Asia, *640*

Scopes trial   Also called the "Monkey Trial," it was a celebrated 1924 contest that pitted Darwinian evolutionists against fundamentalist "Creationists." John T. Scopes, a teacher charged with defying Tennessee law by teaching evolution, was found guilty and fined $100, *651*

Review Questions

1. The introduction suggests that the prohibition of alcohol encouraged people to flaunt other conventions. To what extent were the cultural shifts of the 1920s a rebellion against tradition?

2. How did traditionalists respond to these social and cultural transformations? Was the fundamental tension, as the chapter suggests, between rural and urban cultures? Or was it between classes or ethnic groups?

3. How did technological changes such as radio, the automobile, and the airplane influence culture? How did "mass culture" touch the lives of Americans? Did it improve life or diminish it?

4. How did the 1920s liberate women, African Americans, and minorities?

PEARSON myhistorylab Connections

Reinforce what you learned in this chapter by studying the many documents, images, maps, review tools, and videos available at **www.myhistorylab.com**.

Read and Review

✓●─[Study and Review *Chapter 24*

●●●─[Read the Document Margaret Sanger, *Happiness in Marriage*, p. 647

●●●─[Read the Document *Advertisements from 1925 and 1927*, p. 649

((●─[Hear the Audio *Prohibition is a Failure*, p. 653

●●●─[Read the Document *Creed of Klanswomen*, p. 654

●●●─[Read the Document *Bartolomeo Vanzetti, Court Statement*, p. 656

●●─[View the Image *Downtown Scene with Cars, 1911*, p. 660

Research and Explore

◉●─[Watch the Video *The Harlem Renaissance*, p. 659

◉●─[Watch the Video *The rise and fall of the automobile economy*, p. 661

── ((●─[**Hear** the **Audio** ──

Hear the audio file for Chapter 24 at
www.myhistorylab.com.

Will you get a job?

In June, 2009 Kyle Daley graduated from UCLA with a 3.5 average. He applied for 600 jobs, mostly entry-level positions in large corporations. He got two interviews but no job. He was not alone. In 2010 the Labor Department reported that nearly 11 percent of recent college graduates were without jobs, the highest rate on record. Because two-thirds had taken out student loans averaging $23,200, many considered bankruptcy.

Daley and his age cohort had grown up during the most prosperous decades the American nation had ever witnessed. But it all came crashing down in 2008. The enormous hot-air balloon that was the U.S. housing market burst. Worldwide financial markets, tethered to U.S. mortgages, fell precipitously. Major investment firms declared bankruptcy. Others, deemed to be "too big to fail," were saved in free fall only by an infusion of taxpayer money.

From "Normalcy" to Economic Collapse: 1921–1933

25

During the Depression, thousands of young men rode freight trains from one city to another, looking for work, as depicted in *Private Car* (1932), by Leconte Stewart.

CONTENTS

((•—[**Hear** the **Audio** **Chapter 25 at www.myhistorylab.com**

Massive layoffs ensued. "I don't remember any time, maybe even the Great Depression, when things went down so fast," observed Paul Volker, the eighty-one-year-old former chairman of the Federal Reserve.

The Great Depression had similarly been preceded by an era of economic prosperity. In 1924 Commerce Secretary Herbert Hoover had proclaimed "a new era" in which cutthroat competition was being superseded by cooperative associations of producers. This heralded "infinite possibilities of moral progress." Such words perhaps sounded hollow, coming in the wake of a Harding administration disgraced by scandal. By 1924 Calvin Coolidge was president, to be succeeded by Hoover in 1929; both presided over a nation that basked in the dawn of a prosperous new era, though a few dark war clouds could be seen in the distance. Many Americans, giddy over their stock market winnings, placed more and more bets on Wall Street. When it all went bust in 1929, many found themselves mired in the depths of the Great Depression. ■

Harding and "Normalcy"

Warren G. Harding was a newspaperman by trade, publisher of the *Marion Star*, with previous political experience as a legislator and lieutenant governor in his home state, Ohio, and as a U.S. senator. No president, before or since, looked more like a statesman; few were less suited for running the country.

Harding's genial nature and lack of strong convictions made him attractive to many of the politicos after eight years of the headstrong Wilson. During the campaign he exasperated sophisticates by his ignorance and imprecision. He coined the famous vulgarism *normalcy* as a substitute for the word *normality*; referred, during a speech before a group of actors, to Shakespeare's play *Charles the Fifth*; and committed numerous other blunders. "Why does he not get a private secretary who can clothe . . . his 'ideas' in the language customarily used by educated men?" one Boston gentleman demanded of Senator Lodge, who was strongly supporting Harding. Lodge, ordinarily a stickler for linguistic exactitude, replied acidly that he found Harding a paragon by comparison with Wilson, "a man who wrote English very well without ever saying anything." A large majority of the voters, untroubled by the candidate's lack of erudition, shared Lodge's confidence that Harding would be a vast improvement over Wilson.

Warren G. Harding looked presidential, and his voice was suitably deep and resonant. Yet he lacked mental agility and discipline. Republican Senator Frank Brandegee explained Harding's nomination by proclaiming him "the best of the second-raters," and thus the natural compromise between contending factions in the party.

Harding has often been characterized as lazy and incompetent. In fact, he was hardworking and politically shrewd; his major weaknesses were indecisiveness and an unwillingness to offend. He turned the most important government departments over to efficient administrators of impeccable reputation: Charles Evans Hughes, the secretary of state; Herbert Hoover in the Commerce Department; Andrew Mellon in the Treasury; and Henry C. Wallace in Agriculture. He kept track of what these men did but seldom initiated policy in their areas. However, Harding gave many lesser offices, and a few of major importance, to the unsavory "Ohio Gang" headed by Harry M. Daugherty, whom he made attorney general.

The president was too kindly, too well-intentioned, and too unambitious to be dishonest. He appointed corrupt officials like Daugherty, Secretary of the Interior Albert B. Fall, Director of the Mint "Ed" Scobey, and Charles R. Forbes, head of the new Veterans Bureau, out of a sense of personal obligation or because they were old friends who shared his taste for poker and liquor. Before 1921 he had enjoyed holding office; he was adept at mouthing platitudes, a loyal party man who seldom questioned the decisions of his superiors. In the lonely eminence of the White House, whence, as President Harry Truman later said, the buck cannot be passed, he found only misery. "The White House is a prison," he complained. "I can't get away from the men who dog my footsteps. I am in jail."

"The Business of the United States is Business"

Secretary of the Treasury Mellon, multimillionaire banker and master of the aluminum industry, dominated the administration's domestic policy. Mellon set out to lower the taxes of the rich, reverse the low-tariff policies of the Wilson period, and reduce the national debt by cutting expenses and administrating the government more efficiently.

In principle his program had considerable merit. Tax rates designed to check consumer spending in time of war and to raise the huge sum needed to defeat the Central Powers were undoubtedly hampering economic expansion in the early 1920s. Certain industries that had sprung up in the United States during the Great War were suffering from German and Japanese competition now that the fighting had ended. Rigid regulation necessary during a national crisis could well be dispensed with in peacetime. And efficiency and economy in government are always desirable.

Yet Mellon carried his policies to unreasonable extremes. He proposed eliminating inheritance taxes and reducing the tax on high incomes by two-thirds, but he opposed lower rates for taxpayers earning less than $66,000 a year, apparently not realizing that economic expansion required greater mass consumption as well. Freeing the rich from "oppressive" taxation, he argued, would enable them to invest more in potentially productive enterprises, the success of which would create jobs for ordinary people. Little wonder that Mellon's admirers called him the greatest secretary of the treasury since Alexander Hamilton.

Mellon succeeded in balancing the budget and reducing the national debt by an average of over $500 million a year. So committed were the Republican leaders to retrenchment that they even resisted the demands of veterans, organized in the politically potent American Legion, for an "adjusted compensation" bonus.

That the business community heartily approved the policies of Harding and Coolidge is not surprising. Both presidents were uncritical advocates of the business point of view. "We want less government in business and more business in government," Harding pontificated, to which Coolidge added, "The business of the United States is business." Harding and Coolidge used their power of appointment to convert regulatory bodies like the Interstate Commerce Commission (ICC) and the Federal Reserve Board into pro-business agencies that ceased almost entirely to restrict the activities of the industries they were supposed to be controlling. The ICC became almost the reverse of what it had been in the Progressive Era. The Federal Trade Commission, in the words of one bemused academic, seemed to be trying to commit hara-kiri.

Big oil's plans to drill in the Teapot Dome oil reserves led to a major scandal in the Harding administration. (See also Re-Viewing the Past, *There Will Be Blood*, pp. 668–669.)

••••[Read the **Document** Purinton, *Big Ideas from Big Business* at **www.myhistorylab.com**

The Harding Scandals

At least Mellon was honest. The Ohio gang used its power in the most corrupt way imaginable. Jesse Smith, a crony of Attorney General Daugherty, was what today would be called an influence peddler. When he was exposed in 1923, he committed suicide. Charles R. Forbes of the Veterans Bureau siphoned millions of dollars appropriated for the construction of hospitals into his own pocket. When he was found out, he fled to Europe. Later he returned, stood trial, and was sentenced to two years in prison. His assistant, Charles F. Cramer, committed suicide.

Daugherty himself was implicated in the fraudulent return of German assets seized by the alien property custodian to their original owners. He escaped imprisonment only by refusing to testify on the ground that he might incriminate himself.

The worst scandal involved Secretary of the Interior Albert B. Fall, a former senator. In 1921 Fall arranged with the complaisant Secretary of the Navy Edwin Denby for the transfer to the Interior Department of government oil reserves being held for the future use of the navy. He then leased these properties to private oil companies. Edward L. Doheny's Pan-American Petroleum Company got the Elk Hills reserve in California; the Teapot Dome reserve in Wyoming was turned over to Harry F. Sinclair's Mammoth Oil Company. When critics protested, Fall explained that it was necessary to develop the Elk Hills and Teapot Dome properties because adjoining private drillers were draining off the navy's oil. Nevertheless, in 1923 the Senate ordered a full-scale investigation, conducted by Senator Thomas J. Walsh of Montana. It soon came out that Doheny had "lent" Fall $100,000 in hard cash, handed over secretly in a "little black bag." Sinclair had given Fall over $300,000 in cash and negotiable securities. (For more on Doheny and Fall, see Re-Viewing the Past, *There Will Be Blood*, pp. 668–669.)

••••[Read the **Document** *Executive Orders and Senate Resolutions on Teapot Dome* at **www.myhistorylab.com**

There Will Be Blood

In 2008 Daniel Day-Lewis won the Academy Award for his portrayal of Daniel Plainview in *There Will Be Blood*, a movie about wildcatting oil exploration in California in the early 1900s. Day-Lewis portrayed Plainview as a remorseless predator who lied with fluency and cheated with sincerity. He coaxed and coerced property owners into granting him oil leases on his own terms. When he didn't get what he wanted, he lashed out in violence. When a man claimed to be his long-lost brother, Plainview responded with cautious hospitality; but when he learned that the man was an imposter, he put a bullet through his head.

Day-Lewis's Plainview fixed his coal-black eyes onto people like a fighter-pilot locking onto a target. His unctuous voice, punctuated with a crisp, formal diction, bored through opponents like a lubricated drill biting through rock. A reviewer for the *New York Times* called Day-Lewis's performance "among the greatest I've ever seen." Day-Lewis filled Plainview "with so much rage and purpose you wait for him to blow," the reviewer added. The movie makes a strong case for adding Daniel Plainview to a rogue's gallery of fictional capitalist obsessives: Herman Melville's Ahab, Orson Welles's Citizen Kane, and Michael Douglas's Gordon Gekko ("Greed is good").

By the usual conventions of Hollywood, the evil Plainview would be vanquished by a white-hatted hero. But in *There Will Be Blood* no good guys ride to the rescue because there were no good guys: *Everyone* is after money. The problem was that Plainview scarfed it all up, leaving none for anyone else.

In the absence of a conflict between good and evil, the movie turns on the question: What made Plainview so bad?

Certainly, he was long-suffering. The movie begins with him in a mine shaft, hacking away at rock with a pick and scrabbling through the shards on his hands and knees, looking without success for a glint of gold or silver. When he fell down the shaft and broke his leg, he climbed out by himself. These powerfully discouraging scenes, which take up the first twenty minutes of the movie, include no dialogue whatsoever: Plainview's struggle was a solitary one.

This provides a motivational clue. Plainview hated everyone—with the exception of his son. "I see the worst in people," he declared. "I've built my hatreds up over the years, little by little." He crushed enemies not because he craved wealth but because he could not abide their getting the better of him. Which raises the larger question: Were the obsessions of Daniel Plainview characteristic of the industrial and financial magnates of the age?

Plainview, "born in Fond du Lac, Wisconsin," was based on California oil magnate, Edward L. Doheny, himself born in Fond du Lac. The son of a poor Irish immigrant, Doheny left home at a young age and prospected for gold and silver in New Mexico. He had little luck. His wife and children went hungry; she became an alcoholic and committed suicide. In 1891 Doheny gave up prospecting and went to Los Angeles to find a job. One day he spotted a man with a cart whose wheels were coated in tar. Doheny asked what had happened, and the man mentioned a tar pit at the corner of Patton and State Streets, near what is now Dodger Stadium.

Doheny acquired the oil rights to the area and began digging, shoveling dirt and tar into buckets and hauling it to the surface. At the depth of 155 feet, he was nearly killed by toxic fumes; then he studied a diagram of an oil rig and built a crude derrick. He used a sharpened eucalyptus tree as the drill. At 460 feet, he struck oil. Within a few years, he had built

Edward L. Doheny, California oil magnate.

Daniel Day-Lewis as Daniel Plainview.

Doheny's first oil strike at Signal Hill near Los Angeles.

scores of derricks throughout Los Angeles. The growth of the city that became synonymous with the automobile was literally fueled by the oil that lay beneath it. By 1920 southern California had become the world's leading oil-producer, and Doheny had become rich.

There Will Be Blood omitted the next stage in Doheny's life. In 1900 he went to Mexico and worked out a deal with the dictator Profirio Diaz for the oil rights to some promising regions of the undeveloped country. In 1910, Doheny hit several enormous gushers; soon his company was the largest oil producer in the world. His chief competitor in Mexico was Weetman Pearson, an English engineer and builder who had also wangled a lucrative deal out of Diaz. (Pearson was knighted for providing the oil that powered the royal navy during World War I; his many business enterprises included the firm that published the book you are now reading.)

Doheny was a tough and even ruthless businessman; he made many enemies. But it was not until the 1920s that he attained notoriety. He was among the oilmen who secured from Albert B. Fall, Harding's interior secretary, the right to drill in oil fields that were kept as an emergency reserve for the navy. On learning that Fall was in financial difficulties, Doheny sent his son Ned to Fall's apartment with $100,000 in cash. Fall accepted the money.

Several years later Doheny and his son were among those indicted for bribing Fall. In a Senate hearing Doheny professed his innocence. He had not bribed a government official; he had helped a friend. The amount of the gift—$100,000—was "a bagatelle to me," the equivalent of "the ordinary individual" giving $25 to a down-and-out neighbor. The statement drew gasps from the audience. Doheny, though acquitted, became the era's exemplar of greed and corruption.

There Will Be Blood ends with Plainview living alone in an enormous mansion. When an old antagonist stops by, seeking a handout, Plainview, drunk and enraged, murders him. The scene was filmed in the Beverly Hills mansion that Doheny had built for his son. In 1929 a deranged family friend who lived in the mansion shot and killed Ned before turning the gun on himself. It was some measure of Doheny's shattered reputation that rumors long circulated that Doheny had himself murdered both men. One recent historian has argued that Doheny was responsible for the deaths if only because his greed poisoned everything around him.

There Will Be Blood came out just before the great financial collapse of 2008–2009, when wildcatting financiers inflicted several trillion dollars' damage upon the global economy. It is tempting to see in such behavior a heart of darkness, such as the film imputed to Doheny. But we must remember that while Doheny was no paragon of propriety, he was no murderer. In painting him with the oily hues of a Daniel Plainview, Hollywood transformed the oil magnate into caricature. Indeed, Hollywood's search for box-office gushers is itself reminiscent of Day-Lewis's character. And if, like Plainview, it plays fast and loose with the literal truth, can it really be blamed?

Questions for Discussion

- Doheny pursued wealth with obsessive determination. In *Wall Street* (1987), the character Gordon Gekko declares that "Greed is good." How does greed promote economic growth? How does it become a destructive force?
- Did Doheny benefit society and, if so, how? How did he harm it?

The Greystone mansion, built by Edward Doheny, consisted of eighty-five rooms, a bowling alley, two movie theaters, a library, a billiard room, and many secret bars.

Although the three culprits in the **Teapot Dome scandal** escaped conviction on the charge of conspiring to defraud the government, Sinclair was sentenced to nine months in jail for contempt of the Senate and for tampering with a jury, and Fall was fined $100,000 and given a year in prison for accepting a bribe. In 1927 the Supreme Court revoked the leases and the two reserves were returned to the government.

The public still knew little of the scandals when, in June 1923, Harding left Washington on a speaking tour that included a visit to Alaska. His health was poor and his spirits low, for he had begun to understand how his "Goddamn friends" had betrayed him. On the return trip from Alaska, he came down with what his physician, an incompetent crony whom he had made surgeon general of the United States, diagnosed as ptomaine poisoning resulting from his having eaten a tainted Japanese crab. In fact the president had suffered a heart attack. He died in San Francisco on August 2.

Few presidents have been more deeply mourned by the people at the moment of their passing. Harding's kindly nature, his very ordinariness, increased his human appeal. Three million people viewed his coffin as it passed across the country. When the scandals came to light, sadness turned to scorn and contempt. The poet E. E. Cummings came closer to catching the final judgment of Harding's contemporaries than has any historian:

> *the first president to be loved by his*
> *"bitterest enemies" is dead*
> *the only man woman or child who wrote*
> *a simple declarative sentence with seven grammatical*
> *errors "is dead"*
> *beautiful Warren Gamaliel Harding*
> *"is" dead*
> *he's*
> *"dead"*
> *if he wouldn't have eaten them Yapanese Craps*
> *somebody might hardly never not have been*
> *unsorry, perhaps*

Source: "the first president to be loved by his." Copyright 1931, © 1959, 1991 by the Trustees for the E. E. Cummings Trust. Copyright © 1979 by George James Firmage, from *Complete Poems: 1904–1962* by E. E. Cummings, edited by George J. Firmage. Used by permission of Liveright Publishing Corporation.

Coolidge Prosperity

Had he lived, Harding might well have been defeated in 1924 because of the scandals. Vice President Coolidge, unconnected with the troubles and not the type to surround himself with cronies of any kind, seemed the ideal person to clean out the corrupt officials. Coolidge was a taciturn, extremely conservative New Englander with a long record in Massachusetts politics climaxed by his inept but much admired suppression of the Boston police strike while governor.

Calvin Coolidge's quiet presidential style was a sharp contrast to the outspoken Warren Harding. When Coolidge died in 1933, humorist Dorothy Parker remarked, "How could they tell?"

Harding had referred to him as "that little fellow from Massachusetts." Coolidge preferred to follow public opinion and hope for the best.

Coolidge defused his predecessor's scandals by replacing Harding's Attorney General Daugherty with Harlan Fiske Stone, dean of the Columbia University Law School. Soon Coolidge became the darling of the conservatives. His admiration for businessmen and his devotion to laissez-faire knew no limit. "The man who builds a factory builds a temple," he said in all seriousness. "The Government can do more to remedy the economic ills of the people by a system of rigid economy in public expenditures than can be accomplished through any other action." Andrew Mellon, whom he kept on as secretary of the Treasury, became his mentor in economic affairs.

Coolidge won the 1924 Republican nomination easily. The Democrats, badly split, required 103 ballots to choose a candidate. The southern wing, dry, anti-immigrant, pro-Klan, had fixed on William G. McAdoo, Wilson's secretary of the Treasury. The eastern, urban, wet element supported Governor Alfred E. Smith of New York, child of the slums, a Catholic who had compiled a distinguished record in social welfare legislation. After days of futile politicking, the party compromised on John W. Davis, a conservative corporation lawyer closely allied with the Morgan banking interests.

Dismayed by the conservatism of Coolidge and Davis, Robert M. La Follette, backed by the farm bloc, the Socialist party, the American Federation of Labor, and numbers of intellectuals, entered the race as the candidate of a new Progressive party. The Progressives adopted a neopopulist platform calling for the nationalization of railroads, the direct election of the president, the protection of labor's right to bargain collectively, and other reforms.

The situation was almost exactly the opposite of 1912, when one conservative had run against two liberals and had been swamped. But times had changed. Coolidge received 15.7 million votes, Davis 8.4 million, La Follette 4.8 million. Conservatism was clearly the dominant mood of the country.

While Coolidge reigned, complacency was the order of the day. "Mr. Coolidge's genius for inactivity is developed to a very high point," the correspondent Walter Lippmann wrote. "It is a grim, determined, alert inactivity, which keeps Mr. Coolidge occupied constantly."[1] "The country," the president reported to Congress in 1928, "can regard the present with satisfaction, and anticipate the future with optimism."

Peace without a Sword

Presidents Harding and Coolidge handled foreign relations in much the same way they managed domestic affairs. Harding deferred to senatorial prejudice against executive domination in the area and let Secretary of State Charles Evans Hughes make policy. Coolidge adopted a similar course. In directing foreign relations, they faced the obstacle of a resurgent isolationism. The bloodiness and apparent senselessness of the Great War convinced millions that the only way to be sure it would not happen again was to "steer clear" of "entanglements." That these famous words had been used by Washington and Jefferson in vastly different contexts did not deter the isolationists of the 1920s from attributing to them the same authority they gave to Scripture. On the other hand, far-flung American economic interests, as well as the need for both raw materials for industry and foreign markets for America's growing surpluses of agricultural and manufactured goods, made close attention to and involvement in developments all over the world unavoidable.

Isolationist sentiments, therefore, did not deter the government from seeking to advance American interests abroad. The Open Door concept remained predominant; the State Department worked to obtain opportunities in underdeveloped countries for exporters and investors, hoping both to stimulate the American economy and to bring stability to

"backward" nations. Although this policy sometimes roused local resentments because of the tendency of the United States to support entrenched elites while the mass of peasants and city workers lived in poverty, it also resulted in a further retreat from active interventionism.

The first important diplomatic event of the period revealed a great deal about American foreign policy after the Great War. During the war, Japan had greatly increased its influence in East Asia, especially in Manchuria, the northeastern province of warlord-dominated China. To maintain the Open Door in China, it would be necessary to check Japanese expansion. But there was little hope of restoring the old spheres of influence, which the mass of Chinese people bitterly resented. In addition, Japan, the United States, and Great Britain were engaged in expensive naval building programs, a competition none of them really wanted but from which all dared not withdraw unilaterally.

In November 1921, hoping to reach a general agreement with China, Japan, and the Europeans that would keep China open to the commerce of all and slow the armaments race, Secretary of State Hughes convened a conference in Washington. By the following February the Washington Conference had drafted three major treaties and a number of lesser agreements.

In the Five-Power Treaty, the United States, Great Britain, France, Japan, and Italy agreed to stop building battleships for ten years and to reduce their fleets of battleships ships to a fixed ratio, with Great Britain and the United States limited to 525,000 tons, Japan to 315,000 tons, and France and Italy to 175,000 tons. The new ratio was expected to produce a balance of forces in the Pacific.

The Four-Power Treaty, signed by the United States, Great Britain, Japan, and France, committed these nations to respect one another's interests in the islands of the Pacific and to confer in the event that any other country launched an attack in the area.

All the conferees signed the Nine-Power Treaty, agreeing to respect China's independence and to maintain the Open Door. On the surface, this was of monumental importance to the United States since it seemed to mean that Japan had given up its territorial ambitions on the Asian mainland and that both the Japanese and the Europeans had formally endorsed the Open Door concept.

By taking the lead in drafting these agreements, the United States regained some of the moral influence it had lost by not joining the League of Nations. The treaties, however, were uniformly toothless. The signers of the Four-Power Treaty agreed only to consult in case of aggression in the Pacific; they made no promises to help one another or to restrict their own freedom of

[1]Coolidge was physically delicate, plagued by chronic stomach trouble. He required ten or eleven hours of sleep a day.

action. As President Harding assured the Senate, "there [was] no commitment to armed force, no alliance, no written or moral obligation to join in defense."

The naval disarmament treaty said nothing about the number of other warships that the powers might build, about the far more important question of land and air forces, or about the underlying industrial and financial structures that controlled the ability of the nations to make war. In addition, the 5:5:3 ratio actually enabled the Japanese to dominate the western Pacific. It made the Philippine Islands indefensible and exposed Hawaii to possible attack. In a sense these American bases became hostages of Japan. Yet Congress was so unconcerned about Japanese sensibilities that it refused to grant any immigration quota to Japan under the National Origins Act of 1924, even though the formula applied to other nations would have allowed only 100 Japanese a year to enter the country. The law, Secretary Hughes warned, produced in Japan "a sense of injury and antagonism instead of friendship and cooperation."

Hughes did not think war a likely result, but Japanese resentment of "white imperialism" played into the hands of the military party in that nation. Many Japanese army and navy officers considered war with the United States inevitable.

As for the key Nine-Power Treaty, Japan did not abandon its territorial ambitions in China, and China remained so riven by conflict among the warlords and so resentful of the "imperialists" that the economic advantages of the Open Door turned out to be small indeed.

The United States entered into all these agreements without realizing their full implications and not really prepared to play an active part in East Asian affairs. "We have no favorites in the present dog fight in China," the head of the Far Eastern division of the State Department wrote of the civil war going on there in 1924. "They all look alike to us." The Japanese soon realized that the United States would not do much to defend its interests in China.

The Peace Movement

The Americans of the 1920s wanted peace but would neither surrender their prejudices and dislikes nor build the defenses necessary to make it safe to indulge these passions. "The people have had all the war, all the taxation, and all the military service that they want," President Coolidge announced in 1925.

Peace societies flourished, among them the Carnegie Endowment for International Peace, designed "to hasten the abolition of war, the foulest blot upon our civilization," and the Woodrow Wilson Foundation, aimed at helping "the liberal forces of

mankind throughout the world . . . who intend to promote peace by the means of justice." In 1923 Edward W. Bok, retired editor of the *Ladies' Home Journal,* offered a prize of $100,000 for the best workable plan for preserving international peace. He was flooded with suggestions. Former Assistant Secretary of the Navy Franklin D. Roosevelt drafted one while recovering from an attack of polio. Such was the temper of the times that he felt constrained to include in the preamble this statement:

> We seek not to become involved as a nation in the purely regional affairs of groups of other nations, nor to give to the representatives of other peoples the right to compel us to enter upon undertakings calling for a leading up to the use of armed force without our full and free consent, given through our constitutional procedure.

So great was the opposition to international cooperation that the United States refused to accept membership on the World Court, although this tribunal could settle disputes only when the nations involved agreed. Too many peace lovers believed that their goal could be attained simply by pointing out the moral and practical disadvantages of war.

The culmination of this illusory faith in preventing war by criticizing it came with the signing of the Kellogg-Briand Pact in 1928. The treaty was born in the fertile brain of French Foreign Minister Aristide Briand, who was eager to collect allies against possible attack by a resurgent Germany. In 1927 Briand proposed to Secretary of State Frank B. Kellogg that their countries agree never to go to war with each other. Kellogg found the idea as repugnant as any conventional alliance, but American isolationists and pacifists found the suggestion fascinating. They plagued Kellogg with demands that he negotiate such a treaty.

To extricate himself from this situation, Kellogg suggested that the pact be broadened to include all nations. Now Briand was angry. Like Kellogg, he saw how meaningless such a treaty would be, especially when Kellogg insisted that it be hedged with a proviso that "every nation is free at all times . . . to defend its territory from attack and it alone is competent to decide when circumstances require war in self-defense." Nevertheless, Briand too found public pressures irresistible. In August 1928, at Paris, diplomats from fifteen nations bestowed upon one another an "international kiss," condemning "recourse to war for the solution of international controversies" and renouncing war "as an instrument of national policy." Seldom has so unrealistic a promise been made by so many intelligent people. Yet most Americans considered the Kellogg-Briand Pact a milestone in the history of civilization: The Senate, habitually so suspicious of international commitments, ratified it eighty-five to one.

The Good Neighbor Policy

The conflict between the desire to avoid foreign entanglements and the desire to advance American economic interests is well-illustrated by events in Latin America. In dealing with this part of the world, Harding and Coolidge performed neither better nor worse than Wilson had. In the face of continued radicalism and instability in Mexico, which caused Americans with interests in land and oil rights to suffer heavy losses, President Coolidge acted with forbearance. The Mexicans were able to complete their social and economic revolution in the 1920s without significant interference by the United States.

Under Coolidge's successor, Herbert Hoover, the United States began at last to treat Latin American nations as equals. Hoover reversed Wilson's policy of trying to teach them "to elect good men." The Clark Memorandum (1930), written by Undersecretary of State J. Reuben Clark, disassociated the right of intervention in Latin America from the Roosevelt Corollary. The corollary had been an improper extension of the Monroe Doctrine, Clark declared. The right of the United States to intervene depended rather on "the doctrine of self-preservation."

The distinction seemed slight to Latin Americans, but since it seemed unlikely that the existence of the United States could be threatened in the area, it was important. By 1934 the marines who had been occupying Nicaragua, Haiti, and the Dominican Republic had all been withdrawn and the United States had renounced the right to intervene in Cuban affairs. Instead of functioning as the policeman for the region, the United States would be its **"good neighbor."** Unfortunately, the United States did little to try to improve social and economic conditions in the Caribbean region, so the underlying envy and resentment of "rich Uncle Sam" did not disappear.

The Totalitarian Challenge

The futility and danger of isolationism were exposed in September 1931 when the Japanese, long dominant in Chinese Manchuria, marched their army in and converted the province into a puppet state

The League of Nations covenant, the Kellogg Pact, the Nine-Power Treaty—all were mere scraps of paper. They did nothing to prevent Japan's invasion of Manchuria in 1931.

named Manchukuo. This violated both the Kellogg-Briand and Nine-Power pacts. China, now controlled by General Chiang Kai-shek, appealed to the League of Nations and to the United States for help. Neither would intervene. When League officials asked about the possibility of American cooperation in some kind of police action, President Hoover refused to consider either economic or military reprisals. The United States was not a world policeman, he said. The Nine-Power and Kellogg-Briand treaties were "solely moral instruments."

The League sent a commission to Manchuria to investigate. Henry L. Stimson, Hoover's secretary of state, announced (the Stimson Doctrine) that the United States would never recognize the legality of seizures made in violation of American treaty rights. This served only to irritate the Japanese.

In January 1932 Japan attacked Shanghai, the bloody battle marked by the indiscriminate bombing of residential districts. When the League at last officially condemned their aggressions, the Japanese withdrew from the organization and extended their control of northern China. The lesson of Manchuria was not lost on Adolf Hitler, who became chancellor of Germany on January 30, 1933.

It is easy, in surveying the diplomatic events of 1920–1929, to condemn the United States and the European democracies for their unwillingness to stand up for principles, their refusal to resist when Japan and later Germany and Italy embarked on the aggressions that led to World War II. It is also proper to place some of the blame for the troubles of the era on the United States and the European democracies, which controlled much of the world's resources and were primarily interested in holding on to what they had.

War Debts and Reparations

The democracies did not take a strong stand against Japan in part because they were quarreling about other matters. Particularly divisive was the controversy over war debts—those of Germany to the Allies and those of the Allies to the United States. The United States had lent more than $10 billion to its comrades-in-arms. Since most of this money had been spent on weapons and other supplies in the United States, it might well have been considered part of America's contribution to the war effort. The public, however, demanded full repayment—with interest. "These were loans, not contributions," Secretary of the Treasury Mellon firmly declared. Even when the Foreign Debt Commission scaled down the interest rate from 5 percent to about 2 percent, the total, to be repaid over a period of sixty-two years, amounted to more than $22 billion.

Repayment of such a sum was virtually impossible. In the first place, the money had not been put to productive use. Dollars lent to build factories or roads might be expected to earn profits for the borrower, but those devoted to the purchase of shells only destroyed wealth. Furthermore, the American protective tariff reduced the ability of the Allies to earn the dollars needed to pay the debts.

The Allies tried to load their obligations to the United States, along with the other costs of the war, on the backs of the Germans. They demanded that the Germans pay reparations amounting to $33 billion. If this sum were collected, they declared, they could rebuild their economies and obtain the international exchange needed to pay their debts to the United States. But Germany was reluctant even to try to pay such huge reparations, and when Germany defaulted, so did the Allies.

Everyone was bitterly resentful: the Germans because they felt they were being bled white; the Americans, as Senator Hiram Johnson of California would have it, because the wily Europeans were treating the United States as "an international sucker"; and the Allies because, as the French said, *"l'oncle Shylock"* (a play on the names Uncle Sam and Shylock, the moneylender in Shakespeare's *Merchant of Venice)* was demanding his pound of flesh with interest. Clemenceau wrote President Coolidge in 1926, "Come see the endless lists of dead in our villages."

Everyone shared the blame: the Germans because they resorted to a runaway inflation that reduced the mark to less than one trillionth of its prewar value, at least in part in hopes of avoiding their international obligations; the Americans because they refused to recognize the connection between the tariff and the debt question; and the Allies because they made little effort to pay even a reasonable proportion of their obligations.

In 1924 an international agreement, the Dawes Plan, provided Germany with a $200 million loan designed to stabilize its currency. Germany agreed to pay about $250 million a year in reparations. In 1929 the Young Plan further scaled down the reparations bill. In practice, the Allies paid the United States about what they collected from Germany. Since Germany got the money largely from private American loans, the United States would have served itself and the rest of the world far better had it written off the war debts at the start. In any case, in the late 1920s Americans stopped lending money to Germany, the Great Depression struck, Germany defaulted on its reparations payments, and the Allies then gave up all pretense of meeting their obligations to the United States. The last token payments were made in 1933. All that remained was a heritage of mistrust and hostility.

The Election of 1928

Meanwhile, dramatic changes had occurred in the United States. The climax of Coolidge prosperity came in 1928. The president—somewhat cryptically, as was his wont—decided not to run again, and Secretary of Commerce Hoover, whom he detested, easily won the Republican nomination. Hoover was the intellectual leader, almost the philosopher, of the New Era. American capitalists, he believed, had learned to curb their selfish instincts. Voluntary trade associations could create "codes of business practice and ethics that would eliminate abuses and make for higher standards."

Although stiff, uncommunicative, and entirely without experience in elective office, Hoover made an admirable candidate in 1928. His roots in the Midwest and West (Iowa-born, he was raised in Oregon and educated at Stanford University in California) neatly balanced his outstanding reputation among eastern business tycoons. He took a "modern" approach to both capital and labor; businessmen should cooperate with one another and with their workers too. He opposed both unionbusting and trustbusting. His career as a mining engineer had given him a wide knowledge of the world, yet he had become highly critical of Europe.

The Democrats, having had their fill of factionalism in 1924, could no longer deny the nomination to Governor Al Smith. Superficially, Smith was Hoover's antithesis. Born and raised in New York's Lower East Side slums, affable, witty, determinedly casual of

Herbert Hoover relaxes during the 1928 presidential campaign. "That man has been offering me advice for the last five years," President Coolidge said of his secretary of commerce, "all of it bad."

manner, he had been schooled in machine politics by Tammany Hall. He was a Catholic, Hoover a Quaker, a wet where Hoover supported prohibition; he dealt easily with people of every race and nationality, while Hoover had little interest in and less knowledge of African Americans and immigrants. However, like Hoover, Smith managed to combine a basic conservatism with humanitarian concern for the underprivileged. As adept in administration as Hoover, he was equally uncritical of the American capitalist system.

In the election Hoover won a smashing triumph, 444 to 87 in the Electoral College, 21.4 million to 14 million in the popular vote. All the usually Democratic border states and even North Carolina, Florida, and Texas went to the Republicans, along with the entire West and the Northeast save for Massachusetts and Rhode Island.

After this defeat the Democratic party appeared on the verge of extinction. Nothing could have been further from the truth. The religious question and his big-city roots had hurt Smith, but the chief reason he lost was prosperity—and the good times were soon to end. Hoover's overwhelming victory also concealed a political realignment that was taking place. Working-class voters in the cities, largely Catholic and unimpressed by Coolidge prosperity, had swung heavily to the Democrats. In 1924 the twelve largest cities had

been solidly Republican; in 1928 all went Democratic. In agricultural states like Iowa, Smith ran far better than Davis had in 1924, for Coolidge's vetoes of bills designed to raise farm prices had caused considerable resentment. A new coalition of urban workers and dissatisfied farmers was in the making.

View the **Image** *A Heavy Load for Al (1928)* at **www.myhistorylab.com**

Economic Problems

The American economic system of the 1920s had grave flaws. Certain industries did not share in the good times. The coal business, suffering from the competition of petroleum, entered a period of decline. Cotton and woolen textiles also lagged because of the competition of new synthetics, principally rayon. Industry began to be plagued by falling profit margins and chronic unemployment.

The movement toward consolidation in industry, somewhat checked during the latter part of the Progressive Era, resumed; by 1929, 200 corporations controlled nearly half the nation's corporate assets. General Motors, Ford, and Chrysler turned out nearly 90 percent of all American cars and trucks. Four tobacco companies produced over 90 percent of the cigarettes. One percent of all financial institutions controlled 46 percent of the nation's banking business. Even retail merchandising, traditionally the domain of the small shopkeeper, reflected the trend. The A & P food chain expanded from 400 stores in 1912 to 17,500 in 1928. The Woolworth chain of five-and-ten-cent stores experienced similar growth.

Most large manufacturers, aware that bad public relations resulting from the unbridled use of monopolistic power outweighed any immediate economic gain, sought stability and "fair" prices rather than the maximum profit possible at the moment. "Regulated" competition was the order of the day, oligopoly (a market controlled by a small group of firms) the typical situation. The trade association movement flourished; producers formed voluntary organizations to exchange information, discuss policies toward government and the public, and "administer" prices in their industry. Usually the largest corporation, such as U.S. Steel in the iron and steel business, became the "price leader," its competitors, some themselves giants, following slavishly.

The success of the trade associations depended in part on the attitude of the federal government, for such organizations might well have been attacked under the antitrust laws. Their defenders, including President Harding, argued that the associations made business more efficient and prevented violent gyrations of prices and production. Secretary of Commerce Hoover put the facilities of his department at the disposal of the associations. "We are passing from a period of extremely individualistic action into a period of associational activities," Hoover stated. After Coolidge became president, the antitrust division of the Justice Department itself encouraged the trade associations to cooperate in ways that had previously been considered violations of the Sherman Act.

Even more important to the trade associations were the good times. With profits high and markets expanding, the most powerful producers could afford to share the bounty with smaller, less efficient competitors.

The weakest element in the economy was agriculture. Farm prices slumped and farmers' costs mounted. Besides having to purchase expensive machinery in order to compete, farmers were confronted by high foreign tariffs and in some cases quotas on the importation of foodstuffs. As crop yields per acre rose, chiefly because of the increased use of chemical fertilizers, agricultural prices fell further.

Despite the efforts of the farm bloc, the government did little to improve the situation. President Harding opposed direct aid to agriculture as a matter of principle. "Every farmer is a captain of industry," he declared. "The elimination of competition among them would be impossible without sacrificing that fine individualism that still keeps the farm the real reservoir from which the nation draws so many of the finest elements of its citizenship." During his administration Congress strengthened the laws regulating railroad rates and grain exchanges and made it easier for farmers to borrow money, but it did nothing directly to increase agricultural income. Nor did the high tariffs on agricultural produce have much effect. Being forced to sell their surpluses abroad, farmers found that world prices depressed domestic prices despite the tariff wall.

Thus the unprecedented prosperity rested on unstable foundations. The problem was mainly one of maldistribution of resources. Productive capacity raced ahead of buying power. Too large a share of the profits was going into too few pockets. The 27,000 families with the highest annual incomes in 1929 received as much money as the 11 million with annual incomes of under $1,500, the minimum sum required at that time to maintain a family decently. High earnings and low taxes permitted huge sums to pile up in the hands of individuals who did not invest the money productively. A good deal of it went into stock market speculation, which led to the "big bull market" and eventually to the Great Depression.

The Stock Market Crash of 1929

In the spring of 1928, prices on the New York Stock Exchange, already at a historic high, began to surge. As the presidential campaign gathered momentum, the market increased its upward pace, stimulated by

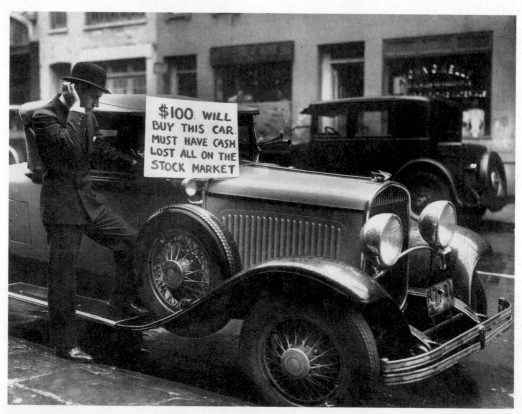

Walter Thompson saw his assets evaporate during the stock market collapse in 1929. Desperate for cash (like nearly everyone else) he offered his snappy roadster for $100.

the candidates' efforts to outdo each other in praising the marvels of the American economic system. "Glamour" stocks skyrocketed—Radio Corporation of America rose from under 100 to 400 between March and November. A few conservative brokers expressed alarm, warning that most stocks were grossly overpriced. The majority scoffed at such talk. "Be a bull on America," they urged. "Never sell the United States short."

During the first half of 1929 stock prices climbed still higher. A mania for speculation swept the country, thousands of small investors putting their savings in common stocks. Then, in September, the market wavered. Amid volatile fluctuations stock averages eased downward. Most analysts contended that the stock exchange was "digesting" previous gains. A Harvard economist expressed the prevailing view when he said that stock prices had reached a "permanently high plateau" and would soon resume their advance.

On October 24 a wave of selling sent prices spinning. Nearly 13 million shares changed hands—a record. Bankers and politicians rallied to check the decline, as they had during the Panic of 1907. J. P. Morgan, Jr., rivaled the efforts of his father in that earlier crisis. President Hoover assured the people that "the business of the country . . . is on a sound and prosperous basis." But on October 29, the bottom seemed to drop out. More than 16 million shares were sold, prices plummeting. The boom was over.

Hoover and the Depression

The collapse of the stock market did not cause the Depression; stocks rallied late in the year, and business activity did not begin to decline significantly until the spring of 1930. The Great Depression was a worldwide phenomenon caused chiefly by economic imbalances resulting from the chaos of the Great War. In the United States too much wealth had fallen into too few hands, with the result that consumers were unable to buy all the goods produced. The trouble came to a head mainly because of the easy-credit policies of the Federal Reserve Board and the Mellon tax structure, which favored the rich. Its effects were so profound and prolonged because the politicians (and for that matter the professional economists) did not fully understand what was happening or what to do about it.

The chronic problem of underconsumption operated to speed the downward spiral. Unable to rid themselves of mounting inventories, manufacturers closed plants and laid off workers, thereby causing demand to shrink further. Automobile output fell from 4.5 million units in 1929 to 1.1 million in 1932. When Ford closed his Detroit plants in 1931, some 75,000 workers lost their jobs, and the decline in auto

production affected a host of suppliers and middlemen as well.

The financial system cracked under the strain. More than 1,300 banks closed their doors in 1930, 3,700 more during the next two years. Each failure deprived thousands of persons of funds that might have been used to buy goods; when the Bank of the United States in New York City became insolvent in December 1930, 400,000 depositors found their savings immobilized. And of course the industrial depression worsened the depression in agriculture by further reducing the demand for American foodstuffs. Every economic indicator reflected the collapse. New investments declined from $10 billion in 1929 to $1 billion in 1932, and the national income fell from over $80 billion to under $50 billion in the same brief period. Unemployment, under 1 million at the height of the boom, rose to at least 13 million.

President Hoover was an intelligent man, experienced in business matters and knowledgeable in economics. Secretary of the Treasury Mellon believed that the economy should be allowed to slide unchecked until the cycle had found its bottom. "Let the slump liquidate itself," Mellon urged. "Liquidate labor, liquidate stocks, liquidate the farmers. . . . People will work harder, live a more moral life. Values will be adjusted, and enterprising people will pick up the wrecks from less competent people." Hoover realized that such a policy would cause unbearable hardship for millions. He rejected Mellon's advice to let the Depression run its course.

Hoover's program for ending the Depression evolved gradually. At first he called on businessmen to maintain prices and wages. The government should cut taxes in order to increase consumers' spendable income, institute public works programs to stimulate production and create jobs for the unemployed, lower interest rates to make it easier for businesses to borrow in order to expand, and make loans to banks and industrial corporations threatened with collapse and to homeowners unable to meet mortgage payments. The president also proposed measures making it easier for farmers to borrow money, and he suggested that the government should support cooperative farm marketing schemes designed to solve the problem of overproduction. He called for an expansion of state and local relief programs and urged all who could afford it to give more to charity. Above all he tried to restore public confidence: The economy was basically healthy; the Depression was only a minor downturn; prosperity was "just around the corner."

Although Hoover's plans were theoretically sound, they failed to check the economic slide, in part because of curious limitations in his conception of how they should be implemented. He placed far too much reliance on his powers of persuasion and the willingness of citizens to act in the public interest without legal compulsion. He urged manufacturers to maintain wages and keep their factories in operation, but the manufacturers, under the harsh pressure of economic realities, soon slashed wages and curtailed output sharply. He permitted the Federal Farm Board (created under the Agricultural Marketing Act of 1929) to establish semipublic stabilization corporations with authority to buy up surplus wheat and cotton, but he refused to consider crop or acreage controls. The stabilization corporations poured out hundreds of millions of dollars without checking falling agricultural prices because farmers increased production faster than the corporations could buy up the excess for disposal abroad.

Hoover resisted proposals to shift responsibility from state and local agencies to the federal government, despite the fact—soon obvious—that they lacked the resources to cope with the emergency. By 1932 the federal government, with Hoover's approval, was spending $500 million a year on public works projects, but because of the decline in state and municipal construction, the total public outlay fell nearly $1 billion below what it had been in 1930. More serious was his refusal, on constitutional grounds, to allow federal funds to be used for the relief of individuals. State and municipal agencies and private charities must take care of the needy.

Unfortunately the Depression was drying up the sources of private charities just as the demands on these organizations were expanding. State and municipal agencies were swamped just when their capacities to tax and borrow were shrinking. By 1932 more than 40,600 Boston families were on relief (compared with 7,400 families in 1929); in Chicago 700,000 persons—40 percent of the workforce—were unemployed. Only the national government possessed the power and the credit to deal adequately with the crisis.

Yet Hoover would not act. He set up a committee to coordinate local relief activities but insisted on preserving what he called "the principles of individual and local responsibility." For the federal government to take over relief would "lead to the super-state where every man becomes the servant of the state and real liberty is lost."

Federal loans to commercial enterprises were constitutional, he believed, because the money could be put to productive use and eventually repaid. When drought destroyed the crops of farmers in the South and Southwest in 1930, the government lent them money to buy seed and even food for their livestock, but Hoover would permit no direct relief for the farmers themselves. In 1932 he approved the creation of the Reconstruction Finance Corporation (RFC) to lend money to banks, railroads, and insurance companies. The RFC represented an important extension of national authority, yet it was thoroughly in line with Hoover's philosophy. Its loans, secured by solid

collateral, were commercial transactions, not gifts; the agency did almost nothing for individuals in need of relief. The same could be said of the Glass-Steagall Banking Act of 1932, which eased the tight credit situation by permitting Federal Reserve banks to accept corporate stocks and bonds as security for loans. The public grew increasingly resentful of the president's doctrinaire adherence to principle while breadlines lengthened and millions of willing workers searched fruitlessly for jobs.

As time passed and the Depression worsened, Hoover put more stress on the importance of balancing the federal budget, reasoning that since citizens had to live within their limited means in hard times, the government should set a good example. This policy was counterproductive; by reducing its expenditures the government made the Depression worse, which reduced federal revenue further. By June 1931 the budget was nearly $500 million in the red.

Hoover understood the value of pumping money into a stagnant economy. He might have made a virtue of necessity. The difficulty lay in the fact that nearly all "informed" opinion believed that a balanced budget was essential to recovery. The most prestigious economists insisted on it, and so did business leaders, labor leaders, and even most socialists. When Hoover said, "prosperity cannot be restored by raids on the public Treasury," he was mistaken, but it is equally wrong to criticize him for failing to understand what almost no one understood in the 1930s.

Much of the contemporary criticism of Hoover and a good deal of that heaped on him by later historians was unfair. Yet his record as president shows that he was too rigidly wedded to a particular theory of government to cope effectively with the problems of the day. Since these problems were in a sense insoluble—no one possessed enough knowledge to understand entirely what was wrong or enough authority to enforce corrective measures—flexibility and a willingness to experiment were essential to any program aimed at restoring prosperity. Hoover lacked these qualities. He was his own worst enemy, being too uncompromising to get on well with the politicians and too aloof to win the confidence and affection of ordinary people. He had too much faith in himself and his plans. When he failed to achieve the results he anticipated, he attracted, despite his devotion to duty and his concern for the welfare of the country, not sympathy but scorn.

Watch the Video *Prosperity of the 1920s and the Great Depression* at **www.myhistorylab.com**

The Economy Hits Bottom

During the spring of 1932, as the economy sounded the depths, thousands of Americans faced starvation. In Philadelphia during an eleven-day period when no relief funds were available, hundreds of families existed on stale bread, thin soup, and garbage. In the nation as a whole, only about one-quarter of the unemployed were receiving any public aid. In Birmingham, Alabama, landlords in poor districts gave up trying to collect rents, preferring, one Alabama congressman told a Senate committee, "to have somebody living there free of charge rather than to have the house . . . burned up for fuel [by scavengers]." Many people were evicted, and they often gathered in ramshackle communities constructed of packing boxes, rusty sheet metal, and similar refuse on swamps, garbage dumps, and other wasteland. People began to call these places "Hoovervilles."

Thousands of tramps roamed the countryside begging and scavenging for food. At the same time, food prices fell so low that farmers burned corn for fuel. Iowa and Nebraska farmers organized "farm holiday" movements, refusing to ship their crops to market in protest against the thirty-one-cent-a-bushel corn and thirty-eight-cent wheat. They blocked roads and rail lines, dumped milk, overturned trucks, and established picket lines to enforce their boycott. The world seemed to have been turned upside down. Professor Felix Frankfurter of the Harvard Law School remarked only half humorously that henceforth the terms BC and AD would mean "Before Crash" and "After Depression."

The national mood ranged from apathy to resentment. In 1931 federal immigration agents and local groups in the Southwest began rounding up Mexican-Americans and deporting them. Some of those returned to Mexico had entered the United States illegally; others had come in properly. Unemployed Mexicans were ejected because they might become public charges, those with jobs because they were presumably taking bread from the mouths of citizens. "Capitalism is dying," the socialist theologian Reinhold Niebuhr remarked in 1932, "and . . . it ought to die."

In June and July 1932, 20,000 Great War veterans marched on Washington to demand immediate payment of their "adjusted compensation" bonuses. When Congress rejected their appeal, some 2,000 refused to leave, settling in a jerrybuilt camp of shacks and tents at Anacostia Flats, a swamp bordering the Potomac. President Hoover, alarmed, charged incorrectly that the **Bonus Army** was largely composed of criminals and radicals and sent troops into the Flats to disperse it with bayonets, tear gas, and tanks. The task was accomplished amid much confusion; fortunately no one was killed. The protest had been aimless and not entirely justified, yet the spectacle of the U.S. government chasing unarmed veterans with tanks appalled the nation.

The unprecedented severity of the Depression led some persons to favor radical economic and political changes. The disparity between the lots of the rich and

Evicted from their homes, many unemployed people gravitated to vacant industrial property, where they erected hovels from scraps of lumber, tarpaper, and cardboard. This shantytown is outside of Seattle.

the poor, always a challenge to democracy, became more striking and engendered considerable bitterness. "Unless something is done to provide employment," two labor leaders warned Hoover, "disorder . . . is sure to arise. . . . There is a growing demand that the entire business and social structure be changed because of the general dissatisfaction with the present system."

The communist party gained few converts among farmers and industrial workers, but a considerable number of intellectuals, alienated by the trends of the 1920s, responded positively to the communists' emphasis on economic planning and the total mobilization of the state to achieve social goals. Even the cracker-barrel humorist Will Rogers was impressed by reports of the absence of serious unemployment in Russia. "All roads lead to Moscow," the former muckraker Lincoln Steffens wrote.

A crowd of homeless men in New York City wait for the municipal lodging house to open.

View the Image *Depression Breadlines in New York City* at **www.myhistorylab.com**

View the Image *Burning Bonus Army Shacks, 1932* at **www.myhistorylab.com**

The Depression and Its Victims

Depression is a word used by economists but also by psychologists, and the depression of the 1930s had profound psychological effects on its victims as well as the obvious economic ones. Almost without exception people who lost their jobs first searched energetically for new ones, but when they remained unemployed for more than a few months they sank gradually into despair. E. Wight Bakke, a Yale sociologist who interviewed hundreds of unemployed men in the United States and England during the Depression, described the final stage of decline as "permanent readjustment," by which he meant that the long-term jobless simply gave up. The settlement house worker Lillian Wald came to a similar conclusion. Unemployed people at her famous Henry Street settlement, she noticed, had lost both "ambition and pride."

Simple discouragement alone does not explain why so many of the jobless reacted this way. People who had worked all their adult lives often became ashamed of themselves when they could not find a job. Professor Bakke reported that half the unemployed people in New Haven that he interviewed never applied for public assistance no matter how desperate their circumstances. A purely physiological factor was often involved as well. When money ran low, people had to cut down on relatively expensive foods

like fruit, meat, and dairy products. In New York City, for example, milk consumption fell by a million quarts a day. In nutritional terms people consumed more carbohydrates and less food rich in energy-building vitamins and proteins. Often they became listless.

The Depression affected the families of the jobless in many ways. It caused a dramatic drop in the birthrate, from 27.7 per thousand population in 1920 to 18.4 per thousand in the early 1930s, the lowest in American history. Sometimes it strengthened family ties. Some unemployed men spent more time with their children and helped their wives with cooking and housework. Others, however, became impatient when their children demanded attention, refused to help around the house, sulked, or took to drink.

The influence of wives in families struck by unemployment tended to increase, and in this respect women suffered less psychologically from the Depression. They were usually too busy trying to make ends meet to become apathetic. But the way they used this influence varied. Some wives were sympathetic, others scornful, when the "breadwinner" came home with empty hands. When the wife of an unemployed man managed to find a job, the result could be either gratitude and pride or bitter resentment on the man's part, resentment or a sense of liberation on the woman's. If there is any generalization about the effects of the Depression on family relations it is probably an obvious one—where relationships were close and loving they became stronger, where they were not, the results could be disastrous.

The Election of 1932

As the end of his term approached, President Hoover seemed to grow daily more petulant and pessimistic. The Depression, coming after twelve years of

unemployment insurance, and conservation and public power projects. In 1928, while Hoover was carrying New York against Smith by a wide margin, Roosevelt won election by 25,000 votes. In 1930 he swept the state by a 700,000-vote majority, double the previous record. He also had the advantage of the Roosevelt name (he was a distant cousin of the inimitable TR), and his sunny, magnetic personality contrasted favorably with that of the glum and colorless Hoover.

Roosevelt was far from being a radical. Although he had supported the League of Nations while campaigning for the vice presidency in 1920, during the 1920s he had not seriously challenged the basic tenets of Coolidge prosperity. He never had much difficulty adjusting his views to prevailing attitudes. For a time he even served as head of the American Construction Council, a trade association. Indeed, his life before the Depression gave little indication that he understood the aspirations of ordinary people or had any deep commitment to social reform.

Roosevelt was born to wealth and social status in Dutchess County, New York, in 1882. Pampered in childhood by a doting yet domineering mother, he was educated at the exclusive Groton School and then at Harvard. Ambition as much as the desire to render public service motivated his career in politics; even after an attack of polio in 1921 had badly crippled both his legs, he refused to abandon his hopes for high office. During the 1920s he was a hardworking member of the liberal wing of his party. He supported Smith for president in 1924 and 1928.

To some observers Roosevelt seemed rather a lightweight intellectually. When he ran for the vice presidency, the *Chicago Tribune* commented, "If he is Theodore Roosevelt, Elihu Root is Gene Debs, and Bryan is a brewer." Twelve years later many critics judged him too irresolute, too amiable, too eager to

A vigorous-looking Franklin D. Roosevelt campaigns for the presidency in 1932. His vice-presidential running mate, John N. Garner, and the conveniently placed post allowed the handicapped candidate to stand when greeting voters along the way.

Republican rule, probably ensured a Democratic victory in any case, but his attitude as the election neared alienated many voters and turned defeat into rout.

Confident of victory, the Democrats chose Governor Franklin Delano Roosevelt of New York as their presidential candidate. Roosevelt owed his nomination chiefly to his success as governor. Under his administration, New York had led the nation in providing relief for the needy and had enacted an impressive program of old-age pensions,

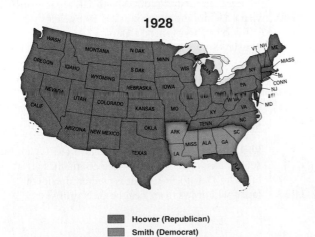

1928

Hoover (Republican)

Smith (Democrat)

1932

Roosevelt (Democrat)

Hoover (Republican)

The Roosevelt Political Revolution, 1932 In 1928, Hoover carried every state apart from the Deep South and Massachusetts; but in 1932, Franklin Roosevelt swept to a landslide victory.

please all factions to be a forceful leader. Herbert Hoover thought he was "ignorant but well-meaning," and the political analyst Walter Lippmann, in a now-famous observation, called him "a pleasant man who, without any important qualifications for the job, would very much like to be President."

Despite his physical handicap—he could walk only a few steps, and then only with the aid of steel braces and two canes—Roosevelt was a marvelous campaigner. He traveled back and forth across the country, radiating confidence and good humor even when directing his sharpest barbs at the Republicans. Like every great political leader, he took as much from the people as he gave them, understanding the causes of their confusion and sensing their needs. "I have looked into the faces of thousands of Americans," he told a friend. "They have the frightened look of lost children. . . . They are saying: 'We're caught in something we don't understand; perhaps this fellow can help us out.'"

On matters such as farm policy, the tariff, and government spending, Roosevelt equivocated, contradicted himself, or remained silent. Nevertheless Roosevelt's basic position was unmistakable. There must be a "re-appraisal of values," a "New Deal." Instead of adhering to conventional limits on the extent of federal power, the government should do whatever was necessary to protect the unfortunate and advance the public good. Lacking concrete answers, Roosevelt advocated a point of view rather than a plan: "The country needs bold, persistent experimentation. It is common sense to take a method and try it. If it fails, admit it frankly and try another. But above all, try something."

The popularity of this approach was demonstrated in November. Hoover, who had lost only eight states in 1928, won only six, all in the Northeast, in 1932. Roosevelt amassed 22.8 million votes to Hoover's 15.8 million and carried the Electoral College, 472 to 59.

During the interval between the election and Roosevelt's inauguration in March 1933, the Great Depression reached its nadir. The holdover "lame duck" Congress, last of its kind, proved incapable of effective action.[2] President Hoover, perhaps understandably, hesitated to institute changes without the cooperation of his successor. Roosevelt, for equally plausible reasons, refused to accept responsibility before assuming power officially. The nation, curiously apathetic in the face of so much suffering, drifted aimlessly, like a sailboat in a flat calm.

●●●─┐**Read** the **Document** Hoover, *New York Campaign Speech* at www.myhistorylab.com

─────────────

[2]The Twentieth Amendment (1933) provided for convening new Congresses in January instead of the following December. It also advanced the date of the president's inauguration from March 4 to January 20.

Chapter Review

Milestones

1921–1922	Washington Conference tries to slow arms race		Young Plan further reduces German reparations
1923	President Harding dies; Coolidge becomes president	1930	Clark Memorandum renounces Roosevelt Corollary to Monroe Doctrine
	Teapot Dome and other Harding scandals are exposed		Hawley-Smoot tariff raises duties on foreign manufactures
1924	Dawes Plan restructures German reparations payments	1931	Ten-year Dust Bowl begins in South and Midwest Japan invades Manchuria
	National Origins Act establishes immigration quotas		Hoover imposes moratorium on war debts
	Coolidge is elected president	1932	Federal troops disperse Bonus Army marchers in Washington, DC
1928	Fifteen nations sign Kellogg-Briand Pact to "outlaw" war		Reconstruction Finance Corporation (RFC) lends to banks, railroads, insurance companies
	Herbert Hoover is elected president		Franklin Delano Roosevelt is elected president
1929	New York Stock Exchange crash ends big bull market; Great Depression begins	1933	Japan withdraws from League of Nations

Key Terms

Bonus Army A gathering of 20,000 Great War veterans in Washington, DC in June 1932, to demand immediate payment of their "adjusted compensation" bonuses voted by Congress in 1924. Congress rejected their demands, and President Hoover ordered U.S. troops to drive them from the capital, *679*

"good neighbor" President Herbert Hoover's policy to promote better relations between the United States and nations in the Western Hemisphere; it declared America's intention to disclaim the right to intervention pronounced in the **Platt Amendment** and the **Roosevelt Corollary**, *673*

Teapot Dome scandal A scandal during the administration of Warren Harding in which the Secretary of the Interior, Albert Fall, accepted bribes from oil companies that then leased the Teapot Dome federal oil reserve in Wyoming, *670*

Review Questions

1. The introduction draws a parallel between the crash of the stock market in 1929 and the U.S. mortgage market in 2008–2009 as explanations of subsequent economic crises. What were the main differences?
2. What were the similarities in the policies of Harding, Coolidge, and Hoover? The differences?
3. What factors explained the prosperity of the 1920s? In what ways was that prosperity shaky?
4. During the 1920s and early 1930s, what role did the United States play in Latin America? In the worsening situations in Europe and Asia?
5. How did the election of 1932 constitute a political "revolution"?

PEARSON myhistorylab Connections

Reinforce what you learned in this chapter by studying the many documents, images, maps, review tools, and videos available at **www.myhistorylab.com**.

Read and Review

✓• Study and Review *Chapter 25*

••• Read the Document Purinton, *Big Ideas from Big Business,* p. 667

••• Read the Document *Executive Orders and Senate Resolutions on Teapot Dome,* p. 667

• View the Image *A Heavy Load for Al (1928),* p. 675

• View the Image *Depression Breadlines in New York City,* p. 680

• View the Image *Burning Bonus Army Shacks, 1932,* p. 680

••• Read the Document Hoover, *New York Campaign Speech,* p. 682

Research and Explore

• Watch the Video *Prosperity of the 1920s and the Great Depression,* p. 678

((•• Hear the Audio

Hear the audio file for Chapter 25 at
www.myhistorylab.com.

Do you have health insurance?

In March 2010, Congress narrowly passed a major health reform law. It requires most employers to provide employees with health insurance and allows parents to extend coverage of their children to age twenty-six. It also creates a fund of nearly a trillion dollars to pay for health insurance for many people not covered by employer-paid policies until 2020.

President Barack Obama, who fought hard for this legislation, compared the battle to the one waged by

Franklin D. Roosevelt sixty-five years earlier over guaranteed incomes for the elderly. "When FDR proposed Social Security, he was accused of being a Socialist," Obama observed. Michelle Bachmann, a Republican congresswoman from Minnesota, opposed the health insurance proposal for that very reason: "If you look at FDR and Barack Obama, this is really the final leap to socialism." Ann Coulter, a conservative pundit who denounced the health insurance plan, went so far as to denounce Social

The New Deal: 1933–1941

26

((•—[Hear the Audio **Chapter 26 at www.myhistorylab.com**

■ Alexandre Hogue's *The Crucified Land* (1939) symbolizes the nation's plight during the Great Depression. Was FDR the new savior?

Security as an elaborate fraud that "would have landed its innovators in a secure federal prison" had they not been government officials.

President Franklin D. Roosevelt signed the Social Security Act in 1935, the cornerstone of his New Deal to counteract the Great Depression. Other New Deal initiatives sought to put the unemployed to work on government projects; to use federal funds to help farmers by raising the price of agricultural products; to reorganize banks, and to alter federal regulation of corporations.

These measures generated opposition. Conservatives regarded much of the New Deal as an unconstitutional infringement of private rights; populists and Marxists denounced the New Deal as a band-aid that failed to address the root causes of poverty. But times were bad. The nation, as Alexandre Hogue suggested in the accompanying painting, was in desperate trouble. Through it all, Roosevelt won the allegiance of voters who regarded him almost as an economic savior and the New Deal as gospel. ■

The Hundred Days

As the date of Franklin Roosevelt's inauguration approached, the banking system completely disintegrated. Starting in the rural West and spreading to major cities like Detroit and Baltimore, a financial panic swept the land. Depositors lined up before the doors of even the soundest institutions, desperate to withdraw their savings. Hundreds of banks were forced to close. In February, to check the panic, the governor of Michigan declared a "bank holiday," shutting every bank in the state for eight days. Maryland, Kentucky, California, and a number of other states followed suit; by inauguration day four-fifths of the states had suspended all banking operations. Other issues loomed, especially war clouds over Europe and east Asia, but few Americans could look much beyond their own immediate, and increasingly dire, economic prospects.

Something drastic had to be done. The most conservative business leaders were as ready for government intervention as the most advanced radicals. Partisanship, while not disappearing, was for once subordinated to broad national needs. A sign of this change came in February, even before Roosevelt took office, when Congress submitted to the states the Twenty-First Amendment, putting an end to prohibition. Before the end of the year the necessary three-quarters of the states had ratified it, and the prohibition era was over.

But it was unquestionably Franklin D. Roosevelt who provided the spark that reenergized the American people. His inaugural address reassured the

A 1933 banner celebrates the repeal of prohibition.

country and at the same time stirred it to action. "The only thing we have to fear is fear itself. . . . This Nation asks for action, and action now. . . . I assume unhesitatingly the leadership of this great army of our people. . . ." Many such lines punctuated the brief address, which concluded with a stern pledge: "In the event that Congress shall fail . . . I shall not evade the clear course of duty that will then confront me. I shall ask the Congress for the one remaining instrument to meet the crisis—broad Executive power to wage a war against the emergency."

The inaugural address captured the heart of the country; almost half a million letters of congratulation poured into the White House. When Roosevelt summoned Congress into a special session on March 9, the legislators outdid one another to enact his proposals into law. "I had as soon start a mutiny in the face of a foreign foe as . . . against the program of the President," one representative declared. In the following "hundred days" serious opposition, in the sense of an organized group committed to resisting the administration, simply did not exist.

Roosevelt had the power and the will to act but no comprehensive plan of action. He and his eager congressional collaborators proceeded in a dozen directions at once, sometimes wisely, sometimes not, often at cross-purposes with themselves and one another. One of the first administration measures was the Economy Act, which reduced the salaries of federal employees by 15 percent and cut various veterans' benefits. Such belt-tightening measures could only make the Depression worse. But most **New Deal** programs were designed to stimulate the economy. All in all, an impressive body of new legislation was placed on the statute books.

On March 5 Roosevelt declared a nationwide bank holiday and placed an embargo on the exportation of gold. To explain the complexities of the banking problem to the public, Roosevelt delivered the first of his "fireside chats" over a national radio network. "I want to talk for a few minutes with the people of the United States about banking," he explained. His warmth and steadiness reassured millions. A plan for reopening the banks under Treasury Department licenses was devised, and soon most of them were functioning again, public confidence in their solvency restored.

In April Roosevelt took the country off the gold standard, hoping thereby to cause prices to rise. Before the session ended, Congress established the Federal Deposit Insurance Corporation (FDIC) to guarantee bank deposits. It also forced the separation of investment banking and commercial banking concerns while extending the power of the Federal Reserve Board over both types of institutions, and it created the Home Owners Loan Corporation

(HOLC) to refinance mortgages and prevent foreclosures. It passed the Federal Securities Act requiring promoters to make public full financial information about new stock issues and giving the Federal Trade Commission the right to regulate such transactions.

Watch the Video *FDR's Inauguration* at **www.myhistorylab.com**

The National Recovery Administration (NRA)

Problems of unemployment and industrial stagnation had high priority during the hundred days Congress appropriated $500 million for relief of the needy, and it created the **Civilian Conservation Corps (CCC)** to provide jobs for men between the ages of eighteen and twenty-five in reforestation and other conservation projects. To stimulate industry, Congress passed one of its most controversial measures, the National Industrial Recovery Act (NIRA). Besides establishing the Public Works Administration with authority to spend $3.3 billion, this law permitted manufacturers to draw up industry-wide codes of "fair business practices." Under the law producers could agree to raise prices and limit production without violating the antitrust laws. The law gave workers the protection of minimum wage and maximum hours regulations and guaranteed them the right "to organize and bargain collectively through representatives of their own choosing," an immense stimulus to the union movement.

The NIRA was a variant on the idea of the corporate state. This concept envisaged a system of industry-wide organizations of capitalists and workers (supervised by the government) that would resolve conflicts internally, thereby avoiding wasteful economic competition and dangerous social clashes. It was an outgrowth of the trade association idea, although Hoover, who had supported voluntary associations, denounced it because of its compulsory aspects. It was also similar to experiments being carried out by the fascist dictator Benito Mussolini in Italy and by the Nazis in Adolf Hitler's Germany. It did not, of course, turn America into a fascist state, but it did herald an increasing concentration of economic power in the hands of interest groups, both industrialists' organizations and labor unions.

The act created a government agency, the **National Recovery Administration (NRA)**, to supervise the drafting and operation of the business codes. Drafting posed difficult problems, first because each industry insisted on tailoring the agreements to its special needs and second because most manufacturers were unwilling to accept all the provisions of Section 7a of the law, which guaranteed workers the right to unionize and bargain collectively. While thousands of employers agreed to the pledge "We Do Our Part" in order to receive the Blue Eagle symbol of NRA, many were more interested in the monopolistic aspects of the act than in boosting wages and encouraging unionization. In practice, the largest manufacturers in each industry drew up the codes.

The effects of the NIRA were both more and less than the designers of the system had intended. In a sense it tried to accomplish the impossible—to change the very nature of business ethics and control the everyday activities of millions of individual enterprises. At the practical level, it did not end the Depression. There was a brief upturn in the spring of 1933, but the expected revival of industry did not take place; in nearly every case the dominant producers in each industry used their power to raise prices and limit production rather than to hire more workers and increase output.

Beginning with the cotton textile code, however, the agreements succeeded in doing away with the centuries old problem of child labor in industry. They established the principle of federal regulation of wages and hours and led to the organization of thousands of workers, even in industries where unions had seldom been

Constance King and Mae Chinn hang an NRA poster—including a Chinese translation—encouraging shoppers to patronize businesses that adhered to the NRA guidelines.

significant. Within a year John L. Lewis's United Mine Workers expanded from 150,000 members to half a million. About 100,000 automobile workers joined unions, as did a comparable number of steelworkers.

Labor leaders used the NIRA to persuade workers that Roosevelt wanted them to join unions—which was something of an overstatement. In 1935, because the craft-oriented AFL had displayed little enthusiasm for enrolling unskilled workers on an industry-wide basis, John L. Lewis, together with officials of the garment trade unions, formed the Committee for Industrial Organization (CIO) and set out to rally workers in each of these mass-production industries into one union without regard for craft lines. Since a union containing all the workers in a factory was easier to organize and direct than separate craft unions, this was a far more effective way of unionizing factory labor. The AFL expelled these unions, however, and in 1938 the CIO became the Congress of Industrial Organizations. Soon it rivaled the AFL in size and importance.

View the Image *PWA in Action Poster* at
www.myhistorylab.com

The Agricultural Adjustment Administration (AAA)

Roosevelt was more concerned about the plight of the farmers than that of any other group because he believed that the nation was becoming overcommitted to industry. The Agricultural Adjustment Act of May 1933 combined compulsory restrictions on production with government payments to growers of wheat, cotton, tobacco, pork, and a few other staple crops. The money for these payments was raised by levying processing taxes on middlemen such as flour millers. The object was to lift agricultural prices to "parity" with industrial prices, the ratio in most cases being based on the levels of 1909–1914, when farmers had been reasonably prosperous. In return for withdrawing part of their land from cultivation, farmers received "rental" payments from the **Agricultural Adjustment Act (AAA)**.

Since the 1933 crops were growing when the law was passed, Secretary of Agriculture Henry A. Wallace, son of Harding's secretary of agriculture and himself an experienced farmer and plant geneticist, decided to pay farmers to destroy the crops in the field. Cotton planters plowed up 10 million acres, receiving $100 million in return. Six million baby pigs and 200,000 pregnant sows were slaughtered. Such ruthlessness appalled observers, particularly when they thought of the millions of hungry Americans who could have eaten all that pork. Thereafter, limitation of acreage proved sufficient to raise some agricultural

prices. Tobacco growers benefited, and so did those who raised corn and hogs. The price of wheat also rose, though more because of bad harvests than because of the AAA program. But dairy farmers and cattlemen were hurt by the law, as were the railroads (which had less freight to haul) and, of course, consumers. Many farmers insisted that the NRA was raising the cost of manufactured goods more than the AAA was raising the prices they received for their crops. "While the farmer is losing his pants to his creditors," one Iowan complained, "NRA is rolling up his shirt. [Soon] we'll have a nudist colony."

A far more serious weakness of the program was its effect on tenant farmers and sharecroppers, many of whom lost their livelihoods when owners took land out of production to obtain AAA payments. In addition many landowners substituted machinery for labor. In the Cotton Belt farmers purchased more than 100,000 tractors during the 1930s. Each could do the work of several tenant or sharecropping families. Yet acreage restrictions and mortgage relief helped thousands of others. The law was a remarkable attempt to bring order to the chaotic agricultural economy. One New Deal official called it "the greatest single experiment in economic planning under capitalist conditions ever attempted by a democracy in times of peace." This was an overstatement. The AAA was a drastic change of American policy, but foreign producers of coffee, sugar, tea, rubber, and other staples had adopted the same techniques of restricting output and subsidizing growers well before the United States did.

Read the Document *An Attack on New Deal Farm Policies* at
www.myhistorylab.com

The Dust Bowl

A protracted drought compounded the plight of the farmers, especially in dry sections of the Midwest. During the first third of the twentieth century, midwestern farmers perfected dryland techniques. This entailed "dragging" the fields after rainfall to improve absorption, raking them repeatedly to eliminate water-devouring weeds, and plowing the soil deeply and frequently to allow rain to sink in quickly. The use of tractors, combines, plows, and trucks during the 1920s made possible this intensive working of the fields. Farmers planted the driest areas in winter wheat, which required little moisture; in Nebraska and Iowa, most farmers planted corn.

Then came the dust storms. During the winter of 1933–1934, bitter cold killed off the winter wheat and heavy storms pulverized the soil. By March 1934 driving winds whipped across the Great Plains. In April storms from the Dakotas belched great clouds

A huge dust cloud engulfs Dodge City, Kansas in 1935.
Source: Kansas State Historical Society.

of dust through Nebraska and Kansas. In May, after the fields had been plowed, more windstorms scattered the seeds and topsoil.

The summer of 1934 was dry, especially in the Dakotas and western Kansas. These farmers were accustomed to dry weather, but the topsoil had been loosened through dryland farming. Strong winds scooped up the dried-out dirt and blew it in heaving clouds throughout the plains. Dust, forced into people's lungs, induced "dust pneumonia," a respiratory ailment that sometimes proved fatal.

The winds devastated wheat and corn. Over 30 percent of the crops in much of North Dakota, South Dakota, Nebraska, Kansas, and the Oklahoma panhandle failed. Two years later, another drought produced similar results. Coming in the midst of the Great Depression, this second calamity proved more than many farmers could bear. Tens of thousands abandoned their farms

The Tennessee Valley Authority (TVA)

Although Roosevelt could do little about the midwestern droughts, he did propose a major initiative to alter the economic infrastructure of the upper South. During the Great War the government had constructed a hydroelectric plant at Muscle Shoals, Alabama, to provide power for factories manufacturing synthetic nitrate explosives. After 1920 farm

groups and public power enthusiasts, led by Senator George W. Norris of Nebraska, had blocked administration plans to turn these facilities over to private capitalists, but their efforts to have the site operated by the government had been defeated by presidential vetoes.

During his first hundred days, Roosevelt proposed a **Tennessee Valley Authority (TVA)** to implement a broad experiment in social planning. Besides expanding the hydroelectric plants at Muscle Shoals and developing nitrate manufacturing in order to produce cheap fertilizers, he envisioned a coordinated program of soil conservation, reforestation, and industrialization.

Over the objections of private power companies, led by Wendell L. Willkie of the Commonwealth and Southern Corporation, Congress passed the TVA Act in May 1933. This law created a board authorized to build dams, power plants, and transmission lines and to sell fertilizers and electricity to individuals and local communities. The board could undertake flood control, soil conservation, and reforestation projects and improve the navigation of the river. Although the TVA never became the comprehensive regional planning organization some of its sponsors had anticipated, it improved the standard of living of millions of inhabitants of the valley. In addition to producing electricity and fertilizers and providing a "yardstick"

The Tennessee Valley Authority Although the Tennessee Valley Authority (TVA) never fully became the regional planning organization its sponsors had anticipated, the TVA nevertheless was able to expand the hydroelectric plants at Muscle Shoals, Alabama, and build dams, power plants, and transmission lines to service the surrounding area.

whereby the efficiency—and thus the rates—of private power companies could be tested, it took on other functions ranging from the eradication of malaria to the development of recreational facilities.

See the Map *The Tennessee Valley Authority* at www.myhistorylab.com

The New Deal Spirit

By the end of the hundred days the country had made up its mind about Roosevelt's New Deal, and despite the vicissitudes of the next decade, it never changed it. A large majority labeled the New Deal a solid success. Considerable recovery had taken place, but more basic was the fact that Roosevelt, recruiting an army of officials to staff the new government agencies, had infused his administration with a spirit of bustle and optimism. The director of the presidential Secret Service unit, returning to the White House on inauguration day after escorting Herbert Hoover to the railroad station, found the executive mansion "transformed during my absence into a gay place, full of people who oozed confidence."

Although Roosevelt was not much of an intellectual, his openness to suggestion made him eager to draw on the ideas and energies of experts of all sorts. New Deal agencies soon teemed with college professors and young lawyers without political experience.

The New Deal lacked any consistent ideological base. While the so-called Brain Trust (a group headed by Raymond Moley, a Columbia political scientist, which included Columbia economists

Rexford G. Tugwell and Adolf A. Berle Jr., and a number of others) attracted a great deal of attention, theorists never impressed Roosevelt much. His New Deal drew on the old populist tradition, as seen in its antipathy to bankers and its willingness to adopt schemes for inflating the currency; on the New Nationalism of Theodore Roosevelt, in its dislike of competition and its de-emphasis of the antitrust laws; and on the ideas of social workers trained in the Progressive Era. Techniques developed by the Wilsonians also found a place in the system: Louis D. Brandeis had considerable influence on Roosevelt's financial reforms, and New Deal labor policy was an outgrowth of the experience of the War Labor Board of 1917–1918.

Within the administrative maze that Roosevelt created, rival bureaucrats battled to enforce their views. The "spenders," led by Tugwell, clashed with those favoring strict economy, who gathered around Lewis Douglas, director of the budget. Roosevelt mediated between the factions. Washington became a battleground for dozens of special interest groups: the Farm Bureau Federation, the unions, the trade associations, and the silver miners. While the system was superior to that of Roosevelt's predecessors—who had allowed one interest, big business, to predominate—it slighted the unorganized majority. The NRA aimed frankly at raising the prices paid by consumers of manufactured goods; the AAA processing tax came ultimately from the pocketbooks of ordinary citizens.

Table 26.1 First New Deal and First Hundred Days (March–June, 1933)

Legislation	Purpose
Banking Act	Provided federal loans to private bankers
Beer-Wine Revenue Act	Repealed Prohibition
Civilian Conservation Corps (CCC)	Created jobs for unemployed young men
Federal Emergency Relief Act (FERA)	Gave federal money to states and localities to provide relief of poor
Agricultural Adjustment Act (AAA)	Raised farm prices by restricting production
Tennessee Valley Authority (TVA)	Massive construction project that generated employment—and electricity—in Tennessee Valley
National Industrial Recovery Act (NIRA)	Created structure for business and labor to cooperate to make particular industries more profitable

The Unemployed

At least 9 million persons were still without work in 1934 and hundreds of thousands of them were in real need. Malcolm Little, later famous as the radical black leader, Malcolm X, recalled 1934 as the worst year of the Great Depression. Then nine, he never had enough to eat. He and his friends would hang out near a bakery, where they could buy a sack of day-old bread and cookies for a nickel. But often, failing to scrape together even a nickel, they went without food all day. Then his mother pulled up some dandelions, boiled them in a pot, and served them for dinner.

Yet the Democrats confounded the political experts, including their own, by increasing their already large majorities in both houses of Congress in the 1934 elections. All the evidence indicates that most of the jobless continued to support the administration. Their loyalty can best be explained by Roosevelt's unemployment policies.

In May 1933 Congress had established the Federal Emergency Relief Administration (FERA) and given it $500 million to be dispensed through state relief organizations. Roosevelt appointed Harry L. Hopkins, an eccentric but brilliant and dedicated social worker, to direct the FERA. Hopkins insisted that the unemployed needed jobs, not handouts. In November he persuaded Roosevelt to create the Civil Works Administration (CWA) and swiftly put 4 million people to work building and repairing roads and public buildings, teaching, decorating the walls of post offices with

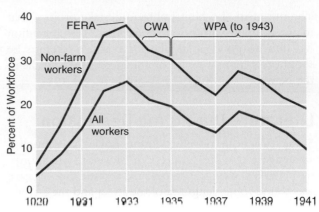

Unemployment and Federal Action, 1929–1941 Unemployment of nonfarm workers reached nearly 40 percent by early 1933. The Federal Emergency Relief Act (FERA) and Civil Works Administration (CWA) (both in 1933) and the Works Progress Administration (WPA) (1935) put millions back to work.

murals, and utilizing their special skills in dozens of other ways.

The cost of this program frightened Roosevelt—Hopkins spent about $1 billion in less than five months—and he soon abolished the CWA. But an extensive public works program was continued throughout 1934 under the FERA. Despite charges that many of the projects were "boondoggles," thousands of roads, bridges, schools, and other structures were built or refurbished.

In May 1935 Roosevelt put Hopkins in charge of the **Works Progress Administration (WPA)**. By the time this agency was disbanded in 1943 it had found employment for 8.5 million people. Besides building public works, the WPA made important cultural contributions. It developed the Federal Theatre Project, which put actors, directors, and stagehands to work; the Federal Writers' Project, which turned out valuable guidebooks, collected local lore, and published about 1,000 books and pamphlets; and the Federal Art Project, which employed painters and sculptors. In addition, the National Youth Administration created part-time jobs for more than 2 million high school and college students.

At no time during the New Deal years did unemployment fall below 10 percent of the workforce, and in some places it was much higher. Unemployment in Boston, for instance, ranged between 20 and 30 percent throughout the 1930s. The WPA did not go far enough, chiefly because Roosevelt could not escape his fear of drastically unbalancing the budget. Halfway measures did not stimulate the economy.

Isaac Soyer's *Employment Agency* (1937) captured the isolation and loss of self-esteem that accompanied joblessness.

Source: Isaac Soyer (1907–1981), *Employment Agency*, 1937, Oil on canvas, 34 ¼ × 45 in. (87 × 114.3 cm.). Collection of the Whitney Museum of American Art, New York.

The president also hesitated to undertake projects that might compete with private enterprises. Yet his caution did him no good politically; the business interests he sought to placate were becoming increasingly hostile to the New Deal.

Literature During the Depression

Some American novelists found Soviet communism attractive and wrote "proletarian" novels in which ordinary workers were the heroes, and stylistic niceties gave way to the rough language of the street and the factory. Most of these books are of little artistic merit, and none achieved great commercial success. The best of the Depression writers avoided the party line, although they were critical of many aspects of American life.

One was John Dos Passos, author of the trilogy *U.S.A.* (1930–1936), a massive, intricately constructed work with an anti-capitalist and deeply pessimistic point of view. It portrayed American society between 1900 and 1930 in broad perspective, interweaving the stories of five major characters and a galaxy of lesser figures.

Dos Passos's method was relentless, cold, and methodical—utterly realistic. He displayed no sympathy for his characters or their world. *U.S.A.* was a monument to the despair and anger of liberals confronted with the Depression. After the Depression, however, Dos Passos rapidly abandoned his radical views.

The novel that best portrayed the desperate plight of the millions impoverished by the Depression was John Steinbeck's *The Grapes of Wrath* (1939), which described the fate of the Joads, an Oklahoma farm family driven by drought and bad times to abandon their land and become migratory laborers in California. Steinbeck captured the patient bewilderment of the downtrodden, the brutality bred of fear that characterized their exploiters, and the furious resentments of the radicals of the 1930s. He depicted the parching blackness of the Oklahoma dust bowl, the grandeur of California, the backbreaking toil of the migrant fruit pickers, and the ultimate indignation of a people repeatedly degraded: "In the eyes of the hungry there is a growing wrath. In the souls of the people the grapes of wrath are filling and growing heavy, growing heavy for the vintage."

Like so many other writers of the 1930s, Steinbeck was an angry man. "There is a crime here that goes beyond denunciation," he wrote. He had the compassion that Dos Passos lacked, and this quality raised *The Grapes of Wrath* to the level of great tragedy. In other works, such as *Tortilla Flat* (1935) and *The Long Valley* (1938), Steinbeck described the life of California cannery workers and ranchers with moving warmth without becoming overly sentimental.

William Faulkner, probably the finest American novelist of the era, responded in still another way. Born in 1897, within a year of Fitzgerald and Hemingway, he attained literary maturity only in the 1930s. Suddenly, between 1929 and 1932, he burst into prominence with four major novels: *The Sound and the Fury, As I Lay Dying, Sanctuary,* and *Light in August.*

No contemporary excelled him as a commentator on the multiple dilemmas of life. His characters are possessed, driven to pursue high ideals yet weighted down with awareness of their inadequacies and their sinfulness. They are imprisoned in their surroundings however they may strive to escape them.

Faulkner was essentially a pessimist. His characters continually experience emotions too intense to be bearable, often too profound and too subtle for the natures he had given them. Nevertheless his stature was beyond question, and unlike so many other novelists of the period he maintained a high level in his later years.

Three Extremists: Long, Coughlin, and Townsend

Roosevelt's moderation and the desperation of the poor roused extremists both on the left and on the right. The most formidable was Louisiana's Senator Huey Long, the "Kingfish." Raised on a farm in northern Louisiana, Long was successively a traveling salesman, a lawyer, state railroad commissioner, governor, and, after 1930, U.S. senator. By 1933 his rule in Louisiana was absolute. Long was certainly a demagogue—yet the plight of all poor people concerned him deeply. More important, he tried to do something about it.

Long did not question segregation or white supremacy, nor did he suggest that Louisiana blacks should be allowed to vote. He used the word *nigger* with total unselfconsciousness, even when addressing northern black leaders. But he treated black-baiters with scathing contempt.

As a reformer, Long stood in the populist tradition; he hated bankers and "the interests." He believed that poor people, regardless of color, should have a chance to earn a decent living and get an education. His arguments were simplistic, patronizing, possibly insincere, but effective. "Don't say I'm working for niggers," he told one northern journalist. "I'm for the poor man— all poor men. Black and white, they all gotta have a chance. . . . 'Every Man a King'—that's my slogan."

Raffish, totally unrestrained, yet shrewd—a fellow southern politician called him "the smartest lunatic I ever saw"—Long had supported the New Deal at the start. But partly because he thought Roosevelt too conservative and partly because of his own ambition, he soon broke with the administration. While Roosevelt was probably more hostile to the big financiers than to any other interest, Long denounced him as "a phoney" and a stooge of Wall Street. "I can take him," he boasted in a typical sally.

"His mother's watching him, and she won't let him go too far, but I ain't got no mother left, and if I had, she'd think anything I said was all right."

By 1935 Long's "Share Our Wealth" movement had a membership of over 4.6 million. His program called for the confiscation of family fortunes of more than $5 million and a tax of 100 percent on incomes over $1 million a year, the money to be used to buy every family a "homestead" (a house, a car, and other necessities) and provide an annual family income of $2,000 to $3,000, plus old-age pensions, educational benefits, and veterans' pensions. As the 1936 election approached, he planned to organize a third party to split the liberal vote. He assumed that the Republicans would win the election and so botch the job of fighting the Depression that he could sweep the country in 1940.

Less powerful than Long but more widely influential was Father Charles E. Coughlin, the "Radio Priest." A genial Canadian of Irish lineage, Coughlin in 1926 began broadcasting a weekly religious message over station WJR in Detroit. His mellifluous voice rhetoric attracted a huge national audience, and the Depression gave him a secular cause. In 1933 he had been an eager New Dealer, but his dislike of New Deal financial policies—he believed that inflating the currency would end the Depression—and his need for ever more sensational ideas to hold his radio audience led him to turn against the New Deal. By 1935 he was calling Roosevelt a "great betrayer and liar."

Although Coughlin's National Union for Social Justice was especially appealing to Catholics, it attracted people of every faith, particularly in the lower-middle-class districts of the big cities. Some of his talks caused

more than a million people to send him messages of congratulation; contributions amounting to $500,000 a year flooded his headquarters. Coughlin attacked bankers, New Deal planners, Roosevelt's farm program, and the alleged sympathy of the administration for communists and Jews, both of which Coughlin denounced in his weekly talks. His program resembled fascism more than any leftist philosophy, but he posed a threat, especially in combination with Long, to the continuation of Democratic rule.

Another rapidly growing movement alarmed the Democrats in 1934–1935: Dr. Francis E. Townsend's campaign for "old-age revolving pensions." Townsend, a retired California physician, colorless and low-keyed, had an oversimplified and therefore appealing "solution" to the nation's troubles. The pitiful state of thousands of elderly persons, whose job prospects were even dimmer than those of the mass of the unemployed, he found shocking. He advocated paying every person aged sixty years and over a pension of $200 a month, the only conditions being that the pensioners not hold jobs and that they spend the entire sum within thirty days. Their purchases, he argued, would stimulate production, thereby creating new jobs and revitalizing the economy. A stiff transactions tax, collected whenever any commodity changed hands, would pay for the program.

Economists quickly pointed out that with about 10 million persons eligible for the Townsend pensions, the cost would amount to $24 billion a year—roughly half the national income. But among the elderly the scheme proved extremely popular. Townsend Clubs, their proceedings conducted in the spirit of revivalist camp meetings, flourished everywhere, and the *Townsend National Weekly* reached a circulation of over 200,000. Although most Townsendites were anything but radical politically, their plan, like Long's Share Our Wealth scheme, would have revolutionized the distribution of wealth in the country. The movement marked the emergence of a new force in American society. With medical advances lengthening the average life span, the percentage of old people in the population was rising. The breakdown of close family ties in an increasingly mobile society now caused many of these citizens to be cast adrift to live out their last years poor, sick, idle, and alone.

With the possible exception of Long, the extremists had little understanding of practical affairs. (It could be said that Townsend knew what to do with money but not how to get it, and Coughlin knew how to

Charles E. Coughlin, the "Radio Priest," was the father of conservative "talk radio."

get money but not what to do with it.) Collectively they represented a threat to Roosevelt; their success helped to make the president see that he must move boldly to restore good times or face serious political trouble in 1936.

Political imperatives had much to do with Roosevelt's decisions, and the influence of Justice Brandeis and his disciples, notably Felix Frankfurter, was great. They urged Roosevelt to abandon his probusiness programs, especially the NRA, and stress restoring competition and taxing corporations more heavily. The fact that most businessmen were turning away from him encouraged the president to accept this advice; so did the Supreme Court's decision in *Schecter v. United States* (May 1935), which declared the National Industrial Recovery Act unconstitutional. (The case involved the provisions of the NRA Live Poultry Code; the Court voided the act on the grounds that Congress had delegated too much legislative power to the code authorities and that the defendants, four brothers engaged in slaughtering chickens in New York City, were not engaged in interstate commerce.)

Read the **Document** Coughlin, *A Third Party (1936)* at **www.myhistorylab.com**

The Second New Deal

Existing laws had failed to end the Depression. Conservatives roundly denounced Roosevelt, and extremists were luring away some of his supporters. Voters, heartened by the partial success of early New Deal measures, were clamoring for further reforms. But the Supreme Court had declared many key New Deal measures unconstitutional. For these many reasons, Roosevelt, in June 1935, launched what historians call the Second New Deal.

There followed the "second hundred days," one of the most productive periods in the history of American legislation. The National Labor Relations Act—commonly known as the **Wagner Act**—restored the labor guarantees wiped out by the *Schechter* decision. It gave workers the right to bargain collectively and prohibited employers from interfering with union organizational activities in their factories. A National Labor Relations Board (NLRB) was established to supervise plant elections and designate successful unions as official bargaining agents when a majority of the workers approved. It was difficult to force some big corporations to bargain "in good faith," as the law required, but the NLRB could conduct investigations of employer practices and issue cease and desist orders when "unfair" activities came to light.

The **Social Security Act** of August 1935 set up a system of old-age insurance, financed partly by a tax on wages (paid by workers) and partly by a tax on payrolls (paid by employers). It created a state-federal system of unemployment insurance, similarly financed. Liberal critics considered this Social Security system inadequate because it did not cover agricultural workers, domestics, self-employed persons, and some other groups particularly in need of its benefits. Health insurance was not included, and because the size of pensions depended on the amount earned, the lowest-paid workers could not count on much support after reaching sixty-five. Yet the law was of major significance. Over the years the pension payments were increased and the classes of workers covered expanded.

The Rural Electrification Administration (REA), created by executive order, also began to function during this remarkable period. The REA lent money at low interest rates to utility companies and to farmer cooperatives interested in bringing electricity to rural areas. When the REA went into operation, only one farm in ten had electricity; by 1950 only one in ten did not.

Another important measure was the Wealth Tax Act of August 1935, which, while not the "soak the rich" measure both its supporters and its opponents claimed, raised taxes on large incomes considerably. Estate and gift taxes were also increased. Stiffer taxes

Monopoly, patented in 1935, was an instant best-seller: Players risk all their assets in an attempt to secure a real estate monopoly—and thus great wealth.

Table 26.2 Second New Deal (1935–1938)

Legislation	Purpose
Emergency Relief Appropriations Act (1935)	Created Works Progress Administration (WPA) to give jobs to blacks, white-collar workers, and even artists and writers
Rural Electrification Administration (1935)	Extended electric power lines to rural areas
Social Security Act (1935)	Devised system to provide unemployment insurance and pensions for elderly
Wagner Act (1935)	Guaranteed the rights of unions to organize and negotiate for members
Fair Labor Standards Act (1938)	Set minimum hourly wages and maximum hours of work

on corporate profits reflected the Brandeis group's desire to penalize corporate giantism. Much of the opposition to other New Deal legislation arose from the fact that after these changes in the tax laws were made, the well-to-do had to bear a larger share of the cost of *all* government activities.

Whether the Second New Deal was more radical than the first depends largely on the vantage point from which it is considered. Measures like the Social Security Act had greater long-range effect on American life than the legislation of the first hundred days but were fundamentally less revolutionary than laws like the National Industrial Recovery Act and the Agricultural Adjustment Act, which attempted to establish a planned economy.

Herbert Hoover epitomized the attitude of conservatives when he called the New Deal "the most stupendous invasion of the whole spirit of Liberty that the nation has witnessed." Undoubtedly many opponents of the New Deal sincerely believed that it was undermining the foundations of American freedom. The cost of the New Deal also alarmed them. By 1936 some members of the administration had fallen under the influence of the British economist John Maynard Keynes, who argued that the world Depression could be conquered if governments would deliberately unbalance their budgets by reducing interest rates and taxes and by increasing expenditures to stimulate consumption and investment.

Roosevelt never accepted Keynes's theories; he conferred with the economist in 1934 but could not grasp the "rigmarole of figures" with which Keynes deluged him. Nevertheless the imperatives of the Depression forced him to spend more than the government was collecting in taxes; thus he adopted in part the Keynesian approach. Conservative businessmen considered him financially irresponsible, and the fact that deficit spending seemed to be good politics made them seethe with rage.

The Election of 1936

The election of 1936 loomed as a showdown. "America is in peril," the Republican platform declared. The GOP candidate, Governor Alfred M. Landon of Kansas, was a former follower of Theodore Roosevelt, a foe of the Ku Klux Klan in the 1920s, and a believer in government regulation of business. But he was a poor speaker, colorless, and handicapped by the reactionary views of many of his backers. Against the charm and political astuteness of Roosevelt, Landon's arguments—chiefly that he could administer the government more efficiently than the president—made little impression. He won the support of some anti-New Deal Democrats, among them two former presidential candidates, Al Smith and John W. Davis, but this was not enough.

On election day the country gave the president a tremendous vote of confidence. He carried every state but Maine and Vermont. The Republicans elected only eighty-nine members of the House of Representatives and their strength in the Senate fell to sixteen, an all-time low. In dozens of city and state elections, Democratic candidates also made large gains. Both Roosevelt's personality and his program had captivated the land. He seemed irresistible, the most powerfully entrenched president in the history of the United States.

Roosevelt did not win in 1936 because of the inadequacies of his foes. Having abandoned his efforts to hold the businessmen, whom he now denounced as "economic royalists," he appealed for the votes of workers and the underprivileged. The new labor unions gratefully poured thousands of dollars into the campaign to reelect him. Black voters switched to the Democrats in record numbers. Farmers liked Roosevelt because of his evident concern for their welfare: When the Supreme Court declared the Agricultural Adjustment Act unconstitutional (*United States v. Butler*, 1936), he immediately rushed through a new law, the Soil Conservation and Domestic Allotment Act, which accomplished the same objective by paying farmers to divert land from commercial crops to soil-building plants like clover and soybeans. Countless elderly persons backed Roosevelt out of gratitude for the Social Security Act.

●●●┌**Read** the **Document** FDR, *Fireside Chat* at
www.myhistorylab.com

Roosevelt Tries to Undermine the Supreme Court

On January 20, in his second inaugural address, Roosevelt spoke of the plight of millions of citizens "denied the greater part of what the very lowest standards of today call the necessities of life." A third of the nation, he added without exaggeration, was "ill-housed, ill-clad, ill-nourished." He interpreted his landslide victory as a mandate for further reforms, and with his prestige and his immense congressional majorities, nothing appeared to stand in his way. Nothing, that is, except the Supreme Court.

Throughout Roosevelt's first term the Court had stood almost immovable against increasing the scope of federal authority and broadening the general power of government, state as well as national, to cope with the exigencies of the Depression. Of the nine justices, only Louis Brandeis, Benjamin N. Cardozo, and Harlan Fiske Stone viewed the New Deal sympathetically. Four others—James C. McReynolds, Willis Van Devanter, Pierce Butler, and George Sutherland—were intransigent conservatives. Chief Justice Charles Evans Hughes and Justice Owen J. Roberts, while more open-minded, tended to side with the conservatives on many questions.

Much of the early New Deal legislation, pushed through Congress at top speed during the hundred days, had been drafted without proper regard for the Constitution. Even the liberal justices considered the National Industrial Recovery Act unconstitutional (the *Schechter* decision was unanimous).

In 1937 all the major measures of the second hundred days appeared doomed. The Wagner Act had little chance of winning approval, experts predicted. Lawyers were advising employers to ignore the Social Security Act, so confident that the Court would declare it unconstitutional.

Faced with this situation, Roosevelt decided to ask Congress to shift the balance on the Court by increasing the number of justices, thinly disguising the purpose of his plan by making it part of a general reorganization of the judiciary. A member of the Court who reached the age of seventy would have the option of retiring at full pay. Should such a justice choose not to retire, the president was to appoint an additional justice, up to a maximum of six, to ease the burden of work for the aged jurists who remained on the bench.

Roosevelt knew that this measure would run into resistance, but he expected that the huge Democratic majorities in Congress could override any opposition and that the public would back him solidly. No astute politician had erred so badly in estimating the effects of an action since Stephen A. Douglas introduced the Kansas-Nebraska bill in 1854.

Although polls showed the public fairly evenly divided on the "court-packing" bill, the opposition was vocal and influential. To the expected denunciations of conservatives were added the complaints of liberals fearful that the principle of court packing might in the future be used to subvert civil liberties. What, Senator Norris asked, would have been the reaction if a man like Harding had proposed such a measure? Opposition in Congress was immediate and intense; many who had cheerfully supported every New Deal bill came out against the plan. The press denounced it, and so did most local bar associations. Chief Justice Hughes released a devastating critique; even the liberal Brandeis—the oldest judge on the court—rejected the bill out of hand.

For months Roosevelt stubbornly refused to concede defeat, but in July 1937 he had to yield. Minor administrative reforms of the judiciary were enacted, but the size of the Court remained unchanged.

The struggle did result in saving the legislation of the Second New Deal. Alarmed by the threat to the Court, Justices Hughes and Roberts, never entirely committed to the conservative position, beat a strategic retreat on a series of specific issues. While the debate was raging in Congress, they sided with the liberals in upholding first a minimum wage law of the state of Washington that was little different from a New York act the Court had recently rejected, then the Wagner Act, and then the Social Security Act. In May Justice Van Devanter retired and Roosevelt replaced him with Senator Hugo Black of Alabama, a New Dealer. The conservative justices thereupon gave up the fight, and soon Roosevelt was able to appoint enough new judges to give the Court a large pro-New Deal majority. No further measure of significance was declared unconstitutional during his presidency. The Court fight hurt Roosevelt severely. His prestige never fully recovered. Conservative Democrats who had feared to oppose him because of his supposedly invulnerable popularity took heart and began to join with the Republicans on key issues. When the president summoned a special session of Congress in November 1937 and submitted a program of "must" legislation, not one of his bills was passed.

The New Deal Winds Down

The Court fight marked the beginning of the end of the New Deal. With unemployment high, wages low, and workers relatively powerless against their employers, most Americans had liked New Deal labor legislation and sympathized with the industrial unions whose growth it stimulated. The NRA, the Wagner Act, and the CIO's organization of industries like steel and automobiles changed the power structure within the economy. What amounted to a revolution in the lives of wage earners had occurred. Aside from the obvious changes—higher wages, shorter hours, paid vacations, insurance of various kinds—unionization had meant fair methods of settling disputes about work practices and a measure of job security based on seniority for tens of thousands of workers. The CIO in particular had done much to increase the influence of labor in politics and to bring blacks and other minorities into the labor movement.

In 1937 a series of "sit-down strikes" broke out, beginning at the General Motors plant in Flint, Michigan. Striking workers barricaded themselves inside the factories; when police and strikebreakers tried to dislodge them, they drove them off with barrages of soda bottles, tools, spare parts, and crockery. The tolerant attitude of the Roosevelt administration ensured the strikers against government intervention. "It is illegal," Roosevelt said of the General Motors strike, "but shooting it out . . . [is not] the answer.. . . Why can't those fellows in General Motors meet with the committee of workers?" Fearful that all-out efforts to clear their plants would result in the destruction of expensive machinery, most employers capitulated to the workers' demands. All the automobile manufacturers but Henry Ford quickly came to terms with the United Automobile Workers.

The major steel companies, led by U.S. Steel, recognized the CIO and granted higher wages and a forty-hour week. The auto and steel unions alone boasted more than 725,000 members by late 1937; other CIO units conquered the rubber industry, the electrical industry, the textile industry, and many more.

These gains and the aggressive way in which the unions pursued their objectives gave many members of the middle class second thoughts concerning the justice of labor's demands. Sit-down strikes, the disregard of unions for the "rights" of nonunion workers, and the violence that accompanied some strikes seemed to many not merely unreasonable but also a threat to social order. The enthusiasm of such people for all reform cooled rapidly.

While the sit-down strikes and the Court fight were going on, the New Deal suffered another heavy blow. Business conditions had been gradually improving since 1933. Heartened by the trend, Roosevelt, who had never fully grasped the importance of government spending in stimulating recovery, cut back sharply on the relief program in June 1937, with disastrous results. Between August and October the economy slipped downward like sand through a chute. Stock prices plummeted; unemployment rose by 2 million; industrial production slumped. This "Roosevelt recession" further damaged the president's reputation, and for many months he aggravated the situation by

adopting an almost Hoover-like attitude. "Everything will work out all right if we just sit tight and keep quiet," he actually said.

While the president hesitated, rival theorists within his administration warred. The Keynesians, led by WPA head Harry Hopkins, Marriner Eccles of the Federal Reserve, and Secretary of the Interior Harold Ickes, clamored for stepped-up government spending. The conservatives, led by Treasury Secretary Henry Morgenthau Jr., advocated retrenchment. Perhaps confused by the conflict, Roosevelt seemed incapable of decisive action.

In April 1938 Roosevelt again committed himself to heavy deficit spending. At his urging Congress passed a $3.75 billion public works bill. Two major pieces of legislation were also enacted at about this time. A new AAA program (February 1938) set marketing quotas and acreage limitations for growers of staples like wheat, cotton, and tobacco and authorized the Commodity Credit Corporation to lend money to farmers on their surplus crops.

The second measure, the Fair Labor Standards Act, abolished child labor and established a national minimum wage of 40 cents an hour and a maximum workweek of 40 hours, with time and a half for overtime. Although the law failed to cover many of the poorest-paid types of labor, its passage meant wage increases for 750,000 workers. In later years many more classes of workers were brought within its protection, and the minimum wage was repeatedly increased.

These measures further alienated conservatives without dramatically improving economic conditions. The resistance of many Democratic members of Congress to additional economic and social "experiments" hardened. As the 1938 elections approached, Roosevelt decided to go to the voters in an effort to strengthen party discipline and reenergize the New Deal. He singled out a number of conservative Democratic senators, notably Walter F. George of Georgia, Millard F. Tydings of Maryland, and "Cotton Ed" Smith of South Carolina, and tried to "purge" them by backing other Democrats in the primaries.

The purge failed. Southern voters liked Roosevelt but resented his interference in local politics. Smith dodged the issue of liberalism by stressing the question of white supremacy. Tydings emphasized Roosevelt's "invasion" of Maryland. In Georgia the president's enemies compared his campaign against George to General Sherman's march across the state during the Civil War. All three senators were easily renominated and then reelected in November. In the nation at large the Republicans made important gains for the first time since Roosevelt had taken office. The Democrats maintained nominal control of both houses of Congress, but the conservative coalition, while unable

The 1937 poster advertises the spread of electricity to rural parts of the nation, one of the many building programs of the New Deal. Indisputably, the New Deal visibly changed the nation; but did it succeed in reviving the economy?

Few issues in the nation's history have been more controversial. At the time and for decades afterward conservative historians such as Edgar E. Robinson denounced the New Deal as an economic failure that infringed on individual rights. Most liberals—foremost among them Arthur M. Schlesinger, Jr. (1957–1960)—acknowledged that the New Deal did not end the Depression but it did restrain corporations and address the needs of most workers, farmers, and consumers. That such people benefited from its actions was proven by how many of them voted for FDR, time and again.

William Leuchtenburg (1963) approved of much of the New Deal, but claimed that it left sharecroppers, slum dwellers, and most blacks "outside of the new equilibrium." It was but a "halfway revolution." A few years later Barton Bernstein (1968) led the far left in a blistering attack: "The New Deal failed to solve the problem of depression, it failed to raise the impoverished, it failed to redistribute income, it failed to extend equality and generally countenanced racial discrimination and segregation." The New Deal, in short, was no revolution at all.

In subsequent decades historians were more inclined to assess the New Deal in light of what was possible at the time. David Kennedy (1999), while acknowledging the New Deal's many failures, was struck by the "the boldness of its vision."

The financial crisis that hit in 2008 and 2009, triggered by inadequate government supervision of mortgage lending and complicated financial investments, caused many historians to champion the regulatory initiatives of the New Deal.

A 1937 poster shows the impact of electrification projects on remote farm homes.

Source: Edgar E. Robinson, *The Roosevelt Leadership* (1955); Arthur M. Schlesinger Jr., *The Age of Roosevelt*, 3 volumes (1957–1960); William Leuchtenburg, *Franklin D. Roosevelt and the New Deal, 1932–1940* (1963); Barton Bernstein, *Towards a New Past* (1968); David M. Kennedy, *Freedom from Fear* (1999).

■ ■ ■ ■ ■

to muster the votes to do away with accomplished reforms, succeeded in blocking additional legislation.

Significance of the New Deal

After World War II broke out in 1939, the Great Depression was swept away on a wave of orders from the beleaguered European democracies. For this prosperity, Roosevelt received much undeserved credit. His New Deal had not returned the country to full employment. Despite the aid given to the jobless, the generation of workers born between 1900 and 1910 who entered the 1930s as unskilled laborers had their careers permanently stunted by the Depression.

Far fewer rose to middle-class status than at any time since the 1830s and 1840s.

Roosevelt's willingness to experiment with different means of combating the Depression made sense because no one really knew what to do; however, his uncertainty about the ultimate objectives of the New Deal was counterproductive. He vacillated between seeking to stimulate the economy by deficit spending and trying to balance the budget, between a narrow "America first" economic nationalism and a broad-gauged international approach, between regulating monopolies and trust-busting, and between helping the underprivileged and bolstering those already strong. At times he acted on the assumptions that the

To hold back immense volumes of water, the Hoover Dam, seen from above, consisted of 2.5 million cubic yards of concrete which, at the base, was thicker than two football fields set end-to-end.

United States had a "mature" economy and that the major problem was overproduction. At other times he appeared to think that the answer to the Depression was more production. He could never make up his mind whether to try to rally liberals to his cause without regard for party or to run the government as a partisan leader, conciliating the conservative Democrats.

Roosevelt's fondness for establishing new agencies to deal with specific problems vastly increased the federal bureaucracy, indirectly added to the influence of lobbyists, and made it more difficult to monitor government activities. His cavalier attitude toward constitutional limitations on executive power, which he justified as being necessary in a national emergency, set in motion trends that so increased the prestige and authority of the presidency that the balance among the executive, legislative, and judicial branches was threatened.

Yet these are criticisms after the fact. By 1939 the country was committed to the idea that the federal government should accept responsibility for the national welfare and act to meet specific problems in every necessary way. What was most significant was not the proliferation of new agencies or the expansion of federal power. These were continuations of trends already a century old when the New Deal began. The importance of the "Roosevelt revolution" was that it removed the issue from politics. "Never again," the Republican presidential candidate was to say in 1952, "shall we allow a depression in the United States."

Because of New Deal decisions, many formerly unregulated areas of American life became subject to federal authority: the stock exchange, agricultural prices and production, labor relations, old-age pensions, relief of the needy. By encouraging the growth of unions, the New Deal probably helped workers obtain a larger share of the profits of industry. By putting a floor under the income of many farmers, it checked the decline of agricultural living standards, though not that of the agricultural population. The Social Security program, with all its inadequacies, lessened the impact of bad times on an increasingly large proportion of the population and provided immense psychological benefits to all.

Watch the Video *Responding to the Great Depression: What New Deal?* at **www.myhistorylab.com**

Women as New Dealers: The Network

Largely because of the influence of Eleanor Roosevelt and Molly Dewson, head of the Women's Division of the Democratic National Committee, the Roosevelt administration employed far more women in positions of importance than any earlier one. Secretary of Labor Frances Perkins, the first woman appointed to a Cabinet post, had been active in labor relations for more than twenty years, as secretary of the Consumers' League during the progressive period, as a factory inspector immediately after the Great War, and as chair of the New York State Industrial Commission. As secretary of labor she helped draft New Deal labor legislation and kept Roosevelt informed on various labor problems outside the government.

In addition to Perkins, there were dozens of other women New Dealers. Dewson and Eleanor Roosevelt headed an informal but effective "network"—women in key posts who were always seeking to place reform-minded women in government jobs.

Through her newspaper column "My Day" and as a speaker on public issues, Eleanor Roosevelt became a major political force, especially in the area of civil rights, where the administration needed constant prodding.

She particularly identified with efforts to obtain better treatment for blacks, in and out of government. Her best-known action occurred in 1939 after the Daughters of the American Revolution (DAR) refused to permit the use of their Washington auditorium for a concert by the black contralto Marian Anderson. Eleanor Roosevelt resigned from the DAR in protest, and after the president arranged for Anderson to sing at the Lincoln Memorial, she persuaded a small army of dignitaries to sponsor the concert. An interracial crowd of 75,000 people attended the performance. The *Chicago Defender*, an influential black newspaper, noted that the First Lady "stood like the Rock of Gibraltar against pernicious encroachments on the rights of minorities." (A disgruntled white

Eleanor Roosevelt dispenses soup to the needy. As a wealthy young socialite, she exhibited little interest in public matters. But after she discovered that Franklin was having an affair with her own social secretary, Lucy Mercer, Eleanor began to change. Her marriage, she confided to a friend, ceased to have any "fundamental love to draw on." She found new purpose by throwing herself into social and political reform.

Southerner made the same point differently: "She goes round telling the Negroes they are as good as anyone else.")

Blacks During the New Deal

The shift of black voters from the Republican to the Democratic party during the New Deal years was one of the most significant political turnarounds in American history. In 1932 when things were at their worst, fewer African Americans defected from the Republican party than the members of any other traditionally Republican group. Four years later, however, blacks voted for Roosevelt in overwhelming numbers.

Blacks supported the New Deal for the same reasons that whites did, but how the New Deal affected blacks in general and racial attitudes specifically are more complicated questions. Claiming that he dared not antagonize southern congressmen, whose votes he needed for his recovery programs, Roosevelt did nothing about civil rights before 1941 and relatively little thereafter. For the same reason, many southern white liberals hesitated to support racial integration for fear that other liberal causes could be injured as a result.

Many of the early New Deal programs treated blacks as second-class citizens. Blacks were often paid at lower rates than whites under NRA codes (and so joked that NRA stood for "Negro Run Around" and "Negroes Ruined Again"). The early farm programs shortchanged black tenants and sharecroppers. Blacks in the Civilian Conservation Corps were assigned to all-black camps. TVA developments were rigidly segregated, and almost no blacks got jobs in TVA offices. New Deal urban housing projects inadvertently but nonetheless effectively increased the concentration of blacks in particular neighborhoods. Because the Social Security Act excluded agricultural laborers and domestic servants, it did nothing for hundreds of thousands of poor black workers or for Mexican American farmhands in the Southwest. In 1939 unemployment was twice as high among blacks as among whites, and whites' wages were double the level of blacks' wages.

The fact that members of racial minorities got less than they deserved did not keep most of them from becoming New Dealers: Half a loaf was more than any American government had given blacks since the time of Ulysses S. Grant.

Black sharecroppers evicted from their tenant farms were photographed by Arthur Rothstein along a Missouri road in 1939. Rothstein was one of a group of outstanding photographers who created a unique "sociological and economic survey" of the nation between 1936 and 1942 under the aegis of the Farm Security Administration.

Aside from the direct benefits, African Americans profited in other ways. Secretary of the Interior Harold L. Ickes appointed Charles Forman as a special assistant assigned "to keep the government honest when it came to race." In 1936 Roosevelt appointed Mary McLeod Bethune, founder of Bethune-Cookman College, as head of the Division of Negro Affairs in the National Youth Administration (NYA). She developed educational and occupational training programs for disadvantaged African American youths. Bethune, along with Forman, William Hastie, another black lawyer in Ickes's department, and a few others made up an informal "Black Cabinet" that lobbied throughout the Washington bureaucracy on behalf of better opportunities for blacks.

In the labor movement the new CIO unions accepted black members, and this was particularly significant because these unions were organizing industries—steel, automobiles, and mining among others—that employed large numbers of blacks. Thus, while black Americans suffered horribly during the Depression, New Deal efforts to counteract its effects brought them some relief and a measure of hope. And this became increasingly true with the passage of time. During Roosevelt's second term, blacks found far less to criticize than had been the case earlier.

A New Deal for Indians

New Deal policy toward American Indians built on earlier trends but carried them further. During the Harding and Coolidge administrations more Indian land had passed into the hands of whites, and agents of the Bureau of Indian Affairs had tried to suppress elements of Indian culture that they considered "pagan" or "lascivious." In 1924 Congress finally granted citizenship to all Indians, but it was still generally agreed by whites that Indians should be treated as wards of the state. Assimilation had failed; Indian languages and religious practices, patterns of family life, Indian arts and crafts had all resisted generations of efforts to "civilize" the tribes.

Government policy took a new direction in 1933 when President Roosevelt named John Collier commissioner of Indian affairs. In the 1920s Collier had studied the Indians of the Southwest and been appalled by what he learned. He became executive secretary of the American Indian Defense Association and, in 1925, editor of a reform-oriented magazine, *American Indian Life*. By the time he was appointed commissioner, the Depression had reduced perhaps a third of the 320,000 Indians living on reservations to penury.

Collier tried to revive the spirits of these people. He was particularly eager to encourage the revival of tribal governments that could represent the Indians in dealings with the United States government and function as community service centers.

In part because of Collier's urging, Congress passed the Indian Reorganization Act of 1934. This law did away with the Dawes Act allotment system and enabled Indians to establish tribal governments with powers like those of cities, and it encouraged Indians to return individually owned lands to tribal control. About 4 million of the 90 million acres of Indian land lost under the allotment system were returned to the tribes.

In truth the problem was more complicated than Collier had imagined. Indians who owned profitable allotments, such as those in Oklahoma who held valuable oil and mineral rights, did not relish turning over their land to tribal control. In New Mexico the Navajos, whose lands had relatively little commercial value, nonetheless voted decisively against going back to the communal system. All told, 77 of 269 tribes voted against communal holdings.

Collier resigned in 1945, and in the 1950s Congress "terminated" most government efforts aimed at preserving Indian cultures. Nevertheless, like so many of its programs, the New Deal's Indian policy was a bold effort to deal constructively with a long-standing national problem.

The Role of Roosevelt

How much of the credit for New Deal policies belongs personally to Franklin D. Roosevelt is debatable. He had little to do with many of the details and some of the broad principles behind the New Deal. His knowledge of economics was skimpy, his understanding of many social problems superficial, and his political philosophy distressingly vague. The British leader Anthony Eden described him as "a conjurer, skillfully juggling with balls of dynamite, whose nature he failed to understand."

Nevertheless, every aspect of the New Deal bears the brand of Roosevelt's remarkable personality. Rexford Tugwell left one of the best-balanced judgments of the president. "Roosevelt was not really very

A miner greets the president. Franklin's "first-class temperament" compensated for his "second-class intellect," Justice Oliver Wendell Holmes famously observed.

much at home with ideas," Tugwell explained. But he was always open to new facts, and something within him "forbade inaction when there was something to be done." Roosevelt constructed the coalition that made the program possible; his humanitarianism made it a reform movement of major significance. Although considered by many a terrible administrator because he encouraged rivalry among his subordinates, assigned different agencies overlapping responsibilities, failed to discharge many incompetents, and frequently put off making difficult decisions, he was in fact one of the most effective chief executives in the nation's history. His seemingly haphazard practice of dividing authority among competing administrators unleashed the energies and sparked the imaginations of his aides.

Like Andrew Jackson, Roosevelt maximized his role as leader of all the people. His informal biweekly press conferences kept the public in touch with developments and himself in tune with popular thinking. His "fireside chats" convinced millions that he was personally interested in each citizen's life and welfare, as in a way he was. At a time when the size and complexity of the government made it impossible for any one person to direct the nation's destiny, Roosevelt managed the minor miracle of personifying that government to 130 million people. Under Hoover, a single clerk was able to handle the routine mail that flowed into the office of the president from ordinary citizens. Under Roosevelt, the task required a staff of fifty.

While the New Deal was still evolving, contemporaries recognized Roosevelt's right to a place beside Washington, Jefferson, and Lincoln among the great presidents. Yet as his second term drew toward its close, some of his most important work still lay in the future.

The Triumph of Isolationism

Franklin Roosevelt was at heart an internationalist, but like most world leaders in the 1930s, he placed revival of his own country's limping economy ahead of general world recovery. In April 1933 he took the United States off the gold standard, hoping that devaluing the dollar would make it easier to sell American goods abroad. The following month the World Economic Conference met in London. Delegates from sixty-four nations sought ways to increase world trade, perhaps by a general reduction of tariffs and the stabilization of currencies. After flirting with the idea of currency stabilization, Roosevelt threw a bombshell into the conference by announcing that the United States would not return to the gold standard. His decision increased international ill feeling, and the conference collapsed. The German

"... and the Wolf chewed up the children and spit out their bones ... But those were **Foreign Children** and it really didn't matter."

Dr. Seuss ©1941

For a time Dr. Seuss—Theodor Seuss Geisel—drew political cartoons. This one, published in October, 1941, makes fun of isolationists. The woman, wearing an "America First" sweater, is oblivious to the threat of Hitler, "Adolf the Wolf." Dr. Seuss's 1958 children's story–"Yertle the Turtle"—denounces tyranny. "You stay in your place while I sit here and rule," declares Yertle, atop a pile of turtles.

financier Hjalmar Schacht announced smugly that Roosevelt was adopting the maxim of the great *Führer*, Adolf Hitler: "Take your economic fate in your own hands."

Against this background, vital changes in American foreign policy took place. Unable to persuade the country to take positive action against aggressors, internationalists like Secretary of State Stimson had begun in 1931 to work for a discretionary arms embargo law to be applied by the president in time of war against whichever side had broken the peace. By early 1933 Stimson had obtained Hoover's backing for an embargo bill, as well as the support of President-elect Roosevelt. First the munitions manufacturers and then the isolationists pounced on it, and in the resulting debate it was amended to make the embargo apply to *all* belligerents.

Instead of providing an effective if essentially negative tool for influencing international affairs, a blanket embargo would intensify America's ostrich-like isolationism. Stimson's policy would have permitted arms shipments to China but not to Japan, which might have discouraged the Japanese from attacking. As amended, the embargo would have automatically applied to both sides, thus removing the United States as an influence in the conflict. Although Roosevelt accepted the change, the internationalists in Congress did not, and when they withdrew their support the measure died.

The danger of another world war mounted steadily as Germany, Italy, and Japan repeatedly resorted to force to achieve their expansionist aims. In March 1935 Hitler instituted universal military training and denounced the settlement at Versailles. In May Mussolini massed troops in Italian Somaliland, using a trivial border clash as a pretext for threatening the ancient kingdom of Ethiopia.

Congress responded by passing a series of **neutrality acts** to prevent the United States from being drawn into a wider war. The Neutrality Act of 1935 forbade the sale of munitions to all belligerents whenever the president should proclaim that a state of war existed. Americans who took passage on belligerent ships after such a proclamation had been issued would do so at their own risk. Roosevelt would have preferred a discretionary embargo or no new legislation at all, but he dared not rouse the ire of the isolationists by vetoing the bill.

In October 1935 Italy invaded Ethiopia and Roosevelt invoked the new neutrality law. Secretary of State Cordell Hull asked American exporters to support a "moral embargo" on the sale of oil and other products not covered by the act. His plea was ignored; oil shipments to Italy tripled between October and January. Italy quickly overran and annexed Ethiopia. In February 1936 Congress passed a second neutrality act forbidding all loans to belligerents.

Then, in the summer of 1936, civil war broke out in Spain. The rebels, led by the reactionary General Francisco Franco and strongly backed by Italy and Germany, sought to overthrow the somewhat leftist Spanish Republic. Here, clearly, was a clash between democracy and fascism, and the neutrality laws did not apply to civil wars. However, Roosevelt now became more fearful of involvement than some isolationists. The president believed that American interference might cause the conflict in Spain to become a global war, and he was wary of antagonizing the substantial number of American Catholics who were sympathetic to the Franco regime. At his urging Congress passed another neutrality act broadening the arms embargo to cover civil wars.

Isolationism now reached its peak. A public opinion poll revealed in March 1937 that 94 percent of the people thought American policy should be directed at keeping out of all foreign wars rather than trying to prevent wars from breaking out. In April Congress passed still another neutrality law. It continued the embargo on munitions and loans, forbade Americans to travel on belligerent ships, and gave the president discretionary authority to place the sale of other goods to belligerents on a cash-and-carry basis.

This played into the hands of the aggressors. While German planes and cannons were turning the tide in Spain, the United States was denying the hard-pressed Spanish loyalists even a case of cartridges.

In January 1938 the House narrowly defeated the Ludlow amendment, which would have prohibited Congress from declaring war without the prior approval of the nation's voters.

"With every surrender the prospects of a European war grow darker," Claude G. Bowers, the American ambassador to Spain, warned. The *New York Herald Tribune* pointed out that the neutrality legislation was literally reactionary—designed to keep the United States out of the war of 1914–1918, not the conflict looming on the horizon. President Roosevelt, in part because of domestic problems such as the Supreme Court packing struggle and the wave of sit-down strikes, and in part because of his own vacillation, seemed to have lost control over the formulation of American foreign policy. The American people, like wild creatures before a forest fire, were rushing in blind panic from the conflagration.

War Again in Asia and Europe

There were limits beyond which Americans would not go. In July 1937 the Japanese resumed their conquest of China, pressing ahead on a broad front. Roosevelt believed that invoking the neutrality law would only help the well-armed Japanese. Taking advantage of the fact that neither side had formally declared war, he allowed the shipment of arms and supplies to both sides.

Then the president went further. Speaking in Chicago in October, he condemned nations—he mentioned none by name—who were "creating a state of international anarchy and instability from which there is no escape through mere isolation or neutrality." The way to deal with "the epidemic of world lawlessness" was to "quarantine" it. Evidently Roosevelt had no specific plan in mind; nevertheless the "quarantine speech" produced a windy burst of isolationist rhetoric that forced him to back down. "It's a terrible thing," he said, "to look over your shoulder when you are trying to lead—and to find no one there."

Roosevelt came gradually to the conclusion that resisting aggression was more important than keeping out of war, but when he did, the need to keep the country united led him at times to be less than candid in his public statements. Hitler's annexation of Austria in March 1938 caused him deep concern. The Nazis' vicious anti-Semitism had caused many of Germany's 500,000 Jewish citizens to seek refuge abroad. Now 190,000 Austrian Jews were under Nazi control. When Roosevelt learned that the Germans were burning synagogues, expelling Jewish children

In 1939 Hitler reviews goose-stepping troops during a celebration of his 50th birthday.

from schools, and otherwise mistreating innocent people, he said that he "could scarcely believe that such things could occur." But public opinion opposed changing the immigration law so that more refugees could be admitted, and the president did nothing.

In September 1938 Hitler demanded that Czechoslovakia cede the German-speaking Sudetenland to the Reich. British Prime Minister Neville Chamberlain and French Premier Edouard Daladier, in a conference with Hitler at Munich, yielded to Hitler's threats and promises and persuaded the Czechs to surrender the region. Roosevelt failed again to speak out. But when the Nazis seized the rest of Czechoslovakia in March 1939, Roosevelt called for "methods short of war" to demonstrate America's determination to check the fascists.

When Hitler threatened Poland in the spring of 1939, demanding the free city of Danzig and the Polish Corridor separating East Prussia from the rest of Germany, and when Mussolini invaded Albania, Roosevelt urged Congress to repeal the 1937 neutrality act so that the United States could sell arms to Britain and France in the event of war. Congress refused. "Captain," Vice President Garner told Roosevelt after counting noses in the Senate, "you haven't got the votes," and the president did not press the issue.

In August 1939 Germany and the Soviet Union signed a nonaggression pact, prelude to their joint assault on Poland. On September 1 Hitler's troops invaded Poland, at last provoking Great Britain and France to declare war. Roosevelt immediately asked Congress to repeal the arms embargo. In November, in a vote that followed party lines closely, the Democratic majority pushed through a law permitting the sale of arms and other contraband on a cash-and-carry basis. Short-term loans were authorized, but American vessels were forbidden to carry any products to the belligerents. Since the Allies controlled the seas, cash-and-carry gave them a tremendous advantage.

The German attack on Poland effected a basic change in American thinking. Keeping out of the war remained an almost universal hope, but preventing a Nazi victory became the ultimate, if not always conscious, objective of many citizens. In Roosevelt's case it was perfectly conscious, although he dared not express his feelings candidly because of isolationist strength in Congress and the country. He moved slowly, responding to rather than directing the course of events.

Cash-and-carry did not stop the Nazis. Poland fell in less than a month; then, after a winter lull that cynics called the "phony war," Hitler loosed his armored divisions. Between April 9 and June 22 he taught the world the awful meaning of *Blitzkrieg*—lightning war, spearheaded by tanks and supporting aircraft. Denmark, Norway, the Netherlands, Belgium, and France were successively overwhelmed. The British army, pinned against the sea at Dunkirk, saved itself from annihilation only by fleeing across the English Channel. After the French submitted to his harsh terms on June 22, Hitler controlled nearly all of western Europe.

Roosevelt responded to these disasters in a number of ways. In the fall of 1939, reacting to warnings from Albert Einstein and other scientists that the Germans were trying to develop an atomic bomb, he committed federal funds to a top-secret atomic bomb program, which came to be known as the **Manhattan Project**. Even as the British and French were falling back, he sold them, without legal authority, surplus government arms. When Italy entered the war against France, the president called the invasion a stab in the

Japanese Expansion, 1920–1941 The Japanese empire, which conquered Korea early in the twentieth century, seized Manchuria in 1931; Jehol, north of Beijing, in 1933; and the rest of China after 1937.

German Expansion, 1936–1939 In March 1936, Hitler's forces reoccupied the Rhineland. In 1938 Germany annexed Austria and wrested the Sudetenland from Czechoslovakia, and in 1939 occupied the remaining Czech lands.

back. During the first five months of 1940 he asked Congress to appropriate over $4 billion for national defense. To strengthen national unity he named Henry L. Stimson secretary of war[1] and another Republican, Frank Knox, secretary of the navy.

After the fall of France, Hitler attempted to bomb and starve the British into submission. The epic air battles over England during the summer of 1940 ended in a decisive defeat for the Nazis, but the Royal Navy, which had only about 100 destroyers, could not control German submarine attacks on shipping. Far more destroyers were needed. In this desperate hour, Prime Minister Winston Churchill, who had replaced Chamberlain in May 1940, asked Roosevelt for fifty old American destroyers to fill the gap.

The navy had 240 destroyers in commission and more than fifty under construction. But direct loan or sale of the vessels would have violated both international and American laws. Any attempt to obtain new legislation would have roused fears that the United States was going down the path that had led it into World War I. Long delay if not outright defeat would have resulted. Roosevelt therefore arranged to "trade" the destroyers for six British naval bases in the Caribbean. In addition, Great Britain leased bases in Bermuda and Newfoundland to the United States.

The destroyers-for-bases deal was a masterful achievement. It helped save Great Britain, and at the same time it circumvented isolationist prejudices since the president could present it as a shrewd bargain that bolstered America's defenses. A string of island bastions in the Atlantic was more valuable than fifty old destroyers.

Lines were hardening throughout the world. In September 1940, despite last-ditch isolationist resistance, Congress enacted the first peacetime draft in American history. Some 1.2 million draftees were summoned for one year of service, and 800,000 reservists were called to active duty. That same month Japan signed a mutual-assistance pact with Germany and Italy. This Rome-Berlin-Tokyo coalition—the **Axis Powers**—fused the conflicts in Europe and Asia, turning the struggle into a global war.

A Third Term for FDR

In the midst of these events the 1940 presidential election took place. Why Roosevelt decided to run for a third term is a much-debated question. Partisanship had something to do with it, for no other Democrat seemed so likely to carry the country. Nor would the president have been human had he not been tempted to hold on to power, especially in such critical times. His conviction that no one else could keep a rein on the isolationists was probably decisive. In any case, he was easily renominated. Vice President Garner, who had become disenchanted with Roosevelt and the New Deal, did not seek a third term; at Roosevelt's dictation, the party chose Secretary of Agriculture Henry A. Wallace to replace him.

By using concern about the European war to justify running for a tradition-breaking third term, Roosevelt brought down on his head the hatred of conservative Republicans and the isolationists of both major parties, just when they thought they would be rid of him. The Republicans nominated the darkest of dark horses, Wendell L. Willkie of Indiana, the

---

[1]Stimson had held this post from 1911 to 1913 in the Taft Cabinet!

utility magnate who had led the fight against the TVA in 1933.

Despite his political inexperience and Wall Street connections, Willkie made an appealing candidate. He was an energetic, charming, openhearted man. His rough-hewn, rural manner (one Democrat called him "a simple, barefoot Wall Street lawyer") won him wide support in farm districts. Willkie had difficulty, however, finding issues on which to oppose Roosevelt. The New Deal reforms were too popular and too much in line with his own thinking to invite attack. He believed as strongly as the president that America could no longer ignore the Nazi threat.

In the end Willkie focused his campaign on Roosevelt's conduct of foreign relations. While rejecting the isolationist position, Willkie charged that Roosevelt intended to make the United States a participant in the war. "If you reelect him," he told one audience, "you may expect war in April 1941," to which Roosevelt retorted (disingenuously, since he knew he was not a free agent in the situation), "I have said this before, but I shall say it again and again and again: Your boys are not going to be sent into any foreign wars." In November Roosevelt carried the country handily, though by a smaller majority than in 1932 or 1936. The popular vote was 27 million to 22 million, the electoral count 449 to 82.

The Undeclared War

The election encouraged Roosevelt to act more boldly. When Prime Minister Churchill informed him that the cash-and-carry system would no longer suffice because Great Britain was rapidly exhausting its financial resources, he decided at once to provide the British with whatever they needed. Instead of proposing to lend them money, a step certain to rouse memories of the vexatious war debt controversies, he devised the lend-lease program, one of his most ingenious and imaginative creations.

First he delivered a "fireside chat" that stressed the evil intentions of the Nazis and the dangers that a German victory would create for America. Aiding Britain should be looked at simply as a form of self-defense. "As planes and ships and guns and shells are produced," he said, American defense experts would decide "how much shall be sent abroad and how much shall remain at home." When the radio talk provoked a favorable public response, Roosevelt went to Congress in January 1941 with a plan calling for the expenditure of $7 billion for war materials that the president could sell, lend, lease, exchange, or transfer to any country whose defense he deemed vital to that of the United States. After two months of debate, Congress gave him what he had asked for.

Although the wording of the **Lend-Lease Act** obscured its immediate purpose, the saving of Great Britain, the president was frank in explaining his plan. He did not minimize the dangers involved, yet his mastery of practical politics was never more in evidence. To counter Irish American prejudices against the English, he pointed out that the Irish Republic would surely fall under Nazi domination if Hitler won the war. He coupled his demand for heavy military expenditures with his enunciation of the idealistic "Four Freedoms"—freedom of speech, freedom of religion, freedom from want, and freedom from fear—for which, he said, the war was being fought.

After the enactment of lend-lease, aid short of war was no longer seriously debated. The American navy began to patrol the North Atlantic, shadowing German submarines and radioing their locations to British warships and planes. In April 1941 U.S. forces occupied Greenland; in May the president declared a state of unlimited national emergency. After Hitler invaded the Soviet Union in June, Roosevelt moved slowly, for anti-Soviet feeling in the United States was intense.[2] But it was obviously to the nation's advantage to help any country that was resisting Hitler's armies. In November, $1 billion in lend-lease aid was put at the disposal of the Soviet Union.

Meanwhile, Iceland was occupied in July 1941, and the draft law was extended in August—by the margin of a single vote in the House of Representatives. In September the German submarine *U–652* fired a torpedo at the destroyer *Greer* in the North Atlantic. The *Greer*, which had provoked the attack by tracking *U–652* and flashing its position to a British plane, avoided the torpedo and dropped nineteen depth charges in an effort to sink the submarine.

Roosevelt (nothing he ever did provided more ammunition for his critics) announced that the *Greer* had been innocently "carrying mail to Iceland." He called the U-boats "the rattlesnakes of the Atlantic" and ordered the navy to "shoot on sight" any German craft in the waters south and west of Iceland and to convoy merchant vessels as far as that island. After the sinking of the destroyer *Reuben James* on October 30, Congress voted to allow the arming of American merchant ships and to permit them to carry cargoes to Allied ports. For all practical purposes, though not yet officially, the United States had gone to war.

---

[2]During the 1930s the Soviet Union took a far firmer stand against the fascists than any other power, but after joining Hitler in swallowing up Poland, it attacked and defeated Finland during the winter of 1939–1940 and annexed the Baltic states. These acts virtually destroyed the small communist movement in the United States.

Cinderella Man

As *Cinderella Man* (2005) opens, boxer James J. Braddock (Russell Crowe) lands a right-hook that sends his opponent sprawling to the canvas—a knockout. Braddock raises his hands in triumph. The crowd roars and a jazz band blares. After the match, Braddock's agent peels off a wad of bills—$8,000—Braddock's winnings. This is just the beginning, the agent tells Braddock, because he has a shot at the heavyweight title.

When Braddock arrives at his home in New Jersey, his wife, Mae (Renée Zellweger) leaps into his arms. "I'm so proud of you," she says. Three children race out of the house and mob their father. Later, as Braddock prepares for bed, he sets his gold watch and thick wallet onto a polished wood dresser. The year is 1928.

Abruptly, the scene dissolves. A cheap, unfinished dresser comes into focus. The watch and wallet are gone. Braddock, unshaven, looks wearily around a squalid hovel. The children, on mattresses in shadows, cough and wheeze. The year is 1933.

Braddock, like much of the nation, has fallen on hard times, his savings wiped out by the Depression. Worse, he has broken his powerful right hand and, desperate for money, resumed boxing before it healed.

During a bout in Mount Vernon, Braddock again breaks his hand but tries to finish the match so he can earn his $50 fee. The fans jeer and the boxing commission revokes his license. He tries to work at the dockyards but often there is no work to be had. The grocer refuses credit. The milkman stops deliveries. The power company shuts off the gas and electricity. His children, underfed and chilled, become sick. Braddock returns to Madison Square Garden, hat in hand, and begs for money. He also applies and receives federal assistance—welfare—at $6.40 a week. Compared to Braddock, Cinderella had it easy.

Then Braddock's agent, an unlikely fairy godmother, shows up with an extraordinary proposition. A huge, young bruiser and leading contender for the heavyweight title— "Corn" Griffin—had been scheduled to fight the next evening at Madison Square Garden. But Griffin's opponent has backed out at the last minute. Rather than cancel the fight, Madison Square Garden has offered Braddock $250 to serve as Griffin's punching bag. Desperate, Braddock accepts.

What happens the next day—June 14, 1934—is the stuff of fairy tales. Braddock borrows boxing boots and heads to Madison Square Garden. He can't afford dinner; his agent, aghast, fetches a bowl of hash minutes before the fight. When Braddock enters the ring, his robe bears another boxer's name.

After the opening bell, Griffin, a thick-necked bull of a man, charges Braddock and pounds him mercilessly. Braddock, sustained only by raw courage—and a tough chin, survives the first two rounds. Then, in the third, he surprises Griffin with a thunderous hook, knocking the giant out cold.

Because Griffin was the top contender, Braddock himself is placed on the list of contenders. He proceeds to score one upset after another until he's next in line to face Max Baer (Craig Bierko), the heavyweight champion whose fearsome right has killed two boxers. The manager of Madison Square Garden requires Braddock to sign a waiver absolving it of responsibility should Braddock also perish at Baer's hands. At a restaurant, Baer runs into Mae and warns her against letting her husband into the ring, adding that she's too pretty to become a widow. "Maybe I'd comfort you after he's gone," he says with a leer.

On June 13, 1935, the night of the fight, as Mae goes to church to pray, reporters speculate on whether Braddock can last a single round against the champ. The betting odds against Braddock are the worst in memory. But a movie named after a fairy tale must have a happy ending, and *Cinderella Man* comes through. After fifteen harrowing rounds, Braddock wins a unanimous decision. In 364 days, he has gone from impoverished "bum" to heavyweight champion of the world.

"This is a true story," declared director Ron Howard. Yet fairy tales, by definition, are make-believe; and Hollywood, by reputation, believes in nothing as fervently as the dollar. Thus viewers are entitled to ask: Does *Cinderella Man* tell the actual story of James J. Braddock?

The surprising answer, given the implausibility of the plot, is yes, up to a point. And that point begins with the Baer-Braddock fight: Madison Square Garden did not warn Braddock of the danger of fighting Baer or oblige him to sign a waiver.

Russell Crowe and Renée Zellweger embrace in *Cinderella Man*.

Max Baer (left) and James J. Braddock eye each other during the heavyweight championship fight on June 13, 1935. Note the "Star of David" on Baer's trunks.

Also, the fight was no slugfest. The *New York Times* dubbed it "one of the worst heavyweight championship contests" in boxing history. Reporters assumed that Baer failed to take the early rounds seriously, lost others on foolish fouls, and realized too late that he was behind. Baer, too, was no unfeeling monster. He never teased Mae Braddock or gloated over killing two fighters in the ring. He even raised money for the first boxer's widow. Most interesting is the movie's error of omission, or, more precisely, of suppression. It makes no mention of the fact that Baer proudly trumpeted his Jewish ancestry. Baer had a large Star of David stitched onto his trunks, an image that appears in the movie once, briefly and from a distance.

Why did director Howard evade the truth about Baer? The likely answer is that Howard knew that fairy tales require villains as well as heroes. *Cinderella Man*'s Braddock looms larger for slaying the Big Bad Baer.

In fact, the real enemy was the Great Depression. Braddock understood this. When asked how he managed to turn his career around, he explained, "I was fighting for milk." Damon Runyon, the writer who first called Braddock "Cinderella Man," recognized that the boxer's story took on mythic proportions because it encapsulated the aspirations of an entire nation.

But the movie misses the point that many ethnic groups had their own boxing champions. After Braddock had upset Griffin, he fought Joe Louis, the Brown Bomber. While the movie rightly shows Irish Americans praying for Braddock, it neglects the millions of African Americans who also gathered around radios, praying for Louis. Jewish fans, similarly, identified with Baer, cherishing his 1933 defeat of the German boxer, Max Schmeling, Hitler's favorite. When Braddock defeated Baer, many Jews were devastated.

In 1936, the *Chicago Defender*, an African American newspaper, wrote that history would be kind to Braddock. "Years from today you will read that Jim Braddock was the one champion who would not and did not draw the color line," it noted. But it concluded that Braddock did so for mercenary reasons: "The facts are that Braddock needs money and he more than anyone else knows that only with Joe Louis in one corner can he draw a purse benefiting a champion's appearance." Three years later, when Louis defeated Braddock to win the heavyweight title, the fight at Chicago's Comiskey Park attracted the largest mixed crowd of blacks and whites in boxing history.

Madison Square Garden, keenly aware of the ethnic appeal of boxing, worked hard to ensure that nearly every major immigrant group had someone to cheer for on fight night. Boxing promoters were among the first to learn that in sports, as in entertainment more generally, segregation did not pay.

Cinderella Man depicts, with considerable accuracy, a simple and good man's triumph over adversity. His story was, indeed, the stuff of myth. But in its earnest attempt to universalize Braddock's appeal, the movie obscures the ethnic divisions that characterized so much of American life during the first half of the twentieth century.

Question for Discussion

■ Do you think the Depression encouraged solidarity among Americans of different races and ethnicities, because everyone could empathize with each other's suffering? Or did it exacerbate tensions by pitting different groups against each other in search of scarce jobs?

Chapter Review

Milestones

1933	FDR becomes president
	Hitler is elected German chancellor
	FDR proclaims Good Neighbor Policy
	Banking Act gives FDR broad powers
	Civilian Conservation Corps (CCC) employs 250,000 young men
	Federal Emergency Relief Act (FERA) funds relief programs
	Agricultural Adjustment Act (AAA) seeks relief for farmers
	Tennessee Valley Authority (TVA) plans dams and power plants
	National Industrial Recovery Act (NIRA) establishes Public Works Administration (PWA) and National Recovery Administration (NRA)
	Banking Act establishes Federal Deposit Insurance Corporation (FDIC)
	Civil Works Administration puts 4 million to work
	Twenty-First Amendment ends prohibition
1934	Indian Reorganization Act gives tribes more autonomy
	Securities and Exchange Commission (SEC) regulates stocks and bonds
	Federal Communications Commission (FCC) regulates interstate and foreign communication
	Federal Housing Administration (FHA) gives housing loans
1935	Emergency Relief Appropriation Act creates Works Project Administration (WPA)

	Rural Electrification Administration brings electricity to farms
	Supreme Court rules NIRA unconstitutional in *Schechter v. United States*
	National Labor Relations Act (Wagner-Connery) encourages unionization
	Social Security Act guarantees pensions and other benefits
	Neutrality Act forbids wartime arms sales to belligerents
	Italy invades and annexes Ethiopia
	Walter Millis publishes isolationist *The Road to War: America, 1914–1917*
1936	FDR is reelected president in record landslide
	Supreme Court declares AAA unconstitutional
1937	Roosevelt tries to pack Supreme Court
	Japanese in China seize Beijing, Shanghai, Nanking
1938	Fair Labor Standards Act abolishes child labor, sets minimum wage
	House of Representatives defeats Ludlow (isolationist) Amendment
	Britain and France appease Hitler at Munich
1939	Germany invades Poland; World War II begins
1940	Hitler conquers Denmark, Norway, the Netherlands, Belgium, France
	FDR is reelected to third term
	Axis Powers sign Rome-Berlin-Tokyo pact
	Isolationists form America First Committee
1941	Lend-Lease Act helps Britain

Key Terms

Agricultural Adjustment Act (AAA)   New Deal legislation that raised farm prices by restricting output of staple crops. It restricted production and paid subsidies to growers; declared unconstitutional in 1936, *688*

Axis Powers   A term for the alliance between Nazi Germany and Italy after 1936 and, after 1940, Japan, *706*

Blitzkrieg   A German tactic in World War II, translated as "lightning war," involving the coordinated attack of air and armored firepower, *705*

Civilian Conservation Corps (CCC)   A New Deal program to provide government jobs in reforestation, flood control, and other conservation projects to young men between ages eighteen and twenty-five, *687*

Lend-Lease Act   A military aid measure, proposed by President Franklin D. Roosevelt in 1941 and adopted by Congress, empowering the president

to sell, lend, lease, or transfer $7 billion of war material to any country whose defense he declared as vital to that of the United States, *707*

Manhattan Project   The code name for the extensive United States military project, established in 1942, to produce fissionable uranium and plutonium, and to design and build an atomic bomb. Costing nearly $2 billion, the effort culminated in the destruction of Hiroshima and Nagasaki in August 1945, *705*

National Recovery Administration (NRA)   A New Deal agency, established in 1933, to promote economic recovery, that promulgated industry-wide codes to control production, prices, and wages, *687*

neutrality acts   Legislation affirming nonbelligerency in the event of war. In relation to American history, such legislation was passed in 1794 to preclude American entanglement in the Napoleonic Wars; similar laws were passed just before and after World War I, especially during the 1930s, *704*

New Deal   A broad program of legislation proposed by President Franklin D. Roosevelt to promote recovery from the Great Depression and provide relief for those in distress, *686*

Social Security Act   A component of Franklin Roosevelt's **New Deal**, it established in 1935 a system of old-age, unemployment, and survivors' insurance funded by wage and payroll taxes, *694*

Tennessee Valley Authority (TVA)   A **New Deal** agency that built and operated dams and power plants on the Tennessee River; it also promoted flood control, soil conservation, and reforestation, *689*

Wagner Act   Officially the National Labor Relations Act and sometimes called Labor's Magna Carta, it gave workers the right to organize and bargain collectively. It also created the National Labor Relations Board to supervise union elections and stop unfair labor practices by employers, *694*

Works Progress Administration (WPA)   A **New Deal** agency, established in 1935 and run by Harry Hopkins, that spent $11 billion on federal works projects and provided employment for 8.5 million persons, *691*

Review Questions

1. The introduction of this chapter compares the 2010 health insurance law with that establishing Social Security in 1935. In what ways is the comparison an apt one? How did the measures and times differ? Was Social Security a form of socialism?

2. Compare the First and Second New Deals. What were the similarities and differences?

3. What was the impact of the Great Depression on art, literature, and popular culture? How did it affect women and minority groups? Labor?

4. How did the New Deal expand the role of the federal government?

5. Why did Asia and Europe slip into war in the 1930s? How did the United States respond during that decade and why?

PEARSON **myhistorylab** Connections

Reinforce what you learned in this chapter by studying the many documents, images, maps, review tools, and videos available at **www.myhistorylab.com**.

Read and Review

✓ Study and Review *Chapter 26*

View the Image *PWA in Action Poster*, p. 688

Read the Document *An Attack on New Deal Farm Policies*, p. 688

See the Map *The Tennessee Valley Authority*, p. 690

Read the Document *Coughlin, A Third Party (1936)*, p. 694

Read the Document *FDR, Fireside Chat*, p. 695

Research and Explore

Watch the Video *FDR's Inauguration*, p. 687

Watch the Video *Responding to the Great Depression: Whose New Deal?*, p. 699

((•— Hear the Audio

Hear the audio file for Chapter 26 at
www.myhistorylab.com.

Does the war in Afghanistan touch your life?

Although all young American men are required to register for the military draft, none has actually been drafted since the 1970s. (Registration exists in the event of a national military emergency.) In place of conscription, the Department of Defense has recruited all-volunteer military services. In times of peace, most generals prefer a volunteer army: Professional soldiers are better trained and often more attentive to orders; but in times of war, when recruiting officers struggle to fill quotas and tours-of-duty are extended, many generals call for a return to the draft.

By 2010, a heated debate among officers surfaced in the *Armed Forces Journal.* Most defended the professional army, noting that the quality of recruits was higher than in two decades, partly because the economic downturn had resulted in a scarcity of jobs. But other officers called for a return to the "citizen soldiers" envisioned by Washington and Jefferson. One reason was that wars fought by conscripts ensured that the nation as a whole engaged in the war effort. The *Seattle Times* observed that although the Iraq war had gone on far longer than World War II, "life for most Americans has

War and Peace: 1941–1945   27

((•— Hear the Audio **Chapter 27 at www.myhistorylab.com**

■ Ed Reep's *Anzio Harbor Under Bombardment* was sketched out as American troops invaded Sicily in 1942. Initially, Reep was too frightened to work on the frontlines, but eventually he painted while under fire.

clicked along without personal loss or even higher federal taxes." "Marines are at war," one general complained, "America is at the mall."

Such remarks underscored how different the current conflicts in Iraq and Afghanistan are from World War II, a monstrous global war among advanced industrial nations. Of every five American males between the ages of twenty and twenty-five, four served in World War II. At the beginning of World War II, 4 million Americans paid income tax; by its end, 43 million did so. Over 85 million Americans—half the nation's population—spent $185 billion to buy war bonds. Food and gasoline were rationed. World War II required the mobilization of the entire

nation. Even painters such as Ed Reep (see the accompanying artwork) and 100 other artists were conscripted into the war effort. Their job was to paint the war as experienced by the citizen-soldiers who fought it.

World War II transformed society, too. In the absence of so many young men, women assumed new roles and worked at different types of jobs. African Americans, Hispanics, American Indians, and other minorities found new opportunities even as they encountered persistent discrimination. Americans of Japanese extraction were relocated against their will to isolated camps. Technological change—culminating in the atom bomb—transformed everyone's lives. It was a war unlike any other. ■

The Road to Pearl Harbor

Neither the United States nor Japan wanted war. Roosevelt considered Germany by far the more dangerous enemy and was alarmed by the possibility of simultaneously fighting German armies in Europe and Japanese forces in the Pacific. In the spring of 1941 Secretary of State Cordell Hull conferred in Washington with the Japanese ambassador, Kichisaburo Nomura, in an effort to resolve their differences. Hull showed little appreciation of the political and military situation in East Asia. He demanded that Japan withdraw from China.

Japan might well have accepted limited annexations in the area in return for the removal of American trade restrictions, but Hull seemed bent on converting the Japanese to pacifism by exhortation. He insisted on total withdrawal, to which even the moderates in Japan would not agree. When Hitler invaded the Soviet Union, thereby removing the threat of Russian intervention in East Asia, Japan decided to complete its conquest of China and occupy French Indochina even at the risk of war with the United States. Roosevelt retaliated (July 1941) by freezing Japanese assets in the United States and clamping an embargo on oil. He hoped that the Japanese war machine, deprived of American oil, would grind to a halt.

Now the ultranationalist war party in Japan assumed control. Nomura was instructed to tell Hull that Japan would refrain from further expansion if the United States and Great Britain would cut off all aid to China and lift the economic blockade. Japan promised to pull out of Indochina once "a just peace" had been established with China. When the United States rejected these demands, the Japanese prepared to assault the Dutch East Indies, British Malaya, and the Philippines. To immobilize the U.S. Pacific fleet, they planned a surprise air attack on the Hawaiian naval base at Pearl Harbor.

An American cryptanalyst, Colonel William F. Friedman, had cracked the Japanese diplomatic code: The Japanese were making plans to attack in early December. But in the hectic rush of events, both military and civilian authorities failed to make effective use of the information collected. They expected the blow to fall somewhere in East Asia, possibly the Philippines.

The garrison at Pearl Harbor was alerted against "a surprise aggressive move in any direction." The commanders there, Admiral Husband E. Kimmel and General Walter C. Short, believing an attack impossible, took precautions only against Japanese sabotage.

Japan's surprise attack on Pearl Harbor on December 7, 1941, killed more than 2,400 American sailors and soldiers and thrust the United States into World War II. President Roosevelt asked Congress for a declaration of war the next day, calling the attack "a date that will live in infamy."

Thus when planes from Japanese aircraft carriers swooped down upon Pearl Harbor on the morning of December 7, they found easy targets. In less than two hours they reduced the Pacific fleet to a smoking ruin: two battleships destroyed, six others heavily battered, nearly a dozen lesser vessels put out of action. More than 150 planes were wrecked; over 2,400 soldiers and sailors were killed and 1,100 wounded.

Never had American armed forces suffered a more devastating or shameful defeat. The official blame was placed chiefly on Admiral Kimmel and General Short. They might well have been more alert, but responsibility for the disaster was widespread. Military and civilian officials in Washington had failed to pass on all that they knew to Hawaii or even to one another. On the other hand, the crucial intelligence about the coming attack that the code breakers provided was mixed with masses of other information and was extremely difficult to evaluate.

On December 8 Congress declared war on Japan. Formal war with Germany and Italy was still not inevitable—isolationists were far more ready to resist the "yellow peril" in Asia than to fight in Europe. The Axis Powers, however, honored their treaty obligations to Japan and on December 11 declared war on the United States. America was now fully engaged in another great war, World War II. (The Great War fought by the previous generation was now identified as World War I.)

Mobilizing the Home Front

World War II placed immense strains on the American economy and produced immense results. About 15 million men and women entered the armed services; they, and in part the millions more in Allied uniforms, had to be fed, clothed, housed, and supplied with equipment ranging from typewriters and paper clips to rifles, grenades, tanks, and airplanes. Congress granted wide emergency powers to the president. It refrained from excessive meddling in administrative problems and in military strategy. However, while the Democrats retained control of both houses throughout the war, their margins were relatively narrow. A coalition of conservatives in both parties frequently prevented the president from having his way and exercised close control over expenditures.

Roosevelt was an inspiring war leader but not a very good administrator. Any honest account of the war on the home front must reveal glaring examples of confusion, inefficiency, and pointless bickering. The squabbling and waste characteristic of the early New Deal period made relatively little difference— what mattered then was raising the nation's spirits and keeping people occupied; efficiency was less than essential, however desirable. But in wartime, the nation's fate, perhaps that of the entire free

A poster encourages women to work in munitions to support the war effort.

world, depended on delivering weapons and supplies to the battlefronts.

The confusion attending economic mobilization can easily be overstressed. Nearly all of Roosevelt's basic decisions were sensible and humane: to pay a large part of the cost of the war by collecting taxes rather than by borrowing and to base taxation on ability to pay; to ration scarce raw materials and consumer goods; to regulate prices and wages. If these decisions were not always translated into action with perfect effectiveness, they operated in the direction of efficiency and the public good.

Roosevelt's greatest accomplishment was his inspiring of industrialists, workers, and farmers with a sense of national purpose. In this respect his function duplicated his earlier role in fighting the Depression, and he performed it with even greater success.

The tremendous economic expansion can be seen in the official production statistics. In 1939 the United States was still mired in the Great Depression. The gross national product amounted to about $91.3 billion. In 1945, after allowing for changes in the price level, it was $166.6 billion. More specifically, manufacturing output nearly doubled and agricultural output rose 22 percent. In 1939 the United States turned out fewer than 6,000 airplanes, in 1944 more than 96,000. Shipyards produced 237,000 tons of vessels in 1939, 10 million tons in 1943.

This growth was especially notable in the South and Southwest. This region got a preponderance of the new army camps built for the war as well as a large share of the new defense plants. Southern productive capacity increased by about 50 percent, and southern per capita output, while still low, crept closer to the national average.

Wartime experience proved that the Keynesian economists were correct in saying that government spending would spark economic growth. About 8 million people were unemployed in June 1940. After Pearl Harbor, unemployment virtually disappeared, and by 1945 the civilian workforce had increased by nearly 7 million. Military mobilization had begun well before December 1941, by which time 1.6 million men were already under arms. Economic mobilization proceeded much more slowly, mainly because the president refused to centralize authority. For months after Pearl Harbor various civilian agencies squabbled with the military over everything from the allocation of scarce raw materials to the technical specifications of weapons. Roosevelt refused to settle these conflicts.

Texaco, which produced this poster, used a racist caricature to discourage absenteeism among American workers during the war.

The War Economy

Yet by early 1943 the nation's economic machinery had been converted to a wartime footing and was functioning effectively. Supreme Court Justice James F. Byrnes resigned from the Court to become a sort of "economic czar." His Office of War Mobilization had complete control over priorities and prices. Rents, food prices, and wages were strictly regulated, and items in short supply were rationed to consumers. While wages and prices had soared during 1942, after April 1943 they leveled off. Thereafter the cost of living scarcely changed until controls were lifted after the war.

Expanded industrial production together with conscription caused a labor shortage that increased the bargaining power of workers. At the same time, the national emergency required some limitation on the workers' right to take advantage of this power. After Pearl Harbor Roosevelt created a National War Labor Board (NWLB) to arbitrate disputes and stabilize wage rates, and he banned all changes in wages without NWLB approval.

Prosperity and stiffer government controls added significantly to the strength of organized labor; indeed, the war had more to do with institutionalizing collective bargaining than the New Deal. As workers recognized the benefits of union membership, they flocked into the organizations. Strikes declined sharply, but some crippling work stoppages did occur. In May 1943, after John L. Lewis's United Mine Workers walked out of the pits, the government seized the coal mines. This strike led Congress to pass, over Roosevelt's veto, the Smith-Connally War Labor Disputes Act, which gave the president the power to take over any war plant threatened by a strike and outlawed strikes against seized plants. Although strikes persisted—the loss in hours of labor zoomed to 38 million in 1945—when Roosevelt asked for a labor draft law, Congress refused to go along.

Wages and prices remained in fair balance. Overtime work fattened paychecks, and a new stress in labor contracts on paid vacations, premium pay for night work, and various forms of employer-subsidized health insurance were added benefits. The war effort had almost no adverse effect on the standard of living of the average citizen, a vivid demonstration of the productivity of the American economy. The manufacture of automobiles ceased and pleasure driving became next to impossible because of gasoline rationing, but most civilian activities went on much as they had before Pearl Harbor. Because of the need to conserve cloth, skirts were shortened, cuffs disappeared from men's trousers, and the vest passed out of style. Plastics replaced metals in toys, containers, and other products. While items such as meat, sugar, and shoes were rationed, they were doled out in amounts adequate for the needs of most persons. Americans had both guns and butter; belt-tightening of the type experienced by the other belligerents was unheard of.

The federal government spent twice as much money between 1941 and 1945 as in its entire previous history. This made heavy borrowing necessary. The national debt, which stood at less than $49 billion in 1941, increased by more than that amount each year between 1942 and 1945 and totaled nearly $260 billion when the war ended. However, more than 40 percent of the total was met by taxation, a far larger proportion than in any earlier war.

This policy helped to check inflation by siphoning off money that would otherwise have competed for scarce consumer goods. Heavy excise taxes on amusements and luxuries further discouraged spending, as did the government's war bond campaigns, which persuaded patriotic citizens to lend part of their income to Uncle Sam. High taxes on incomes (up to 94 percent) and on excess profits (95 percent) convinced people that no one was profiting inordinately from the war effort.

The income tax, which had never before touched the mass of white-collar and industrial workers, was extended downward until nearly everyone had to pay it. To collect efficiently the relatively small sums paid by most persons, Congress adopted the payroll-deduction system proposed by Beardsley Ruml, chairman of the Federal Reserve Bank of New York. Employers withheld the taxes owed by workers from their paychecks and turned the money over to the government.

The steeply graduated tax rates, combined with a general increase in the income of workers and farmers, effected a substantial shift in the distribution of wealth in the United States. The poor became richer, while the rich, if not actually poorer, collected a smaller proportion of the national income. The wealthiest 1 percent of the population had received 13.4 percent of the national income in 1935 and 11.5 percent in 1941. In 1944 this group received 6.7 percent.

🔊 View the Image *Ration Stamps WWII* at **www.myhistorylab.com**

War and Social Change

Enormous social effects stemmed from this shift, but World War II altered the patterns of American life in so many ways that it would be wrong to ascribe the transformations to any single source. Never was the population more fluid. The millions who put on uniforms found themselves transported first to training camps in every section of the country and then to battlefields scattered from Europe and Africa to the far reaches of the Pacific. Burgeoning new defense plants, influenced by a government policy of locating them in "uncongested areas," drew other millions to places like Hanford, Washington, and Oak Ridge, Tennessee, where great atomic energy installations were constructed, and to the aircraft factories of California and other states. As in earlier periods the trend was from east to west and from the rural south to northern cities. The population of California increased by more than 50 percent in the 1940s; the population of other far western states rose almost as much.

During the war the marriage rate rose steeply, from 75 per thousand adult women in 1939 to 118 in 1946. A kind of backlog existed because many people had been forced to put off marrying and having children for financial reasons during the Great Depression. Now wartime prosperity put an end to that problem at the same time that large numbers of young couples were feeling the need to put down roots before the husbands went off to risk death in distant lands. The population of the United States had increased by only 3 million during the Depression decade of the 1930s; during the next *five* years it rose by 6.5 million.

Minorities in Time of War: Blacks, Hispanics, and Indians

The war affected black Americans in many ways. Several factors helped improve their lives. One was their own growing tendency to demand fair treatment. Another was the reaction of Americans to Hitler's barbaric treatment of millions of Jews, an outgrowth of his doctrine of "Aryan" superiority. These barbarities compelled millions of white citizens to reexamine their views about race. If the nation expected African Americans to risk their lives for the common good, how could it continue to treat them as second-class citizens? Black leaders pointed out the inconsistency between fighting for democracy abroad and ignoring it at home. "We want democracy in Alabama," the NAACP announced, and this argument too had some effect on white thinking.

Blacks in the armed forces were treated more fairly than they had been in World War I. They were enlisted

"above and beyond the call of duty"

DORIE MILLER
*Received the Navy Cross
at Pearl Harbor, May 27, 1942*

A poster commemorates Doris "Dorie" Miller, a mess attendant aboard the USS *West Virginia* at Pearl Harbor. Before the ship sank, Miller manned an antiaircraft machine gun and shot down several Japanese planes. He won the Navy Cross for courage, the first awarded to an African American.

for the first time in the air force and the marines, and they were given more responsible positions in the army and navy. The army commissioned its first black general. Some 600 black pilots won their wings. Altogether about a million served, about half of them overseas. The extensive and honorable performance of these units could not be ignored by the white majority.

However, segregation in the armed services was maintained. In some cases German prisoners of war were seated in front of black American soldiers at camp movies. Such practices led frequently to rioting and even to local mutinies among black recruits. The navy continued to confine black and Hispanic sailors to demeaning, noncombat tasks, and black soldiers were often provided with inferior recreational facilities and otherwise mistreated in and around army camps, especially those in the South. In 1943 William Hastie, a former New Dealer who was serving as an adviser on racial matters to Secretary of War Stimson, resigned in protest because of the "reactionary policies and discriminatory practices of the Army and Air Forces in matters affecting Negroes."

However, economic realities operated significantly to the advantage of black civilians. More of them had been unemployed in proportion to their numbers than any other group; now the labor shortage brought employment for all. More than 5 million blacks moved from rural areas to cities between 1940 and 1945 in search of work. At least a million of them found defense jobs in the North and on the West Coast, often developing valuable skills that had been difficult for blacks to acquire before the war because of the discriminatory policies of trade unions and many employers. The black population of Los Angeles, San Francisco, Denver, Buffalo, Milwaukee, and half a dozen other large industrial cities more than doubled in that brief period. The migrants were mostly forced to live in urban ghettoes, but their very concentration (and the fact that outside the South blacks could vote freely) made them important politically.

These gains failed to satisfy black leaders. The NAACP, which increased its membership from 50,000 in 1940 to almost 405,000 in 1946, adopted a more militant stance than in World War I. Discrimination in defense plants seemed far less tolerable than it had in 1917–1918. A. Philip Randolph, president of the Brotherhood of Sleeping Car Porters, organized a march of blacks on Washington in 1941 to demand equal opportunity for black workers. Fearing possible violence and the wrath of southern congressmen, Roosevelt tried to persuade Randolph to call off the march. "It would make the country look bad" and "help the Germans," he claimed. But Randolph persisted, and Roosevelt finally agreed to issue an order prohibiting discrimination in plants with defense contracts.

Prejudice and mistreatment did not cease. In areas around defense plants white resentment of the black "invasion" mounted. By 1943, 50,000 new blacks had crowded into Detroit. A wave of strikes disrupted production at U.S. Rubber and several former automobile plants where white workers laid down their tools to protest the hiring of blacks. In June a race riot marked by looting and bloody fighting raged for three days. By the time federal troops restored order, twenty-five blacks and nine whites had been killed. Rioting also erupted in New York and many other cities.

In Los Angeles the attacks were upon Hispanic residents. Wartime employment needs resulted in a reversal of the Depression policy of forcing Mexicans out of the Southwest, and many thousands flocked north in search of work. Most had to accept menial jobs. But work was plentiful, and they, as well as resident Spanish-speaking Americans, experienced rising living standards.

A larger proportion of Mexican American men served in the armed forces than the national average, but some young civilian Hispanics in the Los Angeles region adopted a kind of civilian dress known as a zoot suit. These "uniforms" consisted of broad-brimmed

In 2007 acclaimed filmmaker Ken Burns released a documentary on World War II. It triggered an angry response from Hispanic Americans who claimed that their role had been ignored. Arnold Garcia, an editor for the *American Statesman* of Austin, Texas, published a Memorial Day tribute to Hispanic servicemen, including his father, Arnulfo Garcia, pictured here, who was inducted into the U.S. Army in 1944. Arnold Garcia wrote that his father had regarded World War II as the "best thing" that had ever happened to him because it had conferred the rights and respect other Americans took for granted. "The Struggle for Latino civil rights was every bit as epic—albeit not as bloody—as World War II," Arnold Garcia wrote.

fedoras, long coats, and pegged trousers. "Zoot suiters" tended to have money in their pockets, and their behavior (like their costume) was not always as circumspect as many local residents would have preferred. A grand jury undertook an investigation, and the Los Angeles City Council even debated banning the wearing of zoot suits. In 1943 rioting broke out when sailors on shore leave, apparently resenting these prosperous-appearing "foreign" civilians, began roaming the area attacking anyone they could find in a zoot suit.

The willingness of white leaders to tolerate attacks on blacks and Hispanics at a time when national unity was so necessary was particularly frustrating. For example, blood plasma from blacks and whites was kept separately even though the two "varieties" were indistinguishable and the process of storing plasma had been devised by a black doctor, Charles Drew.

Blacks became increasingly embittered. Roy Wilkins, head of the NAACP, put it this way in 1942: "No Negro leader with a constituency can face his members today and ask full support for the war in the light of the atmosphere the government has created." Many black newspaper editors were so critical of the administration that conservatives demanded they be indicted for sedition.

Roosevelt would have none of that, but the militants annoyed him; he felt that they should hold their demands in abeyance until the war had been won. Apparently he failed to realize the depth of black anger, and in this he was no different from the majority of whites. A revolution was in the making, yet in 1942 a poll revealed that a solid majority of whites still believed that black Americans were satisfied with their place in society. The riots of 1943 undoubtedly disabused some of them of this illusion.

Concern about national unity did lead to a reaction against the New Deal policy of encouraging Indians to preserve their ancient cultures and develop self-governing communities. There was even talk of going back to the allotment system and trying to assimilate Indians into the larger society. John Collier resigned as commissioner of Indian affairs in disgust in 1945. In fact, the war encouraged assimilation in several ways. More than 24,000 Indians served in the armed forces, an experience that brought them into contact with new people, new places, and new ideas. Many thousands more left the reservations to work in defense industries in cities all over the country.

Read the **Document** Randolph, *Why Should We March* at **www.myhistorylab.com**

Watch the **Video** *The desegregation of the military and blacks in combat* at **www.myhistorylab.com**

The Treatment of German and Italian Americans

Although World War II affected the American people far more drastically than had World War I, it produced much less intolerance and fewer examples of the repression of individual freedom of opinion. People seemed able to distinguish between Italian fascism and Italian Americans and between the government of Nazi Germany and Americans of German descent in a way that had escaped their parents. The fact that few Italian Americans admired Mussolini and that nearly all German Americans were vigorously anti-Nazi helps explain this. So does the fact that both groups were well-organized and prepared to use their considerable political power if necessary to protect themselves from abuse. Nevertheless, U.S. military authorities arrested some 14,000 Germans and Italians as security risks.

Americans went to war in 1941 without illusions and without enthusiasm, determined to win but expecting only to preserve what they had. They therefore found it easier to tolerate dissent, to view the dangers they faced realistically, and to concentrate on the real foreign enemy without venting their feelings on domestic scapegoats. The nation's 100,000 conscientious objectors met with little hostility.

Internment of Japanese Americans

The relatively tolerant treatment of most Americans of German and Italian descent makes the nation's policies toward American citizens of Japanese extraction all the more difficult to comprehend. Generals on the West Coast were understandably unnerved by the Japanese attack on Pearl Harbor and warned that people of Japanese descent might engage in sabotage or espionage for Japan. "The Japanese race is an enemy race," General John L. Dewitt claimed. The 112,000 Americans of Japanese ancestry, the majority of them native-born citizens, were "potential enemies." "The very fact that no sabotage has taken place to date," Dewitt observed, "is a disturbing and confirming indication that such action will be taken." This is like arguing that a driver with a perfect record is all the more likely to career into a tree at any moment. Secretary of War Stimson proposed the relocation of the West Coast people of Japanese extraction, including American citizens, to **internment camps** in Wyoming, Arizona, and other interior states. President Roosevelt concurred but weakly suggested, "Be as responsible as you can."

The Japanese were properly indignant but also baffled, in some cases hurt more than angry. "We didn't feel Japanese. We felt American," one woman, the mother of three small children, recalled many years later. Some Japanese Americans challenged military authorities. Gordon Hirabayashi, an American citizen and senior at the University of Washington, refused to report for transportation to an internment camp. After being convicted and sentenced to prison, he decided to appeal. Previous Supreme Courts had ruled that the government could deprive Americans of their freedoms during war only when the "military necessity" was compelling. By the time the Supreme Court ruled on his and similar cases, the Japanese military had been thrown back in the Pacific; no invasion was even conceivable. Yet the justices worried that if they declared the internment policy to be unconstitutional, they would appear, "out of step" with the nation, as Justice Felix Frankfurter put it. In June 1943, the Court upheld the conviction of Hirabayashi. Finally, in *Ex parte Endo*, it forbade the internment of loyal Japanese American citizens. Unfortunately the latter decision was not handed down until December 1944.

A Japanese girl in California, tagged for relocation to an internment camp, clutches her doll.

Women's Contributions to the War Effort

With economic activity on the rise and millions of men going off to war, a sudden need for more women workers developed. The trends of the 1920s—more women workers and more of them married—soon accelerated. By 1944, 6.5 million additional women had entered the workforce, and at the peak of war production in 1945, more than 19 million women were employed, many of them in well-paying industrial jobs. Additional thousands were serving in the armed forces: 100,000 in the Women's Auxiliary Army Corps, others in navy, marine, and air corps auxiliaries.

At first there was considerable resistance to what was happening. About one husband in three objected in principle to his wife taking a job. Many employers in so-called heavy industry and in other fields traditionally dominated by men doubted that women could handle such tasks.

Unions frequently made the same point, usually without much evidence. A Seattle official of the International Brotherhood of Boilermakers and Iron Shipbuilders said of women job applicants, "They don't understand. . . . If one of these girls pressed the trigger on the yard rivet guns, she'd be going one way and the rivet the other." Actually, many women were

Japanese Relocation from the West Coast, 1942–1945 Japanese and Japanese Americans who lived in the West Coast Military Area were ordered to report to various "assembly centers," from which they were then deported to inland internment or isolation camps.

soon doing "men's work" in the shipyards. The Seattle taxicab union objected to women drivers on the ground that "drivers are forced to do things and go places that would be embarrassing for a woman to do."

These male attitudes lost force in the face of the escalating demand for labor. That employers usually did not have to pay women as much as men made them attractive, as did the fact that they were not subject to the draft. A breakthrough occurred when the big Detroit automobile manufacturers agreed to employ women on their wartime production lines. Soon women were working not only as riveters and cab drivers but also as welders, as machine tool operators, and in dozens of other occupations formerly the exclusive domain of men.

Women took wartime jobs for many reasons other than the obvious economic ones. Patriotism, of course, was important, but so were the excitement of entering an entirely new world, the desire for independence, even loneliness. "It's thrilling work, and exciting, and something women have never done before," one woman reported. She was talking about driving a taxi.

Black women workers had a particularly difficult time: employers often hesitating to hire them because they were black, and black men looking down on them

because they were women. But the need for willing hands was infinite. Sybil Lewis of Sapula, Oklahoma, went to Los Angeles and found a job as a waitress in a black restaurant. Then she responded to a notice of a training program at Lockheed Aircraft, took the course, and became a riveter making airplane gas tanks. When an unfriendly foreman gave her a less attractive assignment, she moved on to Douglas Aircraft. By 1943 she was working as a welder in a shipyard.

Few wartime jobs were easy, and for women there were special burdens, not the least of which was the prejudice of many of the men they worked with. For married women there was housework to do after a long day. One War Manpower Commission bureaucrat figured out that Detroit defense plants were losing 100,000 woman-hours a month because of employees taking a day off to do the family laundry. Although the government made some effort to provide day-care facilities, there were never nearly enough; this was one reason why relatively few women with small children entered the labor market during the war.

The war also affected the lives of women who did not take jobs. Families by the tens and hundreds of thousands pulled up stakes and moved to the centers of war production, such as Detroit and southern

California. Housing was always in short supply in these areas, and while the men went off to the familiar surroundings of yard and factory, their wives had to cope with cramped quarters, ration books, the absence of friends and relatives, the problems encountered by their children in strange schools and playgrounds, and sometimes with outdoor toilets. With so many people living among strangers and in unstable circumstances it is not surprising that crime, juvenile delinquency, and prostitution increased, as indeed they did in other parts of the country too.

Newly married wives of soldiers and sailors (known generally as "war brides") often followed their husbands to training camps, where life was often as difficult as it was around defense plants. Those who did not follow their husbands faced other problems—adjusting to being married without having had much experience of marriage, loneliness, and worry. Whatever their own behavior, war brides quickly learned that society applied a double standard to infidelity, especially when it involved a man presumably risking his life in some far-off land. There was a general relaxation of sexual inhibitions, part of a decades-long trend but accelerated by the war. So many hasty marriages, followed by long periods of separation, also brought a rise in divorces, from about 170 per thousand marriages in 1941 to 310 per thousand in 1945.

Of course "ordinary" housewives also had to deal with shortages, ration books, and other inconveniences during the war. In addition most took on other duties and bore other burdens, such as tending "victory gardens" and preserving their harvests, using crowded public transportation when there was no gas for the family car, mending and patching old clothes when new ones were unavailable, participating in salvage drives, and doing volunteer work for hospitals, the Red Cross, or various civil defense and servicemen's centers.

View the Image *Rosie the Riveter* at
www.myhistorylab.com

Allied Strategy: Europe First

Only days after Pearl Harbor, Prime Minister Churchill and his military chiefs met in Washington with Roosevelt and his advisers. In every quarter of the globe, disaster threatened. The Japanese were gobbling up East Asia. Hitler's armies, checked outside Leningrad and Moscow, were preparing for a massive attack in the direction of Stalingrad, on the Volga River. German divisions under General Erwin Rommel were beginning a drive across North Africa toward the Suez Canal. U-boats were taking a heavy toll in the North Atlantic. British and American leaders believed that eventually

they could muster enough force to smash their enemies, but whether or not the troops already in action could hold out until this force arrived was an open question.

The decision of the strategists was to concentrate first against the Germans. Japan's conquests were in remote and, from the point of view of the **Allies**, relatively unimportant regions. If the Soviet Union surrendered, Hitler's position in Europe might prove impregnable.

But how to strike at Hitler? American leaders wanted to attack German positions in France, at least by 1943. The Soviets, with their backs to the wall and bearing the full weight of the German war machine, heartily agreed. Churchill, however, was more concerned with protecting Britain's overseas possessions than with easing the pressure on the Soviet Union. He advocated instead air bombardment of German industry combined with an attempt to drive the Germans out of North Africa, and his argument carried the day.

During the summer of 1942 Allied planes began to bomb German cities. In a crescendo through 1943 and 1944, British and American bombers pulverized the centers of Nazi might. While air attacks did not destroy the German army's capacity to fight, they hampered war production, tangled communications, and brought the war home to the German people in awesome fashion. Humanitarians deplored the heavy loss of life among the civilian population, but the response of the realists was that Hitler had begun indiscriminate bombing, and victory depended on smashing the German war machine.

In November 1942 an Allied army commanded by General Dwight D. Eisenhower struck at French North

The firebombing of Hamburg (painted here by Floyd Davis, who flew with the Anglo American mission in 1943) killed 50,000 and destroyed Hamburg.

The Liberation of Europe After November, 1942, Allied armies pushed the German-Italian armies back on three fronts: the Soviets, from the East; and American-British armies from North Africa and then, after the Normandy invasion, from France.

Africa. After the fall of France, the Nazis had set up a puppet regime in those parts of France not occupied by their troops, with headquarters at Vichy in central France. This collaborationist Vichy government controlled French North Africa. But the North African commandant, Admiral Jean Darlan, agreed to switch sides when Eisenhower's forces landed. After a brief show of resistance, the French surrendered.

Eisenhower now pressed forward quickly against the Germans in North Africa. In February 1943 at Kasserine Pass in the desert south of Tunis, American tanks met Rommel's Afrika Korps. The battle ended in a standoff, but with British troops closing in from their Egyptian bases to the East, the Germans were soon trapped and crushed. In May, after Rommel had been recalled to Germany, his army surrendered.

In July 1943, while air attacks on Germany continued and the Russians slowly pushed the Germans back from the gates of Stalingrad, the Allies invaded Sicily from Africa. In September they advanced to the Italian mainland. Mussolini had already fallen from power and his successor, Marshal Pietro Badoglio, surrendered. However, the German troops in Italy threw up an almost impregnable defense across the rugged Italian peninsula. The Anglo American army inched forward, paying heavily for every advance. Monte Cassino, halfway between Naples and Rome, did not fall until May 1944, the capital itself not until June; months of hard fighting remained before the country was cleared of Germans. The Italian campaign was an Allied disappointment even though it weakened the enemy.

See the Map *World War II in Europe* at **www.myhistorylab.com**

Germany Overwhelmed

By the time the Allies had taken Rome, the mighty army needed to invade France had been collected in England under Eisenhower's command. On **D-Day**, June 6, 1944, the assault forces stormed ashore at five points along the coast of Normandy, supported by a great armada and thousands of planes and paratroops. Against fierce but ill-coordinated German resistance, they established a beachhead: Within a few weeks a million troops were on French soil. (See Re-Viewing the Past, *Saving Private Ryan*, pp. 726–727.)

Thereafter victory was assured, though nearly a year of hard fighting lay ahead. In August the American Third Army under General George S. Patton, an eccentric but brilliant field commander, erupted southward into Brittany and then veered east toward Paris. Another Allied army invaded France from the Mediterranean in mid-August and advanced rapidly north. Free French troops were given the honor of liberating Paris on August 25. Belgium was cleared by British and Canadian units a few days later. By mid-September the Allies were fighting on the edge of Germany itself.

The front now stretched from the Netherlands along the borders of Belgium, Luxembourg, and France all the way to Switzerland. If the Allies had mounted a massive assault at any one point, as the British commander, Field Marshal Bernard Montgomery, urged, the struggle might have been brought to a quick conclusion. Although the two armies were roughly equal in size, the Allies had complete control of the air and twenty times as many tanks as the foe. The pressure of the advancing Russians on the eastern front made it difficult for the Germans to reinforce their troops in the west. But General Eisenhower believed a concentrated attack was too risky. He prepared instead for a general advance.

While he was regrouping, the Germans on December 16 launched a counterattack, planned by Hitler himself, against the Allied center in the Ardennes Forest. The Germans hoped to break through to the Belgian port of Antwerp, thereby splitting the Allied armies in two. The plan was foolhardy and therefore unexpected, and it almost succeeded. The Germans drove a salient ("the bulge") about fifty miles into Belgium. But once the element of surprise had been overcome, their chance of breaking through to the sea was lost. Eisenhower concentrated first on preventing them from broadening the break in his lines and then on blunting the point of their advance. By late January 1945 the old line had been reestablished.

The Battle of the Bulge cost the United States 77,000 casualties and delayed Eisenhower's offensive, but it exhausted the Germans' last reserves. The Allies then pressed forward to the Rhine, winning a bridgehead on the far bank of the river on March 7. Thereafter, one German city fell almost daily. With the Soviets racing westward against crumbling resistance, the end could not be long delayed. In April, American and Soviet forces made contact at the Elbe River. A few days later, with Soviet shells reducing his capital to rubble, Hitler, by then probably insane, took his own life in his Berlin air raid shelter. On May 8 Germany surrendered.

As the Americans drove swiftly forward in the late stages of the war, they began to overrun Nazi concentration camps where millions of Jews and others had been murdered. The Americans were horrified by what they discovered, but they should not have been surprised. Word of this holocaust, in which 12 million people (half of them Jews) were slaughtered, had reached the United States much earlier. At first the news had been dismissed as propaganda, then discounted as grossly exaggerated. Hitler was known to hate Jews and to have persecuted them, but that he could order the murder of millions of innocent people, even children, seemed beyond belief. By 1943, however, the truth could not be denied.

Little could be done about those already in the camps, but there were thousands of refugees in occupied Europe who might have been spirited to safety. President Roosevelt declined to make the effort; he refused to bomb the Auschwitz death camp in Poland or the rail lines used to bring victims to its gas chambers on the grounds that the destruction of German

Senator Alben Barkley of Kentucky views emaciated bodies at Buchenwald, Germany, one of several dozen Nazi concentration camps created to exterminate Jews—and others whom the Nazis deemed "undesirable."

Table 27.1 Turning Points of the War in Europe

Summer 1942	British bombing of German cities brings war home to Germany
November 1942	U.S./British invasion of North Africa, defeat of Rommel
February 1943	Germans turned back at Stalingrad, beginning of German retreat from Soviet Union
July 1943	U.S./British invasion of Sicily
June 1944	D-Day: U.S./British invasion of northern France
January 1945	Battle of the Bulge: Last-ditch German offensive defeated
May 8, 1945	Germany surrenders

soldiers and military equipment took precedence over any other objective. Thus, when American journalists entered the camps with the advancing troops, saw the heaps of still-unburied corpses, and talked with the emaciated survivors, their reports caused a storm of protest in America.

Watch the **Video** *Nazi Murder Mills;* WARNING: This clip is very graphic at **www.myhistorylab.com**

The Naval War in the Pacific

Defeating Germany first had not meant abandoning the Pacific region entirely to the Japanese. While armies were being trained and matériel accumulated for the European struggle, much of the available American strength was diverted to maintaining vital communications in East Asia and preventing further Japanese expansion.

The navy's aircraft carriers had escaped destruction at Pearl Harbor, a stroke of immense good fortune because, without most tacticians realizing it, the airplane had revolutionized naval warfare. Commanders discovered that carrier-based planes were far more effective against warships than the heaviest naval artillery because of their greater range and more concentrated firepower. Battleships made excellent gun platforms from which to pound shore installations and support land operations, but against other vessels aircraft were of prime importance.

This truth was demonstrated in May 1942 in the Battle of the Coral Sea. Having captured an empire in a few months without the loss of any warship larger than a destroyer, the Japanese believed the war already won. This led them to overextend themselves.

The Coral Sea lies northeast of Australia and south of New Guinea and the Solomon Islands. Japanese

Midway, a tiny Pacific island, mattered only because of its airfield. The Japanese sent a naval task force to invade the island, but in June 1942 U.S. warplanes sank several of the Japanese aircraft carriers accompanying the invasion force. With air cover gone, Japan called off the invasion. Midway marked a turning point in the war in the Pacific.

RE-VIEWING THE PAST
Saving Private Ryan

Steven Spielberg's *Saving Private Ryan* (1998), starring Tom Hanks, has been widely praised as the most realistic combat movie ever made. This judgment is based chiefly on its re-creation of the June 6, 1944, Allied assault on Omaha Beach during the invasion of Normandy. The camera focuses on Hanks, rain dripping from his helmet, huddled in a crowded landing vessel. Explosions rumble in the distance. The ship plows through heavy seas toward a blackened brow of land (see accompanying photograph). Around him, men vomit. Explosions become louder and sharper. Nearby ships strike mines and blow up; others are obliterated by shellfire. Hanks's landing craft lurches to avoid the mayhem. Like hail against a tin roof, gunfire riddles the landing craft. Some of the men are hit, and the others hunch lower, still vomiting. A deafening din envelops the ship as its bow opens. A curtain of bullets cuts down the men in front. Hanks and several others leap into the sea, but the ship has stopped far short of the beach. They sink. As bullets tear through the water, ripping into those still submerged, Hanks struggles to the surface. He swims, weaponless, toward the beach.

He has crossed the threshold of hell, and over the next fifteen minutes viewers descend with him the rest of the way.

Saving Private Ryan differs from other combat films not in the graphic horror of the bloodshed, but in its randomness. The audience expects Hanks to survive the opening scenes of the movie in which he stars, and he does. But all other bets are off: a valiant exploit, a kind gesture, a handsome face—none of these influences the grim lottery of battle. A medic frenziedly works on a severely wounded man, injecting morphine, compressing arteries, and binding wounds. Then more bullets splatter his patient beyond recognition. "Why can't you bastards give us a chance?" the

medic screams. That is the point: When huge armies converge, hurling high explosives and steel at each other, one's chances of survival are unaffected by ethics or aesthetics.

But having made this point with heart-pounding emphasis, the movie subverts it. Hanks, unnerved and dispirited, initially hunkers down in the relative safety of the seawall. But then he does his job, rallying his men. They blast a hole through obstacles, crawl toward the concrete fortifications above, penetrate trench defenses, blow up bunkers, and seize the hill. Many perish in the effort; Hanks, an infantry captain, is among the survivors.

Then comes a new mission that occupies the remainder of the movie. George C. Marshall, U.S. Army Chief of Staff, has learned of a Mrs. Ryan who has been notified on a single day that three of her sons were killed in action. Her fourth son, James, a private in the 101st Airborne, has just parachuted into Normandy behind German lines. Marshall orders that Private Ryan be returned to safety. This mission is given to Hanks and the eight surviving members of his platoon. They march inland, encounter snipers, ambushes, and, in the final scenes, a large detachment of German armored vehicles. But they also find Ryan (played by Matt Damon).

Along the way, the movie asks many provocative questions, such as whether war improves those who fight. "I think this is all good for me, sir," one earnest soldier confides to Hanks. "Really," Hanks says with a faint smile, "how is that?" The soldier cites Ralph Waldo Emerson: "War educates the senses. Calls into action the will. Perfects the physical constitution." "Emerson had a way of finding the bright side, " Hanks deadpans, and the movie endorses his cynicism. Delirious and catatonic soldiers stumble across the battlefield. Others, terrified and jittery, shoot enemy soldiers who have surrendered. A sniper, intoning Old Testament verses, takes aim at unsuspecting enemies. Hanks's hand twitches uncontrollably, a physical manifestation of a disordered soul. War, demonstrably, has not made men better.

Except it has made men better in one sense, and that may be all that matters: Hanks and his men have repeatedly demonstrated a willingness to give up their lives for others. Indeed, the movie's central dilemma concerns the moral arithmetic of sacrifice. Is it right to risk eight men to save one? To send a thousand men to near certain death in an initial assault at Omaha Beach to improve the chances of those that follow? To make one generation endure hell so that another may have freedom? The movie provides no ready answers. But in nearly the final scene it does issue a challenge. Hanks, mortally wounded, is lying amidst the corpses of his platoon, and he beckons to Ryan, who is unhurt. "Earn this," Hanks says, vaguely gesturing to the others.

Actual photograph of American troops approach code-named Omaha Beach at Normandy.

Tom Hanks, Matt Damon, and Edward Burns in *Saving Private Ryan*.

Saving Private Ryan was part of a wave of nostalgic appreciation during the 1990s for the generation that had won World War II. A spate of books, movies, and TV documentaries were other expressions of this phenomenon. On accepting the Oscar for his film, Spielberg thanked his father, a World War II vet, "for showing me that there is honor in looking back and respecting the past."

But respect for the past entails getting it right, and the movie makes some significant errors and omissions. For one, it suggests that the men huddled at the base of the seawall blew up the concrete bunkers on their own. This was not possible. In fact, commanders of destroyers took their ships close to the beaches and fired countless heavy shells into the fortifications, allowing the infantry to move up the hills.

The movie also shows the German soldiers as uniformly expert and professional. But the German army had been decimated by losses in the Soviet Union. The army manning the Normandy defenses included many units composed mostly of old men, boys, or conscripted soldiers from Poland or the Soviet Union. Many surrendered as soon as they encountered American soldiers.

Of the movie's implausible elements, the premise that the U.S. Army high command ordered a special mission to pluck a grieving mother's son from danger was based on fact. A real Mrs. Niland received telegrams on the same day informing her that three of her sons had been killed in action. Her fourth son, "Fritz," had parachuted into Normandy with the 101st Airborne. The army did in fact snatch him from the front line and return him to safety.

The movie provides a fair rendering of many other elements of the battle: the inaccuracy of aerial bombing, which missed most of the beach fortifications; the confusion caused when hundreds of landing craft failed to reach their destination; the destruction of scores of gliders, which crashed into high hedgerows while attempting to land behind German lines.

On the other hand, many men at Omaha Beach, like those depicted in the movie, were shattered by the experience. One private, nearly hit by a shell, recalled that he burst into tears. "My buddies got me behind a burned-out craft, where I cried for what seemed like hours. I cried until tears would no longer come. To this day I've never shed another." Other men confessed that, after the terror of a firefight, their platoon shot Germans who had raised their arms in surrender. "In my opinion any enemy shot during this intense action had waited too long to surrender," one G.I. declared.

Yet through it all, some men, like the captain portrayed by Hanks, drew heroism from some unfathomed depths of the soul. One real soldier at Omaha Beach remembered "a captain and two lieutenants who demonstrated courage beyond belief as they struggled to bring order to the chaos around them."

Saving Private Ryan is not a fully accurate representation of the attack on Omaha Beach, but it depicts—realistically and memorably—how soldiers conferred meaning on the heedless calculus of modern warfare.

Questions for Discussion

- Do generals have the right to order some men to near certain death in order to save others? To save a nation?

- Do soldiers have the right to disobey such orders? Why or why not?

mastery of these waters would cut Australia off from Hawaii and thus from American aid. Admiral Isoroku Yamamoto had dispatched a large fleet of troopships screened by many warships to attack Port Moresby, on the southern New Guinea coast. On May 7–8 planes from the American carriers *Lexington* and *Yorktown* struck the convoy's screen, sinking a small carrier and damaging a large one. Superficially, the battle seemed a victory for the Japanese, for their planes mortally wounded the *Lexington* and sank two other ships, but the troop transports had been forced to turn back—Port Moresby was saved. Although large numbers of cruisers and destroyers took part in the action, none came within sight or gun range of an enemy ship. All the destruction was wrought by carrier aircraft.

Encouraged by the Coral Sea "victory," Yamamoto decided to force the American fleet into a showdown battle by assaulting the Midway Islands, west of Hawaii. His armada never reached its destination. Between June 4 and 7 control of the central Pacific was decided entirely by airpower. American dive bombers sent four large Japanese carriers to the bottom. About 300 Japanese planes were destroyed. The United States lost only the *Yorktown* and a destroyer. Thereafter the initiative in the Pacific war shifted to the Americans, but victory came slowly and at painful cost.

American land forces were under the command of Douglas MacArthur, a brilliant but egocentric general whose judgment was sometimes distorted by his intense concern for his own reputation. MacArthur was in command of American troops in the Philippine Islands when the Japanese struck in December 1941. After his heroic but hopeless defense of Manila and the Bataan peninsula, President Roosevelt had him evacuated by PT boat to escape capture; those under MacArthur's command endured horrific conditions as prisoners of Japan.

Thereafter MacArthur was obsessed with the idea of personally leading an American army back to the Philippines. Although many strategists believed that the islands should be bypassed in the drive on the Japanese homeland, in the end MacArthur convinced the Joint Chiefs of Staff, who determined strategy. Two separate drives were undertaken, one from New Guinea toward the Philippines under MacArthur, the other through the central Pacific toward Tokyo under Admiral Chester W. Nimitz.

⊙ See the **Map** *World War II in the Pacific* at **www.myhistorylab.com**

Island Hopping

Before commencing this two-pronged advance, the Americans had to eject the Japanese from the Solomon Islands in order to protect Australia from a

"You know that sheer hell is going on on that island. It rolls over the water. You can hear the thunder," wrote Richard M. Gibney, who painted *Landing on Tarawa* (1943).

flank attack. Beginning in August 1942, a series of land, sea, and air battles raged around Guadalcanal Island in this archipelago. Once again American airpower was decisive, although the bravery and skill of the ground forces that actually won the island must not be underemphasized. American pilots, better trained and with tougher planes than the Japanese, had a relatively easier task. They inflicted losses five to six times heavier on the enemy than they sustained themselves. Japanese airpower disintegrated during the long battle, and this in turn helped the fleet to take a heavy toll on the Japanese navy. By February 1943 Guadalcanal had been secured.

Table 27.2 Turning Points of World War II in the Pacific

December 7, 1941	Japanese sneak-attack on Pearl Harbor; United States declares war
May 1942	Japanese win Battle of the Coral Sea, but invasion of Australia foiled
June 1942	United States wins Battle of Midway; Japanese advance toward Hawaii turned back
February 1943	United States takes Guadalcanal, along the southernmost periphery of Japanese power
February 1945	United States retakes Philippines
June 1945	United States takes Okinawa, near Japanese islands
August 1945	United States drops atomic bombs on Hiroshima and Nagasaki; Japan surrenders

In the autumn of 1943 the American drives toward Japan and the Philippines got under way at last. In the central Pacific campaign the Guadalcanal action was repeated on a smaller but equally bloody scale from Tarawa in the Gilbert Islands to Kwajelein and Eniwetok in the Marshalls. The Japanese soldiers on these islands fought for every foot of ground. They had to be blasted and burned from tunnels and concrete pillboxes with hand grenades, flamethrowers, and dynamite. They almost never surrendered. But Admiral Nimitz's forces were in every case victorious. By midsummer of 1944 this arm of the American advance had taken Saipan and Guam in the Marianas. Now land based bombers were within range of Tokyo.

Meanwhile, MacArthur was leapfrogging along the New Guinea coast toward the Philippines. In October 1944 he made good his promise to return to the islands, landing on Leyte, south of Luzon. Two great naval clashes in Philippine waters, the Battle of the Philippine Sea (June 1944) and the Battle for Leyte Gulf (October 1944), completed the destruction of Japan's sea power and reduced its air force to a band of fanatical suicide pilots called *kamikazes*, who tried to crash bomb-laden planes into American warships and airstrips. The *kamikazes* caused much damage but could not turn the tide. In February 1945 MacArthur liberated Manila.

The end was now inevitable. B-29 Superfortress bombers from the Marianas rained high explosives and firebombs on Japan. The islands of Iwo Jima and Okinawa, only a few hundred miles from Tokyo, fell to the Americans in March and June 1945. But

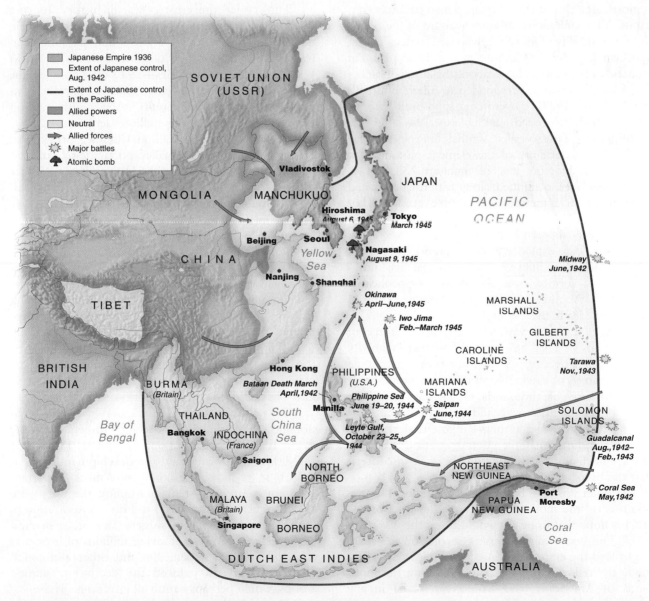

World War II Pacific Theatre After the Battle of Midway (June, 1942), the United States began to seize one Pacific island after another, with one task force pushing west from Pearl Harbor, and another moving north from Australia.

such was the tenacity of the Japanese soldiers that it seemed possible that it would take another year of fighting and perhaps a million more American casualties to subdue the home Japanese islands.

Building the Atom Bomb

At this point came the most controversial decision of the entire war, and it was made by a newcomer on the world scene. In November 1944 Roosevelt had been elected to a fourth term, easily defeating Thomas E. Dewey. Instead of renominating Henry A. Wallace for vice president, whom conservatives considered too radical, the Democratic convention had nominated Senator Harry S Truman of Missouri, a reliable party man well-liked by professional politicians. Then, in April 1945, President Roosevelt died of a cerebral hemorrhage. Thus it was Truman, a man painfully conscious of his limitations yet equally aware of the power and responsibility of his office, who had to decide what to do when, in July 1945, American scientists placed in his hands a new and awful weapon, the atomic bomb.

After Roosevelt had responded to Albert Einstein's warning in 1939, government-sponsored atomic research had proceeded rapidly, especially after the establishment of the so-called Manhattan Project in May 1943. The manufacture of the element plutonium at Hanford, Washington, and of uranium 235 at Oak Ridge, Tennessee, continued, along with the design and construction of a transportable atomic bomb at Los Alamos, New Mexico, under the direction of J. Robert Oppenheimer. Almost $2 billion was spent before a successful bomb was exploded at Alamogordo, in the New Mexican desert, on July 16, 1945. As that first mushroom cloud formed over the desert, Oppenheimer recalled the prophetic words of the *Bhagavad Gita*: "I am become death, the shatterer of worlds."

Should a bomb with the destructive force of 20,000 tons of TNT be employed against Japan? By striking a major city, its dreadful power could be demonstrated convincingly, yet doing so would bring death to tens of thousands of Japanese civilians. Many of the scientists who had made the bomb now argued against its use. Others suggested alerting the Japanese and then staging a demonstration explosion at sea, but that idea was discarded because of concern that the bomb might fail to explode.

Truman was torn between his awareness that the bomb was "the most terrible thing ever discovered" and his hope that using it "would bring the war to an end." The bomb might cause a revolution in Japan, might lead the emperor to intervene, might even persuade the military to give up. Considering the thousands of Americans who would surely die in any conventional invasion of Japan and, on a less humane level, influenced by a desire to end the Pacific war

before the Soviet Union could intervene effectively and thus claim a role in the peacemaking, the president chose to go ahead. The moral soundness of Truman's decision has been debated ever since. (See Debating the Past, "Should A-Bombs Have Been Dropped on Japan?", p. 731.) On August 6 the Superfortress *Enola Gay* dropped an atomic bomb on Hiroshima, killing about 78,000 persons (including twenty American prisoners of war) and injuring nearly 100,000 more out of a population of 344,000. Over 96 percent of the buildings in the city were destroyed or damaged. Three days later, while the stunned Japanese still hesitated, a second atomic bomb, the only other one that had so far been assembled, blasted Nagasaki. This second drop was less defensible morally, but it had the desired result. On August 15 Japan surrendered.

Thus ended the greatest war in history. Its cost was beyond calculation. No accurate count could be made even of the dead; we know only that the total was in the neighborhood of 20 million. As in World War I, American casualties—291,000 battle deaths and 671,000 wounded—were smaller than those of the other major belligerents. About 7.5 million Soviets died in battle, 3.5 million Germans, 1.2 million Japanese, and 2.2 million Chinese; Britain and France, despite much smaller populations, suffered losses almost as large as did the United States. And far more than in World War I, American resources, human and matériel, had made victory possible.

No one could account the war a benefit to humanity, but in the late summer of 1945 the future looked bright. Fascism was dead. The successful wartime diplomatic dealings of Roosevelt, Churchill, and the Soviet dictator, Joseph Stalin, encouraged many to hope that the communists were ready to cooperate in rebuilding Europe. In the United States isolationism had disappeared; the message of Wendell Willkie's best-selling *One World*, written after a globe-circling tour made by the 1940 Republican presidential candidate at the behest of President Roosevelt in 1942, appeared to have been absorbed by the majority of the people.

Out of the death and destruction had come technological developments that seemed to herald a better world as well as a peaceful one. Enormous advances in the design of airplanes and the development of radar (which some authorities think was more important than any weapons system in winning the war) were about to revolutionize travel and the transportation of goods. Improvements in surgery and other medical advances gave promise of saving millions of lives, and the development of penicillin and other antibiotics, which had greatly reduced the death rate among troops, would perhaps banish all infectious diseases.

Above all, there was the power of the atom. The force that seared Hiroshima and Nagasaki could be

Should A-Bombs Have Been Dropped on Japan?

Hiroshima lies in ruins after it was destroyed by an atomic bomb.

Robert J. C. Butow's (1954) analysis of Japanese sources proved that the devastation of Hiroshima and Nagasaki had led to Japan's surrender. If there had been no atom bomb, the United States would probably have been forced to invade the islands. According to military estimates cited at the time, an invasion would have resulted in a hundreds of thousands of American casualties. Biographers such as David McCullough (1992) and Alonzo L. Hamby (1995) agreed that, given public and congressional opinion, Truman had little choice but to end the war as quickly as possible and with the fewest American casualties.

But historian Gar Alperovitz (1965) proposed that Truman had been influenced more by a desire to intimidate Stalin than to force the surrender of Japan. This position was strengthened by subsequently declassified documents indicating that few U.S. military analysts anticipated losses as high as those reported in Butow and other sources. John Dower (1986) discovered evidence in Japanese sources that the Soviet declaration of war, which came in the wake of Hiroshima, shattered the confidence of the Japanese high command as much as the atomic bombs. Soviet entry alone might have ended the war. Dower insisted that Americans rushed to use atomic weapons against Japan because of their "sheer visceral hatred" of the Japanese.

The revisionist hypothesis—that Japan might have surrendered without the atomic bombs—is belied by exhaustive last-ditch Japanese preparations for defending the home islands. Whether this information justifies this first—and to date, only—use of nuclear weapons will forever remain a source of debate.

Source: Robert J. C. Butow, *Japan's Decision to Surrender* (1954); Alonzo L. Hamby, *Man of the People* (1995); David McCullough, *Truman* (1992); Gar Alperovitz, *Atomic Diplomacy* (1965) and *The Decision to Use the Atomic Bomb and the Architecture of an American Myth* (1995); John W. Dower, *War Without Mercy* (1986).

■ ■ ■ ■ ■

harnessed to serve peaceful needs, the scientists promised, with results that might free humanity forever from poverty and toil. The period of reconstruction would be prolonged, but with all the great powers adhering to the new United Nations charter, drafted at San Francisco in June 1945, international cooperation could be counted on to ease the burdens of the victims of war and help the poor and underdeveloped parts of the world toward economic and political independence. Such at least was the hope of millions in the victorious summer of 1945.

●●●┤Read the Document Einstein, *Letter to President Roosevelt* at www.myhistorylab.com

Wartime Diplomacy

The hope for a new era of international cooperation was not to be realized, in large part because of a conflict that developed between the Soviet Union and the western Allies. During the course of World War II every instrument of mass persuasion in the country had been directed toward convincing the people that the Soviets were fighting America's battle as well as their own. Even before Pearl Harbor, former Ambassador Joseph E. Davies wrote in his best-selling *Mission to Moscow* (1941) that the communist leaders were "devoted to the cause of peace for both ideological and practical reasons." Of Stalin, who had ruthlessly executed thousands of his former comrades, Davies wrote the following: "His brown eye is exceedingly kind and gentle. A child would like to sit in his lap and a dog would sidle up to him."

Such views of the character of Joseph Stalin were naive, to say the least, but the United States and the Soviet Union agreed emphatically on the need to defeat Hitler. The Soviets repeatedly expressed a willingness to cooperate with the Allies in dealing with postwar problems. The Soviet Union was one of the twenty-six signers of the Declaration of the United Nations (January 1942), in which the Allies promised to eschew territorial aggrandizement after the war, to respect the right of all peoples to determine their own form of government, to work for freer trade and international economic cooperation, and to force the disarmament of the aggressor nations.[1]

In May 1943 the Soviet Union dissolved the Comintern, its official agency for the promulgation of world revolution. The following October, during a conference in Moscow with the Allies, Soviet Foreign Minister V. M. Molotov joined in setting up a European Advisory Commission to divide Germany into occupation zones after the war. That December, at a conference held in Tehran, Iran, Roosevelt, Churchill, and Stalin discussed plans for a new league of nations. When Roosevelt described the kind of world organization he envisaged, the Soviet dictator offered a number of constructive suggestions.

Between August and October 1944, Allied representatives met at Dumbarton Oaks, outside Washington. The chief Soviet delegate, Andrei A. Gromyko, opposed limiting the use of the veto by the great powers on the future **United Nations (UN)** Security Council, but he did not take a deliberately obstructionist position. At a conference held at Yalta in the Crimea in February 1945 Stalin joined Roosevelt and Churchill in the call for a meeting in April at San Francisco to draft a charter for the UN. "We argued freely and frankly across the table," Roosevelt reported later. "But at the end, on every point, unanimous agreement was reached. I may say we achieved a unity of thought and a way of getting along together." Privately Roosevelt characterized Stalin as "a very interesting man" whose rough exterior clothed an "old-fashioned elegant European

manner." He referred to him almost affectionately as "that old buzzard" and on one occasion called him "Uncle Joe" to his face. At Yalta, Stalin gave Roosevelt a portrait photograph, with a long Cyrillic inscription in his small, tightly written hand.

The UN charter drafted at the 50-nation San Francisco Conference gave each UN member a seat in the General Assembly, a body designed for discussion rather than action. The locus of authority in the new organization resided in the Security Council, "the castle of the great powers." This consisted of five permanent members (the United States, the Soviet Union, Great Britain, France, and China) and six others elected for two-year terms.

The Security Council was charged with responsibility for maintaining world peace, but any great power could block UN action whenever it wished to do so. The United States insisted on this veto power as strongly as the Soviet Union did. In effect the charter paid lip service to the Wilsonian ideal of a powerful international police force, but it incorporated the limitations that Henry Cabot Lodge had proposed in his 1919 reservation to Article X of the League Covenant, which relieved the United States from the obligation of enforcing collective security without the approval of Congress.

Allied Suspicion of Stalin

Long before the war in Europe ended, however, the Allies had clashed over important policy matters. Since later world tensions developed from decisions made at this time, an understanding of the disagreements is essential for evaluating several subsequent decades.

Much depends on one's view of the postwar Soviet system. If the Soviet government under Stalin was bent on world domination, events fall readily into one pattern of interpretation. If, having at enormous cost endured an unprovoked assault by the Nazis, it was seeking only to protect itself against the possibility of another invasion, these events are best explained differently. Because the United States has opened nearly all its diplomatic records, we know a great deal about how American foreign policy was formulated and about the mixed motives and mistaken judgments of American leaders. This helps explain why many scholars have been critical of American policy and the "cold warriors" who made and directed it. The Soviet Union, for many years, did not let even its own historians into its archives.

It is clear, however, that the Soviets resented the British-American delay in opening up a second front. They were fighting for survival against the full power of the German armies; any American invasion of northern France, even an unsuccessful one, would have relieved some of the pressure. Roosevelt and Churchill would not move until they were ready, and Stalin had

[1]These were the principles first laid down in the so-called Atlantic Charter, drafted by Roosevelt and Churchill at a meeting on the USS *Augusta* off Newfoundland in August 1941.

to accept their decision. At the same time, Stalin never concealed his determination to protect his country from future attack by extending its frontier after the war. He warned the Allies repeatedly that he would not tolerate any unfriendly government along the western boundary of the Soviet Union.

Most Allied leaders, including Roosevelt, admitted privately during the war that the Soviet Union would annex territory and possess preponderant power in Eastern Europe after the defeat of Germany, but they never said this publicly. They believed that the Soviets would allow free governments to be created in countries like Poland and Bulgaria. "The Poles," Winston Churchill said early in 1945, "will have their future in their own hands, with the single limitation that they must honestly follow . . . a policy friendly to Russia. This is surely reasonable."

Churchill, Roosevelt, and Stalin meet at the Yalta, U.S.S.R., conference in February 1945. By April 1945, Roosevelt was dead.

However reasonable, Churchill's statement was impractical. The Polish question was a terribly difficult one. The war, after all, had been triggered by the German attack on Poland; the British in particular felt a moral obligation to restore that nation to its prewar independence. During the war a Polish government in exile was set up in London, and its leaders were determined—especially after the discovery in 1943 of the murder of some 5,000 Polish officers several years earlier at Katyn, in Russia, presumably by the Soviet secret police—to make no concessions to Soviet territorial demands. Public opinion in Poland (and indeed in all the states along Russia's western frontier) was not so much anti-Soviet as anti-Russian. Yet the Soviet Union's legitimate interests (to say nothing of its power in the area) could not be ignored.

Yalta and Potsdam

At the **Yalta Conference**, Roosevelt and Churchill agreed to Soviet annexation of large sections of eastern Poland. In return they demanded that free elections be held in Poland itself. "I want this election to be . . . beyond question," Roosevelt told Stalin. "It should be like Caesar's wife." In a feeble attempt at a joke he added, "I did not know her but they said she was pure." Stalin agreed, almost certainly without intending to keep his promise. The elections were never held; Poland was run by a pro-Soviet puppet regime.

Stalin apparently could not understand why the Allies were so concerned about the fate of a small country remote from their strategic spheres. That they professed to be concerned seemed to him an indication that they had some secret, devious purpose. He could see no difference (and "revisionist" American historians agree with him) between the Soviet Union's

dominating Poland and maintaining a government there that did not reflect the wishes of a majority of the Polish people and the United States' dominating many Latin American nations and supporting unpopular regimes within them. Roosevelt, however, was worried about the political effects that Soviet control of Poland might have in the United States. Polish Americans would be furious if the United States allowed the Soviets to control their homeland.

But had Roosevelt described the difficulties to the Polish Americans and the rest of the American people more frankly, their reaction might have been less angry. In any case, when he realized that Stalin was going to act as he pleased, Roosevelt was furious. "We can't do business with Stalin," he said shortly before his death in April 1945. "He has broken every one of the promises he made at Yalta." In July 1945, following the surrender of Germany, the new president, Harry Truman, met with Stalin and Churchill at Potsdam, outside Berlin.[2] At the **Potsdam Conference** they agreed to try the Nazi leaders as war criminals, made plans for exacting reparations from Germany, and confirmed the division of the country into four zones to be occupied separately by American, Soviet, British, and French troops. Berlin, deep in the Soviet zone, had itself been split into four sectors. Stalin rejected all arguments that he loosen his hold on Eastern Europe, and Truman (who received news of the successful testing of the atom bomb while at Potsdam) made no concessions. But he was impressed by Stalin. The dictator was "smart as hell," he wrote in his diary. "Stalin was an SOB," the plainspoken president explained to some officers while returning to the United States from

---

[2]Clement R. Attlee replaced Churchill during the conference after his Labour party won the British elections.

Potsdam on the cruiser *Augusta*. Then he added, "Of course he thinks I'm one too."

On both sides suspicions were mounting, positions hardening. Yet all the advantages seemed to be with the United States. Was this not, as Henry Luce, the publisher of *Time* had declared, "the American century," an era when American power and American ideals would shape the course of events the world over? Besides its army, navy, and air force and its immense industrial potential, alone among the nations the United States possessed the atomic bomb. When Stalin's actions made it clear that he intended to control Eastern Europe and to exert influence elsewhere in the world, most Americans first reacted somewhat

in the manner of a mastiff being worried by a yapping terrier: Their resentment was tempered by amazement. It took time for them to realize that the war had caused a fundamental change in international politics. The United States might be the strongest country in the world, but the western European nations, victor and vanquished alike, were reduced to their own and America's surprise to the status of second-class powers. The Soviet Union, on the other hand, had gained more influence than it had held under the czars and regained the territory it had lost as a result of World War I and the communist revolution.

Watch the Video *The Big Three Conference at Yalta* at www.myhistorylab.com

Chapter Review

Milestones

1941	Roosevelt prohibits discrimination in defense plants (Fair Employment Practices Committee)
	Japan attacks Pearl Harbor
	Roosevelt and Churchill draft Atlantic Charter
1942	Executive Order 9066 sends Japanese Americans to relocation camps
	Japanese take Philippines
	Carrier-based planes dominate Battle of Coral Sea
	U.S. airpower takes control of central Pacific at Battle of Midway
	U.S. troops invade North Africa
1943	Oppenheimer directs Manhattan Project to make atom bomb
	Race riots rage in Detroit and Los Angeles

	Allies invade Italy
	Roosevelt, Churchill, Stalin meet at Tehran, Iran
1944	Allies invade Normandy, France (D-Day)
	Battle of the Bulge exhausts German reserves
1945	Big Three meet at Yalta Conference
	Fifty nations draft UN Charter at San Francisco
	Roosevelt dies; Truman becomes president
	Germany surrenders (V-E Day)
	United States tests atom bomb at Alamogordo, New Mexico
	Truman, Churchill, Stalin meet at Potsdam
	United States drops atom bombs on Hiroshima and Nagasaki, Japan
	Japan surrenders (V-J Day)

Key Terms

Allies   In the context of United States history, a term that refers to the nations that opposed the **Axis Powers**, chiefly Nazi Germany, Italy, and Japan, during World War II. The Allies included Britain, France (except during the Nazi occupation, 1940–1944), the Soviet Union (1941–1945), the United States (1941–1945), and China, *722*

D-Day   June 6, 1944, the day Allied troops crossed the English Channel, landed on the coast of Normandy, and opened a second front in Western Europe during World War II. The "D" stands for "disembarkation"—to leave a ship and go ashore, *724*

internment camps   Detainment centers, mostly located in western states, that held approximately 110,000 Japanese aliens and American citizens of Japanese origin during World War II, *720*

Potsdam Conference   A wartime conference (April 1945) held in occupied Germany where Allied leaders divided Germany and Berlin into four occupation zones, agreed to try Nazi leaders as war criminals, and planned the exacting of reparations from Germany, *733*

United Nations (UN)   An international organization, founded in 1945, that sought to promote discussion and negotiation and thereby avoid war; it was joined by nearly all nations, *732*

Yalta Conference   A wartime conference (February 1945) held in the Russian Crimea, where the **Allies**—Franklin Roosevelt, Winston Churchill (Britain), and Josef Stalin (Soviet Union)—agreed to final plans for the defeat and joint occupation of Germany; it also provided for free elections in Poland, but such elections were never held, *733*

Review Questions

1. What did the U.S. government do to mobilize for war? How did the war affect women and minority groups?
2. Why did FDR order that American citizens of Japanese ancestry be placed in internment camps? What was the Supreme Court's response to the constitutionality of this decision?
3. Why, since Japan attacked first, did FDR decide to commit most American resources to defeating the Germans in Europe? What were the key phases of the war in Europe? Of the war in the Pacific?
4. What role did science and technology play in the war?
5. Should Truman have used atomic bombs against Japan? Why had American relations with the Soviet Union deteriorated by 1945?

PEARSON myhistorylab Connections

Reinforce what you learned in this chapter by studying the many documents, images, maps, review tools, and videos available at **www.myhistorylab.com**.

Read and Review

✔ Study and Review *Chapter 27*

View the Image *Ration Stamps WWII*, p. 717

Read the Document Randolph, *Why Should We March*, p. 719

View the Image *Rosie the Riveter*, p. 722

See the Map *World War II in Europe*, p. 723

See the Map *World War II in the Pacific*, p. 728

Read the Document Einstein, *Letter to President Roosevelt*, p. 731

Research and Explore

Watch the Video *The desegregation of the military and blacks in combat*, p. 719

Watch the Video *Nazi Murder Mills;* WARNING: This clip is very graphic, p. 725

Watch the Video *The Big Three Conference at Yalta*, p. 734

((•—[Hear the Audio

Hear the audio file for Chapter 27 at
www.myhistorylab.com.

Do you ever drive too fast?

In 2009 over 10,000 people between the ages of sixteen and twenty-four were killed in motor vehicle accidents—the leading cause of death among young people. Each month nearly as many Americans died in car crashes as perished at the World Trade Center on September 11, 2001. American traffic fatalities totaled 34,000.

But it could have been worse—and once was. During the decade of the 1970s, a half million Americans died in traffic accidents—over 50,000 each year. In 1972—the worst ever—54,589 were killed, more than the total American deaths in the Korean War. Since Henry Ford first rolled out the Model-T, over three and a half million Americans have died on the nation's roads and highways. Despite the carnage, automobiles have become so much a part of American life that few can imagine living without them.

The ascendancy of the automobile over mass transit was well-established during the 1930s. But World War II put more Americans in motion than ever before. Afterwards, car ownership soared. Designers produced faster and heavier cars for "a wartime generation" that was far "bigger, taller and more active" than its predecessors. The war influenced automotive design in other ways. The 1955 Chevy

((•—Hear the Audio **Chapter 28 at www.myhistorylab.com**

■ The Chevy Nomad, 1955, exemplified the "breathless but unverbalizable consequence of the live culture of the Technological Century," or so gushed British art critic Reyner Banham.

Nomad, pictured here, was the brainchild of Edward Cole, designer of the M-5 tank in 1941. He used a similar V-8 engine to power the Nomad. He highlighted the car's link to the war by adding "gun sights" and a jet airplane as the hood ornament. Driving cars such as this one, Americans hurtled along the new superhighways that the federal government built in part for military purposes.

The American nation, too, was hurtling into a new era of Cold War confrontation with the Soviet Union—"cold" because the prospect of real war between the two superpowers had become unimaginably destructive. In both countries new weapons loomed larger, each more menacing than the last. By 1960, hundreds of millions of

people could be wiped out in an instant. The Cold War between the superpowers turned hot in Korea, the Middle East, and Latin America. Real foreign spies exacerbated fears of domestic subversion.

Postwar complacency soon gave way to racial confrontation at home. African Americans who had helped defeat Nazi racism accelerated demands for fair treatment. First they challenged Jim Crow segregation in the courts. When these initiatives encountered segregationist roadblocks, African Americans turned to nonviolent protests that they knew would likely trigger violent responses.

From 1946 through 1960, Americans lived dangerously in a postwar era of menacing uncertainty. ■

The Postwar Economy

Economists had feared that the flood of millions of veterans into the job market would cause serious unemployment. But the widespread craving for cars—bigger, faster, and "loaded" with features such as radios and air-conditioners—fueled the postwar economic boom. During the decade of the 1920s American factories had produced 31 million cars. In the 1950s, 58 million rolled off the assembly lines; during the 1960s, 77 million were made. The proliferation of cars contributed to the expansion of related industries, especially oil. Gasoline consumption first touched 15 billion gallons in 1931; it soared to 35 billion gallons in 1950 and to 92 billion in 1970. A new business, the motel industry (the word, typically American, was a combination of *motor* and *hotel*) developed to service the millions of tourists and business travelers who burned all this fuel.

Although the car industry was the leading postwar economic sector, war-weary Americans also bought new houses, washing machines, and countless other products. Unable to buy such goods during the war, they used their war-enforced savings to go on a shopping spree that kept factories operating at capacity.

In addition, the government made an unprecedented educational opportunity available to veterans. Instead of a general bonus, which would have stimulated consumption and inflation, in 1944 Congress passed the *GI Bill of Rights*, which made subsidies available to veterans so they could continue their educations, learn new trades, or start new businesses. After the war nearly 8 million veterans took advantage of the education and training grants, greatly to their long-term advantage, and thus to the country's.

Economic prosperity in the decades after World War II allowed the federal government to increase its military and economic commitments abroad without raising taxes.

Truman Becomes President

When Harry S Truman received the news of Roosevelt's death in 1945, he claimed that he felt as though "the moon, the stars, and all the planets" had

Levittown, New York, in 1949 epitomizes the postwar housing boom.

An ad in *Life* magazine features the Dodge Coronet, a car suitable for soldiers.

suddenly fallen upon him. Although he could not have been quite as surprised as he indicated (Roosevelt was known to have been in extremely poor health), he was acutely conscious of his own limitations.

Truman was born in Missouri in 1884. After his service in a World War I artillery unit, he opened a men's clothing store in Kansas City. The store failed in the postwar depression. Truman then became a minor cog in the political machine of Democratic boss Tom Pendergast. In 1934 Truman was elected to the U.S. Senate, where he proved to be a loyal but obscure New Dealer. He first attracted national attention during World War II when his "watchdog" committee on defense spending, working with devotion and efficiency, saved the government immense sums. This led to his nomination and election as vice president.

As president, Truman sought to carry on in the Roosevelt tradition. Curiously, he was at the same time humble and cocky, even brash—both idealistic and cold-bloodedly political. He adopted liberal objectives only to pursue them sometimes by rash, even repressive means. Too often he insulted opponents instead of convincing or appeasing them. Complications tended to confuse him, in which case he either dug in his heels or struck out blindly, usually with unfortunate results. On balance, however, he was a strong and, in many ways, successful president.

But he lost a major battle early on. In June 1947, the new Congress passed the **Taft-Hartley Act**. It outlawed the closed shop (a provision written into many labor contracts requiring new workers to join the union before they could be employed). Most important, it authorized the president to seek court injunctions to prevent strikes that, in his opinion, endangered the national interest.

Truman vetoed the bill, but Congress overrode it. The Taft-Hartley Act made the task of unionizing industries more difficult, but it did not seriously hamper existing unions.

The Containment Policy

Although he was vice president during much of World War II, Truman had been excluded from all foreign policy discussions. He was not granted full security clearance and thus knew little about the Manhattan project. "They didn't tell me anything about what was going on," Truman complained. While FDR had concluded at Yalta that he could charm or otherwise personally cope with the Soviet dictator, Truman early resolved to deal with Stalin firmly.

Repeatedly Stalin made it clear that he had no intention of even consulting with Western leaders about his domination of Eastern Europe, and he seemed intent on extending his power deep into war-devastated central Europe. The Soviet Union also controlled Outer Mongolia, parts of Manchuria, and northern Korea, and it had annexed the Kurile Islands and regained the southern half of Sakhalin Island from Japan. It was fomenting trouble in Iran. By January 1946 Truman had decided to stop "babying" the Russians. "Only one language do they understand," he noted in a memorandum. "How many [military] divisions have you?"

Truman's problem—and it would bedevil American policymakers for years—was that Stalin had far more divisions than anyone else. Truman, a seasoned politician, had swiftly responded to the postwar clamor to "bring the boys home." In the two years following the surrender of Japan, the armed forces of the United States had dwindled from 6 million to 1.5 million. Stalin, who kept domestic foes out of office by shooting them, ignored domestic pressure to demobilize the Red Army, estimated by U.S. intelligence at twice the size of the American army.

Stalin and the mighty Red Army evoked the image of Hitler's troops pouring across the north European plains. Like Hitler, Stalin was a cruel dictator who championed an ideology of world conquest. Averill Harriman, American ambassador to the Soviet Union, warned that communist ideology exerted an "outward thrust" more dangerous than Nazism. George Kennan, a scholarly foreign officer who also had served

ПОД ВОДИТЕЛЬСТВОМ ВЕЛИКОГО СТАЛИНА—ВПЕРЕД К КОММУНИЗМУ!

A propaganda poster enshrining Stalin proclaims that he has led his people "Forward to Communism!"

in Moscow, thought that ideology was more symptom than cause. Marxism, he wrote, provided the intellectual "fig-leaf of morality and respectability" for naked Soviet aggression. In an influential article, "The Sources of Soviet Conduct," published anonymously in the July 1947 issue of *Foreign Affairs,* Kennan argued that the instability and illegitimacy of the Soviet regime generated explosive internal pressures. These forces, vented outward, would cause the Soviet Union to expand "constantly, wherever it is permitted to move" until it filled "every nook and cranny available to it in the basin of world power." A policy of "long-term, patient but firm and vigilant containment" was the best means of dealing with the Soviet Union.

"The Sources of Soviet Conduct" was powerfully argued, but the article was ambiguous and imprecise in crucial aspects. Exactly how the Soviets were to be "contained" and the parts of the world to which the policy should be applied were not spelled out. At the outset containment was less a plan of action than a plea for the resolve to act.

The Atom Bomb: A "Winning" Weapon?

Although Truman authorized use of the atom bomb to force the surrender of Japan, he had hoped that a demonstration of the weapon's power also would

inhibit Stalin and serve as a counterweight to the Red Army. Stalin, however, refused to be intimidated. "Atomic bombs are meant to frighten those with weak nerves," he told his advisers. His resolve had been stiffened as a result of Soviet espionage. Stalin knew that the American atomic arsenal—slightly more than a dozen bombs in 1947—was insufficient to destroy the Soviet Union's military machine.

The atomic bomb was a doubtful deterrent for another reason. Sobering accounts of the devastation of Hiroshima and Nagasaki and the suffering of the victims of radiation poisoning left many Americans uneasy. J. Robert Oppenheimer, director of the atom bomb design team, informed government officials that most scientists in the Manhattan Project would not continue such work. "I feel we have blood on our hands," he told President Truman. "Never mind," Truman snapped. "It'll all come out in the wash." Yet even Truman came to doubt whether the American people would again "permit" their president to use atomic weapons for aggressive purposes.

In November 1945 the United States suggested that the UN supervise all nuclear energy production, and the General Assembly created an Atomic Energy Commission to study the question. In June 1946 Commissioner Bernard Baruch offered a plan for the eventual outlawing of atomic weapons. Under this proposal UN inspectors operating without restriction anywhere in the world would ensure that no country made bombs clandestinely. When, at an unspecified date, the system was established successfully, the United States would destroy its stockpile of bombs.

Most Americans thought the Baruch plan magnanimous, and some considered it positively foolhardy, but the Soviets rejected it. They would neither permit UN inspectors in the Soviet Union nor surrender the Soviet Union's veto power over Security Council actions dealing with atomic energy. They demanded that the United States destroy its bombs at once. American leaders did not comply; they believed that the atom bomb would be, in Baruch's words, their "winning weapon" for years to come. Exactly how it would be used, no one could say.

Watch the **Video** *Duck and Cover* at **www.myhistorylab.com**

A Turning Point in Greece

The strategy of containment began to take shape early in 1947 as a result of a crisis in Greece. Greek communists, waging a guerrilla war against the monarchy, were receiving aid from communist Yugoslavia and Bulgaria. Great Britain had been assisting the monarchists but could no longer afford this drain on its resources. In February 1947 the British informed President Truman that they would cut off aid to Greece.

The British predicament forced American policymakers to confront the fact that their European allies had not been able to rebuild their war-weakened economies. The communist "Iron Curtain" (a phrase coined by Winston Churchill) seemed about to fall down on another nation. That the Soviet Union was actually discouraging the rebels out of fear of American intervention in the area the policymakers ignored. As Undersecretary of State Dean Acheson put it, the "corruption" of Greece might "infect" the entire Middle East and then spread through Asia Minor and Egypt to Italy and France.

Truman therefore asked Congress to approve what became known as the **Truman Doctrine**. If Greece or Turkey fell to the communists, he said, all of the Middle East might be lost. To prevent this "unspeakable tragedy," he asked for $400 million in military and economic aid to Greece and Turkey. "It must be the policy of the United States to support free peoples who are resisting attempted subjugation by armed minorities or by outside pressures," he said.

By exaggerating the consequences of inaction and by justifying his request on ideological grounds, Truman obtained his objective. The result was the establishment of a right-wing, military-dominated government in Greece. In addition, by not limiting his request to the specific problem posed by the situation

in Greece, Truman caused considerable concern in many countries.

The threat to Western Europe certainly loomed large in 1947. With the region, in the words of Winston Churchill (the great phrase-maker of the era), "a rubble-heap, a charnel house, a breeding-ground of pestilence and hate," the entire continent seemed in danger of falling into communist hands without the Soviet Union raising a finger.

Read the **Document** *Truman Doctrine, 1947* at **www.myhistorylab.com**

The Marshall Plan and the Lesson of History

In a 1946 speech entitled "The Lesson of History," George C. Marshall, army chief of staff during World War II, reminded Americans that their isolationism had contributed to Hitler's unchecked early aggression. This time, Marshall noted, the people of the United States must be prepared to act against foreign aggressors. In 1947 Marshall was named secretary of state. He outlined an extraordinary plan by which the United States would finance the reconstruction of the European economy. "Hunger, poverty, desperation, and chaos" were the real enemies of freedom and democracy, Marshall said. The need was to restore "the confidence of the European people in the economic future of their own countries." Even the Soviet Union and Soviet-bloc nations would be eligible for American aid.

The European powers eagerly seized upon what became known as the **Marshall Plan**, a massive infusion of American aid to rebuild Europe after World War II. European leaders set up a sixteen-nation Committee for European Economic Cooperation, which soon submitted plans calling for up to $22.4 billion in American assistance.

The Soviet Union and its European satellites were tempted by the offer and sent representatives to the initial planning meetings. But Stalin grew anxious that his satellite states would be drawn into the orbit of the United States. He recalled his delegates and demanded that Soviet bloc nations do likewise. Those who hesitated were ordered to report to the Kremlin. "I went to Moscow as the Foreign Minister of an independent sovereign state," Jan Masaryk of Czechoslovakia commented bitterly. "I returned as a lackey of the Soviet government."

In February 1948 a communist coup took over the Czechoslovak government; Masaryk fell (or more likely was pushed) out a window to his death. These strong-arm tactics brought to mind the Nazi takeover of Czechoslovakia a decade earlier and helped persuade Congress to appropriate over $13 billion for the Marshall aid program. Results exceeded all expectations. By 1951 Western Europe was booming.

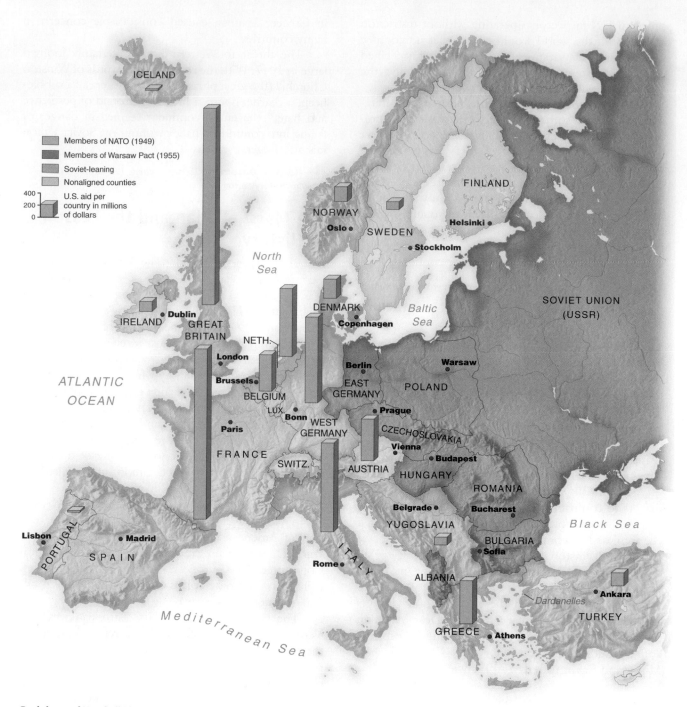

Recipients of Marshall Plan Aid, 1948–1952 Marshall Plan aid was originally offered to the Soviet Union and communist bloc states. Stalin, however, refused to accept American aid and ordered Soviet satellites to refuse, too. All did, except Yugoslavia, whose disobedience infuriated Stalin.

But Europe was now divided in two. In the West, where American-influenced governments were elected, private property was respected if often taxed heavily, and corporations gained influence and power. In the East, where the Soviet Union imposed its will and political system on client states, deep-seated resentment festered among subject peoples.

In March 1948 Great Britain, France, Belgium, the Netherlands, and Luxembourg signed an alliance aimed at social, cultural, and economic collaboration.

The Western nations abandoned their understandable but counterproductive policy of crushing Germany economically. They announced plans for creating a single West German Republic with a large degree of autonomy.

In June 1948 the Soviet Union retaliated by closing off surface access to Berlin from the west. For a time it seemed that the Allies must either fight their way into the city or abandon it to the communists. Unwilling to adopt either alternative, Truman

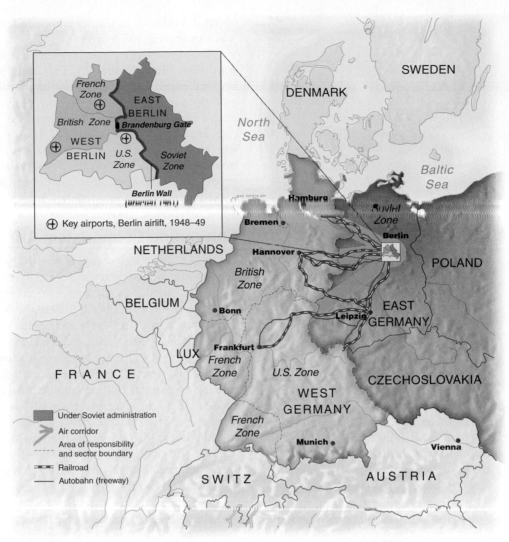

Air Relief to Berlin, 1948–1949 Americans countered Stalin's attempt to starve West Berlin to force it to be merged into communist East Germany by a massive airlift of foodstuffs, fuel, and medical supplies.

decided to fly supplies to the capital from Frankfurt, Hannover, and Hamburg. American C-47 and C-54 transports shuttled back and forth in fair weather and foul, carrying enough food, fuel, and other goods necessary to maintain more than 2 million West Berliners. The **Berlin airlift** put the Soviets in an uncomfortable position; if they were determined to keep supplies from West Berlin, they would have to start the fighting. They were not prepared to do so. In May 1949 they lifted the blockade.

American generals intensified preparation of contingency plans in the event of a Soviet attack.

The Election of 1948

In the spring of 1948 President Truman's fortunes were at low ebb. Public opinion polls suggested that a majority of the people considered him incompetent or worse. The Republicans seemed so sure to win the 1948 presidential election that many prominent

Democrats began to talk of denying Truman the nomination. Two of FDR's sons came out for General Eisenhower as the Democratic candidate. Governor Dewey, who again won the Republican nomination, ran confidently (even complacently), certain that he would carry the country.

Truman's position seemed hopeless because he had alienated both southern conservatives and northern liberals. The Southerners were particularly distressed because in 1946 the president had established a Committee on Civil Rights, which had recommended antilynching and antipoll tax legislation and the creation of a permanent Fair Employment Practices Commission. When the Democratic convention adopted a civil rights plank, the southern delegates walked out. Southern conservatives then founded the States' Rights ("Dixiecrat") party and nominated J. Strom Thurmond of South Carolina for president.

As for the liberals, in 1947 a group that believed Truman's containment policy a threat to world peace

In 1948 the strongly Republican *Chicago Daily Tribune* printed its postelection headlines before all the returns were in. For Truman, it was the perfect climax to his hard-won victory.

organized a new Progressive party and nominated former Vice President Henry A. Wallace. With two minor candidates sure to cut into the Democratic vote, the president's chances seemed minuscule.

Promising to "give 'em hell," Truman launched an aggressive whistle-stop campaign. Traveling by rail, he made several hundred informal but hard-hitting speeches. He excoriated the "do-nothing" Republican Congress, which had rejected his program and passed the Taft-Hartley Act, and he warned labor, farmers, and consumers that if Dewey won, Republican "gluttons of privilege" would do away with all the gains of the New Deal years.

Millions were moved by Truman's arguments and by his courageous fight against great odds. The success of the Berlin airlift during the presidential campaign helped him considerably, as did disaffection among normally Republican midwestern farmers. The Progressive party fell increasingly into the hands of communist sympathizers, driving away many liberals who might otherwise have supported Wallace.

Dewey's smug, lackluster speeches failed to attract independents. One party satirized his campaign by boiling it down to four platitudes: "Agriculture is important." "Our rivers are full of fish." "You cannot have freedom without liberty." "The future lies ahead." The president reinvigorated the New Deal coalition and won an amazing upset victory on election day. He collected 24.1 million votes to Dewey's 21.9 million, the two minor candidates being held to

about 2.3 million. In the Electoral College his margin was a thumping 303 to 189.

Truman's victory encouraged him to press forward with what he called his **Fair Deal** program. He urged Congress to raise the minimum wage, fund an ambitious public housing program, develop a national health insurance system, and repeal the Taft-Hartley Act. However, relatively little of Truman's Fair Deal was enacted into law. Congress approved a federal housing program and measures increasing the minimum wage and Social Security benefits, but these were merely extensions of New Deal legislation.

Containing Communism Abroad

During Truman's second term the confrontation between the United States and the Soviet Union dominated the headlines. To strengthen ties with the European democracies, in April 1949 the North Atlantic Treaty was signed in Washington. The United States, Great Britain, France, Italy, Belgium, the Netherlands, Luxembourg, Denmark, Norway, Portugal, Iceland, and Canada[1] agreed "that an armed attack against one or more of them in Europe or North America shall be considered an attack against them all" and that in the event of such an attack each would take "individually and in concert with the other Parties, such action as it deems necessary, including the use of armed force." The pact established the **North Atlantic Treaty Organization (NATO)**.

In September 1949 the Soviet Union detonated an atomic bomb. Truman had expressed doubts that the Soviets could build such sophisticated weapons. But when the explosion was confirmed, he called for rapid expansion of the American nuclear arsenal. He also asked his advisers to determine whether the United States should develop a new weapon thousands of times more destructive than atomic bombs. The "super" or hydrogen bomb would replicate the fusion process on the surface of the sun. The Atomic Energy Commission argued that there was no military use for hydrogen bombs, which would destroy hundreds of square miles as well as precipitate a dangerous arms race with the Soviet Union. The Joint Chiefs of Staff disagreed. Even if the hydrogen bomb could not be used in battle, they argued, its mere existence would intimidate enemies; and, the military men added, the Soviets would themselves build a hydrogen bomb whether or not the United States did so. (Unbeknownst to American leaders, Stalin had

---

[1]In 1952, Greece and Turkey joined the alliance, and in 1954 so did West Germany.

already ordered development of the hydrogen bomb.) On January 31, 1950, Truman publicly announced that "though none wants to use it" he had no choice but to proceed with a hydrogen bomb.

In Asia the effort to contain communism in China had failed utterly. After World War II, Nationalists under Chiang Kai-shek (sometimes spelled Jiang Jieshi) dominated the south; communists under Mao Zedong controlled much of the north. Truman tried to bring Chiang's Nationalists and Mao's communists together. He sent General Marshall to China to seek a settlement, but neither Chiang nor Mao would make significant concessions. In January 1947 Truman recalled Marshall and named him secretary of state. Soon thereafter civil war, suspended during the Japanese occupation, erupted in China.

By the end of 1949 communist armies had administered a crushing defeat to the nationalists. The remnants of Chiang Kai-shek's forces fled to the island of Formosa, now called Taiwan. Mao ruled China. The "loss" of China to communism strengthened right-wing elements in the Republican party. They charged that Truman had not backed the Nationalists strongly enough and that he had stupidly underestimated Mao's dedication to the cause of world revolution.

Despite a superficial plausibility, neither charge made much sense. American opinion would not have supported military intervention, and such intervention unquestionably would have alienated the Chinese people. That *any* American action could have changed the outcome in China is unlikely. The United States probably gave the Nationalists too much aid rather than too little.

Containment had relied on American money, materials, and know-how, but not on American soldiers. In early 1950, Truman proposed to pare the budget by further reducing the nation's armed forces. Truman also called for a thorough review of the concept of containment. Dean Acheson, who recently had succeeded George Marshall as secretary of state, supervised the study. In March, it was submitted to the National Security Council, assigned a numerical designation (NSC-68), classified top secret, and sent to the nation's military and diplomatic leaders for review.

NSC-68 called for an enormous military expansion. The Soviet Union, it declared, was engaged in a worldwide assault on freedom: "A defeat of free institutions anywhere is a defeat everywhere." Instead of relying on other nations, the United States itself must develop sufficient military forces to stop communism from spreading *anywhere in the world*. Military spending therefore had to be increased from $14 billion to nearly $50 billion. If the Soviet Union failed to keep up with the American expenditures, it would no longer pose a military threat, and if it attempted to match the high levels of American military spending, its less efficient economic system would collapse from the strain.

The document was submitted to Truman on April 7, 1950. He had planned significant cuts to the defense budget; the prospect of increasing it by 350 percent appalled him. Within a few months, however, events in Korea changed his mind.

Hot War in Korea

After World War II the province of Korea was taken from Japan and divided at 38° north latitude into the Democratic People's Republic in the north, backed by the Soviet Union, and the Republic of Korea in the south, backed by the United States and the UN. Both powers withdrew their troops from the peninsula. The Soviets left behind a well-armed local force, but the Republic of Korea's army was small and ill-trained.

American strategists, while seeking to "contain" communism in East Asia, had decided that military involvement on the Asian mainland made little sense. America's first line of defense was to be its island bases in Japan and the Philippines. In a speech in January 1950 Acheson deliberately excluded Korea from what he described as the "defensive perimeter" of the United States in Asia. It was up to the South Koreans, backed by the UN, to protect themselves, Acheson said. This encouraged the North Koreans to attack. In June 1950, when their armored divisions, led by 150 Soviet-made tanks, rumbled across the thirty-eighth parallel, the South Koreans failed to stop them.

Truman was at his family home in Independence, Missouri, when Acheson telephoned with the news of the North Korean attack. "Dean," Truman explained, "we've got to stop the sons of bitches no matter what." Truman hastened to Washington. On the flight, he recalled how the communists in Korea were acting "just as Hitler, Mussolini, and the Japanese had acted ten, fifteen, and twenty years earlier." "If this were allowed to go unchallenged," he concluded, "it would mean a third world war, just as similar incidents had brought on the Second World War." With the backing of the UN Security Council (but without asking Congress to declare war), he sent American planes into battle.[2] Ground troops soon followed. Truman also ordered the adoption of NSC-68 "as soon as feasible."

---

[2]The Soviet Union, which could have vetoed this action, was at the moment boycotting the Security Council because the UN had refused to give the Mao Zedong regime China's seat on that body.

The Chinese counteroffensive of November 1950 caught the Americans by surprise and cut off many units. Here, a U.S. Marine rests during the retreat that winter.

Nominally the Korean War was a struggle between the invaders and the United Nations. General MacArthur, placed in command, flew the blue UN flag over his headquarters, and sixteen nations supplied troops for his army. However, more than 90 percent of the forces were American. At first the North Koreans pushed them back rapidly, but in September a front was stabilized around the port of Pusan, at the southern tip of Korea. Then MacArthur executed a brilliant amphibious invasion, landing at the west coast city of Inchon, fifty miles south of the thirty-eighth parallel. Their lines of supply destroyed, the North Koreans retreated in disorder. By October the battlefront had moved north of the 1945 boundary.

General MacArthur now proposed the conquest of North Korea, even if it meant bombing "privileged sanctuaries" on the Chinese side of the Korean border. A few of Truman's civilian advisers, the most important being George Kennan, opposed advancing into North Korea, fearing intervention not only by the Red Chinese but also by the Soviets. "When we start walking inland from the tip of Korea, we have about a 10,000 mile walk if we keep going," Kennan pointed out.

Truman authorized MacArthur to advance as far as the Yalu River, the boundary between North Korea and China. It was an unfortunate decision, an example of how power, once unleashed, so often gets out of hand. As the advance progressed, ominous reports came from north of the Yalu. Mao's Foreign Minister warned that the Chinese would not "supinely" tolerate seeing their neighbors being "savagely invaded by imperialists." Chinese "volunteers" began to turn up among the captives taken by UN units.

Alarmed, Truman flew to Wake Island, in the Pacific, to confer with MacArthur. The general, who had a low opinion of Asian soldiers, assured him that the Chinese would not dare to intervene. If they did, he added, his army would crush them easily; the war would be over by Christmas.

Seldom has a general miscalculated so badly. Ignoring intelligence reports and dividing his advancing units, he drove toward the Yalu recklessly. Suddenly, on November 26, thirty-three Chinese divisions, hidden along the interior mountains of Korea, smashed through the center of MacArthur's lines. Overnight a triumphant advance became a bloody, disorganized retreat. MacArthur now spoke of the "bottomless well of Chinese manpower" and justified his earlier confidence by claiming that he was fighting "an entirely new war."

The UN army rallied south of the thirty-eighth parallel, and MacArthur then urged that he be permitted to bomb Chinese installations north of the Yalu. He also suggested a naval blockade of the coast of China and the use of Chinese Nationalist troops. Truman rejected these proposals on the ground that they would lead to a third world war. MacArthur, who tended to ignore the larger political aspects of the conflict, attempted to rouse Congress and the public against the president by openly criticizing administration policy. Truman ordered him to be silent. When the general persisted in his criticisms, Truman fired him.

At first the Korean "police action" had been popular in the United States, but as the months passed and the casualties mounted, many citizens became disillusioned and angry. Military men backed the president almost unanimously. General Omar N. Bradley, chairman of the Joint Chiefs of Staff, said that a showdown with communist China "would involve us in the wrong war, at the wrong place, at the wrong time and with the wrong enemy." In June 1951 the communists agreed to discuss an armistice

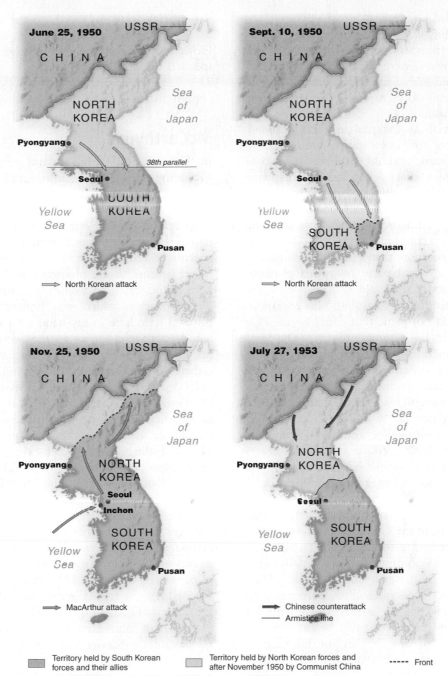

Korean War, 1950–1953 In June, North Korea nearly overran South Korea (top maps). But in September MacArthur counterattacked at Inchon and advanced far into North Korea (bottom left). The intervention of the Chinese in November led to a stalemate (bottom right).

in Korea, although the negotiations dragged on interminably. The war was unresolved when Truman left office: by the time it was over, it had produced 157,000 American casualties, including 54,200 dead.

If the Korean War persuaded Truman to adopt NSC-68, it also exposed the failings of the policy. By conceiving of communism as a monolithic force it tended to make it so, driving Red China and the Soviet Union into each other's arms. By committing American military forces to potential trouble spots throughout the world, it increased the likelihood they would prevail in none.

See the **Map** *The Korean War, 1950–1953* at **www.myhistorylab.com**

The Communist Issue at Home

The Korean War highlighted the paradox that, at the pinnacle of its power, the influence of the United States in world affairs was declining. Its monopoly on nuclear weapons had been lost. China had passed into the communist orbit. Elsewhere in Asia and throughout Africa, new nations, formerly colonial possessions of the Western powers, were adopting a "neutralist" position in the Cold War. Despite the billions poured into armaments and foreign aid, national security seemed far from ensured.

Internal as well as external dangers loomed. Alarming examples of communist espionage in Canada, Great Britain, and the United States convinced many citizens that clever conspirators were everywhere at work undermining American security. Both the Republicans and conservative Democratic critics of Truman's domestic policies were charging that he was "soft" on communists.

There were never more than 100,000 communists in the United States, and party membership plummeted after the start of the Cold War. However, the possibility that a handful of spies could do enormous damage fueled a kind of panic that could be used for partisan purposes. In 1947, hoping to defuse the communists-in-government issue by being more zealous in pursuit of spies than his critics, Truman established a Loyalty Review Board to check up on government employees. The program made even sympathy for a long list of vaguely defined "totalitarian" or "subversive" organizations grounds for dismissal. During the following ten years about 2,700 government workers were discharged, only a relative handful of them for legitimate reasons. A much larger number resigned.

In 1948 Whittaker Chambers, an editor of *Time* who had formerly been a communist, charged that Alger Hiss, president of the Carnegie Endowment for International Peace and a former State Department official, had been a communist in the 1930s. Hiss denied the charge and sued Chambers for libel. Chambers then produced microfilms purporting to show that Hiss had copied classified documents for dispatch to Moscow. Hiss could not be indicted for espionage because of the statute of limitations; instead he was charged with perjury. In January 1950, he was convicted and sentenced to a five-year jail term.

If a distinguished official such as Hiss had been disloyal, anything seemed possible. The case fed the fears of those who believed in the existence of a powerful communist underground in the United States. The disclosure in February 1950 that a British scientist, Klaus Fuchs, had betrayed atomic secrets to the Soviets heightened these fears, as did the arrest and conviction of his American associate, Harry Gold, and two other Americans, Julius and Ethel Rosenberg, on the same charge.

Although they were not major spies and the information they revealed was not crucial, the Rosenbergs were executed, to the consternation of many liberals in the United States and elsewhere. However, information gathered by other spies had speeded the Soviet development of nuclear weapons. This fact encouraged some Republicans to press the communists-in-government issue hard.

McCarthyism

In February 1950 an obscure senator, Joseph R. McCarthy of Wisconsin, introduced this theme in a speech to the even less well-known Ohio County Republican Women's Club of Wheeling, West Virginia. "The reason we find ourselves in a position of impotency," he stated, "is not because our only powerful potential enemy has sent men to invade our shores, but rather because of the traitorous actions of those who have been treated so well by this nation." The State Department, he added, was "infested" with communists. "I have here in my hand a list of 205—a list of names that were known to the Secretary of State as being members of the Communist party and who nevertheless are still working and shaping . . . policy."[3]

Why this speech caused a sensation has never been satisfactorily explained. McCarthy had no shred of evidence to back up these statements, as a Senate committee headed by the conservative Democrat Millard Tydings of Maryland soon demonstrated. He never exposed a single spy or secret American communist. One reporter quipped that McCarthy could not tell Karl Marx from Groucho Marx.

But because of the government loyalty program, the Hiss case, and other recent events, thousands of people were too eager to believe McCarthy to listen to reason. Within a few weeks he was the most talked of person in Congress. Inhibited neither by scruples nor by logic, he lashed out in every direction, attacking international experts like Professor Owen Lattimore of Johns Hopkins University and diplomats such as John S. Service and John Carter Vincent, who were already under attack for having courageously pointed out the deficiencies of the Chiang Kai-shek regime during the Chinese civil war.

When McCarthy's victims indignantly denied his charges, he distracted the public with still more sensational accusations directed at other innocents. Even General Marshall, whose patriotism was beyond question, was subjected to McCarthy's abuse. The general, he said, was "steeped in falsehood," part of a "conspiracy so immense and an

---

[3]McCarthy was speaking from rough notes, and no one made an accurate record of his words. The exact number mentioned has long been in dispute. On other occasions he said there were fifty-seven and eighty-one "card-carrying" communists in the State Department.

infamy so black as to dwarf any previous venture in the history of man."

McCarthy was totally unscrupulous. The "big lie" was his most effective weapon: The enormity of his charges and the status of his targets convinced thousands that there must be some truth in what he was saying. Nevertheless, his crude tactics would have failed if the public had not been so worried about communism. The worries were caused by the reality of Soviet military power, the attack on Korea, the loss of the nuclear monopoly, and the stories about spies, some of them true.

Read the **Document** McCarthy, *Wheeling, West Virginia, Speech* at **www.myhistorylab.com**

Dwight D. Eisenhower

As the 1952 presidential election approached, Truman's popularity was again at low ebb; he chose not to seek reelection. In choosing their candidate, the Republicans passed over the twice-defeated Dewey and their most prominent leader, Senator Robert A. Taft of Ohio, an outspoken conservative, and nominated General Dwight D. Eisenhower.

Eisenhower's popularity did not grow merely out of his achievements in World War II. Although a West Pointer (class of 1915), he struck most persons as anything but warlike. After the bristly, combative Truman, his genial personality and evident desire to avoid controversy proved widely appealing. In his reluctance to seek political office, Eisenhower reminded the country of George Washington, whereas his seeming ignorance of current political issues was no more a handicap to his campaign than the similar ignorance of Jackson and Grant in their times. People "liked Ike" because his management of the Allied armies suggested that he would be equally competent as head of the complex federal government. Eisenhower's campaign was also the first to use television effectively. It featured what came to be known as "spots," twenty-second tapes of candidate Eisenhower responding to questions about his opinions on issues, important and trivial. Eisenhower's promise during the campaign to go to Korea if elected to try to bring the war to an end was a political masterstroke.

The Democrats nominated Governor Adlai E. Stevenson of Illinois, whose grandfather had been vice president under Grover Cleveland. Stevenson's unpretentiousness was appealing, and his witty, urbane speeches captivated intellectuals. In retrospect, however, it is clear that he had not the remotest chance of defeating the popular Eisenhower.

The result was a Republican landslide: Eisenhower received almost 34 million votes to Stevenson's

Many critics lampooned Eisenhower for his banal amusements. A popular bumper sticker read: "BEN HOGAN [a famous golfer] FOR PRESIDENT. IF WE'RE GOING TO HAVE A GOLFER FOR PRESIDENT, LET'S HAVE A GOOD ONE." Others have viewed Eisenhower's passion for golf as characteristic of his presidential style: methodical, prudent, and, when in the rough, disarmingly shrewd.

27 million, and in the Electoral College his margin was 442 to 89.

On the surface, Eisenhower seemed the antithesis of Truman. The Republicans had charged the Democratic administration with being wasteful and extravagant, and Eisenhower planned to run his administration on sound business principles. He spoke scornfully of "creeping socialism," called for more local control of government affairs, and promised to reduce federal spending to balance the budget and cut taxes. He believed that by battling with Congress and pressure groups over the details of legislation, his immediate predecessors had sacrificed part of their status as chief representative of the American people. Like Washington, he tried to avoid being caught up in narrow partisan conflicts. But like Washington, he was not always able to do so.

Eisenhower's somewhat doctrinaire belief in decentralization and private enterprise reduced the effectiveness of his social welfare measures—an extension of Social Security—but on balance, he proved to be an excellent politician. He knew how to be flexible without compromising his basic values. His "conservatism" became first "dynamic conservatism" and then "progressive moderation." He summarized his attitude by saying, "In all those things that deal with people, be liberal, be human."

Yet his policies toward illegal Mexican immigrants and native Americans proved less than humane. In 1954 he authorized Operation Wetback, which rounded up and deported nearly a million illegal Mexican immigrants. He also sought to weaken New Deal policies that strengthened Native American tribes as political entities. Indian leaders resisted this change, and the policy ended in 1961.

The Eisenhower-Dulles Foreign Policy

The American people, troubled and uncertain over the stalemate in Korea, counted on Eisenhower to find a way to employ the nation's immense strength constructively. The new president shared the general feeling that a change of tactics in foreign affairs was needed. He counted on his secretary of state to solve the practical problems.

His choice, John Foster Dulles, was a lawyer with considerable diplomatic experience. He had been an outspoken critic of Truman's policy of containment. In a May 1952 article in *Life* entitled "A Policy of Boldness," he argued that global military containment was both expensive and ineffective: "We cannot build a 20,000-mile Maginot Line or match the Red armies man for man, gun for gun, and tank for tank at any particular time or place their general staff selects." Instead of waiting for the communist powers to make a move and then "containing" them, the United States would build so many powerful nuclear weapons that the Soviet Union or communist China wouldn't dare take provocative actions. An immense arsenal of nuclear bombs, loaded on the nation's formidable fleet of bombers, would ensure a **massive retaliation** against any aggressor. Such a "new look" military would be cheaper to maintain than a large standing army, and it would prevent the United States from being caught up in "local" conflicts like the Korean War.

Korea offered the first test of his views. After Eisenhower's post-election trip to Korea failed to bring an end to the war, Dulles signaled his willingness to use tactical nuclear weapons in Korea by showily transferring nuclear warheads from the United States mainland to bomber units stationed in East Asia. He also issued a calculatedly vague warning about tough new measures. Several weeks later, in July 1953, the Chinese signed an armistice that ended hostilities but left Korea divided. The administration interpreted the

An eleven-megaton hydrogen bomb is detonated over Bikini Atoll in March 1954. One megaton had the explosive power of 1 million tons of TNT. (The bomb that had destroyed Hiroshima had the equivalent of 12,500 tons of TNT.) An earlier atom bomb test at Bikini Island prompted a French fashion designer to give the name "bikini" to his explosively provocative bathing suit.

softening of the Chinese position as proof that the nuclear threat had worked. (Dulles was apparently mistaken about the effectiveness of his nuclear threat. In recent years, Chinese officials have said that they were unaware that Eisenhower and Dulles were considering use of nuclear bombs to end the Korean War.)

Emboldened by his apparent triumph, Dulles again brandished the nation's nuclear arsenal. Chiang Kai-shek had stationed 90,000 soldiers—one-third of his army—in Quemoy and Matsu, two small islands located a few miles from mainland China. In 1954 the Chinese communists began shelling the islands, presumably in preparation to invade them. Chiang appealed for American protection, warning that loss of the islands would bring about the collapse of Nationalist China. Dulles concurred that the consequences throughout East Asia would be "catastrophic." At a press conference in 1955 Eisenhower announced his willingness to use nuclear weapons to defend the islands, "just exactly as you would use a bullet or anything else." The Chinese communists backed down.

Massive retaliation succeeded in reducing the defense budget by allowing Eisenhower to pare a half million men from the armed forces. On balance, however, Dulles's strategy was flawed, and many of his schemes were preposterous. Above all, massive retaliation was an extremely dangerous policy when the Soviet Union possessed nuclear weapons as powerful as those of the United States.

McCarthy Self-Destructs

Although the State Department was now controlled by Dulles, a Republican and hard-line anticommunist, Senator McCarthy refused to moderate his attacks on the department. In 1953 television newscaster Edwin R. Murrow cast doubt on McCarthy's methods; soon he and McCarthy were verbally pummeling each other on television.

But McCarthy finally overreached himself. Early in 1954 he turned his guns on the army, accusing Pentagon officials of trying to blackmail his committee. The resulting Army-McCarthy hearings, televised before the country, and Murrow's increasingly sharp criticisms, proved the senator's undoing. For weeks his dark scowl, his blind combativeness, and his disregard for every human value stood exposed for millions to see. When the hearings ended in June 1954 after some million words of testimony, his spell had been broken.

The Senate, with President Eisenhower (who despised McCarthy but who considered it beneath his dignity as president to "get into the gutter with that guy") applying pressure behind the scenes, at last moved to censure him in December 1954. This reproof completed the destruction of his influence. Although he continued to issue statements and wild charges, the country no longer listened. In 1957 he died of cirrhosis of the liver.

((•–[Hear the Audio *Joseph P. McCarthy Speech* at
www.myhistorylab.com

Asian Policy After Korea

Shortly after an armistice was finally arranged in Korea in July 1953, new trouble erupted far to the south in the former French colony of Indochina. Nationalist rebels led by the communist Ho Chi Minh had been harassing the French in Vietnam, one of the three puppet kingdoms (the others were Laos and Cambodia) fashioned by France in Indochina after the defeat of the Japanese. When China recognized the rebels, who were known as the Vietminh, and supplied them with arms, President Truman countered with economic and military assistance to the French, and President Eisenhower continued and expanded this assistance.

Senator Joe McCarthy and his aide Roy Cohn (left) listen to testimony at the Army-McCarthy hearings in April 1954. Cohn, a tough, young lawyer who had made a reputation prosecuting suspected communists in Manhattan, intimidated some people by threatening to make public their homosexuality; yet he was himself a homosexual who steadfastly denied it. In 1986 he died of AIDS. Tony Kushner's Pulitzer Prize-winning play *Angels in America* (1993) told Cohn's story.

Early in 1954 Ho Chi Minh's troops trapped and besieged a French army in the remote stronghold of Dien Bien Phu. In May the garrison surrendered. Several months later France, Great Britain, the Soviet Union, and China signed an agreement dividing Vietnam along the seventeenth parallel. France withdrew from the area. The northern sector became the Democratic Republic of Vietnam, controlled by Ho Chi Minh; the southern sector remained in the hands of the emperor, Bao Dai. An election to settle the future of all Vietnam was scheduled for 1956.

When it seemed likely that the communists would win that election, Ngo Dinh Diem, a conservative anticommunist, overthrew Bao Dai and became president of South Vietnam. The United States supplied his government liberally with aid. The planned election was never held, and Vietnam remained divided.

Dulles responded to the diplomatic setback in Vietnam by establishing the Southeast Asia Treaty Organization (SEATO), but only three Asian nations—the Philippine Republic (which the United

States granted independence in 1947), Thailand, and Pakistan—joined this alliance.[4]

Israel and the Middle East

Truman and Eisenhower had intervened in the Far East because of a direct communist threat. But as the American love affair with cars turned into an obsession, United States policymakers became increasingly attentive to the Middle East, where seas of oil had been recently discovered. Iran, Iraq, Kuwait, and Saudi Arabia sat upon nearly 60 percent of the world's known reserves.

After World War II, Zionists, who had long sought to promote Jewish immigration to Palestine, intensified their efforts. The slaughter of six million European Jews by the Nazis strengthened Jewish claims to a homeland and intensified pressure to allow hundreds of thousands of Jewish refugees to immigrate to Palestine, which was governed by Great Britain according to a League of Nations mandate. But the influx of Jewish settlers, and their calls for creation of a Jewish state (Israel), provoked Palestinian and Arab leaders. Fighting broke out. President Truman angered Arab leaders by endorsing the partition of the region into an Israeli and a Palestinian state. In 1947, the United Nations voted for partition and on May 14, 1948, the State of Israel was established. Within hours, Truman recognized its sovereignty.

Then Arab armies from Egypt, Jordan, Iraq, Syria, and Lebanon attacked Israel. Although badly outnumbered, the Israelis were better organized and better armed than the Arabs and drove them off with relative ease. Nearly a million local Arabs were displaced, causing a desperate refugee problem in nearby countries.

President Truman had consistently placed support for Israel before other considerations in the Middle East, partly because of the conviction that survivors of the Nazi holocaust were entitled to a country of their own and partly because of the political importance of the Jewish vote in the United States. Dulles and Eisenhower tried to restore balance and mollify the Arabs by deemphasizing American support of Israel. Gas-hungry Americans could ill afford to alienate the Arab world.

In 1952 a revolution in Egypt overthrew the dissolute King Farouk. Colonel Gamal Abdel Nasser emerged as the strongman of Egypt. The United States was prepared to lend Nasser money to build a huge dam on the Nile at Aswan that would provide irrigation and electric power for much of the region. However, Eisenhower would not sell Egypt arms, but the communists would.

For this reason Nasser drifted toward the communist orbit. When Eisenhower then decided not to finance the Aswan Dam, Nasser responded by nationalizing the Suez Canal. This move galvanized the British and French. In conjunction with the French, and without consulting the United States, the British in 1956 decided to take back the canal by force. The Israelis, alarmed by repeated Arab hit-and-run raids, also attacked Egypt.

Events moved swiftly. Israeli armored columns crushed the Egyptian army in the Sinai Peninsula in a matter of days. France and Britain occupied Port Said at the northern end of the canal. Nasser sank ships to block the channel. In the UN the Soviet Union and the United States introduced resolutions calling for a cease-fire. Both were vetoed by Britain and France.

Then the Soviet Union threatened to send "volunteers" to help defend Egypt and launch atomic missiles against France and Great Britain if they did not withdraw. Eisenhower also demanded that the invaders pull out of Egypt. In London large crowds demonstrated against their own government. On November 6, only nine days after the first Israeli units had invaded Egypt, Prime Minister Anthony Eden, haggard and shaken, announced a cease-fire. Israel withdrew its troops. The crisis subsided as rapidly as it had arisen.

The United States had won a measure of respect in the Arab countries, but at what cost? Its major allies had been humiliated. Their ill-timed attack had enabled the Soviet Union to recover much of the prestige it had lost as a result of its brutal suppression of a Hungarian revolt that had broken out a week before the Suez fiasco.

When the Soviet Union seemed likely to profit from its "defense" of Egypt in the crisis, the president announced the Eisenhower Doctrine (January 1957), which stated that the United States was "prepared to use armed force" anywhere in the Middle East against "aggression from any country controlled by international communism." In practice, the Eisenhower Doctrine amounted to little more than a restatement of the containment policy.

Eisenhower and Khrushchev

In 1956 Eisenhower was reelected, defeating Adlai Stevenson even more decisively than he had in 1952. Despite evident satisfaction with their leader, however, the American people were in a sober mood.

---

[4]The other signatories were Great Britain, France, the United States, Australia, and New Zealand.

Vice President Richard M. Nixon and Soviet leader Nikita Khrushchev engage in a "kitchen debate" over the future of capitalism at a Moscow trade fair in 1959. Although the encounter did little to advance United States-Soviet relations, it established Nixon's credentials as a tough negotiator.

Hopes of pushing back the Soviet Union with clever stratagems and moral fervor were fading. Although the United States detonated the first hydrogen bomb in November 1952, the Soviets followed suit within six months. The Cold War between the superpowers had become yet more chilling.

Stalin died in March 1953, and after a period of internal conflict within the Kremlin, Nikita Khrushchev emerged as the new master of the Soviet Union. Khrushchev was perhaps the most confusing (and, arguably, confused) figure of the Cold War. Crude and bibulous, prone to violent tantrums and tearful histrionics, he delighted in shocking people with words and gestures. In the most famous of these, he pounded his shoe on the table during a debate at the United Nations. He appealed to the anti-Western prejudices of countries just emerging from the yoke of colonialism, offering them economic aid and pointing to Soviet achievements in science and technology as proof that communism would vanquish the capitalist system without troubling to destroy it by force. Although a product of the Soviet system, Khrushchev recognized its deep failings and resolved to purge it of Stalinism. He released political prisoners from Stalin's gulags, or political prison camps, and told wide-eyed party functionaries that Stalin had committed monstrous crimes.

Eisenhower, a seasoned analyst of military capabilities, understood that Khrushchev's antics were meant to conceal the Soviet Union's many weaknesses: the bitter opposition to Soviet rule among peoples of Eastern Europe; the deficiencies of the overcentralized Soviet economy, especially in agriculture; and the bureaucratic stultification of its armed forces. The Soviet Union had kept up a good pace in the nuclear arms race but had not attained nuclear parity. Thousands of American airplanes were based in Europe, northern Africa, and Turkey, placing most Soviet targets within easy range. Heavy Soviet bombers, on the other hand, faced the daunting prospect of lumbering thousands of miles over the Arctic and Pacific Oceans to reach American targets, harried all the while by lightning-fast fighter planes. The United States would win (whatever that meant) any nuclear war.

But this advantage disappeared in the exhaust trail of a Soviet rocket, launched on October 4, 1957, that carried a 184-pound capsule named *Sputnik* far above the atmosphere into earth orbit. Soon, American policymakers knew, Soviet missiles capable of reaching American soil would be tipped with nuclear warheads. The nation's far-flung network of bomber defenses had become obsolete, and with it the strategy of massive retaliation.

Table 28.1 The Cold War Escalates

Year	Event	Significance
1947	George Kennan's "Sources of Soviet Conduct"	Outlines rationale for "containment" of Soviet Union
1947	Truman Doctrine	United States supports Greece and Turkey against communist threats
1948	Marshall Plan	United States provides economic aid to Western Europe
1949	Soviet Union detonates atom bomb	Truman calls for development of hydrogen bomb
1950	North Korea invades South Korea	Truman intervenes, as does communist China
1950	NSC-68 adopted	Truman authorizes worldwide expansion of U.S. military to stop Soviet aggression anywhere
1952	United States detonates hydrogen bomb	Soviet Union follows suit, 1953
1953	NSC-68 replaced with "Massive retaliation"	Dulles-Eisenhower signal willingness to start a nuclear war to defend American interests
1957	Soviet Union launches *Sputnik*	Shows Soviet capacity to hit American targets with nuclear weapons

Several weeks later Khrushchev rubbed hard at the rawest sore in the American psyche: the anguished memory of Pearl Harbor. In an interview with publisher William Randolph Hearst, Jr., Khrushchev blustered that the Soviet Union could launch ten or twenty intercontinental missiles with nuclear warheads "tomorrow." While critics at home flayed Eisenhower for allowing a "missile gap" with the Soviet Union, the president testily reassured the American people that they had little to fear, but otherwise remained silent.

As a prudent military man, however, Eisenhower refused to take chances. He secretly authorized high-altitude American planes to spy on key Soviet military installations. On May 1, 1960, high over Sverdlovsk, an industrial center deep in the Soviet Union, an American U–2 spy plane was shot down by antiaircraft fire. The pilot of the plane survived the crash, and he confessed to being a spy. His cameras contained aerial photographs of Soviet military installations. When Eisenhower assumed full responsibility for the mission, Khrushchev accused the United States of "piratical" and "cowardly" acts of

aggression. He also told the United Nations that the Soviet Union was turning out nuclear missiles "like sausages from an automatic machine."

Latin America Aroused

Events in Latin America compounded Eisenhower's difficulties. During World War II the United States, needing Latin American raw materials, had supplied its southern neighbors liberally with economic aid. In the period following victory a hemispheric mutual defense pact was signed at Rio de Janeiro in September 1947, and the following year the Organization of American States (OAS) came into being. In the OAS, decisions were reached by a two-thirds vote; the United States had neither a veto nor any special position.

But as the Cold War progressed, the United States neglected Latin America. Economic problems plagued the region, and in most nations reactionary governments reigned. Radical Latin Americans accused the United States of supporting cliques of wealthy tyrants, whereas conservatives blamed insufficient American economic aid for the plight of the poor.

Eisenhower, eager to improve relations, stepped up economic assistance. Resistance to communism nonetheless continued to receive first priority. In 1954 the government of Jacobo Arbenz Guzman in Guatemala began to import Soviet weapons. The United States promptly dispatched arms to neighboring Honduras. Within a month an army led by an exiled Guatemalan officer marched into the country from Honduras and overthrew Arbenz. Elsewhere in Latin America, Eisenhower, as Truman had before him, continued to support regimes that were kept in power by the local military.

The depth of Latin American resentment of the United States became clear in the spring of 1958, when Vice President Nixon made what was supposed to be a goodwill tour of South America. Everywhere he was met with hostility. In Lima, Peru, he was mobbed; in Caracas, Venezuela, students pelted him with eggs and stones. He had to abandon the remainder of his trip. For the first time the American people gained some inkling of Latin American opinion and the social and economic troubles that lay behind it.

Events in Cuba demonstrated that there was no easy solution to Latin American problems. In 1959 a revolutionary movement headed by Fidel Castro overthrew Fulgencio Batista, one of the most noxious of the Latin American dictators. Eisenhower recognized the Castro government at once, but the Cuban leader soon began to criticize the United States in highly colored speeches. Castro confiscated American property without providing adequate compensation, suppressed civil liberties, and entered into close relations with the Soviet Union. After he negotiated a trade agreement with the Soviet Union in February 1960, which enabled the Russians to obtain Cuban sugar at bargain rates, the United States retaliated by prohibiting the importation of Cuban sugar into America.

Khrushchev then announced that if the United States intervened in Cuba, he would defend the country with atomic weapons. "The Monroe Doctrine has outlived its time," Khrushchev warned. Shortly before the end of his second term, Eisenhower broke off diplomatic relations with Cuba.

Fighting the Cold War at Home

The looming Soviet threat brought the Cold War closer to the American people than ever before. Such fears provided public support for increased spending on defense. In 1955 Eisenhower worried that a Soviet nuclear attack would plunge American cities into chaos. The roads out of threatened cities "would be the breeder of a deadly congestion within hours of an attack," he noted. He therefore backed a federally-funded highway system; this would not only facilitate the evacuation of cities but would also allow the army to mobilize more rapidly. The National Interstate and Defense Highway Act of 1956 became the largest public works project in the nation's history.

The Soviet Union's success in building atomic and hydrogen bombs, and especially in launching an orbiting satellite before the United States, also prompted Eisenhower to initiate a sweeping reform of the nation's schools. "The defense of the nation depends upon the mastery of modern techniques developed from complex scientific principles," he declared. In 1958 he signed the National Defense Education Act. It provided federal aid to promote study of science, mathematics and foreign languages in large, comprehensive (and sometimes anonymous) high schools.

This interchange near Seattle was part of the interstate highway system advanced by Eisenhower to facilitate both military transports and civilian evacuations.

"Godless" communism posed an ideological as well as military threat. In 1954 the Reverend George Docherty warned his Presbyterian congregation in Washington, DC, that "little Muscovites" in the Soviet Union were pledging allegiance to "hammer and sickle" atheism. But an "atheistic American," he intoned, was "a contradiction in terms." Later that day Eisenhower, commenting on the sermon, told a radio audience that whatever their "personal creed," Americans still "believed in a higher power." A few months later he signed a law that added the phrase "one nation under God" to the Pledge of Allegiance. The next year, Congress added "In God We Trust" to the nation's currency.

Blacks Challenge Segregation

Another front in the Cold War concerned race relations. How could African and Asian leaders be persuaded to reject communism and follow the example of the United States when American blacks were treated so poorly? American diplomats winced when the finance minister of Ghana was refused a meal at the Howard Johnson's, a chain restaurant, in Dover, Delaware. "Colored people are not allowed to eat in here," the manager explained to the African leader. Vice President Nixon, no liberal on racial matters but an ardent enemy of communism, declared, "In the world-wide struggle in which we are engaged, racial prejudice is a gun we point at ourselves."

But racial confrontations remained in the news. During and after World War II, like a glacier, slowly but with massive force, a demand for change had developed in the South. Its roots lay in southern industrialization, in the shift from small sharecropping holdings to large commercial farms, in the vast wartime expenditures of the federal government on aircraft factories and army bases in the region; in the impact of the GI Bill on southern colleges and universities, and in the gradual development of a southern black middle class.

Black soldiers who had served abroad demanded that they be treated with respect when they returned home. In 1947 Jackie Robinson, a black officer who had been court-martialed—and acquitted—for refusing to move to the back of a segregated military bus during World War II, was ready to integrate major league baseball. When his team—the Brooklyn Dodgers—checked into the Ben Franklin Hotel in Philadelphia, he was refused a room. A week later the Dodgers went to Pittsburgh. When he took his position at second base, the Pirates refused to come onto the field. Only under threat of forfeiting the game would they play against Robinson.

In this photo opportunity, Phillies manager Ben Chapman refused to shake Jackie Robinson's hand. Instead, he leaned toward Robinson and said quietly, "Jackie, you know, you're a good ballplayer, but you're still a nigger to me." Robinson replied by leading the Dodgers to the pennant and winning Rookie of the Year honors.

Ordinary blacks, too, demanded fairer treatment. More insisted on their right to vote—and many got it. In 1940 only 2 percent of African Americans in the south were registered to vote; by 1947, that had increased to 12 percent. But white resistance remained formidable. In 1946 Eugene Talmadge, behind in the polls, won his race for governor by promising that if he were elected "no Negro will vote in Georgia for four years." One black man who succeeded in registering was gunned down in front of his house.

The NAACP (the National Association for the Advancement of Colored People) decided that the time had come to challenge segregation in the courts. Thurgood Marshall, the organization's chief staff lawyer, went from state to state filing legal challenges to the "separate but equal" principle laid down in *Plessy v. Ferguson* in 1896 (see Chapter 20.) In 1938 the Supreme Court had ordered the University of Missouri law school to admit a black student because no law school for blacks existed in the state. This decision gradually forced some southern states to admit blacks to advanced programs. "You can't build a cyclotron

Angry jeers from whites rain down on Elizabeth Eckford, one of the first black students to arrive for registration at Little Rock's Central High School in 1957. State troops turned black students away from the school until President Eisenhower overruled the state decision and called in the National Guard to enforce integration.

for one student," the president of the University of Oklahoma confessed when the Court, in 1948, ordered Oklahoma to provide equal facilities. Two years later, when Texas actually attempted to create a separate law school for a single black applicant, the Court ruled that truly equal education could not be provided under such circumstances.

In 1953 President Eisenhower appointed California's Governor Earl Warren chief justice of the U.S. Supreme Court. Convinced that the Court must take the offensive in the cause of civil rights, Warren succeeded in welding his associates into a unit on this question. In 1954 an NAACP-sponsored case, *Brown v. Board of Education of Topeka*, came up for decision. Marshall submitted a mass of sociological evidence to show that the mere fact of segregation made equal education impossible and did serious psychological damage to both black and white children. Speaking for a unanimous Court, Warren reversed

the *Plessy* decision. "In the field of public education, the doctrine of 'separate but equal' has no place," he declared. "Separate educational facilities are inherently unequal." The next year the Court ordered the states to end segregation "with all deliberate speed."

Flouting the Court's decision, few districts in the southern and border states integrated their schools. As late as September 1956, barely 700 of the South's 10,000 school districts had been desegregated.

White citizens' councils dedicated to all-out opposition sprang up throughout the South. When the school board of Clinton, Tennessee, integrated the local high school in September 1956, a mob rioted in protest, shouting "Kill the niggers!" and destroying the property of blacks. The school was kept open with the help of the National Guard until segregationists blew up the building with dynamite. In Virginia the governor announced a plan for "massive resistance" to integration that denied state aid to local school systems that wished to desegregate. When the University of Alabama admitted a single black woman in 1956, riots broke out. University officials forced the student to withdraw temporarily and then expelled her when she complained more forcefully than they deemed proper.

President Eisenhower thought equality for blacks could not be obtained by government edict. He said that the Court's ruling must be obeyed, but he did little to discourage southern resistance to desegregation. "I am convinced that the Supreme Court decision set back progress in the South at least fifteen years," he remarked to one of his advisers. "The fellow who tries to tell me you can do these things by force is just plain nuts."

However, in 1957 events compelled him to act. When the school board of Little Rock, Arkansas, opened Central High School to a handful of black students, the governor of the state, Orval M. Faubus, called out the National Guard to prevent them from entering the school. Unruly crowds taunted the students and their parents. Eisenhower could not ignore the direct flouting of federal authority. After the mayor of Little Rock sent him a telegram saying, in part, "situation is out of control and police cannot disperse the mob," Eisenhower dispatched 1,000 paratroopers to Little Rock and summoned 10,000 National Guardsmen to federal duty, thus removing them from Faubus's control. The black students then began to attend class. A token force of soldiers was stationed at Central High for the entire school year to protect them.

Read the **Document** *Brown v. Board of Education of Topeka, Kansas* at **www.myhistorylab.com**

Watch the **Video** *How did the civil rights movement change American schools?* at **www.myhistorylab.com**

Direct Action Protests: The Montgomery Bus Boycott

While Marshall and the NAACP were dismantling the legal superstructure of segregation, its institutional foundations remained. Blacks increasingly took action on their own.

This change first came to national attention during the Eisenhower administration in the rigidly segregated city of Montgomery, Alabama. On Friday, December 1, 1955, Rosa Parks, a seamstress at the Montgomery Fair department store, boarded a bus on her way home from her job. She dutifully took a seat toward the rear as custom and law required. As white workers and shoppers filled the forward section, the driver ordered her to give up her place to a white passenger. Parks, who was also secretary of the

Montgomery NAACP chapter, refused. She had decided, she later recalled, that "I would have to know once and for all what rights I had as a human being and a citizen."

She was arrested. Over the weekend, Montgomery's black leaders organized a boycott. "Don't ride the bus . . . Monday," their mimeographed notice ran. "If you work, take a cab, or share a ride, or walk." Monday dawned bitterly cold, but the boycott was a total success.

Most Montgomery blacks could not afford to miss a single day's wages, so the protracted struggle to get to work was difficult to maintain. Black-owned taxis reduced their rates sharply, and when the city declared this illegal, car pools were quickly organized. Few African Americans owned cars. Although nearly everyone who did volunteered, there were never more than 350 cars available to the more than 10,000 people who needed rides to their jobs and back every day. Nevertheless, the boycott went on.

Late in February the Montgomery authorities obtained indictments of 115 leaders of the boycott, but this move backfired because it focused national attention on the situation. A young clergyman, the Reverend Martin Luther King, Jr., was emerging as the leader of the boycott. A gifted speaker, he became an overnight celebrity. (See American Lives, "Martin Luther King, Jr.," p. 759.) Money poured in from all over the country to support the movement. The boycott lasted for over a year. Finally the Supreme Court declared the local law enforcing racial separation unconstitutional: Montgomery had to desegregate its public transportation system.

This success encouraged blacks elsewhere in the South to band together against segregation. A new organization founded in 1957, the **Southern Christian Leadership Conference (SCLC)**, headed by King, moved to the forefront of the civil rights movement. Other organizations joined the struggle, notably the Congress of Racial Equality (CORE), which had been founded in 1942. The direct action movement was becoming a broad-based nationwide civil rights movement.

The Election of 1960

As the end of his momentous second term approached, Eisenhower somewhat reluctantly endorsed Vice President Richard Nixon as the Republican candidate to succeed him. Nixon had originally skyrocketed to national prominence by exploiting the public fear of communist subversion. "Traitors in the high councils of our government,"

Martin Luther King, Jr.

Well after midnight on December 2, 1955, Jo Ann Robinson, an English professor at Alabama State in Montgomery, was working feverishly in her office with several other women. Eight hours earlier, Rosa Parks had been arrested for violating Montgomery's segregation laws. Robinson had called an emergency meeting of the Women's Political Council. Now they were drafting a leaflet to mobilize the black community: "Another Negro woman has been arrested and thrown into jail because she refused to get up out of her seat and give it to a white person," they wrote. "The next time it may be you." The next day they distributed the leaflet throughout the black community.

On Monday morning, the buses were nearly empty. That afternoon Montgomery's black leaders met to discuss strategy for the meeting that evening. One minister urged that they keep their plans secret. E. D. Nixon, a railroad porter and president of the local NAACP, jumped to his feet: "How do you think you can run a bus boycott in secret?" Then he lost his temper. "You ministers have lived off these wash-women for the last hundred years and ain't never done nothing for them." The ministers, he insisted, should stand up and be men.

As Nixon was finishing his diatribe, the new minister in town strode into the room. Young, well-dressed Martin Luther King, Jr. was regarded as something of a dandy. Now, all eyes turned to the dapper latecomer.

The Rev. Martin Luther King, Jr., Coretta Scott King, and their children share a moment of calm in Montgomery, 1956. That year, while King was addressing a mass meeting, his house was bombed; Coretta and the children were unhurt.

"Brother Nixon," King declared, "I'm not a coward." He called on the ministers to act in open and use their names. On the spot someone proposed that King be named president of the protest movement. Nearly everyone agreed.

That evening, hundreds of Montgomery blacks filled the largest Baptist church, with hundreds more spilling onto the lawn and street. A loudspeaker was set up. Inside, after Parks and others had described the events of the previous week, King strode to the podium. He outlined the situation, and then, slipping into a preaching mode, began to roll off one booming phrase after another. "And you know, my friends, there comes a time when people get tired of being trampled over by the iron feet of oppression," he said in a deep voice. By the time he finished, his words were drowned out by the stomping of feet and the roars of the crowd outside. As if he feared that the passions he had unloosed were too volatile, he reminded the crowd, "We are a Christian people." This protest, he insisted, would not condone violence.

King's rhetorical mastery stunned nearly everyone. He was only twenty-six, and had served as a pastor for only a year.

His father had been minister of the largest Baptist church in Atlanta, and Martin's circumstances as a child had been comfortable. He briefly attended a special school run by Atlanta University, then the local public high school before going to Morehouse College in Atlanta. After a period of indecision he decided to follow in his father's footsteps and become a minister.

He attended Crozer seminary in Pennsylvania. After finishing at the top of his class, he went to Boston University, where he earned a doctorate in philosophy. (Many years later Boston University concluded that some portions of his dissertation had been plagiarized.) His favorite subject had been homiletics—the delivery of effective sermons. He resolved to become a successful preacher in a big-city church.

In 1953 King married Coretta Scott; the next year he was appointed pastor at Dexter Avenue Baptist Church in Montgomery.

But in the first week of December, 1955, his life had taken an unexpected turn. He would be given the task of forging into a single movement the disparate elements of the black community: well-educated and influential women such as those on the Women's Political Council, working-class militants such as E. D. Nixon, impatient young men, and a wide variety of conservative ministers. He would adapt the passive nonviolence tactics used by Indian nationalist Mohandas Gandhi to gain independence from Britain, and apply them to very different circumstances in the American South. He would use the language of Christian brotherhood to reach out to whites. He would lead the movement that would change the nation.

But that was in the future. In December 1955, a convergence of fateful circumstances had pushed him into leadership of a bus boycott. Twelve years later, he would be dead, victim of an assassin's bullet.

John F. Kennedy, comfortable and assured, was more telegenic than Richard M. Nixon in the 1960 debates.

boat. When the boat was sliced in two by a Japanese destroyer, Kennedy showed personal courage in rescuing his men. Besides wealth, intelligence, good looks, and charm, Kennedy had the advantage of his Irish-Catholic ancestry, a valuable asset in heavily Catholic Massachusetts. After three terms in the House, he moved on to the Senate in 1952.

After his landslide reelection in 1958, only Kennedy's religion seemed to limit his political future. (His relentless womanizing was not the sort of topic that then attracted journalistic attention.) No Catholic had ever been elected president, and the defeat of Alfred E. Smith in 1928 had convinced most students of politics (including Smith) that none ever would be elected. Nevertheless, influenced by Kennedy's victories in the Wisconsin and West Virginia primaries—the latter establishing him as an effective campaigner in a predominantly Protestant region—the Democratic convention nominated him.

Kennedy had not been a particularly liberal congressman. He was not involved in the civil rights

he charged in 1950, "have made sure that the deck is stacked on the Soviet side of the diplomatic tables." In 1947 he was an obscure young congressman from California; in 1950 he won a seat in the Senate; two years later Eisenhower chose him as his running mate.

Nixon projected an image of almost frantic earnestness, yet he pursued a flexible course more suggestive of calculation than sincerity. Reporters generally had a low opinion of Nixon, and independent voters seldom found him attractive. He was always controversial, distrusted by liberals even when he supported liberal measures. Yet often his calculations were shrewd; he proved to be a formidable politician.

The Democrats nominated Senator John F. Kennedy of Massachusetts. His chief rival for the nomination, Lyndon B. Johnson of Texas, the Senate majority leader, became his running mate. Kennedy was the son of Joseph P. Kennedy, a wealthy businessman who had served as ambassador to Great Britain under Franklin Roosevelt. An indifferent student at Harvard, Kennedy in his junior year—1939—traveled with his father to Europe. When Hitler attacked Poland a few months later, Kennedy had a topic for his senior thesis: "Appeasement at Munich," in which he chastised British and American leaders in the 1920s and 1930s for a lack of foresight and resolve. Published in 1940 as *Why England Slept*, the book received favorable reviews and was briefly a best seller. During World War II, Kennedy served in the Pacific, captaining a torpedo

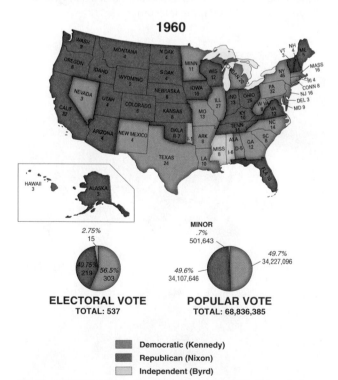

1960

2.75% 15	MINOR .7% 501,643
40.75% 219 56.5% 303	49.6% 34,107,646 49.7% 34,227,096
ELECTORAL VOTE TOTAL: 537	**POPULAR VOTE** TOTAL: 68,836,385

■ Democratic (Kennedy)
■ Republican (Nixon)
▢ Independent (Byrd)

Election of 1960 Like nearly all Democrats since the Compromise of 1877, Kennedy carried most of the South. White Southerners opposed the party of Lincoln, and few black Southerners had been registered to vote.

movement (which was not a major issue in the presidential campaign). He enthusiastically endorsed the Cold War and indicted the Eisenhower administration for falling behind the Soviet Union in the race to build missiles. He admitted frankly that he liked Senator Joseph McCarthy and thought that "he may have something" in his campaign against supposed communists in government. However, as a presidential candidate, he sought to appear more forward-looking. He stressed his youth and "vigor" (a favorite word) and promised to open a **New Frontier** for the country. Nixon ran on the Eisenhower record, which he promised to extend in liberal directions.

A series of television debates between the candidates helped Kennedy by enabling him to demonstrate his maturity and mastery of the issues. Although both candidates laudably avoided it, the religious issue was important. His Catholicism helped Kennedy in eastern urban areas but injured him in many farm districts and throughout the West. Kennedy's victory, 303 to 219 in the Electoral College, was paper-thin in the popular vote, 34,227,000 to 34,109,000.

The years since the end of World War II had been dominated by the prospect of war more terrible than anyone could imagine. By the end of 1960 Eisenhower was less concerned about a communist victory than the impact of the arms race on America itself. By then defense expenditures devoured one-tenth of the nation's GNP. In his final speech as president, Eisenhower warned of the "grave implications" resulting from "the conjunction of an immense military establishment and a large arms industry." What Eisenhower called the **military-industrial complex** potentially endangered "the very structure of our society." Could the nation mount a worldwide defense of democracy without endangering that democracy at home?

Watch the Video *Kennedy-Nixon Debate* at **www.myhistorylab.com**

Chapter Review

Milestones

1944	Congress provides subsidies to veterans in GI Bill of Rights	**1952**	Dwight D. Eisenhower is elected president
1946	UN creates Atomic Energy Commission	**1953**	John Foster Dulles institutes "New Look" nuclear-based foreign policy
1947	Taft-Hartley Act regulates unions and labor disputes		Korean War ends with armistice
1947	Truman announces Truman Doctrine to stop communism's spread	**1954**	Senate holds Army–McCarthy hearings
			United States helps overthrow Arbenz in Guatemala
	George Kennan ("X") urges containment policy in *Sources of Soviet Conduct*		French are defeated in Indochina after siege of Dien Bien Phu
1948	Marshall Plan provides funds to rebuild Europe		Supreme Court orders school desegregation in *Brown v. Board of Education of Topeka*
	Harry S Truman is elected president		
	State of Israel is created as Jewish homeland; Arabs declare war		Egypt nationalizes Suez Canal in Suez Crisis
1948–1949	United States supplies West Berlin during Berlin airlift	**1955**	The Rev. Martin Luther King, Jr., leads Montgomery Bus Boycotts
1949	United States and eleven other nations form North Atlantic Treaty Organization (NATO)	**1956**	Eisenhower is reelected president
		1957	M. L. King, Jr., and followers form Southern Christian Leadership Conference
	Soviet Union detonates atom bomb		National Guard enforces desegregation of Central High School in Little Rock, Arkansas
1950	North Korea invades South Korea		
	NSC-68 calls for massive military buildup	**1959**	Fidel Castro overthrows Fulgencio Batista, takes power in Cuba
	Alger Hiss is convicted of perjury		
	McCarran Act restricts "subversive" activity	**1960**	John F. Kennedy is first Roman Catholic to be elected president
	Senator Joseph McCarthy charges that the State Department is riddled with communists		
	UN counterattack in Korea is driven back by Red Chinese army		

Key Terms

Berlin airlift   U.S. effort to deliver supplies including 2 million tons of food and coal by air to West Berlin in 1948–1949 in response to the Soviet blockade of the city, *743*

Brown v. Board of Education of Topeka   The 1954 Supreme Court decision that held that racially segregated education, which prevailed in much of the South, was unconstitutional. The ruling overturned the doctrine of "separate but equal" that had provided the legal justification for racial segregation ever since the 1896 *Plessy v. Ferguson* Supreme Court decision, *757*

Fair Deal   President Harry Truman's 1949 program for expanded economic opportunity and civil rights, *744*

Marshall Plan   A proposal, propounded in 1947 by Secretary of State George Marshall, to use American aid to rebuild the war-torn economies of European nations. Adopted by Congress in 1948 as the European Recovery Program, it pumped some $13 billion into Europe during the next five years, *741*

massive retaliation   The "New Look" military policy of the Dwight D. Eisenhower and Secretary of State John Foster Dulles relying on nuclear weapons to inhibit communist aggression during the 1950s, *750*

military-industrial complex   A term, popularized by President Dwight D. Eisenhower in his 1961 farewell address, for the concert of interests among the U.S. military and its chief corporate contractors, *761*

New Frontier   President John F. Kennedy's term for a revitalized national agenda, particularly in relation to foreign policy and space exploration, *761*

North Atlantic Treaty Organization (NATO)   A military mutual-defense pact, formed in 1948, by the United States, Canada, and ten European nations, including Great Britain, France, and West Germany; the Soviet Union countered with the formation of the Warsaw Pact among communist regimes in Eastern Europe, *744*

NSC-68   A secret policy statement, proposed by the National Security Council in 1950, calling for a large, ongoing military commitment to contain Soviet communism; it was accepted by President Harry Truman after the North Korean invasion of South Korea, *745*

Southern Christian Leadership Conference (SCLC)   A civil rights organization, founded in 1957 by Martin Luther King, Jr. and his followers, that espoused Christian nonviolence but organized mass protests to challenge segregation and discrimination; it played a major role in support of the **Civil Rights Act of 1964** and the **Voting Rights Act of 1965**, *758*

Taft-Hartley Act   A 1947 federal law that outlawed the closed shop and secondary boycotts and obliged union leaders to sign affidavits declaring that they were not communists, *739*

Truman Doctrine   A foreign policy, articulated by President Harry Truman in 1947, that provided financial aid to Greek and Turkish governments then under threat by communists rebels, *741*

Review Questions

1. The late 1940s and 1950s are often characterized as a period of complacency and consensus. Yet this chapter holds that, in foreign and domestic affairs, it was a period of "menacing uncertainty." What constituted the chief elements of menace?

2. Throughout the period from 1946 to 1960, American presidents sought to "contain" communism. How did Eisenhower's "massive retaliation" differ from Truman's worldwide "NSC-68" containment? How did Sputnik influence the Cold War?

3. Why did Truman intervene in Korea, and why did the war end in stalemate?

4. What was the impact of the Cold War on American society?

5. Why did the civil rights movement gain momentum after 1945? On what grounds did the Supreme Court overturn the "separate but equal" ruling in *Brown v. Board of Education* (1954)? Why did African Americans subsequently resort to "direct action" protests?

PEARSON myhistorylab Connections

Reinforce what you learned in this chapter by studying the many documents, images, maps, review tools, and videos available at **www.myhistorylab.com**.

Read and Review

✓● Study and Review *Chapter 28*

●●● Read the Document *Truman Doctrine, 1947,* p. 741

◉ See the Map *The Korean War, 1950–1953,* p. 747

●●● Read the Document McCarthy, *Wheeling, West Virginia, Speech,* p. 749

((●● Hear the Audio *Joseph P. McCarthy Speech,* p. 751

●●● Read the Document *Brown v. Board of Education of Topeka, Kansas,* p. 758

Research and Explore

◉ Watch the Video *Duck and Cover,* p. 741

◉ Watch the Video *How did the civil rights movement change American schools?,* p. 758

◉ Watch the Video *Kennedy-Nixon Debate,* p. 761

((●● Hear the Audio

Hear the audio file for Chapter 28 at
www.myhistorylab.com.

How do you get out of a deep hole?

On December 2, 2009, as polls revealed growing dissatisfaction with the wars in Iraq and Afghanistan, President Barack Obama promised to withdraw all U.S. troops from Iraq within two years. But he announced that he would send an additional 30,000 troops to Afghanistan, where the situation had deteriorated.

"I do not make this decision lightly," he said, noting that he had opposed the war in Iraq. But Afghanistan, he insisted, was different. It had been the home of the Al Qaeda terrorists who attacked on September 11, 2001.

By sending more troops to Afghanistan now, Obama believed the military would defeat Al Qaeda more quickly. "There are those who suggest that Afghanistan is another Vietnam," he conceded. "I believe this argument depends on a false reading of history."

Because nothing in the past is exactly like anything else, all historical analogies are flawed. But the history of Vietnam suggests that once soldiers have fought and died for a cause, the task of getting out of a war—short of victory—is not an easy one.

From Camelot to Watergate: 1961–1975

29

((•—[Hear the Audio **Chapter 29 at www.myhistorylab.com**

■ Robert McCall's depiction of an American attack on Moscow appeared as the cover of the *Saturday Evening Post* on October 13, 1962. Within two weeks, the United States and the Soviet Union would be at the brink of a nuclear war.

Just before President John F. Kennedy sent the first American troops to Vietnam in 1961, he confided doubts to an aide: "The troops will march in; the bands will play; the crowds will cheer. . . Then we will be told we have to send more troops. It's like taking a drink. The effect wears off, and you have to take another."

By 1963, despite the infusion of some 16,000 U.S. soldiers, South Vietnam was crumbling. In 1965, with a communist takeover imminent, Lyndon Johnson, Kennedy's successor, increased U.S. troop levels to nearly a half million. Yet victory remained elusive. In 1969, his successor,

Richard M. Nixon, promised to bring an honorable peace to Vietnam; but American troops remained for another four years.

The long war in Vietnam exposed deep fissures within the nation. Racial divisions widened into gaping holes. Student protests drew violent responses. Nixon's heated rhetoric and illegal campaign tactics heightened tensions. And less than a year after he resigned, communist North Vietnam completed its conquest of South Vietnam. For the United States, the war ended in failure. ■

Kennedy in Camelot

Having lampooned the Eisenhower administration as stodgy and unimaginative, President Kennedy made a show of his style and wit. He flouted convention by naming Robert, his younger brother, attorney general: "I can't see that it's wrong to give him a little legal experience before he goes out to practice law." Kennedy also prided himself on being a man of letters, winner of a Pulitzer Prize for *Profiles in Courage*. He quoted Robert Frost and Dante. He played and replayed recordings of Winston Churchill, hoping to imprint the great orator's sonorous cadences on his own broad Bostonian vowels. At the instigation of his elegant wife, Jacqueline, Kennedy surrounded himself with the finest intellects at glittering White House galas to honor Nobel Prize winners and celebrated artists.

Kennedy's youthful senior staff boasted impressive scholarly credentials. His national security adviser, McGeorge Bundy, had been dean of the faculty at Harvard (and the first undergraduate at Yale to receive perfect scores in three college entrance examinations). Secretary of Defense Robert McNamara also had taught at Harvard before becoming the first nonfamily member to head the Ford Motor Company. The administration constituted, as journalist David Halberstam observed later, and somewhat ruefully, "the best and the brightest."

Kennedy's campaign slogan—"Let's get this country moving again"—was embodied in his own active life. He played rugged games of touch football with the press corps and romped with his young children in the Oval Office. In an article for *Sports Illustrated* entitled "The Soft American" published just after the election, Kennedy complained that television, movies, and a comfortable lifestyle had made too many young people flabby. His earliest presidential initiative was a physical fitness campaign in the schools.

Kennedy's image of youthful vigor was enhanced by the beauty and presence of Jacqueline, whose wide-eyed diffidence was universally admired as regal bearing. The image was enhanced by Lerner and Loewe's musical *Camelot*, which opened a few weeks before the inauguration. Its evocation of King Arthur, who sought to lead his virile young knights in challenges great and good, suggested the Kennedy White House. (The musical became a favorite of the president; he often listened to cast recordings before going to sleep.) All Washington seemed aglow with excitement and energy. In the words of the administration's chief chronicler, Arthur M. Schlesinger Jr. (another former Harvard professor): "Never had girls seemed so pretty, tunes so melodious, and evenings so blithe and unconstrained."

Never, too, had the substance of an administration been so closely identified with the style of its president. But the dazzle was misleading. Although quick-witted and intelligent, Kennedy was no intellectual. His favorite reading was the James Bond spy novels of Ian Fleming. He never admitted it publicly, but much of *Profiles in Courage* had been ghostwritten by his speechwriter.

Nor did the president embody physical fitness. Congenital back problems, aggravated by war injuries, forced Kennedy to use crutches or a cane in private and to take heavy doses of painkillers and amphetamines. The president's permanent "tan" did not result from outdoor exercise, as the public assumed, but from Addison's disease, an often fatal failure of the adrenal glands for which Kennedy gave himself daily injections of cortisone. Though he publicly denied it, Kennedy was chronically ill throughout his presidency.

The president nevertheless engaged in many extramarital sexual affairs. Reporters covering the White House were aware of his often brazen indiscretions, but chose not to intrude on what they regarded as the president's private life.

The Cuban Crises

"The torch has been passed to a new generation of Americans," Kennedy declared in his inaugural address. Its chief task was to stop the spread of communism. While Eisenhower had relied on the nation's nuclear arsenal to intimidate the Kremlin, Kennedy proposed to challenge communist aggression whenever and wherever it occurred. "We shall pay any price, bear any burden, meet any hardship, support any friend, oppose any foe to assure the survival and the success of liberty," Kennedy intoned. A new breed of cold warrior, Kennedy called on young men and women to serve in the Peace Corps, an organization that he created to mobilize American idealism and technical skills to help developing nations. His was a call for commitment—and action.

Perhaps seduced by his own rhetoric, Kennedy blundered almost immediately. Anti-Castro exiles were eager to organize an invasion of their homeland, reasoning that the Cuban people would rise up against Castro and communism as soon as "democratic" forces provided the necessary leadership. Under Eisenhower the CIA had begun training some 2,000 Cuban exiles in Nicaragua. Kennedy was of two minds about the proposed invasion. Some in his administration opposed it strongly, but his closest advisers, including his brother Robert, urged him to give his approval. In the end he did.

The invaders, 1,400 strong, struck in April 1961. They landed at the Bay of Pigs, on Cuba's southern

"Ich bin ein Berliner" (I am a Berliner), Kennedy declared from a balcony in West Berlin in June, 1961, and his words brought a roar of approval from the West Berliners. Gesturing toward the Berlin wall, he called it "the most obvious and vivid demonstration of the failures of the Communist system."

coast. But the Cuban people failed to flock to their lines, and soon Castro's army pinned the invaders down and forced them to surrender. Because American involvement could not be disguised, the affair exposed the United States to all the criticism that a straightforward assault would have produced, without accomplishing the overthrow of Castro. Worse, it made Kennedy appear impulsive as well as unprincipled. Castro tightened his connections with the Soviet Union.

In June, Kennedy met with Soviet Premier Khrushchev in Vienna. Furious over the invasion of Cuba, Khrushchev blustered about grabbing West Berlin. In August, he abruptly closed the border between East and West Berlin and erected the **Berlin wall**—a barrier of concrete blocks and barbed wire across the city to stop the flow of East Germans into the noncommunist zone. At the same time, the Soviets resumed nuclear testing. Khrushchev ordered detonation of a series of gigantic hydrogen bombs, including one with a power 3,000 times that of the bomb that had devastated Hiroshima.

Kennedy followed suit: He announced plans to build thousands of nuclear missiles, known as Minutemen, capable of hitting targets on the other side of the world. He expanded the space program, vowing that an American would land on the moon within ten years. The president called on Congress to pass a large increase in military spending.

In secret, Kennedy also resolved to destroy Castro. He ordered military leaders to plan for a full-scale invasion of Cuba. (One of the training maneuvers was code-named ORTSAC—Castro spelled backward.) He also instructed the CIA to undertake "massive activity" against Castro's regime. The CIA devised Operation Mongoose, a plan to slip spies, saboteurs, and assassins into Cuba. Although never officially endorsed by the president, Mongoose operated under the oversight of Robert Kennedy. Its attempts to assassinate Castro failed.

In 1962 Khrushchev precipitated the most dangerous confrontation of the Cold War. To forestall the anticipated American invasion of Cuba, he moved tanks, heavy bombers, and 42,000 Soviet troops and technicians to the island. His most fateful step was to sneak several dozen guided nuclear missiles into the country and prepare them for launching. The missiles could have hit most of the eastern United States with nuclear warheads.

On October 14 American spy planes spotted the launching pads and missiles. The president faced a dreadful decision. After the **Bay of Pigs fiasco**, he could not again appear to back down to the communists. But if he invaded Cuba or bombed the Soviet bases and missile sites, Khrushchev would likely seize West Berlin or bomb U.S. missile sites in Turkey. Either action might lead to a full-scale nuclear war and millions of deaths.

On October 22 Kennedy addressed the nation on television. The Soviet buildup was "a deliberately provocative and unjustified change in the status quo." He ordered the American navy to stop and search all vessels headed for Cuba and to turn back any containing "offensive" weapons. Kennedy called on Khrushchev to dismantle the missile bases and remove from the island all weapons capable of striking the United States. Any Cuban-based nuclear attack would result, he warned, in "a full retaliatory response upon the Soviet Union."

For days, while the world watched in horror, Soviet ships steamed toward Cuba and work on the missile launching pads continued. An American spy plane was shot down over Cuba. Khrushchev sent a desperate telegram, suggesting that he was near the breaking point. Robert Kennedy and others engaged in frantic negotiations through intermediaries. Then Khrushchev backed down. He recalled the ships,

This photograph, taken by an American U-2 spy plane and released during the Cuban missile crisis, shows the installation of liquid-fueled Soviet missiles. Khrushchev expected that the missiles could be kept secret. "Our military specialists informed us that strategic missiles can be reliably concealed in the palm forests of Cuba," one of Khrushchev's advisers recalled. Khrushchev, who assumed that the missiles would be harder to spot if they were in a horizontal position, ordered them to be placed in an upright position only at night. This was a mistake: The U-2 was easily able to detect the missiles in their horizontal position.

withdrew the missiles, and reduced his military establishment in Cuba to modest proportions. In response, Kennedy lifted the blockade. He also promised not to invade Cuba, thus ensuring Castro's survival; Kennedy further agreed to withdraw U.S. missiles from Turkey, though this latter concession was not made public at the time.

Immediately the president was hailed for his steady nerve and consummate statesmanship; the Cuban missile crisis was widely regarded as his finest hour. Yet in retrospect it appears that he may have overreacted. The Soviet nuclear threat had been exaggerated. After *Sputnik*, the Soviet long-range missile program flopped, though this was not known at the time. By the summer of 1962 a "missile gap" existed, but it was overwhelmingly in favor of the United States, whose nuclear forces outnumbered those of the Soviet Union by a ratio of seventeen to one. Khrushchev's decision to put medium-range missiles in Cuba signified Soviet weakness rather than impending aggression. Both Kennedy and Khrushchev were sobered by the **Cuban missile crisis**; afterward neither spoke so glibly about superpower confrontation. They signed a treaty outlawing nuclear testing in the atmosphere. But Khrushchev's bluff had been called— a public humiliation from which he never recovered. Within two years, hard-liners in the Kremlin forced him out of office. He was replaced by Leonid Brezhnev, an old-style Stalinist who inaugurated an intensive program of long-range missile development. The nuclear arms race moved to new terrain, uncertain and unimaginably dangerous.

JFK's Vietnam War

Truman's attempt to prevent Ho Chi Minh's communist insurgents from seizing Vietnam failed when the French army surrendered to Ho's troops at Dien Bien Phu in 1954. Eisenhower, equally unwilling to accept a communist victory, then supported creation of an anticommunist South Vietnam, headed by Ngo Dinh Diem, a Vietnamese nationalist who hated the communists. While the United States poured millions of dollars into strengthening Diem's South Vietnam, and especially its army, Ho Chi Minh consolidated his rule in North Vietnam. Those Viet Minh units that remained in the South—they came to be known as Vietcong— were instructed to form secret cells and bide their time. During the late 1950s they gained in strength and militancy.

In May 1959 Ho decided that the time had come to overthrow Diem. Vietcong guerrillas infiltrated thousands of villages, ambushed South Vietnamese convoys, and assassinated government officials. Soon the Vietcong controlled large sections of the countryside, some almost within sight of the capital city of Saigon.

By the time Kennedy took office, Diem's government was tottering. As a senator, Kennedy had endorsed Diem and the attempt to build a noncommunist South Vietnam. He called it the "cornerstone of the Free World in Southeast Asia, the keystone in the arch, the finger in the dike." After the Bay of Pigs debacle, furthermore, Kennedy worried that his credibility with Khrushchev had been damaged. "If he thinks I'm inexperienced and have no guts," he told an aide, "we won't get anywhere with him. So we have to act." Vietnam, he added, "looks like the place."

Kennedy sharply increased the American military and economic commitment to South Vietnam. At the end of 1961 there were 3,200 American military personnel in the country; within two years, there were more than 16,000, and 120 American soldiers had been killed. Despite the expanded effort, by the summer of

In the summer of 1963, Buddhist monks protested against the rule of Diem (and his brother, the Catholic archbishop of Vietnam) by setting themselves on fire.

1963 Diem's regime was in ruins. An ardent Catholic, he cracked down on the Buddhists, who, joined by students, protested his repression. Thousands were arrested, and some were shot. In protest, several Buddhist monks became martyrs by setting themselves on fire in public.

Unable to persuade Diem to moderate his policies, Kennedy sent word to dissident Vietnamese generals of his willingness to support them if they ousted Diem. On November 1 several of these generals surrounded the presidential palace with troops and tanks, seized Diem, and killed him. Kennedy, though appalled by Diem's death, recognized the new junta. The decision to overthrow Diem was fateful; it committed the United States to finding a solution to a worsening situation in Vietnam.

"We Shall Overcome": The Civil Rights Movement

Kennedy initially approached the race question with exceeding caution. His razor-thin victory had depended on the votes both of African Americans in northern cities and white Democrats in the Deep South. As president, his visible support for one group would alienate the other. So Kennedy temporized, urging leaders on both sides to show restraint. This proved impossible. The civil rights movement had already intensified its protests.

In February 1960 four African American college students in Greensboro, North Carolina, sat down at a lunch counter at a Woolworth's store. "We do not serve Negroes," they were told. They returned with more and more demonstrators. By the end of the week over a thousand protesters descended on Woolworth's, led by a phalanx of football players from the nearby black college who cleared the way through a throng of Confederate flag-wavers. "Who do you think you are?" a white demanded. "We the Union army," a football player retorted.

This "sit-in" tactic was not new. The Congress of Racial Equality (CORE) had staged sit-ins in Chicago restaurants back in 1943. But the Greensboro students sparked a national movement; students in dozens of other southern towns and cities copied their example. Soon more than fifty sit-ins were in progress in southern cities. By the end of 1961 over 70,000 people had participated in such demonstrations. Still another new organization, the **Student Nonviolent Coordinating Committee (SNCC)**, was founded by black college students in 1960 to provide a focus for the sit-in movement and to conduct voter registration drives in the South, actions that more than any other roused the fury of southern segregationists.

In May 1961 black and white foes of segregation organized a "freedom ride" to test the effectiveness of federal regulations prohibiting discrimination in interstate transportation. Boarding two buses in Washington, an integrated group of thirteen volunteers took off across the South toward New Orleans. In Alabama they ran into trouble. At Anniston racists set fire to one of the buses, and in Birmingham they were assaulted by a mob. But violence did not stop the freedom riders. Other groups followed, many deliberately seeking arrest to test local segregation ordinances. The resultant court cases repeatedly broke down legal racial barriers throughout the South.

This protracted struggle eventually yielded practical and moral benefits for southern whites as well as blacks. Gradually all but the most unwavering defenders of segregation changed their attitudes. But this took time, and many blacks were unwilling to wait.

Some blacks, contemptuous of white prejudices, were urging their fellows to reject "American" society and all it stood for. In the North, black nationalism became a potent force. Elijah Muhammad, leader of the Black Muslim movement, loathed whites so intensely that he demanded that a part of the United States be set aside exclusively for blacks. He urged his followers to be industrious, thrifty, and abstemious— and to view all whites with suspicion and hatred.

"This white government has ruled us and given us plenty hell, but the time has arrived that you taste a little of your own hell," Muhammad said. He scorned

Whites pour mustard and ketchup over black students (and one white) who were integrating a lunch-counter.

Martin Luther King, Jr., and others who advocated Christian nonviolence. "What fool can love his enemy?" Muhammad asked. Another important Black Muslim, Malcolm X, put it this way in a 1960 speech: "For the white man to ask the black man if he hates him is just like the rapist asking the raped, or the wolf asking the sheep, 'Do you hate me?'" "If someone puts a hand on you," he advised blacks on another occasion, "send him to the cemetery."

Ordinary southern blacks became increasingly impatient. In the face of brutal repression by local police, many began to question Martin Luther King's tactic of nonviolent protest. After leading a series of demonstrations in Birmingham, Alabama, in 1963, King was thrown in jail. When local white clergymen, professing themselves sympathetic to the blacks' objectives, nonetheless urged an end to "untimely" protests, which (they claimed) "incite hatred and violence," King wrote his now-famous "Letter from Birmingham Jail," which contained this moving explanation of why he and his followers were unwilling to wait any longer for justice:

> [W]hen you take a cross-country drive and find it necessary to sleep night after night in the uncomfortable corners of your automobile because no motel will accept you; when you are humiliated day in and day out by nagging signs reading "white" and "colored"; when your first name becomes "nigger" and your middle name becomes "boy" . . . then you will understand why we find it so difficult to wait.

Source: Copyright 1963 Dr. Martin Luther King Jr; copyright renewed 1991 Coretta Scott King.

The brutal repression of the Birmingham demonstrations, captured in newspaper photos and on television broadcasts, brought a flood of recruits and money to the protesters' cause. Pushed by all these developments, President Kennedy reluctantly began to change his policy. His administration had from the start given lip service to desegregation and encouraged activists' efforts to register black voters in the South, but when confrontations arose the president hesitated, arguing that it was up to local officials to enforce the law. After Birmingham, however, Kennedy supported a modest civil rights bill.

When this measure ran into stiff opposition in Congress, blacks organized a demonstration in Washington, attended by 200,000 people. At this gathering, King delivered his "I Have a Dream" address, looking forward to a time when racial prejudice no longer existed and people of all religions and colors could join hands and say, "Free at last! Free at last!" Kennedy sympathized with the Washington gathering but feared it would make passage of the civil rights bill more difficult. As in other areas, he was not a forceful advocate of his own proposals.

Watch the **Video** *Civil Rights March on Washington* at **www.myhistorylab.com**

Watch the **Video** *Civil Rights Movement* at **www.myhistorylab.com**

Read the **Document** Charles Sherrod, *SNCC Memorandum (1961)* at **www.myhistorylab.com**

Tragedy In Dallas: JFK Assassinated

Through it all, Kennedy retained his hold on public opinion. In the fall of 1963 most observers believed he would win a second term. Then, while visiting Dallas, Texas, on November 22, he was shot in the head by an assassin, Lee Harvey Oswald, and died almost instantly.

Kennedy's assassination precipitated an extraordinary series of events. Oswald had fired on the president with a rifle from an upper story of a warehouse. No one saw him pull the trigger. He was apprehended largely because he panicked and killed a policeman across town later in the day. He denied his guilt, but a mass of evidence connected him with the assassination of the president. Before he could be brought to trial, however, he was himself murdered by Jack Ruby, the owner of a Dallas nightclub. The incident took place in full view of television cameras, while Oswald was being transferred from one place of detention to another.

Each day brought new revelations. Oswald had defected briefly to the Soviet Union in 1959, then had returned to the United States and formed a pro-Castro organization in New Orleans. Many concluded that some nefarious conspiracy lay at the root of the tragedy. Oswald, the argument ran, was a pawn—either of communists or anticommunists (the conspiracy theories lost none of their appeal for being contradictory)—whose murder was designed to

JFK and Jacqueline Kennedy ride in a motorcade with Texas Governor John Connolly and his wife in Dallas, November 22, 1963. Several minutes later, Kennedy was shot and killed; Connolly was wounded.

shield from exposure the masterminds who had engineered the assassination. A special commission headed by Chief Justice Earl Warren was convened to analyze the evidence. After a lengthy investigation, it concluded that Oswald had acted alone.

Instead of dampening charges of conspiracy, the report of the Warren Commission provoked new doubts. As word leaked out about the earlier CIA assassination attempts against Castro, the failure of the Warren Report even to mention Operation Mongoose made the commission suspect, all the more so since several members, including Allen Dulles, former director of the CIA, had known of the operation. (On the day of Kennedy's assassination, a CIA agent in Paris gave a Cuban who had volunteered to assassinate Castro a ballpoint pen containing a poisoned hypodermic needle.) In fact, there is little solid evidence to suggest that Oswald was part of a wider conspiracy. But the decision of Dulles and other commissioners to protect CIA secrets engendered skepticism.

One measure of Kennedy's hold on the public imagination was the outpouring of grief that attended his death. Kennedy had given hope to people who had none. Young black civil rights activist Anne Moody, who later wrote *Coming of Age in Mississippi*, was working as a waitress in a segregated restaurant. "Tears were burning my cheeks," she recalled. Her boss, a Greek immigrant, gently suggested she take the rest of the day off. When she looked up, there were tears in his eyes too.

Lyndon Baines Johnson: The Great Society

John F. Kennedy's death made Lyndon B. Johnson president. From 1949 until his election as vice president, Johnson had been a senator from Texas and, for most of that time, Senate Democratic leader. He could be heavy-handed or subtle, and also devious, domineering, persistent, and obliging. Many people swore by him; few had the fortitude to swear at him. Above all he knew what to do with political power. "Some men want power so they can strut around to 'Hail to the Chief,'" he said, "I wanted it to use it."

Johnson, who had consciously modeled his career after that of Franklin D. Roosevelt, considered social welfare legislation his specialty. The contrast with Kennedy could not have been sharper. In his inaugural address, Kennedy had made no mention of domestic issues. Kennedy's plans for federal aid for education, urban renewal, a higher minimum wage, and medical care for the aged were blocked in Congress by Republicans and southern Democrats. The same coalition also defeated his chief economic initiative—a broad tax cut to stimulate the economy.

But Kennedy had reacted to these defeats mildly, almost wistfully. He thought the machinery of the federal government was cumbersome and ineffective.

Johnson knew how to make it work. On becoming president, he pushed hard for Kennedy's programs. Early in his career Johnson had voted against a bill making lynching a federal crime, and he also had opposed bills outlawing state poll taxes and establishing the federal Fair Employment Practices Commission. But after he became an important figure in national affairs, he consistently championed racial equality. Now he made it the centerpiece of his domestic policy. "Civil righters are going to have to wear sneakers to keep up with me," he boasted. Bills long buried in committee sailed through Congress. Early in 1964 Kennedy's tax cut was passed. A few months later, an expanded version of another Kennedy proposal became law as the **Civil Rights Act of 1964**.

The much-strengthened Civil Rights Act outlawed discrimination by employers against blacks and also against women. It broke down legal barriers to black voting in the southern states and outlawed racial segregation of all sorts in places of public accommodation, such as movie theaters, hotels, and restaurants. In addition, unlike presidents Eisenhower and Kennedy, Johnson established agencies to enforce civil rights legislation.

Johnson's success in steering the Civil Rights Act through Congress confirmed his belief that he could be a reformer in the tradition of Franklin Roosevelt. He declared war on poverty and set out to create a **Great Society** in which poverty no longer would exist.

In 1937 Roosevelt had been accused of exaggeration for claiming that one-third of the nation was "ill-housed, ill-clad, ill-nourished." In fact Roosevelt had underestimated the extent of poverty. Wartime economic growth reduced the percentage of poor people in the country substantially, but in 1960 between 20 and 25 percent of all American families—about 40 million people—were living below the poverty line, a government standard of minimum subsistence based on income and family size.

The presence of so many poor people in an affluent society was deplorable but not difficult to explain. In any community a certain number of people cannot support themselves because of physical, mental, or emotional problems. The United States also included entire regions, the best known being Appalachia, that had been bypassed by economic development and no longer provided their inhabitants with adequate economic opportunities.

Moreover, prosperity and advancing technology had changed the definition of poverty. Telephones, radios and electric refrigerators, and other goods

LBJ cultivated the masculine image of a Texas cowboy. Biographers have suggested that Johnson was torn between the expectations of his father, a crude local politician who flouted polite society, and those of his mother, a refined woman who insisted that her son read poetry and practice the violin. Johnson later told biographer Doris Kearns Goodwin that he persisted in Vietnam because he worried that critics would accuse him of being "an unmanly man. A man without a spine."

unimaginable to the most affluent Americans of the 1860s, were necessities a hundred years later. But as living standards rose, so did job requirements. A strong back and a willingness to work no longer guaranteed a decent living. Technology was changing the labor market. Educated workers with special skills and good verbal abilities easily found well-paid jobs. Those who had no special skills or were poorly educated went without work.

The Economic Opportunity Act of 1964 created a mixture of programs, among them a Job Corps similar to the New Deal Civilian Conservation Corps, a community action program to finance local antipoverty efforts, and a system for training the unskilled unemployed and for lending money to small businesses in poor areas. The programs combined the progressive concept of government aid for those in need with the conservative idea of individual responsibility.

Buttressed by his legislative triumphs, Johnson sought election as president in his own right in 1964. He achieved this ambition in unparalleled fashion. His championing of civil rights won him the almost unanimous support of blacks; his tax policy attracted the well-to-do and the business interests; his war on poverty held the allegiance of labor and

other traditionally Democratic groups. His down-home southern antecedents counterbalanced his liberalism on the race question in the eyes of many white southerners.

The Republicans played into his hands by nominating the conservative Senator Barry M. Goldwater of Arizona, whose objective in Congress had been "not to pass laws but to repeal them." As a presidential candidate he favored such laissez-faire policies as cutting back on the Social Security system and doing away with the Tennessee Valley Authority. A large majority of voters found Goldwater out-of-date on economic questions and dangerously aggressive on foreign affairs.

In November, Johnson won a sweeping victory, collecting over 61 percent of the popular vote and carrying the whole country except Goldwater's Arizona and five states in the Deep South, where many conservatives were voting more against Johnson's civil rights policies than in favor of Goldwater. Goldwater had voted against the Civil Rights Act of 1964 and was opposed to government-mandated school integration. (Mapping the Past, "School Segregation after the *Brown* Decision," explores the status of school integration in the decade after the Supreme Court's *Brown* decision.)

School Segregation After the *Brown* Decision

The 1954 *Brown v. Board of Education* decision prohibited racial segregation in the nation's public schools. But many states and school districts ignored federal court orders to comply with the desegregation order. Although Eisenhower put down Arkansas Governor Orval Faubus's public challenge to federal authority in 1957, he did little else to ensure compliance with *Brown*. President Kennedy, similarly, was reluctant to alienate white southern voters. He named to the federal judiciary staunch supporters of school segregation. One of his appointees, E. Gordon West of Louisiana, called the *Brown* ruling "one of the truly regrettable decisions of all time."

The accompanying maps show the slow progress of school desegregation in the South. In 1954, 3,870 southern school districts had both white and black students. (The South here includes Alabama, Arkansas, Florida, Georgia, Kentucky, Oklahoma, Louisiana, Mississippi, North Carolina, South Carolina, Tennessee, Texas, and Virginia.) In only three of these districts did any white and black students attend school together: Arkansas (two) and Texas (one). Only one of the twenty-three school districts in Maryland was desegregated. The percentage of African American students attending schools with whites in the South was slightly above zero.

In 1964 compliance with the Supreme Court's ruling had improved somewhat in the border states, but little in the Deep South. Of the 2,586 school districts in the South that now had black and white students (the number of school districts had declined as a result of consolidation), 1,150 reported that they were desegregated. Only 3 of Louisiana's 67 districts were desegregated, 4 of Mississippi's 150 districts, and 9 of Alabama's 118 districts.

In Alabama, Arkansas, Mississippi, Georgia, Florida, South Carolina, and North Carolina, fewer than 4 percent of black and white children attended school together.

African Americans attending schools with whites in the South and border states, 1954 and 1964

Percentage

0   4   10   20   57   68

Data not available

More substantive progress had occurred in the border regions, where black and white students were far more likely to attend school together. In Kentucky, for example, 68 percent of the black students attended school with whites; figures in other southern states were Maryland 51 percent, West Virginia 63 percent, Missouri 42 percent, and

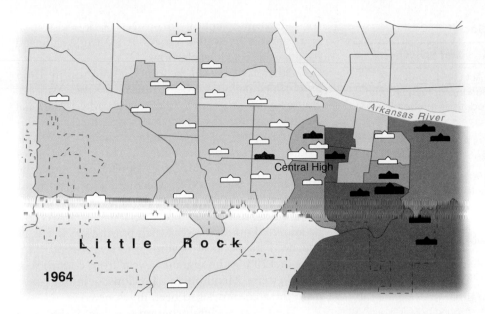

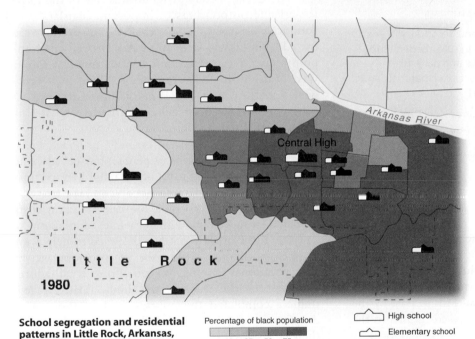

School segregation and residential patterns in Little Rock, Arkansas, 1964 and 1980

Percentage of black population

10 25 50 75

High school

Elementary school

Percentage of black students
100 50 0

ensure admission of the black students, Faubus ordered the closing of both of Little Rock's high schools. In subsequent years, more subtle means were found to discourage the desegregation of Little Rock schools.

In 1964, all of the schools in Little Rock remained segregated (see the accompanying map). African Americans lived mostly in the eastern section of Little Rock, and their children attended all-black elementary schools and an all-black high school. White students attended all-white schools, including Central High.

By 1980, however, the schools of Little Rock had become fully desegregated (see the accompanying map). This map shows that not only did all schools include both white and black students, but that the proportion of black and white students varied little among the schools. The balance was achieved mostly by busing black students into formerly white schools. But the map also shows that Little Rock was itself becoming predominantly black. Busing to achieve racial balance caused many whites to leave Little Rock and move to the mostly white suburbs. By 1980 Central High, which had been exclusively white in 1957, was two-thirds black. The same was true of most of the other schools in Little Rock. School officials worried that Little Rock schools would soon be nearly all black.

Similar patterns were evident in the North, too. Supreme Court rulings might change the law of the land, but the attitudes of the people were less malleable. Judicial opinions could change, too. In 2007, the Supreme Court struck down desegregation efforts that used race as the sole factor in assigning pupils to schools.

Oklahoma 31 percent. Nearly 8 percent of black and white children in Texas also attended school together. But overall, compliance had been slow and incomplete.

The Struggle for School Desegregation in Little Rock, 1964–1980

The most celebrated resistance to *Brown* had occurred in 1957 when Arkansas Governor Orval Faubus ordered state militia to prevent a handful of black students from being admitted to all-white Central High. After President Eisenhower sent the 101st Airborne Division to Little Rock to

Questions for Discussion

■ Which southern states resisted desegregation for the longest period?

■ The maps of Little Rock show a shift from fully segregated schools in 1964 to desegregated schools in 1980. What demographic shift does a comparison of the two maps indicate?

Table 29.1 Making a "Great Society"

Assisted Group	Legislation and Provisions
African Americans	Civil Rights Act (1964): Outlawed discrimination in employment, public accommodations, and federally-funded programs
	Voting Rights Act (1965): Federal registrars sent to the South
Elderly	Medicare (1965): Federally-funded medical care for elderly
Low-income people	Economic Opportunity Act (1964): Federally-funded antipoverty programs and agencies
	Medicaid (1965): Federally-funded health care for welfare recipients
	Housing and Urban Development Act: Federally-funded housing projects and rent support
Students	Elementary and Secondary Education Act (1965): Federal support for public and parochial schools for texts and materials, and for Head Start
	Higher Education Act (1965): Federally-funded loans and scholarships for college students

Quickly Johnson pressed ahead with his Great Society program. In January 1965 he proposed a compulsory hospital insurance system, known as **Medicare**, for all persons over the age of sixty-five. As amended by Congress, the Medicare Act consisted of Part A, hospital insurance for the elderly (funded by increased Social Security taxes), and a voluntary plan, Part B, covering doctors' bills (paid for in part by the government). The law also provided for grants to the states to help pay the medical expenses of poor people, even those below the age of sixty-five. This part of the system was called Medicaid. Before the passage of the Medicare Act, about half of Americans over sixty-five years old had no medical insurance.

Next, Congress passed the Elementary and Secondary Education Act in 1965, which supplied federal funds to school districts; the Higher Education Act (1965), which provided financial aid to college students; and Head Start, a program to prepare poor preschoolers for elementary school. It also incidentally improved the children's health by providing medical examinations and nutritious meals.

Still another important reform was the **Voting Rights Act of 1965**, pressed through Congress by President Johnson after more brutal repressions of civil rights demonstrators in the South. This law provided for federal intervention to protect black registration and voting in six southern states. It applied to state and local as well as federal elections.

Other laws passed at Johnson's urging in 1965 and 1966 included the creation of the National Endowment for the Arts and the National Endowment for the Humanities and measures supporting scientific research, highway safety, crime control, slum clearance, clean air, and the preservation of historic sites. Of particular significance was the Immigration Act of 1965, which did away with most provisions of the national-origin system of admitting newcomers. Instead, 290,000 persons a year were to be admitted on the basis of such priorities as job skills and need for political asylum. The law also placed a limit of 120,000 immigrants a year from countries in the Western Hemisphere. Previously, immigration from these countries had been unrestricted.

The Great Society program was one of the most remarkable outpourings of important legislation in American history. The results, however, were mixed. The 1965 Education Act proved a disappointment. Too many local school districts found ways of using the federal money to cover their ordinary expenses, and the sums actually devoted to programs for the poor failed to improve most students' performances significantly.

Medicare and Medicaid certainly provided medical treatment for millions of people, but because the patients no longer paid most of the bills, doctors, hospitals, and drug companies were able to raise fees and prices without fear of losing business. Medical costs escalated far more rapidly than the rate of inflation.

The Job Corps, which was designed to help poor people get better-paying jobs by providing them with vocational training, was an almost total failure. The cost of the training was high, relatively few trainees completed the courses, and of those who did, few found jobs in which they could make use of their new skills.

On balance, the achievements of the Great Society were far below what President Johnson had promised and his supporters had envisioned. The same, of course, can be said of most ambitious reform programs—of Reconstruction; of the Progressive movement; and certainly of the New Deal, to which Johnson had contributed as a young man. Despite his long political experience, Johnson tried to accomplish too many things too quickly. He relied too heavily on the techniques of political manipulation. Perhaps he was carried away by his unexpected power—that he would ever become president must have seemed to a man of his political acumen most unlikely after he failed to win the nomination in 1960. He seized too avidly this opportunity to make history. Without the crisis atmosphere that had appeared to justify hasty experimentation during the New Deal years, the public judged the results of the Great Society and the president who had shaped it skeptically.

⊙ See the Map *Impact of the Voting Rights Act of 1965* at www.myhistorylab.com

New Racial Turmoil

One reason for skepticism was that the adoption of the Great Society coincided with increasing racial polarization. Black militancy, building steadily during World War II and the postwar years, burst forth powerfully in the mid-1960s. An important illustration was the response of Black Muslims to Malcolm X's 1964 decision to abandon the organization. A trip to the Middle East had exposed him to Islamic doctrines of racial equality and the brotherhood of man. In response he founded the Organization of Afro-American Unity. In 1965, while making a speech in favor of racial harmony, he was assassinated by Black Muslim fanatics.

Even Martin Luther King, Jr., the herald of nonviolent resistance, became more aggressive. "We are not asking, we are demanding the ballot," he said in January 1965. A few weeks after Malcolm's death, King led a march from Selma, Alabama, to Montgomery as part of a campaign to force Alabama authorities to allow blacks to register to vote. King chose Selma because the county in which it was located had a black

Police watch as the Watts section of Los Angeles burns during riots in August, 1965.

majority but only 325 registered black voters. He expected the authorities to react brutally, thus attracting public sympathy for the marchers, and he was not disappointed. His marchers were assaulted by state policemen who wielded clubs and tossed canisters of tear gas.

Many African Americans lost patience with nonviolence. "The time for running has come to an end," declared Stokely Carmichael, chairman of the Student Nonviolent Coordinating Committee (SNCC). "It's time we stand up and take over." He began chanting "Black Power!" and other African-Americans chimed in. Black Power caught on swiftly among militants. This troubled white liberals, who feared that Black Power would antagonize white conservatives. They argued that since blacks made up only about 11 percent of the population, any attempt to obtain racial justice through the use of naked power was sure to fail.

Meanwhile, black anger erupted in a series of destructive urban riots. The most important occurred in Watts, a ghetto of Los Angeles, in August 1965. A trivial incident brought thousands into the streets. The neighborhood almost literally exploded: For six days Watts was swept by fire, looting, and bloody fighting between local residents and nearly 15,000 National Guardsmen, called up to assist the police. The following two summers saw similar outbursts in scores of cities.

Then, in April 1968, Martin Luther King, Jr., was murdered in Memphis, Tennessee, by a white man,

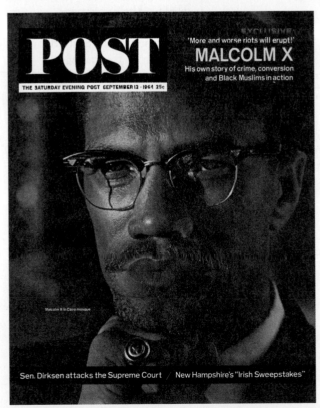

POST

'More and worse riots will erupt!'
MALCOLM X
His own story of crime, conversion and Black Muslims in action

THE SATURDAY EVENING POST SEPTEMBER 12 · 1964 25¢

Malcolm X in Cairo mosque

Sen. Dirksen attacks the Supreme Court / New Hampshire's "Irish Sweepstakes"

Malcolm X, featured on the cover of the *Saturday Evening Post*, broke with the Black Muslims in 1964.

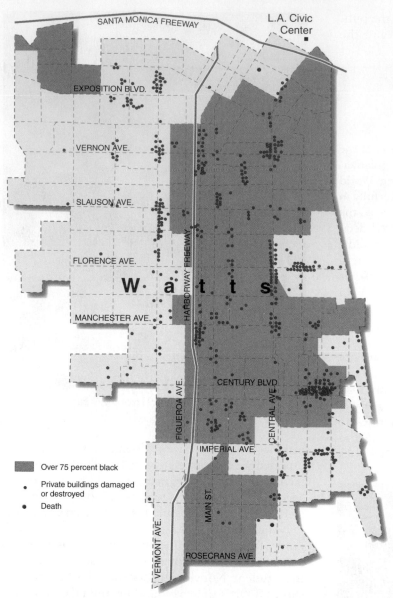

SANTA MONICA FREEWAY

L.A. Civic Center

EXPOSITION BLVD.

VERNON AVE.

SLAUSON AVE.

FLORENCE AVE.

HARBORWAY FREEWAY

W a t t s

MANCHESTER AVE.

FIGUEROA AVE.

CENTURY BLVD

CENTRAL AVE.

IMPERIAL AVE.

■ Over 75 percent black

• Private buildings damaged or destroyed

● Death

MAIN ST.

VERMONT AVE.

ROSECRANS AVE.

Violence and Segregation in Watts, Los Angeles, August 11, 1965 During the race riots that began on this day, hundreds of buildings in the predominantly black ghetto of Watts were destroyed, and some people were killed. Among the complaints of residents was that two superhighways—the Santa Monica Freeway and the Harborway Freeway—turned Watts into a prison for those who lacked automobiles.

bottles and bricks and sometimes shot at, while above the roar of the flames and the hiss of steam rose the apocalyptic chant, "Burn, baby, burn!"

The most frightening aspect of the riots was their tendency to polarize society on racial lines. Whites fled to the suburbs in droves. Advocates of Black Power became more determined to separate themselves from white influence; they exasperated white supporters of school desegregation by demanding schools of their own. Extremists formed the Black Panther party and collected weapons to resist the police. "Shoot, don't loot," the radical H. Rap Brown advised all who would listen. "Violence is as American as cherry pie," he added.

⊚〚**Watch** the **Video** *Malcolm X* at **www.myhistorylab.com**

••●〚**Read** the **Document** *Watts Riots 1967* at **www.myhistorylab.com**

••●〚**Read** the **Document** *Black Power 1967* at **www.myhistorylab.com**

From the "Beat Movement" to Student Radicalism

The increased militancy of many American blacks paralleled the emergence of an increasingly strident attitude among many young people as the "conformist" decade of the 1950s gave way to the "activist" 1960s.

This common characterization, however, is overdrawn. The roots of 1960s' dissent were firmly planted in the 1950s. J. D. Salinger, perhaps the most popular writer of the decade and the particular favorite of college students—*The Catcher in the Rye* (1951) sold nearly 2 million copies—wrote about young people whose self-absorption was a product of their alienation from society. Allen Ginsberg's dark, desperate *Howl*, written in 1955, perhaps the most widely read poem of the postwar era, underscored generational differences. "I saw the best minds of my generation destroyed by madness, starving hysterical naked," the poem begins; and it ends with an almost frantic assault on that "sphinx of cement and aluminum," the fire god Moloch, the devourer of children. In *On the Road* (1957), Jack Kerouac, founder of the **beat** (for "beatific") **school**, described a manic, drug-laced flight from traditional values and institutions. In *Catch-22* (1955), Joseph Heller produced a war novel at once farcical and an indignant denunciation of the stupidity and waste of warfare.

James Earl Ray. Blacks in more than a hundred cities unleashed their anger in outbursts of burning and looting. The death of King appeared to destroy the hope that his peaceful appeal to reason and right could solve the problems of racism.

The victims of racism employed violence not so much to force change as to obtain psychic release; it was a way of getting rid of what they could not stomach, a kind of vomiting. Thus the riots concentrated in the ghettos themselves, smashing, Samson-like, the source of degradation even when this meant self-destruction. When fires broke out in black districts, the firefighters who tried to extinguish them were often showered with

Timothy Leary, "The Johnny Appleseed of LSD," asserted that psychedelic drugs and sexual rapture—"ecstasy"—could promote political freedom, as the cover for his book on the subject suggested.

But if the "beats" were a fringe group of poets and musicians, their successors in the 1960s—generally known as hippies—could be found in large groups in every big city in the United States and Europe. They were so "turned off" by the modern world that they retreated from it, finding refuge in communes, drugs, and mystical religions. They were disgusted by the dishonesty and sordid antics of so many of the politicians, horrified by the brutality of Vietnam, appalled by racism, and contemptuous of the smugness they encountered in colleges and universities. But they rejected activism. Theirs was a world of folk songs and blaring acid rock music, of "be-ins," "love-ins," casual sex, and drugs. Their slogan, "Make love, not war," was more a general pacifist pronouncement than a specific criticism of events in Vietnam. At rock concerts they listened where earlier generations had danced. Timothy Leary, a Harvard psychologist who became known as the "Johnny Appleseed of LSD," advised them to "Tune in, turn on, drop out."

But the 1960s also witnessed the emergence of a new activism. Many students were frustrated by persistent racism and bigotry, but they regarded these as symptoms of a right-wing "power elite" of corporate executives and military and political leaders—a concept outlined in a book of that title by Columbia sociologist C. Wright Mills. In 1962 a small group of students in the **Students for a Democratic Society (SDS)** put together a manifesto for action at a meeting at Port Huron, Michigan: "We are the people of this generation . . . looking uncomfortably to the world we inherit," the Port Huron Statement began. Their main

A young man perches in a tree with a guitar at Woodstock, a drug- and water-logged music festival that attracted 500,000 to rural New York in 1968.

concerns were racial bigotry, the bomb, and the "disturbing paradoxes" associated with these concerns. SDS sought to wrest power from the "military-industrial" complex and institute a radical socialist government. They proposed to radicalize college students; how this was to be accomplished, they did not say.

But SDS grew, powered by rising college enrollments and a seemingly unending list of local campus issues. The first great student outburst convulsed the University of California at Berkeley in the fall of 1964. Angry students, many veterans of the 1964 fight for black rights in the South, staged sit-down strikes in university buildings to protest the prohibition of political canvassing on the campus. This free speech movement disrupted the institution over a period of weeks. Hundreds were arrested, the state legislature threatened reprisals, the faculty became involved in the controversy, and the crisis led to the resignation of the president of the University of California, Clark Kerr.

But what transformed student activism from being a local campus irritation to a mass political movement was the decision by Lyndon Johnson to escalate the war in Vietnam.

((•─ Hear the Audio Timothy Leary, *Going Out* (1966) at **www.myhistorylab.com**

 Watch the Video *Protests Against the Vietnam War* at **www.myhistorylab.com**

Johnson Escalates the War

After Diem's assassination in 1963, the situation in South Vietnam worsened. One military coup followed another, and political instability aggravated military incapacity. President Johnson nevertheless felt that he had no choice but to prop up the South Vietnamese regime. "If I don't go in now," he told an adviser, "they'll be all over me in Congress. They won't be talking about my civil rights bill, or education, or beautification. No sir, they'll push Vietnam up my ass every time."

Johnson decided to punish North Vietnam directly for prosecuting the war in the South. In early 1964 he secretly ordered American warships to escort the South Vietnamese navy on commando missions far into the Gulf of Tonkin. After one such mission, American destroyers were fired on by North Vietnamese gunboats. Several nights later during a heavy storm, American ships reported that they were being fired on, though the enemy was never spotted. Using this Tonkin "incident" as pretext, Johnson demanded, and in an air of crisis obtained, an authorization from Congress to "repel any armed attack against the forces of the United States and to prevent further aggression." With this blank check, known as the **Gulf of Tonkin Resolution**, and buttressed by his sweeping defeat of Goldwater in 1964, Johnson authorized air attacks in North Vietnam. By the summer of

From 1965 to 1968, American troops in Vietnam conducted "search and destroy" missions to shatter the insurgents. Here a soldier watches as a village is burned.

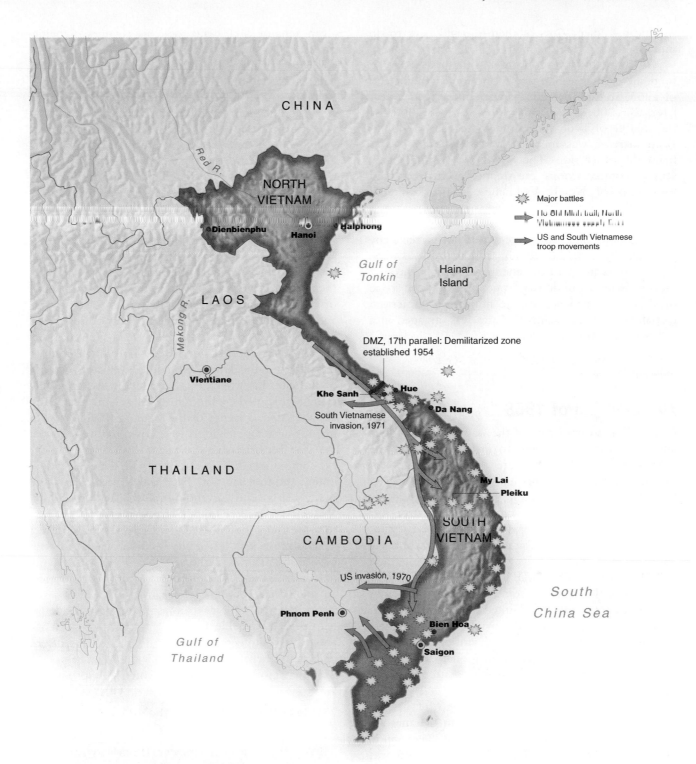

The Vietnam War, 1961–1975 As American bombing and "search and destroy" missions spread throughout South Vietnam, North Vietnamese supply lines moved westward, into Laos and Cambodia. U.S. troops and bombers attacked there as well. This destabilized Cambodia, which fell to the brutal Khmer Rouge communists in 1975.

1965, American bombers were conducting some 5,000 raids each month.

But the hail of bombs on North Vietnam had little effect on the struggle in the South. Worse, the Vietcong expanded the areas under their control. After a fact-finding mission in the war zone, McGeorge

Bundy concluded that the prospects were grim for South Vietnam. "The energy and persistence of the Vietcong are astonishing," he reported. "They have accepted extraordinary losses and they come back for more. They show skill in their sneak attacks and ferocity when cornered." If the war was to be won,

American soldiers—lots of them—would have to do much of the fighting themselves.

In July 1965 Johnson ordered the first of several huge increases in American ground forces. By the end of 1965, 184,000 Americans were in the field; a year later, 385,000; and after another year, 485,000. By the middle of 1968 the number exceeded 538,000. Each increase was met by corresponding increases from the other side. The Soviet Union and China sent no combat troops, but stepped up their aid, and thousands of North Vietnamese regulars filtered across the seventeenth parallel to fight with the Vietcong guerrillas.

The new American strategy was not to seize any particular battlefield or terrain as in all previous wars, but to kill as many of the enemy as possible through bloody "search and destroy" operations. As the scope of the action broadened, the number of American casualties rose. The United States was engaged in a full-scale war, one that Congress had never declared.

⬤⬤▸[**Read** the **Document** *The Gulf of Tonkin Resolution Message* at **www.myhistorylab.com**

The Election of 1968

Gradually the opponents of the war gained numbers and strength. They began to include some of the president's advisers. By late 1967 Secretary of Defense McNamara, who had methodically tracked kill ratios, troop replacement rates, and nearly every other conceivable statistic, concluded that "the figures didn't add up" and the war could not be won. Deeply despondent, he resigned, but did not publicly admit his doubts.

Opposition to the war was especially vehement on college campuses, some students objecting because they thought the United States had no business intervening in the Vietnam conflict, others because they feared being drafted, still others because so many students obtained educational deferments, while young men who were unable to attend college were conscripted.

Then, in November 1967, Eugene McCarthy, a low-keyed, introspective senator from Minnesota, announced his candidacy for the 1968 Democratic presidential nomination. Opposition to the war was his issue.

Preventing Johnson from being renominated seemed impossible. Aside from the difficulty of defeating a "reigning" president, there were the domestic achievements of Johnson's Great Society program: the health insurance program for retired people, greatly expanded federal funding of education and public housing, and the Civil Rights Act.

Even Senator McCarthy took his chances of being nominated so lightly that he did not trouble to set up a real organization. He entered the campaign only to "alleviate . . . this sense of political helplessness." Someone, he decided, must step forward to put the Vietnam question before the voters.

Stung by the critics, Johnson ordered General William C. Westmoreland, commander of American forces in Vietnam, to reassure the American people on the course of the war. The general obligingly returned to the United States in late 1967 and told the press that he could see "some light at the end of the tunnel."

Suddenly, early in 1968, on the heels of this announcement, North Vietnamese and Vietcong forces launched a general offensive to correspond with their Lunar New Year (called Tet). Striking thirty-nine of the forty-four provincial capitals, many other towns and cities, and every American base, they caused chaos throughout South Vietnam. They held Hué, the old capital of the country, for weeks. To root insurgents out of Saigon the Americans had to level large sections of the city. Elsewhere the destruction was total, an irony highlighted by the remark of an American officer after the recapture of the village of Ben Tre: "It became necessary to destroy the town to save it."

The **Tet offensive** was essentially a series of raids; the communists did not expect to hold the cities indefinitely, and they did not. Their losses were enormous. Nevertheless the psychological impact in South Vietnam and in the United States made Tet a clear victory for the communists. American pollsters reported an enormous shift of public opinion against further escalation of the fighting. When Westmoreland described Tet as a communist defeat and yet requested an additional 206,000 troops, McCarthy, who was campaigning in the New Hampshire primary, suddenly became a formidable figure. Thousands of students and other volunteers flocked to the state to ring doorbells on his behalf. On primary election day he polled 42 percent of the Democratic vote. This prompted

Table 29.2 Major Events in the Vietnam War, 1961–1968

Year	Event
1961	JFK dispatches thousands of U.S. military "advisers" to South Vietnam
1963	Vietnamese Buddhists rebel; United States supports overthrow of Diem
1964	LBJ obtains Gulf of Tonkin Resolution to expand war
1965	LBJ greatly increases U.S. troop levels
1968	Tet Offensive throughout South Vietnam; LBJ decides not to seek reelection; My Lai Massacre

former attorney general Robert F. Kennedy, brother of the slain president, to declare his candidacy for the Democratic nomination. Like McCarthy, Kennedy opposed Johnson's Vietnam policies but thought his chances of winning were better than McCarthy's.

Confronting this division in the ranks, President Johnson realized he could no longer hope to be an effective president. In a surprising televised announcement, he withdrew from the race. Vice President Hubert H. Humphrey then announced his candidacy, and Johnson threw the weight of his administration behind him.

Kennedy carried several primaries, including California. Immediately after his victory speech in a Los Angeles hotel, however, he was assassinated by Sirhan Sirhan, an Arab nationalist who had been incensed by Kennedy's support of Israel. In effect, Kennedy's death ensured the nomination of Humphrey.

The contest for the Republican nomination was far less dramatic, although its outcome, the nomination of Richard M. Nixon, would have been hard to predict a few years earlier. After his loss to Kennedy in 1960, Nixon ran unsuccessfully for governor of California in 1962, then moved to New York City and joined a prominent law firm. But he remained active in Republican affairs. In 1964 he had campaigned hard for Goldwater. When no other Republican developed extensive support as the 1968 election approached, Nixon entered the race, swept the primaries, and won an easy first-ballot victory at the Republican convention.

Nixon then astounded the country and dismayed liberals by choosing Governor Spiro T. Agnew of Maryland as his running mate. Agnew was a political unknown. ("Spiro who?" jokesters asked.) Nixon chose him primarily to attract southern votes.

Placating the South seemed necessary because Governor George C. Wallace of Alabama was making a determined bid to win enough electoral votes for his American Independent party to prevent any candidate from obtaining a majority. Wallace was flagrantly anti-black and anti-intellectual. (College professors were among his favorite targets. In attacking them he used such well-worn images as "ivory tower folks with pointed heads" and—more inventive—people without "sense enough to park a bicycle straight.") He denounced federal "meddling," the "coddling" of criminals, and the forced integration of schools.

This Republican strategy to win the South heightened the tension surrounding the Democratic convention, which met in Chicago in late August. Humphrey delegates controlled the convention. Several thousand activists, representing a dozen groups and advocating tactics ranging from orderly demonstrations to civil disobedience to indiscriminate violence, descended on Chicago to put pressure on the delegates to repudiate the Johnson Vietnam policy.

In the tense atmosphere that resulted, the party hierarchy overreacted. The mayor of Chicago, Richard J. Daley, whose ability to "influence" election results in a manner favorable to Democrats had often been demonstrated, ringed the convention with policemen to protect it from disruption. This was a reasonable precaution in itself. Inside the building the delegates nominated Humphrey and adopted a war plank satisfactory to Johnson. Outside, however, provoked by the abusive language and violent behavior of radical demonstrators, the police tore into the protesters, in novelist Norman Mailer's graphic phrase, "like a chain saw cutting into wood," while millions watched on television in fascinated horror.

The mayhem in Chicago seemed to benefit Nixon by strengthening the convictions of many voters that the tougher treatment of criminals and dissenters that he and Agnew were calling for was necessary. Those who were critical of the Chicago police tended to blame Humphrey, whom Mayor Daley supported.

Nixon campaigned at a deliberate, dignified pace. He made relatively few public appearances, relying instead on carefully arranged television interviews and taped commercials. He stressed firm enforcement of the law and his desire "to bring us together." As for Vietnam, he would "end the war and win the peace," by just what means he did not say. Agnew, in his blunt, coarse way, assaulted Humphrey, the Democrats, and left-wing dissident groups. (Critics who remembered Nixon's own combative style in the era of Joseph McCarthy called Agnew "Nixon's Nixon.")

But gradually Humphrey gained ground, and on election day the popular vote was close: Nixon slightly less than 31.8 million, Humphrey nearly 31.3 million. Nixon's Electoral College margin, however, was substantial—301 to 191. The remaining 46 electoral votes went to Wallace, whose 9.9 million votes came to 13.5 percent of the total. Together, Nixon and Wallace received 57 percent of the popular vote.

Nixon as President: "Vietnamizing" the War

When he took office in January 1969, Richard Nixon projected an image of calm and deliberate statesmanship; he introduced no startling changes, proposed no important new legislation. Indeed, he accepted more or less uncritically the New Deal approach to managing

Astronaut Buzz Aldrin, a member of the *Apollo* 11 mission, walks on the moon (1969). President Kennedy's goal to put an American on the moon by the end of the decade was achieved during Nixon's administration.

the economy. He considered the solution of the Vietnam problem his chief task. Although he insisted during the 1968 campaign that he would end the war on "honorable" terms if elected, he suggested nothing very different from what Johnson was doing.

In office, Nixon first proposed a phased withdrawal of all non-South Vietnamese troops, to be followed by an internationally supervised election in South Vietnam. The North Vietnamese rejected this scheme and insisted that the United States withdraw its forces unconditionally. The intransigence of the North Vietnamese left the president in a difficult position. Nixon could not compel the foe to end a war it had begun against the French nearly a quarter of a century earlier, and every passing day added to the strength of antiwar sentiment, which, as it expressed itself in ever more emphatic terms, in turn led to deeper divisions in the country. Yet Nixon

could not face up to the consequences of ending the war on the communists' terms.

The president responded to the dilemma by trying to build up the South Vietnamese armed forces so that American troops could pull out without South Vietnam being overrun by the communists. He shipped so many planes to the Vietnamese that within four years they had the fourth-largest air force in the world. He also announced a series of troop cuts.

For a while, events appeared to vindicate Nixon's position. A gradual slowing of military activity in Vietnam had reduced American casualties. Troop withdrawals continued in an orderly fashion. A new lottery system for drafting men for military duty eliminated some of the inequities in the selective service law.

But the war continued. Early in 1970 reports that an American unit had massacred civilians, including

South Vietnamese women and children were among some 300 apparently unarmed civilians killed in the My Lai Massacre in 1968. Lieutenant William Calley was convicted of murder and sentenced to life in prison. After many appeals, he was released in 1974.

dozens of women and children, in a Vietnamese hamlet known as My Lai revived the controversy over the purposes of the war and its corrosive effects on those who were fighting it. The American people, it seemed, were being torn apart by the war: one from another according to each one's interpretation of events; and many within themselves as they tried to balance the war's horrors against their pride, their abhorrence of communism, and their unwillingness to turn their backs on their elected leader.

Nixon wanted to end the war but he did not want to lose it. The war's human, economic, and social costs could only vex his days and threaten his future reputation. When he reduced the level of the fighting, the communists merely waited for further reductions. When he raised it, many Americans denounced him in increasingly massive antiwar protests. If he pulled out of Vietnam and the communists won, other Americans would be outraged.

Perhaps Nixon's error lay in his unwillingness to admit his own uncertainty, something the greatest presidents—one thinks immediately of Lincoln and Franklin Roosevelt—were never afraid to do. Facing a dilemma, he tried to convince the world that he was firmly in control of events, with the result that at times he seemed more like a high school valedictorian declaiming sententiously about

the meaning of life than the mature statesman he so desperately wished to be. Thus he heightened the tensions he sought to relax—in America, in Vietnam, and elsewhere.

The Cambodian "Incursion"

Late in April 1970 Nixon announced that Vietnamization was proceeding more rapidly than he had hoped, that communist power was weakening, and that within a year another 150,000 American soldiers would be extracted from Vietnam. A week later he announced that military intelligence had indicated that the enemy was consolidating its "sanctuaries" in neutral Cambodia and that he was therefore dispatching thousands of American troops to destroy these bases. (American planes had been bombing enemy sites in Cambodia for some time, although this fact was not revealed to the public until 1973.)

To foes of the war, Nixon's decision seemed so appallingly unwise that some of them began to fear that he had become mentally unbalanced. The contradictions between his confident statements about Vietnamization and his alarmist description of powerful enemy forces poised like a dagger thirty-odd miles from Saigon did not seem the product of a reasoning mind.

Nixon's shocking announcement triggered many campus demonstrations. One college where feeling ran high was Kent State University in Ohio. For several days students there clashed with local police; they broke windows and caused other damage to property. When the governor called out the National Guard, angry students showered the soldiers with stones. During a noontime protest on May 4 the guardsmen, who were poorly trained in crowd control, suddenly opened fire. Four students were killed, two of them women who were merely passing by on their way to class.

While the nation reeled from this shock, two students at Jackson State University were killed by Mississippi state policemen. A wave of student strikes followed, closing down hundreds of colleges, including many that had seen no previous unrest. Moderate students by the tens of thousands joined with the radicals.

The almost universal condemnation of the invasion and of the way it had been planned shook Nixon hard. He backtracked, pulling American ground troops out of Cambodia quickly. But he did not change his Vietnam policy, and in fact Cambodia apparently stiffened his determination. As American ground troops were withdrawn, he stepped up air attacks.

The balance of forces remained in uneasy equilibrium through 1971. But late in March 1972 the North Vietnamese again mounted a series of assaults throughout South Vietnam. Nixon responded with heavier bombing, and he ordered the approaches to Haiphong and other North Vietnamese ports sown with mines to cut off the communists' supplies.

Détente with Communism

But in the midst of these aggressive actions, Nixon and his National Security Adviser Henry Kissinger devised a bold diplomatic offensive, executed in nearly complete secrecy—from even the State and Defense Departments! Nixon and Kissinger made an effective though not always harmonious team. Abandoning a lifetime of treating communism as a single worldwide conspiracy that had to be contained at all costs, Nixon decided to deal with China and the Soviet Union as separate powers and, as he put it, to "live together and work together" with both. Nixon and Kissinger called the new policy **détente**, a French term meaning "the relaxation of tensions between governments." But détente was not an expression of friendship so much as an acknowledgment that for decades the policy of containment had driven China and the Soviet Union closer together.

First Nixon sent Kissinger secretly to China and the Soviet Union to prepare the way for summit meetings with the communist leaders. Both the Chinese and the Soviets agreed to the meetings. Then, in February 1972, Nixon and Kissinger, accompanied by a small army of reporters and television crews, flew to Beijing. After much dining, sightseeing, posing for photographers, and consultation with Chinese officials, Nixon agreed to promote economic and cultural exchanges and supported the admission of communist China to the United Nations. (Since the founding of the United Nations, the United States had recognized only the Republic of China— Taiwan.) As a result, exports to communist China increased substantially, reaching $4 billion in 1980. Among other American products, Coca-Cola was introduced to the Chinese, marketed under a name meaning "tasty happiness." Nixon's visit, ending more than twenty years of adamant American refusal to accept the reality of the Chinese revolution, marked a dramatic reversal; as such it was hailed throughout the world.

In May 1972 Nixon and Kissinger flew to Moscow. This

National Guardsmen firing into a crowd of antiwar protesters at Kent State University killed four students and injured eleven others. The shootings triggered massive demonstrations and protests across the nation.

trip also produced striking results. The mere fact that it took place while war still raged in Vietnam was remarkable. More important, however, the meeting resulted in a **Strategic Arms Limitation Treaty (SALT)**. The two powers agreed to stop making nuclear ballistic missiles and to reduce the number of antiballistic missiles in their arsenals to 200. Nixon also agreed to permit large sales of American grain to the Soviet Union.

By the summer of 1972, with the presidential election looming in the fall, Kissinger redoubled his efforts to negotiate an end to the Vietnam war. By October he and the North Vietnamese had hammered out a settlement calling for a cease-fire, the return of American prisoners of war, and the withdrawal of United States forces from Vietnam. Shortly before the presidential election Kissinger announced that peace was "at hand."

Nixon in Triumph

A few days later President Nixon was reelected, defeating the Democratic candidate, Senator George McGovern of South Dakota, in a landslide—521 electoral votes to 17. McGovern carried only Massachusetts and the District of Columbia. McGovern's campaign had been hampered by his tendency to advance poorly thought-out proposals, such as his scheme for funneling money directly to the poor, and by his rather bumbling, low-key oratorical style. The campaign marked the historical breakdown of the coalition that Franklin Roosevelt had fashioned and on which he and his Democratic successors, particularly Truman and Johnson, had ridden to power. Of that coalition, only African Americans voted solidly for McGovern.

Nixon understandably interpreted his convincing triumph as an indication that the citizenry approved of everything he stood for. He had won over hundreds of thousands of voters who had supported Democrats in earlier elections. The "solid South" was again solid, but this time solidly Republican. Nixon's so-called southern strategy of reducing the pressure for school desegregation and otherwise restricting federal efforts on behalf of blacks had a powerful attraction to northern blue-collar workers as well.

Suddenly Nixon loomed as one of the most powerful and successful presidents in American history. His tough-minded but flexible handling of foreign policy questions, even his harsh Vietnamese policy, suggested decisiveness and self-confidence, qualities

President and Mrs. Nixon dine with Chinese communist officials in Beijing in February 1972. Even Nixon's harshest critics conceded that his initiative in reopening United States–China relations was a diplomatic masterstroke.

he had often seemed to lack in his earlier career. His willingness, despite his long history as a militant cold warrior, to negotiate with the communist nations indicated a new flexibility and creativity. His landslide victory appeared to demonstrate that a large majority of the people approved of his way of tackling the major problems of the times.

But Kissinger's agreement with the North Vietnamese came apart when Nguyen Van Thieu, the South Vietnamese president, refused to sign it. Thieu claimed that the agreement, by permitting communist troops to remain in the South, would ensure his ultimate defeat. "Why," he asked Kissinger, "are you rushing to get the Nobel Prize?" To Kissinger's chagrin, Nixon sided with Thieu and resumed the bombing of North Vietnam in December 1972, this time sending the mighty B-52s directly over Hanoi and other cities. The destruction they caused was great, but their effectiveness as a means of forcing concessions from the North Vietnamese was at best debatable, and in these strikes for the first time the United States lost large numbers of the big strategic bombers.

In January 1973 a settlement was finally reached. As with the October "agreement," the North Vietnamese retained control of large sections of the South, and they promised to release American prisoners of war within sixty days. Thieu assented this time, largely because Nixon secretly pledged that the United States would "respond with full force" if North Vietnam resumed its offensive. Within several months most prisoners of war were released, and the last American troops were pulled out of Vietnam. More than 57,000 Americans had died in the long war, and over 300,000 more had been wounded. Nearly a million communist soldiers and 185,000 South Vietnamese soldiers were reported killed.

In 1973, too, Kissinger was named secretary of state; he shared the Nobel Prize for Peace with a North Vietnamese diplomat for negotiating an end to the Vietnam war.

Domestic Policy Under Nixon

When Nixon became president in 1969, the major economic problem he faced was inflation. This was caused primarily by the heavy military expenditures and easy-money policies of the Johnson administration. Nixon cut federal spending and balanced the 1969 budget, while the Federal Reserve Board forced up interest rates to slow the expansion of the money supply. When prices continued to rise, uneasiness mounted and labor unions demanded large wage increases.

In 1970 Congress passed a law giving the president power to regulate prices and wages. Nixon originally opposed this legislation, but in the summer of 1971 he changed his mind and announced a ninety-day price and wage freeze. Then he set up a pay board and a price commission with authority to limit wage and price increases when the freeze ended. These controls did not check inflation completely—and they angered union leaders, who felt that labor was being shortchanged—but they did slow the upward spiral.

In handling other domestic issues, the president was less firm. Like President Kennedy he was primarily interested in foreign affairs. He supported a bold plan for a "minimum income" for poor families, but dropped it when it alarmed his conservative supporters and got nowhere in Congress. But when a groundswell of public support for conserving natural resources and checking pollution led Congress to pass bills creating the **Environmental Protection Agency (EPA)** and the Clean Air Act of 1970, he signed them cheerfully.

Primarily he was concerned with his own political standing. Hoping to strengthen the Republican party in the South, he checked further federal efforts to force school desegregation on reluctant local districts, and he set out to add what he called "strict constructionists" to the Supreme Court, which he believed had swung too far to the left in such areas as race relations and the rights of persons accused of committing crimes. He also proposed mostly conservatives to fill vacancies in the Supreme Court.

After his triumphant reelection and the withdrawal of the last American troops from Vietnam, Nixon resolved to change the direction in which the nation had been moving for decades. He announced that he intended to reduce the interference of the federal government in the affairs of individuals. People should be more self-reliant, he said, and he denounced what he called "permissiveness." Excessive concern for the interests of blacks and other minorities must end. Criminals should be punished "without pity." No person or group should be coddled by the state.

These aims brought Nixon into conflict with liberals in both parties, with the leaders of minority groups, and with those alarmed by the increasing power of the executive. The conflict came to a head over the president's anti-inflation policy. After his second inauguration he ended price and wage controls and called for voluntary "restraints." This approach did not work. Prices soared in the most rapid inflation since the Korean War. In an effort to check the rise, Nixon set a rigid limit on federal expenditures. To keep within the limit, he cut back or abolished a

The Clean Air Act of 1970 mandated reductions in air pollution, arguably the most important environmental legislation passed by the United States during the twentieth century.

large number of social welfare programs and reduced federal grants in support of science and education. He even impounded (refused to spend) funds already appropriated by Congress for purposes of which he disapproved.

The impoundment created a furor on Capitol Hill, but when Congress failed to override his vetoes of bills challenging this policy, it appeared that Nixon was in total command. The White House staff, headed by H. R. Haldeman (called "the Prussian") and John Ehrlichman, dominated the Washington bureaucracy and dealt with legislators as though they were lackeys. Critics began to grumble about a new "imperial presidency." No one seemed capable of checking Nixon.

The Watergate Break-in and Cover-up

On March 19, 1973, James McCord, a former agent of both the Federal Bureau of Investigation and the Central Intelligence Agency accused of burglary, wrote a letter to the judge presiding at his trial. His act precipitated a series of disclosures that first disrupted and then destroyed the Nixon administration.

McCord had been employed during the 1972 presidential campaign as a security officer of the Committee to Re-elect the President (CREEP). At about 1 AM on June 17, 1972, he and four other men had broken into Democratic party headquarters at Watergate, a complex of apartments and offices in Washington. The burglars were members of an unofficial CREEP surveillance group known as "the plumbers." Nixon, who was compelled by a need to conceal information about his administration, had formed the group after the Pentagon Papers, a confidential report on government policy in Vietnam, had been leaked to the press. The "plumbers" had been caught rifling files and installing electronic eavesdropping devices.

Two other Republican campaign officials were soon implicated in the affair. Their arrest aroused suspicions that the Republican party was behind the break-in. Nixon denied it. "I can say categorically," he announced on June 22, "that no one on the White House staff, no one in this Administration presently employed, was involved in this very bizarre incident."

Most people evidently took the president at his word. He was far ahead in the polls and seemed so sure to win reelection that it was hard to believe he would stoop to burglary to discover what the

Democrats were up to. In any case, the affair did not materially affect the election. When brought to trial early in 1973, most of the Watergate burglars pleaded guilty.

McCord, who did not, was convicted by the jury. Before Judge John J. Sirica imposed sentences on the culprits, however, McCord wrote his letter. High Republican officials had known about the burglary in advance and had paid the defendants "hush money" to keep their connection secret, McCord claimed. Perjury had been committed during the trial.

The truth of McCord's charges swiftly became apparent. The head of CREEP, Jeb Stuart Magruder, and President Nixon's lawyer, John W. Dean III, admitted their involvement. Among the disclosures that emerged over the following months were these:

- Large sums of money had been paid to the burglars at the instigation of the White House to ensure their silence.
- Agents of the Nixon administration had burglarized the office of a psychiatrist, seeking evidence against one of his patients, Daniel Ellsberg, who had been charged with leaking the Pentagon Papers to the *New York Times*. (This disclosure led to the immediate dismissal of the charges against Ellsberg.)
- CREEP officials had attempted to disrupt the campaigns of leading Democratic candidates during the 1972 primaries in a number of illegal ways.
- A number of corporations had made large contributions to the Nixon reelection campaign in violation of federal law.
- The Nixon administration had placed wiretaps on the telephones of some of its own officials as well as on those of journalists critical of its policies without first obtaining authorization from the courts.

These revelations led to the dismissal of John Dean and to the resignations of most of Nixon's closest advisers, including Haldeman, Ehrlichman, and Attorney Generals John Mitchell and Richard Kleindienst. They also raised the question of the president's personal connection with the **Watergate scandal**. This he steadfastly denied. He insisted that he would investigate the Watergate affair thoroughly and see that the guilty were punished. He refused, however, to allow investigators to examine White House documents, on grounds of executive privilege, which he continued to assert in very broad terms.

In the teeth of Nixon's denials, John Dean, testifying under oath, stated flatly and in circumstantial detail that the president had ordered him to pay the Watergate burglars to conceal White House involvement; if true, the president had been guilty of obstructing justice, a serious crime.

Dean had been a persuasive witness, but many people were reluctant to believe that a president could lie so cold-bloodedly to the entire country. Therefore, when it came out during later hearings of the Senate committee investigating the Watergate scandal that the president had systematically made secret tape recordings of White House conversations and telephone calls, the disclosure caused a sensation. It seemed obvious that these tapes would settle the question of Nixon's involvement once and for all. Again Nixon refused to allow access to the evidence.

One result of the scandals and of Nixon's attitude was a precipitous decline in his standing in public opinion polls. Calls for his resignation, even for impeachment, began to be heard. Yielding to pressure, he agreed to the appointment of an "independent" special prosecutor to investigate the Watergate affair, and he promised the appointee, Professor Archibald Cox of Harvard Law School, full cooperation.

Cox swiftly aroused the president's ire by seeking access to White House records, including the tapes. When Nixon refused to turn over the tapes, Cox obtained a subpoena from Judge Sirica ordering him to do so. The administration appealed this decision and lost in the appellate court. Then, while the case was headed for the Supreme Court, Nixon ordered the new attorney general, Elliot Richardson, to dismiss Cox. Both Richardson, who had promised the Senate during his confirmation hearings that the special prosecutor would have a free hand, and his chief assistant resigned rather than do as the president directed. The third-ranking officer of the Justice Department carried out Nixon's order.

These events of Saturday, October 20, promptly dubbed the Saturday Night Massacre, caused an outburst of public indignation. Congress was bombarded by thousands of letters and telegrams demanding the president's impeachment. The House Judiciary Committee began an investigation to see if enough evidence for impeachment existed. (The House of Representatives must vote to indict federal officials for impeachment; the actual impeachment trial is conducted by the Senate.)

Once again Nixon backed down. He agreed to turn over the tapes to Judge Sirica with the understanding that relevant materials could be presented to the grand jury investigating the Watergate affair but that nothing would be revealed to the public. He then named a new special prosecutor, Leon Jaworski, and promised him access to whatever White House documents he needed. However, it soon came out that several tapes were missing and that an important section of another had been deliberately erased.

Then Vice President Agnew (defender of law and order, foe of permissiveness) was accused of income tax fraud and of having accepted bribes while serving as Baltimore county executive and governor of Maryland. To escape a jail term Agnew admitted in October that he had been guilty of tax evasion and resigned as vice president.

Acting according to the procedures for presidential and vice-presidential succession of the Twenty-Fifth Amendment, adopted in 1967, President Nixon nominated Representative Gerald R. Ford of Michigan as vice president, and he was confirmed by Congress. Ford had served continuously in Congress since 1949 and as minority leader since 1964. His positions on public issues were close to Nixon's; he was an internationalist in foreign affairs and a conservative and convinced Republican partisan on domestic issues.

The Judgment on Watergate: "Expletive Deleted"

Meanwhile, special prosecutor Jaworski continued his investigation of the Watergate scandals. In March 1974 a grand jury indicted Haldeman; Ehrlichman; former attorney general John Mitchell, who had been head of CREEP at the time of the break-in; and four other White House aides for conspiring to block the Watergate investigation. The jurors also named Nixon an "unindicted co-conspirator," Jaworski having informed them that their power to indict a president was constitutionally questionable. Judge Sirica thereupon turned over the jury's evidence against Nixon to the House Judiciary Committee.

In an effort to check the mounting criticism, late in April Nixon released edited transcripts of the tapes he had turned over to the court the previous November. In addition to much incriminating evidence, the transcripts

When the White House tapes were turned over to the special prosecutor, several crucial sections had been erased. Rosemary Woods, Nixon's personal secretary, attempted to demonstrate how she had accidentally erased the pivotal sections.

provided the public with a fascinating and shocking view of how the president conducted himself in private. In conversations he seemed confused, indecisive, and lacking in any concern for the public interest. His repeated use of foul language, so out of keeping with his public image, offended millions. The phrase "expletive deleted," inserted in place of words considered too vulgar for publication in family newspapers, overnight became a catchword.

With the defendants in the Watergate case demanding access to tapes that they claimed would prove their innocence, Jaworski was compelled either to obtain them or to risk having the charges dismissed on the grounds that the government was withholding evidence. He therefore subpoenaed sixty-four additional tapes. Nixon refused to obey the subpoena. Swiftly the case of *United States v. Richard M. Nixon* went to the Supreme Court.

In the summer of 1974—after so many months of alarms and crises—the Watergate drama reached its climax. The Judiciary Committee, following months of study of the evidence behind closed doors, decided to conduct its deliberations in open session. While millions watched on television, thirty-eight members of the House of Representatives debated the charges and finally adopted three articles of impeachment. They charged the president with obstructing justice, misusing the powers of his office, and failing to obey the committee's subpoenas. Except in the case of the last article, many of the Republicans on the committee joined with the Democrats in voting aye, a clear indication that the full House would vote to impeach.

On the eve of the debates, the Supreme Court had ruled unanimously that the president must turn over the sixty-four subpoenaed tapes to the special prosecutor. Executive privilege had its place, the Court stated, but no person, not even a president, could "withhold evidence that is demonstrably relevant in a criminal trial."

When the subpoenaed tapes were released and transcribed, Nixon's fate was sealed. Three recorded conversations between the president and H. R. Haldeman just after the Watergate break-in proved conclusively that Nixon had tried to obstruct justice by engaging the CIA in an effort to persuade the FBI not to follow up leads in the case on the spurious grounds that national security was involved.

When the House Judiciary Committee members read the new transcripts, all the Republican members who had voted against the impeachment articles reversed themselves. Republican leaders told the president categorically that the House would impeach him and that no more than a handful of senators would vote for acquittal.

•••> Read the **Document** *House Judiciary Committee's Conclusion on Impeachment* at **www.myhistorylab.com**

Nixon Resigns, Ford Becomes President

On August 8, 1974, Nixon announced his resignation. "Dear Mr. Secretary," his terse official letter to Secretary of State Kissinger ran, "I hereby resign the Office of President of the United States. Sincerely, Richard Nixon." The resignation took effect at noon on August 9, when Gerald Ford was sworn in as president. "Our long national nightmare is over," Ford declared.

Within weeks of taking office, Ford pardoned Nixon for whatever crimes he had committed in office, even any, if such existed, as had yet to come to light. Not many Americans wanted to see the ex-president lodged in jail, but pardoning him seemed both illogical and incomprehensible when Nixon had admitted no guilt and had not yet been officially charged with any crime. (Nixon's instant acceptance of the pardon while claiming to have done no wrong was also illogical but not incomprehensible.)

The meaning of "Watergate" became the subject of much speculation. Whether Nixon's crude efforts to dominate Congress, to crush or inhibit dissent, and to subvert the electoral process would have permanently altered the American political system had they succeeded is beyond knowing. However, the orderly way in which these efforts were checked suggests that the system would have survived in any case.

Whether Nixon's resignation marked the end of one era or the beginning of another is a difficult question. Like most critical moments in human history, it seems in retrospect to have been both. Nixon had extricated the United States from Vietnam—though at tremendous cost in lives and money and to little evident purpose. His détente with the Soviet Union and Red China was surely an early sign of the easing of Cold War tensions characteristic of the decades to follow. Moreover, Nixon's assault on liberals, coming just as public disillusionment with the Great Society programs was mounting, put an end to the liberal era that had begun with the reforms of the New Deal.

⟨⊙⟩ Watch the **Video**   Richard Nixon, *I am not a crook* at **www.myhistorylab.com**

Chapter Review

Milestones

1951	J. D. Salinger publishes The Catcher in the Rye
1955	Joseph Heller publishes *Catch-22*
	Allen Ginsberg publishes *Howl*
1957	Jack Kerouac publishes *On the Road*
1960	Black college students found Student Nonviolent Coordinating Committee (SNCC)
	John F. Kennedy elected President
1961	CIA-trained Cuban exiles launch disastrous Bay of Pigs invasion
	Soviets build Berlin wall
	John F. Kennedy founds Peace Corps
	Freedom riders integrate buses in South
1962	Soviet Premier Khrushchev precipitates Cuban missile crisis
	Students for a Democratic Society (SDS) issues Port Huron Statement
1963	United States supports coup to oust President Ngo Dinh Diem of South Vietnam
	Martin Luther King, Jr., gives "I Have a Dream" speech during March on Washington
	Lee Harvey Oswald assassinates President Kennedy; Lyndon Johnson becomes president
1964	Congress endorses escalation of Vietnam War in Gulf of Tonkin Resolution
	Lyndon Johnson is elected president, begins Great Society program
	Congress passes historic Civil Rights Act
	Free speech movement disrupts University of California at Berkeley
1965	Congress passes Immigration Act, ending national quota system
	Medicare Act pays some medical costs for senior citizens and the poor
	Congress funds education with Elementary and Secondary Education Act and Higher Education Act

	Black Muslim fanatics assassinate Malcolm X
1968	Communists strike all over South Vietnam in Tet Offensive
	Lyndon Johnson withdraws as candidate for reelection
	Martin Luther King, Jr., is assassinated
	Robert F. Kennedy is assassinated
	Richard Nixon is elected president
1969	Nixon announces "Vietnamization" of war
	Apollo 11 lands on the moon
1970	Nixon announces "incursion" into Cambodia
	Antiwar student protesters are killed at Kent State University and Jackson State University
	Congress passes Clean Air Act and creates Environmental Protection Agency (EPA)
1972	Nixon's "plumbers" burglarize Democratic national headquarters at Watergate complex
	Nixon and Kissinger visit China and Soviet Union
	United States and Soviet Union sign Strategic Arms Limitation Treaty (SALT)
	Nixon is reelected in landslide
1973	House Judiciary Committee begins impeachment hearings against Nixon
	Vice President Spiro Agnew resigns; Gerald Ford is appointed vice president
	Last American troops leave Vietnam
	Nixon fires Watergate special prosecutor Archibald Cox (Saturday Night Massacre)
1974	Supreme Court orders release of Nixon's White House tapes
	Nixon resigns; Gerald Ford becomes president and pardons Nixon

Key Terms

Bay of Pigs fiasco　A military debacle in April 1961, during an American-organized effort to invade Cuba and drive Fidel Castro, the communist ruler, from power. The invasion force of some 1,500 Cuban exiles was routed at the Bay of Pigs, a major embarrassment for President John F. Kennedy, *767*

beat school　Also known as "beats," "beatniks," or the "beat generation"—nonconformists in the late 1950s who rejected conventional dress and sexual standards and cultivated avant-garde literature and music, *778*

Berlin wall　Erected by East Germany in 1961 and torn down by a Dutch company in 1989, the wall isolated West Berlin from the surrounding areas in communist controlled East Berlin and East Germany, *767*

Civil Rights Act of 1964　Legislation outlawing discrimination in public accommodations and employment on the basis of race, skin color, sex, religion, or national origin, *772*

Cuban missile crisis   The showdown between the United States and the Soviet Union during October 1962, after the Soviet Union had sneaked medium-range nuclear missiles into communist Cuba. After President John F. Kennedy publicly demanded their removal and ordered the blockade of Cuba, Soviet leader Nikita Khrushchev agreed to do so, averting a nuclear war, *768*

détente   A French term, meaning the relaxation of tensions, applied to an easing of Cold War antagonisms during the 1970s. Under President Richard Nixon and foreign affairs adviser Henry Kissinger, détente was a strategy to allow the United States to weaken the bonds between the Soviet Union and communist China, *786*

Environmental Protection Agency (EPA)   A federal agency created in 1970 to oversee environmental monitoring and cleanup programs, *788*

Great Society   The sweeping legislative agenda of President Lyndon Johnson; it sought to end poverty, promote civil rights, and improve housing, health care, and education. The program was criticized as costly and ineffective, *772*

Gulf of Tonkin Resolution   Congressional action, undertaken at President Johnson's request, giving the President the authority to deploy U.S. troops to repel aggression in Southeast Asia. This provided congressional sanction for the escalation of the Vietnam war, *780*

Medicare   A social welfare measure, enacted in 1965, providing hospitalization insurance for people over sixty-five and a voluntary plan to cover doctor bills paid in part by the federal government, *776*

Strategic Arms Limitation Treaty (SALT)   A treaty, signed by the United States and the Soviet Union in 1972, restricting the testing and deployment of nuclear ballistic missiles, the first of several such treaties, *787*

Student Nonviolent Coordinating Committee (SNCC)   A civil rights organization, founded in 1960, that drew heavily on younger activists and college students. After 1965, under the leadership of Stokely Carmichael and then H. Rap Brown, the group advocated "Black Power.", *769*

Students for a Democratic Society (SDS)   An organization created by leftist college students in the early 1960s; it organized protests against racial bigotry, corporate exploitation of workers, and, especially after 1965, the Vietnam war, *779*

Tet offensive   A wide-ranging offensive, launched by North Vietnamese and Vietcong troops throughout South Vietnam in February 1968. It failed to cause the South Vietnamese government to collapse, but persuaded many Americans that the war was not winnable. President Lyndon B. Johnson announced his decision not to run for reelection several months later, *782*

United States v. Richard M. Nixon   A Supreme Court ruling (1974) that obliged President Richard Nixon to turn over to the Watergate special prosecutor sixty-four White House audiotapes; these helped prove that Nixon had known about the cover-up of the Watergate burglary, *792*

Voting Rights Act of 1965   Federal legislation that empowered federal registrars to intervene when southern states and municipalities refused to let African Americans register to vote, *776*

Watergate scandal   A complex scandal involving attempts to cover up illegal actions taken by administration officials and leading to the resignation of President Richard Nixon in 1974, *790*

Review Questions

1. The introduction emphasizes the difficulties JFK, LBJ, and Nixon had in getting out of the "quagmire" that was the Vietnam war. What might they have done differently? Why did they pursue the course they chose?

2. Why did the escalation of the war from 1961 to 1968 fail to produce a victory? How did Nixon change the Vietnam policies of his predecessors? Why didn't they succeed?

3. How did the war affect American society? What effect did student protests have on the war?

4. How did Johnson's Great Society differ from Franklin D. Roosevelt's New Deal? Which aspects of the Great Society proved most successful? Why did others fall short of expectations?

5. What explains the rise of Black Power during the 1960s? Why did the race riots strike just as the federal government was providing tangible assistance on matters of civil rights, racial discrimination, and poverty?

6. Why did Nixon form the "plumbers" and then obstruct justice following the Watergate break-in? Why did Ford pardon Nixon?

myhistorylab Connections

PEARSON

Reinforce what you learned in this chapter by studying the many documents, images, maps, review tools, and videos available at **www.myhistorylab.com**.

Read and Review

✓ **Study** and **Review** *Chapter 29*

Read the Document *Charles Sherrod, SNCC Memorandum (1961), p. 771*

See the **Map** *Impact of the Voting Rights Act of 1965, p. 777*

Read the **Document** *Watts Riots 1967, p. 778*

Read the **Document** *Black Power 1967, p. 778*

Hear the **Audio** *Timothy Leary, Going Out (1966), p. 780*

Read the **Document** *The Gulf of Tonkin Resolution Message, p. 782*

Read the **Document** *House Judiciary Committee's Conclusion on Impeachment, p. 792*

Research and Explore

Watch the **Video** *Civil Rights March on Washington, p. 771*

Watch the **Video** *Civil Rights Movement, p. 771*

Watch the **Video** *Malcolm X, p. 778*

Watch the **Video** *Protests Against the Vietnam War, p. 780*

Watch the **Video** *Richard Nixon, I am not a crook, p. 792*

Hear the **Audio**

Hear the audio file for Chapter 29 at
www.myhistorylab.com.

Do you pay too much for gas?

During the summer of 2008, with the presidential campaign in full swing, gas prices topped $4 a gallon. Republican candidate John McCain, formerly a solid environmentalist, called for laws allowing oil companies to drill for oil in U.S. coastal waters. Sarah Palin, Governor of oil-rich Alaska and McCain's running mate, put it more succinctly: "Drill, Baby, Drill!"

Senator Barack Obama had opposed offshore drilling. Weeks earlier, he had told residents of Jacksonville, Florida, "I intend to keep in place the moratorium here and around the country that prevents oil companies from drilling off Florida's coasts." But as gas prices rose, his lead in the polls slipped. With the election less than two months away, Obama reversed course. Now he supported off-shore drilling. Democratic leaders in Congress, scrambling to clamber onto the offshore drilling bandwagon, pushed through a law ending the quarter-century old ban on drilling for oil in federal waters off the Atlantic and Pacific Coasts.

Running on Empty: 1975–1991

CONTENTS

- The Oil Crisis
- Ford as President
- The Fall of South Vietnam
- Ford versus Carter
- The Carter Presidency
- A National Malaise
- Stagflation: The Weird Economy
- "Constant Decency" in Action
- The Iran Crisis: Origins
- The Iran Crisis: Carter's Dilemma
- The Election of 1980
- Reagan as President
- Four More Years
- "The Reagan Revolution"
- The New Merger Movement
- "A Job for Life": Layoffs Hit Home
- Corporate Restructuring
- Rogue Foreign Policy
- Assessing the Reagan Revolution
- The Election of 1988
- George H. W. Bush as President
- The Collapse of Communism in Eastern Europe
- The War in the Persian Gulf
- Deficits
- *American Lives: Bill Gates*

((•—[Hear the Audio **Chapter 30 at www.myhistorylab.com**

■ William Eggleston, whom many critics regard as "the father of modern color art photography," gives a stark rendering of a closed Arco gas station, from his collection *Troubled Waters* (1980).
Source: Courtesy Eggleston Artistic Trust, Cheim & Read, New York.

Then, in 2010, a British-owned oil rig forty miles off the coast of Louisiana exploded, killing eleven workers and releasing millions of barrels of crude oil into the Gulf of Mexico. The oil spill was the worst environmental disaster in the nation's history. Obama issued a moratorium on new offshore drilling projects.

For much of the twentieth century, the high cost and environmental risks of offshore oil drilling exceeded the projected profits of such ventures. But that changed in 1970s when the flow of crude oil to the United States and the West was cut off; the price of oil soared. Now offshore drilling made economic sense. Because most of the untapped oil lay beneath the oceans, offshore drilling platforms were built in the North Sea, off the coast of Brazil, and in the Gulf of Mexico.

For a nation dependent on the automobile, the 1970s oil shortage plunged the economy into a deep recession. Factories were closed and workers laid off. A new conservatism prevailed, part of a reaction against the costly measures of LBJ's Great Society. The need for cheap oil, moreover, pushed the United States deeper into the labyrinth of Middle Eastern politics. War would follow. ■

797

The Oil Crisis

While most Americans watched, transfixed, as the events of Watergate interred the Nixon presidency, few were aware that a battle on the other side of the world was about to transform their lives. On October 6, 1973, the eve of Yom Kippur, the Jewish Day of Atonement, Egypt and Syria attacked the state of Israel. Six years earlier Israel had trounced the Egyptians with humiliating ease; it had then seized the Sinai peninsula and the West Bank of the Jordan River, an area including Jerusalem. But now Egypt's armored divisions roared into the Sinai and threatened to slice Israel in half; Syrian troops advanced against Israel farther north.

After the Arab oil embargo, gasoline became so scarce that customers were limited to buying ten gallons at a time. This led to long lines at the pumps.

Israeli Prime Minister Golda Meir pleaded with President Nixon for additional arms and aircraft. He responded vigorously, promising that "every last goddamn airplane" would be sent to Israel. "We are going to be condemned by the Arabs one way or the other," Nixon concluded. The United States immediately airlifted scores of fighter planes and other desperately needed material to Israel. The Israelis recrossed the Suez Canal, cut Egyptian supply lines, and forced Egypt's president, Anwar Sadat, to capitulate. But the Arab world then aimed its biggest weapon squarely at the United States: It cut off oil shipments to the West.

Deprived of Middle Eastern oil, the American economy sputtered. The price of oil rose to $12 a barrel, up from $3. This sent prices soaring for nearly everything else. Homes were heated with oil, factories were powered by it, utility plants used it to generate electricity, and farm produce was shipped to markets on gas-fueled trucks. Nylon and other synthetic fibers as well as paints, insecticides, fertilizers, and many plastic products were based on petrochemicals. Above all else, oil was refined into gasoline. By the time of the Yom Kippur War, American car owners were driving more than a trillion miles a year, the major reason why the United States, formerly a major oil exporter, imported one-third of its oil. The Arab oil embargo pushed up gas prices; service stations intermittently ran out of gasoline; long lines formed at those that remained open.

In the spring of 1974, Henry Kissinger negotiated an agreement that required Israel's withdrawal from some territory occupied since the 1967 war; the Arab nations then lifted the oil embargo. But the principal oil exporting nations—Venezuela, Saudi Arabia, Kuwait, Iraq, and Iran—had learned a valuable lesson: If they limited production, they could drive up the price of oil. After the embargo had ended, their cartel, the **Organization of Petroleum Exporting Countries (OPEC)**, announced another price increase. Gasoline prices doubled overnight.

American automakers who had scoffed at bulbous Volkswagen "bugs" and tiny Japanese "boxes" now winced as these foreign competitors claimed the new market for small, fuel-efficient, front-wheel-drive cars. American auto companies were unable to respond to this challenge because their contracts with the United Automobile Workers (UAW) linked wages to consumer prices, which had floated upward with the price of oil. As production costs rose, manufacturers needed to sell more of their behemoth models, loaded with expensive options such as air conditioning, power windows, and stereo systems. They could not profitably sell the small cars the public craved. (In 1982, when Ford belatedly entered the front-wheel drive market, it lost $40 on each car sold.) Because the automobile industry stimulated so many other industries—steel, vinyl, glass, rubber—the nation's manufacturing sector was soon in trouble.

Ford as President

Gerald Ford replaced Nixon as president in the summer of 1974, just as the economy was beginning to deteriorate. At first, the country greeted Ford with a collective sigh of relief. Most observers considered Ford unimaginative, certainly not brilliant. But he was hardworking, and—most important under the circumstances—his record was untouched by scandal.

Ford identified inflation as the chief economic culprit and asked patriotic citizens to signify their willingness to fight it by wearing WIN (Whip Inflation Now) buttons. Almost immediately the economy slumped. Production fell and the unemployment rate rose above 9 percent, about twice the postwar average. The president was forced to ask for tax cuts and other measures aimed at stimulating business activity. This made inflation worse and did little to promote employment. The economic problems were difficult, and Ford was handicapped by the fact that the Democrats had solid control of Congress, but his performance was at best inept.

The Fall of South Vietnam

Depressing news about the economy was compounded by disheartening events in Vietnam. In January 1975, after two years of a bloody "cease-fire" (Hanoi charged Saigon with 301,000 violations; and Saigon charged its adversary with 35,673), North Vietnam attacked just south of the seventeenth parallel, commencing its two-year plan to conquer South Vietnam. The South Vietnamese army retreated, then fled, and finally dissolved with a rapidity that astonished their attackers.

Ford had always supported the Vietnam War. As the military situation deteriorated, he urged Congress to pour more arms into the South to stem the North Vietnamese advance. The legislators flatly refused to do so, and on May 1, 1975, the Viet Cong and North Vietnamese entered Saigon, which they renamed Ho Chi Minh City. The long Vietnam War was finally over.

Ford versus Carter

Ford's uninspiring record on the economy and foreign policy suggested that he would be vulnerable in 1976. That year the Democrats chose Jimmy Carter, a former governor of Georgia, as their candidate. Carter's rise from almost total obscurity was even more spectacular than that of George McGovern in 1972 and was made possible by the same forces: television, the democratization of the delegate-selection process, and the absence of a dominant leader among the Democrats.

Carter had been a naval officer and a substantial peanut farmer and warehouse owner before entering politics. He was elected governor of Georgia in 1970. While governor he won something of a reputation as a southern public official who treated black citizens fairly. (He hung a portrait of Martin Luther King, Jr., in his office.) Carter's political style was informal. During the campaign for delegates he turned his inexperience in national politics to advantage, emphasizing his lack of connection with the Washington establishment rather

The rapid collapse of the South Vietnamese army in 1975 caught many by surprise. Here evacuees form a line on the roof of the U.S. embassy in Saigon, hoping to crowd into the last helicopters leaving the country before the North Vietnamese took over.

than apologizing for it. He repeatedly called attention to his integrity and deep religious faith. "I'll never lie to you," he promised voters, a pledge that no candidate would have bothered to make before Nixon's disgrace. He won the Democratic nomination easily.

Carter sought to make the election a referendum on morality. After Watergate, an atmosphere of scandal permeated Washington, and aspiring journalists and congressmen trained their sights on Kissinger, who remained secretary of state after Nixon's resignation. The most significant of the allegations was his meddling in the affairs of Chile, which in 1970 elected Salvador Allende, a Marxist, as president. "I don't see why we need to stand by and watch a country go communist due to the irresponsibility of its people," Kissinger had quipped. He called on the CIA to "destabilize" Allende's regime. In 1973, Allende was murdered in a military coup and his government toppled. Carter promised an administration of "constant decency" in contrast to Kissinger's penchant for secret diplomacy and covert skullduggery.

In the Republican primaries, Ford was challenged by Ronald Reagan, ex-governor of California, a movie actor turned politician who was the darling of the Republican right wing. Reagan was an excellent speaker, whereas Ford proved somewhat bumbling on the stump. Reagan, too, hammered away at Kissinger, citing his "immoral" détente with communist China. At Reagan's insistence, the Republican platform denounced "secret agreements, hidden from our people"—another jab at Kissinger.

Both Republican candidates gathered substantial blocs of delegates, but Ford staved off the Reagan challenge. That he did not win easily, possessed as he was of the advantage of incumbency, made his chances of election in November appear slim.

When the final contest began, both candidates were vague with respect to issues, a situation that hurt Carter particularly because he had made so much of honesty and straight talk. The election was memorable chiefly for its gaffes: Carter's admission to *Playboy* that he had "lusted after women" in his heart and Ford's declaration in a televised debate, "There is no Soviet domination in Eastern Europe." Voters were left to choose between Carter's seeming ignorance of human frailty and Ford's human frailty of seeming ignorant.

With both candidates stumbling toward the finish line, pundits predicted an extremely close contest, and they were right: Carter won, 297 electoral votes to 241, having carried most of the South, including Texas, and a few large industrial states. He also ran well in districts dominated by labor union members. The wish of the public to punish the party of Richard Nixon probably was a further reason for his victory.

Watch the **Video** *Ford Presidential Campaign Ad: Feeling Good About America* at **www.myhistorylab.com**

The Carter Presidency

Carter shone brightly in comparison with Nixon, and he seemed more forward-looking and imaginative than Ford. He tried to give a tone of democratic simplicity and moral fervor to his administration. After delivering his inaugural address he walked with his wife Rosalynn and their young daughter Amy in the parade from the Capitol to the White House instead of riding in a limousine. They enrolled Amy, a fourth-grader, in a largely black Washington public school. Soon after taking office he held a "call-in"; for two hours he answered questions phoned in by people from all over the country.

Carter's actual administration of his office did not go nearly so well. He put so many Georgians in important posts that his administration took on a parochial character. The administration developed a reputation for submitting complicated proposals to Congress with great fanfare and then failing to follow up on them. Whatever matter Carter was considering at the moment seemed to absorb him totally—other urgent matters were allowed to drift.

A National Malaise

To Carter, the nation's economic woes were symptomatic of a more fundamental flaw in the nation's soul. In a heralded

Georgia governor Jimmy Carter and President Gerald Ford debate in 1976. The campaign featured Carter's candor in a *Playboy* interview: "I've committed adultery in my heart many times." The headline stories often neglected the sentences that followed: "This is something that God recognizes I will do   and I have done it—and God forgives me for it."

This unused Pittsburgh steel mill was demolished in 1982.

television speech he complained that "a moral and spiritual crisis" had sapped people's energies and undermined civic pride: "We've learned that piling up material goods cannot fill the emptiness of lives which have no confidence or purpose." Critics responded that the nation needed a president rather than a preacher, and that sermons on the emptiness of consumption rang hollow to those who had lost their jobs.

The economic downturn, though triggered by the energy shortage, had more fundamental causes. In the prosperous postwar decades, many companies had grown too big and complacent, more attuned to the demands of the corporate bureaucracy than the needs of customers. Workers' boredom lowered productivity Absenteeism at General Motors and Ford had doubled during the 1960s. On an average day in 1970, 5 percent of GM's workforce was missing without explanation, and on Mondays and Fridays 10 percent failed to show up. That year Lee Iacocca, the president of Ford, was unnerved by employee attitudes during his visit to a plant at Wixcom, Indiana: "I see some young guy who's going full-time to school at Wayne State, his mind is elsewhere, and he doesn't give a shit what he builds, he doesn't care and he isn't involved in his job.

We can't change a man like that anymore." Incapable of eliminating slipshod work in Ford plants, Iacocca recommended that dealers improve their repair shops.

Two years later simmering discontents among young workers boiled over at the GM assembly division at Lordstown, Ohio. GM had installed robotic welding machines, streamlined the workforce, and accelerated the assembly line: 100 cars passed through the line each hour—40 more than under the previous system. Without authorization from the national UAW, younger workers refused to work at the faster pace, allowing many chassis to pass through untouched and throwing the factory into chaos. "Significant numbers of American workers," the U.S. Department of Health, Education, and Welfare concluded, had grown dissatisfied with the "dull, repetitive, seemingly meaningless tasks" of the postwar workplace.

Younger workers were growing impatient too with aging union leaders and a system that welded salary increases to seniority. Increasingly the young rejected the postwar accord in which organized labor essentially ceded control of the workplace in return for cost-of-living increases and job security.

Union membership slipped badly from the high point of the mid–1950s, when over one in three nonagricultural workers belonged to unions; by 1978, the proportion had declined to one in four, and by 1990, one in six. During the 1940s and 1950s, most workers voted to join a union, pay dues, and have the organization bargain for them. By 1978, however, union organizers were losing three-fourths of their campaigns to represent workers; and many workers who belonged to unions were opting to get out. Every year, 800 more union shops voted to rescind their affiliation.

Read the **Document** Carter, *Crisis of Confidence (1979)* at www.myhistorylab.com

Stagflation: The Weird Economy

Recessions are part of the natural business cycle: When economies overheat, they eventually cool down. But the economic crisis after 1973 was unsettling because, for the first time in the nation's history, the rising tide of unemployment had failed to extinguish inflation. Millions of workers lost their jobs, yet wages and prices continued to rise. The term **stagflation** (a combination of stagnation and inflation) was coined to describe this anomaly. In 1971 an inflation rate of 5 percent had so alarmed President Nixon that he had imposed a price freeze. By 1975 inflation had soared to 11 percent and by 1979, it peaked at a whopping 13 percent; unemployment ranged from 6 to 10 percent, nearly twice the usual postwar level.

The skyrocketing price of oil caused many to champion nuclear energy. But on March 28, 1979, the failure of a cooling system caused the Three Mile Island nuclear reactor to overheat and generate radioactivity in the Harrisburg region. The reactor was shut down five days later.

inflation, but taxes went up more rapidly because larger dollar incomes put people in higher tax brackets. This "bracket creep" caused resentment and frustration among middle-class families. "Taxpayer revolts" erupted as many people turned against expensive government programs for aiding the poor. Federal borrowing to cover the deficit pushed up interest rates and increased the costs of all businesses that had to borrow.

Soaring mortgage rates made it more difficult to sell homes. The housing slump meant unemployment for thousands of carpenters, bricklayers, and other construction workers and bankruptcy for many builders. Double-digit interest rates also hurt small businesses seeking to expand. Savings and loan institutions were especially hard-hit because they were saddled with countless mortgages made when rates were as low as 4 and 5 percent. Now they had to pay much more than that to hold deposits and offer even higher rates to attract new money.

Bad as inflation was in the mid-1970s, it got worse in 1979 when further instability in the Middle East nearly tripled the price of oil, which now reached $34 a barrel. This sent gasoline far over the $1 a gallon price barrier many had thought inconceivable. Within months Ford stock, at thirty-two in 1978, plummeted to sixteen; its credit rating with Standard and Poor's fell from AAA to an ignominious BBB. Chrysler, the third largest automaker, tottered near bankruptcy and then fell over the edge, saved in mid-fall only by a $1.2 billion federal loan guarantee. From 1978 to 1982, the jobs of one in three autoworkers were eliminated.

Carter had promised to fight inflation by reducing government spending and balancing the budget and to stimulate the economy by cutting taxes, policies that were very much like those of Nixon and Ford. He advanced an admirable if complicated plan for conserving energy and reducing the dependence of the United States on OPEC oil. This plan would raise the tax on gasoline and impose a new tax on "gas guzzlers," cars that got relatively few miles per gallon. But in his typical fashion he did not press hard for these measures.

The federal government made matters worse in several ways. Wages and salaries rose in response to

"Constant Decency" in Action

"It is a new world," Carter declared in his first speech on foreign affairs. In contrast to the shadowy dealings and sly gambits of the Nixon-Kissinger years, he would conduct a foreign policy characterized by "constant decency." The defense of "basic human rights" would come before all other concerns. He then cut off aid to Chile and Argentina because of human rights violations. He also negotiated treaties with Panama that provided for the gradual transfer of the Panama Canal to that nation and guaranteed the canal's neutrality. But he said little about what was going on in a long list of other nations whose citizens' rights were being repressed.

The president also intended to carry forward the Nixon-Kissinger policy of détente, and in 1979 another Strategic Arms Limitation Treaty (SALT II) was signed with the Soviet Union. But the following winter the Soviet Union sent troops into Afghanistan to overthrow the government there. Carter denounced the invasion and warned the Soviets that he would use force if they invaded any of the countries bordering the Persian Gulf. He withdrew the SALT treaty, which he had sent to the Senate for ratification. He also refused to allow American athletes to compete in the 1980 Olympic games in Moscow.

Carter's one striking diplomatic achievement was the so-called **Camp David Accords** between Israel and Egypt. In September 1978 President Anwar Sadat of Egypt and Prime Minister Menachem Begin of Israel came to the United States at Carter's invitation to seek a peace treaty ending the state of war that had existed between their two countries for many years.

For two weeks they conferred at Camp David, the presidential retreat outside the capital, and Carter's mediation had much to do with their successful negotiations. In the treaty Israel promised to withdraw from territory captured from Egypt during the 1967 Israeli-Egypt war. Egypt in turn recognized Israel as a nation, the first Arab country to do so. Peace ensured an uninterrupted supply of Arab oil to the United States. The Camp David Accords were the first and, as it turned out, the last significant agreement between Israel and a major Arab state.

The Iran Crisis: Origins

At this point a dramatic shift in the Middle East thrust Carter into the spotlight as never before. On November 4, 1979, about 400 armed Muslim militants broke into the American embassy compound in Tehran, Iran, and took everyone within the walls captive.

The seizure had roots that ran far back in Iranian history. During World War II, Great Britain, the Soviet Union, and later the United States occupied Iran and forced its pro-German shah into exile, replacing him with his twenty-two-year-old son, Muhammad Reza Pahlavi. But in the early 1950s power shifted to Prime Minister Muhammad Mossadegh, a leftist who sought to finance social reform by nationalizing the mostly American-owned Anglo-Iranian Oil Company.

In 1953, the Iranian army, backed by the CIA, arrested Mossadegh and put the young Pahlavi in power. The fall of Mossadegh ensured a steady flow of cheap oil, but it turned most Iranians against the United States and Shah Pahlavi. His unpopularity led the shah to purchase enormous amounts of American arms. Over the years Iran became the most powerful military force in the region.

Although Iran was an enthusiastic member of the OPEC cartel, the shah was for obvious reasons a firm friend of the United States. In the troubled Middle East, Iran seemed "an island of stability," President Carter said.

The appearance of stability was deceptive. The shah's secret police, the Savak, brutally suppressed liberal opponents. At the same time, Muslim religious leaders were particularly offended by the shah's attempts to introduce Western ideas and technology into Iran. Because his American-supplied army and his American-trained secret police kept the shah in power, his opponents hated the United States almost as much as they hated their autocratic ruler. The shah's rule was not one of "constant decency."

Throughout 1977, riots and demonstrations convulsed Iran. When soldiers fired on protesters, the bloodshed caused more unrest, and that unrest caused even more bloodshed. Over 10,000 civilians were killed; many times that number were wounded. In 1978 the whole country seemed to rise against the shah. Finally, in January 1979, he was forced to flee. A revolutionary government headed by a religious leader, the Ayatollah Ruhollah Khomeini, assumed power. Freedom, he said, was the great enemy of Islam: "[I]t will corrupt our youth . . . pave the way for the oppressor . . . and drag our nation to the bottom." He also claimed that Islam condoned terror: "Islam says: Whatever good there is exists thanks to the sword and in the shadow of the sword! . . . The sword is the key to paradise, which can be opened only for holy warriors."

Khomeini denounced the United States, the "Great Satan," whose support of the shah, he said, had caused the Iranian people untold suffering. When President Carter allowed the shah to come to the United States for medical treatment for cancer, militants in Tehran seized the American embassy.

The Iran Crisis: Carter's Dilemma

The militants announced that the Americans at the embassy would be held hostage until the United States returned the shah to Iran for trial as a traitor. They also demanded that the shah's vast wealth be confiscated and surrendered to the Iranian government. President Carter rejected these demands. Instead Carter froze Iranian assets in the United States and banned trade with Iran until the hostages were freed.

A stalemate developed. Months passed. Even after the shah, who was terminally ill, left the United States for Panama, the Iranians remained adamant. The **Iranian hostage crisis** produced a remarkable emotional response in the United States. For the first

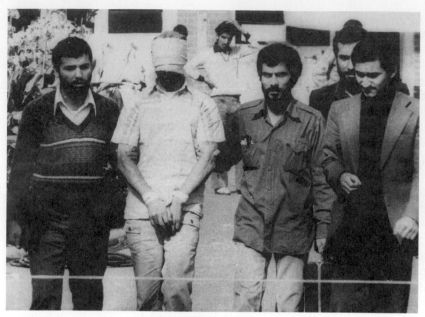

In 1979 Islamic militants hold an American embassy worker in Tehran.

Mahmoud Ahmadinejad, President of the Islamic Republic of Iran, lectures in 2010. When Ahmadinejad spoke at the UN in 2009, many were struck by his resemblance to the young militant (left photo) who held Americans hostage in Iran in 1979. Then, Ahmadinejad was 23. He denied that he was the person in the earlier photo.

time since the Vietnam War the entire country agreed on something.

Nevertheless the hostages languished in Iran. In April 1980 Carter finally ordered a team of marine commandos flown into Iran in Sea Stallion helicopters in a desperate attempt to free the hostages. The raid was a fiasco. Several helicopters broke down when their rotors sucked sand into the engines. Another helicopter crashed and eight commandos were killed. The Iranians made political capital of the incident, gleefully displaying on television the wrecked aircraft and captured American equipment. The stalemate continued. When the shah died in exile in Egypt in July 1980, the Iranians made no move to release the hostages.

The Election of 1980

Despite the failure of the raid and the persistence of stagflation, Carter had more than enough delegates at the Democratic convention to win nomination on the first ballot. His Republican opponent in the campaign that followed was Ronald Reagan. At sixty-nine, Reagan was the oldest person ever nominated for president by a major party. However, his age was not a serious handicap in the campaign; he was physically trim and vigorous and seemed no older than most other prominent politicians.

Reagan had grown up a New Deal Democrat, but during and immediately after World War II he became disillusioned with liberalism. As president of the Screen Actors Guild he attacked the influence of

communists in the movie industry. After his movie career ended (he always insisted that he was typed as "the nice guy who didn't get the girl"), Reagan did publicity for General Electric until 1960, then worked for various conservative causes. Reagan won the undying loyalty of supporters of the Vietnam War, as well as the permanent enmity of the left, by proposing that the United States "level North Vietnam, pave it, paint stripes on it, and make a parking lot out of it." In 1966 he ran for governor of California, and struck a responsive chord by attacking the counterculture. "Hippies," he quipped, "act like Tarzan, look like Jane, and smell like Cheetah." He won the election and was easily reelected.

Both Carter and Reagan spent much of the 1980 campaign explaining why the other was unsuited to be president. Carter defended his record, though without much conviction. Reagan denounced criminals, drug addicts, and all varieties of immorality and spoke in support of patriotism, religion, family life, and other "old-fashioned" virtues. This won him the enthusiastic backing of fundamentalist religious sects and other conservative groups. He also called for increased spending on defense, and he promised to transfer some functions of the federal government to the states and to cut taxes. He insisted at the same time that the budget could be balanced and inflation sharply reduced.

Reagan's tendency to depend on popular magazine articles, half-remembered conversations, and other informal sources for his economic "facts" reflected a mental imprecision that alarmed his critics, but his sunny disposition and easygoing style compared favorably with Carter, who seemed tight-lipped and tense even when flashing his habitual toothy smile. A television debate between Carter and Reagan underscored their personal differences, but Reagan's question to the audience, "Are you better off now than you were four years ago?" had more effect on the election than any policy he said he would pursue.

On election day the voting was light, but Reagan received 8 million more votes than Carter. Dissatisfaction with the economy and the unresolved hostage crisis seem to have determined the result. The Republicans also gained control of the Senate and cut deeply into the Democratic majority in the House of Representatives.

Carter devoted his last weeks in office to the continuing hostage crisis. War had broken out between Iran and Iraq in September. The Iraqi president, Saddam Hussein, had hoped to exploit the chaos following the downfall of the shah to seize oil-rich territory in Iran. Early Iraqi victories prompted the Iranians to free the hostages in return for the release of Iranian assets that had been frozen in the United States. After 444 days in captivity, the fifty-two hostages were set free on January 20, the day Reagan was inaugurated.

Watch the **Video** *Reagan Presidential Campaign Ad: A Bear in the Woods* at **www.myhistorylab.com**

Reagan as President

Reagan hoped to change the direction in which the country was moving. He demanded steep reductions in federal spending and the deficit, to be accomplished by cutting social expenditures such as welfare, food stamps and student loans, and by turning many functions of the federal government over to the states. The marketplace, not federal bureaucratic regulations, should govern most economic decisions.

He asked Congress to lower income taxes by 30 percent. When critics objected that this would increase the deficit, the president and his advisers reasoned that the tax cut would leave people with more money, which they would invest in productive ways. The new investment would generate more goods and jobs—and, ultimately, taxes for the federal government. This scheme became known as **Reaganomics**.

Helped by the votes of conservative Democrats, Reagan won congressional approval of the Budget Reconciliation Act, which reduced government expenditures on domestic programs by $39 billion.

Ronald Reagan rides a horse—a familiar photo opportunity for presidents. (Recall the similar picture of LBJ on page 773.) But Reagan was an amiable cowboy; his smile and sense of humor were his most disarming weapons. In 1966 just after the election, when reporters asked him what sort of governor he would be, Reagan, a former actor, answered, "I don't know. I've never played a governor." Three months into his presidency, moments after he was seriously wounded in an assassination attempt, he took his wife's hand. "Honey," he said, "I forgot to duck." While being wheeled into the operating room, he quipped to the surgeons, "I hope you are all Republicans."

Congress enacted most of the tax cuts the president had asked for, lowering individual income taxes by 25 percent over three years, but it resisted reducing the politically popular "entitlement" programs, such as Social Security and Medicare, which accounted for about half of the budget. Reagan himself refused to reduce the military budget to bring the government's income more nearly in line with its outlays. Instead he called for a military buildup to ensure that the United States would prevail in any war with the Soviet Union, which he called an "evil empire." In particular, he sought to expand and improve the nation's nuclear arsenal. He made no secret of his wish to create so formidable a nuclear force that the Soviets would have to back down in any confrontation. The deficit worsened.

In Central America Reagan sought the overthrow of the left-wing government of Nicaragua and the defeat of communist rebels in El Salvador. He even used American troops to overthrow a Cuban-backed regime on the tiny Caribbean island of Grenada. When criticized for opposing leftist regimes while backing rightist dictators, Jeane Kirkpatrick, U.S. ambassador to the United Nations, explained that "rightist authoritarian regimes can be transformed peacefully into democracies, but totalitarian Marxist ones cannot."

In 1982 the continuing turmoil in the Middle East thrust the Reagan administration into a new crisis. Israel had invaded Lebanon to destroy Palestine Liberation Organization units that were staging raids on northern Israeli settlements. Israeli troops easily overran much of the country, but in the process the Lebanese government disintegrated. Reagan agreed to commit American troops to an international peacekeeping force.

Tragedy resulted in October 1983 when a fanatical Muslim crashed a truck loaded with explosives into a building housing American marines in Beirut. The building collapsed, killing 239 marines. Early the next year, Reagan removed the entire American peacekeeping force from Lebanon.

Four More Years

A sitting president with an extraordinarily high standing in public opinion polls, Reagan was nominated for a second term at the 1984 Republican convention without opposition. The Democratic nomination went to Walter Mondale of Minnesota, who had been vice president under Carter. Mondale electrified the country by choosing Representative Geraldine Ferraro of New York as his running mate. An Italian American and a Catholic, Ferraro was expected to appeal to conservative Democrats who had supported Reagan in 1980 and to win the votes of many Republican women.

Reagan began the campaign with several important advantages. He was especially popular among religious fundamentalists and other social conservatives, and these groups were increasingly vocal. President Nixon had spoken of a "silent majority." By 1980 the kind of people he was referring to were no longer silent. Fundamentalist television preachers were almost all fervent Reaganites and the most successful of them were collecting tens of millions of dollars annually in contributions from viewers. One of these, the Reverend Jerry Falwell, founded the **Moral Majority** and set out to create a new political movement. "Americans are sick and tired of the way the amoral liberals are trying to corrupt our nation," Falwell announced in 1979.

During the first Reagan administration, the Moral Majority had become a powerful political force. Falwell denounced drugs, the "coddling" of criminals, homosexuality, communism, and abortion, all things that Reagan also disliked. Falwell also disapproved of forced busing to integrate schools. In addition,

Success of the Republican "Southern Strategy"   In 1968, Kevin M. Phillips, a key Nixon strategist, proposed a "southern strategy" to create an "emerging Republican majority." Many doubted that the South, which had long been opposed to the party of Lincoln, could be won over. But in presidential elections from 1968 to 1988, far more southern counties voted Republican than Democratic.

Reagan favored government aid to private schools run by church groups, something dear to the Moral Majority despite the constitutional principle of separation of church and state.

Reagan's support was also drawn from blue collar workers and white Southerners, constituencies that had been solidly Democratic during the New Deal and beyond. The president's personality was another important plus—voters continued to admire his informal yet firm style and his stress on patriotism and other "traditional" virtues.

Most polls showed Reagan far in the lead when the campaign began, and this remained true throughout the contest. Nothing Mondale or Ferraro did or said affected the president's popularity. Bad news, even his own mistakes, had so little effect on Reagan's standing that people began to call him "the Teflon president." On election day he got nearly 60 percent of the popular vote and lost only in Minnesota, Mondale's home state, and in the District of Columbia. Reagan's Electoral College margin was overwhelming, 525 to 13.

Of all the elements in the Democratic New Deal coalition, only African Americans, who voted solidly for Mondale, remained loyal. The Democratic strategy of nominating a woman for vice president was a failure; far more women voted for Reagan than for the Mondale-Ferraro ticket.

Reagan's triumph, like the two landslide victories of Dwight Eisenhower in the 1950s, was a personal one. The Republicans made only minor gains in the House of Representatives and actually lost two seats in the Senate.

"The Reagan Revolution"

Reagan's agenda for his second term closely resembled that of his first. In foreign affairs, he ran into continuing congressional resistance to his requests for military support for his anticommunist crusade. This was particularly true after Mikhail S. Gorbachev became the Soviet premier in March 1985. Gorbachev seemed far more moderate and flexible than his predecessors. He began to encourage political debate and criticism in the Soviet Union—the policy known as *glasnost* (openness) and he sought to stimulate the stagnant Soviet economy by decentralizing administration and rewarding individual enterprise (*perestroika*).

Gorbachev also announced that he would continue to honor the unratified SALT II agreement, whereas Reagan, arguing that the Soviet Union had not respected the limits laid down in the pact, seemed bent on pushing ahead with the expansion and modernization of America's nuclear arsenal. Reagan sought funds to develop an elaborate system of missile defenses. He referred to it as the **Strategic Defense Initiative (SDI)**, although it was popularly known as Star Wars, a reference to the 1977 George Lucas film. SDI would consist of a network of computer-controlled space stations that would detect oncoming enemy missiles and destroy them with speculative high-tech weaponry.

When the president realized that the Soviets were eager for an agreement to limit nuclear weapons, he ceased referring to the Soviet Union as an "evil empire." In October 1986 he met with Gorbachev in Iceland in search of an agreement on arms control. The chief sticking point was SDI, which Gorbachev denounced as "space strike" weaponry that might be used to wipe out Soviet cities. Gorbachev proposed instead the elimination of all nuclear weapons—including SDI. Reagan, however, was determined to push Star Wars, and the summit collapsed.

Reagan pressed ahead with the Star Wars defense-in-space system. After NASA's spectacular Apollo program, which sent six expeditions to the moon between 1969 and 1972, the space agency's prestige was beyond measure. The Skylab orbiting space station program (1973–1974) was equally successful. Next, shortly after the beginning of Reagan's first term, the manned space shuttle *Columbia*, launched by rocket into orbit for several days, returned to earth intact, gliding on its stubby, swept-back wings to an appointed landing strip. *Columbia* and other shuttles were soon transporting satellites into space for the government and private companies, and its astronauts were conducting military and scientific experiments of great importance.

Congress, however, balked at the enormous cost of Star Wars. Expense aside, the idea of relying for national defense on the complex technology involved in controlling machines in outer space suffered a further setback in 1986, when the space shuttle *Challenger* exploded shortly after takeoff, killing its seven-member crew. This disaster temporarily put a stop to the program.

Reagan's basic domestic objectives—to reduce the scope of federal activity, particularly in the social welfare area; to lower income taxes; and to increase the strength of the armed forces—remained constant. Despite the tax cuts already made, congressional leaders of both parties agreed to the Income Tax Act of 1986, which reduced the top levy on personal incomes from 50 percent to 28 percent and the tax on corporate profits from 46 percent to 34 percent.

Reagan advanced another of his objectives more gradually. This was his appointment of conservatives to federal judgeships, including Sandra Day O'Connor, the first woman named to the Supreme Court. By 1988 Reagan had appointed three Supreme Court justices and well over half the members of the federal judiciary.

The New Merger Movement

During the Reagan years, the nation began to climb out of the recession of the 1970s. Reagan's policies helped, though often in unpredictable ways. Reagan's relaxed regulation of Wall Street helped precipitate a frenzy of corporate mergers. Deregulation provided the context for the merger movement, but the person most responsible for it was Michael Milken, a shrewd stockbroker of the firm of Drexel Burnham Lambert. Milken specialized in selling "junk bonds," the debt offerings of companies whose existing debts were already high. He persuaded savings and loan associations, insurance companies, pension funds, and other big investors to buy these junk bonds, which, though risky, offered high interest rates. The success of his initial ventures prompted Milken to approach smaller companies, encourage them to borrow immense sums by floating junk bonds, and use the proceeds to acquire larger firms.

In 1985 Ronald Perelman, an aggressive entrepreneur, employed this strategy to perfection. He had recently obtained control of Pantry Pride, a supermarket chain with a net worth of about $145 million. Now he sought to acquire Revlon, a $2 billion cosmetics and health care conglomerate. With Milken's help, Pantry Pride borrowed $1.5 billion and used that capital to buy Revlon. He then paid off Pantry Pride's $1.5 billion in junk bonds ("junk" because the debt so greatly exceeded the $145 million value of Pantry Pride) by selling huge chunks of Revlon. Then he integrated the food component of Revlon into Pantry Pride. The bond purchasers profited handsomely from the high return on the junk bonds, and Perelman made a fortune from his new food conglomerate. That same year the R. J. Reynolds Tobacco Company purchased Nabisco, another food conglomerate, for $4.9 billion. Three years later this new giant,

RJR Nabisco, was itself taken over by Kohlberg, Kravis, Roberts, and Company for $24.9 billion.

During the frenzied decade of the 1980s, one-fifth of the *Fortune* 500 companies were taken over, merged, or forced to go private; in all, some 25,000 mergers and acquisitions were successfully undertaken; their total value was nearly a half-trillion dollars. To make their companies less tempting to cash-hungry raiders, many corporations took on whopping debts or acquired unprofitable companies. By the late 1980s, many American corporations were wallowing in red ink. Debt payments were gobbling up 50 percent of the nation's corporate pretax earnings.

"A Job for Life": Layoffs Hit Home

Most corporations coped with the debt in two ways: They sold assets, such as factories, offices, and warehouses; or they cut costs through layoffs. U.S. Steel, whose rusting mills desperately needed an infusion of capital, instead spent $5 billion to acquire Marathon Oil of Ohio; that decision meant that nearly 100,000 steelworkers lost their jobs. No firm was immune, nor any worker secure. "A job for life" had long been IBM's unofficial but endlessly repeated slogan. As late as 1985, it ran an advertisement to reassure employees: "Jobs may come and go—But people shouldn't." Yet during the next nine years a crippled IBM eliminated 80,000 jobs and more than a third of its workforce. During the 1980s, the total number of employees who worked for *Fortune* 500 companies declined by three million; nearly one-third of all positions in middle

Workers at a Nike factory in Indonesia insert soles into sneakers.

management were eliminated. Millions of "organization men" (about one-third of whom now were women) were laid off as the organizations themselves "downsized," the corporate euphemism for wholesale firings.

Many of the jobs went abroad, where labor costs were lower and unions nonexistent. In 1980 Xerox of America, realizing that it could no longer compete with its more efficient Japanese subsidiary, transferred contracts to Japan and laid off tens of thousands of American workers. In 1984 Nike moved sewing operations to Indonesia, where it could hire female workers for fourteen cents an hour. In 1986 the chassis for the Mustang, long a symbol of American automotive style, was built by Mazda in Hiroshima, Japan.

Towering mountains of private corporate debt nearly were overshadowed by the Everest of public debt held by the federal government itself. Reagan's insistence on a sharp cut in personal taxes and a substantial increase in military expenditures produced huge—and growing—annual federal deficits. When Reagan took office, the total federal debt was $900 million; eight years later, it exceeded $2.5 *trillion*. "No one imagined how bad the outcome would be," explained David Stockman, Reagan's budget director. "It got away from us."

Corporate Restructuring

Although few perceived it at the time, the economy was undergoing a transformation of historic dimensions. Much as the depression after 1893 had strengthened the nation's economy by wiping out thousands of inefficient steel and machinery firms, the seismic economic upheavals after 1973 toppled many inefficient manufacturers but created the foundations for more efficient global conglomerates. As weeds grew in the parking lots of the factories of the "Rust Belt" of the Midwest, new technology industries sprouted in the "Silicon Valley" of California, along Route 128 outside of Boston, and in booming cities such as Seattle, Washington, and Austin, Texas.

By the end of the Reagan era, the economy consisted of two separate and increasingly unequal components: a battered sector of traditional heavy industry, characterized by declining wages and diminishing job opportunities; and an advancing high-tech and service sector dominated by aggressive, innovative, and individualistic entrepreneurs. (See American Lives, "Bill Gates," pp. 810–811) The older corporations that survived the shakeout of the 1980s were leaner and better equipped to compete in expanding global markets.

Yet American society was becoming as fractured as the "bipolar" economy from which it drew sustenance.

A worker studies a lighted diagram of an integrated circuit at a California computer factory.

The Reagan tax cuts had disproportionately benefited the wealthy, as had the extraordinary rise of the stock market. Conversely, the economic transformation struck low- or semiskilled wage earners hardest; at the same time, the Reagan administration's shifting of much of the burden of social welfare onto state and local governments reduced benefits to those who lost jobs or could not find work in the strange new economy dominated by information services and bewildering new technologies. At the end of Reagan's second term the standard of living of the poorest fifth of the population (40 million people) was 9 percent lower than it had been in 1979, while that of the wealthiest fifth had risen about 20 percent.

Rogue Foreign Policy

Especially during his second term as president, Reagan paid little attention to the details of administration. Thus two major initiatives unfolded of which Reagan himself claimed little knowledge.

The first concerned Nicaragua. In 1979 leftist rebels had overthrown the dictatorial regime of

Bill Gates

"Project Breakthrough! World's First Minicomputer Kit to Rival Commercial Models." This headline in the January 1975 issue of *Popular Electronics* triggered the neurons in Bill Gates's brain. In an instant, he perceived that the revolution had begun. Most earlier computers cost hundreds of thousands of dollars, filled room-sized air-conditioned vaults, and were found in university science centers, government agencies, and corporate headquarters. But this kit cost only $397. The computer (its name—*Altair*—came from a planet in the TV series *Star Trek*), could fit on a desktop. Gates believed that computers like this would soon be as much a part of life as telephones or automobiles. Armed with the slogan, "A computer on every desktop," Gates resolved to become the Henry Ford of the computer revolution (and to become, like Ford, immensely rich). He was twenty years old.

Gates recognized Altair's fatal flaw: It did little more than cause a few lights to blink in complex ways. It lacked internal instructions to convert electrical signals into letters and numbers. He determined to write instructions—the software—to make the personal computer useful. Gates and Paul Allen, a school friend, telephoned Ed Roberts, the president of MITS, manufacturer of the Altair. They told him they had written operating software for the machine. Roberts was skeptical. Scores of programmers had made such claims, he said, but none had actually done it. He told them to bring their software to the company headquarters in Albuquerque, New Mexico, within two months.

Bill Gates as a young CEO at Microsoft.

Allen and Gates were euphoric, but not for long: They had not even begun to write a program for the Altair. The challenge of doing so in five weeks would have been unimaginable but for one thing: The electronic core of the Altair was the Intel 8080 computer chip, and for years Allen and Gates had been devising machines and software based on the Intel 8008, whose logic was similar to the 8080.

The boys had met in 1967 at Lakeside, an elite private school in Seattle, when Gates was in seventh grade, Allen in ninth. That year, the Lakeside Mothers Club had bought time on a digital training terminal that connected by phone to a company that leased a mainframe computer. Within weeks of its installation, this computer had become Gates's life. He remained in the terminal room after school and late into the evenings, breaking only for Coke and pizza. Sometimes he conked out while staring at the screen; his clothes were perpetually wrinkled and spattered with pizza sauce. "He lived and breathed computers," a friend recalled.

Gates learned programming by writing programs and seeing what worked. His first was for playing tic-tac-toe. He also designed a program for student schedules at Lakeside. He placed "all the good girls in the school" (and very few males of any kind) in his own classes—an early manifestation of his penchant for defeating competitors by conniving to eliminate them.

Although his father was a wealthy corporate attorney and his mother a prominent socialite, Gates was preoccupied with making money. In high school he took a job tabulating automobile traffic data; this required that he count the holes in a roll of paper punched out when automobiles passed over a hose. He designed a computerized machine to count and analyze the data and he formed a company, Traf-O-Data, to build and market the device. But, Traf-O-Data failed to attract many customers—most municipalities and highway departments lost interest when they learned that the company was run by high school students.

Gates, who earned a perfect score on the math portion of the SAT, chose a complex strategy to gain admission to the most competitive colleges. In his application to Harvard, he emphasized his political involvement (he had worked one summer as a congressional page); to Yale, he cited his creativity (a starring role in a dramatic production) and character (a former Boy Scout); and to Princeton, "I positioned myself as a computer nerd." Admitted to all three, he went to Harvard. Allen went to work as a programmer for Honeywell. But when they began work on the Altair operating program, Allen moved into Gates's dormitory and Gates skipped most classes. To save time, they built a simulator based on the published specifications of the Altair and feverishly churned out the operating software.

They completed the program just hours before Allen boarded the plane to Albuquerque. (Allen went because he was older and presumably a more credible "corporate" spokesman.) The next morning, Allen fed long rolls of punched yellow paper tape—the software—into an Altair while company executives looked on skeptically. For fifteen minutes the machine clattered away. Misgivings mounted. Then the teletype printed the word, "READY." Allen typed, "PRINT 2 + 2." The teletype spat out "4." The program worked. Gates and Allen had a deal.

Gates dropped out of Harvard and formed a partnership with Allen. They called their company Microsoft and moved to Albuquerque. They wrote operating programs for personal computers introduced by Apple, Commodore, and Radio Shack. Soon money was pouring into Microsoft. In 1979 they moved Microsoft to Bellevue, Washington, near Seattle. Then came the blockbuster.

In 1980 IBM, the world's foremost manufacturer of mainframe computers, belatedly entered the home computer market. IBM approached Gates to write the operating software for its new, state-of-the-art personal computer. IBM intended to keep the computer's specifications secret so that other manufacturers could not copy its design, but Gates shrewdly proposed that IBM make its specifications public. Doing so would allow the IBM personal computer to become the industry standard, giving IBM the edge in developing peripherals—printers, monitors, keyboards, and various applications. IBM agreed. Now Gates's software, called Microsoft-Disk Operating System (MS-DOS), would run every IBM personal computer as well as every computer made by other companies according to the IBM specifications. In a single stroke, Gates had virtually monopolized the market for PC operating software.

Microsoft's sales jumped from $7.5 million in 1980 to $140 million in 1985. Then Microsoft moved into software applications: word processing, accounting, and games. After Allen was diagnosed with Hodgkin's disease in 1983, he briefly retired and purchased the Portland Trail Blazers basketball team; he became a billionaire. By 1991, Gates was the wealthiest man in the world. In 1994, he and his wife established the Bill and Melinda Gates Foundation; by 2010, it had assets of over $33 billion and gave nearly $2 billion annually to charitable causes, especially education.

Questions for Discussion

- Intelligence, ambition, business sense, or all three? In what ways did Bill Gates's triumph parallel Andrew Carnegie's a century earlier?

- What was the main prerequisite for Gates's triumph?

Anastasio Somoza. Because the victorious Sandinista government was supported by both Cuba and the Soviet Union, Reagan was determined to force it from power. He backed anti-Sandinista elements in Nicaragua known as the Contras and in 1981 persuaded Congress to provide these "freedom fighters" with arms.

But the Contras made little progress, and many Americans feared that aiding them would lead, as it had in Vietnam, to the use of American troops in the fighting. In October 1984 Congress banned further military aid to the Contra rebels. Reagan then sought to persuade other countries and private American groups to help the Contras (as he put it) keep "body and soul together."

Marine Colonel Oliver North, an aide of Reagan's national security adviser, devised a scheme to indirectly funnel federal money to the Contras. He inflated the price of U.S. weapons, sold them to Iran[1], and secretly

---

[1]Earlier in the Iran-Iraq war, when Iran appeared on the verge of defeating Iraq, Reagan had provided $500 million a year in credits to allow Iraq's Saddam Hussein to buy armaments. If either Iran or Iraq won decisively, it could control the flow of Middle Eastern oil. The United States therefore preferred a stalemate.

transferred the profits to the Contras. This plainly violated the congressional ban on such aid.

When North's stratagem came to light in November 1986, he was fired from his job with the security council. Reagan insisted that he knew nothing about the aid to the Contras. Critics pointed out that if he was telling the truth it was almost as bad since that meant that he had not been able to control his own administration.

Meanwhile, the Soviet invasion of Afghanistan in 1980 enraged Charles Wilson, a Democratic congressman from Texas. (Wilson, a womanizer, heavy drinker, and alleged cocaine-user, was played by Tom Hanks in the movie, *Charlie Wilson's War* [2007]). Wilson persuaded his colleagues to allocate money for the *mujahideen*, Muslim warriors who were trying to drive the Soviets out of their country. Within several years the Afghan tribes, especially Islamist radicals known as the Taliban, were covertly receiving hundreds of millions of dollars in weapons. Stinger missiles, which could be moved on mules, proved especially effective at shooting down Soviet helicopters. Provisioned with American weapons, Muslim insurgents ambushed

Mujahideen in Afghanistan stand on top of a Soviet helicopter they shot down with U.S.-supplied Stinger missiles in the early 1980s.

convoys, mined roads, and engaged in various acts of terrorism. Soviet casualties increased, as did the cost of the war. Opposition mounted to communist leaders in the Soviet Union. Soviet generals began referring to the war in Afghanistan as "our Vietnam." In 1989 the Soviets pulled out; in 1996 the Taliban took over Afghanistan and instituted a radical Islamic state.

•••Read the Document Reagan, *Support for the Contras (1984)* at www.myhistorylab.com

Assessing the Reagan Revolution

Reagan was not an able administrator; the **Iran-Contra affair** and financial scandals of his administration did not stick to him because he was seldom close enough to the action to get splattered by it. Reagan articulated, simply and persuasively, a handful of concepts—chiefly the "evil" character of Soviet communism, the need to get government off people's backs—and in so doing created a political climate conducive to change. Reagan was directly responsible for neither of the great transformations of the late twentieth century—the restructuring of American corporations and the collapse of the Soviet Union. Yet his actions and, indeed, his failures to act indisputably influenced them. His decision to increase military spending and undertake the fantastically expensive SDI ("Star Wars") forced Gorbachev to seek an accommodation with the United States. Reagan's tax cuts precipitated unimaginably large federal deficits, and deregulation unloosed a sordid pack of predators who preyed on the economy. Yet the ensuing Darwinian chaos strengthened those corporations that survived and gave them the muscle to prevail in emerging global markets. "We are the change," Reagan declared in his farewell address. What he had done, exactly, he did not say. Yet the statement, however roseate, vague, and self-congratulatory, was not untrue.

The Election of 1988

The issues that had dominated American politics for over a decade—the Soviet threat, the energy crisis, stagflation—were gone. The presidential election of 1988 initially lacked focus. The selection of Vice President George H. W. Bush as the Republican nomination was a foregone conclusion. Bush, the son of a Connecticut senator, had attended an elite private school and Yale. He served as a pilot during World War II and then settled in Texas, where he worked in the family's oil business and became active in Republican politics. From 1971 to 1973 he

served as ambassador to the UN and from 1976 to 1977 as director of the CIA. As Republican presidential hopeful, he trumpeted his experience as vice president; but when the Reagan administration was tarnished by the Iran-Contra scandal, Bush claimed that he had been "out of the loop" and thus free of the scandal.

The Democratic race was far more complicated but scarcely more inspiring. So many lackluster candidates entered the field that wits called them "the seven dwarfs." But eventually Governor Michael Dukakis of Massachusetts, stressing his record as an efficient manager, accumulated delegates steadily and won the nomination.

During the campaign, Bush attacked Dukakis as a liberal governor who had been soft on crime. Lee Atwater, campaign manager for Bush, produced and aired a television advertisement showing prisoners, many of them black, streaming through a revolving door. Dukakis's attempts to shift the focus away from crime failed. The presidential campaign became, in effect, a referendum on crime in which Dukakis failed the toughness test. Bush won 54 percent of the vote and carried the Electoral College, 426 to 112.

George H. W. Bush as President

In 1989 President Bush, having attacked Dukakis for being soft on crime, named a "drug czar" to coordinate various bureaucracies, increased federal funding of local police, and spent $2.5 billion to stop the flow of illegal drugs into the nation. Although the campaign generated plenty of arrests, drugs continued to pour in: As one dealer or trafficker was arrested, another took his place.

Bush also worked to shed the tough image he had cultivated during the campaign. In his inaugural address he said that he hoped to "make kinder the face of the nation and gentler the face of the world." He also displayed a more traditional command of the workings of government and the details of current events than his predecessor. At the same time he pleased right-wing Reagan loyalists by his opposition to abortion and gun control, and by calling for a constitutional amendment prohibiting the burning of the American flag. His standing in the polls soared.

The Collapse of Communism in Eastern Europe

One important reason for this was the flood of good news from abroad. The reforms instituted in the Soviet Union by Gorbachev led to demands from its Eastern

In 1987, President Reagan went to Berlin and addressed the leader of the Soviet Union: "Mr. Gorbachev," he said, "Tear down this wall." Two years later, after Gorbachev had withdrawn Soviet troops from East Germany, Berliners tore down the wall themselves.

European satellites for similar liberalization. Gorbachev responded by announcing that the Soviet Union would not use force to keep communist governments in power in these nations. Swiftly the people of Poland, Hungary, Czechoslovakia, Bulgaria, Romania, East Germany, and the Baltics did away with the repressive regimes that had ruled them throughout the postwar era. Except in Romania, where the dictator Nicolae Ceausescu was executed, all these fundamental changes were carried out peacefully.

Almost overnight the international political climate changed. Soviet-style communism had been discredited. The Soviet bloc was no longer a force. A Soviet attack anywhere was almost unthinkable. The Cold War was over.

President Bush profited from these developments immensely. He expressed moral support for the new governments (and in some cases provided modest financial assistance) but he refrained from embarrassing the Soviets. At a summit meeting in Washington in June 1990 Bush and Gorbachev signed agreements reducing American and Russian stockpiles of long-range nuclear missiles by 30 percent and eliminating chemical weapons.

In 1989 President Bush sent troops to Panama to overthrow General Manuel Noriega, who had refused to yield power when his figurehead presidential candidate lost a national election. Noriega was under indictment in the United States for drug trafficking. After temporarily seeking refuge in the Vatican embassy in Panama, he surrendered to the American forces and was taken to the United States, where he was tried, convicted, and imprisoned.

Meanwhile, in the Soviet Union, nationalist and anticommunist groups demanded more local control of their affairs. President Gorbachev, who opposed this breakup, sought compromise, backing a draft treaty that would increase local autonomy and further privatize the Soviet economy. In August, however, before this treaty could be ratified, hard-line communists attempted a coup. They arrested Gorbachev, who was vacationing in the Crimea, and ordered tanks into Moscow. But Boris Yeltsin, the anticommunist president of the Russian Republic, defied the rebels and roused the people of Moscow. The coup swiftly collapsed. Its leaders were arrested, the communist party was officially disbanded, and the Soviet Union itself was replaced by a federation of states, of which Russia, led by Yeltsin, was the most important. Gorbachev, who had begun the process of liberation, found himself without a job.

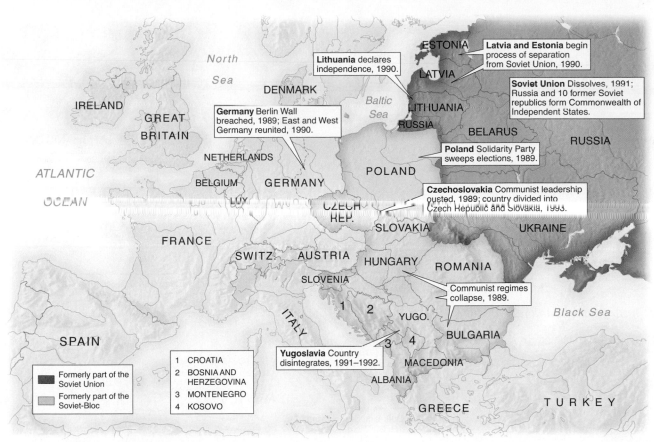

North Sea

Baltic Sea

Lithuania declares independence, 1990.

Latvia and Estonia begin process of separation from Soviet Union, 1990.

ESTONIA

LATVIA

LITHUANIA

Soviet Union Dissolves, 1991; Russia and 10 former Soviet republics form Commonwealth of Independent States.

DENMARK

IRELAND

GREAT BRITAIN

Germany Berlin Wall breached, 1989; East and West Germany reunited, 1990.

RUSSIA

BELARUS

RUSSIA

NETHERLANDS

ATLANTIC OCEAN

BELGIUM   GERMANY

LUX.

POLAND

Poland Solidarity Party sweeps elections, 1989.

CZECH REP.

Czechoslovakia Communist leadership ousted, 1989; country divided into Czech Republic and Slovakia, 1993.

FRANCE

SWITZ. AUSTRIA

SLOVAKIA

UKRAINE

HUNGARY   ROMANIA

SLOVENIA

Communist regimes collapse, 1989.

ITALY

1   2

YUGO.

Black Sea

SPAIN

3   4

BULGARIA

MACEDONIA

Yugoslavia Country disintegrates, 1991–1992.

ALBANIA

Formerly part of the Soviet Union

Formerly part of the Soviet-Bloc

1 CROATIA
2 BOSNIA AND HERZEGOVINA
3 MONTENEGRO
4 KOSOVO

GREECE   TURKEY

The Collapse of Communism in Eastern Europe When Gorbachev withdrew Soviet troops from Eastern Europe, the communist regimes there collapsed rapidly. The Soviet Union itself disintegrated.

The War in the Persian Gulf

Although Reagan had provided economic assistance to Saddam Hussein of Iraq to prevent Iran from winning the Iran-Iraq war, few in the administration were enthusiastic about the Iraqi dictator. For years Saddam had been crushing the Kurds, an ethnic minority in northern Iraq that sought independence. In 1987 the U.S. State Department reported on his "widespread destruction and bulldozing of Kurdish villages." In March 1988, after Kurdish rebels had supported an Iranian advance into Iraq near Halabja, a mostly Kurdish city, Saddam's troops dropped mustard gas, sarin, and other chemical weapons on the city. Some 5,000 civilians died.

In August 1990, Saddam launched an all-out attack on Iraq's tiny neighbor to the south, the oil-rich sheikdom of Kuwait. Saddam hoped to swallow up Kuwait, thus increasing Iraq's already large oil reserves to about 25 percent of the world's total. His soldiers overran Kuwait swiftly, then systematically carried off everything of value they could bring back to Iraq. Within a week Saddam annexed Kuwait and massed troops along the border of neighboring Saudi Arabia.

As the routed Iraqi army fled Kuwait, it ignited (literally) an ecological disaster by setting fire to the Kuwaiti oil fields. Here American soldiers advance past a burning oil well; it took many months before all the wells could be extinguished.

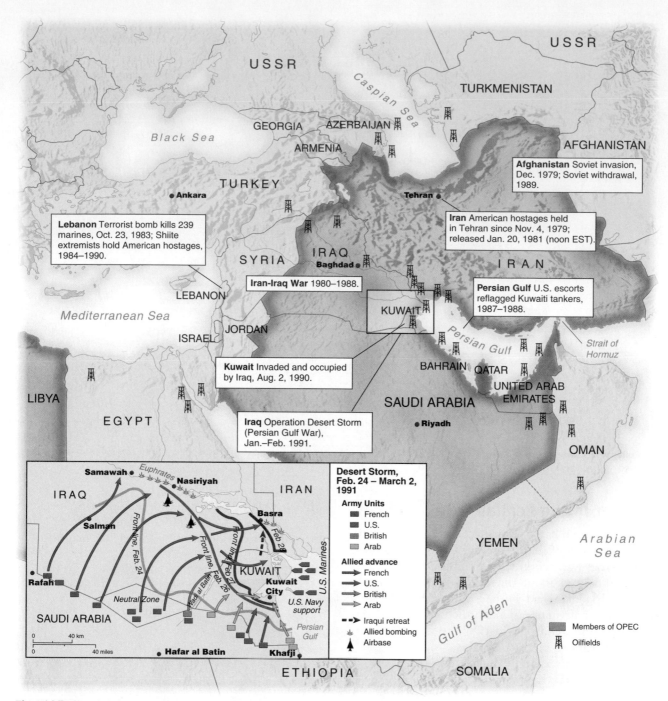

The Middle East In February 1991, combined U.S., British, French, and Arab armies drove Saddam Hussein from Kuwait and invaded Iraq.

The Saudis and the Kuwaitis turned to the United States and other nations for help, and it was quickly given. In a matter of days the UN applied trade sanctions against Iraq, and at the invitation of Saudi Arabia, the United States (along with Great Britain, France, Italy, Egypt, and Syria) moved troops to Saudi bases. Islamist fundamentalists opposed the presence of non-Muslim troops on Saudi soil; but the Saudi ruling family overruled them, fearing an Iraqi invasion.

By November, Bush had increased the American troops in the area from 180,000 to more than 500,000, part of a larger UN operation. On January 17, the Americans unleashed an enormous air attack, directed by General Norman Schwarzkopf. This air assault went on for nearly a month, and it reduced much of Iraq to rubble. The Iraqi forces, aside from firing a number of Scud missiles at Israel and Saudi Arabia and setting fire to hundreds of Kuwaiti oil wells, simply endured the rain of destruction that fell on them daily.

On February 23 Bush issued an ultimatum to Saddam: Pull out of Kuwait or face an invasion. When Saddam ignored the deadline, UN troops (most under U.S. command) attacked. Bush called the assault "Desert Storm." Between February 24 and February 27 they retook Kuwait, killing tens of thousands of Iraqis. Some 4,000 Iraqi tanks and enormous quantities of other military equipment were destroyed.

Bush then stopped the attack, and Saddam agreed to UN terms that included paying reparations to Kuwait, allowing UN inspectors to determine whether Iraq was developing atomic and biological weapons, and agreeing to keep its airplanes out of "no-fly" zones over Kurdish territory and other strategic areas. Polls indicated that about 90 percent of the American people approved both the president's management of the **Persian Gulf War** and his overall performance as chief executive. These were the highest presidential approval ratings ever recorded.

President Bush and most observers expected Saddam to be driven from power in disgrace by his own people. Indeed, Bush publicly urged the Iraqis to do so. The Kurds in northern Iraq and pro-Iranian Muslims in the south then took up arms, but Saddam used the remnants of his army to crush them. He also refused repeatedly to carry out the terms of the peace agreement, chiefly by hindering the UN inspections for weapons of mass destruction. This led critics to argue that Bush should not have stopped the fighting until Baghdad, the Iraqi capital, had been captured and Saddam's army destroyed.

Watch the Video *President Bush on the Gulf War* at www.myhistorylab.com

Deficits

The huge cost of the Persian Gulf War exacerbated the federal deficit. Candidate Bush had promised not to raise taxes, saying in a phrase he would later regret, "Read my lips: No new taxes." As president he recommitted himself to that objective; in fact he even proposed reducing the tax on capital gains. But like his conservative predecessor, Bush could not control the deficit. Congress obstinately resisted closing local military bases or cutting funding for favored defense contractors. Reducing nonmilitary expenditures, especially popular entitlement programs such as Medicare and Social Security, also proved nearly impossible.

The deficit for 1992 hit $290 billion. Bush had no choice but to join with Congress in raising the top income tax rate from 28 percent to 31 percent and levying higher taxes on gasoline, liquor, expensive automobiles, and certain other luxuries. This damaged his credibility and angered conservative Republicans. "Read my lips," critics muttered, "No more Bush."

Another drain on the federal treasury resulted from the demise of hundreds of federally insured savings and loan institutions (S&Ls). S&Ls had traditionally played an important role in nearly every community, and a secure if sleepy niche in the economy: home mortgages. In the 1980s Congress permitted S&Ls to enter the more lucrative but riskier business of commercial loans and stock investments. This attracted a swarm of aggressive investors who acquired S&Ls and invested company assets in high-yield but risky junk bonds and real estate deals.

In October 1987 the stock market crashed, rendering worthless the assets held by many of the S&Ls. Hundreds were plunged into bankruptcy. In 1988 Michael Milken, the junk bond "guru," was indicted on ninety-eight charges of fraud, stock manipulation, and insider trading. He pleaded guilty, agreed to pay $1.3 billion in compensation, and was sent to jail. Drexel Burnham Lambert, his investment firm, filed for bankruptcy. The junk bond market collapsed.

Because S&L deposits were insured by the federal government, taxpayers were forced to cover the losses. The reserve fund for such purposes—$5 billion—was quickly exhausted. In 1991 Congress allocated $70 billion to close the failing S&Ls, liquidate their assets, and pay off depositors. The Justice Department charged nearly a thousand people for criminal involvement in a mess that, according to most estimates, would eventually cost taxpayers $500 billion.

During the preceding two decades, the American nation, like the automobiles that stretched for blocks in line to buy gasoline during the oil embargo, had been running on empty. The federal government was deeply in debt. Corporations had exhausted their cash reserves. Workers lived in fear of the layoff or bank foreclosure notice. Gone were the fanciful expressions of an earlier era—long and wide-bodied chassis, roaring V-8 engines, sweeping tail fins, chromium grills like the jaws of a barracuda. Most cars had become simple boxes, trimmed with plastic, whose efficient four-cylinder engines thrummed steadily.

The nation's aspirations, like its cars, had become smaller, more sensible. Politicians muted their rhetoric, rarely issuing grandiose declarations of war against some intractable foe of humanity. Corporate executives spoke of "downsizing" firms rather than building them into empires. And the American people increasingly hunkered down in their own private spaces, which they locked up and wired with alarms.

Chapter Review

Milestones

1973	Israel, aided by United States, defeats Egypt and Syria
1973–1974	Arabs impose oil embargo
1974–1976	Gerald Ford serves as president after Nixon's resignation
1975	Vietnam War ends when South Vietnam falls
1976	Jimmy Carter is elected president
1978	Egypt and Israel sign Camp David Accords
1979	Jerry Falwell founds the Moral Majority
	Muslim militants seize U.S. Embassy in Tehran, Iran
	United States recognizes People's Republic of China
1980	Soviet troops invade Afghanistan
	U.S. rescue mission in Iran fails
	Ronald Reagan is elected president
1980s	Entrepreneurs' merger movement leads to huge corporate debt
1981	Iran releases U.S. hostages
	Reagan appoints Sandra Day O'Connor to Supreme Court
1981–1988	War persists between Iran and Iraq
1984	Reagan is reelected president
1985	Mikhail Gorbachev becomes premier of the Soviet Union
1986	Reagan secretly sells arms to Iran to finance Nicaraguan Contras
1988	Republican George H. W. Bush elected president
1989	Gorbachev allows Eastern European nations to establish independent democratic governments
1990	Iraq invades Kuwait
1991	UN forces, led by the United States, drive Iraqi forces from Kuwait
	Soviet Union is dissolved; Boris Yeltsin becomes president of Russia

Key Terms

Camp David Accords A 1978 peace treaty between Egypt and Israel, mediated by President Jimmy Carter, signed at Camp David, a presidential retreat near Washington, DC, *803*

Iran-Contra affair Scandal involving high officials in the Reagan administration accused of funding the Contra rebels in Nicaragua in violation of 1984 Congressional laws explicitly prohibiting such aid. The Contra funding came from the secret sale of arms to Iran, *813*

Iranian hostage crisis Protracted crisis that began in 1979 when Islamic militants seized the American embassy in Tehran, Iran, and held scores of its employees hostage. The militants had been enraged by American support for the deposed Shah of Iran. The crisis, which lasted over a year, contributed to President Jimmy Carter's defeat in his reelection campaign in 1980, *803*

Moral Majority A term associated with the organization by that name, founded in 1979 by the Reverend Jerry Falwell to combat "amoral liberals," drug abuse, "coddling" of criminals, homosexuality, communism, and abortion, *806*

Organization of Petroleum Exporting Countries (OPEC) A cartel of oil-producing nations in Asia, Africa, and Latin America that gained substantial power over the world economy in the mid- to late-1970s, *798*

Persian Gulf War The 1991 war following Iraq's takeover of Kuwait; the United States and a coalition of allies defeated the army of Iraqi leader Saddam Hussein but failed to drive him from power, *817*

Reaganomics A label pinned on President Ronald Reagan's policies of tax cuts, social welfare cuts, and increased military spending; it generated huge federal deficits, but also promoted the reorganization of large corporations, *805*

stagflation A term coined in the 1970s to describe the period's economic downturn and simultaneous deflation in prices, *801*

Strategic Defense Initiative (SDI) The concept of a space-based missile defense system—popularly known as "Star Wars," after the movie by that name—proposed by President Ronald Reagan in 1983. Controversial and costly, the concept was never fully realized, *807*

Review Questions

1. The introduction to this chapter suggests that cheap oil (and gas) has long been prominent in American politics. How did the oil shortage of the 1970s affect politics? What was its impact on the economy? In what sense was "stagflation" weird?

2. Did Carter realize his hopes for a foreign policy based on "constant decency"?

3. How did Reagan contribute to corporate restructuring? What was the impact of the merger movement on the American economy generally? What new industries emerged in the late 1980s and 1990s?

4. Why did the Soviet Union collapse? What role, if any, did Reagan play in its demise?

5. Why did George H. W. Bush go to war with Iraq? Why, having defeated the Iraqi army, didn't he seize Baghdad and remove Saddam Hussein from power?

PEARSON myhistorylab™ Connections

Reinforce what you learned in this chapter by studying the many documents, images, maps, review tools, and videos available at **www.myhistorylab.com**.

Read and Review

✓ Study and Review *Chapter 30*

••• Read the Document Carter, *Crisis of Confidence (1979)*, p. 801

••• Read the Document Reagan, *Air Traffic Controllers' Strike (1981)*, p. 808

••• Read the Document Paul Craig Roberts, *The Supply-Side Revolution (1984)*, p. 808

••• Read the Document Reagan, *Support for the Contras (1984)*, p. 813

Research and Explore

◉ Watch the Video *Ford Presidential Campaign Ad: Feeling Good About America*, p. 800

◉ Watch the Video *Reagan Presidential Campaign Ad: A Bear in the Woods*, p. 805

◉ Watch the Video *Ronald Reagan on the Wisdom of the Tax Cut*, p. 808

◉ Watch the Video *President Bush on the Gulf War*, p. 817

((•• Hear the Audio

Hear the audio file for Chapter 30 at
www.myhistorylab.com.

Why do you go to college?

Every year since 1966, the UCLA School of Education has surveyed nearly a quarter of a million first-year college students. A comparison of the results suggests that in some ways, the college-aged Boomers of the late 1960s were not much different from Millennials in 2009. Then as now, the great majority regarded themselves as "middle-of-the-road" in politics. Both groups also over-estimated their academic worth: More than two-thirds considered themselves to be among the top 10 percent of their peers academically.

But the past forty years have witnessed a widening gulf between Boomers (born from 1946 to 1964) and

Millennials (born after 1980). One example relates to life goals. According to the survey, when Boomers were in their freshman year of college, about three-fourths believed that "acquiring a meaningful philoso-phy of life" was "essential" or "very important." Only a third attached similar importance to "being well off financially." But forty years later the percentages had been nearly reversed. Over three-fourths of the Millennials entering college in 2009 believed that "being well off financially" was "essential" or "very important" while only a third thought it equally important to acquire "a meaningful philosophy of

From Boomers to Millennials 31

CONTENTS

((•—[Hear the Audio **Chapter 31 at www.myhistorylab.com**

■ To Millennials, the good life was commonly depicted in material terms: a big house with an expensive automobile, much as shown in this 2006 photograph. But the Age of Bling may have ended two years later, when the economy tanked and college graduates confronted a more austere future.

life." (The figures do not add up to 100 percent because respondents could give opinions for more than one statement.) Millennials are far more likely to seek wealth, while Boomers were more likely to seek "a meaningful philosophy of life."

One explanation is that Boomers came of age during a period of unprecedented economic growth. They were free to ponder the meaning of life because they rarely worried about finding a decent job. They could imagine brave new worlds of gender revolution and institutional transformation, of liberal treatment of criminals and immigrants, of a broader reform of society as a whole.

But the protracted recession after 1973 changed the way people looked at things. An infusion of new peoples, a liberalization of attitudes, and a transformation of institutions all suggested that society was becoming unhinged. A period of retrenchment was in order. Marriage and the family were to be preserved in familiar forms; tougher laws must be passed and criminals punished.

Through it all, the sphere of public life contracted; private concerns—such as making money—took precedence over grand social schemes. And public spaces receded as people retreated to their cars and homes, where they could interact with Facebook friends and virtual realities. ■

The New Immigration

A Pew poll in 2008 unearthed another major attitudinal difference between Boomers and Millennials. When asked whether immigrants strengthened the country with their hard work and talent, or burdened it because they took jobs, housing, and healthcare, the Boomers overwhelmingly (50 percent to 30 percent) regarded immigrants as a burden, while Millennials overwhelmingly (58 percent to 32 percent) thought immigrants strengthened the country. One reason for the attitudinal change is that a far higher proportion of Millennials are themselves immigrants or the children of immigrants.

Immigration is a global phenomenon that has transformed the United States in the past forty years. But while it is possible—and even necessary—to consider the subject in terms of large statistical trends,

Dolores Huerta and César Chávez, leaders of the United Farm Workers, discuss their 1968 strike of grape pickers. They are framed by photographs of Robert Kennedy, campaigning for the Democratic nomination for president, and Mohandas Gandhi, leader of the non-violent protest movement that won independence for India in 1947.

every county and city has its particular immigration narrative. Indeed, as countless population streams have for centuries flowed into that heaving ocean of peoples that is the United States, every family's immigrant history is irreducibly unique, as the American Lives essay about "Barack Obama" demonstrates (see pp. 824–825).

Since 1924, immigration to the United States had been governed by a quota system that ensured that the distribution of new immigrants mirrored the nation's existing ethnic patterns (see Chapter 24, p. 640). But the Immigration Act of 1965 eliminated the old system. It instead gave preference to immigrants with specialized job skills and education, and it allowed family members to rejoin those who had immigrated earlier. In 1986, Congress offered amnesty to illegal immigrants who had long lived in the United States and penalized employers who hired illegal immigrants in the future. Many persons legalized their status under the new law, but the influx of illegal immigrants continued. Together, these laws enabled more than 25 million to immigrate to the United States from 1970 to 2000.

Asians, many of whom possessed skills in high-tech fields, benefited most from the abandonment of the "national origins" system. Of the 9 million Asians who immigrated to the United States during these years, most were from China, South Korea, India, Pakistan, and the Philippines. Following the defeat of South Vietnam and the Khmer Rouge takeover over Cambodia, some 700,000 South Vietnamese and Cambodians received refugee status.

From 1970 to 2000 the largest number of immigrants were Latinos, sometimes called Hispanics (16 million). By 2000, the Latino population of the United States (35 million) for the first time exceeded African Americans (34 million). The overwhelming majority of these Spanish-speaking immigrants were Chicanos—Mexican Americans who settled in the Southwest. (Of the nation's 35 million Hispanics, 11 million lived in California, and nearly 7 million in Texas; over 42 percent of the population of New Mexico was Latino.) In addition, several million Puerto Ricans came to the mainland United States, most of whom settled in well-established Puerto Rican neighborhoods in northeastern cities. About a million Cuban immigrants arrived in Florida during these years.

But immigration was far more complex than the aggregate data suggest. Dearborn, Michigan, headquarters of the Ford Motor Company, is in many ways the prototypical American city. Yet nearly a third of its 100,000 residents are Arab-speaking immigrants from Lebanon, Iraq, Yemen, and Palestine.

Lowell, Massachusetts, whose textile mills employed young women from New England farms during the 1820s and 1830s, is now home to some 20,000 Cambodians, refugees from the regime of Pol Pot, a communist dictator who killed some 2 million of his own people.

About 10,000 Sudanese, refugees from a genocidal war in Africa, have flocked to Omaha, Nebraska, to work in its meatpacking plants. Nearly as many Bosnians, refugees from a civil war in the Balkans, have settled in Boise, Idaho.

Nearly every community had its own immigrant narrative, but some patterns were broadly applicable. As whites left for the suburbs and businesses relocated to the malls, immigrants moved into vacated city housing and established businesses downtown. In Los Angeles, for example, Korea Town, Japan Town, the Latino barrio, and South Central districts sprouted almost overnight.

In many communities, the new immigrants became a significant political force. Latinos elected mayors in Los Angeles, Miami, Denver, and San Antonio. César Chávez, a pivotal figure in the history of Mexican Americans (Chicanos), succeeded in bringing tens of thousands of Mexicans into his United Farm Workers union. In a series of well-publicized strikes and boycotts, Chávez and the UFW forced wage concessions from hundreds of growers in California, Texas, and the Southwest.

But the infusion of immigrants generated concern. In 1992 Patrick Buchanan, campaigning for the Republican nomination for president, warned that the migration of "millions of illegal aliens a year" from Mexico constituted "the greatest invasion" the nation had ever witnessed. By then, about one-third of the Chicanos in the United States had arrived without valid visas, usually by slipping across the long U.S. border with Mexico. Of particular concern was the fact that the Latino poverty rate—which hovered around 10 percent—was twice the national average. In 1994 California passed Proposition 187, which made illegal immigrants ("undocumented aliens") ineligible for social services, public education, and nonemergency medical services. (The U.S. Supreme Court struck the law down as an infringement of federal powers. In 2001 the Supreme Court ruled that immigrants were entitled to all the protections the Constitution afforded citizens.)

Conservatives were not alone in opposing illegal immigration. Loose immigration policies suppressed wage rates; often illegal immigrants were recruited as strike breakers. Many labor leaders blamed the post-1965 influx of immigrants for the decline in union memberships. Chávez argued that illegal immigration

AMERICAN LIVES
Barack Obama

Not many thirty-three-year-olds write a memoir. But Barack Obama, who intended to write a book on race relations, instead explored the meaning of his young life.

The facts were clear enough. He was born on August 4, 1961, in Honolulu, Hawaii. His mother was Stanley (Ann) Dunham, whom a friend described as "Kansas white." His father, Barack Obama, Sr., was a Luo tribesman from Nyanza Province, Kenya who had come to the University of Hawaii on a program to educate potential leaders of newly independent African nations. The couple had met in a Russian-language course at the university the previous year. Within a few months, Dunham was pregnant. Obama told her that he had been married in Kenya but had since divorced. Ann and Obama married in February, 1961. She was eighteen when she had Barack, Jr.

Her husband, however, had lied. Not only was he still married to a Kenyan, but he had one son by her with another

Stanley (Ann) Dunham with her son, Barack Obama, age two.

on the way. In 1962, after graduating from Hawaii, he went to Harvard to pursue a graduate degree, leaving Ann and their son in Hawaii. When she went to visit him at Harvard, she brought the infant along. The trip went badly. Her husband had not told his friends about her or his wife in Kenya. Ann returned to Hawaii; it would be another ten years before she or her son saw his father again.

Ann and her son moved into her parents' two-bedroom apartment in Honolulu. She returned to college and her parents often took care of the boy, whom everyone called Barry. Several years later Ann divorced Obama—by then he had taken yet another wife—and she married an Indonesian geologist at the University of Hawaii. In 1967, Ann, her new husband and six-year-old Barry moved to the outskirts of Jakarta, Indonesia, where the family lived in a stucco house on a dirt lane. Chickens and ducks ran around the backyard and two crocodiles lived in a fenced-in pond on the property. Obama's mother had always encouraged her son to adapt to different peoples, but soon her thinking shifted. Now she realized the vast chasm separating the prospects of young people who grew up in Indonesia compared to the United States.

She enrolled in a correspondence course for elementary school children in the United States. At four each morning, she awakened Barry and together they worked through the materials. After he had completed fourth grade in Jakarta, she sent him to Honolulu to live with her parents, promising to follow within a year.

Barry's grandfather arranged for the boy to attend the elite Punahou Academy. He was one of the few African Americans in the school. When some boys teased him about living in the jungle, he invented stories about how his father was a warrior and an African prince. Obama nearly persuaded himself that this fiction was true.

When his father showed up in Honolulu for a month-long visit, Barry was appalled. What would he tell his friends? But he was also confused. His long-absent father proceeded to boss Ann and her parents and demanded that Barry work harder in school. When Barry's teacher invited his father to give a lecture on Africa, Barry was mortified. But his father's talk was smooth and gripping. Barry's friends were impressed. His father left soon afterwards. Barry never saw him again.

As a teenager, Barry excelled at basketball; his senior year, he was on the Punahou team that won the state championship. He also wrote poetry. But he lacked motivation and managed only a B– average as a senior. He spent most of his time hanging out with slacker friends. Privately, he brooded over his father's estrangement. He coped with doubts about himself by using marijuana, booze, and cocaine. When one of his friends was busted for drug possession, Obama knew it could have been him.

824

Obama at Occidental College in 1980.

His first two years at Occidental College in California were more of the same. He did little work. He was nevertheless popular with nearly everyone, navigating among different social groups with ease. "He was a hot, nice, everything-going-for-him dude," one friend recalled. "You couldn't help but like him." But issues of race weighed upon him and his black friends. After some of them teased him for using the name Barry, he began to ask people to call him Barack.

After his sophomore year, Obama transferred to Columbia University in New York. Denied campus housing as a transfer student, he lived in cheap apartments in Harlem. Then something changed. He studied, ran three miles a day, often fasted on Sundays, gave up drinking and drugs (cigarettes proved more difficult), and kept a journal to record his thoughts and poetry.

Late in the fall of his senior year, he received a phone call from Africa. His father was dead. He had been drunk and drove his car into the stump of a gum tree. Even in death, his father remained a mystery to Obama.

Obama later dreamt that he was on a long bus ride that ended up at a jail. He went in and saw his father in a cell, naked but for a cloth around his waist. As Obama entered the cell, his father teased him for being so thin. Obama embraced him and wept. His father then said that he had always loved his son. Barack suggested that his father accompany him from jail; but his father replied that it would be best if the boy left alone.

When Obama awakened, he was crying.

Perhaps young Barack had at last reconciled with his absent father, enabling him to march toward his destiny with the singular purposefulness that became his trademark. Or

perhaps he sensed that he would have to create a meaningful life through achievement of his own.

Whatever the reason, he did achieve. In 1985, after graduating from Columbia, he took a job as a community organizer in Chicago and established job training programs in schools, fought to remove asbestos in housing projects, and campaigned against drug dealers. Then he was admitted to Harvard Law School, named to the *Harvard Law Review*, and elected its president, the first black to hold this prestigious position. Afterwards he returned to Chicago to write a book; it became *Dreams from My Father* (1995), a memoir from which much of this account is taken. (The publisher has refused permission for any quotes from that book to appear in this one.) He taught constitutional law at the University of Chicago while working for a black law firm with strong connections to Chicago politics. In 1996 he ran for the Illinois state legislature and won. It was the beginning of a meteoric ascent in American politics that culminated in Obama's election as president in 2008.

Questions for Discussion

- President Barack Obama identifies himself as black. Do you agree? What is the definition of race in the contemporary United States?

- What explains Obama's transition from being an indifferent student in high school and college to a disciplined achiever?

undermined his efforts to organize Chicano farm-workers. In 1973 the UFW provided manpower for a "wet line" along the United States border to block illegal immigration from Mexico.

In *Who Are We?* (2004), Harvard political scientist Samuel P. Huntington warned that the massive infusion of Latinos could "divide the United States into two peoples, two cultures, and two languages." Population projections showed that by 2050 whites might become a minority. But Huntington's dichotomy was too simple. Although immigrant groups often lived in distinct neighborhoods—Mexicans on one block and Hondurans on the next—they increasingly reached across national boundaries. Local restaurants offered wide assortments of ethnic fares, outdoor festivals attracted all peoples, and popular music featured a boggling fusion of styles. Most important, immigrants increasingly ceased to think of themselves as belonging to a particular ethnic group. In 2000, nearly 7 million Americans identified themselves as "multiracial." And a rising generation of Millennials regarded immigrants as a national asset rather than a burden.

•••⎯[Read the **Document** *Illegal Immigration Reform and Immigrant Responsibility Act of 1996* at **www.myhistorylab.com**

👁⎯[See the **Map** *Immigration to the U.S., 1945–1990* at **www.myhistorylab.com**

•••⎯[Read the **Document** *LBJ Immigration Act of 1975* at **www.myhistorylab.com**

The Emergence of Modern Feminism

"Boomers"—from the phrase "baby boom"—got that name because so many of their generation were born after World War II, when returning soldiers were reunited with their girlfriends and wives, and when ample job opportunities made it easier to raise families. Boomers' parents married earlier and had children sooner after marriage than at any other time in the twentieth century. By the late 1950s, the birthrate of the United States approached that of teeming India.

A decisive force in the early lives of Boomers was Dr. Benjamin Spock's *Common Sense Guide to Baby and Child Care.* First published in 1946, Spock's manual sold 24 million copies during the next quarter century. Spock's book guided young parents through the common medical crises of parenthood—ear infections, colic, chickenpox—and also counseled them on psychological issues. A mother's most important job, Spock insisted, was to shore up her children's sense of self by providing continuous support and affection. Women who worked outside the home necessarily "neglected" their children. The child who was "mildly neglected," Spock added, was apt to grow up "mildly disturbed." Psychologists such as Marynia Farnham added that a woman's reproductive system influenced her mental processes: Women were naturally attuned to nurturing and childcare. Those women who entered the aggressive "men's world" of work would be at odds with their own psychological inclinations.

Television picked up on this theme and hammered away at it each week in sitcoms such as Robert Young's ironically titled *Father Knows Best* (1954–1962) and Jackie Gleason's equally ironic take on working-class marriage, *The Honeymooners* (1953–1962). Repeatedly irascible or befuddled patriarchs blundered into family matters, only to be gently eased out of harm's way by their understanding and psychologically savvy wives. Even Lucille Ball and Vivian Vance, the screwball housewives in the popular sitcom *I Love Lucy* (1952–1957), had a better grasp of family dynamics than their stumble-bum husbands.

But the reality of the postwar woman was more complicated. Economic expansion generated many new jobs, especially in the burgeoning corporate bureaucracies and retail stores. Women were in high demand because they would work for lower wages than men. Many took jobs, ignoring Spock and cultural conventions. In 1940, only one in four civilian employees was female, one-third of them married. Three decades later, four in ten paid employees were

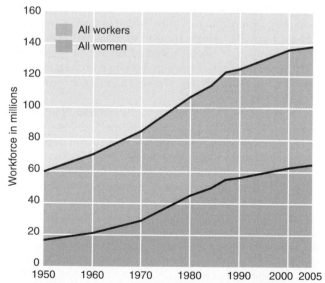

Paid Workforce, 1950–2005, by Gender The number (and percentage) of wage-earning women increased rapidly after 1960. In 1950, for example, fewer than one-third of the paid work force consisted of women; by 2006, the proportion had increased to nearly half.

women, two-thirds of them married. By 1970 perhaps 20 million women—after returning home from work, fixing dinner, putting the children to bed, and doing a load of laundry—collapsed in front of the television set and watched domestic heroines such as Donna Reed vacuuming the house in high heels and pearls, making clothes and cakes from scratch, soothing the fragile psyches of her husband and children, and otherwise living a fantasy that accorded with the views of Spock and others.

When they returned to the office, store, or factory the next day, however, such women were acutely aware of the fact that men in similar jobs were paid more and had better opportunities for advancement. Women noticed, too, that minorities had improved their situations by fighting publicly. Increasingly activists for women's rights adopted similar strategies; they were the founders of the modern women's liberation movement.

One of its leaders was Betty Friedan, an activist journalist in the labor movement during the 1930s and 1940s who shifted to gender issues in later decades. In *The Feminine Mystique* (1963), Friedan argued that advertisers, popular magazines, and other "authorities" brainwashed women into thinking that they could thrive only at home. They were wrong, Friedan insisted. According to her survey of her classmates at Smith College, many housewives were troubled with vague but persistent feelings of anger and discomfort. "The only way for a woman . . . to know herself as a person is by creative work of her own," she wrote. A "problem that had no name" was stifling women's potential.

The Feminine Mystique provided what later came to be known as "consciousness raising" for thousands of women. Over a million copies were quickly sold. Friedan was deluged by hundreds of letters from women who had thought that their unease and depression despite their "happy" family life were both unique and unreasonable. Many now determined to expand their horizons by taking jobs or resuming their education.

Friedan had assumed that if able women acted with determination, employers would recognize their abilities and stop discriminating against them. As feminists were outlining plans to strengthen women's claims to fair treatment in the workplace, they won an unexpected victory. In 1964, during a debate on whether to ban racial discrimination in employment, Virginia Senator Howard Smith, seeking to scuttle the law, proposed that women also be protected from discrimination in hiring and promotion. Several congresswomen immediately endorsed the idea and proposed an amendment to

that effect. This became Title VII of the Civil Rights Act of 1964.

In 1966 Friedan and other feminists founded the **National Organization for Women (NOW)**. "The time has come for a new movement toward true equality for all women in America and toward a fully equal partnership of the sexes," the leaders announced. "The silken curtain of prejudice and discrimination against women" in government, industry, the professions, religion, education, "and every other field of importance" must be drawn back. In 1967 NOW came out for an equal rights amendment to the Constitution, for changes in the divorce laws, and for the legalization of abortion, the right of "control of one's body."

The **Equal Rights Amendment (ERA)**, which would make it unconstitutional to deny equal rights "on account of sex," had been proposed by the National Woman's party in 1923; by the late 1930s it appeared headed for adoption by Congress. But Eleanor Roosevelt and other women's groups killed the amendment, fearing it would rescind laws that protected poor women and their children. By the late 1960s, however, NOW's campaign for the ERA was yielding dividends. In 1971 the House of Representatives approved the ERA and the Senate followed the next year. By the end of 1972, twenty-two states had raced to go on record to ratify the amendment: What politician could prudently oppose equal rights for women? At the outset of 1973, only sixteen more states needed to ratify ERA before it was added to the Constitution.

Feminist activists soon turned to another major goal: legalization of abortion. The Constitution made no reference to abortion. But during the nineteenth century botched surgical abortions that killed many women prompted the American Medical Association to call for the "general suppression" of the practice. By 1900, every state except Kentucky had passed antiabortion laws. Most states granted exceptions when the woman had been impregnated by rape or incest or when a doctor thought it necessary to save the woman's life. In 1967, for example, Governor Reagan of California, an opponent of abortion, signed a law allowing doctors to perform abortions if childbirth would "gravely impair the physical or mental health of the mother." The number of legal abortions in California increased from 5,018 in 1968 to more than 100,000 by 1972.

In 1970, however, feminist activists persuaded the Hawaii legislature to repeal its criminal abortion statute, the first state to do so. Later that year, another battle was waged in New York. It pitted feminists, liberals, and the medical establishment against

The National Organization for Women holds a rally in Illinois for the Equal Rights Amendment. In 1982, as the deadline for ratification was about to expire, a majority in the Illinois legislature favored the ERA but not by a sufficient margin. The defeat in Illinois meant that the ERA was dead.

conservatives and the Roman Catholic Church. The state assembly repealed its antiabortion law by a single vote. Feminists regarded this as a crucial but sobering victory. If a liberal state such as New York had barely mustered a majority in favor of abortion rights, how long would it take for the campaign to prevail elsewhere?

View the Image *Jimmy Carter Signs the House of Representative Resolution for the Equal Rights Amendment, 1972* at **www.myhistorylab.com**

Roe v. Wade

The question soon became moot; the United States Supreme Court took the decision out of the hands of state legislatures. A key factor was a new concept in constitutional law: the "right to privacy." In the nineteenth century, the Catholic Church had persuaded many state legislatures to ban dissemination of information on contraceptives and birth control.

Connecticut was one such state. But in 1961 Estelle Griswold, head of Planned Parenthood in Connecticut, opened a birth control clinic to challenge the law. In the case of *Griswold v. Connecticut*, the Supreme Court, headed by Earl Warren, struck down the Connecticut statute, contending that it violated couples' "right to privacy." While conceding that no such term appeared in the Constitution, the Court held that various other constitutional provisions—such as freedom of speech and press and prohibitions against unreasonable searches—together provided an "umbrella" of privacy-related rights. This "right to privacy" protected people from unwarranted intrusions by the state.

Then, in 1969, Norma McCorvey asked her doctor for an abortion. She was unmarried, unemployed, twenty-five years old, and pregnant. Her doctor refused. Abortion, he told her, was illegal in Texas unless performed to save the woman's life. McCorvey's

A woman endorses *Roe v. Wade* in New York in 2003, the thirtieth anniversary of the ruling.

lawyer encouraged her to challenge the law. She consented, using the pseudonym "Jane Roe," and her lawyer filed suit against Henry Wade, the Dallas County prosecutor.

In 1973, after McCorvey had the baby, the U.S. Supreme Court rendered a decision in *Roe v. Wade*. Rejecting any "single" theory of life, the justices maintained that a fetus did not have a "right to life" until the final three months of pregnancy, when it could likely survive without the mother. Until then, the mother's right to "privacy" took precedence. The state could not prevent a woman from having an abortion during the first six months of pregnancy. Most abortions were no longer illegal. A major goal of the feminists had been achieved almost overnight.

The *Roe v. Wade* decision resulted in a rapid expansion of abortion facilities. From 1973 to 1980, the number of abortions performed annually increased from 745,000 to 1.5 million. Abortion had become the nation's most common surgical procedure. The new feminist movement had prevailed on a number of issues that would have been unthinkable a decade earlier.

Read the **Document** *Roe v. Wade (January 22, 1973)* at **www.myhistorylab.com**

Conservative Counterattack

But the *Roe v. Wade* decision also energized a grass-roots conservative movement against abortion, often supported by the Catholic Church, the Mormons, and Protestant groups such as Falwell's Moral Majority (see Chapter 30, pp. 806–807). The right-to-life movement endorsed the presidential campaigns of Ronald Reagan and George H. W. Bush, whose Supreme Court appointments generally favored the right-to-life position. In *Webster v. Reproductive Health Services* (1989) and *Planned Parenthood of*

State Laws on Abortion prior to *Roe v. Wade* (1973) Prior to *Roe v. Wade*, only Hawaii, Alaska, and New York had legalized abortion. Louisiana, Pennsylvania, and New Hampshire prohibited all abortions, while every other state allowed abortions only in cases of rape or incest or to preserve the life of the woman.

Abortion Rates by State, 2006 In 2006, 22 percent of all pregnancies were terminated by abortion, while another 15 percent miscarried. The highest abortion rate was in the District of Columbia, where half of all pregnancies were aborted; this was followed by New York (33 percent), New Jersey (31 percent), and Maryland (30 percent). The states with the lowest abortion rates were Utah (7 percent) and South Dakota (9 percent).

Phyllis Schlafly drew much of her support from working-class women who were left vulnerable by the recession after 1973.

Southeastern Pennsylvania v. Casey (1992), the Supreme Court allowed states to impose certain conditions, such as tests of viability and waiting periods, before abortions could be performed. But well into the twenty-first century, *Roe v. Wade* remained the law of the land.

Conservatives were more successful in contesting the ERA, which seemed headed to prompt ratification. In 1973 Phyllis Schlafly, a former vice president of the National Federation of Republican Women and publisher of a conservative newsletter, spearheaded a nationwide campaign against ratification of the ERA. She argued that it would subject young women to the military draft, deprive divorced women of alimony and child custody, and make married women legally responsible for providing 50 percent of household income. As the recession after 1973 dragged the economy down, Schlafly's words struck a responsive chord among anxious housewives and low-wage-earning women who doubted they could survive the recessionary economy on their own. The ratification campaign

Legend:
- States ratifying ERA 1972
- States ratifying ERA 1973
- States ratifying ERA 1974–77
- States ratifying ERA 1972, later rescinding ERA
- States unratified
- ALASKA
- HAWAII

Failure of the Equal Rights Amendment, 1972–1982 The states that failed to ratify ERA were mostly in the South and the predominantly Mormon Rockies. The states that NOW regarded as pivotal were Illinois, North Carolina, and Virginia.

lost momentum and stalled, falling just three states short. By 1980, the ERA was dead.[1]

The Rise of Gay and Lesbian Rights

The rhetoric of "minority rights" and the example of activists in other movements during the 1960s encouraged gay rights activists to demand that society cease harassing and discriminating against *them*. In 1969, New York City police raided the Stonewall Inn, a popular gay bar in Greenwich Village and arrested the occupants—most of them gays—for "solicitation" of illegal sexual acts. The crowd outside threw rocks and bottles and the police were forced to retreat. The Stonewall riot lasted for several days and marked a turning point

in the history of gays and lesbians. No longer would gays in Greenwich Village remain "in the closet"—hidden from view. Public advocacy of their cause strengthened it immeasurably.

As gay and lesbian relationships became the subject of public discussion rather than private innuendo, gay activists embarked on numerous campaigns to eliminate discrimination against gays. Gay psychiatrists challenged the American Psychiatric Association's longstanding judgment that homosexuality was a treatable mental illness. In 1973 the association's board of directors agreed to remove homosexuality from the standard manual of psychiatric disorders. Disgruntled traditionalists challenged the decision and forced the directors to put the matter up for a vote of the entire membership. In 1974 the members upheld the directors. The next year the American Psychological Association concurred. Homosexuality was not a mental illness.

Gay and lesbian activists also filed suits to eliminate discrimination against gays in education, housing, education, and employment. In response to such

---

[1]Various Supreme Court decisions, such as *Reed v. Reed* (1971), struck down laws that failed to provide "equal protection" of men and women or applied arbitrary standards in making legal distinctions between the rights of men and women.

Harvey Milk was the first openly gay candidate to be elected to office in California.

pressures, the U.S. Civil Service Commission rescinded its ban on hiring homosexuals. Now gays chose to run openly for public office. In 1977, Harvey Milk, the first openly gay man to run for office in California, was elected supervisor in San Francisco. The next year he led the fight against a California law that would fire gay teachers. Former California governor Ronald Reagan opposed the bill as a violation of human rights, as did President Jimmy Carter; the proposition was defeated by a million votes. Three weeks later Milk was assassinated; he became a martyr to the gay rights movement (Sean Penn played the starring role in *Milk* [2008], a sympathetic account of the activist's life.)

••◦—Read the **Document** *The Gay Liberation Front, Come Out (1970)* at **www.myhistorylab.com**

AIDS

But by the late 1970s, as gays were openly acknowledging and celebrating their sexual identity, many were being struck down by a lethal new disease. World health officials had spotted the outbreak of yet another viral epidemic in central Africa; but no one noticed that this virus had mutated into a more lethal strain and was spreading to Europe and North America. On June 5, 1981, the Centers for Disease Control (CDC) alerted American health officials to an outbreak of a rare bacterial infection in Los Angeles. What made the outbreak distinctive was that this particular infection, usually found in infants or older people with fragile immune systems, had struck five healthy young men. All were homosexuals. Within months, all died.

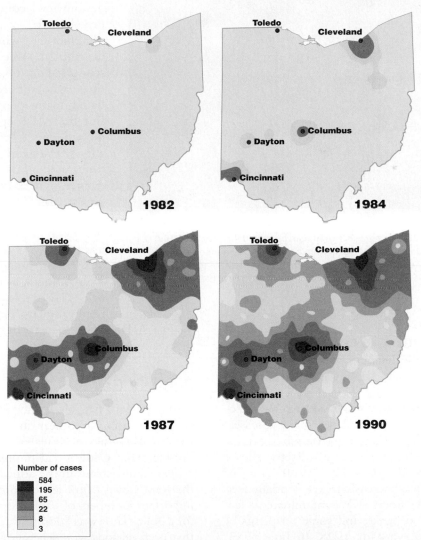

Number of cases

584
195
65
22
8
3

The Spread of AIDS in Ohio, 1982–1990 AIDS first appeared in large cities, such as Cleveland (1982 map), where gays could mix more anonymously. By 1984, AIDS had spread to every major city in Ohio; thereafter, it dispersed through much of the state.

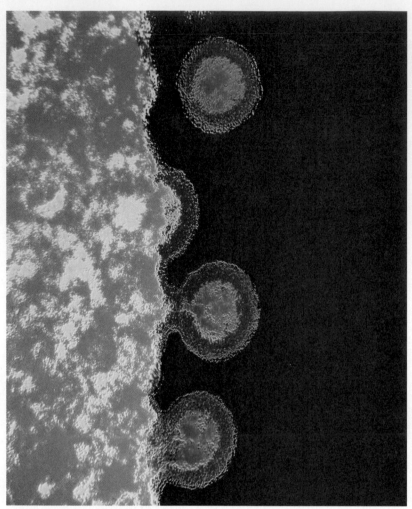

In this electron microscopic photograph, two human immunodeficiency virus (HIV) cells, in different stages of budding, are emerging from an infected T-lymphocyte human blood cell (pink). The HIV cell that has almost broken free includes RNA (green—the cell's genetic code) and it will reinfect other T-cells. T-cells are part of the body's immune system.

Not until 1985, when the square-jawed romantic actor Rock Hudson confirmed that he was dying of AIDS, did the subject command widespread public attention. President Reagan, an old friend of Hudson's, publicly acknowledged that the disease constituted a grave health crisis. Congress approved Reagan's call for a substantial increase in AIDS funding. But Reagan's appeal was belated and insufficient. By then, nearly 21,000 Americans had died; by 1999, the total number of AIDS-related deaths approached 400,000.

The AIDS epidemic affected public policy and private behavior. A nationwide educational campaign urged "safe" sex, especially the use of condoms, which by 1990 were distributed free in many high schools. Fear of the disease, and of those who suffered from it, exacerbated many people's homophobia. But the AIDS epidemic also forced most people to confront homosexuality directly and perhaps for the first time, and thus contributed to a deeper understanding of the complexity of human nature. After Hudson's revelation, for example, the *New York Times* commenced using "gay" and "lesbian," the terms then preferred by the people so identified, instead of "homosexual." Gay and lesbian organizations, the vanguard in the initial war against AIDS, continued to fight for social acceptance and legal rights.

By 1982 the CDC called this new disease **acquired immunodeficiency syndrome (AIDS)**. The CDC learned that AIDS was caused by the **human immunodeficiency virus (HIV)**, a lethal virus that destroys the body's defenses against infection, making victims susceptible to many diseases. HIV spreads when an infected person's body fluids come in contact with someone else's. By the end of 1982, the CDC had documented 900 cases of AIDS; the disease was increasing exponentially (see the maps on p. 833). Soon HIV contaminated a few of the nation's blood banks, and some recipients of transfusions came down with AIDS. In June 1983, when the federal budget approached $1 trillion, Congress finally voted $12 million for AIDS research and treatment.

Publicly Gay

Although gays had always served in the military—Milk had been an officer in the navy during the Korean War—they were technically banned. In 1992 President Bill Clinton had promised to end the ban on gays and lesbians in the armed services, but when the Joint Chiefs of the armed forces and a number of important members of Congress objected, he settled for a policy known as "don't ask, don't tell," meaning that such persons would be allowed to enlist only if they did not openly proclaim their sexual preferences. In 2010 Congress voted to openly admit gays and lesbians to the armed forces.

In 2004, San Francisco granted the first same-sex marriage license to Phyllis Lyon, 79, and Del Martin, 83, longtime activists. Because California did not allow same-sex marriages, San Francisco officials explained that theirs was an act of "civil disobedience."

acceptance of same-sex marriage as essential for wider acceptance. They noted that gay and lesbian couples formed bonds that were as close and loving as those of heterosexual couples. Why, gay and lesbian couples asked, should they not be allowed to adopt children or receive the legal protections and benefits of marriage? Conservative groups argued that religious texts and moral traditions had defined marriage as heterosexual. "Any sex outside of the marriage bond between a man and a woman is violating God's law," Jerry Falwell declared. In 2006 conservatives, backed by President George W. Bush, proposed an amendment to the Constitution that would define marriage as "a union between a man and a woman." The measure fell just short of passage in the Senate.

Another long-term objective was same-sex marriage. Some gay and lesbian leaders disagreed; Milk, for example, maintained that gay liberation entailed breaking free from heterosexual conventions, including marriage. But other activists regarded

In 2000 Vermont became the first state to recognize same-sex civil unions, providing gay and lesbian couples with some of the legal rights of marriage. In

Table 31.1 Gender Activist Victories and Conservative Responses

Year	Activist Victory	Consequence	Conservative Response (after 1972)
1964	Title VII, Civil Rights Act of 1964	Prohibited employers from discriminating on account of sex; enforced by federal government	
1965	*Griswold v. Connecticut*	Supreme Court asserted a "right to privacy" to allow dissemination of information on birth control	
1972	Equal Rights Amendment (ERA) approved by Congress	Extended the equal rights protections of Fourteenth Amendment to women	Phyllis Schlafly inaugurated "Stop ERA" campaign (1973), which blocked ratification
1973	*Roe v. Wade*	Supreme Court legalized most abortions	Jerry Falwell's Moral Majority founded; helped elect Ronald Reagan president (1980); named more conservative Supreme Court justices
2000	Vermont recognized same-sex unions	Paved way for a half-dozen states to approve same-sex marriage	George W. Bush-backed proposed constitutional amendment to limit marriage to heterosexuals narrowly defeated in Senate (2006)

2004 Massachusetts was the first state to recognize same-sex marriage; within the next five years, a half dozen states passed similar laws. When Washington, DC approved a same-sex marriage law, the Catholic Archdiocese of Washington, DC protested the decision by revising health care benefits of its agencies to avoid covering same-sex couples. But by 2010, according to most opinion polls, a solid majority of Americans favored same-sex marriage. And by a hefty margin, Millennials were far more likely to endorse same-sex marriage than any other age group, including Boomers.

Crime and Punishment

Civil rights protesters who intentionally violated laws rather than work within the law to change it; feminists who flouted conventional gender roles and asserted a right to abortion; gays and lesbians who claimed a right to serve openly in the military and enter into same-sex marriages—all were evidence, at least in the opinion of some, that the nation had lost its moral bearings. Such misgivings had spiked in the late 1960s, as antiwar protests closed down college campuses and race riots ravaged cities. Violent crime increased. Many called for restoration of "law and order." The phrase had been used repeatedly by Nixon and Agnew, whose own troubles with the law caused the phrase to temporarily slip from view. But during the 1970s and 1980s conservative activists, borrowing strategies from activist movements on the left, succeeded in implementing many of the goals of the "law and order" movement. They elected officials who passed tougher laws, hired more police, and built additional prisons.

The shift toward capital punishment was symptomatic. During the 1960s only a handful of criminals were executed. When the Supreme Court ruled

Narcotics policemen in Bridgeport, Connecticut, arrest a suspect for selling crack near housing projects in 1994.

in 1972 in the *Furman* decision that jury-imposed capital punishment was racially biased and thus unconstitutional, the matter seemed moot: No criminal had been executed since 1967. The practice simply had fallen from favor. But in response to the conservative demand for tough legislation against criminals, legislators rewrote capital punishment statutes in light of the *Furman* decision, depriving juries of discretion in sentencing. The Supreme Court upheld these laws and capital punishment resumed in 1976. Since then, over a thousand convicts have been executed.

Increasingly conservative state legislatures imposed tougher sentences and made it more difficult for prisoners to obtain parole. In 1973 New York State passed laws that mandated harsh sentences for repeat drug offenders. In 1977 California replaced its parole system with mandatory sentencing, which denied convicts the prospect of early release. Ten other states adopted similar parole restrictions. Nationwide, the proportion of convicts serving long, mandatory sentences increased sharply.

Another manifestation of the crackdown on crime was the increase in the nation's prison population. In 1973 the nation's prisons—state and federal—held about 200,000 convicts. By 1990 the number of prisoners exceeded 750,000, and by 2004, 2 million. This required the construction of a 1,000-bed prison every week. In 1995, for the first time, states spent more on prisons than on higher education. By 2010, the United States incarcerated more people than any country in the world, except perhaps communist China, which did not disclose such information.

Read the **Document** *United States of America v. Timothy James McVeigh—Sentencing (August 14, 1997)* at **www.myhistorylab.com**

Crack and Urban Gangs

Several factors intensified the problem of violent crime, especially in the inner cities. One was a shift in drug use. During the 1960s marijuana had become commonly available, especially on college campuses; this was followed by cocaine, which was far more powerful and addictive but so expensive that few could afford it.

During the 1980s growers of coca leaves in Peru and Bolivia greatly expanded production. Drug traffickers in Colombia devised sophisticated systems to transport cocaine to the United States. The price of cocaine dropped from $120 an ounce in 1981 to $50 in 1988.

Still more important was the proliferation of a cocaine-based compound called "crack" because it

crackled when smoked. Crack was sold in $10 vials. Many users found that it gave an intense spasm of pleasure that overrode all other desires.

The lucrative crack trade led to bitter turf wars in the inner cities; dealers hired neighborhood youths, organized them into gangs, armed them with automatic weapons, and told them to drive competitors away. The term "drive-by shooting" entered the vocabulary. A survey of Los Angeles county in the early 1990s found that more than 150,000 young people belonged to 1,000 gangs. Violence had become a fact of life. In 1985, before crack had seized hold of the inner city, there were 147 murders in Washington, DC; in 1991, the figure skyrocketed to 482.

Black on black murder had become a significant cause of death for African Americans in their twenties. In 1988 Monsta' Kody Scott, who at age eleven pumped shotgun blasts into rival gang members, returned after prison to his Los Angeles neighborhood. He was horrified: Gangs no longer merely shot their rivals but sprayed them with automatic weapons, seventy-five rounds to a clip, or blew them away with small rockets. By 2010, 30 percent of African American men in their twenties were in prison, or on probation or parole. The recurrent refrain of rap performers—that America was a prison—had become, for many, an everyday reality.

Violence and Popular Culture

Conservatives—and plenty of liberals—were also dismayed by the violence of popular culture. They cited as proof the lurid violence of the movie industry, pointing out that in *Public Enemy*, reputedly the most violent film of the 1930s, and *Death Wish*, a controversial vigilante fantasy of 1974, the body count reached eight. But three movies released during the late 1980s—*Robocop*, *Die Hard*, and *Rambo III*—each produced a death tally of sixty or more, nearly one every two minutes. The trend culminated in *Natural Born Killers* (1994), director Oliver Stone's unimaginably violent "spoof" of media violence. Television imitated the movies as the networks crammed violent crime shows into prime time. In 1991 an exhaustive survey found that by the age of eighteen, the average viewer had witnessed some 40,000 murders on TV.

Popular music also acquired a new edge. In 1981 Warner Brothers launched a television channel featuring pop songs set to video. Music TV (MTV) was an instant success; within three years, some 24 million tuned in every day. Michael Jackson's video extravaganza, *Thriller* (1984), transformed the genre. Its surreal images, disjointed editing, and frenzied music set a new standard. Pop music acquired a harder beat and more explicit lyrics. In 1988 the American Academy of Pediatrics expressed concern that teenagers on the average spent two hours a day watching rock videos. Over half featured violence and three-fourths contained sexually suggestive material.

A new sound called "rap" then emerged from the ghetto. Rap consisted of unpredictably metered lyrics set against an exaggeratedly heavy downbeat. Rap performers did not play musical instruments or sing songs so much as convey, in words and gestures, an attitude of defiant, raw rage against whatever challenged their sense of manhood: other young males; women, whom they derided in coarse sexual epithets; and the police. Predictably, raps such as "Cop Killer" and "Illegal Search" contributed to the charge that rap condoned violence and crime.

"I call it crime rhyme," explained rapper Ice-T, "rhyme about actual street events." Some "gangsta" rappers dressed in stylized prison garb—beltless pants and "do-rags." Several major rappers were murdered, and others ran afoul of the law.

The appeal of rap quickly spread beyond black audiences. When Dr. Dre (Andrew Young), founder of a gangsta rap group and head of a record firm, discovered that whites bought more rap CDs than blacks, he promoted the career of a young white rapper, Eminem. Born Marshall Bruce Mathers III, Eminem attracted attention with songs such as "Murder, Murder," "Kill You," "Drug Ballad," and "Criminal." He bashed women, gays, his wife, and nearly everyone else. His lyrics were of such surpassing offensiveness that he became an overnight celebrity and instant millionaire. His fans, whom he treated with scorn, were delighted by the universality of his contempt. The list of those suing him included his mother.

By the 1990s improvements in computer graphics led to the development of increasingly realistic—and violent—video games. "Grand Theft Auto," which by 2005 had sold over 35 million copies and generated over $2 billion, was the subject of a *60 Minutes* special. Journalist Ed Bradley described the game this way: "See a car you like? Steal it. A cop in your way? Blow him away." Bradley recounted the story of Devin Moore, an eighteen-year-old who played the game "day and night" for years. On June 7, 2003, he stole a car; when apprehended he grabbed a gun, killed three policemen, and fled in a police cruiser. When finally caught he said, "Life is like a video game. Everybody's got to die sometime."

Several states passed laws prohibiting the sale or rental of violent video games to anyone under the age of eighteen. (Governor Arnold Schwarzenegger, former star of the extraordinarily violent "Conan" and "Terminator" films, signed the California law.) But federal courts struck down such laws as incompatible with the Constitutional right of free speech.

The violation of social norms has long been part of adolescence. In the 1830s boys devoured "Davy Crockett" tales that championed sadistic violence and bawdy sexual antics; even during the presumably "conformist" decade of the 1950s young people enjoyed the scatological humor of *Mad Magazine*, the suggestive gyrations of Elvis Presley, and the rebellious sexual innuendo of nearly all types of popular music. Anthropologists have suggested that in Western societies adolescence is a transitional stage in which young people delight in "cultural inversions" that turn the social order upside down.

Most consumers of pop violence in the 1990s and early years of the 2000s, like the readers of the Crockett comics or *Mad Magazine*, had little difficulty distinguishing between cultural fantasies and everyday life. But for those who had grown up in ghettos where gangs ruled the streets and where friends and relatives were commonly swallowed up by the criminal justice system, the culture of violence seemed to legitimate the meanness of everyday life. Violence and criminality had become so much a part of popular culture, and popular culture of adolescent life, that some retreated wholly to imaginative worlds conjured by movies, video and computer games, TV, and pop music. To them, the world of parents and teachers seemed duller and less responsive—less *real*—than the one inside their heads.

America, it seemed, had become seemingly filled with menace. At night, few ventured downtown and many avoided public places. Car alarm systems became standard. The popular phrase—"your home is your castle"—took on an eerie reality. Americans reinforced doors with steel, nailed windows shut, and increasingly hunkered down in their own private spaces, which they locked up and wired with alarms.

From Main Street to Mall to Internet

In 1960 civil rights protesters picketed six stores in Richmond, Virginia. Within several decades, all of the stores had closed. So had most of the luncheonettes, 5 & 10 cent stores, bus stations, and community swimming pools that had been sites of civil rights protests during the late 1950s and early

In 2007 a storm approaches the mostly abandoned main street of Robert Lee, county seat of Coke County, Texas.

1960s. Civil rights leaders targeted such facilities because they sought equal access to public spaces downtown, where community life was transacted. There people worked, bought clothing and cars, got their hair cut and cavities filled, paid taxes and filed for driver's licenses, ate meals and brokered deals, watched movies and attended ball games, and engaged in countless other activities. Thirty years later, however, many downtown business districts had been all but abandoned.

Some blamed the civil rights movement itself. Inner-city protests and the desegregation of city schools, they said, caused many whites to flee to the suburbs. Others cited the rise in crime in the late 1960s. But "white flight" commenced in the late 1940s, long before the civil rights movement and busing disputes, before the race riots and crack infestations. (See the map of St. Louis on p. 840.) Postwar federal policies played a major role in the demographic upheaval that transformed the cities

and gave rise to the suburbs. The G. I. Bill of 1946 offered veterans cheap home mortgages. Real estate developers bought huge tracts of land and built inexpensive houses designed especially for returning veterans. Postwar lending policies of the Federal Housing Authority also contributed to the rise of the suburbs, chiefly by rejecting loans in older residential urban areas. Eisenhower's decision to pump money into highway construction (rather than subways and railway infrastructure) also contributed to the growth of suburbs.

Retailers followed consumers, renting space in strip malls along the busy roadways that reached out to the suburbs. Then came the shopping malls. In 1946 there were only eight shopping malls in the nation; by 1972, over 13,000. Mall managers anchored their complexes with national retailers such as Sears and JCPenney. Because such companies bought in large quantities, their stores outpriced locally owned competitors on Main Street.

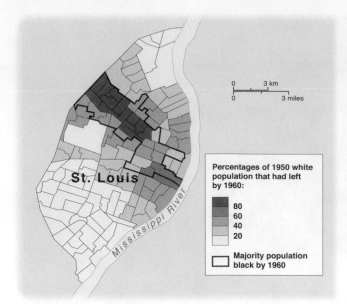

Racial Shifts in St. Louis During the 1950s During the 1950s, the white population of St. Louis declined by more than 200,000, while the black population increased by 100,000. Much of the central core was almost entirely black.

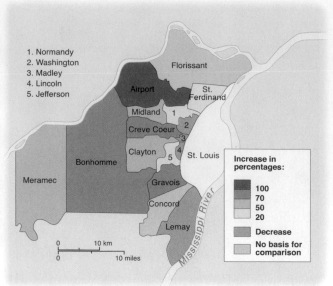

Growth of Suburban St. Louis, 1950–1960 During the 1950s, the suburban townships in St. Louis county west of the city gained nearly 300,000 people, an increase of 73 percent. More than 99 percent of the suburban residents were white.

Main Street faded. By the 1980s, retailers such as Sam Walton took the logic of price competition several steps farther. Because the chain stores in the malls sold the same nationally advertised brands, he reasoned that all shoppers wanted was the lowest price. Walton therefore dispensed with the customary amenities of shopping—attractive displays, pleasant décor, professional salespeople—and built "big box" stores that were little more than shopper-accessible warehouses. Then came another shift. Early in the twenty-first century, shoppers who wearied of pushing carts through dimly lit warehouses and standing in line to pay now had an alternative: They could shop via the Internet, which by 2010 accounted for nearly 10 percent of all retail sales.

The transformation of retailing—from downtown to the suburbs to the Internet—was symptomatic of a more general shift from public to private spaces. In the 1950s, people were free to go downtown whenever they wished, to open nearly any type of business that suited their fancy, to give political speeches or distribute leaflets. Mall owners and big-box managers, on the other hand, set the hours and conditions of operation, restricted political expression and access (most recently by banning unchaperoned teenagers on weekends) and by offering leases (or products) that fit prescribed marketing plans.

Within a half century, shopping had not only become more private, but it also was less social. Big-box stores replaced commissioned salespeople with low-paid checkers. In the past decade improvements in scanner technology have allowed retailers to dispense even with checkers. And an increasing number of online consumers shop at home. Increasingly, shopping entails no social interaction whatsoever.

A similar shift from public interaction to private pursuits has characterized many other daily activities. For much of their lives, Boomers regularly visited local banks to make deposits and cash checks. But during the recession of the 1970s banks closed many branches and in subsequent decades hundreds of banks were merged. More branches were closed and tens of thousands of tellers laid off. Rather than drive to distant branches and wait in long lines, banking customers learned to use ATMs and bank online. Banking for Boomers had been a social occasion; for Millennials it became an interaction with a machine.

By the 1970s and 1980s, many service sector jobs had disappeared: milkmen who delivered fresh dairy products; door-to-door salespeople who demonstrated cosmetics, appliances, and encyclopedias; "service station" attendants who pumped gas and checked the oil; bakery owners and candy makers who sold goods they had made themselves. Then in the 1990s, person-to-person interactions in daily life occurred even less frequently. With the advent of the Internet and improved software, many people became their own travel agent, tax preparer, financial adviser, grocer, cosmetician, medical assistant, and bookseller.

From Community to Facebook

Religious institutions have long constituted the bulwark of communities, and the postwar period witnessed a remarkable expansion. By 1990, membership in all churches and synagogues surpassed 148 million, an increase of 60 million during the previous four decades. (The total population during the period increased by nearly 100 million.) With the large influx of Hispanic immigrants, membership in the Roman Catholic Church more than doubled. Membership in mainstream Protestant churches generally declined, but rose solidly in fundamentalist and evangelical churches, such as the Southern Baptist, Pentecostal, Holiness, Assemblies of God, and Church of God in Christ. The Jehovah's Witnesses and the Mormon Church grew as well. In 1990 two-thirds of all Americans reported that they belonged to a church, the highest percentage by far among the major industrial nations of the West.

The Crystal Cathedral was erected in 1980 in Garden Grove, California, by Dr. Robert H. Schuller, a televangelist whose weekly broadcasts were seen by tens of millions of viewers. Designed by Phillip Johnson, the cathedral is made of over 10,000 glass panes.

But the membership numbers were misleading. Since 1970, church attendance among persons younger than sixty has declined about 20 percent. The UCLA survey cited in the introduction to this chapter found that in 1968, 9 percent of entering college freshmen said they never attended church; by 2000, that percentage had more than doubled. By the 1970s, moreover, millions of Americans went to church by turning on the TV. "Televangelists" such as Rex Humbard, Oral Roberts, Jerry Falwell, Pat Robertson, and Jim and Tammy Bakker founded their own churches and educational institutions, supported by direct appeals to viewers. A few established their own colleges, such as Falwell's Liberty University, Oral Roberts University, and Robertson's CBN University (renamed Regent University in 1990). A number of scandals involving prominent televangelists caused disillusionment and widespread defections. On the other hand, the rapid spread of cable television greatly increased the number of available channels, enabling scores of new evangelists to reach out to viewers. Community-based ministers saw congregations shrink; thousands of churches closed their doors for good. Some churches devised "healing rituals" to ease their abandonment of formerly sacred space.

Participation in team sports fell at about the same rate as church attendance. By the first decade of the twenty-first century, more young people played basketball and soccer than in the past, but far fewer played softball, baseball, football, tennis, and league bowling. The fields on which young Boomers often spent much of their lives had been sold to developers or fenced in and locked.

The lack of exercise among Millennials became a source of national concern. In 2010 Surgeon General Regina Benjamin announced that one in three American children was obese. One reason, Benjamin explained, was that youngsters between ages eight to eighteen averaged seven hours and thirty-eight minutes a day on electronic media—watching TV, talking on cell phones, playing video games, and logged into the Internet. That year, First Lady Michelle Obama inaugurated a nationwide antiobesity campaign named—appropriately— "Let's move!"

Some Millennials exercised *while* engaged with electronic media. (Multitasking became a redundant adjective for the Millennial generation.) Since 2000, membership in gyms skyrocketed. And often Millennials could be seen pounding away on treadmills or other exercise machines, staring at TV monitors or listening to music with an earpiece. Not all Millennials are sedentary; but many are nearly always plugged in.

The rise of online learning is an illustration of the transformation of social activities into solitary Internet pursuits. By 2009, over 4 million Americans enrolled in online courses, twice as many as in 2003. For many, especially full-time employees, ease of access compensated for the lack of face-to-face contact with other students. Tim Scott, a twenty-five-year-old clerk in a drugstore who enrolled in technology courses at the University of Phoenix, explained, "This is pretty much the only way I could get a college degree." Online education spread to all walks of life. Some people took courses to learn new languages and career skills, such as "Dental Anthropology," "Clown Education," or "Golf Course Management." Others logged in to learn new hobbies, such as "building a kayak," "paragliding in the Alps," or "Salsa dancing." Employees were required to take mandatory online courses on company policies and sexual harassment. Although surveys suggest that most online learners prefer classes in which they interact with real people in a classroom, the fact was that often regular classrooms had themselves become anonymous and impersonal. As Harvard Professor Clayton Christensen observed, "Anything beyond the 10th row in a large lecture hall is distance learning."

One reason distance online education took off was that it spared commuting students the hassle of driving to college and finding parking. Such experiences underscored the extent to which cars had become the predominant mode of transportation, another shift from the earlier social context of mass transit to the mostly solitary experience of driving. Bus and train ridership was declining well before the advent of the Boomers; but the postwar population shift to the suburbs accelerated the ascendancy of cars over mass transit. As more drivers—nearly always alone—clogged the highways, traffic jams grew longer. By 2005, the average American spent thirty-eight hours a year stuck in traffic. Although many found repose within the solitary confines of a car, others coped with the loneliness of driving by chatting on their cell phones or texting friends. (A Pew poll in 2010 found that one in three texting teenagers did so while driving a car.)

The postwar suburban home itself was conceived as a private refuge from the hustle and bustle of downtown. But over time suburban homes became still more private. Newer houses were set farther back from the curb; high fences and thick hedges discouraged the over-the-barbecue conviviality of the 1950s suburbs. By the 1990s, many well-to-do people moved into privately owned "gated communities," surrounded by high fences and patrolled by private security guards. Only residents and specified guests were allowed in.

In *Second Life*, multi-player online game, these two avatars engage in virtual courtship.

The trend toward increased privacy could be seen even within the home. Young Boomers generally ate dinner in a family dining room and played cards and board games afterwards in the living room. By the mid 1950s, television-watching had become a family affair, and a child's dreaded punishment was to be sent to his or her room after dinner. During the 1980s and 1990s, however, homes became larger and families smaller. Most Millennials had their own bedrooms. By 1975 fewer than half of Americans ate dinner with their whole family; and by 2000, that number was fewer than one-third. Family members instead retreated to their own rooms to watch their own television shows or log onto the Internet. (In 2010 the average number of TV sets per household—2.93—exceeded the number of *people* per household—2.88.) For Millennials, the worst punishment was to be deprived of the Internet or their Blackberries.

Millennials withdrew to the privacy of their rooms in order to socialize. David Greenfield of the Center for Internet Studies explained that the Internet was "a socially connecting device that's socially isolating at the same time." For their part, most Millennials thought the Internet improved social relations. "I've outsourced my social life exclusively to Facebook," one Millennial explained in 2009. "My time on Facebook substitutes for face time and has made my life more organized and efficient." In 2010 Facebook reported that the average college student had over 400 Facebook friends. Plenty of users greatly exceeded this average, prompting Facebook in 2008 to rule that friendship rosters would be capped at 5,000. Social connections in excess of 5,000, Facebook officials reasoned, were probably not "actual friends." While bemoaning the cutoff, Jeffrey Wolfe, a real estate broker in San Francisco with 4,417 friends, conceded that keeping up with them could be demanding: "Normally I start hitting it about 10 o'clock at night, and if I do it right, I can be done by 1 a.m."

Some worried that Millennials spent so much time attending to their own circle of Facebook friends (however great in circumference) or logging onto sites dedicated to Lady Gaga, labrador retrievers, or Legos, that they often failed to encounter people with ideas or perspectives different from their own. But others endorsed the Internet as an ideal if somewhat odd way to meet strangers and exchange opinions. *Second Life*, a virtual 3D world populated by some 18 million "residents," was among the innumerable interactive games that allowed strangers to converse and imaginatively interact. In 2009 Linden Lab, the San Francisco company behind the concept, noted that residents had logged over a billion hours on the site and spent a billion dollars buying unreal things (mostly clothing and cars) for their virtual personas, or avatars. One Stanford researcher explained how he had experienced "the most sexually charged non-sexual experience I've ever had" when his avatar was propositioned by another avatar in a "private room" (!).

Virtual communities possessed both the advantages and disadvantages of anonymity. "On the Internet, no one knows you're a dog," as a *New Yorker* cartoon's canine narrator remarked. A 2001 study found that half of the female Avatars in *Second Life* were actually men. Anonymity may help protect people who wish to articulate ideas and explore behaviors that might generate disapproval in "real" settings.

But the anonymity of the Internet also carries risks. Sexual predators target teen chat rooms and social-networking sites. Anonymity, too, allows people to vent frustrations, prejudices, and spite without concern for consequences. In 2006, Lori Drew, a mother in O'Fallon, Missouri, sought to teach a lesson to Megan Meier, a fourteen-year-old whom Drew believed had been spreading rumors about Drew's daughter. Drew created a fictitious MySpace persona of a sixteen-year-old named "Josh," who friended Meier, gained her confidence, and acquired her secrets. But then "Josh" turned on Meier, advising, "The world would be a better place without you." Twenty minutes later, Meier hanged herself in her bedroom closet.

Drew was convicted of a misdemeanor for violating the terms of her MySpace agreement; but a federal judge set the ruling aside: Violation of an Internet agreement did not constitute criminal behavior. State legislatures in Missouri and California immediately passed "anti-cyberbullying" laws. In 2009 Congresswoman Linda Sanchez introduced the "Megan Meier Cyberbullying Prevention Act," but constitutional experts predicted that such laws would be struck down as infringements on free speech and privacy rights.

But what did privacy mean? During the previous four decades, Boomers and Millennials had repeatedly debated and redefined the concepts of private and public. Feminists had asserted a "right to privacy," including a right to an abortion; but the Moral Majority had insisted on the superior "right to life" of the fetus. Gays and lesbians had sought freedom from government harassment; but they also sought public acceptance through adoption of same-sex marriage laws and open acknowledgement of their service in the military. President Reagan and conservatives campaigned to "get government off our backs" and yet they expanded the government's role in prosecuting behavior deemed deviant or immoral. And if public physical spaces were disappearing, Millennials increasingly participated, often from the solitude of a bedroom or study, in a bogglingly public world of the Internet, blithely posting their innermost thoughts on social networking sites.

Greying of the Boomers

On January 1, 2011, when the first Boomer turned sixty-five, nearly one-seventh of the American population was over sixty-five, the customary retirement age. Demographic projections indicated that by the time the Millennials reached sixty-five, one-fifth of the population would be over sixty-five.

The aging of the nation's population had serious economic implications. A substantial proportion of the nation's wealth was shifting from economically productive purposes (educating the young, building and maintaining infrastructure, and creating new businesses and technology) to the less productive task of providing health care and pensions for the elderly.

Of particular concern was the viability of Social Security, the New Deal program that provided pensions for the elderly. In theory, workers and employers paid into the Social Security Trust Fund; when workers retired, they would draw their "savings" from the Trust Fund. But under pressure from seniors—the highest-voting proportion of the population—Congress increased old-age benefits. As of 2010, the Social Security Trust Fund had $2 trillion in assets, but the projected cost of Social Security by 2050 exceeded $7 trillion. The difference would have to be covered by the contributions made by working Millennials, many of whom worried that the fund would be gone by the time they retired. A 2009 poll by the American Association of Retired Persons (AARP) found that only 31 percent of Americans between the ages of eighteen and thirty-nine believe that Social Security will be available to them on retirement.

In 1980, sixty-year-old John A. Garraty, co-author of this book, completed his first twenty-four-mile marathon in New York City. He completed his last marathon when he was seventy-two.

Medical advances during the late twentieth century led to an increase in the life span: An American born in 1900 could expect to live to be fifty, while one born in 2000 was projected to live to seventy-seven. But this good news further complicated the transition from Boomers to Millennials.

Compounding the difficulty were attitudinal differences between the generations, such as those cited elsewhere in this chapter. The 2008 Pew poll also found that 75 percent of Millennials had profiles on a social networking site, compared to 30 percent of Boomers; that 38 percent of Millennials had a tattoo, compared to 15 percent of Boomers; and that 23 percent of Millennials had body piercings other than an ear lobe, compared to fewer than 1 percent of Boomers. How Millennials will treat aging Boomers is anyone's guess.

Chapter Review

Milestones

1946	Dr. Benjamin Spock publishes *Common Sense Guide to Baby and Child Care*
1947	Construction begins on Levittown, New York, first tract-house suburb
1960	FDA approves sale of birth control pills
1963	Betty Friedan publishes *The Feminine Mystique*
1965	Congress passes Immigration Act that ends "national origins" quotas
	Supreme Court affirms "right to privacy" in *Griswold v. Connecticut*
	César Chávez organizes boycott to support grape pickers
1969	Stonewall riots mark public assertion of rights of homosexuals
1973	Supreme Court legalizes abortion in *Roe v. Wade*
1979	Jerry Falwell founds the Moral Majority
1982	Center for Disease Control identifies new disease, AIDS
1989	Supreme Court limits abortion rights in *Webster v. Reproductive Health Services*
2000	Vermont recognies same-sex unions
2010	Michelle Obama introduces anti-obesity campaign

Key Terms

acquired immunodeficiency syndrome (AIDS) A deadly, and very often sexually transmitted disease that emerged in the 1980s and that at first spread chiefly among injection drug users and gay male populations, but soon affected all communities. The disease is a complex of deadly pathologies resulting from infection with the **human immunodeficiency virus (HIV)**. By 2000, AIDS deaths in the United States had surpassed 40,000, *834*

Equal Rights Amendment (ERA) A proposed amendment to the U.S. Constitution to outlaw discrimination on the basis of sex. Although first proposed in 1923, the amendment was not passed by Congress until 1972; but the ratification movement fell short and the ERA was not added to the Constitution, *827*

human immunodeficiency virus (HIV) A virus, usually spread through sexual contact, that attacks the immune system, sometimes fatally. HIV, which causes **acquired immunodeficiency syndrome (AIDS)**, first appeared in the United States in the 1980s, *834*

National Organization for Women (NOW) An organization, founded in 1966 by Betty Friedan and other feminists, to promote equal rights for women, changes in divorce laws, and legalization of abortion, *827*

Review Questions

1. The introduction to this chapter argues that young Boomers were more inclined to look for a "meaningful philosophy of life," while young Millennials were more interested in being "well-off financially." Do you agree? What evidence from the chapter supports your position? What refutes it?

2. What accounted for the emergence of modern feminism in the 1960s? Did it succeed in changing gender roles and if so, how? What explained the emergence of gay and lesbian activism?

3. What were the main components of the conservative movement after 1970? How did it influence culture and society?

4. How did the cultural shift from "downtown" to the suburbs change society more generally? In what sense has life become more or less "private"?

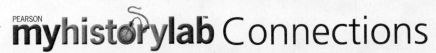

myhistorylab Connections

Reinforce what you learned in this chapter by studying the many documents, images, maps, review tools, and videos available at **www.myhistorylab.com**.

Read and Review

✓• Study and Review *Chapter 31*

⚫•⎼Read the Document *Illegal Immigration Reform and Immigrant Responsibility Act of 1996, p. 826*

👁•⎼See the Map *Immigration to the U.S., 1945–1990, p. 826*

⚙•⎼View the Image *Jimmy Carter Signs the House of Representative Resolution for the Equal Rights Amendment, 1972, p. 828*

⚫•⎼Read the Document *Roe v. Wade (January 22, 1973), p. 829*

⚫•⎼Read the Document *The Gay Liberation Front, Come Out (1970), p. 833*

Research and Explore

⚫•⎼Read the Document *LBJ Immigration Act of 1975, p. 826*

⚫•⎼Read the Document *United States of America v. Timothy James McVeigh—Sentencing (August 14, 1997), p. 837*

((•⎼ **Hear** the **Audio**

Hear the audio file for Chapter 31 at
www.myhistorylab.com.

What will happen to you?

"Those who fail to learn from the past are doomed to repeat it"—This cliché, a favorite of history teachers, contains some truth. The book you are reading, for example, provides some solid guidance: Governments that ignore the wishes of the people probably won't long endure; wars are easier to start than to stop; and investments that seem to be "too good to be true" probably are. But apart from such common-sense observations, history provides few clues about the future.

The first decade of the twenty-first century proves this point emphatically. In 2000 Americans were mostly optimistic, and for good reason. After the dissolution of the Soviet Union in 1991, the United States had no significant enemies. A new era of peace was dawning. Successive presidents reduced the nation's armed forces by nearly a million men and women; defense spending (as a proportion of the GNP) was nearly cut in half. Three decades of deficits had come to an end: In 2000 the U.S. Treasury operated at a $250 billion *surplus*. The Congressional Budget Office projected a $4 *trillion* federal surplus for the coming decade.

Shocks and Responses: 1992–Present

32

((•─ **Hear** the **Audio** **Chapter 32 at www.myhistorylab.com**

■ A U.S. military convoy travels from Kabul to southern Afghanistan; the photo was taken by Second Lieutenant Chris Vongsawat.

It didn't happen. The terrorist attack of September 11, 2001, which virtually no one predicted, shattered hopes for peace. Within two years, American soldiers were fighting fierce battles in Afghanistan and Iraq. By the end of the decade, over 5,000 U.S. servicemen and women would be dead and many thousands more wounded.

By then, too, an economic earthquake had nearly toppled the nation's major financial institutions. By late 2008 political and economic leaders were spending trillions to prop up banks, investment houses, and insurance firms that "were too big to fail." The federal deficit for the decade approached *$4 trillion.*

More bad news was to come. In early 2010 an oil rig owned by British Petroleum blew up, killing eleven men who had been working on the rig and releasing millions of barrels of oil into the Gulf of Mexico. Thousands of miles of coastal wetlands and beaches and untold numbers of water birds, shrimp and fish were fouled with oil. President Obama called it the nation's worst environmental disaster ever.

By then, *Time* magazine had already pronounced these years "The Decade from Hell." But no one had any inkling of this in 1992. ■

A New Face: Bill Clinton

In 1946 William (Bill) Clinton was born William Jefferson Blythe IV, but his father died in a car accident before he was born. Though his stepfather was an abusive alcoholic, at age fifteen Bill legally took his stepfather's name. He graduated from Georgetown, won a Rhodes scholarship to study at Oxford University, and graduated from Yale Law School. He returned to Arkansas and was soon elected state attorney general.

In 1977 Clinton and his wife, Hillary Rodham, joined with James McDougal, a banker, to secure a loan to build vacation homes in the Ozarks. But the development, which they named Whitewater, eventually became insolvent. McDougal illegally covered the debts with a loan from a savings and loan company he had acquired. In 1989 the savings and loan failed, costing the federal government $60 million to reimburse depositors. In 1992 federal investigators claimed that the Clintons had been "potential beneficiaries" of McDougal's illegal activities.

By this time Clinton, now governor of Arkansas, was campaigning in the New Hampshire primary for the Democratic nomination for president. Few voters could make much sense of the financial mess known as the "Whitewater scandal," nor did they have much opportunity to do so: Another, far more explosive story threatened to sink the Clinton campaign. It came out that Clinton had for many years engaged in an extramarital affair with one Gennifer Flowers; Clinton's standing in the polls tumbled.

Hillary Rodham Clinton appeared with her husband on CBS's *60 Minutes* to address the allegations. Bill Clinton indignantly denied Flowers's statements but then issued an earnest if ambiguous appeal for forgiveness. "I have acknowledged causing pain in my marriage," he said. "I think most Americans will know what we're saying; they'll get it." Clinton was right, early evidence of his ability to address the American people directly, but on his own—carefully worded—terms. He finished second in New Hampshire, captured most of the remaining primaries, and won the Democratic nomination with

Young Bill Clinton (left) shakes hands with President John F. Kennedy. "The torch has been passed to a new generation of Americans," Kennedy had declared in his inaugural. "Ask not what your country can do for you—ask what you can do for your country," JFK added. Thirty years later, Clinton's inaugural echoed Kennedy's: "Today, a generation raised in the shadows of the Cold War assumes new responsibilities," Clinton declared. "I challenge a new generation of young Americans to a season of service."

ease. His choice of running mate—Senator Al Gore of Tennessee, a Vietnam veteran, family man, and environmentalist—helped the ticket considerably.

The Election of 1992

While Clinton tiptoed through a minefield of personal scandals, President George (Herbert Walker) Bush rested secure in the belief that, after crushing Saddam Hussein and the Iraqi army in the Gulf War, the 1992 election campaign would be little more than a victory lap. But he encountered unexpectedly stiff opposition within the Republican party. Patrick Buchanan, an outspoken conservative, did well enough to alarm White House strategists. Then Ross Perot, a billionaire Texan, announced his independent candidacy. Perot charged that both major parties were out of touch with "the people." He promised to spend $100 million of his own money on his campaign. Perot's platform had both conservative and liberal planks. He would "take the shackles off of American business," avoid raising taxes, and cut government spending by "getting rid of waste." He also supported gun control, backed a woman's right to an abortion, promised to get rid of political action committees, and called for an all-out effort to "restructure" the health care system.

Polls quickly revealed that Perot was popular in California, Texas, and other key states that Bush was counting on winning easily. At the Republican convention in August, Bush was nominated without opposition.

Clinton accused Bush of failing to deal effectively with the lingering economic recession and promised to undertake public works projects, to encourage private investment, and to improve the nation's education and health insurance systems. Bush played down the seriousness of the recession, but his jaunty comments offended those who had lost their jobs.

On election day, more than 100 million citizens voted. About 44 million voted for Clinton, 38 million for Bush, and 20 million for Perot. Clinton was elected with 370 electoral votes to Bush's 168. Perot did not win any electoral votes.

Watch the **Video** *Bill Clinton Sells Himself to America: Presidential Campaign Ad, 1992* at **www.myhistorylab.com**

A New Start: Clinton as President

Clinton first used his executive authority to strengthen the Supreme Court majority in favor of upholding the landmark case of *Roe v. Wade*. The majority included three conservative justices who had been appointed by Reagan and Bush. Clinton appointed Ruth Bader Ginsberg, a judge known to believe that abortion was constitutional. Clinton indicated that he would veto any bill limiting abortion rights. He also reversed important Bush policies by signing a revived family leave bill into law and by authorizing the use of fetal tissue for research purposes.

The first major test of the president's will came when he submitted his first budget to Congress. He hoped to reduce the deficit by roughly $500 billion in five years, half by spending cuts, half by new taxes. The proposal for a tax increase raised a storm of protest. A number of congressional Democrats refused to go along with Clinton's budget, and since the Republicans in Congress voted solidly against any increase in taxes, the president was forced to accept major changes. Even so, the final bill passed by the narrowest of margins. Clinton rightly claimed a victory.

He then turned to his long-awaited proposal to reform the nation's expensive and incomplete health insurance system. A committee headed by his wife had been working for months with no indication that a plan acceptable to the medical profession, the health insurance industry, and ordinary citizens was likely to come from its deliberations. The plan that finally emerged seemed even more complicated and possibly more costly than the existing system. It never came to a vote in Congress.

View the **Image** *Bill Clinton and Al Gore on the South Lawn of the White House, 1993* at **www.myhistorylab.com**

Watch the **Video** *Bill Clinton First Inauguration* at **www.myhistorylab.com**

Emergence of the Republican Majority

The Whitewater scandal, which Clinton had managed to brush aside during the campaign, gnawed at his presidency. Public pressure forced Attorney General Janet Reno to appoint a special prosecutor. She named Kenneth W. Starr, a Republican lawyer, to investigate Whitewater and other alleged misdeeds of the Clintons.

More troubles followed. Paula Corbin Jones, a State of Arkansas employee, charged that Clinton, while governor, had invited her to his hotel room and asked her to engage in oral sex. Clinton's attorney denied the accusation and sought to have the case dismissed on the grounds that a president could not be sued while in office. The case commenced a tortuous route through the courts.

Eager to take advantage of Clinton's troubles, Republicans looked to the 1994 congressional elections. Led by Congressman Newt Gingrich of Georgia, they offered voters an ambitious program to stimulate the economy by reducing both the federal debt and the federal income tax. Federally administered welfare programs were to be replaced by block grants to the states. Many measures protecting the environment, such as those making businesses responsible for cleaning up their waste, were to be repealed.

On election day, the Republicans gained control of both houses of Congress. Under the firm direction of Gingrich, now Speaker, the House approved nearly all of the provisions of this **Contract with America**. This appalled Clinton, who vetoed the 1995 budget drafted by the Republicans. When neither side agreed to a compromise, the government for a time ran out of money and shut down all but essential services.

The Election of 1996

The public tended to blame Congress, and particularly Speaker Gingrich, for the shutdown. The president's approval rating rose. But the main issue of the day was the economy, and the upturn during and after 1991 benefited Clinton enormously. By the fall of 1996, unemployment had fallen well below 6 percent, and inflation below 3 percent. The Dow Jones Industrial Average of leading stocks soared past 6,000, more than triple the average in 1987. Clinton was renominated for a second term without opposition.

A number of Republicans competed in the presidential primaries, but after a slow start Bob Dole of Kansas, the Senate majority leader, won the nomination. Dole had been a senator for more than thirty years, but despite his experience he was a poor campaigner, stiff and monotone. His main proposal was a steep reduction of the deficit and a 15-percent income tax cut. Pressed to explain how this could be done without drastic cuts in popular social programs, especially Social Security and Medicare, he gave a distressingly vague reply. Clinton, a charismatic campaigner, stressed preparing for the twenty-first century and took, in general, an optimistic view of the economy.

On election day Clinton won an impressive victory, sweeping the Northeast, all the Midwest except Indiana, the upper Mississippi Valley, and the Far West. He divided the South with Dole, who carried a band of states running north from Texas. Clinton's Electoral College margin was substantial, 379 to 159.

The Republicans, however, retained control of both houses of Congress. Many retained, as well, an unquenchable hatred of Clinton.

Clinton Impeached

Although President Clinton steadfastly denied allegations of womanizing, in January 1998 a judge ordered him to testify in Paula Corbin Jones's lawsuit against him. Jones, who sought to strengthen her suit by showing that Clinton had a history of propositioning women, also subpoenaed a former White House intern. Her name was Monica Lewinsky.

Lewinsky and Clinton were separately asked if they had had an affair, and each denied the charge. When word of their alleged relationship was leaked to the press, Clinton declared in a TV news conference, "I did not have sexual relations with that woman, Miss Lewinsky." Hillary Clinton denounced the allegations as part of a "vast right-wing conspiracy" against her husband.

Unbeknown to the Clintons, however, Lewinsky had been confiding to Linda Tripp, a former White House employee, and Tripp had secretly tape-recorded some twenty hours of their conversations. Tripp turned these tapes over to special prosecutor Starr, whose investigations of the Clintons' roles in the Whitewater scandal had broadened into a more general inquiry. In the tapes Lewinsky provided intimate details of repeated sexual encounters with the president. Clinton and Lewinsky appeared to have lied under oath. Starr threatened to indict Lewinsky for perjury. In return for immunity from prosecution, she admitted that she had engaged in sexual relations with the president and that he and his aides had encouraged her to give misleading testimony in the Jones case.

When called in August to testify on videotape before the Starr grand jury, Clinton conceded that he had engaged in "inappropriate intimate contact" with Lewinsky. But he insisted, "I have not had sex with her as I defined it." When pressed to supply his own definition, he responded with legalistic obfuscation: "My understanding of this definition is it covers contact by the person being deposed with the enumerated areas, if the contact is done with an intent to arouse or gratify." Because Clinton had not intended to arouse or gratify Lewinsky, he had not "had sex" with her. He allowed that this definition was "rather strange."

More legalisms followed. When asked if he had ever been alone with her, he responded, "It depends on how you define alone." When asked if his lawyer had been correct when he had assured the judge in

A seemingly anonymous well-wisher from the crowd greets President Bill Clinton. When Clinton was later investigated for having an affair with Monica Lewinsky, a former White House intern, this photograph of the two surfaced. Clinton's lack of discretion struck many as self-destructive.

January that "there is absolutely no sex of any kind," Clinton said that the statement was not untrue because "it depends on what the meaning of the word 'is' is."

Clinton's testimony infuriated Starr, who made public Lewinsky's humiliatingly detailed testimony and announced that Clinton's deceptive testimony warranted consideration by the House of Representatives for impeachment.

But throughout Clinton's legal battles, opinion polls indicated that two in three Americans approved of his performance as president. Buoyed by the vibrant economy, most Americans blamed the scandal on the intrusive Starr nearly as much as the evasive Clinton. The November election proved disastrous for the Republicans, who nearly lost their majority in the House.

Clinton's troubles, however, were by no means over. Republican leaders in the House impeached Clinton on the grounds that he had committed perjury and had obstructed justice by inducing Lewinsky and others to give false testimony in the Jones case. The vote closely followed party lines.

The impeachment trial in the Senate began in January 1999. Chief Justice William Rehnquist presided. The Republicans numbered fifty-five, enough to control the proceedings but twelve short of the two-thirds necessary to convict the president and remove him from office. Democrats, while publicly critical of Clinton's behavior, maintained that his indiscretions did not constitute "high crimes and misdemeanors" as specified in the Constitution for removal from office. They prevailed. The article

accusing Clinton of perjury was defeated by a vote of fifty-five to forty-five; on the article alleging obstruction of justice, the vote was fifty to fifty. Clinton remained president.

Read the **Document** Bill Clinton, *Answers to the Articles of Impeachment* at **www.myhistorylab.com**

Clinton's Legacy

One reason why Clinton survived was the health of the economy. Few wanted to rock the ship of state when it was stuffed with cash. Until the final months, the Clinton years coincided with the longest economic boom in the nation's history. Clinton deserves considerable credit for the remarkable prosperity of the era. His reducing the federal deficit drove interest rates down, spurring investment and economic growth. By August 1998 unemployment had fallen to 4.5 percent, the lowest level since the 1960s; inflation had eased to a minuscule 1 percent, the lowest level since the 1950s. In 1998 the federal government operated at its first surplus since 1969. In the 2000 fiscal year, the surplus hit $237 billion.

Clinton also supported globalization of the economy. He successfully promoted the **North American Free Trade Agreement (NAFTA)** to reduce tariff barriers; Congress approved NAFTA in 1993. During the last half of the 1990s, the United States led all industrial nations in the rate of growth of its real gross domestic product. But the new global economy harmed many. Some union leaders bitterly asked how their members could compete

In 1993, Clinton succeeded in brokering a deal between Israeli prime minister Yitzhak Rabin (left) and Palestinian leader Yasir Arafat. It was supposed to lead to the formation of a Palestinian state. The assassination of Rabin by a Jewish extremist shattered the agreement.

against convict labor in China or sweatshop workers in Indonesia or Malaysia. Others complained that the emphasis on worldwide economic growth was generating an environmental calamity. International protests against the World Trade Organization culminated in the disruption of its 2000 meeting in Seattle, when thousands of protesters went on a rampage, setting fires and looting stores.

Clinton's record in foreign affairs was mixed. In 1993 he failed in an effort to assemble an international force to prevent "ethnic cleansing" by Serbian troops against Muslims in Bosnia, formerly part of Yugoslavia. In 1999 critics predicted another debacle when Clinton proposed a NATO effort to prevent General Slobodan Milosevic of Yugoslavia from crushing the predominantly Muslim province of

Kosovo, which was attempting to secede. But after several months of intense NATO bombing of Serbia, Milosevic withdrew from Kosovo. Within a year, he was forced out of office and into prison, awaiting trial for war crimes before a UN tribunal.

Clinton labored, as had his predecessors in the White House, to broker peace between Israel and the Palestinians; like his predecessors, he failed. In 1993 Yitzhak Rabin, Israeli prime minister, and Yassir Arafat, leader of the Palestine Liberation Organization, signed an agreement preparing for a Palestinian state. But extremists on both sides shattered the fragile accord. In 1995 Rabin was assassinated by a Jewish zealot. Palestinians, enraged by the construction of Israeli settlements in Palestinian territory, stepped up their campaign of suicide bombings.

Israel retaliated with tank and helicopter attacks on suspected terrorist strongholds. The negotiations collapsed. Arafat unleashed a new wave of uprisings, and hardliners, headed by Ariel Sharon, took charge of Israel. Violence intensified on both sides.

Whatever the successes and shortcomings of his administration, the Clinton presidency will always be linked to his relationship with a White House intern and the impeachment proceedings that ensued. Though by no means the first president to stray from matrimonial propriety, Clinton's behavior, in an era when the media thrived on scandal, was symptomatic of an almost willful self destructiveness.

The Economic Boom and the Internet

A significant part of the prosperity of the 1990s came from new technologies such as cellular phones and genetic engineering. But the most important was the development of a revolutionary form of communication: the Internet. Developed in the 1970s by U.S. military and academic institutions to coordinate research, the Internet initially proved an awkward means of linking information. Data in one computer did not readily relate to that elsewhere. The Internet was a communication system that lacked a common language.

That was remedied in the early 1990s by Tim Berners-Lee, a British physicist working at a research institute in Switzerland. He devised the software that became the grammar—the "protocols"—of the Internet "language." With this language, the Internet became the World Wide Web (WWW), a conduit for a stream of electronic impulses flowing among hundreds of millions of computers.

The number of Web sites increased exponentially. In 1995 Bill Gates's Microsoft entered the picture with its Windows operating system, which made the computer easy to use. It created a Web browser—Microsoft Internet Explorer—and embedded its software in the Windows 95 bundle. This provoked howls of protest from Netscape as well as from other service providers: America Online, CompuServe, and Prodigy. Microsoft, they complained, was threatening to monopolize access to and use of the Internet. (A federal judge concurred, ordering that Microsoft be broken up; his ruling was overturned on appeal in 2001.)

In the meantime, Jeff Bezos dreamed of using the Internet to sell books. In 1995 his company, Amazon.com, sold its first book. Within six years, its annual sales approached $3 billion. Bezos became one of the richest men in the nation.

If Bezos could use the Web for selling books, others imagined they could sell everything from pet food to pornography (eBay, an Internet auction house, had an online catalog consisting of three million items). Many start-up companies (dot-coms, in the slang of the day) consisted of little more than the hopes of the founders. "Venture capitalists," independent investors seeking to fund emerging "tech" companies, sensed a glittering new economic frontier somewhere down the Internet superhighway, and they poured billions into start-up dot-coms. In 1999 some 200 Internet companies "went public," selling shares in the major stock exchanges. They raised $20 billion easily. The prices of dot-com stocks kept on climbing though few generated profits; some lacked any revenue whatsoever.

In the spring of 2000, with the stock market still surging, a selling wave hit the tech stocks and spilled over to other companies. Stock prices plummeted. In all, some $2 trillion in stock funds disappeared. As the 2000 election approached, many feared that the economy was nearing a recession.

The 2000 Election: George W. Bush Wins by One Vote

During the 2000 campaign, Vice President Al Gore secured the Democratic nomination and chose as running mate Senator Joseph Lieberman of Connecticut, an observant Jew and outspoken critic of Clinton during the impeachment proceedings.

The leading contender was George W. Bush, son of former President Bush. Like his father, Bush graduated from Yale and worked in the family oil business. He headed a group that bought the Texas Rangers baseball team. Although some doubted Bush's abilities, his visible success with the Rangers catapulted him into Texas politics. An effective and personable campaigner, he was elected governor in 1994. Six years later he defeated Senator John McCain of Arizona in a battle for the Republican nomination for president. Bush selected as running mate Dick Cheney, who had served as defense secretary in his father's administration.

Consumer activist and environmentalist Ralph Nader also entered the presidential race, running on the Green party ticket. This worried Gore, author of *Earth in the Balance*; he had hoped to carry the environmentalist vote.

The main issue was what to do with the federal surplus, which by some projections would soon exceed $1 trillion. Bush called for a substantial tax cut; Gore wanted to increase spending on education and shore up the Social Security system.

Gore, though knowledgeable, seemed stiff, and he occasionally indulged in self-serving bombast, as when he claimed to have "invented" the Internet. Bush's principal offense was against the English language. "Rarely is the question asked," he once declaimed, "Is our children learning?" His poetic flights of fancy did not stay long aloft, as when he evoked American aspirations for "wings to take dream" and endorsed economic growth to "make the pie higher." However exaggerated or garbled their messages, the candidates spent a record $1 billion getting it to the voters.

Having been inundated with advertisements, many on election night breathed a sigh of relief that the election was finally over. They were wrong. By midnight it appeared that Bush had 246 electoral votes, and Gore, 267, with 270 necessary to win; but Florida, with 25 electoral votes, had not been decided. As returns trickled in, the television networks reversed themselves and declared Florida—and the election—"too close to call." Bush's lead there was 1,784 out of nearly 6 million cast.

After a machine recount, Bush's margin in Florida was reduced to several hundred votes, with Democrats complaining that a punch-card ballot used in some communities was confusing, depriving Gore of thousands of votes; worse, the machines routinely failed to count incompletely punched ballots. Gore's lawyers demanded that the ballots in several predominantly Democratic counties be counted by hand. Republicans countered that Democrats had no right to change voting procedures after the election. They demanded that the hand recounts cease.

The entire election ended up in the courts. On December 12, more than a month after the election, the Supreme Court ruled by a five to four vote that the selective hand recounts violated the Constitution's guarantee of equal protection. Bush's victory stood.

Nationwide, Gore received 51 million votes, Bush, 50.5 million. Nader, who did not win any electoral votes, received nearly 3 million.

The New Terrorism

After the fall of the Soviet Union, American military might seemed unassailable. Military dictators who had been kept afloat by the Soviets or the Americans—and often from both simultaneously—now were obliged

The gaping hole in the destroyer USS *Cole*, in the port of Aden, Yemen, was caused by suicide bombers on October 12, 2000. The attack was linked to Osama bin Laden's al-Qaeda terrorist network, based in Afghanistan.

to seek the support of the people they had long ruled. This further destabilized the Middle East. The military leaders of Egypt and hereditary rulers of Saudi Arabia, for example, sought to retain the support of Islamic clerics while refraining from accepting an Islamic theocracy—direct rule by Islamic rulers. Arab leaders cultivated popular support by denouncing Israel, which refused to return land seized in the 1967 war. The United States encouraged Israel to trade that land for peace. But few Israelis believed the promises of Arab leaders who had steadfastly called for the annihilation of Israel and had funded terrorism. Insofar as Israel relied ultimately on American support, Arab rage was increasingly directed at the United States.

During these years, Islamist terrorists emerged throughout the Middle East, usually in response to the repression of radical Islamic clerics. In 1998 a new figure surfaced from among such groups: Osama bin Laden, son of a Saudi oil billionaire. In 1998, bin Laden published a *fatwa*—a religious edict—to Islamic peoples throughout the world: "To kill Americans and their allies, both civil and military, is an individual duty of every Muslim who is able . . ." By now, bin Laden was protected by an extremist Islamic group, the Taliban, that ruled Afghanistan. (The United States had provided military assistance to the Taliban in its ultimately successful campaign to drive the Soviet Union out of the country a decade earlier. See Chapter 30.) Six months later, bin Laden's terrorist organization—al-Qaeda—had planned and ordered the bombings of the U.S. embassies in Nairobi and Dar es Salaam in Africa, which killed hundreds of people. Worse was to follow.

September 11, 2001

At 8:40 on the morning of September 11, 2001, Madeline Amy Sweeney, an attendant on American Airlines Flight 11, placed a cell phone call from the galley of the plane to her supervisor in Boston. In a whisper, she said that four Arab men had slashed the throats of two attendants, forced their way into the cockpit, and taken over the plane. She gave him their seat numbers so that their identities could be determined from the passenger log. The supervisor asked if she knew where the plane was headed. She looked out the window and noted that it was descending rapidly. "I see water and buildings." Then she paused: "Oh my God." The water was the Hudson River, and the buildings were the skyscrapers of lower Manhattan, foremost among them the 110-story twin towers of the World Trade Center.

The hijackers pushed the throttle to full, and the Boeing 767 was traveling at 500 miles per hour at 8:46 when it slammed into the ninety-sixth floor of the north tower. A fireball, fed by 10,000 gallons of jet fuel, instantly engulfed eight or nine stories.

Fifteen minutes later a second airliner came into view over Manhattan harbor, banked sharply, and plowed into the eightieth floor of the south tower. New York mayor Rudolph Giuliani, who had raced to the scene, asked Fire Chief Peter Ganci, "What should I communicate to people?" "Tell them to get in the stairways," Ganci replied. "I think we can save everyone below the fire." The World Trade Center employed 50,000. As thousands fled the buildings, hundreds of firefighters, Ganci among them, charged up the stairs to rescue those who were trapped.

At 9:30 the White House received word that another hijacked airliner was barreling toward Washington, DC. Secret Service agents rushed Vice President Cheney to an emergency command bunker far below the White House. At 9:35 the airliner plunged into the Pentagon and burst into flames. Cheney telephoned President Bush, who was in Sarasota, Florida. The nation was under attack. Bush authorized the Air Force to shoot down any other hijacked airliners. A few minutes later a fourth hijacked airliner crashed into a field in Pennsylvania after passengers had declared their intention—again by cell phone—to retake the plane.

While television viewers absorbed these shocks, they watched as the upper floors of the World Trade Center towers blackened, like charred matches. At 9:59, the south tower collapsed, followed by the north tower a half hour later, pulverizing millions of tons of concrete and glass and enveloping lower Manhattan in choking dust. Nearly three thousand lay dead in the mountain of rubble, including Chief Ganci and 350 firemen; several hundred more perished at the Pentagon and in the crash of the airliner in Pennsylvania.

Teams of four or five Arabic-speaking men had hijacked each of the planes. Several of the hijackers were quickly linked to the al-Qaeda terrorist network run by bin Laden, who had previously been indicted (but not captured) for the 1998 bombing of U.S. embassies in East Africa and the 2000 attack on the USS *Cole*. Bin Laden operated with impunity in Afghanistan.

That evening President Bush addressed the nation. He spoke simply and with force. "We will find these people," he said of the terrorists. "They will pay." Any government harboring the terrorists—an obvious reference to the Taliban—would be held

A second jetliner approaches the south tower of the World Trade Center on September 11, 2001. The north tower had already been hit and was engulfed in flames and smoke.

equally responsible for the attack. Bin Laden, in a video recorded from an undisclosed location, denied involvement in the attack but praised those who carried it out.

Several weeks later, Bush declared that bin Laden would be taken "dead or alive." The president also offered a $25 million reward for his death or capture, an evocation of swift frontier justice that suited the national mood. Within the United States, thousands of Arabs were rounded up and detained; those with visa and immigration violations were imprisoned.

Then more trouble arrived at the capital, this time in the mail. Several letters addressed to government officials included threatening messages and a white powder consisting of billions of anthrax spores, which could prove fatal if touched or inhaled. Thousands of government employees took antibiotics as a precaution, but some spores had seeped out of the envelopes and killed five postal workers and mail recipients.

Bush responded to these multiple threats by creating a Cabinet position, the Office of Homeland

Security, and naming Pennsylvania Governor Tom Ridge to direct it. Repeatedly Ridge issued vague warnings of imminent terrorist attacks. How exactly Americans were to protect themselves, he did not say.

Read the **Document**   George W. Bush, *Address to Congress (September 20, 2001)* at **www.myhistorylab.com**

America Fights Back: War in Afghanistan

Bush had declared a **war on terror**, a war unlike any other the nation had fought. Al-Qaeda had secret terrorist cells in many countries. Bin Laden was ensconced in remote Afghanistan, protected by thousands of Taliban soldiers who had inflicted heavy losses on Soviet invaders in the 1980s. The source of the anthrax letters proved even more problematic, because the spores resembled a strain developed in American military laboratories. (In 2008, an American scientist who had worked in a federal biotech weapons lab committed suicide shortly after the FBI prepared to file charges against him as the sole culprit.)

Bush's challenge was all the greater because of his own stated opposition to ill-defined and far-flung military operations. He had chastised the Clinton-Gore administration for "extending our troops all around the world." He underscored his reticence for such ventures by naming Colin Powell secretary of state. Powell, who had been sobered by his experiences in Vietnam, maintained that U.S. troops should only be deployed when their political objective was clear, military advantage overwhelming, and means of disengaging secure. This became known as the Powell doctrine, and Bush had endorsed it during the campaign. But the proposed war against terror adhered to none of its precepts. Now such scruples did not matter; the president had little choice but to fight.

Powell urged European, Asian, and even Islamic states to crack down on terrorist cells in their countries and to provide assistance in the U.S. military campaign against the Taliban; he also persuaded anti-Taliban factions within Afghanistan to join forces to topple the regime. On September 20 Bush ordered the Taliban to surrender bin Laden and top al-Qaeda leaders; when the Taliban refused, Bush unleashed missiles and warplanes against Taliban installations and defenses, much like the campaign that had ended Serbian aggression against ethnic Muslims in Kosovo.

For several weeks, Taliban soldiers cowered in bunkers as bombs thudded nearby; but they defended their positions when anti-Taliban forces attacked. Then small teams of elite American soldiers, armed with hand-held computers and satellite-linked navigational devices, joined with anti-Taliban contingents, marking Taliban positions with laser spotters and communicating with high-altitude bombers. These planes, circling at 30,000 feet, dropped electronically guided bombs on Taliban troops with uncanny (but not infallible) accuracy. Within weeks the Taliban were driven from power. Only one American soldier was killed by hostile fire. The United States had won the first battles in the war against terror.

The Second Iraq War

In January 2002, after the Taliban had been crushed, President Bush declared that he would not "wait on events while dangers gather." The United States would take "preemptive actions"—war—against regimes that threatened it. He identified Iran, North Korea, and Iraq as an **axis of evil** that warranted scrutiny. Immediately after September 11, he secretly initiated plans to attack Iraq, ruled by Saddam Hussein.

Secretary of State Powell advised Bush not to attack Iraq. If Saddam were driven from power, Powell warned, Bush would become "the proud owner of 25 million people—you'll own it all." Vice President Cheney, Defense Secretary Donald Rumsfeld, and others in the administration insisted that the Iraqis would welcome liberation and embrace democracy. A free Iraq, they added, would stimulate democratic reforms throughout the Middle East, as had happened in Eastern Europe following the collapse of the Soviet Union. Bush agreed.

In September, Bush sought congressional support for an attack on Iraq. "The Iraqi regime possesses chemical and biological weapons," he declared, adding that Saddam also sought nuclear weapons. Congress voted overwhelmingly for the war appropriation.

Bush then called on the United Nations to join the United States. That Saddam had used chemical weapons during the Iran-Iraq war and also against the Kurds was beyond dispute; but following Saddam's defeat in 1991, UN inspectors had destroyed thousands of tons of Iraqi chemical weapons. They doubted that more such weapons had been stockpiled. Bush saw this as proof that Saddam had hoodwinked the inspectors. When the Security Council delayed taking action, Bush formed a coalition to oust Saddam. The United States was joined by Great Britain, Italy, Spain, and a few other countries.

On March 20, 2003, American missiles and bombs pounded Saddam's defenses. The "Shock and Awe" campaign to liberate Iraq had begun. Two armored columns roared across the Kuwaiti border into Iraq, passing burned-out Iraqi tanks from the first Gulf War. British forces moved along the coast toward the oil port of Basra. Television reporters, perched atop Humvees and armored personnel carriers, provided live coverage. The first night, American units advanced halfway to Baghdad.

On April 4, the U.S. Army seized the Baghdad International Airport. That day, television footage aired on Al Jazeera, an Arab television network, showed a man—apparently Saddam—walking through Baghdad and exhorting the Iraqis: "Resist them, O courageous citizens of Baghdad. Our martyrs will go to paradise, and their dead will go to hell." The next morning, some 800 American soldiers in tanks and armored vehicles blasted their way into downtown Baghdad. While some Iraqis poured into the streets to celebrate, others looted offices,

"Mission Accomplished" proclaimed the banner on the USS *Abraham Lincoln*, where on May 1, 2004, President George W. Bush declared, "Major combat operations in Iraq have ended." But the war continued for years.

museums, stores, and hospitals. Saddam disappeared and his government evaporated. By mid-April, the Pentagon declared that major combat operations had come to an end.

But Iraq was in chaos. There were too few U.S. troops to preserve order. Islamist radicals, enraged by the American occupation, joined with Saddam's supporters in ambushing occupation forces. The insurgents rammed trucks filled with explosives into police stations, wired cell phones to artillery shells, and detonated them as Americans approached. Others sabotaged oil pipelines and power generators.

2004: Bush Wins a Second Term

The war became the main issue of the presidential campaign. In December 2003 American soldiers captured Saddam, hiding in an underground bunker. Bush's approval rating soared.

By January, however, Senator John Kerry, a Democratic senator from Massachusetts, was gaining in the polls. The son of a diplomat and a graduate of Yale, Kerry appeared accomplished and steady. He had commanded a patrol boat during the Vietnam War and was decorated for courage under fire. In

Do Historians Ever Get It Right?

The *Debating the Past* essays in previous chapters have offered hundreds of interpretations, many of them contradictory. Why, if historians are looking at the same past, do they see it so differently?

Consider the accompanying photograph. It shows a cityscape as reflected on the many windows of a new skyscraper. Each pane of glass has its own angle of reflection, imposing unique distortions on the scene; note that one window—all black—is open, about to receive a pipe. Historians, too, look at the past from different perspectives, and sometimes crucial pieces of evidence are missing.

Well into the twentieth century, most historians believed that their collective labors—more research, more books—were leading to a composite picture that provided a fuller and clearer rendering of the past. But some historians have doubted whether their profession can sharpen the picture's focus, or whether a coherent vista of "the past" even existed. If our own lives are a jumble of motivations and confusions, how can one paint a portrait of an entire people?

In an exhaustive study of the American Historical Association, Peter Novick (1988) further demonstrated that while historians have long championed objectivity in principle, their research has been riddled with bias. Ignorant of their cultural blinders, historians grope in search of historical truths they can never see.

By undercutting their profession's claims of "truth," Novick's book made historians more susceptible to an idea that was sweeping through literature departments. Known as "deconstruction" or "textualism" and derived from French philosopher Jacques Derrida, it held that "there is nothing outside the text." (Or, to use the metaphor of the photograph, there is nothing beyond the reflections.) No one could reasonably claim to know what a novelist meant by any novel, or what any statesman or historical figure meant by the words he or she spoke or wrote. By extension, no historian can explain what any historical record meant to the people of the times it reflected. Inspired by such observations, Robert F. Berkhofer Jr. (1995) repudiated the very idea of a grand historical narrative, partly because readers would interpret that narrative in their own ways.

Raising Berkhofer's contention at the end of a book that purports to provide just such a narrative may seem perverse. But his point contains an obvious truth: Readers of any work of history, this one included, will make of it what they will.

Source: Peter Novick, *That Noble Dream* (1988); Robert F. Berkhofer Jr., *Beyond the Great Story* (1995); Jacques Derrida, *Deconstruction in a Nutshell* (1997).

April, he won the Democratic nomination. He chose Senator John Edwards of North Carolina, a wealthy trial lawyer, as his running mate.

In Iraq, the situation deteriorated further. In April the *60 Minutes* news program revealed that American captors had tortured Iraqi captives in the Abu Ghraib prison. Photographs of American soldiers, including women, taunting naked Muslim men fueled the insurgency. Casualties mounted. The cost of the occupation spiraled upward. Worse, American forces failed to find any Iraqi weapons of mass destruction.

At the Democratic convention in July, Kerry emphasized his military service in Vietnam. "As president," Kerry declared, "I will fight a smarter, more effective war on terror." He criticized Bush for attacking Iraq before capturing Osama bin Laden, who remained at large. He also chided the president for initiating war with insufficient international support, and not sending enough troops to preserve order and rebuild Iraq.

Bush mobilized conservatives and religious fundamentalists by proposing a constitutional amendment that would define marriage as the union between a man and a woman. Kerry endorsed gay rights but endlessly qualified earlier statements in support of same-sex marriage.

Bush also pounced on Kerry's war record. Some Vietnam veterans seized on the fact that in 1971 Kerry had told a congressional committee that the Vietnam War was wrong and immoral. How, these veterans asked, could an antiwar activist serve as commander-in-chief?

Republicans also portrayed Kerry as opportunistic. If Kerry and Edwards thought the war was a mistake, why did they vote for the original war resolution in the Senate? Kerry became entangled in long-winded explanations. "I actually voted for the $87 billion before I voted against it," he said. Bush gleefully seized on this "flip-flop" and dubbed Kerry "Flipper." During a debate with Bush, Kerry conceded that he had "made a mistake" in explaining his position on Iraq. "But the president made a mistake in invading Iraq. Which is worse?"

"You know where I stand," Bush had declared at nearly every campaign stop, and in the end a majority of voters stood with him. The election, one of the most divisive in recent decades, brought 12 million more voters to the polls than in 2000. Kerry received 57 million votes, 3 million more than Ronald Reagan in his 1984 landslide. But Bush got over 60 million, a record. He also prevailed in the Electoral College, 286 to 252.

Crime: Good News and Bad

The crime wave, which had assumed tsunami dimensions during the 1980s, subsided during the 1990s. By 2009, the homicide rate nationwide was 40 percent below 1991. In many big cities the decline was astonishing. In 1990, for example, 5,641 felonies were committed in New York City's twenty-fourth precinct, near Central Park; in 2009 the number of felonies there had declined to 987. Television shows such as *Hill Street Blues* (1981–1987) and *L.A. Law* (1986–1994), which had chronicled the gritty side of urban life during the crack epidemic of the 1980s, gave way to *Seinfeld* (1989–1998), *Friends* (1994–2004), *Sex and the City* (1998–2004), and other shows that emphasized the vitality and cultural diversity of city life. No longer overwhelmed with crime, cities especially attracted young adults—the children of parents who had fled to the suburbs.

Various explanations were offered for the drop in crime. Some insisted that the "law and order" campaigns of the previous three decades had put the worst criminals in prison, others cited the general health of the economy, and still others credited *Roe v. Wade* (1973) and the legalization of abortion with reducing the number of unwanted children.

But if urban crime was down, violence repeatedly jolted the nation. On April 20, 1999, two teenagers wearing trench coats and armed with automatic weapons went on a rampage at Columbine High School in Littleton, Colorado. Before shooting themselves to death, they killed twelve students and a teacher and wounded more than thirty. On October 2, 2006, a thirty-two-year-old truck driver took a dozen Amish schoolgirls hostage and shot and killed six of them. A week earlier, in two separate incidents, a gunman took six girls hostage at Platte Canyon High School at Bailey, Colorado, and shot and killed one; and a fifteen-year-old student at Weston High School in Cazenovia, Wisconsin, shot and killed his principal.

Perhaps inspired by these attacks, a deranged student at Virginia Tech in February 2007 bought a .22 caliber Walther P22 pistol on the Internet. The next month he bought a Glock 19 rapid-fire semi-automatic pistol and acquired ammunition from online vendors and from Wal-Mart and Dick's Sporting Goods. On April 16 he went to another dorm and shot and killed a female student and the resident advisor. After reloading, he entered Norris Hall, an engineering building, chained all three entry doors closed, climbed the stairs to the second floor, and walked up and down the hallway, taking aim at students and teachers and shooting them. Then he put a pistol to his head and committed suicide. The shooting spree at Norris lasted less than ten minutes: He shot over sixty people, killing thirty-three.

The massacre at Virginia Tech was the worst mass killing in recent American history. But each year, about 14,000 Americans are killed with guns. The spate of shootings reignited a heated debate. Proponents of gun control deplored the easy access to such lethal weapons. The National Rifle Association and other defenders of the right to bear arms, affirmed by the Second Amendment to the Constitution, blamed criminals for the mayhem. They insisted that law-abiding citizens needed guns to defend themselves from such evildoers. In 2010 the Supreme Court struck down municipal laws banning handguns in Chicago and the District of Columbia (*McDonald v. Chicago*).

Hurricane Katrina

The Bush presidency was largely shadowed by two events over which he initially had little control: the terrorist attack of September 11, 2001, and Hurricane Katrina, which swept across Florida and into the warm waters of the Gulf Coast in August 2005. On the morning of August 28, the National Weather Service released so dire a warning about Katrina—"devastating damage," "most of the area will be uninhabitable for weeks"—that some broadcasters refused to read it, thinking it might be a hoax. State and federal officials ordered mandatory evacuation of the Louisiana coastline.

Millions fled in their cars, clogging the highways. But of the half million residents of New Orleans, 100,000 remained, many of them poor African Americans who lacked access to automobiles. As rain started to fall that evening, some 10,000 took refuge in the New Orleans Superdome stadium.

Early the next morning Katrina crashed ashore. Within minutes, it destroyed nearly every building in Plaquemines Parish. Winds approaching 150 miles per hour ripped two holes in the Superdome. By afternoon, the hurricane had moved north, dumping more water along the way, swelling the rivers, streams, and canals that emptied into the Gulf. Within hours, rising waters spilled over the banks and collapsed canals.

Downtown New Orleans after Hurricane Katrina.

Then the levees at Lake Pontchartrain broke, flooding much of New Orleans.

Rural areas were hit equally hard. Waters rose so rapidly that thousands sought refuge on their roofs; many drowned when rising waters trapped them in attics. At St. Rita's Nursing Home in St. Bernard Parish, water rose to the ceiling of the one-story building in twenty minutes. Frantic workers attempted to float bed-ridden elderly out of windows on mattresses; within an hour thirty-five were dead.

By that evening, much of New Orleans was underwater. Some 25,000 people crowded into the Superdome. Food and water grew scarce. Fights broke out. When officials locked the Superdome's doors, the thousands left outside went to the nearby Convention Center, surged past security guards, and took possession of the complex.

At first, no one comprehended the dimensions of the catastrophe. Communication systems failed. The winds knocked out power and phone lines and cell phone towers; those cell phone towers that remained standing were overloaded. Over the next three days, the situation worsened. Over a million people had been displaced from their homes. In the heat and humidity, dead bodies, sewage, rotting food and plants, and factory effluents combined to form a fetid and toxic inland sea. The Convention Center, which now housed 20,000, descended into anarchy. There were reports of rape and murder. Throughout the storm-devastated region, looting became widespread; public order collapsed.

"Mr. President, we need your help," declared Louisiana Governor Kathleen Blanco. But TV crews arrived on the scene long before assistance from the Federal Emergency and Management Agency (FEMA). Television viewers were outraged to see footage of the dead floating in pools of filth or abandoned in wheelchairs.

Yet Michael Chertoff, secretary of Homeland Security (which oversaw FEMA), expressed satisfaction with its efforts. "Considering the dire circumstances that we have in New Orleans, virtually a city that has been destroyed—things are going relatively well," he declared. By then, more than 1,300 were dead.

Many shared in the blame. For decades, engineers had warned that the levees and canals in New Orleans could fail, but little was done to strengthen them. Environmentalists had complained of the overdevelopment and erosion of the coastal marshes and wetlands whose vegetation sponged up excess water, but their warnings, too, had been mostly ignored. Officials in New Orleans had neglected to devise an evacuation plan for those without cars; worse, one-sixth of the police force abandoned the city before the

storm struck. Mayor C. Ray Nagin inexplicably took refuge in the twenty-seven-story Hyatt; when he ventured down the stairs—the elevators ceased working when power failed—his statements were emotional and confused. In Washington, FEMA director Michael Brown was so worried about making a mistake that he failed to do much at all—the worse mistake possible. Bush erred in publicly complimenting the beleaguered FEMA director: "Brownie, you're doing a heck of a job," a statement so obviously at variance with public perception that it became an instant joke. Within a week Brown was demoted; soon afterward he resigned.

Katrina was not the worst natural disaster in the nation's history. In 1900 a hurricane destroyed Galveston, then the largest city in Texas, killing 10,000. In 1906 an earthquake hit San Francisco, ignited hundreds of fires that burned 500 blocks of the city, and killed 700—a larger proportion of the population than perished in Katrina. But apart from Katrina's terrible human toll, the hurricane pointed up the nation's vulnerability. If Homeland Security could not get buses or water to New Orleans in a timely fashion, how could it protect the nation from determined terrorists or respond effectively should they mount another attack?

Iraq Insurgency and Bush's "Surge"

Bush faltered during Katrina partly because he was distracted by Iraq. Ironically, the chaos left in the wake of Katrina in many ways paralleled the collapse of civil society in Iraq after Saddam. (A further irony: Half of the Louisiana National Guard was missing during Katrina because it had been sent to restore order in Iraq.) Iraq certainly needed all the help it could get. Insurgents blew up police stations and marketplaces; saboteurs destroyed power facilities and cut oil pipelines; and rival religious sects, tribes, warlords, and criminal gangs pushed the country toward anarchy.

While coalition forces attempted to halt the violence, political officials laid the foundations for a new Iraqi government. On June 28, 2004, the coalition transferred nominal authority to an Iraqi Governing Council whose chief task was to organize the election of a National Assembly to draft a constitution. On January 30, 2005, nearly 8 million Iraqis went to the polls, almost two-thirds of the eligible voters.

The election, though fraught with irregularities, offered a glimpse of the democratic Iraq that Bush hoped would initiate a broader transformation of the Middle East. But the election also underscored the divisions within Iraq. In the north, the Kurdish

In 2006 an Iraqi tribunal convicted Saddam Hussein of murdering his own people and sentenced him to death by hanging. What might have been a defining moment in the emergence of a new Iraq was marred when he was rushed to the gallows and taunted by his executioners.

majority won most of the seats, but Kurdish leaders sought to form their own state and secede. In the south, the Shiites embraced a messianic strain of Islam and had strong ties to the radical Islamic clerics who ruled Iran. The Sunnis, adherents of the version of Islam that prevailed in most of the Arab world from Saudi Arabia through North Africa, dominated the region around Baghdad. Post-Saddam Iraq was on the verge of fracturing into separate nations.

Complicating matters further was the decision by terrorists to wreck the new government by driving a deeper wedge between Sunnis and Shiites. On February 22, 2006, insurgents blew up the golden dome of the Askariya Mosque in Sammara, a Shiite shrine. Enraged Shiites attacked Sunni mosques and clerics, triggering an endless cycle of reprisals. Some Iraqi military and police officers formed extralegal death squads to eliminate Sunni leaders and terrorize their followers. Sunni militias responded in kind.

In the fall of 2006, an Iraqi tribunal convicted Saddam of killing 148 Shiites, the first of several planned trials to chronicle his regime's genocide. But on December 30, 2006, the Iraqi government dispatched Saddam to the gallows. Instead of marking

the triumph of law over tyranny, the executioners resembled the Shiite death squads: Hangmen taunted Saddam and chanted the name of Muqtada Al Sadr, a Shiite cleric whose militias caused much of the chaos.

Through it all, American officials groped their way through the bewildering labyrinth of Iraqi politics and religion. U.S. policies seemed to offend everyone. Often the only apparent issue uniting Iraqi factions was their condemnation of "infidel" troops in Iraq. Yet thoughtful Iraqis conceded that in the absence of American soldiers, Iraq would likely fracture, plunging the country into full-scale civil war and perhaps setting the entire Middle East ablaze. Bush decided to persist.

Attacks on security forces and civilians intensified and casualties mounted. As the 2006 U.S. congressional elections approached, the war was costing $2 billion a week; the annual U.S. deficit soared to a half trillion dollars. Democrats, most of whom had voted for the war, increasingly withdrew their support. Some Republicans, too, defected from the president's position.

When the midterm votes were counted, the Republicans were decisively defeated. Democrats now controlled Congress—and the budget. Several days

On March 20, 2003, American, British, and NATO forces commenced the assault to drive Saddam Hussein from power. It marked the beginning of the second Gulf War, also known as "Operation Iraqi Freedom." Saddam was swiftly driven from power, but by March 20, 2010, the seventh anniversary of the war, Americans were still fighting in Iraq and Afghanistan. By then, over 5,000 United States service personnel had died, including over 100 women; over 25,000 had been wounded. The following soldiers are a random sample of that group, chosen because they died on the March 20 anniversary of the onset of the war.

Francisco ("Paquito") Martinez, 20

Francisco G. Martinez.

"Paquito" Martinez was born on December 16, 1984 in San Juan, Puerto Rico. He was the son of Francisco Martinez, an army soldier and air force airman, and Carmen R. Hernandez. In 2000 Paquito moved to Ft. Worth, Texas, where he joined his father, "Paco," and his stepmother Maria. His father worked as a computer software engineer. Paquito enjoyed skateboarding, drawing, poetry and Web design. He sang and performed in a rock band that played minge, grundge, and heavy metal. An "army brat," he vowed never to follow his father into military service. But several months after graduating from Eastern Hills High School in 2002, "Paquito" enlisted. He thought he might eventually go into computer-based graphic design.

In 2003 he was stationed in Korea. The next year he was sent to Iraq. He soon had doubts about the war. "I will serve myself, my family, my friends, and my loved ones," he blogged. "I won't serve my country, nor will I serve its leaders."

Later that year he completed a video entitled "Peacefull." Grass sways in the foreground; a hill sits in the distance. In editing the video, Martinez drained it of color: http://www.mfconsulting.com/fm5/videos/peacefull-raw1.asf

The text is sparse:

take this time to breathe
open your mind
feel your worries flow free

Then a monarch butterfly, in dazzling yellows and orange, wafts across the scene.

life is what you make of it

This last phrase was a rendering of a *Meditation* of René Descartes, the seventeenth-century French philosopher. The video was set to Moby's haunting song, "When It's Cold I'd Like to Die."

On March 20, 2005, while on patrol in Tamin, Iraq, a sniper shot Martinez in the hip, severing an artery; despite trauma surgery, he died within an hour.

Curtis E. Glawson Jr., 24

Curtis E. Glawson Jr.

Curtis E. Glawson was born on June 10, 1982, in Detroit, Michigan. His parents—Yolanda and Curtis Sr.—were both career soldiers. As a child Curtis traveled with his parents from one base to another in Germany, New Mexico, Georgia, and Alabama. He learned to adapt to different people and cultures and made friends quickly; his smile was electric.

Glawson was fast and agile and he excelled in sports. When not engaged in football, baseball, basketball and running, he enjoyed sports-related video games. He was a passionate fan of all Detroit (and Michigan) sports teams: the Tigers, Lions, Pistons, Red Wings, and the Wolverines. Friends called him Mr. ESPN.

In 2000 Glawson graduated from Daleville high school in Alabama, near Fort Rucker. He immediately enlisted in the army. That fall he was sent to Fort Jackson, South Carolina, where he received advanced training in mechanics. Certified as a light truck mechanic, he was subsequently stationed in Afghanistan, Uzbekistan, and Korea.

In Korea, he met Hyunjung Jang; the couple married at the United States embassy in Seoul in September, 2005.

In February, 2007 he was sent to Baghdad in Iraq. Once, when his unit made a wrong turn, they encountered a group of preteens armed with AK-47 automatic weapons. Although he grew increasingly nervous about his missions, he relished his work. When his mother urged him to beg off dangerous assignments, he replied, "No, momma, I can't do that. I have a job to do."

On the morning of March 20, 2007, Glawson was sent to retrieve a truck that broke down in the outskirts of Baghdad. He went out, fixed it, and brought it back to the motor pool. Later that afternoon, his platoon sergeant asked if Curtis could rescue another disabled vehicle in a dangerous sector. "I'm good to go, sergeant," Glawson replied. "Are you sure?" the officer asked, looking him in the eye. "Always ready, sergeant," Glawson replied.

That journey proved to be his last. As the road wound toward the dusty hills outside Baghdad, an **Improvised explosive device (IED)** blew up his vehicle. Glawson was killed instantly. He wanted to be remembered as a loving son, husband, brother, friend, and dedicated soldier.

Wayne R. Cornell, 26

Wayne R. Cornell.

Wayne Cornell was born August 3, 1980, in Grand Island, Nebraska. His father, Larry Cornell, was a Vietnam veteran and an electrician; his mother, Patricia, worked in a factory. When Wayne was three his parents divorced. Several years later his mother married Ronald Perrie, who became a major influence in Wayne's life.

At an early age, Wayne was attracted to martial arts. He later specialized in Hapkido, a Korean variant, and attained third degree black belt in Tae Kwon Do. In 1999 he graduated from Silver Lake High School in Roseland, Nebraska.

For a time Cornell considered becoming a police officer. But military service ran deep in the family; in addition to his father, Cornell's grandfather had served in World War II and his great-grandfather in World War I. In 2001 Wayne enlisted in the National Guard and was stationed in Hastings, Nebraska. The next year he married Patricia Warburton; the couple had three children: Dameion, Zoie, and Sadie—the third born three months after Wayne's death. He did tours in Bosnia and Afghanistan. He was also a volunteer fireman and emergency medical technician in Holstein, Nebraska.

In 2005 Cornell joined the U.S. Army and was stationed in Fort Riley, Kansas. Soon thereafter he was sent to Iraq, where he served as a sergeant. "He embraced the responsibilities, consequences and sacrifices" that went with military service, his sister, JaDeen, recalled. His family said that he never expressed opinions on the war.

On March 20, 2007, while on a patrol on the outskirts of Baghdad, an IED blew up near his vehicle. He was killed. (This explosion was separate from the one that killed Glawson that same day.)

Daniel J. Geary, 22

Daniel J. Geary.

Daniel Geary was born on September 12, 1986, the son of Michael Geary, machine foreman, and Agnes Geary, machine operator, in Rome, New York. Daniel was the fourth of seven children. When he was eight, he smelled smoke and pulled his four-year-old sister from a room that was engulfed in flames.

As a teenager, Geary enjoyed paintball, working on his Chevy Sebring, and bowling. At sixteen, he bowled his first perfect game. He attended Rome Free Academy, a public high school, but dropped out a few weeks before graduation. For a time, he was unsure of what to do with his life. He landed a job at the Turning Stone Casino in Rome, owned by the Oneida Indians. Several months later, however, he resolved to get his diploma. "I was never more proud of him," his mother recalled. In 2006 he returned to school, joined the officer training program, and decided on a career in the military. In June, shortly before receiving his diploma, he enlisted in the Marines and soon subscribed to its motto wholeheartedly: *semper fidelis* (always faithful).

In September, Geary reported to Camp Lejeune, North Carolina, where he met his fiancée. In November, 2008, after a tour of duty on a ship in the Indian Ocean, he was sent to Kandahar, Afghanistan. He was impressed by the mountains that towered above ancient valleys. "Other than people trying to shoot me and blow me up," he told his mother, "you can't believe how beautiful it is over here."

On March 19, 2009, he was part of a team of Marines that caught an enemy bomber near a police station. The next day the team returned to the station to encourage the local police to work harder to capture insurgents. While the others were meeting inside, Geary stood guard, manning a machine gun in a Humvee. Then a car with police markings came through the gate, approached the Humvee and blew up, killing Geary instantly.

Question for Discussion

■ These four soldiers are among the millions who made the American nation but whose names so often are missing from historical accounts. What other unsung heroes are missing from this book?

after the election Bush dismissed Defense Secretary Rumsfeld, acknowledging voter "displeasure with the lack of progress in Iraq." But the president vowed to remain. "America's going to stand with you," Bush promised Iraqi leaders.

Democrats named Nancy Pelosi Speaker of the House of Representatives, the first woman to hold that position. Insofar as the speaker follows the vice president in chain of succession, Pelosi became the highest-ranking woman ever to hold office in the United States. In January 2007, when Bush called for a modest increase in troop levels in Iraq, Pelosi and some prominent Democrats opposed the measure. The Democratic leadership in Congress voted to reduce funding for the war, actions Bush vetoed.

In January, 2007 Bush named General David Petraeus to command a **"surge"** in American troop levels in Iraq. Petraeus advanced a doctrine summarized by the phrase: clear, hold, and build. The troops were to remove insurgents from a region, establish military control over it, and build stronger ties with the Iraqi people. Initially, Petraeus made little progress. The losses among American military personnel mounted (see American Lives, "Four Heroes," pp. 866–867). Petraeus shifted more military tasks to the Iraqis and reduced operations that would likely lead to high civilian casualties. He also worked to bring former Sunni leaders into the Iraqi government. By the spring of 2008, the violence in Iraq had declined; the "surge" appeared to be working.

2008: McCain v. Obama

By the spring of 2008 John McCain, a Republican senator from Arizona, was far ahead in the race for the Republican nomination. McCain had piloted a navy fighter-bomber during the Vietnam war. After his plane was shot down over North Vietnam, he was held as a prisoner-of-war for six years; occasionally he was tortured. Now seventy-one, McCain if elected would be the oldest person to serve as a first-term president. (Reagan was sixty-nine when first elected president and seventy-three when reelected.) Although McCain's positions were similar to those of Bush, McCain had often criticized the president and described himself as a "maverick."

True to his own label, he surprised pundits by naming Sarah Palin, the little-known governor of Alaska, as running mate. Her youth (forty-four) counterbalanced McCain's age. Palin also exhibited a down-to-earth feistiness. "What's the difference between a pitbull and a hockey mom?" she asked during her acceptance speech. Her reply—"Lipstick"—brought roars from delighted conservatives. As her joke suggested, Palin was a new type of feminist: a former beauty queen who hunted and fished; an ardent defender of traditional family values who pursued an extravagantly ambitious career.

Among Democrats, Hillary Clinton, now a senator from New York, emerged as frontrunner. But she was soon eclipsed by Barack Obama, a first-term senator from Illinois (see Chapter 31, American Lives, "Barack Obama," pp. 824–825). Clinton had voted for the war in Iraq while Obama opposed it; otherwise they agreed on most issues. During the primary campaign, Obama exuded an almost serene self-possession while Clinton often seemed ill-at-ease. Obama won the Democratic nomination and named Joe Biden, a senator from Delaware, as his running-mate.

During the general election McCain pointed out that Obama had failed to serve even a single full term as U.S. senator: Obama, he claimed, was unqualified for the presidency. But McCain's choice of Palin deprived McCain of his strongest issue. Palin had served as governor for only two and a half years; before that she was mayor of tiny Wasilla, Alaska. When critics questioned her experience in foreign affairs, her breezy reply—"You can actually see Russia from land here in Alaska"—cast doubt on McCain's judgment.

Obama criticized the Republican administration for waging war against Iraq, thereby diverting resources that might have crushed the main 9/11 culprits: the Taliban in Afghanistan and Osama bin Laden, who remained at large. Obama proposed moving troops from Iraq to Afghanistan. He also advocated a major expansion of federally backed health care. McCain sought to send more troops to Iraq: The "war on terror" did not allow retreats. He also criticized Obama's health-care proposal as a major step toward socialized medicine.

McCain, a conservative, accepted public support to help finance his campaign, while Obama, a liberal, rejected public financing—the first candidate to do so. (The campaign finance reform law of 1976, passed after the Watergate scandal, limited the amount that could be spent in publicly supported campaigns.) Obama proceeded to raise a staggering $750 million, much of it from small contributors, and vastly outspent McCain. Obama also demonstrated an ability to mobilize and energize young people, especially through new electronic media. (See the introduction to Chapter 9, pp. 246–247.) By late summer, he was ahead in the polls.

But as the campaign was heating up, a tremor rocked the foundations of the global economic system.

Republican candidates John McCain and Sarah Palin campaign at Franklin & Marshall University in 2008.

Alarming financial news pushed the campaign out of the headlines.

Watch the Video *The Historical Significance of the 2008 Presidential Election* at **www.myhistorylab.com**

Financial Meltdown

The fault lines of the 2008–2009 crisis extended to the 1990s. At that time the economy appeared to have recovered from the recession that began in 1973. But while the stock market soared, wages lagged far behind. Consumers, reasoning that the Cold War was over and the economy healthy, went on a spending spree. Within a decade their savings were gone. By 2005, for the first time since the Great Depression, the American people spent more than they earned. Mostly they bought houses. But how, without savings, could they afford down payments? Politicians, bankers, and financial "wizards" had devised several solutions. In 2002 President George W. Bush declared that the government should "encourage folks to own their own home."

Homeowners, he believed, were more responsible citizens than renters. Democrats, too, regarded home ownership as a crucial step out of poverty. Leaders in both parties advocated easier lending requirements and prodded the huge federally owned mortgage companies to issue more mortgages. Private mortgage companies followed suit. They reasoned that as house prices increased, the ability of homeowners to repay loans mattered less: A repossessed house could be sold for more than the original mortgage loan.

Granted easier credit, millions of Americans for the first time bought homes. In 1994, 64 percent of U.S. families owned homes; by 2004, the percentage had increased to 69 percent, the highest ever. Housing prices soared. Many homeowners bought bigger ones—"McMansions," in the slang of the day. By 2008, one in every five new houses had three or more garages.

Soon banks and mortgage companies had exhausted their capital. Large international investment banks such as Goldman Sachs, Lehman Brothers, and

All of the homes in this new neighborhood of Brentwood, California are for sale, evidence of the collapse of the mortgage market in 2008–2009.

Bear Stearns more than filled the void. They bought tens of thousands of mortgages from the original banks and lending institutions. Lending banks used this revenue to loan out more mortgages—thereby generating more profits (and bonuses). International investment firms chopped up the mortgages like sausages, clumped them into complicated investment bundles, and sold the bundles to investors worldwide. Credit-rating companies, such as Moody's and Standard and Poor's, pronounced the bundles to be sound investments. And many investors bought insurance from the American Insurance Group (AIG) to protect them if the bundles somehow went bad. AIG, perceiving little risk, failed to set aside much money to cover potential losses.

By late 2008, however, millions of homeowners were swamped with bills they could not pay. Total household debt in the United States exceeded

Table 32.1 Causes of the 2008–2009 Financial Crisis

Consumers exhaust savings to buy houses
The president and Congress call on federally owned mortgage companies to relax lending requirements
Global investment bankers devise complicated bundles of mortgages and market them globally
Credit-rating agencies grade these mortgage investments as solid and AIG insures them
Lending banks issue mortgages greatly in excess of available reserves
Millions of homeowners fall into debt and cannot make mortgage payments
Collapse of mortgage investments brings down investment banks
Capital evaporates, leading to layoffs and threatening a second Great Depression

$14.5 *trillion*—twenty times more than in 1974. Nearly 10 percent of all American mortgages were delinquent or in foreclosure. Goldman Sachs quietly placed bets that the mortgage bundles it had mass-marketed would lose their value!

Investors suddenly caught on and dumped their mortgage bundles. Panic selling hit financial markets worldwide. Almost overnight, Bear Stearns collapsed and Lehman Brothers went bankrupt. The Dow Jones Industrial Average plunged from over 14,000 to under 9,000; stocks lost $8 trillion. Pension funds, corporate reserves, and personal accounts for retirement and college education lost one-third of their value. AIG, swamped with claims, neared bankruptcy. Its failure would take down many of the world's major banks and investment firms.

Nearly all banks and investment houses ran low on capital; many struggled to stave off bankruptcy. Few could make new loans. But most businesses, hospitals, schools, state and municipal governments relied on short-term loans, which were repaid as revenues came in. In the absence of these customary loans, few employers could pay bills or cover payrolls. A global calamity loomed.

In the final months of 2008, Bush and his chief financial advisers raced to avert catastrophe. Ben Bernanke, head of the Federal Reserve and a scholar of the Great Depression, pleaded with Congress to authorize over $700 billion to buy up the "toxic" mortgage bundles, an indirect way of preserving the banks and global investment firms that had issued them. He also proposed to pump hundreds of billions directly into Goldman Sachs, AIG, and scores of other investment banks. Such companies, he warned, were "too big to fail." Congress seethed at using taxpayers' money to bail out avaricious corporate executives; but political leaders could not risk a second Great Depression. Congress passed the emergency bail-out bills with few modifications.

"Yes We Can": Obama Elected President

The economic crisis caught nearly everyone by surprise. Much of the blame fell on Republicans, whose support for deregulation of financial markets dated from the Reagan era. McCain was especially hurt by the economic meltdown. On September 15, 2008, the day after Lehman Brothers declared bankruptcy, McCain downplayed the crisis, claiming "The fundamentals of our economy are strong." Within a few hours, the stock market fell 500 points. He appeared to be out of touch.

Obama's oft-repeated (albeit vague) insistence on change now acquired new meaning. When confronted with "impossible odds," he insisted, "Americans have responded with a simple creed: Yes we can." The nation was ready for change. On election day, Obama won by over 8 million votes; his victory in the Electoral College was by a 365 to 173 margin.

McCain generously acknowledged the historic character of the election. "I recognize the special significance it has for African Americans and the special pride that must be theirs tonight," he noted. Obama's victory stunned foreigners. Chinese leaders and intellectuals took it for granted that "America could not accept a black president," reported Wang Jisi of Peking University. Nelson Mandela, the black leader of the movement that toppled white rule in South Africa, claimed that Obama's election inspired everyone who wanted "to change the world for a better place." Gordon Brown, prime minister of Great Britain, called Obama's election "a moment that will live in history as long as history books are written."

Obama as President

Only a few weeks after Obama, his wife Michelle, and their two daughters had moved into the White House, he was awarded the Nobel Prize "for his extraordinary efforts to strengthen international diplomacy and cooperation between peoples." Abashed at receiving an award in the expectation that he would earn it, Obama gave the $1.4 million prize to charity. Nevertheless, Obama's intentions of changing the course of American foreign policy were evident. He closed CIA-run secret prisons and banned torture and other means of coercion during interrogation of suspected terrorists. He named Hillary Clinton secretary of state and promised to work more closely with the international community.

In Iraq, Obama proceeded cautiously. He asked Robert Gates, secretary of defense under Bush, to remain in that capacity in his administration. He also announced a plan to withdraw most American troops from Iraq by the fall of 2010.

During his first months as president, however, Obama was mostly absorbed in the financial crisis. Despite repeated promises of change, he retained many of Bush's chief financial advisers; nearly all were Wall Street insiders. Critics grumbled that it made little sense to ask those who had broken the economy to put it back together. But Obama had little choice. No one else understood the complicated mathematical

President-elect Barack Obama, his daughters, and wife, Michelle, celebrate his victory in November, 2008.

models on which modern trading was based; unfortunately, few Wall Street executives understood them either. Macroeconomics, some economists maintained, had become an elaborate exercise in chaos theory.

By late March 2009 the Dow Jones had fallen below 6,600, down from 14,000 seventeen months earlier. Chrysler declared bankruptcy, followed by General Motors several months later. Huge layoffs ensued. Unemployment rose steadily, surpassing 10 percent for the first time in several decades. Obama pumped another $700 billion into the struggling economy.

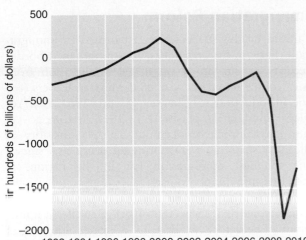

Annual Federal Deficit (and Surplus), 1992–2010 After years of deficits, the federal government operated at a $250 billion surplus in 2000. But the war on terror after 9/11 resulted in massive deficits, which were exacerbated by the financial meltdown after 2008.

that once the stimulus money had been exhausted, employment, wages, and prices would again fall and the nation would slip into a recession—or worse. Others pointed to the projected $1.8 trillion deficit for 2009 and predicted rampant inflation. Insofar as no one had forecast the financial meltdown of 2008–2009, most political leaders discounted *all* economic predictions and simply hoped for the best.

✓•⎯Study and **Review** *The Connection Between Obama & Lincoln* at www.myhistorylab.com

Health Care Reform

Obama now moved ahead on his promise to reform health care. Veteran politicians and pundits smiled at his bold words. In 1993 President Clinton, a formidable politician, had mounted a major campaign to enact a health care reform spearheaded by his wife, Hillary. They failed.

Then word leaked out that hundreds of millions of dollars had been paid in bonuses to executives of Goldman Sachs, AIG, and many of the big banks that had been saved by federal bailouts. Obama railed against their ill-timed greed and slapped the companies with nuisance taxes, but he could do little else. He needed the big financial institutions to help jolt the economy back to life.

By the fall of 2009, the strategy appeared to be working. Employment increased and the stock market rose. Some banks repaid their government loans. Talk of economic collapse abated, partly because predictions varied widely. Some economists insisted

But by 2009 nearly everyone agreed that medical costs had spun out of control. In 1990, per capital medical expenditures were $3,000; by 2009, they exceeded $8,000. That year, though nearly 18 percent of the nation's gross domestic product went for medical care, some 46 million Americans lacked any coverage whatsoever. When struck by serious illness, they were denied treatment or were hit with staggering bills. More than half of the nation's personal bankruptcies were precipitated by illness.

Fingers pointed in every direction. Doctors blamed lawyers, whose success at winning huge malpractice settlements drove up the cost of malpractice insurance premiums. Lawyers blamed the

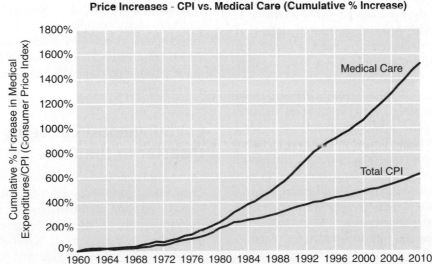

Price Increases - CPI vs. Medical Care (Cumulative % Increase)

The Increasing Cost of Health Care, 1960-2008 (% increase) By the 1990s, health care cost increases greatly exceeded the increase in the Consumer Price Index.

medical profession for failing to weed out incompetent doctors. Nearly everyone blamed the insurance companies, which earned large profits by processing forms. A major factor was Medicare itself: By pushing so much money into health care, the federal government, which paid for nearly half of all health care expenses, increased the price of health care services and goods. Technological improvements, too, rendered medical treatment more costly.

Obama's goal was twofold: to provide health care to Americans who lacked it and to reduce health care costs. Some advocated a government-run system, such as Franklin Roosevelt had done with old age pensions through Social Security. Many European governments operated health care systems along similar lines. But opposition to socialized medicine in the United States was intense. Polls showed that few Americans wanted their doctors to be employees of the federal government.

Supported by Democratic leaders in Congress, Obama proposed a system that combined private and public health insurance. Elderly and poor Americans would continue to be covered by the government; private insurers would continue to insure millions of Americans, but they could not kick people out of their systems when they became ill; companies with more than fifty employees would be required to provide health care insurance for employees and their families or else face stiff penalties; most other persons would be eligible for publicly supported health insurance.

Republicans almost uniformly denounced the plan; they insisted that Americans did not want the federal government to control health care. Republicans instead recommended tax incentives or state initiatives to encourage private employers to broaden coverage. Republicans added that the federal government, with a looming annual deficit of $1.8 trillion, would be hard-pressed to pay for Medicare in the future; to embark on a major new commitment was madness.

The Democrats, despite strong majorities in both houses of Congress, were themselves divided on Obama's plan. The final compromise provided for his reform to be phased in over ten years at a cost of $1 trillion, and coverage would not be universal: By 2019, 24 million people would still lack health insurance, about a third of them illegal immigrants.

In March 2010, Congress approved the measure—the vote in the House was 220 to 207. No Republican voted for the bill. Obama had nevertheless engineered the first major health care reform since 1965, when President Lyndon Johnson signed Medicare into law.

Immigration Reform

Buoyed by this success, Obama turned to immigration. Early in his presidency, he strengthened border security to cut down on illegal immigration from Mexico, an action that angered Mexican leaders (see the introduction to Chapter 11, pp. 296–297). Yet illegal immigration persisted. In 2010 Arizona governor Jan Brewer, complaining that "the majority of illegal trespassers" were "bringing drugs in," signed the toughest immigration law in the nation. It required immigrants to carry alien registration forms at all times and authorized police to stop and question anyone they suspected of being an illegal immigrant. Legislators in dozens of states introduced similar bills. Obama denounced such laws as a form of racial profiling and ordered the Justice Department to take legal action against the Arizona bill. He also called for a federal initiative to prevent states from acting "irresponsibly."

Obama also steered toward a compromise. He rejected state plans for rounding up and deporting the nation's 11 million illegal immigrants; he also opposed liberal proposals to declare an "amnesty" against illegal immigrants and grant them immediate citizenship. Instead he proposed a "practical, common-sense" solution—a "pathway to citizenship." Illegal immigrants would be granted citizenship only after they admitted they had broken the law, paid a fine and back taxes, and provided evidence of a willingness to assimilate, such as by learning English. As with health care reform, Obama outlined few specifics, preferring to allow Congress to shape the plan.

Republicans bristled; without more effective policing of the border, Obama's "reform" would encourage more illegal immigrants to pour into the country. Many complained that Obama was courting Hispanic voters just a few months ahead of the 2010 congressional elections. The prospects for quick passage of comprehensive immigration reform seemed poor.

Environmental Concerns and Disaster in the Gulf

During his first weeks in office, Obama had pledged a "new era of global cooperation on climate change." Nearly everyone assumed that he intended to push for ratification of the 1997 agreement, signed by more than 130 nations at Kyoto, Japan, to reduce emissions of carbon dioxide and other atmospheric pollutants. The Senate had opposed the Kyoto accords because developing nations—including

In 2010 protesters in Washington DC demanded that the Obama administration support liberalized immigration policies.

China, the worst air polluter in the world—were exempted from its costly provisions. President Clinton never submitted the treaty for ratification. In 2001, President George W. Bush withdrew the United States from subsequent negotiations. But in 2006 the mayors of over 200 U.S. cities, struggling with smog and air pollution, signed a Climate Protection Agreement pledging to meet the Kyoto targets for greenhouse gas reductions by 2012. But if Obama intended to move in the direction of the Kyoto agreements, the economic crisis of 2008–2009 changed his mind. With the nation's economy in recession, Obama thought it unwise to impose new environmental restrictions. In late 2009 he quietly withdrew support for an international arrangement on atmospheric pollutants.

By then, political economic realities had already caused Obama to backtrack on another environmental issue. Originally an opponent of oil drilling off the Atlantic coast, he changed his position during the 2008 presidential campaign: The nation needed cheap oil and gasoline (see introduction, Chapter 30, pp. 796–797). On April 21, 2010, disaster struck in the Gulf of Mexico. Workers aboard a British Petroleum (BP) oil platform forty-one miles off the coast of Louisiana were drilling for oil at a depth of 5,000 feet. This was not exceptional; for over a decade, global oil companies had been sinking hundreds of wells into the Gulf of Mexico, which generated one-fourth of all oil produced in the United States. But that day, a drill hit a pocket of methane gas under high pressure; it shot upward through the

A brown pelican surveys the ecological damage caused by the BP oil spill in the Gulf of Mexico in 2010.

drilling pipe and exploded, blasting eleven workers from the platform and engulfing it in flames. (The bodies of the workers were not found.) Oil gushed from the damaged pipe, an upsetting image captured by underwater cameras and transmitted by streaming video on the Web. The world watched in horror as BP's repeated attempts to cap the well failed; weeks passed as hundreds of millions of gallons of oil spewed into the Gulf, fouling marshes and beaches, killing fish, birds, and aquatic life. Obama called it the "worst environmental disaster America has faced."

Pressure built on him to "do something." Exactly what was unclear. "He can't put on scuba gear and go down and stop this well," observed New York City mayor Michael Bloomberg, a Republican. Obama forced BP to set aside $20 billion to cover damage claims and sacked the director of the Minerals Management Service for failing to adequately inspect the off-shore platforms. He also declared a six-month moratorium on deepwater drilling, pending the inspection of existing platforms.

But this provoked howls of protest. Opponents of the moratorium included both of Louisiana's senators and its governor, Bobby Jindal, who noted that the oil industry accounted for 17 percent of Louisiana's jobs and much of the state's revenue. "The last thing we need is to enact public policies that will certainly destroy thousands of existing jobs," Jindal added. Such opposition underscored the dilemma confronting a nation whose thirst for cheap oil was unquenchable. The exhaustion of oil reserves beneath the earth's landmass necessitated offshore drilling; but the environmental risks of deep-sea drilling were all too apparent.

Obama resurrected his campaign goal of promoting alternative sources of energy, such as solar and wind power. But such solutions seemed to lie far in the future. Whether the disaster in the Gulf of Mexico would reinvigorate the environmental movement remained to be seen.

Afghanistan, Again

The economic crisis and the environmental calamity in the Gulf of Mexico notwithstanding, Afghanistan loomed as the dominant issue for Obama's presidency. Few could have imagined such a development in December 2001, when the war in Afghanistan appeared to be over. The Taliban had been driven from power; most of its leaders had been killed or captured or they had fled to Pakistan. Bush shifted his attention to driving Saddam Hussein from power in Iraq; a United Nations commission was given the task of building a new Afghan government.

In late 2001, the commission summoned Afghan leaders who eventually chose Hamid Karzai as interim leader of the nation. Karzai had helped channel American aid to the Taliban when it was fighting the Soviet Union; he later became a staunch opponent of the Taliban and worked with Americans to forge a coalition in opposition to it. As interim leader, Karzai relied on United Nations troops—one-half of them provided by the United States—to enforce the new government's authority.

For a time it appeared that a new Afghanistan was emerging. Hundreds of schools, hospitals, and roads

were built; women were granted new rights. In 2004 Karzai defeated twenty-two opponents to become the first democratically elected president of the Islamic Republic of Afghanistan.

But much of the progress was illusory. Karzai's government was weak and riddled with corruption. In the southern sections of Afghanistan, Islamic radicals resurfaced and the former Taliban slipped back into the country, calling on Muslims to fight "infidel" troops. In the north, tribal leaders jockeyed to expand their power. Nearly everywhere, criminal militias vied for control of the lucrative opium trade.

By late 2006 the Taliban initiated a concerted effort to topple Karzai's government. It named its own "shadow" governors as rulers of Afghanistan's provinces. Al-Qaeda, the terrorist group behind 9/11, also mounted its own attacks, as did rebel war-

An Army helicopter arrives to evacuate soldiers wounded after their armored vehicle hit an improvised explosive device (IED) in the Tangi Valley in Afghanistan.

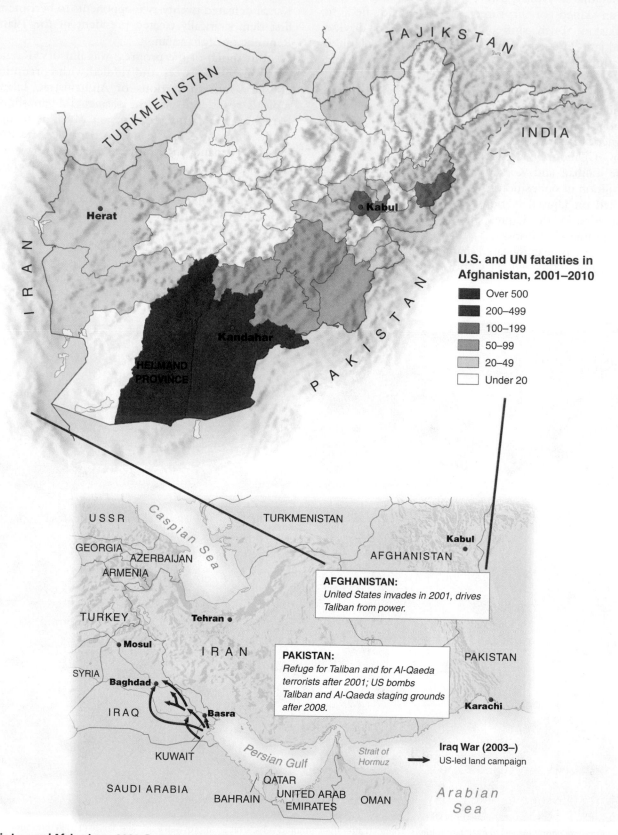

U.S. and UN fatalities in Afghanistan, 2001–2010

- Over 500
- 200–499
- 100–199
- 50–99
- 20–49
- Under 20

AFGHANISTAN:
United States invades in 2001, drives Taliban from power.

PAKISTAN:
Refuge for Taliban and for Al-Qaeda terrorists after 2001; US bombs Taliban and Al-Qaeda staging grounds after 2008.

Iraq War (2003–)
US-led land campaign

War in Iraq and Afghanistan, 2001–Present Since 2003, the United States has fought two major wars in Central Asia: in Afghanistan, first to drive the Taliban from power and later to suppress an insurgency; and in Iraq, first to crush Saddam Hussein and later to install a democratic government. In Afghanistan, American losses have been heaviest in the southern provinces bordering Pakistan.

lords and crime leaders. Increasingly insurgents borrowed techniques that had proven effective in Iraq, especially suicide bombers and roadside bombs. Afghanistan was slipping into chaos.

The election scheduled for the fall of 2009 made matters worse. The first round was marred by voting fraud, which UN observers confirmed. During the final campaign the chief opposition candidate withdrew, charging Karzai's government with rigging the outcome. Karzai "won" by default. Enemies of Karzai's regime exploited the controversy.

By late 2009 Obama, who had opposed the "surge" in Iraq, sent another 30,000 troops to Afghanistan. American forces increasingly relied on drones—unmanned planes—to drop guided bombs on suspected enemies in Afghanistan and Pakistan. When the bombs missed the targets and killed civilians, riots ensued and UN casualties mounted.

For some time, General Stanley McChrystal, commander of the United Nations troops, had chafed at rules of engagement designed to limit civilian casualties. Obama's administration, McChrystal's aides complained to reporters for *Rolling Stone*, was weak and ineffective. The article appeared in June 2010, the month with the heaviest losses of the war. Obama sacked McChrystal for insubordination, replacing him with David Petraeus, architect of the "surge" in Iraq. "We have arrived at a critical point," Petraeus declared on July 4, 2010. "We are in this to win."

A month later secret government documents, leaked to the press, revealed that while Pakistan had pledged to support the war on terror, its intelligence service helped the Taliban plan attacks on American soldiers. Insurgents in Iraq and Afghanistan persisted in blowing up crowded marketplaces, mosques, and government offices. Prospects for victory in the region remained bleak; no one could even imagine what it would look like.

The Persistent Past and Imponderable Future

But the previous eighteen years had shown that human events rarely unfold in predictable ways. The 9/11 terrorist attack, the subsequent wars in Iraq and Afghanistan, the near-collapse of the economy in 2008–2009, Hurricane Katrina, and the massive oil spill in the Gulf of Mexico all shocked the American people. And the surprises were not all bad. No one in 1992 could have predicted that the tidal wave of crime would recede the following

decade. For that matter, the relative absence of racial references during the 2008 campaign that resulted in the election of the nation's first African American president would have been unimaginable decades earlier.

But if the past does not enable us to predict the future, what do we ever "learn" from history? Consider an analogy with seismology, the study of earthquakes. Seismologists cannot predict exactly when and where any earthquake will strike, but their study of the underlying forces—the shift and collision of tectonic plates—helps explain the phenomenon. Historians similarly cannot predict the future course of human events. But the study of history can provide insights on the underlying forces that generate historical change. No one predicted, for example, that a particular deep-sea oil well would explode and release millions of barrels of oil into the Gulf of Mexico in the summer of 2010; but the American nation's voracious thirst for oil—a result of many developments during the previous century—led to the demand for the exploitation of deep-water oil resources. Similarly, in the first decades of the twenty-first century Americans fought and died in Iraq and Afghanistan because of a wide variety of historical forces, ranging from a commitment to democratic values and human rights to a demand for cheap Middle Eastern oil. History does not predict the future, which emerges through the convergence of infinite actions and reactions. But history can help reveal the various forces that are heaving beneath the surface of time.

This book was conceived as a reminder that the past is never truly past. It radiates through time. It touches our lives, just as what we do today will influence the future. By connecting to the past, we better understand ourselves and perhaps gain an inkling of what will become of us.

Just about everything that happens in one part of the modern world is in some way related to everything else that is going on. Far too many things are happening for anyone to sort out which is going to have what effect on tomorrow's events, let alone those that occur a year from now. "Then" (whether tomorrow or next year) historians will be able to study those particular events and puzzle out their chief causes—but not "now."

Yet "now" is where we happen to be, and thus this book, so full of events and their causes and results, must end inconclusively. No one knows what will happen next. But not knowing what will happen is one reason why life is so interesting.

Chapter Summary

Milestones

1992	Democrat Bill Clinton is elected president
1993	Ruth Bader Ginsberg becomes second woman justice of the Supreme Court
1994	Republicans win control of both houses of Congress
	Congress defeats Clinton's health care reform plan
1996	Democrat Bill Clinton is reelected president; Republicans retain control of Congress
	Measure revamping federal welfare system is passed by Congress and signed by President Clinton
1998	The House of Representatives impeaches Clinton
1999	Clinton acquitted by Senate, Clinton remains in office
	NATO troops, including Americans, are sent to Kosovo to stop Serbian "ethnic cleansing"
	Gun violence in schools escalates; twelve die at Columbine High School in Colorado
2000	Republican George W. Bush is elected president when Supreme Court halts Florida recounts
2001	Terrorists hijack airliners and fly them into the twin towers of the World Trade Center in New York and the Pentagon, killing 3,000
	United States drives Taliban from power in Afghanistan

2002	President Bush prepares for war as he accuses Saddam Hussein of Iraq of developing weapons of mass destruction
2003	United States and United Kingdom attack and defeat Iraq and capture Saddam Hussein
2004	Republican George W. Bush is reelected president
2005	Hurricane Katrina devastates New Orleans and Gulf Coast region
2007	Democrat Nancy Pelosi becomes first woman Speaker of the House
2008	Deranged student kills thirty-three at Virginia Tech
	Democrat Barack Obama is first African American to be elected president
	Collapse of U.S. mortgage markets triggers global financial crisis
2009	Obama implements troop surge in Afghanistan
2010	Congress approves health care bill
	BP-owned rig explodes, killing eleven and spewing oil into the Gulf of Mexico
	Arizona passes law to crack down on illegal immigrants; national debate ensues
	Republicans take control of House of Representatives

Key Terms

axis of evil   A pejorative phrase, coined by President George W. Bush in 2002, referring to states that supported terrorism and sought weapons of mass destruction. He specifically identified Iraq, Iran, and North Korea, *859*

Contract with America   A pledge, signed by many Republicans running for Congress in 1994, to support conservative reforms limiting federal power and expenditures. Championed by House Speaker Newt Gingrich, it contributed to a Republican electoral victory; but opposition by President Bill Clinton, a Democrat, prevented passage of much of the contract's legislative agenda, *852*

improvised explosive device (IED)   Also known as "roadside bombs," IEDs are homemade bombs that usually consist of captured artillery shells that are wired to a detonator. Either they are exploded remotely or by suicide bombers. IEDs accounted for over a third of the casualties sustained by American and United Nations forces in the Iraq and Afghanistan wars, *867*

North American Free Trade Agreement (NAFTA)   A 1993 accord signed by Canada, Mexico, and the United States to reduce and eventually eliminate barriers to trade, including tariffs, among the signatories, *853*

"surge"   The sudden increase in troop strength that appeared to have been used successfully against the Iraq insurgency in 2007. President Barack Obama similarly adopted a surge in 2009 to stabilize a deteriorating situation in Afghanistan, *868*

war on terror   Initially, a worldwide campaign to catch and prosecute those guilty of the September 11, 2001, attacks; as terrorist attacks spread throughout the world, the war became defined far more broadly, *858*

Review Questions

1. The introduction divides this chapter into two different narrative arcs: the first one—from 1992 to 2001—is mostly positive; the second, from 9/11 through 2010, is said to constitute—as Time magazine put it—"The Decade from Hell." What were the "positive" aspects of the period from 1992 to 2001? The "negative" components of the subsequent one? How is this characterization too simple?

2. Bill Clinton was hardly the first president to commit adultery. Why did his indiscretions lead to charges that resulted in an impeachment proceeding? Did his actions constitute "high crimes and misdemeanors"? What were the major achievements of the Clinton presidency?

3. The section of this chapter on the disputed 2000 presidential election is subtitled: "George W. Bush Wins by One Vote." What does that mean? Why did Bush win the election?

4. Why did Islamist terrorists attack on 9/11? Why did George W. Bush go to war against Afghanistan shortly afterwards? Why did he then invade Iraq? What issues in Iraq made it difficult to withdraw United States troops?

5. Hurricane Katrina was a natural disaster. To what extent, however, did human actions—and inactions—aggravate the calamity?

6. Why did global financial markets nearly collapse from 2008–2009? What caused the financial meltdown? What impact did it have on Americans?

7. What factors contributed to Barack Obama being elected president? What were the major elements of his health care reform act and how did he get it through Congress?

8. Why did Obama send American troops back into Afghanistan?

myhistorylab Connections

Reinforce what you learned in this chapter by studying the many documents, images, maps, review tools, and videos available at **www.myhistorylab.com**.

Read and Review

✓ **Study** and **Review** Chapter 32

View the Image *Bill Clinton and Al Gore on the South Lawn of the White House, 1993*, p. 851

Read the Document Bill Clinton, *Answers to the Articles of Impeachment*, p. 853

Read the Document George W. Bush, *Address to Congress (September 20, 2001)*, p. 858

Research and Explore

Watch the Video *Bill Clinton Sells Himself to America: Presidential Campaign Ad, 1992*, p. 851

Watch the Video *Bill Clinton First Inauguration*, p. 851

Watch the Video *The Historical Significance of the 2008 Presidential Election*, p. 869

✓ **Study** and **Review** *The Connection Between Obama & Lincoln*, p. 873

((•—Hear the Audio

Hear the audio file for Chapter 32 at
www.myhistorylab.com.

APPENDIX:
The Declaration of Independence

In Congress, July 4, 1776

The Unanimous Declaration of the Thirteen United States of America,

When, in the course of human events, it becomes necessary for one people to dissolve the political bonds which have connected them with another, and to assume, among the powers of the earth, the separate and equal station to which the laws of nature and of nature's God entitle them, a decent respect to the opinions of mankind requires that they should declare the causes which impel them to the separation.

We hold these truths to be self-evident: That all men are created equal; that they are endowed by their Creator with certain unalienable rights; that among these are life, liberty, and the pursuit of happiness; that, to secure these rights, governments are instituted among men, deriving their just powers from the consent of the governed; that whenever any form of government becomes destructive of these ends, it is the right of the people to alter or to abolish it, and to institute new government, laying its foundation on such principles, and organizing its powers in such form, as to them shall seem most likely to effect their safety and happiness. Prudence, indeed, will dictate that governments long established should not be changed for light and transient causes; and accordingly all experience hath shown that mankind are more disposed to suffer, while evils are sufferable, than to right themselves by abolishing the forms to which they are accustomed. But when a long train of abuses and usurpations, pursuing invariably the same object, evinces a design to reduce them under absolute despotism, it is their right, it is their duty, to throw off such government, and to provide new guards for their future security. Such has been the patient sufferance of these colonies; and such is now the necessity which constrains them to alter their former systems of government. The history of the present King of Great Britain is a history of repeated injuries and usurpations, all having in direct object the establishment of an absolute tyranny over these states. To prove this, let facts be submitted to a candid world.

He has refused his assent to laws, the most wholesome and necessary for the public good.

He has forbidden his governors to pass laws of immediate and pressing importance, unless suspended in their operation till his assent should be obtained; and, when so suspended, he has utterly neglected to attend to them.

He has refused to pass other laws for the accommodation of large districts of people, unless those people would relinquish the right of representation in the legislature, a right inestimable to them, and formidable to tyrants only.

He has called together legislative bodies at places unusual, uncomfortable, and distant from the depository of their public records, for the sole purpose of fatiguing them into compliance with his measures.

He has dissolved representative houses repeatedly, for opposing, with manly firmness, his invasions on the rights of the people.

He has refused for a long time, after such dissolutions, to cause others to be elected; whereby the legislative powers, incapable of annihilation, have returned to the people at large for their exercise; the state remaining, in the mean time, exposed to all the dangers of invasions from without and convulsions within.

He has endeavored to prevent the population of these states; for that purpose obstructing the laws for naturalization of foreigners; refusing to pass others to encourage their migration hither, and raising the conditions of new appropriations of lands.

He has obstructed the administration of justice, by refusing his assent to laws for establishing judiciary powers.

He has made judges dependent on his will alone, for the tenure of their offices, and the amount and payment of their salaries.

He has erected a multitude of new offices, and sent hither swarms of officers to harass our people and eat out their substance.

He has kept among us, in times of peace, standing armies, without the consent of our legislatures.

He has affected to render the military independent of, and superior to, the civil power.

He has combined with others to subject us to a jurisdiction foreign to our constitution, and unacknowledged by our laws, giving his assent to their acts of pretended legislation:

For quartering large bodies of armed troops among us;

For protecting them, by a mock trial, from punishment for any murder which they should commit on the inhabitants of these states;

For cutting off our trade with all parts of the world;

For imposing taxes on us without our consent;

For depriving us, in many cases, of the benefits of trial by jury;

For transporting us beyond seas, to be tried for pretended offenses;

For abolishing the free system of English laws in a neighboring province, establishing therein an arbitrary government, and enlarging its boundaries, so as to render it at once an example and fit instrument for introducing the same absolute rule into these colonies;

For taking away our charters, abolishing our most valuable laws, and altering fundamentally the forms of our governments;

For suspending our own legislatures, and declaring themselves invested with power to legislate for us in all cases whatsoever.

He has abdicated government here, by declaring us out of his protection and waging war against us.

He has plundered our seas, ravaged our coasts, burned our towns, and destroyed the lives of our people.

He is at this time transporting large armies of foreign mercenaries to complete the works of death, desolation, and tyranny already begun with circumstances of cruelty and perfidy scarcely paralleled in the most barbarous ages, and totally unworthy the head of a civilized nation.

He has constrained our fellow-citizens, taken captive on the high seas, to bear arms against their country, to become the executioners of their friends and brethren, or to fall themselves by their hands.

He has excited domestic insurrection among us, and has endeavored to bring on the inhabitants of our frontiers the merciless Indian savages, whose known rule of warfare is an undistinguished destruction of all ages, sexes, and conditions.

In every stage of these oppressions we have petitioned for redress in the most humble terms; our repeated petitions have been answered only by repeated injury. A prince, whose character is thus marked by every act which may define a tyrant, is unfit to be the ruler of a free people.

Nor have we been wanting in our attentions to our British brethren. We have warned them, from time to time, of attempts by their legislature to extend an unwarrantable jurisdiction over us. We have reminded them of the circumstances of our emigration and settlement here. We have appealed to their native justice and magnanimity; and we have conjured them, by the ties of our common kindred, to disavow these usurpations, which would inevitably interrupt our connections and correspondence. They, too, have been deaf to the voice of justice and of consanguinity. We must, therefore, acquiesce in the necessity which denounces our separation, and hold them, as we hold the rest of mankind, enemies in war, in peace friends.

We, therefore, the representatives of the United States of America, in General Congress assembled, appealing to the Supreme Judge of the world for the rectitude of our intentions, do, in the name and by the authority of the good people of these colonies, solemnly publish and declare, that these United Colonies are, and of right ought to be, FREE AND INDEPENDENT STATES; that they are absolved from all allegiance to the British crown, and that all political connection between them and the state of Great Britain is, and ought to be, totally dissolved; and that, as free and independent states, they have full power to levy war, conclude peace, contract alliances, establish commerce, and do all other acts and things which independent states may of right do. And for the support of this declaration, with a firm reliance on the protection of Divine Providence, we mutually pledge to each other our lives, our fortunes, and our sacred honor.

John Hancock

New Hampshire
Josiah Bartlett
William Whipple
Matthew Thornton

Massachusetts
John Adams
Samuel Adams
Robert Treat Paine
Elbridge Gerry

New York
William Floyd
Philip Livingston
Francis Lewis
Lewis Morris

Rhode Island
Stephen Hopkins
William Ellery

New Jersey
Richard Stockton
John Witherspoon
Francis Hopkinson
John Hart
Abraham Clark

Pennsylvania
Robert Morris
Benjamin Rush
Benjamin Franklin
John Morton
George Clymer
James Smith
George Taylor
James Wilson
George Ross

Delaware
Caeser Rodney
George Read
Thomas McKean

Maryland
Samuel Chase
William Paca
Thomas Stone
Charles Carroll
of Carrollton

North Carolina
William Hooper
Joseph Hewes
John Penn

Virginia
George Wythe
Richard Henry Lee
Thomas Jefferson
Benjamin Harrison
Thomas Nelson, Jr.
Francis Lightfoot Lee
Carter Braxton

South Carolina
Edward Rutledge
Thomas Heyward, Jr.
Thomas Lynch, Jr.
Arthur Middleton

Connecticut
Roger Sherman
Samuel Huntington
William Williams
Oliver Wolcott

Georgia
Button Gwinnett
Lyman Hall
George Walton

Preamble

We the People of the United States, in Order to form a more perfect Union, establish Justice, insure domestic Tranquility, provide for the common defence, promote the general Welfare, and secure the Blessings of Liberty to ourselves and our Posterity, do ordain and establish this Constitution for the United States of America.

Article I

Section 1

All legislative Powers herein granted shall be vested in a Congress of the United States, which shall consist of a Senate and House of Representatives.

Section 2

The House of Representatives shall be composed of Members chosen every second Year by the People of the several States, and the Electors in each State shall have the Qualifications requisite for Electors of the most numerous Branch of the State Legislature.

No Person shall be a Representative who shall not have attained to the Age of twenty five Years, and been seven Years a Citizen of the United States, and who shall not, when elected, be an inhabitant of that State in which he shall be chosen.

Representatives and direct Taxes shall be apportioned among the several States which may be included within this Union, according to their respective Numbers, *which shall be determined by adding to the whole Number of free Persons, including those bound to Service for a Term of Years, and excluding Indians not taxed, three fifths of all other Persons.* The actual Enumeration shall be made within three Years after the first Meeting of the Congress of the United States, and within every subsequent Term of ten Years, in such Manner as they shall by Law direct. The Number of Representatives shall not exceed one for every thirty Thousand, but each State shall have at Least one Representative; *and until such enumeration shall be made, the State of New Hampshire shall be entitled to chuse three, Massachusetts eight, Rhode-Island and Providence Plantations one, Connecticut five, New York six, New Jersey four, Pennsylvania eight, Delaware one, Maryland six, Virginia ten, North Carolina five, South Carolina five, and Georgia three.*

When vacancies happen in the Representation from any State, the Executive Authority thereof shall issue Writs of Election to fill such Vacancies.

The House of Representatives shall chuse their Speaker and other Officers; and shall have the sole Power of Impeachment.

---

*Passages no longer in effect are printed in italic type.

Section 3

The Senate of the United States shall be composed of two Senators from each State, *chosen by the Legislature thereof,* for six Years; and each Senator shall have one Vote.

Immediately after they shall be assembled in Consequence of the first Election, they shall be divided as equally as may be into three Classes. The Seats of the Senators of the first Class shall be vacated at the Expiration of the second Year, of the second Class at the Expiration of the fourth Year, and of the third Class at the Expiration of the sixth Year so that one third may be chosen every second Year; and if Vacancies happen by Resignation, or otherwise, during the Recess of the Legislature of any state, the Executive thereof may make temporary Appointments until the next Meeting of the Legislature, which shall then fill such Vacancies.

No Person shall be a Senator who shall not have attained to the Age of thirty Years, and been nine Years a Citizen of the United States, and who shall not, when elected, be an Inhabitant of that State for which he shall be chosen.

The Vice President of the United States shall be President of the Senate, but shall have no Vote, unless they be equally divided.

The Senate shall chuse their other Officers, and also a President *pro tempore*, in the Absence of the Vice President, or when he shall exercise the Office of President of the United States.

The Senate shall have the sole Power to try all Impeachments. When sitting for that Purpose, they shall be on Oath or Affirmation. When the President of the United States is tried the Chief Justice shall preside: And no Person shall be convicted without the Concurrence of two thirds of the Members present.

Judgment in Cases of Impeachment shall not extend further than to removal from Office, and disqualification to hold and enjoy any Office of honor, Trust or Profit under the United States: but the Party convicted shall nevertheless be liable and subject to Indictment, Trial, Judgment and Punishment, according to Law.

Section 4

The Times, Places and Manner of holding Elections for Senators and Representatives, shall be prescribed in each State by the Legislature thereof; but the Congress may at any time by Law make or alter such Regulations, except as to the Places of chusing Senators.

The Congress shall assemble at least once in every Year, *and such Meeting shall be on the first Monday in December, unless they shall by Law appoint a different Day.*

Section 5

Each House shall be the Judge of the Elections, Returns and Qualifications of its own Members, and a Majority of each shall constitute a Quorum to do Business; but a smaller

Number may adjourn from day to day, and may be authorized to compel the Attendance of absent Members, in such Manner, and under such Penalties as each House may provide.

Each House may determine the Rules of its Proceedings, punish its Members for disorderly Behaviour, and, with the Concurrence of two thirds, expel a Member.

Each House shall keep a Journal of its Proceedings, and from time to time publish the same, excepting such Parts as may in their Judgment require Secrecy; and the Yeas and Nays of the Members of either House on any question shall, at the Desire of one fifth of those Present, be entered on the Journal.

Neither House, during the Session of Congress, shall, without the Consent of the other, adjourn for more than three days, nor to any other Place than that in which the two Houses shall be sitting.

Section 6

The Senators and Representatives shall receive a Compensation for their Services, to be ascertained by Law, and paid out of the Treasury of the United States. They shall in all Cases, except Treason, Felony and Breach of the Peace, be privileged from Arrest during their Attendance at the Session of their respective Houses, and in going to and returning from the same; and for any Speech or Debate in either House, they shall not be questioned in any other Place.

No Senator or Representative shall, during the Time for which he was elected, be appointed to any civil Office under the Authority of the United States, which shall have been created, or the Emoluments whereof shall have been encreased during such time, and no Person holding any Office under the United States, shall be a Member of either House during his Continuance in Office.

Section 7

All Bills for raising Revenue shall originate in the House of Representatives; but the Senate may propose or concur with Amendments as on other Bills.

Every Bill which shall have passed the House of Representatives and the Senate, shall, before it become a Law, be presented to the President of the United States; If he approve he shall sign it, but if not he shall return it, with his Objections to the House in which it shall have originated, who shall enter the Objections at large on their Journal, and proceed to reconsider it. If after such Reconsideration two thirds of that House shall agree to pass the Bill, it shall be sent, together with the Objections, to the other House, by which it shall likewise be reconsidered, and if approved by two thirds of that House, it shall become a Law. But in all such Cases the Votes of both Houses shall be determined by yeas and Nays, and the Names of the Persons voting for and against the Bill shall be entered on the Journal of each House respectively. If any Bill shall not be returned by the President within ten Days (Sundays excepted) after it shall have been presented to him, the Same shall be a Law, in like Manner as if he had signed it, unless the Congress by their Adjournment prevent its Return, in which Case it shall not be a Law.

Every Order, Resolution, or Vote to which the Concurrence of the Senate and House of Representatives may be necessary (except on a question of Adjournment) shall be presented to the President of the United States; and before the Same shall take Effect, shall be approved by him, or being disapproved by him, shall be repassed by two thirds of the Senate and House of Representatives, according to the Rules and Limitations prescribed in the Case of a Bill.

Section 8

The Congress shall have Power To lay and collect Taxes, Duties, Imposts and Excises, to pay the Debts and provide for the common Defence and general Welfare of the United States; but all Duties, Imposts and Excises shall be uniform throughout the United States;

To borrow Money on the credit of the United States;

To regulate Commerce with foreign Nations, and among the several States, and with the Indian Tribes;

To establish an uniform Rule of Naturalization, and uniform Laws on the subject of Bankruptcies throughout the United States;

To coin Money, regulate the Value thereof, and of foreign Coin, and fix the Standard of Weights and Measures;

To provide for the Punishment of counterfeiting the Securities and current Coin of the United States;

To establish Post Offices and post Roads;

To promote the Progress of Science and useful Arts, by securing for limited Times to Authors and Inventors the exclusive Right to their respective Writings and Discoveries;

To constitute Tribunals inferior to the supreme Court;

To define and punish Piracies and Felonies committed on the high Seas, and Offences against the Law of Nations;

To declare War, grant Letters of Marque and Reprisal, and make Rules concerning Captures on Land and Water;

To raise and support Armies, but no Appropriation of Money to that Use shall be for a longer Term than two Years;

To provide and maintain a Navy;

To make Rules for the Government and Regulation of the land and naval Forces;

To provide for calling forth the Militia to execute the Laws of the Union, suppress Insurrections and repel Invasions;

To provide for organizing, arming, and disciplining, the Militia, and for governing such Part of them as may be employed in the Service of the United States, reserving to the States respectively, the Appointment of the Officers, and the Authority of training the Militia according to the discipline prescribed by Congress;

To exercise exclusive Legislation in all Cases whatsoever, over such District (not exceeding ten Miles square) as may, by Cession of particular States, and the Acceptance of Congress, become the Seat of the Government of the United States, and to exercise like Authority over all Places purchased by the Consent of the Legislature of the State in which the Same shall be, for the Erection of Forts, Magazines, Arsenals, dock-Yards, and other needful Buildings;—And

To make all Laws which shall be necessary and proper for carrying into Execution the foregoing Powers, and all other Powers vested by this Constitution in the Government of the United States, or in any Department of Officer thereof.

Section 9

The Migration or Importation of such Persons as any of the States now existing shall think proper to admit, shall not be prohibited by the Congress prior to the Year one thousand eight

hundred and eight, but a Tax or duty may be imposed on such Importation, not exceeding ten dollars for each Person.

The Privilege of the Writ of Habeas Corpus shall not be suspended, unless when in Cases of Rebellion or Invasion the public Safety may require it.

No Bill of Attainder or ex post facto Law shall be passed.

No Capitation, or other direct, Tax shall be laid, unless in Proportion to the Census or Enumeration herein before directed to be taken.

No Tax or Duty shall be laid on Articles exported from any State.

No Preference shall be given by any Regulation of Commerce or Revenue to the Ports of one State over those of another: nor shall Vessels bound to, or from, one State, be obliged to enter, clear, or pay Duties in another.

No Money shall be drawn from the Treasury, but in Consequence of Appropriations made by Law; and a regular Statement and Account of the Receipts and Expenditures of all public Money shall be published from time to time.

No Title of Nobility shall be granted by the United States: And no Person holding any Office of Profit or Trust under them, shall, without the Consent of the Congress, accept of any present, Emolument, Office, or Title, of any kind whatever, from any King, Prince, or foreign State.

Section 10

No State shall enter into any Treaty, Alliance, or Confederation; grant Letters of Marque and Reprisal; coin Money; emit Bills of Credit; make any Thing but gold and silver Coin a Tender in Payment of Debts; pass any Bill of Attainder, ex post facto Law, or Law impairing the obligation of Contracts, or grant any Title of Nobility.

No State shall, without the Consent of the Congress, lay any Imposts or Duties on Imports or Exports, except what may be absolutely necessary for executing its inspection Laws: and the net Produce of all Duties and Imposts, laid by any State on Imports or Exports, shall be for the Use of the Treasury of the United States; and all such Laws shall be subject to the Revision and Controul of the Congress.

No State shall, without the Consent of Congress, lay any Duty of Tonnage, keep Troops, or Ships of War in time of Peace, enter into any Agreement or Compact with another State, or with a foreign Power, or engage in War, unless actually invaded, or in such imminent Danger as will not admit of delay.

Article II

Section 1

The executive Power shall be vested in a President of the United States of America. He shall hold his Office during the Term of four Years, and, together with the Vice President, chosen for the same Term, be elected, as follows:

Each State shall appoint, in such Manner as the Legislature thereof may direct, a Number of Electors, equal to the whole Number of Senators and Representatives to which the State may be entitled in the Congress: but no Senator or Representative, or Person holding an Office of Trust or Profit under the United States, shall be appointed an Elector.

The Electors shall meet in their respective States, and vote by Ballot for two Persons, of whom one at least shall not be an Inhabitant of the same State with themselves. And they shall make a List of all the Persons voted for, and of the Number of Votes for each; which List they shall sign and certify, and transmit sealed to the Seat of the Government of the United States, directed to the President of the Senate. The President of the Senate shall, in the Presence of the Senate and House of Representatives, open all the Certificates, and the Votes shall then be counted. The Person having the greatest Number of Votes shall be the President, if such Number be a Majority of the whole number of Electors appointed; and if there be more than one who have such Majority, and have an equal Number of Votes, then the House of Representatives shall immediately chuse by Ballot one of them for President; and if no Person have a Majority, then from the five highest on the List the said House shall in like Manner chuse the President. But in chusing the President, the Votes shall be taken by States, the Representation from each State having one Vote; A quorum for this Purpose shall consist of a Member or Members from two thirds of the States, and a Majority of all the States shall be necessary to a Choice. In every Case, after the Choice of the President, the Person having the greatest Number of Votes of the Electors shall be the Vice President. But if there should remain two or more who have equal Votes, the Senate shall chuse from them by Ballot the Vice President.

The Congress may determine the time of chusing the Electors, and the Day on which they shall give their Votes; which Day shall be the same throughout the United States.

No person except a natural born Citizen, *or a Citizen of the United States, at the time of the Adoption of this Constitution,* shall be eligible to the Office of President; neither shall any Person be eligible to that Office who shall not have attained to the Age of thirty five Years, and been fourteen Years a Resident within the United States.

In Case of the Removal of the President from Office, or of his Death, Resignation, or Inability to discharge the Powers and Duties of the said Office, the Same shall devolve on the Vice President, and the Congress may by Law provide for the Case of Removal, Death, Resignation or Inability, both of the President and Vice President, declaring what Officer shall then act as President, and such Officer shall act accordingly, until the Disability be removed, or a President shall be elected.

The President shall, at stated Times, receive for his Services, a Compensation, which shall neither be encreased nor diminished during the Period for which he shall have been elected, and he shall not receive within that period any other Emolument from the United States, or any of them.

Before he enter on the Execution of his Office, he shall take the following Oath or Affirmation:—"I do solemnly swear (or affirm) that I will faithfully execute the Office of President of the United States, and will to the best of my Ability, preserve, protect and defend the Constitution of the United States."

Section 2

The President shall be Commander in Chief of the Army and Navy of the United States, and of the Militia of the several States, when called into the actual Service of the United

States; he may require the Opinion, in writing, of the principal Officer in each of the executive Departments, upon any Subject relating to the Duties of their respective Offices, and he shall have Power to grant Reprieves and Pardons for Offences against the United States, except in Cases of Impeachment.

He shall have Power, by and with the Advice and Consent of the Senate, to make Treaties, provided two thirds of the Senators present concur; and he shall nominate, and by and with the Advice and Consent of the Senate, shall appoint Ambassadors, other public Ministers and Consuls, Judges of the supreme Court, and all other Officers of the United States, whose Appointments are not herein otherwise provided for, and which shall be established by Law: but the Congress may by Law vest the Appointment of such inferior Officers, as they think proper in the President alone, in the Courts of Law, or in the Heads of Departments.

The President shall have Power to fill up all Vacancies that may happen during the Recess of the Senate, by granting Commissions which shall expire at the End of their next Session.

Section 3

He shall from time to time give to the Congress Information of the State of the Union, and recommend to their Consideration such Measures as he shall judge necessary and expedient; he may, on extraordinary Occasions, convene both Houses, or either of them, and in Case of disagreement between them, with Respect to the Time of Adjournment, he may adjourn them to such Time as he shall think proper; he shall receive Ambassadors and other public Ministers; he shall take Care that the Laws be faithfully executed, and shall Commission all the officers of the United States.

Section 4

The President, Vice President and all civil Officers of the United States, shall be removed from Office on Impeachment for, and Conviction of, Treason, Bribery or other high Crimes and Misdemeanors.

Article III

Section 1

The judicial Power of the United States, shall be vested in one supreme Court, and in such inferior Courts as the Congress may from time to time ordain and establish. The Judges, both of the supreme and inferior Courts, shall hold their offices during good Behaviour, and shall, at stated Times, receive for their Services, a Compensation, which shall not be diminished during their Continuance in Office.

Section 2

The judicial Power shall extend to all Cases, in Law and Equity, arising under this Constitution, the Laws of the United States, and Treaties made, or which shall be made, under their Authority;—to all Cases affecting Ambassadors, other public Ministers and Consuls;—to all Cases of admiralty and maritime Jurisdiction;—to Controversies to which the United States shall be a Party;—to Controversies

between two or more States;—*between a State and Citizens of another State;*—between Citizens of different States;—between Citizens of the same State claiming Lands under Grants of different States, and between a State, or the Citizens thereof, and foreign States, Citizens or Subjects.

In all Cases affecting Ambassadors, other public Ministers and Consuls, and those in which a State shall be Party, the supreme Court shall have original Jurisdiction. In all the other Cases before mentioned, the supreme Court shall have appellate Jurisdiction, both as to Law and Fact, with such Exceptions, and under such Regulations as the Congress shall make.

The Trial of all Crimes, except in Cases of Impeachment, shall be by Jury; and such Trial shall be held in the State where the said Crimes shall have been committed, but when not committed within any State, the Trial shall be at such Place or Places as the Congress may by Law have directed.

Section 3

Treason against the United States, shall consist only in levying War against them, or in adhering to their Enemies, giving them Aid and Comfort. No person shall be convicted of Treason unless on the Testimony of two Witnesses to the same overt Act, or on Confession in open Court.

The Congress shall have Power to declare the Punishment of Treason, but no Attainder of Treason shall work Corruption of Blood, or Forfeiture except during the Life of the Person attainted.

Article IV

Section 1

Full Faith and Credit shall be given in each State to the public Acts, Records, and judicial Proceedings of every other State. And the Congress may by general Laws prescribe the Manner in which such Acts, Records and Proceedings shall be proved, and the Effect thereof.

Section 2

The Citizens of each State shall be entitled to all Privileges and Immunities of Citizens in the several States.

A Person charged in any State with Treason, Felony, or other Crime, who shall flee from Justice, and be found in another State, shall on Demand of the executive Authority of the State from which he fled, be delivered up, to be removed to the State having Jurisdiction of the Crime.

No Person held to Service or Labour in one State, under the Laws thereof, escaping into another, shall, in Consequence of any Law or Regulation therein, be discharged from such Service or Labour, but shall be delivered up on Claim of the Party to whom such Service or Labour may be due.

Section 3

New States may be admitted by the Congress into this Union; but no new State shall be formed or erected within the Jurisdiction of any other State; nor any State be formed by the Junction of two or more States, or Parts of States, without the Consent of the Legislatures of the States concerned as well as of the Congress.

The Congress shall have Power to dispose of and make all needful Rules and Regulations respecting the Territory or other Property belonging to the United States; and nothing in this Constitution shall be so construed as to Prejudice any Claims of the United States, or of any particular States.

Section 4

The United States shall guarantee to every State in this Union a Republican Form of Government, and shall protect each of them against Invasion; and on Application of the Legislature, or of the Executive (when the Legislature cannot be convened) against domestic violence.

Article V

The Congress, whenever two thirds of both Houses shall deem it necessary, shall propose Amendments to this Constitution, or, on the Application of the Legislatures of two thirds of the several States, shall call a Convention for proposing Amendments, which, in either Case, shall be valid to all Intents and Purposes, as Part of this Constitution, when ratified by the Legislatures of three fourths of the several States, or by Conventions in three fourths thereof, as the one or the other Mode of Ratification may be proposed by the Congress; Provided *that no Amendment which may be made prior to the Year One thousand eight hundred and eight shall in any Manner affect the first and fourth Clauses in the Ninth Section of the first Article;* and that no State, without its Consent, shall be deprived of its equal Suffrage in the Senate.

Article VI

All Debts contracted and Engagements entered into, before the Adoption of this Constitution, shall be as valid against the United States under this Constitution, as under the Confederation.

This Constitution, and Laws of the United States which shall be made in Pursuance thereof; and all Treaties made, or which shall be made, under the Authority of the United States, shall be the supreme Law of the Land; and the Judges in every State shall be bound thereby, any Thing in the Constitution or Laws of any State to the Contrary notwithstanding.

The Senators and Representatives before mentioned, and the Members of the several State Legislatures, and all executive and Judicial Officers, both of the United States and of the several States, shall be bound by Oath or Affirmation, to support this Constitution; but no religious Test shall ever be required as a Qualification to any Office of public Trust under the United States.

Article VII

The Ratification of the Conventions of nine States, shall be sufficient for the Establishment of this Constitution between the States so ratifying the Same.

Done in Convention by the Unanimous Consent of the States present the Seventeenth Day of September in the Year of our Lord one thousand seven hundred and Eighty seven and of the Independence of the United States of America the Twelfth[†] IN WITNESS whereof We have hereunto subscribed our Names,

George Washington
President and Deputy from Virginia

Delaware
George Read
Gunning Bedford, Jr.
John Dickinson
Richard Bassett
Jacob Broom

Maryland
James McHenry
Daniel of St. Thomas Jenifer
Daniel Carroll

Virginia
John Blair
James Madison, Jr.

North Carolina
William Blount
Richard Dobbs Spraight
Hugh Williamson

South Carolina
John Rutledge
Charles Cotesworth Pinckney
Charles Pinckney
Pierce Butler

Georgia
William Paterson
William Few
Abraham Baldwin

New Hampshire
John Langdon
Nicholas Gilman

Massachusetts
Nathaniel Gorham
Rufus King

Connecticut
William Samuel Johnson
Roger Sherman

New York
Alexander Hamilton

New Jersey
William Livingston
David Brearley
Jonathan Dayton

Pennsylvania
Benjamin Franklin
Thomas Mifflin
Robert Morris
George Clymer
Thomas FitzSimons
Jared Ingersoll
James Wilson
Gouverneur Morris

[†]The Constitution was submitted on September 17, 1787, by the Constitutional Convention, was ratified by the Convention of several states at various dates up to May 29, 1790, and became effective on March 4, 1789.

the Constitution

Amendment I

Congress shall make no law respecting an establishment of religion, or prohibiting the free exercise thereof; or abridging the freedom of speech, or of the press; or the right of the people peaceably to assemble, and to petition the Government for a redress of grievances.

Amendment II

A well regulated Militia being necessary to the security of a free State, the right of the people to keep and bear Arms, shall not be infringed.

Amendment III

No Soldier shall, in time of peace be quartered in any house, without the consent of the Owner, nor in time of war, but in a manner to be prescribed by law.

Amendment IV

The right of the people to be secure in their persons, houses, papers, and effects, against unreasonable searches and seizures, shall not be violated, and no Warrants shall issue, but upon probable cause, supported by Oath or affirmation, and particularly describing the place to be searched, and the persons or things to be seized.

Amendment V

No person shall be held to answer for a capital, or otherwise infamous crime, unless on a presentment or indictment of a Grand Jury, except in cases arising in the land or naval forces, or in the Militia, when in actual service in time of War or public danger; nor shall any person be subject for the same offense to be twice put in jeopardy of life or limb; nor shall be compelled in any criminal case to be a witness against himself, nor be deprived of life, liberty, or property, without due process of law; nor shall private property be taken for public use, without just compensation.

Amendment VI

In all criminal prosecutions, the accused shall enjoy the right to a speedy and public trial, by an impartial jury of the State and district wherein the crime shall have been committed, which district shall have been previously ascertained by law, and to be informed of the nature and cause of the accusation; to be confronted with the witnesses against him; to have compulsory process for obtaining witnesses in his favor, and to have the Assistance of Counsel for his defence.

Amendment VII

In Suits at common law, where the value in controversy shall exceed twenty dollars, the right of trial by jury shall be preserved, and no fact tried by a jury, shall be otherwise re-examined in any Court of the United States, than according to the rules of the common law.

Amendment VIII

Excessive bail shall not be required, nor excessive fines imposed, nor cruel and unusual punishments inflicted.

Amendment IX

The enumeration in the Constitution, of certain rights, shall not be construed to deny or disparage others retained by the people.

Amendment X[*]

The powers not delegated to the United States by the Constitution, nor prohibited by it to the States, are reserved to the States respectively, or to the people.

Amendment XI

[Adopted 1798]

The Judicial power of the United States shall not be construed to extend to any suit in law or equity, commenced or prosecuted against one of the United States by Citizens of another State, or by Citizens or Subjects of any Foreign State.

Amendment XII

[Adopted 1804]

The Electors shall meet in their respective states, and vote by ballot for President and Vice President, one of whom, at least, shall not be an inhabitant of the same state with themselves; they shall name in their ballots the person voted for as President, and in distinct ballots the person voted for as Vice President, and they shall make distinct lists of all persons

---

[*]The first ten amendments (the Bill of Rights) were ratified and their adoption was certified on December 15, 1791.

voted for as President, and of all persons voted for as Vice President, and of the number of votes for each, which lists they shall sign and certify, and transmit sealed to the seat of the government of the United States, directed to the President of the Senate;—The President of the Senate shall, in the presence of the Senate and House of Representatives, open all the certificates and the votes shall then be counted;—The person having the greatest number of votes for President, shall be the President, if such number be a majority of the whole number of Electors appointed; and if no person have such majority, then from the persons having the highest numbers not exceeding three on the list of those voted for as President, the House of Representatives shall choose immediately, by ballot, the President. But in choosing the President, the votes shall be taken by states, the representation from each state having one vote; a quorum for this purpose shall consist of a member or members from two-thirds of the states, and a majority of all the states shall be necessary to a choice. And if the House of Representatives shall not choose a President whenever the right of choice shall devolve upon them, before *the fourth day of March* next following, then the Vice President shall act as President, as in the case of the death or other constitutional disability of the President.—The person having the greatest number of votes as Vice President, shall be the Vice President, if such number be a majority of the whole number of Electors appointed, and if no person have a majority, then from the two highest numbers on the list, the Senate shall choose the Vice President; a quorum for the purpose shall consist of two-thirds of the whole number of Senators, and a majority of the whole number shall be necessary to a choice. But no person constitutionally ineligible to the office of President shall be eligible to that of Vice President of the United States.

Amendment XIII

[Adopted 1865]

Section 1

Neither slavery nor involuntary servitude, except as a punishment for crime whereof the party shall have been duly convicted, shall exist within the United States, or any place subject to their jurisdiction.

Section 2

Congress shall have power to enforce this article by appropriate legislation.

Amendment XIV

[Adopted 1868]

Section 1

All persons born or naturalized in the United States, and subject to the jurisdiction thereof, are citizens of the United States and of the State wherein they reside. No State shall make or enforce any law which shall abridge the privileges or immunities of citizens of the United States; nor shall any State deprive any person of life, liberty, or property, without due process of law; nor deny to any person within its jurisdiction the equal protection of the laws.

Section 2

Representatives shall be apportioned among the several States according to their respective numbers, counting the whole number of persons in each State, excluding Indians not taxed. But when the right to vote at any election for the choice of electors for President and Vice President of the United States, Representatives in Congress, the Executive and Judicial officers of a State, or the members of the Legislature thereof, is denied to any of the male inhabitants of such State, being twenty-one years of age, and citizens of the United States, or in any way abridged, except for participation in rebellion, or other crime, the basis of representation therein shall be reduced in the proportion which the number of such male citizens shall bear to the whole number of male citizens twenty-one years of age in such State.

Section 3

No person shall be a Senator or Representative in Congress, or elector of President and Vice President, or hold any office, civil or military, under the United States, or under any State, who, having previously taken an oath, as a member of Congress, or as an officer of the United States, or as a member of any State legislature, or as an executive or judicial officer of any State, to support the Constitution of the United States, shall have engaged in insurrection or rebellion against the same, or given aid or comfort to the enemies thereof. But Congress may by a vote of two-thirds of each House, remove such disability.

Section 4

The validity of the public debt of the United States, authorized by law, including debts incurred for payment of pensions and bounties for services in suppressing insurrection or rebellion, shall not be questioned. But neither the United States nor any State shall assume or pay any debt or obligation incurred in aid of insurrection or rebellion against the United States, or any claim for the loss or emancipation of any slave; but all such debts, obligations and claims shall be held illegal and void.

Section 5

The Congress shall have power to enforce, by appropriate legislation, the provisions of this article.

Amendment XV

[Adopted 1870]

Section 1

The right of citizens of the United States to vote shall not be denied or abridged by the United States or by any State on account of race, color, or previous condition of servitude.

Section 2

The Congress shall have power to enforce this article by appropriate legislation.

Amendment XVI

[Adopted 1913]

The Congress shall have power to lay and collect taxes on incomes, from whatever source derived, without apportionment among the several States, and without regard to any census or enumeration.

Amendment XVII

[Adopted 1913]

The Senate of the United States shall be composed of two Senators from each State, elected by the people thereof, for six years; and each Senator shall have one vote. The electors in each State shall have the qualifications requisite for electors of the most numerous branch of the State legislatures.

When vacancies happen in the representation of any State in the Senate, the executive authority of such State shall issue writs of election to fill such vacancies: *Provided,* That the legislature of any State may empower the executive thereof to make temporary appointments until the people fill the vacancies by election as the legislature may direct.

This amendment shall not be so construed as to affect the election or term of any Senator chosen before it becomes valid as part of the Constitution.

Amendment XVIII

[Adopted 1919, repealed 1933]

Section 1

After one year from the ratification of this article the manufacture, sale, or transportation of intoxicating liquors within, the importation thereof into, or the exportation thereof from the United States and all territory subject to the jurisdiction thereof for beverage purposes is hereby prohibited.

Section 2

The Congress and the several States shall have concurrent power to enforce this article by appropriate legislation.

Section 3

This article shall be inoperative unless it shall have been ratified as an amendment to the Constitution by the legislatures of the several States, as provided in the Constitution, within seven years from the date of the submission hereof to the States by the Congress.

Amendment XIX

[Adopted 1920]

The right of citizens of the United States to vote shall not be denied or abridged by the United States or by any State on account of sex.

Congress shall have power to enforce this article by appropriate legislation.

Amendment XX

[Adopted 1933]

Section 1

The terms of the President and Vice President shall end at noon on the 20th day of January, and the terms of Senators and Representatives at noon on the 3d day of January, of the years in which such terms would have ended if this article had not been ratified and the terms of their successors shall then begin.

Section 2

The Congress shall assemble at least once in every year, and such meeting shall begin at noon on the 3d day of January, unless they shall by law appoint a different day.

Section 3

If, at the time fixed for the beginning of the term of the President, the President elect shall have died, the Vice President elect shall become President. If a President shall not have been chosen before the time fixed for the beginning of his term, or if the President elect shall have failed to qualify, then the Vice President elect shall act as President until a President shall have qualified; and the Congress may by law provide for the case wherein neither a President elect nor a Vice President elect shall have qualified, declaring who shall then act as President, or the manner in which one who is to act shall be selected, and such person shall act accordingly until a President or Vice President shall have qualified.

Section 4

The Congress may by law provide for the case of the death of any of the persons from whom the House of Representatives may choose a President whenever the right of choice shall have devolved upon them, and for the case of the death of any of the persons from whom the Senate may choose a Vice President whenever the right of choice shall have devolved upon them.

Section 5

Sections 1 and 2 shall take effect on the 15th day of October following the ratification of this article.

Section 6

This article shall be inoperative unless it shall have been ratified as an amendment to the Constitution by the legislatures of three fourths of the several States within seven years from the date of its submission.

Amendment XXI

[Adopted 1933]

Section 1

The eighteenth article of amendment to the Constitution of the United States is hereby repealed.

Section 2

The transportation or importation into any State, Territory, or possession of the United States for delivery or use therein of intoxicating liquors in violation of the laws thereof, is hereby prohibited.

Section 3

This article shall be inoperative unless it shall have been ratified as an amendment to the Constitution by conventions in the several States, as provided in the Constitution, within seven years from the date of the submission hereof to the States by the Congress.

Amendment XXII

[Adopted 1951]

Section 1

No person shall be elected to the office of the President more than twice, and no person who has held the office of President, or acted as President, for more than two years of a term to which some other person was elected President shall be elected to the office of the President more than once. But this Article shall not apply to any person holding the office of President when this Article was proposed by the Congress, and shall not prevent any person who may be holding the office of President, or acting as President, during the term within which this Article becomes operative from holding the office of President or acting as President during the remainder of such term.

Section 2

This article shall be inoperative unless it shall have been ratified as an amendment to the Constitution by the legislatures of three-fourths of the several States within seven years from the date of its submission to the States by the Congress.

Amendment XXIII

[Adopted 1961]

Section 1

The District constituting the seat of Government of the United States shall appoint in such manner as the Congress shall direct:

A number of electors of President and Vice President equal to the whole number of Senators and Representatives in Congress to which the District would be entitled if it were a State, but in no event more than the least populous State; they shall be in addition to those appointed by the States, but they shall be considered, for the purposes of the election of President and Vice President, to be electors appointed by a State; and they shall meet in the District and perform such duties as provided by the twelfth article of amendment.

Section 2

The Congress shall have power to enforce this article by appropriate legislation.

Amendment XXIV

[Adopted 1964]

Section 1

The right of citizens of the United States to vote in any primary or other election for President or Vice President, for electors for President or Vice President, or for Senator or Representative in Congress, shall not be denied or abridged by the United States or any state by reason of failure to pay any poll tax or other tax.

Section 2

The Congress shall have the power to enforce this article by appropriate legislation.

Amendment XXV

[Adopted 1967]

Section 1

In case of the removal of the President from office or his death or resignation, the Vice President shall become President.

Section 2

Whenever there is a vacancy in the office of the Vice President, the President shall nominate a Vice President who shall take the office upon confirmation by a majority vote of both houses of Congress.

Section 3

Whenever the President transmits to the President pro tempore of the Senate and the Speaker of the House of Representatives his written declaration that he is unable to discharge the powers and duties of his office, and until he transmits to them a written declaration to the contrary, such powers and duties shall be discharged by the Vice President as Acting President.

Section 4

Whenever the Vice President and a majority of either the principal officers of the executive departments or of such other body as Congress may by law provide, transmit to the President pro tempore of the Senate and the Speaker of the House of Representatives their written declaration that the President is unable to discharge the powers and duties of his office, the Vice President shall immediately assume the powers and duties of the office as Acting President.

Thereafter, when the President transmits to the President pro tempore of the Senate and the Speaker of the House of Representatives his written declaration that no inability exists, he shall resume the powers and duties of his office unless the Vice President and a majority of either the principal officers of the executive department or of such other body as Congress may by law provide, transmit within four days to the President pro tempore of the Senate and the Speaker of the House of Representatives their written declaration that the President is unable to discharge the powers and duties of his office. Thereupon Congress shall decide the issue, assembling within

48 hours for that purpose if not in session. If the Congress, within 21 days after receipt of the latter written declaration, or, if Congress is not in session, within 21 days after Congress is required to assemble, determines by two-thirds vote of both houses that the President is unable to discharge the powers and duties of his office, the Vice President shall continue to discharge the same as Acting President; otherwise, the President shall resume the powers and duties of his office.

Amendment XXVI

[Adopted 1971]

Section 1

The right of citizens of the United States, who are 18 years of age or older, to vote shall not be denied or abridged by the United States or any state on account of age.

Section 2

The Congress shall have the power to enforce this article by appropriate legislation.

Amendment XXVII

[Adopted 1992]

No law, varying the compensation for the services of the Senators and Representatives shall take effect, until an election of Representatives shall have intervened.

abolitionism (p. 281) Worldwide movement to end slavery. In the United States the term chiefly applies to the antebellum reformers whose cause culminated in the Civil War.

acquired immunodeficiency syndrome (AIDS) (p. 834) A deadly, and very often sexually transmitted disease that emerged in the 1980s and that at first spread chiefly among injection drug users and gay male populations, but soon affected all communities. The disease is a complex of deadly pathologies resulting from infection with the **human immunodeficiency virus (HIV)**. By 2000, AIDS deaths in the United States had surpassed 40,000.

Agricultural Adjustment Act (AAA) (p. 688) New Deal legislation that raised farm prices by restricting output of staple crops. It restricted production and paid subsidies to growers; declared unconstitutional in 1936.

Albany Plan (p. 87) A proposal, drafted in Albany, New York, in 1754 by Benjamin Franklin of Pennsylvania, for a "plan of union" for the collective defense of the British colonies. Because it held the potential for unifying the colonies against its rule, the British government never adopted the plan.

Alien and Sedition Acts (p. 165) Four laws passed by the Federalist-dominated Congress in 1798 directed against sympathizers to the **French Revolution**—chiefly Thomas Jefferson and his **Republican party**. The laws, which stifled dissent and made it more difficult for immigrants to gain citizenship, had lapsed by 1802.

Allied Powers (p. 613) The military alliance during World War I, chiefly consisting of Britain, France, Russia, and Italy, that opposed the **Central Powers**, chiefly Germany, Austria-Hungary, and Turkey.

Allies (p. 722) In the context of United States history, a term that refers to the nations that opposed the **Axis Powers**, chiefly Nazi Germany, Italy, and Japan, during World War II. The Allies included Britain, France (except during the Nazi occupation, 1940–1944), the Soviet Union (1941–1945), the United States (1941–1945), and China.

American Colonization Society (p. 234) An organization, founded in 1816, that proposed to solve the "Negro problem" by transporting freed slaves from the United States to Africa. Although the society purchased land in Africa (Liberia), few African Americans chose to resettle there.

American Federation of Labor (AFL) (p. 479) A union, formed in 1886, that organized skilled workers along craft lines. It focused on workplace issues rather than political or social reform.

American System (p. 214) Kentucky Senator Henry Clay's plan for national economic development; it included protective tariffs, a national bank, and federal subsidies for railroad and canal construction.

Anaconda Plan (p. 377) General Winfield Scott's strategy for defeating the Confederacy; its central elements included a naval blockade and seizure of the Mississippi River valley.

Antifederalists (p. 149) Critics of the Constitution who initially opposed its ratification. By the late 1790s, they generally endorsed states' rights and sought limitations on federal power.

antinomianism (p. 39) A religious doctrine that affirmed that individuals who possessed saving grace were exempt from the rules of good behavior and from the laws of the community. In puritan New England, such beliefs were generally regarded as heresy.

Arminianism (p. 35) A religious doctrine that held that good works and faith could lead to salvation. In puritan New England, this was regarded as heresy akin to Catholicism because it implied that God's will was contingent on the acts of man.

Articles of Confederation (p. 129) The charter establishing the first government of the United States, ratified in 1781. The Articles placed the coercive powers to tax and regulate trade within the individual state governments; the national government, widely criticized for being weak, was superseded by the government established by the Constitution of the United States, effective in 1789.

Ashcan School (p. 558) Artists in the early twentieth century who used as their subject matter the things and people found in city streets and slums. Ashcan artists often supported progressive political and social reform.

Atlanta Compromise (p. 539) A social policy, propounded by black leader Booker T. Washington in 1895, advocating that blacks concentrate on learning useful skills rather than agitate over segregation, disfranchisement, and discrimination. In Washington's view, black self-help and self-improvement was the surest way to economic advancement.

axis of evil (p. 859) A pejorative phrase, coined by President George W. Bush in 2002, referring to states that supported terrorism and sought weapons of mass destruction. He specifically identified Iraq, Iran, and North Korea.

Axis Powers (p. 706) A term for the alliance between Nazi Germany and Italy after 1936 and, after 1940, Japan.

Bacon's Rebellion (p. 62) An armed uprising in 1676, led by Nathaniel Bacon, against Virginia governor Sir William Berkeley. Initially the rebels attacked Indian settlements but later moved against Berkeley's political faction and burned Jamestown, capital of the colony. After Bacon's death that year, the rebellion collapsed.

Bank of the United States (p. 156) Established as a joint public and private venture in 1791 at the behest of Secretary of Treasury Alexander Hamilton, the Bank of the United States served as a depository of government funds, collected and expended government revenue, and issued notes to serve as a national medium of exchange. The bank's charter expired in 1811. A Second Bank of the United States was chartered in 1816.

Bank war (p. 252) The political dispute over whether to renew the charter of the Second Bank of the United States. In 1832, Congress voted to recharter the bank but President Andrew Jackson vetoed the measure and the charter expired in 1836. He argued that the Bank was unconstitutional, a dangerous monopoly, and vulnerable to control by foreign investors.

Bay of Pigs fiasco (p. 767) A military debacle in April 1961, during an American-organized effort to invade Cuba and drive Fidel Castro, the communist ruler, from power. The invasion force of some 1,500 Cuban exiles was routed at the Bay of Pigs, a major embarrassment for President John F. Kennedy.

beat school (p. 778) Also known as "beats," "beatniks," or the "beat generation"—nonconformists in the late 1950s who rejected conventional dress and sexual standards and cultivated avant-garde literature and music.

Berlin airlift (p. 743) U.S. effort to deliver supplies including 2 million tons of food and coal by air to West Berlin in 1948–1949 in response to the Soviet blockade of the city.

Berlin wall (p. 767) Erected by East Germany in 1961 and torn down by a Dutch company in 1989, the wall isolated West Berlin from the surrounding areas in communist controlled East Berlin and East Germany.

Bill of Rights (p. 154) The first ten amendments to the United States Constitution (adopted in 1791); they protected individual liberties and states' rights against the power of the national government.

Black Codes (p. 407) Special laws passed by southern state and municipal governments after the Civil War that denied free blacks many rights of citizenship.

Bland-Allison Silver Purchase Act (p. 545) An 1878 compromise law that that provided for the limited coinage of silver.

Blitzkrieg (p. 705) A German tactic in World War II, translated as "lightning war," involving the coordinated attack of air and armored firepower.

Bonus Army (p. 679) A gathering of 20,000 Great War veterans in Washington, DC in June 1932, to demand immediate payment of their "adjusted compensation" bonuses voted by Congress in 1924. Congress rejected their demands, and President Hoover ordered U.S. troops to drive them from the capital.

Boston Massacre (p. 105) A violent confrontation between British troops and a Boston mob on March 5, 1770; the soldiers opened fire and killed five, an incident that inflamed sentiment against the British.

Brown v. Board of Education of Topeka (p. 757) The 1954 Supreme Court decision that held that racially segregated education, which prevailed in much of the South, was unconstitutional. The ruling overturned the doctrine of "separate but equal" that had provided the legal justification for racial segregation ever since the 1896 *Plessy v. Ferguson* Supreme Court decision.

Camp David Accords (p. 803) A 1978 peace treaty between Egypt and Israel, mediated by President Jimmy Carter, signed at Camp David, a presidential retreat near Washington, DC.

carpetbaggers (p. 414) A pejorative term for Northerners who went to the South after the Civil War to exploit the new political power of freed blacks and the disenfranchisement of former Confederates.

Central Powers (p. 613) Germany and its World War I allies—Austria-Hungary, Turkey, and Bulgaria.

Chinese Exclusion Act (p. 436) A law passed by Congress in 1882 that prohibited Chinese immigration to the United States; it was overturned in 1943.

Civil Rights Act of 1964 (p. 772) Legislation outlawing discrimination in public accommodations and employment on the basis of race, skin color, sex, religion, or national origin.

civil rights cases (p. 537) A group of cases in 1883 in which the U.S. Supreme Court declared unconstitutional the Civil Rights Act of 1875, which had prohibited racial discrimination in hotels, theaters, and other privately owned facilities. The Court ruled that the **Fourteenth Amendment** barred state governments from discriminating on the basis of race but did not prevent private individuals, businesses, or organizations from doing so.

Civilian Conservation Corps (CCC) (p. 687) A **New Deal** program to provide government jobs in reforestation, flood control, and other conservation projects to young men between ages eighteen and twenty-five.

Clayton Antitrust Act (p. 577) Legislation that strengthened antitrust laws. Passed in 1914, it outlawed interlocking directorates, exempted labor unions from antitrust laws, and limited the use of injunctions in labor disputes.

Coercive Acts (p. 108) A series of laws passed by Parliament in 1774 to punish Boston and Massachusetts for the destruction of tea during the "Boston Tea Party." Many colonists, who regarded these and similar laws as "intolerable," moved closer toward war.

Columbian Exchange (p. 27) The transfer of plants, animals, and diseases from Europe, Africa, and Asia to and from the Americas after Columbus's fateful voyage in 1492.

Common Sense (p. 117) An influential tract, published by Thomas Paine in January 1776, calling for American independence from Great Britain and establishment of a republican government.

Compromise of 1850 (p. 315) Several laws that together sought to settle several outstanding issues involving slavery. They banned the slave trade, but not slavery in Washington, DC; admitted California as a free state; applied popular sovereignty to the remaining Mexican Cession territory; settled the Texas-New Mexico boundary dispute; and passed a more stringent **Fugitive Slave Act**.

Compromise of 1877 (p. 427) A brokered arrangement whereby Republican and Democratic leaders agreed to settle the disputed 1876 presidential election. Democrats allowed returns that ensured the election of Republican Rutherford B. Hayes; and Republicans agreed to withdraw federal troops from the South, ensuring an end to Reconstruction.

Comstock Lode (p. 444) The first major vein of silver ore in the United States, discovered in the late 1850s, near Virginia City, Nevada.

conquistadores (p. 22) The Spanish term for "conquerors," specifically the explorers, adventurers, and soldiers who crushed the native peoples of the Americas.

Conservation (p. 572) The efficient management and use of natural resources, such as forests, grasslands, and rivers; it represents a "middle-of-the-road" policy as opposed to the uncontrolled exploitation of such resources or the preservation those resources from any human exploiters.

Continental army (p. 115) The regular or professional army authorized by the **Second Continental Congress**, mostly under the command of General George Washington during the Revolutionary War.

Contract with America (p. 852) A pledge, signed by many Republicans running for Congress in 1994, to support conservative reforms limiting federal power and expenditures. Championed by House Speaker Newt Gingrich, it contributed to a Republican electoral victory; but opposition by President William Clinton, a Democrat, prevented passage of much of the contract's legislative agenda.

Copperheads (p. 378) Term that initially applied to northern Democrats who resisted Republican war measures and advocated negotiation with the Confederacy. Later in the Civil War, the term became tantamount to an accusation of treason against the Union.

Crittenden Compromise (p. 367) Legislation proposed by Kentucky Senator John Crittenden during the Secession Crisis in 1860–1861. It called for a constitutional amendment recognizing slavery in all territory south of 36°30' (the "Missouri Compromise line") and an ironclad amendment guaranteeing slavery in slave states. President-elect Lincoln and the Republicans rejected the proposals.

crop-lien system (p. 420) A system of agriculture in which local landowners and merchants loaned money to farm workers in return for a portion of the harvest of cash crops. By forcing farmers to plant cash crops, the system discouraged diversified agriculture in the South.

Cuban missile crisis (p. 768) The showdown between the United States and the Soviet Union during October 1962, after the Soviet Union had sneaked medium-range nuclear missiles into communist Cuba. After President John F. Kennedy publicly demanded their removal and ordered the blockade of Cuba, Soviet leader Nikita Khrushchev agreed to do so, averting a nuclear war.

Cult of True Womanhood (p. 271) An ideal of middle-class womanhood in the early nineteenth century that asserted that women were naturally pious, pure, and submissive; exemplars of Christian precepts; and best-suited to supervise the moral development of the family.

D-Day (p. 724) June 6, 1944, the day Allied troops crossed the English Channel, landed on the coast of Normandy, and opened a second front in Western Europe during World War II. The "D" stands for "disembarkation"—to leave a ship and go ashore.

***Dartmouth College v. Woodward* (p. 242)** The 1819 Supreme Court case that held that a state charter—in this case, to Dartmouth College—was a contract and that contracts could not be canceled or altered without the consent of both parties, a ruling that strengthened corporations and encouraged investment.

Dawes Severalty Act of 1887 (p. 441) An 1887 law terminating tribal ownership of land and allotting some parcels of land to individual Indians with the remainder of the land left open for white settlement. It included provisions for Indian education and eventual citizenship. The law led to corruption, exploitation, and the weakening of Indian tribal culture. It was reversed in 1934.

détente (p. 786) A French term, meaning the relaxation of tensions, applied to an easing of Cold War antagonisms during the 1970s. Under President Richard Nixon and foreign affairs adviser Henry Kissinger, détente was a strategy to allow the United States to weaken the bonds between the Soviet Union and communist China.

dollar diplomacy (p. 605) A policy of President William Taft to promote American economic penetration to underdeveloped nations, especially in Latin America; it sought to strengthen American influence without requiring the presence of U.S. troops.

Dred Scott decision (p. 358) The 1857 Supreme Court ruling that held that blacks were not citizens and could not sue in a federal court, and, most important, that Congress had exceeded its

constitutional authority in banning slavery from the territories. By declaring the Missouri Compromise unconstitutional, and making future compromises even more difficult, the decision pushed the nation closer to civil war.

Electoral College (p. 148) An assembly of delegates representing each of the states who choose the president of the United States. This mechanism, established by the U.S. Constitution, was regarded as less volatile than allowing voters to elect the president directly.

Emancipation Proclamation (p. 384) A decree by President Abraham Lincoln that freed all slaves in Confederate states that remained in active rebellion on January 1, 1863, when the proclamation went into effect.

Embargo Act (p. 189) A law passed by Congress in 1807 prohibiting all American exports. President Thomas Jefferson, who proposed the law, sought to pressure Britain and France—then at war with each other—into recognizing neutral rights.

***encomienda* system (p. 22)** A feudal labor arrangement, imposed in the Spanish colonies of the Americas, by which Spanish settlers were granted a certain number of Indian subjects who were obliged to pay tribute in goods and labor.

Enlightenment (p. 88) An intellectual movement of the eighteenth century that celebrated human reason and scientific advances and expressed doubts about the truth claims of sacred texts.

Environmental Protection Agency (EPA) (p. 788) A federal agency created in 1970 to oversee environmental monitoring and cleanup programs.

Equal Rights Amendment (ERA) (p. 827) A proposed amendment to the U.S. Constitution to outlaw discrimination on the basis of sex. Although first proposed in 1923, the amendment was not passed by Congress until 1972; but the ratification movement fell short and the ERA was not added to the Constitution.

Era of Good Feelings (p. 209) A period from 1817 to 1823 in which the disappearance of the **Federalists** enabled the Republicans to govern in a spirit of seemingly nonpartisan harmony.

Espionage Act (p. 623) A law passed in 1917 that made it a crime to obstruct the nation's effort to win World War I.

Fair Deal (p. 744) President Harry Truman's 1949 program for expanded economic opportunity and civil rights.

Farewell Address (p. 163) President Washington's influential 1796 speech in which he deplored the rise of political factions and warned against "permanent alliances" with foreign nations.

Federal Reserve Act (p. 576) A 1913 law establishing a Federal Reserve Board, which controlled the rediscount rate and thus the money supply; this helped regularize the national banking system.

***Federalist Papers* (p. 153)** A series of essays, chiefly written by Alexander Hamilton, James Madison, and John Jay, explaining and defending the national government proposed by the Constitutional Convention of 1787.

Federalists (p. 149) Advocates of a strong national government; they supported ratification of the Constitution and subsequently supported measures to expand federal revenues and functions.

Fifteenth Amendment (p. 414) An amendment (1870), championed by the Republican party, that sought to guarantee the vote to blacks in the South following the Civil War.

First Continental Congress (p. 108) An assembly comprised of delegates from twelve colonies that met in Philadelphia in 1774. It denied Parliament's authority to legislate for the colonies, adopted the Declaration of Rights and Grievances, created a Continental Association to enforce a boycott of British imports, and endorsed a call to take up arms against Britain.

Force Acts (p. 423) Three laws passed by the Republican-dominated Congress in 1870–1871 to protect black voters in the South. The laws placed state elections under federal jurisdiction and imposed fines and imprisonment on those guilty of interfering with any citizen exercising his right to vote.

Fourteen Points (p. 628) A comprehensive plan, proposed by President Woodrow Wilson in January 1918, to negotiate an end to World War I. It called for freedom of the seas, free trade, arms reduction, national self-determination and an end to colonial rule and secret diplomacy.

Fourteenth Amendment (p. 409) An amendment, passed by Congress in 1866 and ratified in 1868, that prohibited states from depriving citizens of the due process or the equal protection of the laws. Although the amendment was a response to discriminatory laws against blacks in the South, it figured prominently in the expansion of individual rights and liberties during the last half of the twentieth century.

Free Soil party (p. 311) A party that emerged in the 1840s in opposition to the expansion of slavery into the territories. Formally organized in 1848, it nominated Martin Van Buren for president. In 1856, Free Soil party members joined with former **Whigs** and other disaffected voters to form the **Republican party**.

Freedmen's Bureau (p. 408) A federal refugee agency to aid former slaves and destitute whites after the Civil War. It provided them food, clothing, and other necessities as well as helped them find work and set up schools.

French and Indian War (p. 92) Fourth in the series of great wars between Britain and France, this conflict (1754–1763) had its focal point in North America and pitted the French and their Indian allies against the British and their Indian allies. Known in Europe as the **Seven Years' War**, this struggle drove the French government from much of North America.

French Revolution (p. 158) The massive and violent social and political upheaval commencing in 1789 that ended the French monarchy, established a republic, expropriated the land and property of the Catholic Church, and culminated in a bloody reign of terror.

Fugitive Slave Act (p. 315) Initially, a 1793 law to encourage the return of runaway slaves; this law was amended, as part of the **Compromise of 1850**, so as to authorize federal commissioners to compel citizens to assist in the return of runaway (fugitive) slaves. The law offended Northerners and its nonenforcement offended Southerners.

Gibbons v. Ogden **(p. 242)** Supreme Court ruling (1824) that held that no state could pass laws affecting interstate trade, thereby ensuring the federal government's supremacy in interstate commerce.

Glorious Revolution (p. 68) The peaceful accession of William II, a Protestant, and Queen Mary to the British throne in 1688, ending the Catholic rule of James II. Many colonists rebelled against governors who had been appointed by James II and demanded greater political rights.

gold rush (p. 309) Term for the gold-mining boom in the U.S. western territories in the late 1840s and 1850s.

"good neighbor" (p. 673) President Herbert Hoover's policy to promote better relations between the United States and nations in the Western Hemisphere; it declared America's intention to disclaim the right to intervention pronounced in the **Platt Amendment** and the **Roosevelt Corollary**.

Great Awakening (p. 85) A widespread evangelical revival movement of the 1740s and 1750s, sparked by the tour of the English evangelical minister George Whitefield. The Awakening spread religious fervor but weakened the authority of established churches.

Great Compromise (p. 149) Resolved the differences between the New Jersey and Virginia delegations to the Constitutional Convention by providing for a bicameral legislature: the Senate, with equal representation for each state, and the House of Representatives, apportioned by population.

Great Society (p. 772) The sweeping legislative agenda of President Lyndon Johnson; it sought to end poverty, promote civil rights, and improve housing, health care, and education. The program was criticized as costly and ineffective.

Gulf of Tonkin Resolution (p. 780) Congressional action, undertaken at President Johnson's request, giving the President the authority to deploy U.S. troops to repel aggression in Southeast Asia. This provided congressional sanction for the escalation of the Vietnam war.

Half-Way Covenant (p. 67) A modification of puritan practice, adopted by many Congregational churches during the 1650s and afterwards, that allowed baptized puritans who had not experienced saving grace to acquire partial church membership and receive sacraments.

Harlem Renaissance (p. 658) A modern artistic and literary movement that celebrated African American life and culture in early twentieth-century Harlem, New York. Among its key figures were Langston Hughes, Richard Wright, and Zora Neale Hurston (literature); Duke Ellington (music); Jacob Lawrence (painting); and Aaron Douglas (sculpture).

Hartford Convention (p. 203) A gathering of New England **Federalists** from December 1814 through January 1815 to channel opposition to Thomas Jefferson and the **War of 1812**. Some participants may have regarded the meeting as preparatory to a secession movement by the New England colonies.

headright (p. 58) A system of land distribution, adopted first in Virginia and later in Maryland, that granted colonists fifty acres for themselves and another fifty for each "head" (or person) they brought with them to the colony. This system was often used in conjunction with indentured servitude to build large plantations and supply them with labor.

Hepburn Act (p. 572) Federal legislation, passed in 1906, that gave the Interstate Commerce Commission sufficient power to inspect railroad companies' records, set maximum rates, and outlaw free passes.

Homestead Act (1862) (p. 389) Federal law granting 160 acres of public land in the West to any settler who would farm and improve it within five years of the grant; it encouraged migration into the Great Plains.

human immunodeficiency virus (HIV) (p. 834) A virus, usually spread through sexual contact, that attacks the immune system, sometimes fatally. HIV, which causes **acquired immunodeficiency syndrome (AIDS)**, first appeared in the United States in the 1980s.

impressment (p. 187) The policy whereby Britain forced people to serve in its navy. The impressment of sailors—even American citizens—on neutral vessels during the Napoleonic Wars outraged Americans and was a major cause of the **War of 1812**.

improvised explosive device (IED) (p. 867) Also known as "roadside bombs," IEDs are homemade bombs that usually consist of captured artillery shells that are wired to a detonator. Either they are exploded remotely or by suicide bombers. IEDs accounted for over a third of the casualties sustained by American and United Nations forces in the Iraq and Afghanistan wars.

indentured servants (p. 58) Individuals working under a form of contract labor that provided them with free passage to America in return for a promise to work for a fixed period, usually seven years. Indentured servitude was the primary labor system in the Chesapeake colonies for most of the seventeenth century.

Industrial Workers of the World (IWW) (p. 559) A militant labor organization, founded in 1905 and inspired by European anarchists, that advocated "abolition of the wage system" and called for a single union of all workers, regardless of trade or skill level; it was repressed during and after World War I.

internment camps (p. 720) Detainment centers, mostly located in western states, that held approximately 110,000 Japanese aliens and American citizens of Japanese origin during World War II.

Interstate Commerce Act (p. 476) Federal law establishing the Interstate Commerce Commission in 1887, the nation's first regulatory agency.

Iran-Contra affair (p. 813) Scandal involving high officials in the Reagan administration accused of funding the Contra rebels in Nicaragua in violation of 1984 Congressional laws explicitly prohibiting such aid. The Contra funding came from the secret sale of arms to Iran.

Iranian hostage crisis (p. 803) Protracted crisis that began in 1979 when Islamic militants seized the American embassy in Tehran, Iran, and held scores of its employees hostage. The militants had been enraged by American support for the deposed Shah of Iran. The crisis, which lasted over a year, contributed to President Jimmy Carter's defeat in his reelection campaign in 1980.

isolationism (p. 586) A national policy that eschews foreign alliances, such as was propounded by George Washington in his "Farewell Address." Isolationism was also embraced by part of the **Monroe Doctrine** of 1823 and after the First World War, when the United States refused to join the **League of Nations** and sought to distance itself during the 1930s from the rumblings of another world war. Isolationism ended as national policy when Japan attacked Pearl Harbor on December 7, 1941.

Jacksonian democracy (p. 318) A political doctrine, chiefly associated with Andrew Jackson, that proclaimed the equality of all adult white males—the common man—and disapproved of anything that smacked of special privilege, such as chartered banks.

Jay's Treaty (p. 162) Named after John Jay, the American negotiator, and ratified in 1795, this treaty eased tensions with Great Britain. By its provisions Britain agreed to evacuate forts on the United States' side of the Great Lakes and submit questions of neutral rights to arbitrators.

joint-stock companies (p. 30) Businesses in which investors pooled capital for specific purposes, such as conducting trade and founding colonies. Examples include the English joint-stock companies that founded the Virginia, Plymouth, and Massachusetts Bay colonies.

judicial review (p. 148) A crucial concept that empowered the Supreme Court to invalidate acts of Congress. Although not explicitly propounded in the U.S. Constitution, Chief Justice John Marshall affirmed in *Marbury v. Madison* (1803) that the right of judicial review was implicit in the Constitution's status as "the supreme Law of the Land."

Kansas-Nebraska Act (p. 353) A compromise law in 1854 that superseded the **Missouri Compromise** and left it to voters in Kansas and Nebraska to determine whether they would be slave or free states. The law exacerbated sectional tensions when voters came to blows over the question of slavery in Kansas.

Kentucky and Virginia Resolves (p. 166) Political declarations in favor of states' rights, written by Thomas Jefferson and James Madison, in opposition to the federal **Alien and Sedition Acts**. These resolutions, passed by the Kentucky and Virginia legislatures in 1798, maintained that states could nullify federal legislation they regarded as unconstitutional.

Knights of Labor (p. 478) A national labor organization, formed in 1869 and headed by Uriah Stephens and Terence Powderly, that promoted union solidarity, political reform, and sociability among members. Its advocacy of the eight-hour day led to violent strikes in 1886 and the organization's subsequent decline.

Know-Nothing party (p. 353) A nativist, anti-immigrant and anti-Catholic party that emerged in response to the flood of Catholic immigrants from Ireland and Germany in the 1840s. The party achieved mostly local successes in the Northeast port cities; but in 1856 former President Millard Fillmore, whose Whig party had dissolved, accepted the nomination of southern Know-Nothings but carried only Maryland, a failure that contributed to the movement's decline.

Ku Klux Klan (p. 423) Founded as a social club in 1866 by a handful of former Confederate soldiers in Tennessee, it became a vigilante group that used violence and intimidation to drive African Americans out of politics. The movement declined in the late 1870s but resurfaced in the 1920s as a political organization that opposed all groups—immigrant, religious, and racial—that challenged Protestant white hegemony.

laissez-faire (p. 471) A French term—literally, "to let alone"—used in economic contexts to signify the absence of governmental interference in or regulation of economic matters.

League of Nations (p. 631) A worldwide assembly of nations, proposed by President Woodrow Wilson, that was included in the Treaty of Versailles ending World War I. The refusal of the United States to join the League limited its effectiveness.

Lecompton constitution (p. 359) A proslavery constitution, drafted in 1857 by delegates for Kansas territory, elected under questionable circumstances, seeking admission to the United States. It was rejected by two territorial governors, supported by President Buchanan, and decisively defeated by Congress.

Leisler's Rebellion (p. 74) An uprising in 1689, led by Jacob Leisler, that wrested control of New York's government following the abdication of King James II. The rebellion ended when Leisler was arrested and executed in 1690.

Lend-Lease Act (p. 707) A military aid measure, proposed by President Franklin D. Roosevelt in 1941 and adopted by Congress, empowering the president to sell, lend, lease, or transfer $7 billion of war material to any country whose defense he declared as vital to that of the United States.

Lewis and Clark expedition (p. 182) An exploration of the Louisiana Territory and the region stretching to the Pacific, commissioned by President Jefferson. Commanded by Meriwether Lewis and William Clark, the enterprise (1804–1806) brought back a wealth of information about the region.

Louisiana Purchase (p. 177) An 1803 agreement whereby the United States purchased France's North American Empire, the vast region drained by the Mississippi and Missouri Rivers, for $15 million; it doubled the size of the nation.

Loyalists (p. 119) Sometimes called Tories, the term for American colonists who refused to take up arms against England in the 1770s.

lyceums (p. 291) Locally sponsored public lectures, often featuring writers, that were popular in the nineteenth century.

Manhattan Project (p. 705) The code name for the extensive United States military project, established in 1942, to produce fissionable uranium and plutonium, and to design and build an atomic bomb. Costing nearly $2 billion, the effort culminated in the destruction of Hiroshima and Nagasaki in August 1945.

manifest destiny (p. 300) Originating in the 1840s, a term that referred to support of the expansion of the United States through the acquisition of Texas, Oregon, and parts of Mexico. The term was also used in the 1890s in reference to the conquest of foreign lands not meant to be incorporated into the United States.

***Marbury v. Madison* (p. 176)** An 1803 Supreme Court ruling that declared the Judiciary Act of 1789 unconstitutional and established the precedent for judicial review of federal laws.

Marshall Plan (p. 741) A proposal, propounded in 1947 by Secretary of State George Marshall, to use American aid to rebuild the war-torn economies of European nations. Adopted by Congress in 1948 as the European Recovery Program, it pumped some $13 billion into Europe during the next five years.

massive retaliation (p. 750) The "New Look" military policy of the Dwight D. Eisenhower and Secretary of State John Foster Dulles relying on nuclear weapons to inhibit communist aggression during the 1950s.

Mayflower Compact (p. 35) An agreement, signed aboard the *Mayflower* among the Pilgrims en route to Plymouth Plantation (1620), to establish a body politic and to obey the rules of the governors they chose.

***McCulloch v. Maryland* (p. 242)** An 1819 Supreme Court ruling that state governments could not tax a federal agency—in this case the second Bank of the United States—for "the power to tax involves the power to destroy." The decision affirmed the doctrine of the implied powers of the federal government.

Medicare (p. 776) A social welfare measure, enacted in 1965, providing hospitalization insurance for people over sixty-five and a voluntary plan to cover doctor bills paid in part by the federal government.

mercantilism (p. 83) A loose system of economic organization designed, through a favorable balance of trade, to guarantee the prosperity of the British empire. Mercantilists advocated possession of colonies as places where the mother country could acquire raw materials not available at home.

Mexican War (p. 305) Fought between the United States and Mexico from May 1846 to February 1848, the Mexican War greatly added to the national domain of the United States; see also **Treaty of Guadalupe Hidalgo**.

military-industrial complex (p. 761) A term, popularized by President Dwight D. Eisenhower in his 1961 farewell address, for the concert of interests among the U.S. military and its chief corporate contractors.

Missouri Compromise (p. 218) A legislative deal, brokered in 1820, that preserved the balance of slave and free states in the Union by admitting Missouri as a slave state and Maine as a free state; it also banned slavery from that part of the Louisiana Territory north of 36°30'.

Monroe Doctrine (p. 206) A foreign policy edict, propounded by President James Monroe in 1823, declaring that the American continents were no longer open to European colonization or exploitation and that the United States would not interfere in the internal affairs of European nations.

Moral Majority (p. 806) A term associated with the organization by that name, founded in 1979 by the Reverend Jerry Falwell to combat "amoral liberals," drug abuse, "coddling" of criminals, homosexuality, communism, and abortion.

muckraker (p. 558) A term for progressive investigative journalists who exposed the seamy side of American life at the turn of the twentieth century by "raking up the muck."

mugwumps (p. 356) A group of eastern Republicans, disgusted with corruption in the party, who campaigned for the Democrats in the 1884 elections. These anticorruption reformers were conservative on the money question and government regulation.

National American Woman Suffrage Association (NAWSA) (p. 567) An organization, founded in 1890, that united the National Woman Suffrage Association, headed by Elizabeth Cady Stanton and Susan B. Anthony, and the American Woman Suffrage Association, headed by Lucy Stone. After ratification of the Nineteenth Amendment granting women the vote in 1920, the NAWSA became the League of Women Voters.

National Association for the Advancement of Colored People (NAACP) (p. 580) A national interracial organization, founded in 1909, that promoted the rights of African Americans. Initially it fought against lynching, but from 1955 through 1977, under the leadership of Roy Wilkins, it launched the campaign that overturned legalized segregation and it backed civil rights legislation. The NAACP remains the nation's largest African American organization.

National Grange of the Patrons of Husbandry (p. 475) A farmers' organization, founded in 1867 by Oliver H. Kelley, that initially provided social and cultural benefits but then supported legislation, known as the Granger laws, providing for railroad regulation.

National Organization for Women (NOW) (p. 827) An organization, founded in 1966 by Betty Friedan and other feminists, to promote equal rights for women, changes in divorce laws, and legalization of abortion.

National Origins Act (p. 640) A federal law, passed in 1929 that curtailed immigration, especially from southern and eastern Europe and Asia.

National Recovery Administration (NRA) (p. 687) A **New Deal** agency, established in 1933, to promote economic recovery, that promulgated industry-wide codes to control production, prices, and wages.

nationalism (p. 134) An affinity for a particular nation; in particular, a sense of national consciousness and loyalty that promotes the interests and attributes of that nation over all others.

Nativism (p. 493) A fear or hatred of immigrants, ethnic minorities, or alien political movements.

Navigation Acts (p. 84) Seventeenth-century Parliamentary statutes to control trade within the British empire so as to benefit Britain and promote its administration of the colonies.

Neolithic revolution (p. 5) The transition from a hunter-gatherer economy to one mostly based on the cultivation of crops.

neutrality acts (p. 704) Legislation affirming nonbelligerency in the event of war. In relation to American history, such legislation was passed in 1794 to preclude American entanglement in the Napoleonic Wars; similar laws were passed just before and after World War I, especially during the 1930s.

New Deal (p. 686) A broad program of legislation proposed by President Franklin D. Roosevelt to promote recovery from the Great Depression and provide relief for those in distress.

New Freedom (p. 575) Democratic candidate Woodrow Wilson's term in the 1912 presidential campaign for a proposed policy that would restore competition by breaking up the trusts and punishing corporations that violated rules of business conduct.

New Frontier (p. 761) President John F. Kennedy's term for a revitalized national agenda, particularly in relation to foreign policy and space exploration.

new immigration (p. 493) Reference to the influx of immigrants to the United States during the late nineteenth and early twentieth century predominantly from southern and eastern Europe.

New Jersey Plan (p. 147) The proposal to the Constitutional Convention of 1787 by New Jersey delegate William Paterson to create a federal legislature in which each state was represented equally. The concept became embodied in the United States Constitution through the Senate, in which each state has two representatives, though this was counterbalanced by the House of Representatives, in which each state's representation is proportional to its population.

New Nationalism (p. 574) Progressive candidate Theodore Roosevelt's term in the 1912 presidential election for an expansion of federal power to regulate big business and enact legislation to promote social justice.

Niagara movement (p. 580) A response by W. E. B. Du Bois and other blacks, following a meeting in Niagara Falls in 1905, in opposition to Booker T. Washington's advocacy of black accommodation to white prejudice; these leaders drafted a political program to achieve equal opportunity, equal justice, and an end to segregation that led to the founding of the **National Association for the Advancement of Colored People (NAACP)**.

North American Free Trade Agreement (NAFTA) (p. 853) A 1993 accord signed by Canada, Mexico, and the United States to reduce and eventually eliminate barriers to trade, including tariffs, among the signatories.

North Atlantic Treaty Organization (NATO) (p. 744) A military mutual-defense pact, formed in 1948, by the United States, Canada, and ten European nations, including Great Britain, France, and West Germany; the Soviet Union countered with the formation of the Warsaw Pact among communist regimes in Eastern Europe.

Northwest Ordinance (p. 135) A 1787 measure of the Continental Congress, passed according to the **Articles of Confederation**, to provide for governance of the region north of the Ohio River and the eventual admission of up to five territories—ultimately the states of Ohio, Indiana, Illinois, Michigan, and Wisconsin. The ordinance also prohibited slavery in the region and reserved lands for Indians.

NSC-68 (p. 745) A secret policy statement, proposed by the National Security Council in 1950, calling for a large, ongoing military commitment to contain Soviet communism; it was accepted by President Harry Truman after the North Korean invasion of South Korea.

nullification (p. 258) A doctrine, forcefully articulated by John C. Calhoun in 1828, asserting that a state could invalidate, within its own boundaries, federal legislation the state regarded as unconstitutional.

Open Door policy (p. 602) A policy, propounded by Secretary of State John Hay in 1899, affirming the territorial integrity of China and a policy of free trade.

Organization of Petroleum Exporting Countries (OPEC) (p. 798) A cartel of oil-producing nations in Asia, Africa, and Latin America that gained substantial power over the world economy in the mid- to late-1970s.

Ostend Manifesto (p. 348) A confidential 1854 dispatch to the U.S. State Department from American diplomats meeting in Ostend, Belgium, suggesting that the United States would be justified in seizing Cuba if Spain refused to sell it to the United States. When word of the document was leaked, Northerners seethed at this "slaveholders' plot" to extend slavery.

Paleolithic revolution (p. 4) Period 750,000 years ago when humans devised simple stone tools, inaugurating life based on hunting and gathering.

Pendleton Act (p. 535) An 1883 law bringing civil service reform to federal employment; it classified many government jobs and required competitive exams for these positions.

People's (Populist) party (p. 542) The People's party of America was an important "third party," founded in 1891, that sought to unite various disaffected groups, especially farmers. The party nominated James B. Weaver for president in 1892 and in 1896 joined with the Democratic party in support of William Jennings Bryan for president.

Persian Gulf War (p. 817) The 1991 war following Iraq's takeover of Kuwait; the United States and a coalition of allies defeated the army of Iraqi leader Saddam Hussein but failed to drive him from power.

Platt Amendment (p. 598) A law, passed in 1901 and superseding the **Teller Amendment**, which stipulated the conditions for the withdrawal of American forces from Cuba; it also transferred ownership of the naval base at Guantanamo Bay to the United States.

Plessy v. Ferguson **(p. 537)** Supreme Court ruling (1896) that held that racial segregation of public accommodations did not infringe on the "equal protection" clause of the Constitution; this "separate but equal" doctrine was overturned by *Brown v. Board of Education* in 1954.

popular sovereignty (p. 310) The principle of allowing people to make political decisions by majority vote. As applied to American history, the term generally refers to the 1848 proposal of Michigan Senator Lewis Cass to allow settlers to determine the status of slavery in the territories.

Potsdam Conference (p. 733) A wartime conference (April 1945) held in occupied Germany where Allied leaders divided Germany and Berlin into four occupation zones, agreed to try Nazi leaders as war criminals, and planned the exacting of reparations from Germany.

pragmatism (p. 524) A philosophical system, chiefly associated with William James, that deemphasized abstraction and assessed ideas and cultural practices based on their practical effects; it helped inspire political and social reform during the late nineteenth century.

predestination (p. 35) The Calvinist belief, accepted by New England puritans, that God had determined who would receive eternal grace at the dawn of time; nothing people did during their lifetime could alter their prospects of salvation.

Progressivism (p. 556) A cluster of movements for various forms of social change—some of them contradictory—during the early twentieth century; progressives generally opposed corruption and inefficiency in government, monopoly power among corporations, and wayward behavior among immigrants and others.

Protestant Reformation (p. 30) A religious movement of the sixteenth century initially focused on eliminating corruption in the Catholic Church; but under the influence of theologians Martin Luther and John Calvin, it indicted Catholic theology and gave rise to various denominations that advanced alternative interpretations.

puritans (p. 35) A term, initially derisive, referring to English religious dissenters who believed that the religious practices and administration of the Church of England too closely resembled those of the Catholic Church; many migrated to Massachusetts Bay after 1630 to establish a religious commonwealth based on the principles of John Calvin and others.

Quakers (p. 42) Adherents of a religious organization founded in England in the 1640s who believed that the Holy Spirit lived in all people; they embraced pacifism and religious tolerance, and rejected formal theology. In the decades after 1670, thousands of Quakers emigrated to New Jersey and Pennsylvania.

Radical Republicans (p. 378, 406) A faction within the Republican party, headed by Thaddeus Stevens and Benjamin Wade, that insisted on black suffrage and federal protection of the civil rights of blacks. After 1867, the Radical Republicans achieved a working majority in Congress and passed legislation promoting Reconstruction.

Reaganomics (p. 805) A label pinned on President Ronald Reagan's policies of tax cuts, social welfare cuts, and increased military spending; it generated huge federal deficits, but also promoted the reorganization of large corporations.

"reconcentration" camps (p. 591) A term that referred to the Spanish refugee camps into which Cuban farmers were herded in 1896 to prevent them from providing assistance to rebels fighting for Cuban independence from Spain.

"red scare" (p. 635) Public hysteria over Bolshevik influence in the United States after World War I; it led to the arrest or deportation of thousands of radicals, labor activists, and ethnic leaders.

Republican party (p. 355) One of the original two political parties, sometimes called "Democratic Republican," it was organized by James Madison and Thomas Jefferson and generally stood for states' rights, an agrarian economy and the interests of farmers and planters over those of financial and commercial groups, who generally supported the **Federalist** party; both of the original parties faded in the 1820s. A new Republican party emerged in the 1850s in opposition to the extension of slavery in the territories. It also adopted most of the old Whig party's economic program. The party nominated John C. Fremont for president in 1856 and Abraham Lincoln in 1860.

romanticism (p. 285) A loosely defined aesthetic movement originating in the late eighteenth century and flowering during the early nineteenth century; it encompassed literature, philosophy, arts, and music and enshrined feeling and intuition over reason.

Sanitary Commission (p. 391) A private and voluntary medical organization, founded in May 1861, that sought to improve the physical and mental well-being of Union soldiers during the Civil War.

scalawags (p. 414) White southern Republicans—mainly small landowning farmers and well-off merchants and planters—who cooperated with the congressionally imposed Reconstruction governments set up in the South following the Civil War.

Scopes trial (p. 651) Also called the "Monkey Trial," it was a celebrated 1924 contest that pitted Darwinian evolutionists against fundamentalist "Creationists." John T. Scopes, a teacher charged with defying Tennessee law by teaching evolution, was found guilty and fined $100.

Second Continental Congress (p. 115) A gathering of American Patriots in May 1775 that organized the **Continental army**, requisitioned soldiers and supplies, and commissioned George Washington to lead it.

Second Great Awakening (p. 274) A wave of religious enthusiasm, commencing in the 1790s and lasting for decades, that stressed the mercy, love, and benevolence of God and emphasized that all people could, through faith and effort, achieve salvation.

second party system (p. 260) A term for the political contention between the Democratic party, as rejuvenated by Andrew Jackson in 1828, and the **Whigs**, who emerged in response to Jackson.

Sedition Act (p. 623) Federal legislation, first passed in 1798 and expired in 1801, that placed limits on freedom of speech during wartime. Another such act was passed in 1918 and led to the imprisonment of Socialist Eugene V. Debs and others during World War I.

Seneca Falls Convention (p. 284) A meeting, held at Seneca Falls, New York in 1848, that affirmed that "all men and women are created equal" and sought the franchise (vote) for women.

settlement houses (p. 506) Community centers, founded by reformers such as Jane Addams and Lillian Wald beginning in the 1880s, that were located in poor urban districts of major cities; the centers sought to Americanize immigrant families and provide them with social services and a political voice.

Seven Years' War (p. 93) The global conflict, sometimes known as the **French and Indian War**, that lasted from 1756 to 1763 and pitted France and its allies against Britain and its allies. Britain ultimately prevailed, forcing France to surrender its claims to Canada and all territory east of the Mississippi River.

Shakers (p. 276) A religious commune founded by Ann Lee in England that came to America in 1774. Shakers practiced celibacy, believed that God was both Mother and Father, and held property in common.

sharecropping (p. 420) A type of agriculture, frequently practiced in the South during and after Reconstruction, in which landowners provided land, tools, housing, and seed to a farmer who provided his labor; the resulting crop was divided between them (i.e., shared).

Shays's rebellion (p. 145) An armed rebellion of western Massachusetts farmers in 1786 to prevent state courts from foreclosing on debtors. Nationalists saw such unrest as proof of the inadequacy of the federal government under the **Articles of Confederation**.

Sherman Antitrust Act (p. 477) A federal law, passed in 1890, that outlawed monopolistic organizations that functioned to restrain trade.

Sherman Silver Purchase Act (p. 545) An 1890 law that obliged the federal government to buy and coin silver, thereby counteracting the deflationary tendencies of the economy at the time; its repeal in 1894, following the Depression of 1893, caused a political uproar.

social Darwinism (p. 472) A belief that Charles Darwin's theory of the evolution of species also applied to social and economic institutions and practices: The "fittest" enterprises or individuals prevailed, while those that were defective naturally faded away; society thus progressed most surely when competition was unrestricted by government.

Social Gospel (p. 505) A doctrine preached by many urban Protestant ministers during the early 1900s that focused on improving living conditions for the city's poor rather than on saving souls; proponents advocated civil service reform, child labor laws, government regulation of big business, and a graduated income tax.

Social Security Act (p. 694) A component of Franklin Roosevelt's **New Deal**, it established in 1935 a system of old-age, unemployment, and survivors' insurance funded by wage and payroll taxes.

Southern Christian Leadership Conference (SCLC) (p. 758) A civil rights organization, founded in 1957 by Martin Luther King, Jr. and his followers, that espoused Christian nonviolence but organized mass protests to challenge segregation and discrimination; it played a major role in support of the **Civil Rights Act of 1964** and the **Voting Rights Act of 1965**.

Specie Circular (p. 260) An edict, issued by President Andrew Jackson in 1836, obliging purchasers of public land to do so with gold coins rather than the paper currency issued by state banks; it caused the speculative boom in real estate to collapse and exacerbated a financial panic the following year.

spoils system (p. 251) A term, usually derisive, whereby newly elected office-holders appoint loyal members of their own party to public office.

Square Deal (p. 571) The phrase, initially employed by President Theodore Roosevelt in 1904, to describe an arbitrated settlement between workers and an employer, but more generally employed as a goal to promote fair business practices and to punish "bad" corporations that used their economic clout unfairly.

stagflation (p. 801) A term coined in the 1970s to describe the period's economic downturn and simultaneous deflation in prices.

Stamp Act Congress (p. 102) A meeting in New York City of delegates of most of the colonial assemblies in America to protest the Stamp Act, a revenue measure passed by Parliament in 1765; it was a precursor to the Continental Congress.

Strategic Arms Limitation Treaty (SALT) (p. 787) A treaty, signed by the United States and the Soviet Union in 1972, restricting the testing and deployment of nuclear ballistic missiles, the first of several such treaties.

Strategic Defense Initiative (SDI) (p. 807) The concept of a space-based missile defense system—popularly known as "Star Wars," after the movie by that name—proposed by President Ronald Reagan in 1983. Controversial and costly, the concept was never fully realized.

Student Nonviolent Coordinating Committee (SNCC) (p. 769) A civil rights organization, founded in 1960, that drew heavily on younger activists and college students. After 1965, under the leadership of Stokely Carmichael and then H. Rap Brown, the group advocated "Black Power."

Students for a Democratic Society (SDS) (p. 779) An organization created by leftist college students in the early 1960s; it organized protests against racial bigotry, corporate exploitation of workers, and, especially after 1965, the Vietnam war.

"surge" (p. 868) The sudden increase in troop strength that appeared to have been used successfully against the Iraq insurgency in 2007. President Barack Obama similarly adopted a surge in 2009 to stabilize a deteriorating situation in Afghanistan.

Taft-Hartley Act (p. 739) A 1947 federal law that outlawed the closed shop and secondary boycotts and obliged union leaders to sign affidavits declaring that they were not communists.

Tariff of Abominations (p. 216) An exceptionally high tariff, passed in 1828, that provoked Vice President John C. Calhoun to write the "South Carolina Exposition and Protest"—a defense of the doctrine of **nullification**.

Teapot Dome scandal (p. 670) A scandal during the administration of Warren Harding in which the Secretary of the Interior, Albert Fall, accepted bribes from oil companies that then leased the Teapot Dome federal oil reserve in Wyoming.

Teller Amendment (p. 592) A rider to the 1898 war resolution with Spain whereby Congress pledged that it did not intend to annex Cuba and that it would recognize Cuban independence from Spain.

temperance movement (p. 280) A reform movement of the nineteenth and early twentieth centuries in which women and ministers played a major role and that advocated moderation in the use of alcoholic beverages, or, preferably, abstinence. The major organizations included the American Temperance Society, the Washingtonian movement, and the Women's Christian Temperance Union (WCTU).

Ten Percent Plan (p. 406) A measure drafted by President Abraham Lincoln in 1863 to readmit states that had seceded once 10 percent of their prewar voters swore allegiance to the Union and adopted state constitutions outlawing slavery.

tenement (p. 497) Four- to six-story residential apartment house, once common in New York and certain other cities, built on a tiny lot with little regard for adequate ventilation or light.

Tennessee Valley Authority (TVA) (p. 689) A New Deal agency that built and operated dams and power plants on the Tennessee River; it also promoted flood control, soil conservation, and reforestation.

Tet offensive (p. 782) A wide-ranging offensive, launched by North Vietnamese and Vietcong troops throughout South Vietnam in February 1968. It failed to cause the South Vietnamese government to collapse, but persuaded many Americans that the war was not winnable. President Lyndon B. Johnson announced his decision not to run for reelection several months later.

Thirteenth Amendment (p. 407) Passed in 1865, this amendment declared an end to slavery and negated the Three-fifths Clause in the Constitution, thereby increasing the representation of the southern states in Congress.

Three-Fifths Compromise (p. 148) The provision in the Constitution that defined slaves, for purposes of representation in the House of Representatives and state tax payments, not as full persons, but as constituting only three-fifths of a person.

Trail of Tears (p. 258) The name for the 1838 forced removal of Cherokee and other Indians from Georgia and the western Appalachians to Indian Territory in Oklahoma and nearby regions.

transcendentalism (p. 286) A diverse and loosely defined philosophy that promoted a mystical, intuitive way of looking at life that subordinated facts to feelings. Transcendentalists argued that humans could transcend reason and intellectual capacities by having faith in themselves and in the fundamental benevolence of the universe. They were complete individualists.

Transcontinental Treaty (p. 206) Also called the Adams-Onís Treaty. Ratified in 1821, it acquired Florida and stretched the western boundary of the Louisiana Territory to the Oregon coast.

Treaty of Guadalupe Hidalgo (p. 309) Signed in 1848, this treaty ended the **Mexican War**, forcing that nation to relinquish all of the land north of the Rio Grande and Gila Rivers, including what would eventually become California, in return for monetary compensations.

Treaty of Tordesillas (p. 22) Negotiated by the pope in 1494, this treaty resolved the territorial claims of Spain and Portugal; in the Western Hemisphere Portugal was granted Brazil, while Spain was granted nearly all of the remaining lands.

triangular trade (p. 71) An oversimplified term for the trade among England, its colonies in the Americas, and slave markets in Africa and the Caribbean.

Truman Doctrine (p. 741) A foreign policy, articulated by President Harry Truman in 1947, that provided financial aid to Greek and Turkish governments then under threat by communists rebels.

Underground Railroad (p. 350) A support system established by antislavery groups in the upper South and the North to help fugitive slaves who had escaped from the South to make their way to Canada.

Underwood Tariff (p. 576) A 1913 reform law that lowered tariff rates and levied the first regular federal income tax.

United Nations (UN) (p. 732) An international organization, founded in 1945, that sought to promote discussion and negotiation and thereby avoid war; it was joined by nearly all nations.

United States v. Richard M. Nixon **(p. 792)** A Supreme Court ruling (1974) that obliged President Richard Nixon to turn over to the Watergate special prosecutor sixty-four White House audiotapes; these helped prove that Nixon had known about the cover-up of the Watergate burglary.

utopian (p. 278) Any of countless schemes to create a perfect society.

Virginia Plan (p. 147) An initiative, proposed by James Madison of Virginia, calling on the Constitutional Convention to declare that seats in the federal legislature would be proportionate to a state's population, a concept that caused smaller states to propose a New Jersey plan in which each state would have the same number of representatives. The controversy was resolved in the Great Compromise.

Voting Rights Act of 1965 (p. 776) Federal legislation that empowered federal registrars to intervene when southern states and municipalities refused to let African Americans register to vote.

Wade-Davis bill (p. 406) An 1864 alternative to Lincoln's "**Ten Percent Plan**," this measure required a majority of voters in a southern state to take a loyalty oath in order to begin the process of Reconstruction and guarantee black equality. It also required the repudiation of the Confederate debt. The president exercised a pocket veto, and it never became law.

Wagner Act (p. 694) Officially the National Labor Relations Act and sometimes called Labor's Magna Carta, it gave workers the right to organize and bargain collectively. It also created the National Labor Relations Board to supervise union elections and stop unfair labor practices by employers.

War Hawks (p. 198) Young congressional leaders who in 1811 and 1812 called for war against Great Britain as the only way to defend the national honor.

War Industries Board (WIB) (p. 621) A federal agency, established during World War I, that reorganized industry for maximum efficiency and productivity.

War of 1812 (p. 198) A war fought by the United States and Britain from 1812 to 1815 over British restrictions on American shipping.

war on terror (p. 858) Initially, a worldwide campaign to catch and prosecute those guilty of the September 11, 2001, attacks; as terrorist attacks spread throughout the world, the war became defined far more broadly.

Watergate scandal (p. 790) A complex scandal involving attempts to cover up illegal actions taken by administration officials and leading to the resignation of President Richard Nixon in 1974.

Whigs (p. 260) Originally a reference to British politicians who sought to exclude the Catholic Duke of York from succession to the throne in the 1760s; in the United States after the 1830s, it referred to a political party that opposed the Jacksonian Democrats and favored a strong role for the national government, especially in promoting economic growth.

Whiskey Rebellion (p. 161) A violent protest by western Pennsylvania farmers who refused to pay the whiskey tax proposed by Alexander Hamilton. In 1794, the rebels threatened to destroy Pittsburgh; by the time the Union army had arrived, the rebels had dispersed.

Wilmot Proviso (p. 310) A proposed amendment to an 1846 appropriations bill that banned slavery from any territory the United States might acquire from Spain. It never passed Congress, but generated a great debate on the authority of the federal government to ban slavery from the territories.

woman suffrage (p. 565) The right of women to vote, ensured by the passage and ratification of the Nineteenth Amendment (1920).

Works Progress Administration (WPA) (p. 691) A New Deal agency, established in 1935 and run by Harry Hopkins, that spent $11 billion on federal works projects and provided employment for 8.5 million persons.

XYZ Affair (p. 165) A political furor caused by French diplomats who in 1797 demanded a bribe before they would enter into negotiations with their American counterparts; some **Federalists**, furious over this assault on national honor, called for war.

Yalta Conference (p. 733) A wartime conference (February 1945) held in the Russian Crimea, where the **Allies**—Franklin Roosevelt, Winston Churchill (Britain), and Josef Stalin (Soviet Union)—agreed to final plans for the defeat and joint occupation of Germany; it also provided for free elections in Poland, but such elections were never held.

Young America movement (p. 348) The confident enthusiasm, infused with a belief in the nation's **"manifest destiny,"** that spread rapidly during the 1850s.

Picture Credits

Index

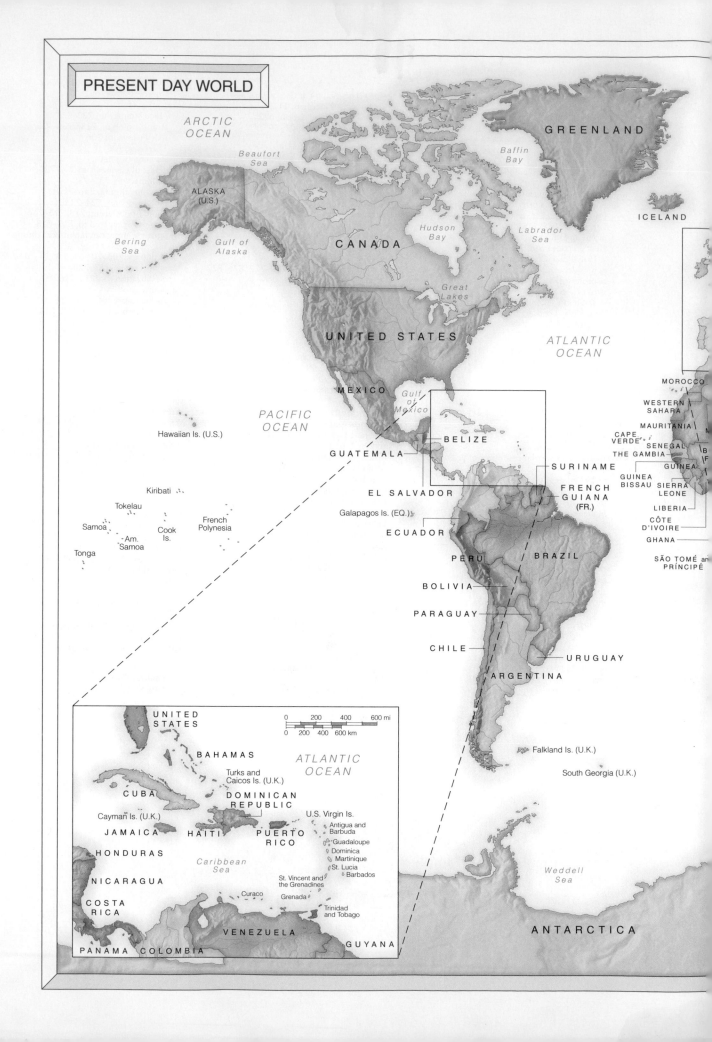

PRESENT DAY WORLD

ARCTIC
OCEAN

GREENLAND

Beaufort
Sea

Baffin
Bay

ALASKA
(U.S.)

ICELAND

Bering
Sea

Gulf of
Alaska

Hudson
Bay

Labrador
Sea

CANADA

Great
Lakes

UNITED STATES

ATLANTIC
OCEAN

MOROCCO

MEXICO

Gulf
of
Mexico

WESTERN
SAHARA

PACIFIC
OCEAN

BELIZE

MAURITANIA

CAPE
VERDE

Hawaiian Is. (U.S.)

GUATEMALA

SENEGAL

THE GAMBIA

SURINAME

GUINEA

Kiribati

EL SALVADOR

FRENCH
GUIANA
(FR.)

GUINEA
BISSAU

SIERRA
LEONE

Tokelau

Galapagos Is. (EQ.)

LIBERIA

Samoa

Cook
Is.

French
Polynesia

ECUADOR

CÔTE
D'IVOIRE

Am.
Samoa

GHANA

Tonga

PERU

BRAZIL

SÃO TOMÉ an
PRÍNCIPÉ

BOLIVIA

PARAGUAY

CHILE

URUGUAY

ARGENTINA

Falkland Is. (U.K.)

South Georgia (U.K.)

UNITED
STATES

0   200   400   600 mi

0   200   400   600 km

BAHAMAS

ATLANTIC
OCEAN

Turks and
Caicos Is. (U.K.)

CUBA

DOMINICAN
REPUBLIC

Cayman Is. (U.K.)

U.S. Virgin Is.

Antigua and
Barbuda

JAMAICA

HAITI

PUERTO
RICO

Guadaloupe

HONDURAS

Dominica

Martinique

Caribbean
Sea

St. Lucia

Weddell
Sea

NICARAGUA

Barbados

St. Vincent and
the Grenadines

COSTA
RICA

Curaco

Grenada

ANTARCTICA

Trinidad
and Tobago

PANAMA

COLOMBIA

VENEZUELA

GUYANA

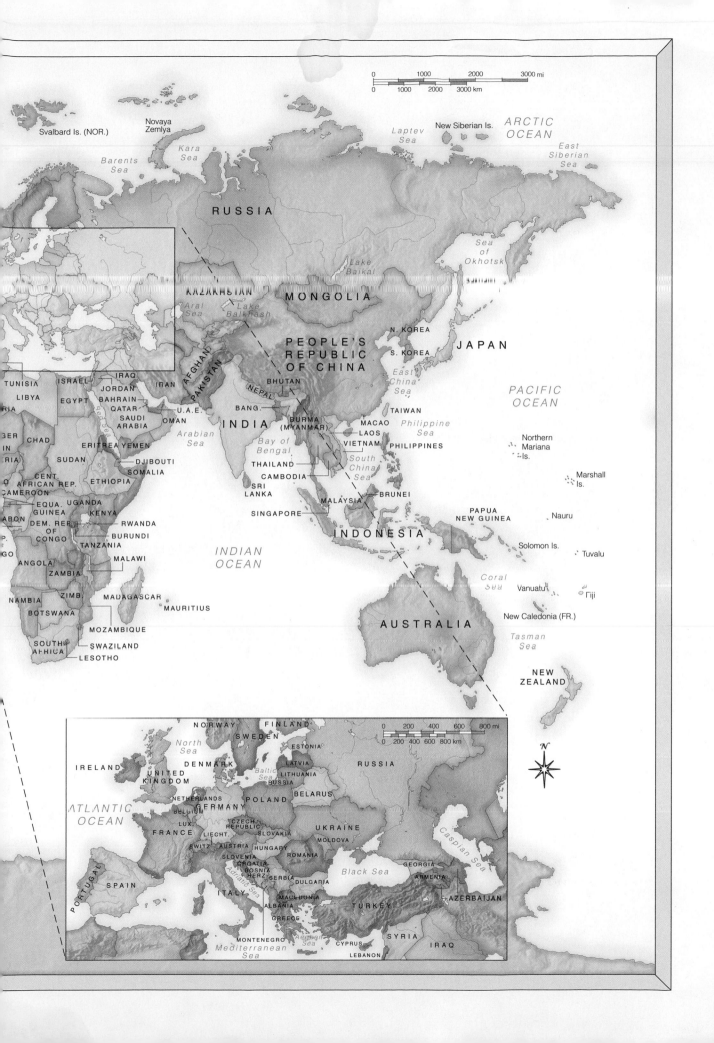

ARCTIC OCEAN

Svalbard Is. (NOR.)

Novaya Zemlya

Kara Sea

Barents Sea

Laptev Sea

New Siberian Is.

East Siberian Sea

RUSSIA

Lake Baikal

Sea of Okhotsk

KAZAKHSTAN

MONGOLIA

Aral Sea

Lake Balkhash

N. KOREA

S. KOREA

JAPAN

PEOPLE'S REPUBLIC OF CHINA

East China Sea

PACIFIC OCEAN

AFGHAN.

PAKISTAN

NEPAL

BHUTAN

TUNISIA

ISRAEL

IRAQ

IRAN

LIBYA

JORDAN

EGYPT

BAHRAIN

QATAR

U.A.E.

SAUDI ARABIA

OMAN

BANG.

BURMA (MYANMAR)

MACAO

TAIWAN

Philippine Sea

LAOS

VIETNAM

PHILIPPINES

Northern Mariana Is.

INDIA

Arabian Sea

Red Sea

CHAD

ERITREA

YEMEN

SUDAN

DJIBOUTI

SOMALIA

CENT. AFRICAN REP.

ETHIOPIA

CAMEROON

EQUA. GUINEA

UGANDA

KENYA

DEM. REP. OF CONGO

RWANDA

BURUNDI

TANZANIA

ANGOLA

ZAMBIA

MALAWI

Bay of Bengal

THAILAND

CAMBODIA

SRI LANKA

MALAYSIA

SINGAPORE

South China Sea

BRUNEI

INDONESIA

PAPUA NEW GUINEA

Marshall Is.

Nauru

Solomon Is.

Tuvalu

NAMIBIA

ZIMB.

BOTSWANA

MADAGASCAR

MAURITIUS

MOZAMBIQUE

SWAZILAND

SOUTH AFRICA

LESOTHO

INDIAN OCEAN

Coral Sea

Vanuatu

Fiji

New Caledonia (FR.)

AUSTRALIA

Tasman Sea

NEW ZEALAND

0 1000 2000 3000 mi
0 1000 2000 3000 km

NORWAY

FINLAND

SWEDEN

North Sea

ESTONIA

IRELAND

DENMARK

LATVIA

LITHUANIA

Baltic Sea

RUSSIA

RUSSIA

UNITED KINGDOM

NETHERLANDS

POLAND

BELARUS

ATLANTIC OCEAN

BELGIUM

GERMANY

LUX.

CZECH REPUBLIC

UKRAINE

FRANCE

LIECHT.

SLOVAKIA

MOLDOVA

SWITZ.

AUSTRIA

HUNGARY

ROMANIA

Caspian Sea

SLOVENIA

CROATIA

BOSNIA HERZ.

SERBIA

BULGARIA

GEORGIA

ARMENIA

PORTUGAL

SPAIN

Adriatic Sea

ITALY

MACEDONIA

Black Sea

AZERBAIJAN

ALBANIA

GREECE

TURKEY

MONTENEGRO

Aegean Sea

CYPRUS

SYRIA

IRAQ

LEBANON

Mediterranean Sea

N

0 200 400 600 800 mi
0 200 400 600 800 km